Praise for

THE AGE OF SACRED TERROR

"*Sacred Terror* is well written and thoughtf̶ ̶ ̶ ̶ ̶ ̶ ̶ ̶ ̶ ̶ ̶ ̶ v on the evolution of modern Islamic radicali̶ ̶ ̶ ̶ ̶ ̶ ̶ ̶ ̶ ̶ ̶ ̶ nd, as in all first-rate books, the clari̶ ̶ ̶ ̶ ̶ ̶ ̶ ̶ ̶ ̶ ̶ ̶ ̶ inst sentiment."
                                                              ̶ ̶y *Standard*

"A lucid, passionate, shockin̶ ̶ ̶ ̶ ̶ ̶ ̶ ̶ ̶ ̶ ̶ terrorism. Anyone interested in how the enemies of t̶ ̶ ̶ ̶ ̶ ̶ ̶ ̶rate will want to read this book."
                                                              —Ian Buruma

"This important book [is] a surprisingly lively—and disturbing—tale of bureaucratic vexation."   —Evan Thomas, *The New York Times Book Review*

"Here's a book that truly connects the dots. It does so in a spare, lucid style with flashes of real brilliance and with admirable fairness to all three administrations—from Bush to Clinton to Bush—that have grappled with a decade of steadily escalating terrorism."   —Strobe Talbott

"Insightful and incisive."   —*The Economist*

"This book should be required reading for [the] national commission created to probe the September 11, 2001, terrorist attacks, particularly for Benjamin and Simon's assessment of the work of the CIA and the 'indefensible' record of the FBI."   —Vernon Loeb, *The Washington Post*

"Benjamin and Simon have done their homework. They have pored over ancient texts and have a sophisticated sense of the full range of ideas presented by Islamic theologians, not just the bumper-sticker version grasped by the popular press and by so many semi-educated Islamists."
                                        —Ellen Laipson, *Foreign Affairs*

"A valuable contribution to our understanding of the American government's reaction to the growth in Islamic terror. The authors make good use of thousands of pages of transcripts from the criminal trials that grew out of the 1993 World Trade Center bombing, the African embassy bombings, and other cases. They also provide an inside, real-life perspective on the attitude toward terrorism that prevailed inside the law-enforcement and national-security establishment during much of the 1990s."

—*National Review*

"In reaching for answers about the birth of terrorism . . . the book demands study. Benjamin and Simon lay out a challenging case."

—*Richmond Times-Dispatch*

"I have yet to read a book as comprehensive and timely as *The Age of Sacred Terror*. . . . This is the real story, based on what we know to date, of the origins of Islamist fascism, the slow response of the civilized world to its aggression, what was done and what wasn't done that might have prevented that movement's most horrific plot from succeeding."

—Joe Conason, Salon.com

"*The Age of Sacred Terror* provides a staggering account of the origins of al-Qaeda, its motives, and its bloody history since the early 1990s. . . . The events of September 11, 2001, changed the world: Ours has truly become the age of sacred terror. This book explains in great and compelling detail how those events were possible, how they might perhaps have been avoided, and how they could occur again. Everyone should read it—and be warned."

—Anthony Pagden

"Insightful and balanced . . . the quality of its writing and its lucid history of the thread of violent intolerance in Islam are likely to keep this book in the forefront."

—*The Boston Globe*

"The book's real value, and why it deserves to be read, is its informed, credible treatment of U.S. policy and, especially, policy processes. . . . If Benjamin and Simon are correct, and they may be, the United States confronts a protracted struggle, perhaps even a Huntingtonian clash of civilizations."

—*Middle East Journal*

"Perhaps the greatest contribution of this important book will be to imbue the war on terror with a new realism. Al Qaeda will strike America again, the authors predict; fighting back will be complicated and the effort will require sustained national and international cooperation. Perhaps this time their prophecies will not go unheeded." —*Newsweek*

"*The Age of Sacred Terror* is a remarkable new book by two of the Clinton White House's counterterrorist directors that delves into the roots of militant Islam and its jihad duties."—Arnaud de Borchgrave, *The Washington Times*

"It's not easy being a Jeremiah—no one wants to hear your gloomy prediction, and you probably don't feel like celebrating when it comes true. Having warned of a terrorist attack long before 9/11, former Clinton NSC staffers Daniel Benjamin and Steve Simon find that systematic anti-Americanism in the Islamic world spells more dark days ahead, unless U.S. policies and PR strategies change." —*Publishers Weekly*

"A thoughtful, well-researched . . . in-depth look at al-Qaeda and Osama bin Laden, and the American response to them. It's worth noting that [Benjamin and Simon] began work on this book more than a year before the attacks, and extra time shows in the depth and breadth of their discussion." —*The Vancouver Sun*

"A valuable account of how the former administration viewed the rise of Islamic terrorism." —*The Dallas Morning News*

"The authors' elucidation of the sources of radical Islamic thought underpinning [bin Laden's] actions is as cogent as it is unsettling. As well, they serve up a compelling look inside the government's response to his emergence as the West's most formidable and intractable enemy. It is instructive reading on how the very nature of cumbersome government puts its citizens at risk." —Montreal *Gazette*

STEVEN SIMON, senior analyst at the RAND Corporation, served on the National Security Council staff as director for global issues from 1994 to 1998 and senior director for counterterrorism from 1998 to 1999. Prior to entering the administration, he held several positions at the U.S. Department of State dealing with regional security and nonproliferation. He holds degrees from Harvard, Columbia, and Princeton and was an international-affairs fellow at Oxford University.

DANIEL BENJAMIN, senior fellow at the Center for Strategic and International Studies, served as director for counterterrorism on the National Security Council staff from 1998 to 1999 and as special assistant and foreign-policy speechwriter for President Clinton from 1994 to 1997. Prior to entering the administration, he was Berlin bureau chief for *The Wall Street Journal* and has been a foreign correspondent for *Time*. He holds degrees from Harvard and Oxford, where he was a Marshall Scholar.

THE AGE OF SACRED TERROR

THE AGE OF
SACRED
TERROR

RADICAL ISLAM'S WAR AGAINST AMERICA

DANIEL BENJAMIN

STEVEN SIMON

RANDOM HOUSE TRADE PAPERBACKS / NEW YORK

FOR HENRIKE

—

FOR VIRGINIA

This book was originally conceived in the late summer of 1999, in Room 302 of the Old Executive Office Building, the strange and wonderful nineteenth-century edifice inside the White House compound where much of the President's staff works. Room 302 was the home of the National Security Council's Directorate of Transnational Threats, which was responsible for issues including international crime, counternarcotics, critical infrastructure (computer security), homeland defense, and counterterrorism. At the time, Steven Simon was senior director and Daniel Benjamin was director for the last of these portfolios.

NSC is for many a familiar acronym but a little-known organization. Established by the National Security Act of 1947, the NSC is a body chaired by the President that brings together the vice president; the secretaries of state, defense, and treasury; the national security adviser; the director of Central Intelligence; the chairman of the Joint Chiefs of Staff; and other senior officials as needed to deliberate on foreign and security policy. In practice, a mention of the NSC is almost always a reference to the staff that serves the President and the national security adviser within the White House on matters ranging from high diplomacy to nuclear arms negotiations to humanitarian affairs. Its official job is to provide policy "coordination"—a task that can involve ensuring that all the executive branch's agencies agree on policy and are working together, or, as has increasingly been the case since Henry Kissinger's tenure as national security adviser in the Nixon administration, it can mean driving the engine of state toward a particular set of goals.

The NSC is that rare thing in Washington, a flat organization. Under the national security adviser and his one or two deputies, it averaged between eighty and a hundred professionals—roughly twenty senior directors and the rest directors—during the second half of the 1990s. In the final three years of the Clinton administration, the Transnational Threats Directorate was unusual in being run by a bureaucrat with an additional title: "national coordinator for counterterrorism, infrastructure protection, and security." The man who held that position was Richard A. Clarke. Although others in the directorate handled important matters relating to terrorism (money laundering, for example), we and Clarke were the only people at the White House working full-time on the issue. Steven Simon, a career State Department civil servant, was detailed to the office from the Bureau of Political-Military Affairs at Foggy Bottom in April 1994; Daniel Benjamin, who had been a journalist and, most recently, had spent three years at the NSC as one of President Clinton's foreign policy speechwriters, joined Transnational Threats in January 1998.

There could hardly be a better vantage point for tracking what was going on in the world of terrorism or how the United States was coping with that world's challenges than TNT, as the office was known. Clarke chaired the government's interagency working group—the Counterterrorism Security Group—which dealt with terrorism in all its aspects, from crisis management to budgeting to policy recommendations for the nation's leaders. We participated in these meetings and, on occasion, chaired them and subgroups of the CSG. Our jobs involved working closely with the agencies that have primary roles in counterterrorism—the CIA, the State Department, the Defense Department, and the Justice Department and FBI— as well as with others such as the Federal Aviation

Administration, the Federal Emergency Management Agency, and the Immigration and Naturalization Service. Our responsibilities included staying current with the torrents of information provided daily by the many parts of the intelligence community, the State Department, the Pentagon, and other government sources concerning Islamist violence, the handful of states that sponsor terror, and other kinds of terrorist groups, ranging from the Colombian FARC and the Peruvian Shining Path to the Sri Lankan Tamil Tigers, the Kurdish PKK, and the Japanese Aum Shinrikyo. We needed to stay informed for reasons that were, organizationally speaking, horizontal and vertical: we had to be able to identify issues of concern with our colleagues from other agencies and keep the national security adviser and, by extension, the President briefed on important developments and supplied with options when decisions were required.

—

Our discussions in the summer and fall of 1999 centered on the changing nature of terrorism. Over the decade, there had been a series of conspiracies, many but not all carried out by Islamic extremists, that departed radically from the norms of terrorism to which the West had become accustomed. Familiar kinds of political reasons for attacks were giving way to religious ones. It seemed to us that the new motivation was related to a new level of violence, a desire to kill on a grand scale that had not been seen before. Even if these new terrorists did not often achieve their aims, their goals were dramatically different. We believed that the trend was ominous and had not been sufficiently recognized by the broader public. Al-Qaeda's nearly simultaneous bombing of two United States embassies in East Africa was a watershed for us.

Each of us was preparing to leave the NSC by the end of 1999. We had both been at the White House for five years, working at an agency where most stayed for a year or two and where, for all the obvious rewards, the personal costs were considerable. (Coincidentally—though not incidentally—both of us had gotten married in the summer of 1998.) The year after the embassy bombings was a series of nonstop crises and near crises, including a significant number of attempts to attack United States facilities and kill Americans. At our homes, the secure phones rang throughout the night as the Situation Room apprised us of threats, attacks against countries around the world, and plane crashes, or read to us one of the increasingly frequent outgoing diplomatic messages regarding terrorism for White House clearance. When we left the administration, Steven Simon was appointed assistant director of the International Institute for Strategic Studies in London. Daniel Benjamin received a senior fellowship at the United States Institute of Peace.

The book we planned to write was intended to provide a descriptive warning about the new terrorism and an analysis of its causes, including the resurgence of forms of religious belief that drive adherents to commit violence, and the circumstances that give rise to such creeds. During 2000, we began exploring these issues in articles in *The New York Times* and lengthier pieces in *Survival,* Britain's equivalent to *Foreign Affairs.* We focused on al-Qaeda, writing that there was a "new, religiously motivated terrorism . . . that [was not] constrained by limits on [its] violence" and that the changes in motivation, tools, and weaponry "could elevate terrorism from the level of tactical nuisance to strategic threat."[1] We were fortunate to have positions in which we had latitude to research the issue because, in general, there was limited interest in terrorism elsewhere in the scholarly and think-tank world. Over the next eighteen months, we applied for a number of foundation grants to pursue this work and came up empty-handed. Centrist and left-of-center institutions appeared to see this line of argument as leading dangerously toward Muslim-bashing, despite our insistence on the distinction between violent Islamists and the vast majority of Muslims, as well as our stated interest in violence in other religious traditions. Right-of-center institutions indicated that terrorism was not a serious enough security issue to be worth their money.

We were more fortunate with our book proposal, which was circulated in October 2000. To our surprise, Random House quickly accepted it. In the spring, we traveled to Pakistan and Egypt to pursue our research. We also continued to try to sound a warning about the threat of al-Qaeda.

During the summer of 2001 we wrote in *The Washington Post* and the *Financial Times* about the need to take action in Afghanistan to force change in or the removal of the Taliban's leadership, and the importance of revising America's approach to Pakistan, which we feared might be headed for a radical Islamist takeover.[2] We noted that the existing state of affairs was benefiting al-Qaeda, which had killed more Americans than any other foreign adversary in the eight years of the Clinton administration. Finally, in an article accepted by the *Los Angeles Times* in July and still awaiting publication two months later, we argued that the threat posed by Usama bin Laden and his followers was being taken all too lightly. A greater awareness was needed that al-Qaeda was intent on killing unprecedented numbers of Americans.

The book we intended to write was overtaken by the catastrophe of September 11. Daniel Benjamin was standing in his kitchen that morning, holding his four-week-old son, when CNN called and asked if he was watching the television. Steven Simon heard the news in a London cab. Neither of us had any doubt about who had committed the atrocity. Yet for all the thought we had devoted to catastrophic terror, we were as horror-stricken as a nation full of people who barely knew the name al-Qaeda. In a heartbeat, the reality of the day shattered the imaginative preparations of several years.

Many of our original themes are still addressed in chapters 1 through 5 and chapter 12, but the events of September 11 required that we write a different book, one that also tried to answer questions about what the United States government has done to combat terror in the last decade and why the nation as a whole was caught off guard as never before. We have strived to be circumspect, and we have researched these years as carefully as we could. This book, however, falls short of being a history. It is a record of United States actions seen from the perspective of individuals who were working in the White House. A fuller view of how America came to suffer the bloodiest surprise in its history will require further scholarly work and, above all, the release of a vast number of documents. The latter is unlikely to occur for years to come.

That is understandable—and unfortunate. We recognize the demands of secrecy: the United States is in a deadly conflict, and its opponent has demonstrated a remarkable ability to turn our assets—from Boeing jets to satellite phones to the open society itself—against us. It would be a terrible mistake to underestimate al-Qaeda's acumen, its ability to identify weaknesses in America's defenses and the sources and methods of our intelligence. Indeed, several months ago, we were astonished to see an article we had published in *Survival* after September 11 cited in a piece of journalism by a jihadist.[3] At the same time, America's national security is in the midst of a transformation to meet the needs of a new era. We face a difficult time doing it correctly without a better airing of the mistakes made in the past.

The United States government provided virtually no official cooperation for this book. Working through the designated press offices, we were granted precisely one interview by currently serving officials. That meeting, with an FBI official, required more than a year to arrange. Requests to the White House for interviews with National Security Advisor Condoleezza Rice and her deputy Stephen Hadley were turned down. So, too, were requests to Director of Central Intelligence George Tenet and others at the CIA. Cooperation from former government officials was much greater. It should be mentioned, however, that former FBI director Louis Freeh declined to be interviewed.

Portions of this book that deal with the period of time we served in the White House have been reviewed by government agencies in keeping with the conditions on the security clearances we held. A number of passages were changed to avoid the release of classified material.

The notes section refers to many of the sources we have consulted. A great deal of our information, however, is derived from the transcripts of the major terrorism trials of the last eight years. These records are a treasure trove. Reading through the nearly fifty thousand pages of testimony, we learned more about the rise of the new terrorism than we ever could have expected. In many instances, we discovered information so crucial that we were amazed that the relevant agencies did not inform us of it

while we were at the NSC. We have not footnoted these proceedings because it would have made the text unwieldy and unreadable. The relevant
cases are

United States of America v. Mohammad A. Salameh et al.
  S593 Cr. 180 (KTD)
United States of America v. Omar Ahmad Ali Abdel Rahman et al.
  S593 Cr. 181 (MBM)
United States of America v. Ramzi Ahmed Yousef, Abdul Hakim Murad,
  Wali Khan Amin Shah
  S1293 Cr. 180 (KTD)
United States of America v. Eyad Ismoil
  S1293 Cr. 180 (KTD)
United States of America v. Usama bin Laden et al.
  S798 Cr. 1023

ACKNOWLEDGMENTS

In writing this book, we have accumulated numerous debts. Many friends read drafts of chapters and offered excellent editorial suggestions: Michael Abramowitz, Bruce Butterworth, Mary de Rosa, Irish Flynn, John Kelsay, and Vinca LaFleur. We benefited from the scholarly advice and help of Steve Cohen, David Cook, Bill Danvers, Norman Eisen, Jeff Ellis, Dennis Gormley, David Levenson, and James Piscatori, and during our travels, from the help of Hannah Bloch, Brooke Unger, and Deborah Wise. For her unerring advice and support, we thank our literary agent, Esther Newberg. Scott Moyers of Random House has been everything we could ask for in an editor—one who has taken the ideas within this book every bit as seriously as we have. We thank Robert Silvers of *The New York Review of Books,* who published an earlier version of chapter 6, and Don Morrison, editor of the European edition of *Time,* who published several essays that allowed us to work out in print some of our ideas for the first time. Herbert Hadad of the office of the United States Attorney for the Southern District of New York helped us obtain valuable court exhibits. We are grateful to Bill Leary, Rod Soubers, and Daniel Sanborn of the National Security Council for shepherding the manuscript through the clearance process.

We cite many secondary sources in this book. Intellectual honesty and admiration requires that we mention several scholars whose work has had a formative influence on our own: Richard Bulliet; John J. Collins; Bruce Hoffman; Saad Eddin Ibrahim; Johannes J. G. Jansen; Mark Juergensmeyer; Gilles Kepel; Bernard Lewis; Rudolf Peters; Alan Richards; and Emmanuel Sivan. In each of their fields, they opened essential doors for us. If we have trespassed in any way, the fault is entirely ours.

—

I have been tremendously fortunate in having superb research assistance from Qais Sultan and Rob Gile at the Center for Strategic and International Studies. Caitlin Williams of CSIS worked unspeakable hours delving into the most stubborn questions and devoted herself to ensuring that both individual phrases as well as whole sections were right.

Two institutions provided the environment and support that were vital for this project. At the United States Institute of Peace, I had the opportunity government officials crave to take stock and develop thoughts accumulated over years. USIP's president, Richard Solomon, and the director of the Randolph Jennings Senior Fellows Program, Joe Klaits, were good friends and generous benefactors. Since the beginning of 2001, I have been fortunate to call the Center for Strategic and International Studies home. CSIS's president, John Hamre, and Kurt Campbell, its senior vice president and director of the international security program, unstintingly supported my work on terrorism, even when it was unfashionable. They saw to it that I had the freedom and research and administrative support necessary to concentrate exclusively on the writing of the book. Stephanie Kaplan, Jessica Cox, and Amanda Pomeroy provided indispensable assistance throughout the last eighteen months.

One debt outweighs all others. From the book's inception to the day we saw the smoke rise over the Pentagon and in the months since, my wife, Henrike, provided the sustenance, intellectual and emotional, without which I could not have completed this project. Her contribution is on every page.

Daniel Benjamin
Washington, D.C. July 2002

—

I am grateful to the International Institute for Strategic Studies for giving me the time this spring to complete the manuscript. My colleagues Dana Allin, editor of *Survival,* and Jonathan Stevenson, editor of *Strategic Survey* and an expert on terrorism in his own right, were generous and wise in their recommendations, and I benefited from David Ucko's thoughts on religion and violence. Ahmad Lutfi, a doctoral candidate at the London School of Economics, proved an indefatigable researcher and was most patient with my Arabic. Sue Watson of IISS kept the office running smoothly during the final frenzy of book preparation, and the library staff, Ellen Peacock, Emma Sullivan, and Sophie Delfolie, were amazingly helpful and efficient. It is my wife, Virginia, to whom I owe the greatest debt and to whom I dedicate this book. The compiler of the biblical Book of Proverbs must have been thinking of her when he wrote: A woman of valor, who can find? Far beyond pearls is her value. Her husband's heart trusts in her and he shall lack no fortune.

Steven Simon
London July 2002

CONTENTS

PART ONE

THE TERROR

CHAPTER 1

DAYBREAK

T HE FIRST KILLING of the Terror was carried out by an Egyptian in Manhattan. The weapon was not a Boeing 767 but a chrome-plated .357 Magnum, and the attack happened in the conference room of a midtown hotel. One man was killed; two others were injured. Years would pass before anyone realized that the event was more than the solitary act of a deranged man.

On November 5, 1990, El-Sayyid Nosair rushed toward the podium in the Morgan D Room of the Marriott East Side Hotel. Just to the side of the microphone, Meir Kahane was signing books and greeting members of the audience for the speech he had just finished. As he neared the front of the room, Nosair aimed his gun and fired. The bullet tore into Kahane's neck and exited through his cheek. As blood poured from his mouth, Kahane raised his hands to his head and fell backward. The shooter spun and ran toward the exit, but just before the door, he was grabbed by a seventy-three-year-old man named Irving Franklin. Nosair kept moving and dragged Franklin a couple of yards before shooting him in the leg to get free. He sprinted from the hotel and jumped in a cab, thinking it was the getaway car he had arranged. It wasn't. Nosair jammed the gun into the back of the cabbie's head and screamed at him to drive. But traffic was moving slowly, and when a student who had been at Kahane's lecture and chased after Nosair jumped in front of the cab, the driver slid out the door and took off. Nosair abandoned the car, too, but he ran into the path of a Postal Service policeman. Nosair shot and wounded the officer, who returned fire, dropping the Egyptian with a neck wound.

As he lay bleeding on the sidewalk, El-Sayyid Nosair was sure he had changed the course of history.

He believed this because of his bizarre reading of Israeli politics. Kahane was a Brooklyn rabbi who founded the Jewish Defense League and then immigrated to Israel and established the Kach party, which was banned from his country's parliament in 1988 because of its blatant racism—the group advocated, for example, the expulsion of Arabs from Israel and the Occupied Territories. Yet Nosair was convinced that Kahane was destined to be the leader of the Jewish state and a force in global affairs: "They were preparing him to dominate, to be the prime minister someday," he would later say. "They were preparing him despite their assertion that they reject his agenda and that he is a racist."

A thirty-four-year-old from the northeastern Egyptian city of Port Said, Nosair had moved to the United States in 1981 with a university degree in engineering in hand. He was not a happy immigrant. His sister in Egypt later related that he disliked America, saying, "He didn't like the morality there."[1] Nonetheless, he stayed, married an American woman, and moved to New Jersey, bouncing from job to job and winding up as a heating and air-conditioning repairman for the City of New York.

To investigators, he seemed mentally disturbed, and a police official described him as depressed. A month after the shooting, a federal investigator said, "Either the man is a lone nut, or he's a lone nut and someone whispered something in his ear knowing he'd do it. Or there's an enormous international conspiracy."[2] Authorities quickly settled on the first hypothesis. Their belief that there was nothing more to the case—and, perhaps, the refusal of Kahane's Orthodox family to allow a full autopsy—

helps explain the shoddiness of the case prosecutors put together. At trial, the jury could not be convinced that it was Nosair who shot Kahane. He was convicted on two counts of assault, first-degree coercion (for his treatment of the cabbie), and a weapons charge and packed off to the state prison at Attica.

Nosair may in fact have been a bit unbalanced, but he was no loner. And he had been preparing himself for the killing for many months.

He studied weaponry and tactics using official U.S. Army manuals and other sensitive documents that his friend Ali Mohamed, a sergeant at Fort Bragg, the home of the U.S. Special Operations Command in North Carolina, brought him on weekend visits. Together with several others from the Farouq Mosque on Atlantic Avenue in Brooklyn, where he worshiped, he was working on his marksmanship. In the spring and summer of 1989, the group would meet early in the morning and drive out on the Long Island Expressway to the Calverton Shooting Range on eastern Long Island. Mohammed Salameh was there, as were Nidal Ayyad and Clement Hampton-El, an African American hospital worker who had converted to Islam. Many wore the same T-shirt in black or gray: on the top was printed "Help Each Other in Goodness and Piety," and on the bottom "A Muslim to a Muslim Is a Brick Wall." In the middle was printed "Services Office" along with a map of a country with "Afghanistan" written in the center. Mahmud Abouhalima—Mahmud the Red, as he was called because of his hair—sported a National Rifle Association cap. The group brought with them a small arsenal: rifles, shotguns, 9-mm and .357-caliber handguns, and AK-47 assault weapons. Ali Mohamed gave pointers.

The men were training for jihad, Islamic holy war. In 1989, most of the world understood *jihad* to mean what was written on the men's T-shirts: Afghanistan, the fight against the Soviet Union. By the time Nosair was visiting the firing range, the Soviet Union had been defeated, though fighting continued against the communist regime in Kabul. But to Nosair and his friends, jihad was more than that. It meant, as he wrote in a notebook, attacking *all* those "who waged war against Allah and his messenger . . . who should be murdered or crucified or . . . their feet should be cut off on opposite sides or they should be exiled from the land." Killing Kahane, he would later boast, was an act of jihad, one in which "God the almighty enabled his extremely brave people, with his great power to destroy one of the top infidels." So, too, was the attempt he reportedly made on the life of Mikhail Gorbachev: he threw a soda can filled with explosives at the Soviet leader's motorcade in 1990, but it did not detonate. And so was the bombing of a gay bar in Greenwich Village in April of the same year, which injured three people and with which he was later linked.

But Nosair had another, more breathtaking vision of jihad. Written in a notebook of his, it called for the "breaking and destruction of the enemies of Allah. And this is by means of destroying exploding, the structure of their civilized pillars such as the touristic infrastructure which they are proud of and their high world buildings which they are proud of and their statues which they endear and the buildings which gather their head[s,] their leaders, and without any announcement for our responsibility of Muslims for what had been done."

El-Sayyid Nosair inaugurated the age of sacred terror with the assassination of a bit player on the world stage, an act wholly uncharacteristic of everything that would follow. But he wrote down the idea for its defining event, the attacks of September 11 and the destruction of the World Trade Center, no later than 1990. The notion of destroying the Twin Towers was almost certainly not Nosair's; the whole speech in which the passage is found was likely something he copied. The language and the horrific grandeur of the imagery mark it as the idea of a man Nosair telephoned regularly in Egypt to apprise of his group's jihad training, and whom he then helped settle in the United States in 1990: Sheikh Omar Ahmad Abdel Rahman. The Blind Sheikh, as he is also known, a cleric revered among Islamist radicals for providing the religious authorization to assassinate Egyptian president Anwar Sadat, had slipped out of Egypt to Sudan in 1990. There, the consular section of the U.S. embassy mistakenly issued him a visa, even though his name was on a watch list. He arrived in America in July of that year and became the central figure of the burgeoning jihadist set in New York and northern New Jersey.

WORLD TRADE CENTER I

Ramzi Yousef was another engineer with history on his mind. Half Palestinian, half Pakistani, he grew up in Kuwait; he had a degree in computer-aided electrical engineering from a polytechnic in Wales and a desire to kill 250,000 people. The number was not random: it was, Yousef would explain, the number killed by the American atomic bombs dropped on Hiroshima and Nagasaki. If he could murder on that scale, he believed, he would teach the United States that it was in a war.

Yousef's ambitions dovetailed with those of the Blind Sheikh. In August 1992, when Rahman decided the time had come to topple the "civilized pillars," he dialed a number in Pakistan, 810604. Shortly thereafter, on September 1, Yousef and another man, Ahmad Ajaj, arrived at Kennedy Airport, having flown from Peshawar via Karachi. Entering the country separately, both were stopped by immigration officials. Ajaj had a poorly forged Swedish passport, and when the authorities opened his suitcase, they found it filled with bomb manuals. He was immediately detained. Yousef, carrying an Iraqi passport that aroused suspicion, instantly requested asylum. He was taken for an interview, but the waiting room was overflowing with applicants. Yousef was photographed, fingerprinted, and given a date to appear in court, an appointment he never kept.

Within two days, he had moved into a Jersey City apartment with Mohammed Salameh, a Palestinian on an expired visa who was a member of the Farouq Mosque jihad group. He contacted Mahmud Abouhalima; Mahmud the Red was the man who drove the getaway car that El-Sayyid Nosair missed, another member of the Long Island shooting party, and the chauffeur and assistant to the Blind Sheikh. Eventually, several others would join in—among them Nidal Ayyad, a chemical engineer, and Eyad

Ismoil, a Jordanian who had come to the United States to attend college, dropped out, and become part of the circle around Rahman. One more person, an Iraqi named Abdul Rahman Yasin, who lived upstairs from Yousef and Salameh, joined the group.

There are two enduring misconceptions about Ramzi Yousef. The first is that he was a lone wolf, a solo operator who got a contract to do a job or, propelled by his own ambitions, simply set out to do it himself. True, he was not a card-carrying member of any renowned terrorist organization. But from the time he landed in the United States to the time he left, he was part of a constant triangular conversation. The phone in his apartment and the one in the home of the Blind Sheikh were frequently connected. And both of them regularly called Pakistan: 810604, the number Rahman had dialed before Yousef's arrival.

The second misunderstanding concerns Yousef's motivations. He is remembered as a something of a bon vivant bomber, a man with ready recommendations for whorehouses around the world and motivations that were a mixture of vanity and secular politics. Undoubtedly, he wanted to make a mark, and he was no puritan. But the image needs adjustment. Yousef met his accomplice Ajaj at Khalden, a terrorist training camp in Afghanistan, where both learned about explosives. When Ajaj was stopped, he was carrying an instructional video on bomb making that began by declaring that there is no alternative to waging holy war against the enemies of God and that depicted the demolition of an American building. He also had a letter of introduction to the camp, in which the unknown author wrote: "The jihad today is an appointed duty and every Muslim has no legal excuse. It is a sin to abandon the jihad, for if one inch of Muslim land is occupied, it is the duty of the Muslims to save that inch. And now the religion of God is under assault and all the Islamic countries are occupied by rulers who do not govern by the revealed word of God." Yousef likely absorbed this thinking at Khalden and perhaps elsewhere. It seems a better assumption that, like many who came later, he took seriously the admonition, written in a dozen training manuals, to camouflage his identity through behavior that made him appear to be an unbeliever.

His first two months in the country were taken up with assembling the crew, surveying the target, and planning. Ramzi seems not to have known how many people were likely to be in the Twin Towers on any given day, but he knew it was the target that gave him the best chance of reaching his goal of a quarter million dead. He pondered what kind of explosive to build. He considered a device with cyanide, thinking that the unprecedented use of a chemical weapon would add to the spectacle of his performance. To release the gas effectively, however, required technology that was beyond his financial means.

Once he settled on the type of main charge he wanted, he wasted no time. For Yousef, the terrorist Prometheus, the explosive would be urea nitrate—a substance used only once before in the United States, and then only in a 1988 pipe bombing. In November, Yousef and his team began working their way through the phone book listings for chemical supply companies, searching for one that would sell them what they needed.

It took them twelve days. City Chemical in Jersey City sold them fifteen hundred pounds of urea, 130 gallons of nitric acid, and a variety of other chemicals. Mixing ingredients was simple: working in the rented apartment where they also lived, they soaked the urea with water in a blue trash can and added the nitric acid. Then they spread out the mash onto newspapers to dry. Each day, when the newest batch was ready, they would load it into Salameh's 1978 Chevy Nova, drive to a self-storage shed they had rented, and deposit it there. They drove out to Liberty State Park in New Jersey and tested the explosive. In all, they needed about three weeks to produce a main charge weighing around fifteen hundred pounds. To make a bigger bang, they added a hundred pounds of aluminum powder, an oxidizing agent that would add to the velocity of the explosion.

As a technician, Ramzi had notable skills, but it was his resourcefulness and determination that distinguished him. The main charge required an initiator, something that would explode and trigger the urea nitrate. Here, he was frustrated. He tried in vain to see if there was some way to get hold of Ajaj's confiscated manuals, speaking in code to the incarcerated Palestinian in a New York prison on a phone connection routed through Texas. Abouhalima bought a pound of smokeless powder, and with this, the crew assembled a fusing system. And Ramzi experimented, mixing nitroglycerin to use as an alternate initiator for insurance. He kept it in a refrigerator, which someone had told him was a way to safely store the volatile liquid.

In fact, cold storage increased the likelihood that the chemical would blow them all up, but they were lucky in this way as in others. At about one A.M. on January 24, 1993, after a meeting at Abouhalima's house, Salameh and Ramzi were driving through Woodbridge Township, New Jersey, when the Nova jumped a curb, tearing apart the undercarriage. The two were banged up—Ramzi badly so—and taken to Rahway Hospital. Salameh was released in the morning, but his passenger remained for five days. The police described the inside of the car as looking as if someone had emptied a garbage can in it and did not examine it too closely. To be safe, Abouhalima visited the car repair shop the next day to clean out anything that might interest the authorities during a second look. Ramzi did not let the mishap slow him down. From his hospital bed, he called in orders for more chemicals.

Salameh, a man who had failed his driving test four times, remained the group's driver. With the Nova gone, Nidal Ayyad, who worked at Allied Signal, used his corporate account to rent a car for Salameh. On February 16, while driving to the storage facility, Salameh got into another accident, this time with a second car. A woman, he claimed, had swerved her car into his. After forty-five minutes of questioning, the police officer let him go.

In mid-February, the bomb was all but complete. The crew still needed a vehicle to deliver the bomb and another one in which to escape. On the twenty-third, Nidal Ayyad, again using his corporate account, rented another car for Salameh to use for the getaway. Finding a van was harder. Members of the crew called around frantically. Ramzi even

clipped a coupon from the phone book. Salameh was the one who succeeded. DIB Leasing, a Ryder outlet in Jersey City, offered him a choice
between a cargo van and a cube van. In perhaps his only sentient act in
the entire conspiracy, Salameh put down a $400 cash deposit and opted
for the Ford Econoline cargo van because it had a lower roof and would
meet the underground height restrictions at the World Trade Center.
Later in the day, he drove Ayyad's rental on one more visit to the Twin
Towers.

Ramzi wanted the biggest explosion possible, so he added one more
ingredient: hydrogen gas. Tanks of the gas would be lashed to the bomb;
when it detonated, they would rupture. A fraction of a second later, he
believed, the flammable gas would ignite, pushing the walls of the building, already stretched by the first explosion, past the breaking point.
Ayyad, calling from his office, found a company that would sell him the
gas. Three cylinders were delivered to the storage shed on the afternoon
of February 25. Later, the bomb was loaded into the van along with the
tanks.

That night, Yousef and Ismoil moved closer to the World Trade Center, staying at the Harbor Motor Inn in Brooklyn, the van parked outside.
The next morning, Salameh followed them in the red Chevy Corsica
Ayyad had rented as they drove the twelve miles to the Twin Towers.
They pulled up on an access road where there was no ticket booth and
delivery trucks routinely stopped in the no-parking zone. After setting the
timer to go off in seven minutes, Yousef and Ismoil got into the Corsica
and started driving out of the complex. A truck stopped in front of them,
standing still for two minutes while Salameh leaned on the horn in desperation. Then they were clear.

At 12:18 P.M. on February 26, the bomb detonated, ripping a 150-
square-foot crater in the nearly foot-thick concrete floor and demolishing
much of the surrounding structure. The blast blew through the con-
course level of the Vista Hotel two floors up, as well as three floors down.
It tore a three-thousand-pound diagonal steel brace off the building,
sending half of it flying some thirty-five feet. The gas enhancement ap-

parently failed.[3] Six people, most of them building workers, were killed while they ate in a lunchroom, and about a thousand were injured. The damage to the building cost $510 million to repair.

———

That night, Ramzi Yousef boarded a Pakistani International Airways flight to Karachi. A few hours later, Ismoil caught a plane to Amman. Abouhalima stayed in the United States, but four days later he panicked. He flew to Jeddah, Saudi Arabia, then to Egypt. Salameh planned to travel to Germany on March 5.

First, though, he had an errand to run. On February 25 the day before the bombing, he reported to the police that the van had been stolen. Two hours after the blast, he showed up at DIB Leasing, informed them of the "theft," and asked for his deposit back. He was told to bring in a police report. He came back again on March 1 and was turned away again. On March 4, the day before he was scheduled to leave the country, the man behind the counter at DIB handed him $200, which Salameh accepted. As he walked away from the office, FBI agents waiting outside arrested him. By a stroke of luck, investigators at the blast site had turned up a piece of the van's frame, a section where the secondary vehicle identification number was stamped. (The secondary VIN, a portion of the seventeen-digit number on the dashboard, helps authorities track stolen cars and vehicles that are used as the Ford van was.) The eight-digit number led the FBI to DIB Leasing. Salemeh's refusal to forget about the deposit was the thread that unraveled the conspiracy.

The FBI interviewed Abdul Rahman Yasin on March 4. He struck the agents as forthcoming. Believing he would be a cooperative witness, they released him. The next morning, he flew to Amman, the first stop on his way to Iraq.

Nidal Ayyad, who had earned his degree at Rutgers, stayed around to be the bombers' spokesman. The day after the blast, he called the New York *Daily News* from his office to claim responsibility and mailed a letter to much the same effect to *The New York Times:*

The following letter from the Liberation Army regarding the operation conducted against the WTC.

We are, the fifth battalion in the Liberation Army, declare our responsibility for the explosion on the mentioned building. This action was done in response for the American political, economical, and military support to Israel, the state of terrorism, and to the rest of the dictator countries in the region.

Our demands are:

1. Stop all military, economical and political aids to Israel.
2. All diplomatic relations with Israel must stop.
3. Not to interfere with any of the Middle East countries' interior affairs.

If our demands are not met, all of our functional groups in the army will continue to execute our missions against military and civilian targets in and out the United States. This will also include some potential nuclear targets. For your own information, our army has more than hundred and fifty suicidal soldiers ready to go ahead. The terrorism that Israel practices (which is supported by America) must be faced with a similar one. The dictatorship and terrorism (also supported by America) that some countries are practicing against their own people must also be faced with terrorism.

The American people must know that the civilians who got killed are not better than those who are getting killed by the American weapons and support.

The American people are responsible for the actions of their government and they must question all of the crimes that their government is committing against other people or they, Americans, will be the targets of our operations that could diminish them. We invite all of the people from all countries and all of the revolutionaries in the world to participate in this action with us to accomplish our just goals.

If then anyone transgresses the prohibition against you, transgress
ye likewise against him.

> Liberation Army, fifth battalion.
> Al-Farrek Al-Rokn, Abu Bakr Al-Makee.

A deleted version of the letter was later found on Ayyad's computer; it
added to the *Times* version an acknowledgment and a warning: "Unfor-
tunately our calculations were not very accurate this time; however, we
promise you that next time, it will be very precise and WTC will continue
to be one of our targets unless our demands have been met."

———

From the perspective of those who backed it, plotted it, and carried it out,
the first attack on the Twin Towers was a failure. Stunned by what was at
the time the worst foreign terrorist attack in U.S. history, most Americans
did not see the February 26 bombing that way. Not until two years later,
when he was captured and regaled law-enforcement officials with his
original plan, were the full dimensions of Ramzi's ambitions revealed, and
even then they received little attention.

Yousef did not aim to *damage* the World Trade Center: he set out to
bring the towers down. Placed correctly, he thought, a large enough
charge would cause one tower to topple into the other, killing everyone
inside. In light of that goal, the jihadists' view was closer to the mark.
Ramzi's attack reversed the law of historic repetition—it was the farce that
preceded the tragedy of September 11. For all his ingenuity, Yousef knew
little about physics, civil engineering, or the structural safeguards built
into the Twin Towers, so he underestimated the amount of explosives
needed to destroy one building. He also did not understand that it was
impossible to tip one tower over into the other. Gravity and the enormous
inertial mass of the building meant that structural failure would result in
pancaking.

What El-Sayyid Nosair began with a bullet, Ramzi Yousef sought to
raise to an altogether new level, where killing by a handful of men equaled
the most lethal strikes ever by a superpower.

TERRSTOP: THE MANHATTAN LANDMARKS

What would the sheikh approve?

After the World Trade Center bombing, Omar Abdel Rahman's followers were eager to strike again, to get it right. Among themselves, they acknowledged that the attack had caused plenty of damage, but it was still "filled with errors," as Siddiq Ali, a Sudanese said. The others agreed it was a screwup. The issue was what to hit next, and the paramount question concerned what targets would be ruled Islamically acceptable by the Blind Sheikh.

There were plenty of ideas. From Attica, El-Sayyid Nosair had been urging his fellow jihadists to mount an attack. I did my part, the man who killed Kahane would tell them when they visited. When are you going to do yours? Nosair put forward suggestions. One was to set off twelve bombs in New York at once, with two reserved to target Dov Hikind, a Jewish member of the city council, and Judge Alvin Schlesinger, who had sentenced Nosair to more than seven years in prison. Another plan Nosair pushed for was the kidnapping of Richard Nixon or Henry Kissinger. Either hostage, he thought, would be an excellent chip in bargaining for the release of the World Trade Center conspirators who had been arrested: Nidal Ayyad, Mohammed Salameh, and Mahmud Abouhalima, the last of whom had been captured in Egypt and tortured before being handed over to the United States.

Siddiq Ali was thinking bigger. He wanted massive, paralyzing attacks. Boom, boom, boom, he would say, and America is on standby. Pick the right targets, and the damage would overwhelm the country. He was not alone in wanting to bring his adoptive nation to its knees—members of the circle had been talking about carrying out their "jihad business" for years. Ibrahim el-Gabrowny, a cousin of Nosair's, wanted to play his part. So did Clement Hampton-El, the African American convert who had traveled to fight in Afghanistan and been wounded in the leg. So did a handful of the others.

When a proposal was brought to him, though, the sheikh became nervous. He feared government surveillance and spoke cryptically. (Among themselves the jihadists spoke about the dangers posed by the "Food and Beverage Industry.") As one of the group would explain, however, "dealings with the sheikh should be only in headlines. The details, he has nothing do with it. This is the sheikh's system. You ask him what is lawful and what is forbidden." His approval would constitute a fatwa, a religious ruling, but there would be no piece of paper, sometimes no more than a muffled signal. Consulting Rahman was a requirement of the faith for the plotters. It also reaffirmed his role—he had done this before in Egypt and, it seems almost certain, before the World Trade Center bombing.

In May 1993 he was asked: Would the United Nations be an illicit target? The strike, he was assured, would be devastating, far more effective than the World Trade Center attack.

"It is not illicit," Rahman replied. "However, will be bad for Muslims. . . . Do inflict damage, inflict damage [but] on the American Army itself."

What about blowing up the New York FBI headquarters, at 26 Federal Plaza?

He hesitated. The timing was bad, just months after the World Trade Center.

But the plan, his followers said, was ready.

"Slow," he responded. Do it, but not just yet.

—

The men not only recognized the sheikh's authority; they had drunk deeply of his rhetoric. They believed, as he did, that there was only one way to rectify the indignities that had befallen the world's Muslims. As he said in a speech in early 1993:

There is no solution for our problems except jihad for the sake of God. . . . There's no solution, there's no treatment, there's no medicine, there's no cure except with what was brought by the Islamic method which is jihad for the sake of God. . . . No, if those who have the right to have something are terrorists then we are terrorists. And we welcome being terrorists. And we do not deny this charge to our-selves. And the Koran makes it, terrorism, among the means to per-form jihad in the sake of Allah, which is to terrorize the enemies of God and who are our enemies, too.

This jihad, Rahman would say, was not a matter of prayer and discus-sion but of bullets and bombs.

They say that he who leaves his job during the day in order to go to the mosque has performed jihad. And he who listens to a religious lecture has performed jihad. What is this? This is distortion to the subject of jihad. Praying, listening, jihad? . . . Coming to the mosques is a good work. And group praying is just praying. Jihad is fighting the enemies. Fighting the enemies for God's sake in order to raise them high in his word. . . . We don't fight our enemy unless we have guns, tanks and airplanes equal to those of the Soviet Union.

About real weapons, however, Siddiq Ali and the rest knew little. Only Emad Salem had experience with arms and explosives. The former Egyp-tian officer had become part of the group in 1991, when he met some of the others at Nosair's trial. As he got to know the jihad circle, he im-pressed them with talk of his military experience as a sniper and com-mando. While driving to a conference in Detroit, he told Sheikh Rahman that he was a mujahid, a holy warrior, because he had fought the Israelis in the 1973 war. And he endured it when Rahman sneered at him, saying that he was no mujahid because he had fought for the infidel government of Egypt. How, Salem asked, could he redeem himself? Turn the barrel of your gun on Mubarak—the Egyptian president—replied the sheikh. He is a tyrant and the "loyal dog of the Americans."

Salem put up with the derision for a reason: the FBI paid him to. He had attended the Nosair trial at the Bureau's behest. He became a mem-ber of the Blind Sheikh's court and, except for a few months, had been a regular informant on the group. In the latter half of 1992 and early 1993,

Salem's relationship with the Bureau was suspended. In part, this happened because he warned agents that he did not ever want to testify, perhaps because he believed it would make him the target of people whom he feared. In part, too, it appears that the Bureau lost interest. If so, the agents who handled him showed poor timing; the period when he went off the payroll coincided with the World Trade Center bombing conspiracy.

Salem was a habitual liar: he told the woman who would become his wife that he had been not only the head of security for the Egyptian president but also a senior official in military intelligence, and that he been wounded in combat. None of it was true; he had most recently been a security guard at the high-end department store Bergdorf Goodman and an engineer at a New York Best Western hotel.[4] Even so, he would insist later on the witness stand that he had warned the Bureau about the plot against the World Trade Center. "It takes a bomb with you guys to wake up and start to move," FBI documents after the attack quoted him as saying to agents.

TERRSTOP, the FBI's name for its operation to stop terrorists in the aftermath of the first World Trade Center attack, was not quite ABSCAM for jihadists, but it was not far off. Salem was the catalyst; without him, the conspiracy would not have gotten off the ground. He provided a safe house in Queens—which the Bureau wired for video surveillance—and made the work plan for building fuel-fertilizer bombs. Together with Siddiq Ali and another conspirator, Amir Abdelgani, a Sudanese driver for a medical delivery service, he surveyed targets, the list of which continually lengthened. The heart of the plan involved destroying the Lincoln and Holland Tunnels, and the conspirators visited them repeatedly to decide where they would park their car bombs and how they would escape in other vehicles, which would be following in another lane. They considered attacking the George Washington Bridge but were unsure of what was needed to bring it down. They scouted stores in midtown Manhattan's Diamond District, whose jewelry retailers and wholesalers are mostly Jewish. The FBI building remained a priority, as did the UN, where Siddiq Ali was making arrangements with an official from the Sudanese mission to get access to the garage.

As the roster of targets lengthened, so did the number of participants. Fares Khallafalla, a young man whose mother described him as "beginning to live the American dream," purchased timers and fertilizers and tried to buy stolen cars for use as bomb vehicles. Mohammed Saleh, a Bronx gas station owner, was enlisted to provide 255 gallons of diesel fuel to mix with the fertilizer. Victor Alvarez, a Puerto Rican convert to Islam who was borderline retarded and a habitual cocaine user, was given the job of procuring a machine gun so the group could fend off police who might try to stop the bomb-laden cars on the way to their destinations. In all, eleven men, including the Blind Sheikh, would eventually be counted as coconspirators.

The preparations in the Queens safe house began in June. As more individuals joined the circle, Siddiq Ali pumped them up. "One billion Muslims," he said, "did not see any action" when the World Trade Center was bombed. The attack was supposed to reverse the world hierarchy and bring the mighty low. But instead "America which [was] hit, became the God of the infidels and liars instead of God the almighty." This plan would be different. "You want to hit something which will paralyze the economy. . . . You bring it to the lowest level."

As they prepared to build the bombs, they bought bags of Scott's Super Turf Builder—probably not what they needed. Though the target list remained nebulous, they began mixing fuel and fertilizer on June 23, 1993. Then the FBI agents burst in.

—

When the case came to court, El-Sayyid Nosair was included among the indictees, all of whom were charged with the unusual crime of seditious conspiracy. Many faced a variety of other counts as well. Among those against Nosair were federal charges for the killing of Meir Kahane.

Through much of the eight-month-long trial, an attorney who sat near him recalls, Nosair paid little attention to the proceedings and occupied

himself by drawing. The man whose sister said he found America morally
deficient drew portrait after portrait of one person: Princess Diana.

BOJINKA

It was a pillar of smoke, like a sign from the Bible, that led the police
to a sixth-floor apartment in the Josefa Building on President Quirino
Avenue. What they found at three A.M. on January 7, 1995, in the one-
bedroom flat above the teeming streets of Manila Bay was not the remains
of a typical kitchen fire.

The firemen had just left, but in the still smoky apartment the police
officers immediately noticed a large cauldron by the sink and an assortment of bottles and jugs. In the bedroom, they found a table covered
with an assortment of Bibles, crucifixes, vestments, pictures of Pope John
Paul II, and Casio timers. On the bedside tables they saw wristwatches
with wires attached to them, and a soldering iron. The pope, the police
knew, would be staying just a couple of hundred yards away, at the nun-
cio's residence on Taft Avenue, when he visited the Philippines in less
than two weeks. Rummaging around the kitchen, they found sections of
pipe. They opened a couple of juice bottles sitting on the counter, sniffed
them, and winced in pain at the noxious odor. The kitchen, they recognized, was a bomb factory. They swept up documents, papers, and a laptop computer that was next to the living room couch. They summoned
their experts to look at the makeshift lab, then they called the Americans.

When word of the apartment fire reached Washington, the religious
articles raised concern. But if there had been a plot to assassinate the
pope, the fire and the scattering of those in the flat had probably disrupted it. Other material seized suggested that something else was going
on. At first, counterterrorism officials were puzzled by a piece of paper
with a series of numbers that no one could figure out. Someone in the
FAA security office finally put it together: the numbers were a sequence of
flights from a listing in an out-of-date *Official Airline Guide*. When computer experts finally cracked some of the coded and encrypted files on the

laptop, the broad outlines of a plot were confirmed: the plan was called Bojinka, and it called for blowing as many as twelve U.S. 747s out of the skies over the Pacific. United Airlines, Delta, and Northwest flights out of Manila, Tokyo, Singapore, Bangkok, Taipei, and Seoul were all targeted. To officials who had been through the bombing of Pan Am 103 and a litany of other terrorist attacks, the plan was staggering, and the shock was magnified by the revelation that the laptop belonged to Ramzi Yousef. Clever enough to elude an international dragnet for two years after the World Trade Center bombing, Yousef, they knew, would not hesitate to kill four thousand people.

The roll of major airplane bombings can be counted on two hands. In the Pan Am 103 case, the most famous, Libyan dictator Moamar Qadhafi's intelligence service had doomed 259 passengers and crew members and eleven more people on the ground. Yousef's plan aimed to reduce that tragedy to a footnote. In the fifty-five years since World War II, there had been wars in Korea, Vietnam, and Iraq, and scores of hurricanes and earthquakes. But there was never a day on which four thousand people, Americans or foreigners under U.S. sovereignty, died a violent death.

As fast as they could make the phone calls, FAA officials used their emergency authority to order up virtually every pertinent security measure in the book at West Coast and Asian airports. From the evidence in the Manila flat, it was impossible to be sure that some bomb kits had not already been assembled and distributed. Takeoffs were delayed while emergency inspections were carried out. A United Airlines aircraft from Bangkok was turned around in midflight because of fears that a device might be on board. No one could say who or where the bombers were. No one knew when the attacks were to start or how to stop them.

—

To prevent a plane from being bombed, nothing is more important than knowing what the explosive device looks like. Nothing from the apartment shed any light on this. The Philippine government was being helpful, but, fearful that bad news might imperil the pope's trip, it was carefully controlling the flow of information to the Americans. The FBI sent a group of agents to meet with senior police officials in Manila. At an initial briefing, the Filipinos told them that it looked like "an Abu Sayyaf type attack," referring to the radical Islamist group in the Philippines, that, among other targets, attacked Catholic churches and clergy.

In the hope of shaking some information loose, the FAA had also dispatched to Manila one of its small cadre of bomb technicians. Cal Walbert sat through the formal briefing the Filipinos had put on. While the FBI agents continued to work through official channels, waiting for the government to show them more, Walbert looked up an acquaintance, a Filipino police major and bomb tech with whom he had worked on a case six years earlier. Walbert asked the major if he could meet with the bomb squad from Manila's Western Police District, which had combed through the Josefa apartment but whose findings had not been made available to the FBI. When they arrived at the station, he asked the squad commander whether any fusing system had been found. The policeman opened his desk drawer and, as if to say, "You mean this?," pulled out one of the Casios with wires attached.

"Really impressive" was the way Walbert described the fusing system. He had rarely seen anything so ingenious.

The next day, together with the FBI, he compiled an inventory of the chemicals from the apartment and saw some of the other materials that had been gathered up—batteries, two-pin connectors, the juice bottles, and an empty bottle of contact lens solution. Then he figured out the bomb assembly, called FAA headquarters, and described it to another explosives expert. At a White House meeting of counterterrorism officials, Irish Flynn, the retired Navy admiral who headed FAA security, held up a schematic, to the astonishment of those assembled.

———

Ramzi had improved. During the two years since the World Trade Center bombing, he had studied texts on chemistry and explosives. Working in the apartment, he had synthesized TATP, triacetonetriperoxide and nitroglycerin, and he also appeared to be making nitrocellulose, otherwise known as gun cotton. A favorite of Palestinian terrorists, TATP is a highly sensitive explosive; anyone carrying it would run the risk of blowing himself up. In fact, no one had ever dared use it on a plane. Nitroglycerin was even more dangerous. In addition, the overall assembly was an unrivaled piece of terrorist tradecraft: with only negligible amounts of metal and no high-density materials, it would be all but impossible to detect using any existing security system. Once the design was clear, the counterterrorism experts began piecing together Yousef's method, and they realized with horror that he had already tested and perfected his system.

A month earlier, a bomb had exploded on a Philippine Air Lines 747 flying from Manila to Tokyo, killing a Japanese businessman. Although the blast damaged the plane's hydraulic system, the aircraft managed a safe emergency landing on Okinawa. Photographs of the dead man's butterflied torso looked like something out of a supermarket tabloid and left American analysts dumbfounded. There was no claim of responsibility and the killing bore no trademarks of known terrorists. The counterterrorism experts reasoned that either the passenger had been singled out for assassination, or one of the Philippines' many rebel groups was sending some kind of message to Manila. With no obvious U.S. angle, the event received little further attention.

Now the mutilated torso made sense. Japanese authorities had been studying the PAL craft and reported finding fragments of a Casio watch, wiring, and the container that held the explosive: a plastic bottle. Yousef, it turned out, had been on the flight, the explosive smuggled aboard in his hand luggage. From interviews with flight attendants, it became clear that he had assembled the bomb in the bathroom during the first leg of the trip, taped it under a seat, and disembarked during a stopover on the Philippine island of Cebu. Haruki Ikegami, the Japanese businessman, had the misfortune to sit in the seat Yousef had left. Yousef had used a small charge, to avoid destroying the plane and arousing too much interest. He only wanted to verify that his device worked. The size of the blast surprised even him.[5]

In the Manila apartment, three complete fusing devices had been found but so had receipts for components for several more. The stock of chemicals suggested that a number of bombs might already have been produced and distributed to Yousef's operatives, who, the laptop showed, intended to hopscotch from one flight to another around the Pacific. The Casios could be programmed for a time and date *three years* in the future.

———

To intercept a bomb of this kind, the aviation authorities' only hope was to keep every bottle, jar, and can off planes that might be targeted. Nothing like this had ever been done before. In mid-January, the FAA fired off a set of security directives ordering the most extensive baggage searches ever and confiscation of all containers. The sole exception was made for bottles of infant formula. Passengers departing from Australia could only hope that their $100 bottles of Shiraz and Cabernet would catch up with them later. Since the bombs might already be on board with timers set, work crews began turning aircraft inside out, ripping out life preservers by the thousand. Fear that the security measures would prompt the bombers to plant their devices aboard foreign airliners flying to America out of the designated airports prompted the FAA and its counterparts to apply the same standards to those planes as well. In the White House, there was discussion of extending the directives to a broader area.

For three weeks, aviation authorities in the United States and Asia-Pacific hectored and cajoled airline officials, demanding that they push their people to unprecedented levels of vigilance and intrusiveness, and industry executives, who could seldom remember the authorities being so agitated, responded. For all the effort, the FAA's leaders feared they were racing the clock and bound to lose, that the collective adrenaline level was unsustainable, airport personnel would tire of the drill, and Yousef might come up with a stratagem for defeating the countermeasures. Meanwhile, the international search for Yousef and his accomplices became one of the most intensive manhunts ever.

In early February, U.S. investigators caught a break. An operative whom Ramzi had only recently signed up had come to the Bangkok airport. Instead of getting on board a plane, though, he planned to deliver his package for air shipment. The aviation security people had foreseen the possibility and sent out a directive requesting that packages brought directly to the airlines for shipment be unwrapped and examined. As the operative watched the security people work their way through the packages, he thought about what he was doing. He turned around and left the airport, went back to his apartment, and poured the explosive down the drain. He then provided the tip that led to Ramzi Yousef.

On February 7, 1995, in Islamabad, a hastily assembled team of all the American officials in town who could handle weapons and kick down doors joined up with Pakistani special forces. They converged on the Su-Casa Guest House, one of a number of B&Bs in a neighborhood filled with the residences of foreign diplomats, representatives of international organizations, and journalists. They burst into Room 16 and apprehended Yousef. The team raced to an airstrip, hustled him on to a waiting jet, and flew him to the United States to stand trial for the World Trade Center bombing and the Bojinka conspiracy.

Even with Ramzi out of action, the FAA could not breathe easy. Bombs and operatives remained unaccounted for. Several months passed before they allowed security procedures to return gradually to normal at most Asian airports; in Manila, many of the most stringent measures were retained.

Astonishingly, the intense security and lengthy delays at airports elicited little interest from the press. Secret briefings on Capitol Hill had been so hair-raisingly effective that not a single congressional staffer succumbed to the temptation to call a reporter.

Ramzi was finished, but where that thread stopped, another became visible. The Bojinka investigation yielded a clue to the recent appearance of outsize terrorist conspiracies. Among the papers found in the Josefa apartment was a business card belonging to Mohammed Jamal Khalifa, a Saudi "businessman" and a brother-in-law of Usama bin

Laden. Khalifa, it turned out, had paid for the apartment on President Quirino Avenue.

A serendipitous mishap, a plume of smoke—these were all that stood in the way of an airborne massacre that would have eclipsed decades of terrorist attacks combined.

THE EMBASSIES

The phone traffic was constant on February 22, 1998. First, a call would come from the satellite phone in Afghanistan. Then, after he finished that conversation, Khalid al-Fawaz would dial a local number in London, the offices of *al-Quds al-Arabi,* an Arabic-language daily. Then Afghanistan would call again. The back-and-forth began before noon and did not end until just about six in the evening, when *al-Quds* called the three-digit regional prefix and the thirteen-digit satellite phone number directly. The newspaper staffer spent half an hour on the line taking dictation.

Satellite phones and journalism have gone hand in hand since before the Gulf War, when an army of reporters lugging INMARSATs descended on Saudi Arabia and Iraq. But no journalist's copy had ridden a signal into the sky and back to earth like the one printed in *al-Quds* on the twenty-third. The piece was actually not a story but a fatwa. It declared that "to kill the Americans and their allies—civilians and military—is an individual duty for every Muslim who can do it in any country in which it is possible to do it." Usama bin Laden had bought his satellite phone a year earlier, just after moving to Afghanistan, a country with no reliable telecommunications.[6]

The transmission of the fatwa, the "Declaration of Jihad Against Jews and Crusaders," marked the beginning of the final stage of an operation wholly worthy of the global age. Most of the surveillance photos and diagrams had been stored on computer disks for several years. The group had had a presence on the ground in Nairobi since 1992, a sort of offshore subsidiary, with proven, secure channels for moving money and identification documents from phony charitable organizations that gave its people an ostensible reason for being in the city. The operatives' morale was high; each of them knew his role. A sleeper cell in the coastal city of Mombasa waited to be awakened for service. A year earlier, when the al-Qaeda leadership issued the order to "militarize" its cells in East Africa, Harun Fazil, the Comoran islander who was effectively in charge of the Nairobi cell, responded with a memo that said, "We, the East Africa crew, do not want to know how work plans are operated because we are not fit for plans. We are just implementers. We, thanks be to God, trust our command and appreciate their work. . . . But the advice here is for work purposes only, because this work we are doing, the return of an Islamic state, is a team effort and not an individual one; we are all participating in it."

The plans for bombing the American embassies in Nairobi and the Tanzanian capital Dar es Salaam were known respectively as Operation Kaaba, after the cubic structure at the center of the Grand Mosque in Mecca, the holiest site of Islam, and Operation al-Aqsa, after the mosque in Jerusalem that is the faith's third holiest spot. As preparations entered their final phases, a constellation of different cells, regional offices spread across half the globe, lit up with activity, each with designated tasks. The hub was in Afghanistan, where bin Laden's peripatetic entourage and phalanx of technicians worked out the plans and chose the teams. The cells in Baku, the capital of Azerbaijan, and London would handle communications and publicity. Nairobi was the key point of production and delivery; locations in Germany, Yemen, and elsewhere would play supporting roles. And, like a team from McKinsey or Boston Consulting, a traveling group of experts would descend upon Nairobi and Dar to oversee the management of critical parts of the process.

Among them, Sheikh Ahmad Salim Swedan took charge of acquiring the bomb vehicles. In Nairobi, he bought a pickup, a Toyota Dyna, and in Dar es Salaam, a Nissan Atlas. Swedan oversaw modifications of the vehicles, such as having a metal frame welded onto the back of the Nissan to hold the bomb. In both purchases, he handed over the money immediately but never showed again to complete paperwork. Abdel Rahman, an

Egyptian with long experience in Afghanistan and Somalia, was bomb-maker-in-chief. He handled the parallel processes in Nairobi and Dar of assembling large quantities of dynamite, which were ground into a powder and repacked in large crates.* In the Dar es Salaam bomb, oxygen tanks were tied to the device to provide fragmentation, shrapnel to kill more people, while in Nairobi, aluminum was used to enhance the blast. The charge to detonate the explosives would come from heavy-duty batteries for truck lights. Abdel Rahman made certain that the wiring was done correctly—through holes drilled in the back wall of the cab to a button on the dashboard.

—

After the publication of the fatwa, the operatives who would deliver the bombs were also chosen. These would be suicide attacks or, in the parlance of the group, "martyrdom operations." Men would drive the vehicles carrying the bombs to the targets, getting as close as they could, and then hit the detonator. In Dar es Salaam, two men would drive from the bomb factory, House 213 in the Illala District, but the passenger would get out after a short distance and return to the house to clean up the evidence. In Nairobi, both men in the truck would drive all the way to the embassy. When they got there, the passenger would jump out and brandish a gun at the guards at the embassy gate and demand they open it. Once the barrier was raised, the vehicle could pull up alongside the building.

The men who took on these missions believed that they were performing heroic acts for their faith. Those who devised the plans may have believed that great rewards awaited the bombers, but their reliance on suicide attacks was based on cost-benefit analyses. As one of bin Laden's closest aides wrote recently, "The method of martyrdom operations [is] the most successful way of inflicting damage against the opponent and the

---

* The grinding of the dynamite would later mystify experts, since it likely diminished the yield of the bombs.

least costly to the mujahidin in terms of casualities."[7] In this case, that meant that if the driver stayed with the truck bomb, moving it as close to the target as possible, the attack would maximize the number of casualties. The driver himself would not be around afterward to name accomplices, minimizing the damage to the organization.

The future martyrs were chosen from the ranks of the training camps. Mohammed al-Owhali, a Saudi from a wealthy family, came to Afghanistan in 1996 and studied explosives and the use of various weapons in the camps. He had excelled and been presented more than once to bin Laden. Once he asked the Saudi for a jihad mission but never heard anything further. Around March 1998 another Saudi in the Afghan camps named Azzam approached al-Owhali and asked him if he was still interested in a mission. He said that he was. The two were sent to a facility outside of Kabul for an additional month's training. Afterward, they were ordered to Yemen to lie low for a while. In the summer, they were recalled to Afghanistan and informed about the details of the operation. They made videotapes, farewell statements about their dedication to the cause of jihad, and flew from Pakistan to Kenya at the beginning of August. Less is known about the Dar es Salaam driver, an Egyptian named Hamdan Khalif Alal—he was called "Ahmed the German" because of his fair hair— except that he had been a trainer in one of the camps and turned up in the Tanzanian capital at the beginning of August.

On August 7, 1998—the eighth anniversary of the arrival of American troops in Saudi Arabia, where they were sent to defend the kingdom against Iraq—the execution of the plot went almost exactly as planned. Before the trucks had even left the bomb factories, the press rollout of the event began, as the al-Qaeda cell in Azerbaijan faxed a claim of responsibility to London for the cell there to distribute. Just after 10:30 in the morning, al-Owhali and Azzam drove into the back parking lot of the U.S. embassy in Nairobi. Al-Owhali jumped out of the pickup. He threw homemade grenades at the guards, but he had left his gun in the truck, and they ran away, leaving the gate down. Azzam started firing al-Owhali's gun from the vehicle. Al-Owhali was supposed to stay near the truck, but he decided that he had performed his task, and that to stay would not be martyrdom but suicide, so he turned and ran. Azzam detonated the bomb at 10:35. In Dar es Salaam, Ahmed the German did the same four minutes later.

For the terrorists, it was a triumph of management and just-in-time-production. No one had ever staged a double truck bombing in which the targets were separated by hundreds of miles. Al-Qaeda did not kill as many Americans as it hoped to—twelve died in Nairobi, none in Dar es Salaam. But the group achieved the dramatic overall boost in productivity it had sought, killing 213 in Kenya and 11 in Tanzania, and wounding roughly 5,000 in the two capitals. Bin Laden had shown himself to be every bit as much a figure of the era of globalization as Davos Man.

THE MILLENNIUM AND THE U.S.S. *COLE*

Success breeds complexity. After the East Africa bombings—and with the ripely symbolic millennium approaching—al-Qaeda was determined to up the ante, launch more coordinated attacks, and prove more forcefully to the Muslim world that the United States could be bloodied. Operational planning became baroque. In preparing global fireworks for the global holiday, conspiracies were nestled one inside the other. The leadership in Afghanistan sought to exploit the jihadist networks in several countries to carry out attacks over a span not of several hundred miles, as in August 1998, but several thousand.

The centerpiece would be in Jordan, which would underscore that bin Laden's fight was not just with the United States but with Christians, Jews, and the moderate regimes of the Muslim world. The four-hundred-room Radisson Hotel in Amman was booked for the holidays. Most of the guests would be Americans, Christians coming to visit biblical sites. Israelis, still enjoying the brief political warming in the Middle East, would also be staying in the hotel. For al-Qaeda, the hotel was an irresistible target. A large Jordanian cell—nearly thirty members, many of Palestinian origin—that was affiliated with the network plotted the bombing.

The group laid the groundwork for a series of secondary attacks, and the targets bespeak an effort to wipe out, so far as possible, nonbelievers in the country on the two thousandth anniversary of the Christian era. The cell had a stock of firearms and intended to use them at Mount Nebo, where Moses is said to have glimpsed the Promised Land before dying. A site on the Jordan River associated with John the Baptist was slated for a similar attack. The group considered hitting two of the border crossings with Israel as well. Taken together, the explosions and gunfire would be worthy of a coup. The impact on Jordan, a country known in the region for its close ties to the United States, would be punishing and, perhaps, destabilizing.

To the south, across the Arabian peninsula in Yemen, preparations for another attack were in the making. American warships had recently started refueling in Aden. In early January, the U.S.S. *The Sullivans,* an Arleigh Burke–class destroyer, one of America's most sophisticated vessels, was scheduled to arrive. A Yemeni cell was getting ready to greet the destroyer with a skiff laden with explosives. The cell had a cache of military-grade materials and was fabricating a shaped charge, which would direct the blast at the armored hull instead of dissipating energy in all directions.

Finally, more than seven thousand miles away, a graduate of the Khalden camp, Ramzi Yousef's alma mater, readied himself in Canada for a trip to the United States. Ahmad Ressam was typical of the Algerians who had migrated to Afghanistan and a contrast with the more educated Saudis and Egyptians. He had been an illegal immigrant in France and then moved to Montreal, where he lived off theft and welfare. In addition to the usual training, he spent six weeks in the advanced explosives course at the Derunta camp, outside Jalalabad. There he and his classmates experimented with chemical agents. They put dogs into enclosed areas, then introduced a mixture of cyanide and sulfuric acid to see how quickly the animals died. Ressam returned to Montreal with orders to carry out an operation and $12,000 for expenses. His local network of Algerian compatriots provided additional funding and a fake passport, and he began purchasing chemicals and circuit boards with which to build a bomb. His target—or at least, his first one—would be Los Angeles International Airport.

For all its many subplots, the millennium conspiracy was not uncoordinated. All the lines of activity converged in the hands of one man, a young Palestinian living in Peshawar whose nom de guerre was Abu Zubayda. Among his many responsibilities, Abu Zubayda acted as an admissions officer for the training camps, which was how he came to know Ressam. In an organization that carefully restricted the flow of information to those with a need to know, he was one of the few who knew a great deal.

Abu Zubayda's many talents, however, were not equal to the vigilance of the Jordanian authorities, whose anxieties had increased after the 1998 embassy bombings. In the summer of 1999, the Jordanians were certain that a plot was in train. They identified several suspects for surveillance, and they were listening when Abu Zubayda gave his contact in Amman the order to carry out the attacks.[8] The Jordanians raided the group's safe house on the outskirts of Amman and were shocked to find a subterranean cache of chemicals: seventy-one large containers of sulfuric acid and nitric acid, enough to flatten the Radisson.

News of the discovery electrified intelligence and law-enforcement personnel around the world. Heightened alertness paid off in Port Angeles, Washington, where the ferry from British Columbia docks: a customs official decided to search the rental car of a nervous-looking Ahmad Ressam. In the trunk were found more than a hundred pounds of bomb-making materials.

The Yemeni cell was undone—briefly—by its own mistakes. The operatives stowed their explosives aboard their skiff and began motoring out into the harbor. But they had overloaded their boat. Before they could get close to their target, the skiff began to sink. They managed to save the boat, and the sight of two men struggling in the water seems to have caught no one's notice.

But this failure was not too dispiriting for the terrorists. Ten months later, the same plan, though this time with a lighter load, was used to attack the U.S.S. *Cole*. The bombing killed seventeen U.S. seamen and tore a hole forty feet high and forty feet wide through the half-inch-thick steel of the ship's hull, nearly sinking it.

SEPTEMBER 11

I will surely cast him [the unbeliever] into the Fire. Would that you knew what the fire is like! It leaves nothing, it spares no one; it burns the skins of men. It is guarded by nineteen keepers.

We have appointed none but angels to guard the Fire, and made their number a subject for dispute among the unbelievers, so that those to whom the Scriptures were given may be convinced and the true believers strengthened in their faith.

—QURAN, SURA 74: 30–31

Between 7:55 and 8:42 in the morning, the four planes took off from East Coast airports. Divided among them were nineteen hijackers. There were fifteen Saudi Arabians, two Emiratis, one Lebanese, and, leading them all, an Egyptian, Muhammad Atta.

American Airlines Flight 11 struck the north face of the north tower, WTC 1, hitting the ninety-fourth through ninety-eighth floors at 8:46 A.M. while traveling 470 miles per hour. The Boeing 767-200, which took off from Boston, was carrying ninety-two people and some ten thousand gallons of jet fuel.[9]

United Airlines Flight 175 struck the south face of the south tower, WTC 2, at 9:02 A.M., going 586 miles per hour, well beyond what it was designed for at that altitude—so fast that had the plane not hit the building, it might have broken up. The impact came between the seventy-eighth and eighty-fourth floors. The aircraft, also a Boeing 767-200 flying out of Boston, had sixty-five people and about ten thousand gallons of jet fuel aboard.

The energy stored in the jet fuel from the two planes was the equiva-

lent of 240 tons of dynamite. To put that in perspective, the United States
military possesses tactical nuclear weapons—artillery shells—that can be
calibrated to deliver this explosive yield of nearly a quarter of a kiloton. Of
course, the attacks did not cause any radioactive fallout, but the energy release was nonetheless extraordinary, off the charts of comparison with all
other terrorist attacks. The bomb that was used to destroy Khobar Towers, the U.S. military housing complex attacked in 1996, is believed by
law-enforcement officials to be probably the biggest ever. Its yield was the
equivalent of two and a half tons of TNT, roughly one one-hundredth as
powerful as the two planes.

The airplanes did not explode like bombs. A fraction of a second after
each one hit, a fireball erupted and expanded for two seconds, consuming
some of the jet fuel. The rest of the burning fuel swept across the floors of
the building, igniting intense fires that engulfed the office furnishings.
Temperatures reached between 1,700 and 2,000 degrees Fahrenheit. Reports said the blaze gave off heat estimated to be "comparable to that produced by a large nuclear generating station." In the northeast corner of
WTC 2, where the hurtling plane had shoveled office equipment as it
plowed through the structure, molten metal streamed down the side of
the building.

—

At 9:40, American Airlines Flight 77 hit the west side of the Pentagon.
The Boeing 757 with sixty-five people aboard had departed from nearby
Dulles Airport and started out on its route to Los Angeles before turning
around and heading back toward Washington. The plane blasted a hole
five stories high and two hundred feet wide, killing 189 people.[10]

—

The World Trade Center was built to withstand enormous stresses, including the pressure of hurricane winds against its vast faces. One can
only speculate, but it is possible that the person behind the controls of
Flight 175 accelerated the speed of the plane so dramatically because he

knew that the building could withstand the impact of a somewhat smaller plane, a 707. He could have known this because the civil engineer in charge of the construction of the Twin Towers, Leslie Robertson, had said as much in the trial of the first group of conspirators arrested for the 1993 bombing. Traveling about 25 percent faster than Flight 11, the plane that hit the south tower probably released about 50 percent more energy on impact.[11] The collision caused tremendous structural damage, destroying about thirty of the fifty-nine columns on the perimeter of the south face of the building.

The towers had considerable redundancy built into them—the load on the destroyed columns shifted to others. Had the impact of the plane been the only trauma to the buildings, they would probably be standing today. The heat of the fires, however, doomed them. The metal framing of the floors, the joists and trusses that connected them to the buildings' tubular perimeter construction, expanded in the heat, creating additional stress on the structure. Some columns may have buckled. Each floor of the building, a steel plate about an acre large covered with four inches of concrete on top, weighed about 3.2 million pounds. On about the eightieth floor of the south tower, in the corner where the molten metal ran down the side, there was a partial collapse. The weight of the falling floor caused the one below to give way, and then the one below that. The building came down in ten seconds. The impact of the 500,000-ton structure's fall registered on seismographs as 2.1 on the Richter scale and was felt by instruments more than 250 miles away.

—

At 10:10 A.M., the fourth plane, United Airlines Flight 93, crashed in a field in Shanksville, Pennsylvania, eighty miles southeast of Pittsburgh. The 757, carrying forty-five people, had been scheduled for an 8:00 A.M. takeoff from Newark Airport, but a forty-minute delay put the hijackers behind schedule, and passengers learned of the attacks on the World Trade Center through cell-phone conversations. In the ensuing struggle between the passengers and hijackers, the plane went down,

killing everyone aboard. The hijackers' target was reportedly the White
House.

—

The north tower began to collapse at 10:28, much as the south tower had.
It had survived for 102 minutes after being struck. About 99 percent of
those who were below the floors hit by the aircraft in both buildings were
safely evacuated. Only a handful from above the impact zone in the south
tower survived; none did from the upper reaches of the north tower. The
heroism of the firemen, police, building staff, and ordinary citizens on
September 11 has justifiably been recounted by every newspaper, and by
every radio and television broadcaster in the country. Two thousand eight
hundred and one people are believed to have died in the World Trade
Center. No one knows how many were evacuated from the buildings. But
if one reckons that the towers typically had forty thousand or more people working inside during the day—not counting visitors—then the number of lives saved was extraordinary. It was possible to save them because
the buildings themselves held up for as long as they did—longer than
most structures would have. The construction of the towers turned out to
be heroic in its own way.

Almost immediately after the attacks, the site where the World Trade
Center had stood became known as Ground Zero. Curiously, it went un-
noted that throughout the Cold War, Ground Zero was widely considered to be the Pentagon, the mostly likely target for a Soviet missile in a
nuclear exchange. A café in the Pentagon courtyard was even named
Ground Zero.

Of course, the Soviets were deterred; the terrorists of al-Qaeda were
not. In picking targets, those who planned the attacks took on the greatest symbols of American military, political, and economic power. Yet by
concentrating their weaponry—our planes—on the World Trade Center,
they moved the bull's-eye of the nation from the headquarters of the U.S.
armed forces to icons of economic and, more important, civilian life. Why
did the terrorists pick the World Trade Center as their foremost target?

The simplest reason is much like the classic one given for the toppling of the Tower of Babel: the Twin Towers and the civilization they represent are an unforgivable challenge to the sovereignty of heaven. Unlike the God of the Old Testament, however, al-Qaeda considered rectifying the moral order a human task.

CHAPTER 2

IBN TAYMIYYA AND HIS CHILDREN

When the trumpet of the Last Judgement sounds the dead all rise from their graves and rush to the Field of Judgement "like men rallying to a Standard." There they take up their station before God, in two mighty crowds separated from each other, the faithful on one side and the unbelieving on the other; and each individual is judged by God. . . .

The bi-partition of the crowd in Islam is unconditional. The faithful and the unbelieving are fated to be separate for ever and to fight each other. The war of religion is a sacred duty and thus, though in a less comprehensive form, the double crowd of the Last Judgement is prefigured in every earthly battle.

—ELIAS CANETTI, *Crowds and Power*[1]

SPEAKING TO THE AMERICAN PEOPLE and listeners around the world in his January 2002 State of the Union Address, President George W. Bush capped his discussion of the nation's new and unexpected war on terrorism by saying: "The enemy of America is not our many Muslim friends; it is not our many Arab friends. Our enemy is a radical network of terrorists, and every government that supports them. We are not deceived by their pretenses to piety."

They are not imbued with the spirit of religion, these terrorists, they only claim to be. The President's message echoed sentiments heard throughout the country in the aftermath of the attacks of September 11, 2001. The destruction of the World Trade Center, the crash into the Pentagon, and the killings aboard four hijacked planes could not have been the work of men who earnestly saw themselves fulfilling God's wishes—they could not be adherents of any of the world's three great monotheistic faiths. Bush returned to the theme repeatedly. "The terrorists are defined by their hatreds: they hate democracy and tolerance and free expression and women and Jews and Christians and all Muslims who disagree with them," he told the members of the German Bundestag during his visit to Berlin in May. "Others killed in the name of racial purity, or the class struggle. These enemies kill in the name of a false religious purity, perverting the faith they claim to hold."

These were words of condemnation but also of reassurance. To millions of American Muslims, the fastest-growing religious community in the country, they sent a message of solidarity and understanding at a time of harassment and alienation. In Germany and other European countries with proportionally larger Muslim populations, they helped calm domestic tensions. To U.S. friends abroad from the Maghreb to Indonesia, they signaled American respect for Islam at a moment when governments friendly to Washington were under fire from large parts of their citizenry, which believed America gave Muslims second-class treatment. For all three audiences, one point was crucial: America was declaring—and rightly—that the vast majority of the world's Muslims should not be tarred with the deeds of the hijackers. These acknowledgments were important not only for atmospherics, but to enable foreign governments to sustain law-enforcement and intelligence cooperation with the United States in the fight against the new breed of terrorists.

There were other benefits to the President's rhetoric, but the sum of all these virtues is not the same as the truth. For the fact is that the attack against America on September 11, 2001, was an act of consummate religious devotion. Those who committed it were deeply pious.

They expressed their motives in indisputably religious terms, and they saw themselves as carrying out the will of God. "Consider that this is a raid on a path," Muhammad Atta wrote in the document that he and his coconspirators used as a kind of final psalm. "As the Prophet said, 'A raid on the path of God . . . is better than this world and what is in it.' " The hijackings were the performance of a sacrament, one intended to restore to the universe a moral order that had been corrupted by the enemies of Islam and their Muslim collaborators.

There is no gainsaying President Bush on this account. He said what needed to be said, held tight the ties that bind America to important allies, and reaffirmed tolerance at home. And, in fact, after the 1998 bombings of U.S. embassies in East Africa, the authors of this book helped draft similar language that President Clinton used to describe the perpetrators of that atrocity. "I want the world to understand that our actions today were not aimed against Islam, the faith of hundreds of millions of good, peace-loving people all around the world, including the United States," he announced after the United States launched its missile strikes against terrorist training camps in Afghanistan and a chemical plant in Sudan. "No religion condones the murder of innocent men, women, and children. But our actions were aimed at fanatics and killers who wrap murder in the cloak of righteousness, and in so doing, profane the great religion in whose name they claim to act."

But neither President's necessary and useful political speech should obscure the realities of September 11: the motivation for the attack was neither political calculation, strategic advantage, nor wanton bloodlust. It was to humiliate and slaughter those who defied the hegemony of God; it was to please Him by reasserting His primacy. It was an act of cosmic war. What appears to be senseless violence actually made a great deal of sense to the terrorists and their sympathizers, for whom this mass killing was an act of redemption.

Only by understanding the religious nature of the attacks of September 11 can we make any sense of their unprecedented scale and their intended effects. And only by doing so will we have any chance of under-

standing the enemy and arriving at a plan to defeat it—a task that began
with the war in Afghanistan but could take a generation to finish.

—

At the Foley Square federal courthouse in lower Manhattan, Room 318 is
reserved for high-security trials. A cavernous room with wood-paneled
walls and dark marble pilasters, it is only a few steps from the gated cross-
walk to the Metropolitan Corrections Center. In case of a disturbance,
guards can be rushed into the courtroom and defendants can be hustled
back to their cells. It is not a place one would ordinarily come to hear a
discussion of medieval Islamic law.

But on February 6, 2001, such a discussion took place in Room 318.
The occasion was the testimony of Jamal Ahmad al-Fadl, a former member of al-Qaeda and an FBI informant who was the first witness in the trial
for the bombing of U.S. embassies in East Africa in 1998. A native of
Sudan, al-Fadl had lived in Saudi Arabia and the United States before
leaving for Pakistan in the late 1980s to join the mujahidin in Afghanistan
and fight against the Soviet Union. By his own testimony, he became a
member of al-Qaeda sometime in 1989–1990, at a military training camp
near the Afghan city of Khost. In the course of his training, al-Fadl learned
how to fire a Kalashnikov and a rocket-propelled grenade launcher (RPG);
he became adept at the use of explosives, including TNT and C-4. At
the end of 1990, al-Fadl moved with Usama bin Laden's organization
to Sudan, where he acted as an al-Qaeda courier, financial front man,
and liaison to Sudanese intelligence. Again by his own account, al-Fadl
fled Sudan in 1996, after bin Laden discovered that he had pocketed
$110,000 in illicit commissions on the sale of goods imported by one of
the Saudi's businesses. Al-Fadl approached a number of countries with
information about bin Laden and Sudan, and eventually walked into an
American embassy—its location has not been disclosed—and announced
that he had information about impending terrorist attacks.[2]

During the trial, al-Fadl recounted how Abu Hajer, a senior bin Laden
lieutenant and the man responsible for procuring material for weapons of

mass destruction for al-Qaeda, instructed members of the group in the teachings of ibn Taymiyya, a medieval Muslim theologian. Al-Fadl did not show himself to be deeply knowledgeable about ibn Taymiyya. Asked for biographical information about the theologian, for example, al-Fadl said he lived "1700 or 1800" years ago, an error of about a thousand years—ibn Taymiyya was born in 1269 C.E. Of ibn Taymiyya's voluminous works on Islamic law and public policy and his hundreds of epistles and fatwas, al-Fadl claimed to have read a single section—dedicated to the concept of jihad—from a larger tract on statecraft.

Despite this limited acquaintance, al-Fadl's remarks made clear that ibn Taymiyya was held in the highest esteem by al-Qaeda, and that the group looked to him as a source of inspiration and justification for their violence. To the prosecutor's question about what Abu Hajer had told him and other al-Qaeda recruits, al-Fadl responded in his poor English,

> He said that our time now is similar like in that time, and he say ibn al Tamiyeh, when a tartar come to Arabic war, Arabic countries that time, he say some Muslims, they help them. And he says ibn al Tamiyeh, he make a fatwah. He said anybody around the tartar, he buy something from them and he sell them something, you should kill him. And also, if when you attack the tartar, if anybody around them, anything, or he's not military or that—if you kill him, you don't have to worry about that. If he's a good person, he go to paradise and if he's a bad person, he go to hell.

In other words, anyone who joins with the "Tartar"—meaning a Muslim apostate—to fight against believing Muslims should be attacked, whether they fight alongside the Tartar or simply do business with him. The warrior need not worry about killing noncombatants, because God will give them their rightful reward.

Al-Fadl's remarks garble what the great Islamic jurist wrote, but the kernel of his testimony does come from ibn Taymiyya. Out of the thought of this medieval preacher, a contemporary of Dante's, a current formed within the ocean of Islamic thought and practice. Alternately slowed and accelerated by social and political circumstances, it gathered tremendous strength in the twentieth century and emerged as a profoundly powerful and disruptive force. To grasp the worldview of al-Qaeda and its leader, Usama bin Laden, it is essential to start with ibn Taymiyya.

——

Taqi al-Din ibn Taymiyya was born in the ancient town of Harran, which today lies in Turkey, a few miles from the border with Syria and about 350 miles northeast of Damascus. Harran sits within the vast Eurasian region that was conquered by the earliest waves of Muslim warriors who emerged from the Arabian peninsula in the seventh century. Six hundred years later, it was in the borderlands of Arab civilization. Ibn Taymiyya's family was forced to flee to Damascus when he was six years old to escape one of a series of Mongol (or Tartar, as they are often called) invasions that swept across Arab lands in the thirteenth century. At the time, Mongol armies from Central Asia had already shattered the Baghdad-based Abbasid empire, which had lasted almost five hundred years. It was said of territories conquered by the Mongol horsemen that "no eye remained open to weep for the dead." This was no exaggeration: Mongol rule, dependent on the threat of collective punishment and insubordination, led to the wholesale destruction of unruly villages with the massacre of every living thing. When Hulagu, a Mongol commander and nephew of Genghis Khan, moved against Baghdad in 1258, he destroyed the elaborate, centuries-old dikes that regulated the waters of the Tigris and supported the intensive cultivation of the surrounding land. As they tried to escape the onslaught, Baghdadis drowned in the flooded plains by the thousands. When the capture of the ancient city was a certainty, the last Abbasid caliph agreed to surrender. Any hope that the capital would be spared was in vain: the Mongols tore down the city's mosques, palaces, libraries, and academies. They put the city to the torch, and butchered those who escaped the flames, killing at least 800,000 men, women, and children. The caliph and his sons were taken out of the city, bundled in carpets, and trampled to death by horses.

Christians, a significant minority in Baghdad, were spared. Within the Mongol empire, Christians enjoyed a place of privilege; many, mostly from Asia Minor, had put their skills at the service of the rulers and were accepted in the upper reaches of society. Rising to become commanders and administrators, they intermarried with the leading families, who embraced some Christian customs and beliefs. Moreover, Christendom viewed the Mongols as potential allies. One hundred years after the failure of the Crusades, both Latin and Byzantine Christians saw the Mongol advance as a hopeful development, one that might help resurrect the dream of rolling back the Muslim conquest.

As the Mongol invaders pressed forward, however, they adopted elements from the cultures they came to dominate, in particular the religion of Islam. In the late thirteenth century, the khan Mahmoud Ghazan formalized this haphazard development by officially converting to Islam, bringing the rest of his tribesmen with him. The tenets of the Mongols' newly adopted faith were blended with long-held pagan beliefs and customs, as well as with the remnants of the Christian practices they had flirted with and were reluctant to abandon.

Warfare between Muslims is condemned in the Quran, but the Mongols' conversion did not stop them from pursuing conquests in the lands of the established Muslim dynasties of the Middle East. Their ruthless and inexorable advance created panic, even desperation, in Syria. For Arabs living through this period, civilization seemed on the brink of destruction. Ibn Taymiyya's own family's flight from the invading Mongol forces would instill in him a searing hatred for the Mongols and all who were like them—Muslims who adulterated Islamic faith with alien practices.

Both ibn Taymiyya's father and grandfather were noted theologians. In Damascus, he demonstrated academic genius and, while still an adolescent, emerged as a tough, uncompromising religious authority. In 1282 he succeeded his father as professor of Hanbali law, one of the four major schools of Sunni Islamic jurisprudence. Contemporary accounts depict him as a broad-shouldered, long-haired zealot, unconventional in behavior and belief. It was said that as he strode to the mosque he would kick over the game boards of backgammon players in the street out of disgust at their frivolity. He attacked his ideological opponents with a vigor that seemed pathological. He made a habit of offending individuals close to the local rulers, and was imprisoned five times for his blistering critiques of colleagues in the religious establishment. He died a prisoner in the Citadel of Damascus, his pens and papers taken away to stop the flow of polemics smuggled out of his cell. The independence that angered the powerful endeared him to the public. Tens of thousands would turn out for his funeral procession.

By his early twenties, ibn Taymiyya was a popular preacher at Damascus's ancient Umayyad Mosque. There and in Cairo, then the center of the Muslim world, he excoriated Muslims who deviated from the true way of Islam. That path was not to be found, ibn Taymiyya held, in the teachings of the contemporary ulema, the religious-scholarly establishment. The clerics had distorted the truth by abandoning an exclusive focus on the Quran and hadith, the traditional accounts of Muhammad's actions and sayings, and dwelling instead on commentaries accumulated over generations. By forsaking the scriptural core of the religion, and tolerating beliefs and practices that the earliest generation of Muslims, the *salaf*, tried to eliminate, religious leaders had lost touch with the essentials of the faith.

Ibn Taymiyya was not so radical as to urge the rejection of Islamic scholarship, but he opposed uncritical adherence to it. His thinking was revolutionary in its opposition to the contemporary view that the final interpretation of Islamic scriptures had been achieved, and that further work would only produce heretical innovation. The ulema of the time deemed the gates of *ijtihad*—the independent interpretation of religious doctrine—closed. For ibn Taymiyya, they were wide open. Only when the individual believer entered them and committed himself to a struggle with the scriptures could Islam be purified. In emphasizing personal engagement with holy writ over the views of the clerical establishment, ibn

Taymiyya is akin to two great figures in Christendom: his near contemporary John Wyclif, who first translated the Bible into English, and Martin Luther.

In his writings, ibn Taymiyya focused on issues of statecraft and good governance, essential ones in his conception of Islam. This was not ground that attracted his fellow religious scholars, who had little stomach for criticizing their rulers; such activities reliably brought a stiff prison sentence. Most paid lip service to the lost ideal of a unified caliphate, a Muslim world ruled from one end to the other by one of the "rightly guided" caliphs, as the first four successors to Muhammad were called.

That was the golden age: one God, one prophet, one scripture, one people, and one ruler. The caliph symbolized the indivisibility of politics and religion, and he exercised his authority through the enforcement of sharia and his pursuit of jihad to enlarge the realm of Islam. He was, moreover, the leader of an ascendant movement destined to conquer the world and thereby redeem it. Division, however, appeared early. The question of who would be the fourth caliph arose when Ali, Muhammad's son-in-law and nephew, was confronted by Muawiya, a warlord from a branch of Muhammad's tribe. The crisis was defused by a compromise, and Muawiya stopped pressing his claim. But some warriors in Ali's camp protested violently. They denied Ali's right to bargain over God's determination that he should be caliph, as much as they rejected Muawiya's arrogance in denying His will. What they found most repugnant was the recourse to mediation by men, which to them represented the elevation of human judgment over the divine. Known as Kharijites, from the Arabic word for *depart* (the name was interpreted by later generations to mean "those who departed from the community of true Muslims"), they began a campaign against Ali, whom they assassinated, and Muawiya that lasted fifty years. Among the many forms of their extremism, the Kharijites imposed unyielding standards of observance on all Muslims and declared an excommunication—they proclaimed *takfir*, or condemnation—against some who otherwise would simply be admonished for their wrongdoings. But for the Kharijites, these offenses warranted the capital punishment normally reserved only for blasphemers. For creating the first great rift in *umma,* the community of believers, the Kharijites would be cursed by mainstream Islam, and they continue to be reviled today. But further, more lasting divisions soon appeared. A single caliph would continue to rule, but his power was limited. The realm of Islam, which had expanded miraculously in the seventh century, came to be fractured and ruled by different rival dynasties—the Abbasids in Iraq, the Fatimids in Egypt, the Almohads in North Africa and Spain, to name a few. After the Abbasids' defeat by the Mongols, the Mamluks, a Turkish dynasty, ruled over Egypt and Syria at the end of the thirteenth century, and they were not disposed to entertain questions about who should properly rule the umma at a time when there was no obvious mandate from heaven.

—

Ibn Taymiyya was enough of a realist to accept that the caliphate of the seventh century was dead, and that the division of the once unified realm of Islam was irreversible. There would no longer be rulers who were at once pope and king, who embodied in one person supreme religious authority and political leadership. The modern notion of separate realms of the religious and the secular would have been inconceivable to ibn Taymiyya, and to all Muslims of his time. Indeed, an integral part of Islam's glory was the figure of the caliph—the divinely mandated leader whose forces led a lightning conquest of much of the known world for the faith. Now ibn Taymiyya searched for new approaches that might preserve the essence of the caliphal concept in a new historical setting. He came to see the relationship between the ruler and his subjects as a contract. The people would offer their obedience to the sultan in return for just rule in accordance with Islamic law. But who, then, would provide the missing religious dimension of leadership? Who would provide day-to-day guidance on matters ranging from what one could eat to how one conducted business to how social relations should be regulated? Ibn Taymiyya's answer was that the clergy would perform this function, in effect sharing the responsibilities of government: the sultan would consult the ulema regularly, and the routine exercise of his authority would be informed by their views.

With this idea, ibn Taymiyya sought nothing less than a redefinition of politics. Generations of caliphs had come and gone since the first, rightly guided ones, and their deference to the ulema had been uneven to say the least. Government had become more and more secularized.

Ibn Taymiyya's refusal to accept the subordination of religion to the state, his insistence on religious observance and genuine coordination between the ruler and the clerical establishment, was an attempt to re-create the essence of a long-lost order in a new age. His were serious demands: a ruler who did not enforce sharia or exhibit scrupulous personal piety would be no better than an apostate, and under Islamic law, Muslims were obligated to rebel against such a leader. To obey a leader who violated the precepts of Islam would be to reject the word of God and be guilty of apostasy oneself.

—

Ibn Taymiyya responded to the Mongols' existential threat to Islamic civilization by building up the bulwarks of his own identity and belief. The harassment of Muslims on the margins of the empire elicited in him a yearning to purify the faith and distinguish between the true Muslims on his side of the boundary and the semi-pagans on the other side. Like many religious thinkers in similar situations, he probably believed divine judgment loomed behind the depredations of the Mongols: the attacks from without were punishment for corruption within, which urgently needed to be removed. And, it seems, his experience of living on a dangerous frontier in a perilous time made him more combative. For all these reasons, ibn Taymiyya was preoccupied with the goal of reestablishing the purity of Islam, and a crucial aspect of this reformation for him was restoring the place of jihad, holy war, at the center of Islamic life. He emphasized the importance of jihad—of actual warfare—in the Quran by pointing to the verses that command Muslims:

Fight in the way of God against those who fight against you, but do
not commit aggression. . . . Slay them wheresoever ye find them and
expel them from whence they have expelled you, for sedition is more
grievous than slaying. . . . Fight against them until sedition is no more
and allegiance is rendered to God alone; but if they make an end, then
no aggression save against the evildoers. (Sura 2:190)

And again:

When the sacred months are over, kill those who ascribe partners to
God wheresoever ye find them; seize them, encompass them, and am-
bush them; then if they repent and observe prayer and pay the alms,
let them go their way. (Sura 9:5)

The mainstream Sunni view in ibn Taymiyya's time was that there
were two kinds of jihad. The first was "offensive" jihad, to expand the ge-
ographical realm of Islam—to subdue infidels beyond existing borders
and bring them the faith. This jihad was a duty of the entire community,
to be carried out by an army of able-bodied men who would fight on behalf of their fellow Muslims. To wage jihad was the obligation of the legitimate political authority, who was enjoined to lead his army on this
holy task at least once a year. He could agree to truces, as Muhammad
did, for as long as ten years if prospects for a successful campaign were
doubtful, but the ruler was required to resume hostilities when the balance of power shifted back in the Muslims' favor. This jihad could be
authorized only by a recognized leader such as the caliph. Freelancing
was prohibited. The second form of jihad was "defensive." If Muslim territory was attacked, jihad was no longer a corporate duty but an individual one. Every male had a duty to join the fight and drive out the
infidel.

Breaking with the authorities of his day, ibn Taymiyya placed jihad on
the same level as the "five pillars" of Islam: prayer, pilgrimage, alms, the
declaration of faith ("There is no God but Allah, and Muhammad is his

prophet"), and the fast of Ramadan. Most clerics did not regard participation in jihad as a sine qua non of piety. Ibn Taymiyya again returned to
scripture: he argued that since prayer and jihad were such important
themes in early, authoritative narratives about Muhammad, clearly these
activities were God's two essential requirements for all conscientious,
able-bodied Muslims. The goal of jihad is God's victory; anyone who op-
poses jihad is therefore an enemy of God.

Elaborating on the ideas of others, ibn Taymiyya took a further step by
holding that the rebellions and heresies that had come to dominate politics after the reign of the rightly guided caliphs might necessitate jihad not
only against external opponents, but also against enemies within the
realm of Islam, in order to preserve the unity of the umma. Traditionally,
jihad had not been considered appropriate for dealing with rebels, who
might, after all, have a legitimate grievance against an impious or irre-
sponsible ruler. Nor was it employed against brigands. Jihad against apostates, however, was another matter: the Quran makes clear that the
punishment for apostasy is death, and already in the early ninth century,
the caliph al-Mamun had recognized the political utility of this distinction and accused his rival (and brother) al-Amin of apostasy to justify
jihad against him. Power, not faith, was at stake, but jihad was nevertheless a useful instrument. Ibn Taymiyya grasped the same principle, but
applied it for more explicitly religious purposes. By asserting that jihad
against apostates within the realm of Islam is justified—by turning jihad
inward and reforging it into a weapon for use against Muslims as well as
infidels—he planted a seed of revolutionary violence in the heart of Islamic thought.

To those in power, ibn Taymiyya's ideas were troublesome but useful.
Twice the ruling sultans enlisted him to incite his fellow Muslims to jihad.
The first time, in 1298, was against so-called Little Armenia, at that time
a Mongol vassal state of Christian faith. The second, more fateful occasion, came in 1303, when the Mamluk sultan ordered ibn Taymiyya to
draft a fatwa that would justify a jihad against the Mongols and then
preach the message with all the fire he could summon in Cairo. The spe-

cific target of the fatwa was to be Muzaffar, prince of Mardin, a fortified Arab city that guarded important trade routes in northern Mesopotamia. Muzaffar, a Muslim, served at the behest of Mongol overlords.

From an Islamic perspective, jihad against the Mongols was not a straightforward matter. Since the khan Mahmoud Ghazan had converted to Islam in 1295, the challenger to Mamluk hegemony in the Middle East had been transformed from pagan to fellow Muslim. Evidence from the period suggests that the Mongol leadership met the barest requirement of conversion at the time, the simple declaration of faith: there is no God but Allah and Muhammad is his prophet. The Mamluk sultan thus faced the conundrum that the Mongols, now Muslims, could not be subjected to jihad. Without the rallying force of a call to jihad, the sultan would be unable to mobilize his subjects to fight the approaching horde. Indeed, in 1299 Mamluk warriors abandoned a battlefield when word spread that the Mongol enemy had converted to Islam.

For ibn Taymiyya, the sultan's request was a perfect opportunity to put his thoughts into action. In his fatwa, he accused Muzaffar of ruling his Muslim subjects not according to sharia, Islamic law, but with infidel laws—the Yasa, the Mongol code of customary law that regulated personal status and set penalties for crimes—thus leading Muslims away from the faith. In short, ibn Taymiyya argued, Muzaffar had committed apostasy, a crime punishable by death.

The fatwa served its purpose. The jihad against the Mongols was successful. This campaign marked the end of the Mongol threat to Syria, and Ghazan died the year after the battle. Disputes over succession, failure to develop bureaucratic institutions, and loss of their military edge combined to diminish Mongol power.

The Mamluk regime survived until 1517, when the Ottoman Turks marched into Egypt. Ibn Taymiyya's work eventually fell out of favor, especially after the collapse of Mamluk power, but his insistence on the believer's experience of the holy texts has echoed down through the ages—louder in some eras, such as the present, than in others. Bundled together with his most famous text, the fatwa against the Mongols, and his assertion that Muslim rulers' legitimacy depends upon their piety and use of sharia in governing, he left behind a set of ideas that adherents centuries later would use to catastrophic effect.

———

In the eighteenth century, a spiritual descendant of ibn Taymiyya emerged in Arabia, then a backwater of the Ottoman Empire: Muhammad ibn Abd al-Wahhab. Ibn Abd al-Wahhab was born in 1703, the son and grandson of judges, in the then teeming town of al-Uyaina. A studious and devout young man, he developed early on a reputation for extreme ideas. He completed his initial religious education in Medina, then visited seminaries in Basra, where he was thrown out after condemning the population for apostasy, and Baghdad. He traveled east to Kurdistan and Iran, where he studied in the academies of Isfahan and Qom.

His experimentation with different approaches to Islam eventually led him to formulate what he regarded as an unadulterated Islam, stripped of innovation and true to his conception of early Muslim practice. Not surprisingly, ibn Abd al-Wahhab was drawn to the works of ibn Taymiyya, and he did much to restore his predecessor's prestige among his own followers, who would be known as Wahhabis, as well as among later activists in Egypt and South Asia inspired by the Wahhabi movement. Ibn Taymiyya's emphasis on the most ancient Islamic sources—the Quran and hadith—fit well with ibn Abd al-Wahhab's desire for a back-to-basics religion that rejected practices introduced after the days of the salaf, the men of old. Ibn Abd al-Wahhab excoriated folk customs such as visiting tombs, leaving food offerings for the dead, or venerating saints, which he took to be "innovation," one of the gravest steps a Muslim could take, for it led inevitably to sin. Against those who committed such offenses, he proclaimed takfir and demanded they be put to death. Muslim society, he believed, had become like the age of barbarism that preceded the Prophet, and renewal and purification were an imperative. According to ibn Abd al-Wahhab's code, delivering a legal ruling on the basis of something other than the Quran and hadith was apostasy, as were vows invoking a being apart from Allah, denial of predestination, profiting from trade, interpreting the Quran in a figurative manner, failing to attend public prayers, and shaving one's beard. And, as ibn Taymiyya had insisted four hundred years earlier, the profession of the double creed—"There is no God but Allah and Muhammad is his prophet"—did not suffice to make a person a Muslim.

In eighteenth-century Arabia, general religious observance was anything but strict, so ibn Abd al-Wahhab was destined to make enemies, especially once he set to vandalizing popular shrines. Finally he exhausted the patience of the local tribal leaders and was run out of al-Uyaina in 1744. He fled to the rustic village of Dariya, not far from modern Riyadh, at the invitation of the sympathetic wife of the ruling sheikh there, Muhammad ibn Saud. Ibn Saud recognized that his guest had made converts as well as enemies and was capable of arousing the Arab tribes' fervor. He hoped to harness ibn Abd al-Wahhab's religious passion and popular appeal to advance his own goal of political and territorial predominance in central Arabia. Ibn Abd al-Wahhab sought ibn Saud's help for his own mission of reform. An alliance of power and faith was born. This new force pressed its ambitions vigorously. By the time of ibn Saud's death in 1765, the entire central Arabian plateau was under their control except for Riyadh, which fell eight years later.

Ibn Abd al-Wahhab died in 1792 at the age of ninety and, in keeping with his abhorrence of the veneration of shrines, was buried in an unmarked grave. Yet his descendants and ibn Saud's continued the campaign to control Arabia. Out of the two-hundred-year religio-political crusade they began came Saudi Wahhabism, Islam's most rigid and puritanical branch. By 1814, they had taken the Hejaz and occupied Mecca. To the north, they raided Damascus. To the east, they reached Qatar and captured al-Hasa (now the Eastern Province), wrecking the Shiite shrines throughout the area. To the south, they seized the towns up to the edge of the Empty Quarter.

Their raids drew the anger of the Ottoman rulers, whose Egyptian governor, Muhammad Ali, and his son Tusun temporarily halted the

Saudi ascendance in a series of battles. The Wahhabi-Saudi alliance surged again in the 1840s and, except for a brief setback toward the end of the nineteenth century, it has maintained control over most of the Arabian peninsula ever since.

A few glimpses from history suggest the ferocity that was bred of this marriage of religious zeal and territorial conquest: in 1802, members of the Ikhwan, the militia of fighters drawn from the tribes of the central Arabian region called the Nejd, destroyed the Prophet's tomb in Medina and, in a fury of iconoclasm, battered the idols that worshipers had placed there. The Ikhwan prevented pilgrims from visiting the holy sites because the visitors were, by Wahhabi lights, defiling them through idolatry. During the subsequent hajj, Wahhabi fighters slaughtered forty members of an Egyptian caravan bringing the black silk *kiswa,* an immense curtain used to cover the Kaaba during pilgrimages to Mecca. That ended a long Egyptian tradition of supplying the kiswa, which the Saudis themselves have provided ever since.

—

For Islamic civilization as a whole, the modern period brought decline and humiliation. This history has been much recounted: after the defeat of the Ottomans at the gates of Vienna in 1683, the territory belonging to Islam was slowly eroded. European power galloped ahead during the industrial revolution, and an inversion resulted: centuries in which Baghdad, Cairo, and Muslim Spain were the preeminent centers of learning and culture ended, and the European ascendancy began. In the late eighteenth and nineteenth centuries, Britain and France extended their empires deep into the heartland of Islam, and Ottoman Turkey became "the sick man of Europe," a great power in decay. Islamic thought reflected this sense of beleaguerment: the concept of jihad took on a new meaning. Now, instead of denoting exclusively actual, physical warfare, it came to mean a struggle against evil impulses within the soul of a believer. Acts of charity, good works in society, and education all came to be seen as part of this effort. This domestication of jihad resembles the pacifist approach of the early Christians and Israelites in certain periods of their history; in a time of weakness, avoiding warfare is a sensible strategy. So the notion of the greater and lesser jihads became widespread: the greater jihad was the internal battle. The lesser was the military jihad, which was denigrated by the establishment of this hierarchy.*

The desire to re-create the golden age of the first generations of Muslims, the salaf, reemerged in the ferment of the late nineteenth and early twentieth century, as nationalism and anticolonial sentiment swept the great European empires. The urge to return to fundamentals, to re-create the age of piety and glory, appeared earliest in Egypt and India, the first two countries with large Muslim populations to feel the full impact of Western culture and political power. At the time, the dominant intellectual discussion was about how the Islamic world might adapt and modernize, and many thinkers sought to show how Islamic practices and values could be reconciled with Western political and social institutions. For modernizers, passages in the the Quran and hadith that dealt with interactions among Muslims could be interpreted in the light of new realities, thus opening the way to reforms in which the challenges of modern life and religious ideals could be reconciled. Reason could show that the

---

* Ibn Taymiyya would not have recognized the modern-day distinction between "greater jihad," the struggle for spiritual excellence, and "lesser jihad," the waging of war against Islam's enemies, cf. Omar A. Farrukh (trans.), *Ibn Taymiyya on Public and Private Law in Islam* (Beirut: Khayats, 1966), 135–61. Along with his contemporaries, he considered the superior form of jihad to be combat against infidels. Spiritual jihad was important as preparation for the more physically demanding kind of jihad. This classical emphasis on jihad as warfare has been adopted enthusiastically by contemporary militants, who reject more recent Sufic and apologetic assertions that spiritual jihad is the authentic jihad.

The last century has seen a trend toward interpretation of the so-called greater jihad as the more genuine form of Islamic struggle. The terminology comes from a hadith of disputed reliability in which Muhammad is reported to have said, upon returning from battle, that he has now returned from the lesser jihad to the greater, spiritual, jihad. Until recently, however, Muslim scholars were unanimous in insisting on the priority jihad had as warfare against the unbeliever. Bernard Lewis made this case most famously, but modern scholarly consensus on the matter is summed up by the new edition of the *Encyclopaedia Islamica,* cf. B. Lewis, Ch. Pellat, J. Schacht, eds., "Djihad," *The Encyclopaedia of Islam* (New Edition), Vol. II (Leiden: E. J. Brill), 538–40. It is worth noting that all of the 199 references to jihad in the most authoritative hadith collection speak of jihad only as warfare, cf. Douglas Streusand, "What Does Jihad Mean?," *Middle East Quarterly,* September 1997.

sequestering of women from the public was un-Islamic, that polygamy could be prohibited, and that bank interest could be earned without being untrue to the faith. The ancient institution of the *shura,* the consultative assembly, could be adapted to justify democracy. Education could produce Muslim leaders who were at home with Western ideas, while knowledgeable about and committed to their Muslim identity.

With the decline of the Ottoman Empire, the standard-bearer of Islam, and its dismemberment after World War I by the victorious Europeans, the search of Egyptian political leaders and social theorists for models that would bring their country to a position of parity with the colonial powers continued amid more dispiriting circumstances. A Cairo intellectual named Rashid Rida (1866–1935) argued that only a *salafiyya* Islam, an Islam purged of impurities and Western influences, could save Muslims from subordination to the colonial powers. Rida was from a landholding family near Tripoli, in what was then Ottoman Syria. He had been educated at a progressive Islamic school that offered both religious instruction and secular education. The late nineteenth century saw greater European economic penetration of Mediterranean lands, which had a profound effect on landowning families like Rida's. The impact was greatest, however, in Egypt, where Rida spent most of his career. Some landowners grasped the opportunity offered by a larger market, but more did not, and suffered. Economic dislocation was accompanied by social disorientation as laws and customs changed in response to European influence. Rida detested the so-called Muslim rulers who substituted Western law for the sharia and "thus abolish supposedly distasteful penalties such as cutting off the hands of thieves or stoning adulterers and prostitutes. They replace them with man-made laws and penalties. He who does that has undeniably become an infidel."[3]

In his writings, Rida employed a Quranic term, *jahiliyya,* that Muhammad had used to characterize the ignorance of Arabian society before Allah's revelation. In the Quran, the word *jahiliyya* connotes barbarity. Rida deployed it for an altogether new purpose: to describe not the darkness of pre-Islamic Arabia, but the Muslim lands of his own age that submitted to man-made law and ignored their patrimony of Islamic law. In 1914, Rida wrote, "The decisive judgment of *kufr* [rejection of Islam] is issued against those who do not rule by God's revelation . . . [and against] those who reconcile their customary usage and interpretation with the Quran."[4] Rida justified his condemnation of secular government by quoting the Quran: "They who do not rule by that which God has revealed are the unbelievers" (Sura 5.44). Rida looked back to the age of the rightly guided caliphs for a model for the Islamic state of the future, and his reasoning would be adopted by generations of Islamists to come.

Rida's belief that only a return to authentic Islam would bring Muslims political and economic power was the idea not of a lone intellectual but rather of a transitional figure—one who cleared the way for future radicalism. Beginning in 1928, a new popular movement, the Muslim Brothers, spread the idea as well. Hassan al-Banna, a teacher from a small town in the Nile delta, formed the group to revive Islam and counter the debilitating effects of British colonial domination. He was driven by a sense of cultural catastrophe: the caliphate had been abolished in Turkey in 1924. Muslim leaders from all over came to meet at al-Azhar, the preeminent Islamic academy in Cairo, in 1926 to discuss reestablishing the institution. They failed, and public dismay was compounded by an official declaration of al-Azhar's scholars that Muslims could not fulfill their Islamic identity in the absence of a true caliphate.

Al-Banna's views clashed with the "Western" thinking that intellectuals in Egypt and elsewhere were beginning to espouse, such as the idea that modern forms of political organization, including Western democracy, which separates religion from politics, were compatible with Islamic principles. Al-Banna rejected this view, proposing instead to establish what he called a comprehensively Islamic "system." Whether this was code for an Islamic state, and therefore a call for revolution, is still a matter of debate. The Muslim Brotherhood credo—"God is our objective; the Quran is our constitution; the Prophet is our leader; Struggle is our way; and death for the sake of God is the highest of our aspirations"—

suggests that he and the other founders of the Brotherhood had more in mind than an Islamic society within a secular state.

By the late 1930s, the group had grown rapidly and pioneered a means of proselytizing through community service. Three hundred Brotherhood branches were in operation, running schools, setting up infirmaries, and indoctrinating members through classes and lectures. Al-Banna was a true man of the twentieth century and understood well the importance of mass communications. The Brothers published a series of widely read newspapers and magazines; after one was shut down, another would open. In the *Majallat al-Ikhwan al-Muslimin,* one of these publications, the Brothers asserted that they "would fight any politician or organization that did not work for the support of Islam or restoration of its glory." Soon they were establishing factories and taking control of trade unions. That was the overt side of the organization. The Brotherhood also began infiltrating members into the armed forces and organizing paramilitary groups, or "phalanges," with the apparent objective of seizing power at some time in the future.

In a pattern that would repeat itself frequently in different countries throughout the rest of the century, these new fundamentalists got the room they needed to spread their message and create this state within a state because of the belief of the government—in this case the Egyptian royal court, then ruling the country during the last phase of its colonial period and the first years of independence—that it could use the religious group to divide and conquer its political opponents. Compared to the secular parties that were agitating for independence and broader political participation, the Muslim Brothers appeared to represent little threat, so their activity usefully challenged other opposition parties.

That changed when the Brothers' growth and clandestine military buildup emboldened them to confront the government and the British presence in Egypt. Beginning in 1948, they attacked British and Jewish businesses (or in some cases, firms that they mistakenly thought were owned by Jews) in an effort to accelerate Britain's withdrawal from Egypt and protest Jewish settlement in Palestine. The nuisance they caused

outweighed their value to the government as a counter to the secular opposition, and King Farouk ordered the Brotherhood dismantled. It responded by assassinating his prime minister, Nuqrashi Pasha, late that
year. The government retaliated by arranging the murder of Hassan al-
Banna, who was gunned down in the street in February 1949. The killing
of their leader and the government's ban sent the Brothers underground.
Instead of discouraging them, though, it strengthened their hatred of
Egypt's rulers. The group, which had some seventy-five thousand members at the time of al-Banna's killing, numbered well into the hundreds of
thousands a decade later.

———

A conservative Islamic reaction to Western colonialism also emerged in
India in the mid-nineteenth century. The emblem of this resurgence was
the Dar ul-Ulum, "Realm of Learning," a seminary second in influence
only to Egypt's al-Azhar. It was established in 1867 at Deoband, in the Indian province of Uttar Pradesh, to propagate the vision of the eighteenth-
century theologian Shah Wali Allah and his Indian Wahhabi disciples.
Dar ul Ulum became the wellspring of South Asian Islamic orthodoxy,
and its alumni and their followers, still known as Deobandis, are committed to a strongly salafi conception of Islam.

Deobandi Islam provided the ideological framework for the ideas of
important thinkers, including Abu al-Ala Maududi, a firebrand journalist
who drew on the legacy of Indian Wahhabism and the writings of Rashid
Rida to make the case for a Muslim society cleansed of Western influence
and of corrupted Muslim traditions.

Muslims had enjoyed political hegemony in much of the Indian sub-
continent for centuries and had established a mutually useful relationship
with the British after their arrival in India in the early eighteenth century.
In the years just after World War I, however, Indian nationalism, primarily
Hindu in its leadership and expression, posed a growing challenge to
British rule. In the course of World War II, Britain made it clear that India
would receive its independence after the end of the conflict, and although

Maududi welcomed Britain's intention to withdraw because it would free Muslims from godless British law and administration, Indian independence raised the unwelcome prospect of Hindu rule over his coreligionists. It seemed to Maududi that either outcome—continued British administration or independence—would crush Muslim hopes for self-realization.

With the birth of Pakistan in 1947, Maududi left his home for the newly independent Muslim state, migrating in the same wave of humanity that carried 6.5 million other Indian Muslims. After settling in Lahore, he agitated for an Islamic state, not a merely Muslim one. What good, he demanded, would it do for Muslims to establish their own state only to be ruled by human law and partake in institutions devised by men? Surely, he reasoned, the purpose of an Islamic state was to live according to God's plan. Maududi made these points using terms invented by the notorious Kharijites more than twelve centuries before. Only God had "absolute sovereignty" and, as ibn Taymiyya insisted, it was not enough for rulers simply to sign up to the Islamic creed. Their legitimacy depended on their personal piety and, most important, their commitment to enforce a Quranic moral order in the lands under their control.

The imposition of this new/old order was a revolutionary task, but—as Maududi wrote, linking together an ancient religion with the political language of the age of communism and fascism—"Islam is a revolutionary ideology." The religion "seeks to alter the social order of the entire world and rebuild it in conformity with its own tenets and ideals. . . . 'Muslims' is the title of that 'International Revolutionary Party' organised by Islam to carry out its revolutionary program. 'Jihad' refers to the revolutionary struggle . . . to achieve this objective." Maududi would become one of the most important intellectual influences on the newly established Pakistan. The organization he had founded in India in 1941, the Jamaat i-Islami, was reestablished as a Pakistani political party with a kind of Leninist organizational structure. The revolution would be led by a sophisticated vanguard that would drive the masses forward into a new, genuinely Islamic order. The foremost religious party in the country, the Jamaat i-Islami commands the loyalty of millions of followers who oppose efforts to liberalize the country's politics. Although the party has never come close to holding power, it has been a formidable source of Islamist ideas and energy, especially as religion became a more important source of legitimacy for both elected and military governments from the 1970s on.

—

When independence finally came to Egypt after World War II, the Cold War had already begun. Countries were taking sides, especially the newly decolonized states of the Middle East, South Asia, and Africa. Despite Rida and the Muslim Brotherhood, Egyptian elites still looked to contemporary models for their new state, not to visions drawn from a distant past. Within this Third World, socialism enjoyed a broad appeal. When Gamal Abdel Nasser and other "Free Officers" deposed King Farouk in the 1952 military coup, the new leaders chose to align themselves with the Soviet Union in foreign relations and to establish a planned economy and police state to control internal affairs. Like most of the newly independent Arab countries, the Egyptian regime was secularist but relied on Islamic groups and symbols—the al-Aqsa Mosque in Jerusalem, the Kaaba in Mecca, great military battles from the centuries past—to strengthen its hold on power. The Muslim Brothers, who had survived their confrontation with the authorities and the death of the charismatic Hassan al-Banna, were hopeful about the new regime and established a tactical alliance with the military officers who had engineered the revolt. But the two groups had irreconcilable visions of Egypt's future. Revolutionary Arab nationalism, not Islamic orthodoxy, was the rallying cry of the Free Officers. When the Brothers realized that Nasser was using them—much as they were trying to use him—they considered assassinating him. In a remarkable foreshadowing of terrorist attacks decades in the future, they devised a plot involving a suicide bomber and an explosive vest. At the time, there were no takers, but the Brothers' determination to act intensified with the announcement of the Suez Canal Evacuation Treaty with Britain, which the Brothers bitterly opposed. Eventually they found a willing assassin in the person of Muhammad Abd al-Latif, a poor tinsmith, who fired several shots in Nasser's direction at one of the regime's mass rallies in Alexandria in 1954. The failed attempt was heard live on radio. The government's response was swift and brutal: hundreds of Muslim Brothers were incarcerated in the regime's concentration camp–like prisons. There they were tortured, and many were executed.

One of the Brothers imprisoned was Sayyid Qutb, a writer and former government official. At first, Nasser's courtship of the Muslim Brothers and the regime's rhetorical call for an Islamic revolution had attracted Qutb. He accepted a post as adviser on curricular reform, met with Nasser, and even became a liaison between the Brothers and the Revolutionary Command Council, Egypt's equivalent of the Politburo. He appears genuinely to have believed that Nasser was committed to establishing an Islamic state. When the break between the Brothers and the regime came, he must have been emotionally crushed, and he soon found himself in unimaginably hellish surroundings. Qutb was sentenced to fifteen years at hard labor. He was briefly released in 1964. The next year, he was rearrested, tried, and hanged. In the brutal world of detention camps and prison hospitals, he developed his essential ideas, producing a large corpus of writings that include a massive commentary on the Quran and numerous essays.

In a century in which some of the most important writing came out of prisons, Qutb, for better or worse, is the Islamic world's answer to Solzhenitsyn, Sartre, and Havel, and he easily ranks with all of them in influence. It was Sayyid Qutb who fused together the core elements of modern Islamism: the Kharijites' takfir, ibn Taymiyya's fatwas and policy prescriptions, Rashid Rida's salafism, Maududi's concept of the contemporary jahiliyya and Hassan al-Banna's political activism. In conditions that proved to him beyond refutation the horror of government by manmade laws, Qutb concluded that the unity of God and His sovereignty meant that human rule—government that legislates its own behavior—is illegitimate. Muslims must answer to God alone. Human government, even one that paid lip service to Islam, was apostate; the very presumption that there could be human rule over Muslims implied a denial of

God's authority over mankind and was therefore heretical. Such a government was the legitimate target of jihad. Only by destroying *jahili*—non-Islamic and therefore barbarous—rule could a truly Islamic society appear, one consistent with the beliefs and practices of the earliest, purest stage of the religion's development. The responsibility of jihad would fall to a vanguard of true believers, who would kill the jahili rulers and lead fellow Muslims into a new golden age. Today, Qutb's works are staples of bookshops throughout the Middle East, and his manifesto, *Signposts,* is one of the most influential works in Arabic of the last half century. Years later it would even become an important text for Shiite revolutionaries in Iran, and passages were translated into Farsi by Ali Khamenei, now the Supreme Leader of the country. Qutb's martyrdom has been an inspiration to successive generations of disciples—for whom there is even a special word in Arabic, *Qutbiyyun,* which can be rendered in English as Qutbites. He is the source.

———

The son of a pious teacher in a rural upper-Egyptian town in Minya province, Qutb traveled in his early years along an intellectual and political trajectory typical of a generation of Egyptian activists. He was at first enamored of the West but grew disenchanted as Egypt pursued a program of secular modernization and still saw its woes multiply after World War II. He was working as a school inspector in 1948 when the Ministry of Education sent him to the United States for a fact-finding mission and to improve his English. Rigidly religious, prudish, and already growing suspicious of the West as morally corrupting, Qutb was destined for an unhappy experience. During his ocean crossing, an encounter one night with an amorous and tipsy woman—from whom he recoiled in shock—got him off to a bad start and became a symbol of the trip, which was more than a year long. In America, he felt engulfed by licentiousness, racism, and a popular admiration for Israel that disgusted him. His visits to New York City and Washington, D.C., and his extended stay in Greeley, Colorado, where he lived while working for his master's degree in education at

Northern Colorado Teachers College, confirmed his judgment that
American culture was empty and foul. His revulsion grew at the sight
of the broad, well-kept lawns of Greeley, which typified for him an obsession with superficial and mindless individualism. He was repelled by
churches that seemed to him to be competing with one another in the
business of saving souls. When he saw men and women dancing to the
current hit "Baby, It's Cold Outside," he reacted with a curdling disdain,
writing that "the hall swarmed with legs." Qutb returned to Egypt filled
with loathing for the United States and convinced that Islam and Western
values were fundamentally antagonistic. "Humanity today," he wrote, "is
living in a large brothel! One has only to glance at its press, films, fashion
shows, beauty contests, ballrooms, wine bars, and broadcasting stations!
Or observe its mad lust for naked flesh, provocative pictures, and sick,
suggestive statements in literature, the arts, and mass media! And add to
all this the system of usury which fuels man's voracity for money and en-
genders vile methods for its accumulation and investment, in addition to
fraud, trickery, and blackmail dressed up in the garb of law."[5]

At the heart of Qutb's thought was a powerful dualism: the barbarous and the godly. Drawing on ibn Taymiyya and Maududi, Qutb transformed the term *jahiliyya* from a shorthand description of the world
of pre-Islamic seventh-century Arabia into something far more charged,
turning it from a pejorative into a metaphysical category. Maududi, whose
works were published in Cairo in 1951, used the word to refer to foreign
ideas and conventions that distorted Islam or denied the rule of God. For
Qutb, jahiliyya was a more oppressive, poisonous, and ubiquitous aspect
of existence. It stood for a moral corruption that was not limited to a
specific place and time but that had darkened all times and places since
the eclipse of Muhammad's ideal community of Muslims in mid-seventh-
century Arabia. "Everything around us is Jahiliyya," Qutb would write,
"people's perceptions and beliefs, habits and customs, the sources of
their culture, arts and literature, and their laws and legislations."[6] Like
ibn Taymiyya and ibn Abd al-Wahhab, Qutb did not shy from condemning "much of what we think of as Islamic culture, Islamic sources or Is-

lamic philosophy," which was "in fact the making of Jahiliyya."[7] He put before Muslims an immense existential choice, for those who wanted to lead a correct Islamic life could not have it both ways: "Islam cannot accept any compromise with Jahiliyya. . . . Either Islam will remain, or Jahiliyya; Islam cannot accept or agree to a situation which is half Islam and half Jahiliyya. In this respect, Islam's stand is very clear. It says that truth is one and cannot be divided; if it is not the truth, than it must be falsehood. The mixing and coexistence of truth and falsehood is impossible. Command belongs to Allah or else to Jahiliyya. The Sharia of Allah with prevail, or else people's desires."[8]

If all around one is jahiliyya, seductive, debasing, and forbidden, how can the ordinary, decent Muslim save his soul? Qutb prescribed harsh measures, demanding a separation from "all the influences of Jahiliyya in which we live and from which we derive our benefits." Given the realities of daily life, this could not be a severance of all ties, but rather a drawing of boundaries and a spiritual removal from one's jahili surroundings. Immersion in the Quran is a crucial first step toward this separation. This internal migration would imitate Muhammad's Hijra, the flight from Mecca to Medina. In this withdrawal would be the genesis of dramatic change. Once the community of true Muslims was strong enough, it would form a revolutionary vanguard. Jihad could then be waged against jahili rulers and the reform of Islamic society would be carried out.

For Qutb, the only path for a truly Islamic society was to accept the unlimited suzerainty of God over communal and personal existence. But the restoration of this absolute sovereignty—Qutb uses the term for God's rule that originated with the Kharijites and that figures prominently in ibn Taymiyya and Maududi—requires the believers to rebel, to wrest power from those who exercise it for human and not divine ends. Qutb leaves no doubt about the scope of this task, which entails "a full revolt against human rulership in all its shapes and forms, systems and arrangements. . . . It means destroying the kingdom of man to establish the kingdom of heaven on earth."[9] This can only be attained through jihad. The Muslim Brothers sought to create their "Islamic system" from the ground up, using the provision of social services and education to bring the masses over to their vision. But this approach was grounded in the illusion that the jahili rulers would eventually cede their positions as Egyptians became more pious.[10] This would never happen, Qutb declared. A radical, violent break was required.

If Qutb's equation of modern secularism with jahiliyya placed contemporary Muslims in a moral universe like that of the seventh century, his view of the West replayed the era of the great Crusades. In fact, for Qutb virtually every confrontation between the worlds of Islam and the West is a repetition of the conflicts of the twelfth and thirteenth centuries. In his writings, "the Crusades" are an ancient and perpetual antagonism, unconfined by specifics of time and place. Whether he speaks of Byzantine resistance to Muslim conquerors in the seventh century or the coming of the colonial powers in the nineteenth century, all are manifestations of the Crusades. If anyone argues that the source of Western enmity toward Islam is Jewish money, British ambition, or American guile, he replies: "All these opinions overlook one vital element . . . the Crusader spirit which runs in the blood of all westerners."[11]

Qutb draws another theme from ibn Taymiyya's well that would influence modern radicals: intense anti-Semitism. In the early and medieval Islamic periods, Jews and Christians were, for the most part, treated relatively well. They were "people of the book"—monotheists whose beliefs were drawn from sacred scriptures, even if they did not accept Muhammad's prophecy. They benefited from certain privileges, in return for paying a poll tax, keeping their religious practices out of sight, abstaining from proselytizing, and, in the case of Jews, wearing distinctive clothing in public. Jews and Christians were officially barred from some professions, the senior ranks of the bureaucracy, and the army. Exceptions to these restrictions were not uncommon and, on the whole, Jews fared better in Muslim lands than in Christian Europe, where atrocious persecution was common.

The Quran offers texts to justify a range of attitudes toward Jews. In some passages, Muhammad sharply criticizes the Jews because they re-

fused his call to Islam. They are accused of subverting and falsifying their
own scripture and rejecting their own prophets, as well as Jesus and, of
course, Muhammad himself. Violent clashes that led to the destruction of
the Jewish community of Medina at the hands of Muhammad and his followers are also depicted. Yet there are also contrasting verses that portray
Jews in a more favorable light, creating a picture of normal interaction between Jewish and Muslim communities in Arabia during Muhammad's
early years. (Ibn Ishaq, one of the first biographers of Muhammad, writing within a century of the Prophet's death, recorded that Jews were initially considered to be part of the umma.)[12] Perhaps the most important
aspect of Muslim-Jewish relations before the twentieth century is how
negative Quranic portrayals of Jews were interpreted. Unlike the Catholic
Church, which until the Second Vatican Council in the 1960s identified
all Jews with those who are alleged by the Gospels to have rejected Jesus
and caused him to be crucified, Muslims did not view the Jews of Medina
as progenitors of a line of eternal traitors, and they bore no special hatred
for Jews of later generations.

In his time, ibn Taymiyya exemplified a trend toward harsher treatment of the Jews and Christians within Mamluk domains. Mamluk rulers,
who came from the Turkish lands north of the Caspian and Black Seas,
were outsiders in the Arab world without a sense of the long history of
Muslim toleration for Jews and the obligation to protect *dhimmi*s, "people of privilege." As outsiders with only a shallow Islamic education, they
were deaf to customary practice, instead taking their cues from passages
in the Quran that stigmatized Christians and Jews and discouraged social
contact. Ibn Taymiyya came of age in an atmosphere of increasing intolerance, and he fostered it. Indeed, he first made a name for himself by demanding the death penalty for a Christian in Damascus who was accused
of insulting the Quran. In his writings about the Jews, he argued that their
cruelty toward the prophets, their rejection of God's truth in the form of
Muhammad's call, their treatment of Jesus, and their untrustworthiness
and stinginess effectively invalidated their status as dhimmis. He issued a
fatwa overturning an existing Islamic law that prohibited Muslims from

cursing or insulting Jewish holy books and insisted upon stringent enforcement of the strictures on Jews regarding clothing, holding positions of civil authority, and exhibiting their religion publicly. It was fortunate for the Jews of Damascus that ibn Taymiyya was not in power since he urged the death sentence for Jews guilty of some of these infractions.

Six hundred and fifty years later, Qutb adopted this stance with malicious vigor, taking it to incredible extremes. Jews, Qutb argued, conspired against Muslims from the earliest days and never ceased their plotting. Even worse, taking a gigantic step further, he contended that "anyone who leads this community away from its religion and its Quran can only be a Jewish agent"—in other words, any source of division, anyone who undermines the relationship between Muslims and their faith is by definition a Jew.[13] The Jews thus become the incarnation of all that is anti-Islamic, and such is their supposed animosity that they will never relent "because the Jews will be satisfied only with destruction of this religion [Islam]." The struggle with the Jews will be a war without rules, since "from such creatures who kill, massacre and defame prophets one can only expect the spilling of human blood and dirty means which would further their machinations and evilness." The Jews pose a danger that is more than physical. In a passage that looks back to *The Protocols of the Elders of Zion* and forward to Usama bin Laden, Qutb warns that the Jews' "satanic usurious activity" will "deliver the proceeds of all human toil into the hands of the great usurious Jewish financial institutions." They will rob the believers and kill them.[14]

———

Qutb's views made their first lethal mark in Egypt ten years after he was hanged in a Cairo prison. For all the energy it mustered for persecuting its religious opponents, the regime failed to improve economic conditions or stand up militarily to Israel. In its inability to deliver basic improvements, Nasser's Egypt set the pattern that created the conditions for a religious revival, as disenchantment with secular nationalism led the discontented to seek another, potentially more nourishing ideology. While the government's Marxist approach fell short, its revolutionary rhetoric caught on. Discontent fueled a popular interest in Islam and a new revolution that would be genuinely Islamic, not the phony version peddled by those in power. There was a growing belief that a return to their authentic heritage—their true identity—would deliver independence, security, and prosperity to Muslims.

As Nasser's successor Anwar Sadat consolidated his power in Egypt during the 1970s, he dismantled his predecessor's domestic program and initiated an economic liberalization. In some quarters, this policy reversal was strongly resisted, especially in Egypt's burgeoning universities, where activists were still committed to Nasser's pan-Arab socialism. To counter the opposition, Sadat lifted legal restrictions and eased police pressure on Islamic student unions, which he believed would drive the Nasserists out of the universities through propaganda and physical violence. This stratagem, much like Farouk's use of the Muslim Brothers, succeeded in the short run. Over the longer term, Sadat's tactics nurtured terrorist groups for whom kicking the leftists off campus was just the beginning.

The first to undertake the cause of the Islamic revolution was Salih Siriyya's Shabab Muhammad, "Muhammad's Young Men." Siriyya, a Palestinian militant, was living in Jordan in 1970 when Yasir Arafat led Palestinian forces in the "Black September" revolt against the government of King Hussein. With the suppression of the revolt by King Hussein's Bedouin army, Siriyya escaped to Iraq. There, he soon came under suspicion, so he fled to Egypt in 1971, where he found a job as an Arab League bureaucrat and fell in with the leadership of the Muslim Brothers. At the time, the Brothers must have seemed timid to Siriyya. Six years after Sayyid Qutb had been put to death in Nasser's drive to destroy the Brothers, they were not going to risk offending the Sadat regime; they stuck to a strategy of grassroots work to build a new Islamic society. For Siriyya, this incrementalism doomed the Brothers to irrelevance. Real change could come only through coup d'etat.

Siriyya cast his spell over a small group of students in Cairo and

Alexandria, formed his own revolutionary cadre, and drew up a plan for toppling Sadat. He resolved to storm the Technical Military Academy in Heliopolis, a suburb of Cairo, and with weapons and vehicles captured there, deploy as many as a hundred militants, including cadets studying at the academy. The fighters would then attack the Arab Socialist Union building in central Cairo, where Sadat was attending an official event. Whether the President and his companions were to be arrested or killed outright remains unclear, like many details of the conspiracy. In the last phase of the coup, Siriyya's forces intended to capture the television station and declare the establishment of the Islamic Republic of Egypt.

The execution of the plan was a botch. The attempt to seize the military academy fizzled quickly when the conspirators came under fire from guards at the academy's armory, and the entire conspiracy collapsed in Heliopolis; Sadat was never in any danger. Siriyya and his top assistant were captured and executed, and twenty-nine members of his band were jailed. Many others, however, were freed and soon gravitated to other radical circles then forming.

One group that rivaled Shabab Muhammad was dubbed al-Takfir wal-Hijra—"Condemn and Emigrate"—by the police and media. As a shorthand description of the group's program, this served the public relations purposes of the Egyptian regime, since it highlighted two aspects of the group's beliefs that were most alienating to ordinary Egyptians. It was also not inaccurate: the group's leader, a charismatic former Muslim Brother and disciple of Sayyid Qutb named Shuqri Mustafa, believed his band's duty was to proclaim the apostasy of Egyptian society—to declare it takfir. In his manifesto, *The Caliphate*, he proclaimed that "all that is seen before you now on earth of men and women, of money, soldiers, arms and ploys, of constitutions and laws, wars and conciliations . . . represents a front for God's enemies, led by evil on earth. . . . Within this reality a man will come who, together with the believers who would follow him, will erase this reality, fight the infidel entity and establish the Islamic body."[15] But the apostate power was still too strong to defeat in battle, so the group had to separate itself from Egyptian society—to emi-

grate internally in imitation of Muhammad's flight from Mecca. Ultimately, the group believed, its members' exemplary living would attract a
mass of penitents, who together could wage jihad against the jahili state.

The group called itself al-Jamaat al-Muslimin, "The Islamic Group,"
because adherents considered themselves to be the only true Muslims in
an overwhelmingly jahili society. They were known also as "the people of
the cave," because of a brief period in which they experimented with a her-
mitlike existence in the desert. They were more frequently called *takfiris*,
"those who condemn," and separation was necessary for them because
anything beyond the barest contact with the barbarousness of contemporary life threatened to corrupt these young, authentic Muslims.[16]

The takfiris were seized with a messianic fervor. Members believed
that Shuqri was the Mahdi, the long-awaited messiah who would be the
savior of Islam; in photographs from that time, he has the Mansonesque
stare of a man certain of his own apocalyptic role. The group's ultimate
objective was the reconstitution of the caliphate, a restoration of the
golden age, and the establishment of Islamic rule over the entire world. It
forecast the emergence of an Islamic superpower that would challenge the
United States and Soviet Union and ultimately replace them as the dominant power on earth. The members shared a sense of profound crisis and
thought they had detected signs of the coming end of time: deep divisions
in society, growing political disorder, and widespread apostasy. The moment required action by the few true Muslims to hasten the beginning of
divine rule.

The takfiris' emergence was possible because of the Sadat government's use of Islamic groups as a counterweight to Nasserite leftists, but as
their leaders became more paranoid and prone to violence, the band became a target of the secret police. Shuqri's conviction that his group was
the only body of true Muslims meant that a decision to leave the group—
and there were many who sought to escape his tyrannical behavior—was
apostasy and punishable by death. As Shuqri began pronouncing sentences on those who wanted to break with the group, disillusioned members decided it was time to cooperate with the police. Internal security

agents had no trouble infiltrating the group. Growing police interest and negative publicity in the press strengthened the takfiris' sense of impending catastrophe.

The pressure increased when Shuqri ordered his followers to carry out death sentences on two particular renegades. The attempt was disrupted by police who were either watching the group or were tipped off by one of the intended victims. Shuqri became a wanted man, vilified in the media and hunted by the authorities. Egyptian security forces were now capturing members of the shrinking group and holding them without charge.

In desperation, Shuqri abandoned the strategy of withdrawal and decided to strike at the enemy. On July 3, 1977, the remnant of the group kidnapped Sheikh al-Dhahabi, a former dean of al-Azhar's secular and religious law faculties who was then the government's minister of religious foundations, the entities that manage the budgets and facilities of mosques and religious schools. The sheikh was chosen because he had inveighed against Islamists in a publication circulated the year before. His larger crime, however, was to be a prominent representative of the establishment clergy, who were paid by the government and could be counted on to support it. Shuqri—like other militants in Egypt—blamed these ulema for cooperating with the regime and thus helping to uphold the jahili state. Because they used their authority to seduce innocent Muslims away from the truth, these clerics were the most egregious of apostates. They diverted Muslims from the text of the Quran, which was in an Arabic that any Egyptian could understand, insisting that a valid understanding of God's word depended above all on the official clergy's exclusive ability to cite the commentaries of the great medieval schools of scriptural interpretation. As far as Shuqri was concerned, the clerics were simply protecting their prerogatives and concealing their intellectual cowardice. Even worse, he argued, this practice set the great commentators up as idols, competing with God and the Prophet. Those who relied upon these jurists were denying the oneness of Allah and deserved death.

For al-Dhahabi's release, Shuqri issued a bizarre set of demands:

200,000 Egyptian pounds, amnesty for his fellow group members, the printing of a communiqué in *The New York Times,* and a government commission to investigate the security services. When the regime refused, al-Dhahabi was executed. Shuqri was hunted down and caught, and his group was eventually dispersed. In the process, however, it made a lasting impression by engaging the security forces in a series of gunfights that left sixty dead or wounded.

When he appeared in court, Shuqri mocked the establishment clerics, their learning, and the state that supported them. He derided the ulema for their interpretation of jihad as an internal struggle to overcome one's evil impulses. Yes, he said, he knew the hadith in which the Prophet returns from the battlefield saying, "We have come home from the small jihad to the great jihad," but we all know it's from the least authoritative hadith compilation and therefore a forgery. The clerics were doubly discredited by the trial proceedings: not only were they being dismissed as puppets of the regime by the takfiri defendants, but the military prosecutors pinned the blame for the takfiri phenomenon on the clergy's failure as educators. How, the prosecutors asked, could the institution responsible for the religious instruction of the country's youth have allowed Shuqri's heretical beliefs to gain such a following in the universities?

The outcome of the trial was never in doubt. Shuqri was executed in 1978 at the age of thirty-seven, along with four other takfiris. But the trial badly discredited the ulema, who were already a weakened force for moderation in an increasingly radicalized Egypt.

—

In the campus ferment of the mid-1970s, another group emerged that shared many of Jamaat i-Islami's goals but operated with different methods and ideology: the Jamaat al-Jihad. The new group was galvanized by two events that occurred after Shuqri Mustafa's execution: the first was Anwar Sadat's decision to make peace with Israel. To these fundamentalists, an agreement with the Jews that validated infidel occupation of Muslim land was inexcusable. The clerics of al-Azhar justified the peace agreement with Israel on scriptural grounds, citing Muhammad's agreement to a truce with his Meccan enemies in 628, but that only served to deepen contempt for the ulema among extremists, who saw them as the lapdogs of an impious ruler. The second was the 1979 enactment of a new secular law regulating family matters, which came after years of foot-dragging by the conservative religious opposition in the National Assembly. This government intrusion into family affairs was in some respects the greater outrage. Among other provisions, the law gave women the right to divorce if their husbands took other wives without their consent. It gave divorced mothers custody of children up to certain ages and entitled them to live in their ex-husband's home until they remarried or other arrangements were made. To Islamists, this guarantee to women of new rights not authorized by sharia was an affront that compromised a husband's authority over his wife and home. Moreover, the new family law's principal advocate was Jihan Sadat, the president's wife; as a woman, the radicals maintained, she had no role in such matters. The legal reform came after years of promises by the Egyptian regime to make national law conform to sharia, so it hardly counted as a good faith effort. These were tremendous provocations, and they inflamed the radicals' perception of an historic catastrophe, that Islam faced a world of unprecedented hostility. Spurred by Islamist successes in student union elections in the universities, student opposition to the government spread. Sadat responded by suspending the student unions, outlawing independent Islamic student associations, and stepping up arrests of young radicals.

The al-Jihad group began life as a more formidable organization than the Shabab Muhammad or al-Takfir wal-Hijra because it was led not by charismatics but by dedicated revolutionaries. Its intellectual guide was Muhammad Abd al-Salam Faraj, an electrical engineer who, like Shuqri Mustafa, had been a Muslim Brother until he was disillusioned by that organization's accommodation to the regime. His father had been a Ministry of Health employee with strong convictions that drew him to the Muslim Brothers and landed him repeatedly in prison. Advancing age cooled his militancy, and he settled in a provincial capital, married well, and earned enough money to send his son to Cairo University.

After his education, Faraj settled in the outskirts of Cairo and around 1980 linked up with two brothers-in-law, Abbud Abd al-Latif al-Zumr, and Tariq Abd al-Mawjud al-Zumr. Theirs was an establishment family that had intermarried with leading clans and been important in politics before Nasser's revolution. One of Abbud's uncles was a general who had fallen in the October War of 1973; another was a member of Parliament. His father had been mayor of his village, and a number of relatives were army officers. Abbud himself was an army colonel, and he would handle security and special operations for the group. In its embryonic stage as a three-man cell, the group began to prepare for an Islamic revolution. This would not be accomplished in the style of Shuqri Mustafa, through the conversion of the masses over a long period of time. The revolution would come from above, led by a vanguard as in Salih Siriyya's vision of a takeover of the state by decapitating the regime.

A second wing of the group, bound to the Cairo cell through ties of friendship and kinship, formed in upper Egypt. The link was Muhammad Zuhdi, a fugitive from the town of Minya who was wanted for antigovernment activity and was hiding out in Cairo's University City dormitories. There, the al-Zumr brothers-in-law introduced him to Faraj. Zuhdi and Faraj shared a desire for action and set to work bringing together activists from the south with those in and around Cairo. Court documents later referred to the resulting organization as Tanzim Muhammad Abd al-Salam Faraj, or Tanzim al-Jihad. Not long after this connection was forged, Tanzim grew with the addition of a new faction led by another university graduate, Kamal al-Said Habib, from the College of Commerce. The last volunteer came from the southern town of Nag Hammadi: First Lieutenant Khalid Ahmed Shawqi al-Islambouli met Zuhdi in 1980 and joined the Tanzim in 1981. Al-Islambouli's family was a rural version of the al-Zumr family. His father was in-house counsel for a sugar factory, his uncle had been a judge, and many of his male relatives had law degrees; one family member served as chairman of the district council and another was a senior army officer. These were not people brought low by poverty or seething with frustrated expectations.

Religious inspiration was provided to the group by Sheikh Omar Abdel Rahman, the Blind Sheikh. At the time, he was in his early forties, a family man with two wives and eight children. Like most of the conspirators from northern Egypt, Rahman came from the outer edges of Cairo, a sprawling region that was neither rural nor as densely urban as central Cairo. Although he had been sightless from childhood, his determination carried him through the doctoral program at al-Azhar, where he won a degree in Quranic exegesis in 1972. This same resolve brought him into conflict with Nasser's state. By his early thirties, he had already served a nine-month sentence in solitary confinement at the notorious Qala prison and been under house arrest. When Sadat came to power and attempted to enlist the Islamic opposition in the battle against the left, Rahman was rehabilitated—against the wishes of the internal security service, which considered the cleric to be trouble in waiting. In 1973, Rahman was permitted to take up a lectureship on the theology faculty of al-Azhar's Asyut campus in southern Egypt. There he met Zuhdi and his fellow Tanzim and, through them, Faraj.

As the group developed, day-to-day leadership was provided by committees, which took decisions in concert with a majlis al-shura, or consultative council. The majlis had one committee for recruitment, another to coordinate logistical support, and a third to manage finances. Cells in Cairo met regularly to plot strategy and coordinate operational matters. The recruitment of new members and the formation of cells were centered in radical mosques: new members were drawn from among the most devout young worshipers. Those selected were invited to more exclusive study sessions with an imam linked to the group. These events were known as retreats—another allusion to the notion of hijra, or migration, away from jahili society. A few participants would then get a smattering of training in unarmed combat and instruction in handling weapons and explosives. The group practiced a fairly sophisticated level of tradecraft—thanks presumably to Abbud—in which information was strictly controlled and cover names and codes were used in communications. They maintained a discipline, summed up by the oath sworn by new recruits to "hear and obey," that provided them with the secrecy to operate in a formidable police state. In addition to its regimentation, al-Jihad had another advantage over the takfiris. The latter's separatist ideology led the group to limit its contact with other Egyptians and thereby preserve its spiritual purity. Al-Jihad, by contrast, did not believe that all of Egyptian society was submerged in the darkness of jahiliyya. Government leaders were the problem, not the Muslims over whom they ruled or even those whose salaries they paid. Since only the regime was designated as apostate—it was left to God to judge whether others in society had deviated from the true path—al-Jihad could recruit government workers, soldiers, intelligence operatives, and reporters. The security risk posed by this wider network was offset by two factors: the group continued to look to family relations or close friends for new members, and there was an opportunity for extended observation of recruits during the indoctrination phase in the mosque. This more flexible assessment of who was jahili and who was not also allowed al-Jihad to penetrate the Egyptian security services. The group's conviction that the evil resided in the government led them to a further conclusion: the Egyptian people would support a revolutionary assault on the power structure of the state. Thus, there was no reason to postpone the slaying of the Pharaoh, as the Islamists called Sadat.

Al-Jihad thinking was set forth in a manifesto called *The Neglected Obligation* (*al-Faridah al-Ghaiba*), written by the group's commissar, Faraj. The book probably dates from 1980, the year he formed the Tanzim, and it is thought that about five hundred copies were privately printed. The title echoes ibn Taymiyya's insistence on the crucial importance of jihad. Muslims satisfy themselves with observation of the five traditional pillars of the faith—declaration of faith, pilgrimage, prayer, alms, and the Ramadan fast—but they forsake what Faraj considered the sixth and most vital one, jihad. The electrician-cum-theologian quotes a

famous hadith concerning a man who converted to Islam in the presence
of Muhammad, went out to fight in a jihad, and was immediately killed
without having the opportunity to do the good and charitable things that
are required of Muslims. When informed of the convert's fate, Muhammad said, "Nevertheless, his reward is great." Faraj took this as scriptural
proof that jihad takes precedence over other duties. Like Shuqri Mustafa,
he was intent on puncturing the notion that there exists a greater jihad of
individual spiritual renewal that takes precedence over the lesser jihad
of killing the enemies of God. Faraj also dismissed the classical legal requirement that only the caliph or emir can authorize jihad: he cited another hadith, in which the Prophet said, "When three go out, make one
an emir." As for the relevance of the ulema's opinion on any of these matters, Faraj was contemptuous: the Muslim commanders who conquered
the world "from Spain to India" were not great scholars; al-Azhar was not
able to keep the French from invading Egypt in the nineteenth century;
and anyone who does not believe that Islam was spread by the sword has
not read the Quran, he declared.

The Neglected Obligation relies explicitly on Qutb and ibn Taymiyya
and reads at times like the record of a debate within the group as it ex-
plores the way forward. Faraj ridicules the gradual approach to change
advocated by the Muslim Brothers. He cites ibn Taymiyya's fatwa against
the Mongols to show that jihad against those who merely call themselves
Muslims is valid and that killing Muslims in pursuit of that goal is legitimate. He argues further that the use of stratagems of deceit for this purpose was approved by authoritative Muslim jurists. Those he invokes to
create the impression of a clerical consensus are a who's who of the greatest jurists and generals of the golden age of Islam. He dismisses contemporary established ulema as nothing more than the salaried puppets of
the state, with no authority over true Muslims.

His tract also provides a fascinating window into the group's debate
about Israel, which he calls the "far enemy." Faraj maintains the "near
enemy," apostate Muslim rulers, must be destroyed first. Then, the purified Islamic community can turn its guns against the "far enemy."

—

They barely had an idea of their original civilization.

—V. S. NAIPAUL, *A Bend in the River*[17]

Ideology tells us a great deal about these radicals, but so does sociology. We have seen how many of the leaders of al-Jihad came from backgrounds that were well-to-do or better. It is tempting to think that the leaders came from these ranks and that their followers were rabble—misfits and marginal characters seduced by a cause. But Saad Eddin Ibrahim, the eminent Egyptian social scientist who interviewed Shabab Muhammad survivors in prison, characterized them as well-educated "model young Egyptians," mostly from cohesive lower-middle-class and middle-class families, where the head of household was a professional. The takfiri members also fit this profile. The statistical breakdown of those involved with al-Jihad is particularly revealing: the group was almost evenly split between students and nonstudents; about 40 percent of the latter were artisans or merchants, 17 percent professionals, 9 percent soldiers or policemen, 4 percent farmers, and only 5 percent unemployed. Of the students in al-Jihad, one-third were in engineering or medicine. In Siriyya's "Military Academy" group, almost all of whom were students, nearly half were also studying those two subjects.

These numbers weaken any thesis that Egypt's Islamist militants are the downtrodden rising up. They may well have class frustrations, and some have argued that the activists come from a stratum of society in which there is an inordinate disparity between education and a sense of entitlement on the one hand and actual opportunity on the other.[18] But what is most striking is the phenomenon of so many well-trained, literate young men assuming the authority of religious interpretation. While his clerical authority was valued by al-Jihad, Sheikh Rahman is the outlier in a group whose chief theorist was an electrician. Qutb, Siriyya, Shuqri, and Faraj— all are autodidacts of one stripe or another. There are few clergy among these fundamentalists, but no shortage of willingness to determine—on the basis of their own learning—what is God's truth. Implicit in this is a dis-regard for generations of learning and religious authority, a repudiation that goes beyond the insistence of ibn Taymiyya on the individual strug-gle with the Quran and hadith.

One explanation for this phenomenon involves several major devel-opments within the Islamic world over the last two centuries. According to Professor Richard Bulliet of Columbia University, a central tendency in the modernization that began with colonialism in the nineteenth century was a weakening of the traditional role of the ulema. The institution of Western legal codes removed clerics from the administration of justice, and in education, even the sons of distinguished religious figures were sent to Western-style schools, which were largely free of ulema. This mar-ginalization was increased by the rise of printing, which weakened the traditional relationship between sheikh and talib, or student. When de-colonization came after World War II, a time when nationalism was flour-ishing, Bulliet says, "The state school system . . . trained people for state service . . . but [state schools] were very cautious about teaching much of anything about Islam because they did not want to instill the reverence for the old authorities. They did not want to have the mullah in schools play-ing a major role in the education. So there was a growing number of liter-ate young Muslims who could read books but who had not been trained in Islam and were not socialized to look at the sheikh as a figure of au-thority. The state took away the old authorities and gave an audience to the new ones, the lawyers, doctors, pharmacists, pedagogues, engineers, economists, who trained at Western schools or Western-curriculum schools, and these men say: Here is what I think." The weakening of traditional authority was also, at least in part, an aspect of the twentieth-century Islamist program. Maududi wrote well before al-Jihad appeared that "every Muslim who is capable and qualified to give a sound opinion on matters of Islamic law, is entitled to interpret the law of God when such interpretations become necessary." With the bonds of tradition removed, all have the ability to argue for their version of the faith—in print, on audiotapes and videotapes, and now on the Internet. Says Bulliet, "At the street level there is no agreement as to what constitutes authority in Islam."

This concatenation of change bears a striking resemblance to another era of upheaval, when literacy was on the rise and established authority was under attack: the Protestant Reformation. From shortly after Martin Luther's defiance of the Catholic Church through the English civil war, there were numerous occasions in which Protestant radicals of one sect or another, certain in their interpretation of the Bible, sought to create states in which God's law ruled—a line runs from the rebellion of Thomas Muenzer in Germany in 1525 to Cromwell's creation of the New Model Army for the "Revolution of the Saints." (In the Pilgrims and the Puritans' Great Migration of the late 1630s, there was a related, but peaceful, effort to depart from the larger, corrupt community and establish a republic of the holy.) A parallel can also be drawn between the Protestants' reduction of the number of sacraments on the basis of what appeared in scripture and the Islamists' effort to revise the pillars of the faith, raising jihad to the highest level of priority.

—

Despite al-Jihad's technical competence as a clandestine group, it stumbled into a premature confrontation with the government. The trigger was the organization's decision to undertake operations in upper Egypt against the Copts, the country's ancient Christian population. The involvement began with the initiative of a separate Islamic group to build a mosque on land owned by a Christian. Despite a court order supporting the Copt's claim that this violated his rights, the Muslim group continued its work. At wits' end, the landowner took the law into his own hands and shot some of the militants at the construction site. This had a volcanic effect in Egypt, where tensions between the minority Christians and the Muslim population had been steadily rising. Al-Jihad decided to take advantage of the violent mood to build up contacts, especially in the military, and develop new sources for weapons and recruits.

The group then went on a spree of armed robberies to fatten its treasury. They targeted Christian-owned jewelry stores, citing the Quran on the right to take spoils won in a war with polytheists. The cash went straight to Faraj. Flush with money and sensing that Egypt was ripe for a new Islamic order, the group began to plan for an assault on key government officials. They cased Sadat's Cairo residence and his villa, a residence of the Coptic leader, Pope Shenouda, the homes of the National Guard and Security Police commanders, and the Ministry of the Interior.

The spiraling violence precipitated government intervention. Sadat directed the security services to start a roundup of Islamic militants, whose opposition to the regime had become clear to the authorities. The police cast a wide net, arresting more than fifteen hundred activists. Virtually all of Faraj's southern Egyptian cells were broken up and leading operatives were apprehended. The group's prospects looked bleak; it would only be a matter of time before the al-Jihad leaders in custody would break under torture.

The conspirators, however, remained a step ahead. On September 23, 1981, Khalid al-Islambouli learned that he had been assigned to participate in the October 6 military parade in commemoration of the 1973 "victory" against Israel. (Egypt's ability to maintain a foothold in the Sinai peninsula had been construed as a triumph even though the war ended with the country's Third Army fully encircled west of the Suez Canal.) Within forty-eight hours, al-Islambouli met with Faraj to propose using the opportunity to kill Sadat and everyone else in the reviewing stand. Faraj recognized that this was al-Jihad's moment. Two members were immediately assigned to the assassination team, and another was brought into the group a few days later. Four colleagues from the south hurried to meet with Faraj, and together they devised a complementary plan for the takeover of the provincial capital of Asyut. Faraj set to work on a design for seizing control of Cairo itself, beginning with the television station. This facility was a priority objective because from it al-Jihad would announce to the world that the evil prince had been slain and that Muslims must now rise up and overthrow their jahili oppressors.

On October 6, the conspiracy began as planned. Al-Islambouli had arranged for his real army squad to be given leave on the day of the parade and replaced by the three-man assassination team. As the truck neared the front of the reviewing stand, he pulled the emergency brake, dismounted with his companions, and sprinted toward the presidential section. There, pressed up against a barrier, they sprayed the assembled notables with automatic-rifle fire. The grainy image of a soldier pumping bullets into Sadat's body as the President groaned *"La, la"* ("No, no") was broadcast worldwide. The exultant killer jumped up and down, shouting, "My name is Khalid Islambouli, I have slain Pharaoh, and I do not fear death!"

The attempt to take over Cairo following the parade-ground killings failed completely, in part because the assassins were captured alive. The conspirators had expected to be shot on the scene; whether they were tortured or just delirious at their success, they revealed enough information to give the security services what they needed to overcome the other plotters—and the militants helped by falling short in their execution of the remainder of the plan. They had intended to steal weapons from an armory, but they botched the attempt to drug the security personnel there. As a result, they never had the firepower required to seize the television station. They also failed to get control of three of the city's vital traffic nodes and pedestrian plazas. In the south, the radicals began their operation late because of poor coordination but still succeeded in briefly taking over the central police headquarters in Asyut and nearly seized a second precinct. Most of the Tanzim were soon tracked down and killed or captured. A small remnant tried to continue the fight from remote hideouts. But the rapid, uncontested transfer of power to Sadat's vice president, Hosni Mubarak, meant that there was no upheaval of any kind, and the state suppressed these scattered efforts with brutal efficiency.

Of the many who faced trial in connection with the events of October 1981, it was the Blind Sheikh whose case proved most significant. He stood accused of having been the group's mufti—essentially, their chaplain. This meant more than offering spiritual succor to his flock: Rahman provided the fatwas that certified the legality of killing the Christian jewelry-store owners and, because he was an apostate, of Anwar Sadat. He was also charged with helping to fence the stolen valuables and producing seditious propaganda tapes for distribution within Egypt.

Much of the testimony in the trials of the jihadists was extracted by torture, Rahman's included. However, the government apparently did not hinder the sheikh's defense counsel, and Rahman made no attempt to conceal his beliefs from the court. Instead, he delivered a virtuoso tirade against the judges, the state, and the law. He scorned the government that presumed to teach that "jihad is that [struggle] against illness, poverty, and ignorance," and he declared that "the word *jihad* in the language of [religious] law and in Islamic conception means fighting for the sake of Allah, to raise the word of Allah. And it is a notion that the umma has agreed upon for fourteen centuries." He insisted on the immutability of sharia, rejecting the supposition that "the different circumstances which the society is going through, according to the claims of the prosecution, allow it to suspend the legal punishments of Allah and his law. It [the prosecution] replaces divine laws with Crusader laws; it does not cut off the hand of the thief, it does not lash the drinker, it does not stone the married adulterer."

Astonishingly, most of the charges against Rahman were ultimately dismissed. He was found to have preached that apostate rulers must be overthrown but not to have specified that Sadat or any other leader should be executed. Likewise, Rahman was judged to have justified theft from Christians during jihad, but it was not proven that he authorized the specific attacks on Copts that were carried out by his congregants. The judges found that Rahman had simply acted within his writ as an *alim*, a member of the clerical establishment, in saying and doing these things. The exoneration seems bizarre, especially in light of his continued involvement with terrorists over the subsequent decade. After the Sadat assassination and while still in Egypt, he was implicated in the murders of the speaker of the parliament, Rifaat al-Mahgoub, and the secular writer Farag Foda. He is thought to have been involved in plots to kill the Nobel Prize–winning author Naguib Mahfouz and Sadat's successor, Hosni

Mubarak. And, of course, he played a central role in planning attacks against the United States in 1993, helping to select targets and authorizing bombings. As strange as his 1982 acquittal in Egypt may seem in retrospect, it was a powerful demonstration of the ideological affinities between the ulema and the terrorists. Clerical authorities could not contradict the underlying premise of the terrorists and their spiritual mentors, including Rahman, that rulers who deliberately forsake the sharia and reject their obligation to make it the law of the land deserve to die. As the Quran declares, "They who do not judge by that which God has revealed are the unbelievers."

To be sure, the vast majority of ulema would not agree to an explicit call for the death of a coreligionist. But this truth obscures a larger one. Muslims the world over look to the clerical establishment in Egypt for guidance in religious matters, and these authorities share some fundamental presuppositions, if not the conclusions, of the radical agenda. The strong insistence of many clergy on implementation of sharia in general and a ban on interest in particular; on censoring of sexual imagery and language in the media; on modesty in women's dress; and on the elimination of nightclubs and gambling have created a milieu that validates what the terrorists themselves are saying. When Rahman declares that "the lands of Muslims will not become bordellos for sinners of every race and color," who among his peers is going to argue with him? And if they did not subscribe to his conclusion that "America is behind all these un-Islamic governments"—those that reject sharia and foster such barbarities—and that a "revengeful God would scratch America from the face of the earth," what would happen to their credibility? The lesson of Rahman's 1982 acquittal in a Cairo courtroom is that there is a strong connection between the subculture of terrorism and a broader culture in which the basis for terrorist violence is well established and legally unassailable.

—

One characteristic of Egyptian religious terrorism has been the belief that a decisive blow against the government would somehow precipitate an uprising against the government. Shuqri Mustafa expected that his group's actions would lead ineluctably to revolution. Al-Jihad thought that the masses could be roused to action once the Cairo television station was seized. Their belief was that the faithful were eager to throw off the yoke of jahiliyya, and that a single dramatic act would cause an extraordinary change in history. This conviction reappears among other groups of Islamists who seek radical change. In Syria, the year after Sadat's assassination, the idea surfaced again. The Muslim Brothers in that country— the group had long since spread from Egypt throughout the Arab world—had been growing restive during the 1970s like their Egyptian counterparts.

The Brothers' strongholds were in the Sunni-dominated northern cities of Aleppo, Homs, and Hama. In 1979, the group went on a killing spree at a military academy in Aleppo, murdering sixty-nine cadets. The cadets were Alawites, members of a minority sect related to the Shiites that had dominated Syria for over thirty years and is considered by radical Sunnis, like the Brothers, to be heretical.[19] (Hafiz al-Assad, the long-time dictator, was an Alawite, as are his son Bashar and most of the country's military leadership.) The massacre was followed by a series of assassinations of Syrian officials, bombings of regional Baath party headquarters, and, finally, shoot-outs with security forces in downtown Damascus. When Egypt moved to put down its religious opposition, it was mindful of its own place at the center of the Arab world and showed relative restraint. Syria, a hermit regime on the periphery, decided that it did not need to follow suit. Al-Assad sent his brother Rifaat and a sizable military force northward in February 1982. There were no trials. Rifaat's forces ringed the ancient city of Hama with artillery and shelled it for three weeks. Afterward, military and internal security personnel were dispatched to comb through the rubble for surviving Brothers and their sympathizers. The best estimates are that eighteen thousand people were killed in Hama. Rifaat then proceeded to Aleppo and Homs, where it is said that casualties were even greater.

Since Syrian authorities did not rely on the due process of law and there is no independent press in the country, we cannot know precisely what motivated the rebels. We can assume, however, that they were linked with the Egyptian movement, and shared its inspiration, doctrine, and objectives. The Syrian Brothers were likely seeking to spark the same divinely assisted revolution as were the radical offshoots of the Egyptian Brothers. Their fantasy of triggering a break in history through their actions is not far afield from Timothy McVeigh's notion that his blow against a symbol of the U.S. government's authority would spur a broad-based popular revolt in America against the nation's Jewish—read "infidel"—rulers. These terrorists see themselves in a metaphysical battle, in which an attack by the true believers against God's enemies will draw Him directly into the battle.

—

On November 20, 1979, at 5:30 in the morning, the imam of the Grand Mosque in Mecca was about to usher in the new year with special prayers when he was interrupted. A young Saudi man, dressed like a desert prophet and named Juhayman bin Muhammad bin Sayf al-Utaybi, stood up before fifty thousand stunned worshipers and declared his brother-in-law Muhammad bin Abd Allah al-Qahtani to be the Mahdi, Islam's long-awaited messiah. "The Mahdi and his men," shouted al-Utaybi into the microphone, "will seek shelter and protection in the Holy Mosque because they are persecuted everywhere until they have no recourse but the Holy Mosque."

Shots were fired, but the imam managed to escape and notify the authorities. For the next three hours, officials were at a loss about how to respond, and in that time, Juhayman actually convinced many in the throng that the Mahdi had truly arrived. When it dawned on local officials that the radicals were linked to the security forces, they realized they faced a crisis. Al-Utaybi was a veteran of the Saudi Arabian National Guard (SANG), a military unit formed from the fierce Bedouin tribes of the Wahhabi heartland. These troops were the best equipped in the kingdom because it was their job to put down insurrections in the ranks of the regular army units or in the streets. Traditionally, the commander of this praetorian guard is the kingdom's crown prince. (Abdullah, the current crown prince and de facto Saudi leader since King Fahd's incapacitation, led the SANG for many years.) But whoever was supposed to be watching the watchers had failed. National Guard troops had infiltrated weapons, ammunition, gas masks, and provisions into the mosque compound over a period of weeks before the new year. When al-Utaybi and his followers made their move, the National Guard units that were present reportedly refused to fire on them.[20]

Al-Utaybi began his takeover at the dawn hour of New Year's Day, the first day of the month of Muharram, fourteen hundred years after Muhammad's Hijra from Mecca to Medina. The year 1000 had been a time of mass hysteria for Christians across Europe, and the approach of the year 1000 in the Islamic calendar, as an Ottoman official recorded, brought a period of unnerving anticipation and "signs," including a revolt, fires, and an outbreak of plague. The first day of the year 1400 after the Hijra was also laden with millennial significance. According to one well-known tradition, the Mahdi would reveal himself on this day. The portents of his coming were compelling: Muhammad bin Abd Allah al-Qahtani was a descendant of Muhammad's tribe, a descendant of the Prophet himself. "His and his father's names were the same as Muhammad's and his father's, and he had come to Mecca from the north," as a hadith had predicted.

Al-Utaybi was inspired by both ibn Taymiyya and the revered ibn Abd al-Wahhab, and he made this debt explicit in demands that were bellowed over the mosque's public-address system throughout the crisis and in a 190-page compendium of letters that circulated secretly throughout the kingdom.[21] Islam, the rebels declared, was in a disastrous state. The Saudi government was guilty of failing to rule under sharia. It governed arbitrarily and introduced innovations that undermined the faith, much like its counterparts in the capitals of other Islamic countries. "All Muslims are living under imposed rulers who do not uphold the religion," the document asserted. "We owe obedience only to those who lead by God's book. Those who lead the Muslims with differing laws and systems and who only take from religion what suits them have no claim on our obedience and their mandate to rule is nil."[22] The Saudi rulers were apostates, like the Dajjal, the deceiver or false messiah who lures Muslims from the path of God. "Anyone with eyesight can see today how they represent religion as a form of humiliation, insult, and mockery. These rulers have subjected Muslims to their interests and made religion into a way of acquiring their materialistic interests. They have brought upon Muslims all evil and corruption." Also damningly, the al-Saud had entered into an alliance with Christians, allowing foreign military and civilian personnel to tread on the sacred soil of Arabia. These Christians were plundering Islam's legacy and impoverishing Muslims while enriching themselves and their apostate accomplices within the House of al-Saud. According to some traditions, the redeemer—by implication, al-Qahtani—would slay the Dajjal and establish a just kingdom, where poverty had been abolished and the Sunna ("Path") of Muhammad reinstated.

Outside the mosque, the Saudis were in disarray. With the trustworthiness of the country's best officers and men impossible to gauge, regular army troops were thrown into the battle. But these forces had only rudimentary skills and lacked the weaponry, specialized combat training, and experience to root out hundreds of fanatical, heavily armed men from the dark cellars of the gigantic complex. The use of overwhelming firepower was out of the question; the Custodian of the Two Holy Mosques, as the Saudi monarch calls himself, was scarcely in a position to destroy Islam's most sacred structure in order to save it. The militants' resolve, preparation, and strong defensive position made an infantry assault suicidal.

The official ulema reacted with horror at the takeover, and some of them issued a fatwa authorizing the use of force against "the wild beast" al-Utaybi and the Mahdists. Yet they were in an embarrassing position. They themselves had decried the infiltration of foreign ideas and technologies, they resented the advent of secular domestic institutions such as the Justice Ministry, and they disapproved of Saudi alliances with other countries. In expressing their opposition to the royal program of modernization, they, like their counterparts in Egypt, legitimated the radical agenda and inadvertently encouraged a mood of violent pessimism. The ulema, however, both depended on the regime for their status and influence and rejected rebellion as unjustifiable under Islam.

With time and royal credibility being lost, the Saudi leadership decided to call on the French for "technical" assistance. Paris obliged by deploying to Mecca the Groupe d'Intervention de la Gendarmerie Nationale, a national paramilitary law-enforcement agency. The results have not been officially documented, but informed observers report that the French advisers offered the Saudis two options: use nerve gas against the fighters, or flood the mosque substructures and insert a high-voltage cable to electrocute them en masse. There are conflicting accounts of which method the Saudis chose—secretive in the best of times, they have been extraordinarily unwilling to talk about any aspect of the takeover— but the government forces got the upper hand. Bitter hand-to-hand fighting continued in the mosque cellars until December 5, 1979, more than two weeks after the takeover began, when al-Utaybi and his surviving cohort were taken into custody and paraded before television cameras. He and al-Qahtani were subsequently decapitated, along with more than sixty of his surviving coconspirators, in the largest mass execution in Saudi history. And rumors circulated for some time after that al-Utaybi— the John the Baptist figure in this drama—or the savior al-Qahtani was alive and in hiding.

The claim that the messiah had come was not unprecedented. From the testimony of those who knew him, it is clear Shuqri Mustafa thought he was the Mahdi, and he intimated as much at his trial. In his writings, as in Faraj's, the complete absence of any thought about the day after the jihadists strike their blow—after Pharaoh is slain—reinforces the sense that these men were possessed by an apocalyptic mind-set.

A verse especially favored by all of these conspirators, Sura 9:14 of the Quran, says, "Fight them and God will punish them at your hands. . . . God will make you victorious over them." The militants take this to mean that the warrior need only strike the first blow in the conflict, which is taking place both on earth and in heaven: God will finish the job. A gloss quoted by the terrorists on the verse says that "God has changed the law of nature to punish unbelievers [at Sodom and Gomorrah] and will do the same today."

———

The uprising in the Grand Mosque showed what a strong hold violent messianic ideas had on a few hundred Saudis. In the decades since, it has become evident that new apocalyptic myths are capturing the imagination of readers in much of the Middle East. These stories and novels mix themes from the Quran and the Bible with *Star Wars* imagery. The works appear in Middle Eastern bookshops, and although it is difficult to gauge how large a readership they have, shopkeepers say they sell well. The end-of-the-world motif meshes well with the deep pessimism and anger that permeate most of the Islamic world because of the perception of chronic economic failure and political weakness.

A young scholar of Islam at Rice University, David Cook is a pioneer in studying this new literature.* Among the writers he has considered is Muhammad Isa Saud, who, writing in the late 1990s, predicted that the messiah "will emerge at the festival of the hajj in 1419 [1998–99], and in Muharram 1420 [1999–2000] he will proclaim the return of the caliphate. If the issue is delayed, it will not be beyond 1425 [2004–2005] . . . and in 2000 there will be the battle of the Mediterranean and in 2001 will be Armageddon, which will be preceded by or be close to a great nuclear battle between France and America in which Paris will be destroyed, and the sea will swallow up New York." Another apocalyptic writer, Bashir Muhammad, writes that the United States is actually the mysterious tribe

* We are grateful to Professor Cook for his insights and for sharing with us the manuscript of his forthcoming book, *Between Hope and Hatred: Contemporary Muslim Apocalyptic Literature,* as well as his article "America: The Second 'Ad: Prophecies About the Downfall of the United States," from which we have drawn the quotations from contemporary Muslim apocalyptic literature.

of Ad. In the Quran, Ad is a city destroyed by God as punishment for its repudiation of his authority.[23] Bashir Muhammad interprets scriptural references to Ad to show that it was an extraordinarily advanced society, with sophisticated weaponry including nuclear arms, a panoply of cultural achievements, a permissive attitude toward homosexuality, and skyscrapers. The tribe's arrogance is unbounded; to the writer, the signs that it is the United States are unmistakable.

Yet another installment in this genre maintains that America is the Dajjal, the deceiver of early Islamic apocalyptic texts. He aims to rule the world, but as the end of time approaches, he will be thwarted. In the overheated prose typical of these stories:

> All of this will not happen despite the Jews, the Dajjal, their helpers and their slaves from the infidel Masonic collaborationist governments, and their ignorant masses . . . the U.S. will be slaughtered—which will break the Dajjal's strong arm, and necessitate his disappearance for a time. . . . Then he will go to Europe and lead Russia in its war against the united Islamic state led by the true caliph, the Mahdi. But the true conflict is between the Jewish Zionists who ride a horse called the Crusaders—this conflict will be between the Islamic community and their enemies the Jews and the Christians, who are one.
>
> From this will develop the great apocalyptic war, the War of Armageddon among the Jews and Christians. The Dajjal will appear [in person] after it, after the Muslim conquest of Rome and all of Europe and America as well, since it will be his [the Dajjal's] plan that both the Crusader and the Islamic armies perish during the course of this battle. Then he will appear with his secret army of hypocrites—those are most of his followers—the Masons and the other Jewish secret organizations, and a special army of the children of fornication which are numerous today in the immoral prostrate West.

The reader, of course, will not be disappointed. The climactic battle will ultimately be won by the Mahdi. Drawing on the Book of Revelation, these apocalyptic fantasists identify America as "the first head of the beast that leads the other six heads" to be struck by God. Destruction comes in as many ways, depending on the writer. In one version, devastation will arrive in the form of an enormous earthquake predicted in the Quran for the end of days.[24] In this scenario, New York City is singled out for complete annihilation:

> Since in New York especially there are more Jews than in other places, and in it is their wealth, their banks, their political foundations which control the entire world (the U.N., the Security Council, the International Monetary Fund, the World Bank, and the principal media networks), so there is no evil greater than in New York in any other place on the inhabited earth, and for this reason their portion of the punishment will be greater in measure and it will be a total uprooting.

After the destruction of New York, the conflict swings back and forth, until a last battle involving nuclear and chemical weapons annihilates America and the Jews. To cap this epic, the rest of the world freely converts to Islam and peace envelops all.

Several threads run through these visions of religious violence. The participants fight in another dimension, where absolute good and evil contend for primacy. Historical time is drawing to a close and a battle is about to be joined that will lead to the appearance of the messiah or God's ultimate triumph. Time becomes compressed. The enemy of centuries ago is indistinguishable from the enemy of today, and all the characters take on the outsize proportions of the mythic.

—

Intellectual history is replete with cases of ideas long eclipsed reappearing and capturing the imagination. The appropriation and reinvention, after some fourteen hundred years, of classical republicanism by Machiavelli and his followers—which, through various leaps, wound up influencing America's founding fathers—is one case. The resurrection in the twentieth century of ibn Taymiyya's thinking about governance and piety, apostasy and jihad is another. The process was carried out by a strange assortment of individuals. Among them were serious intellectuals, deeply affected by the currents of contemporary politics, men such as Rida, Qutb, and Maududi. Others, hard men like Siriyya, Faraj, and al-Islambouli, combined varying degrees of interest in theory with a readiness to commit violence. Others, including Shuqri Mustafa and Juhayman al-Utaybi, evinced a messianic zeal, a furious otherworldliness that is the most foreign of all these qualities to our twenty-first-century sensibilities. All of them, however, drank deeply from the headwaters of jihad in the Mamluk empire of the fourteenth century.

Their ideas, moreover, all feed into the eruption of jihadist Islamism that has confronted the West, and America in particular, over the last decade. In Usama bin Laden, all these streams converge—Qutb's uncompromising opposition to the world of jahiliyya, al-Utaybi's Wahhabi fervor and millennialism, and more than a generation of theorizing and of vilification of secular rulers in the lands of Islam and the West. The perception of a world in crisis, of a battle waged simultaneously on earth and in heaven, and of the ability to hasten divine intervention through human acts—all these come together in al-Qaeda and the monumental violence of September 11, 2001.

CHAPTER 3

THE WARRIOR PRINCE

FOR THE MOST HUNTED MAN of his era, Usama bin Muhammad bin Awad bin Laden has a biography that is astonishingly vague. The facts of his early life, in particular, remain largely unknown. This obscurity is all the more surprising because bin Laden is a scion of one of the wealthiest, best-known families in Saudi Arabia.

The bin Ladens are Saudi citizens but are not Saudi in origin. They are a family of the Hadramawt, a region of southeastern Yemen that is one of the ancient places of the earth, mentioned in the tenth chapter of Genesis in the recitation of the descendants of Noah and the lands they peopled. In the 1930s, Usama's father, Muhammad bin Awad bin Laden, an illiterate peasant, left his impoverished village and traveled with his brother to Saudi Arabia, where he found work as a porter. He set up his own construction firm, which rapidly grew into a large concern. The elder bin Laden ingratiated himself with the royal family and secured a sizable part of the Saudi construction market. He was roadbuilder-in-chief for a nation that had virtually no paved highways, and, under King Faisal, he served as minister of public works. Within the kingdom, Saudi Binladin Group projects have included several royal palaces and the renovations of the Mosque of the Prophet in Medina and the Grand Mosque in Mecca, the latter a vast, costly project that enlarged the structure, which holds some fifty thousand people. (The firm has also handled the renovations of the al-Aqsa Mosque in Jerusalem in the 1960s, and Usama has boasted of its responsibility for improvements on the three holiest sites of Islam.) In 2002, the company tore down the 230-year-old Ottoman fortress in Mecca as part of a $500 million development project to build high-rises and a luxury hotel. Another large contract in the 1990s involved building a military base for U.S. service personnel, who were relocated deep in the Saudi desert after the 1995 bombing of Khobar Towers. Today, the annual revenues of the family-held company are estimated to be in the vicinity of $5 billion, it employs more than 35,000 people, and its operations have broadened to include everything from selling soft drinks to building the Kuala Lumpur airport. The company has counted among its business partners companies ranging from General Electric to Citigroup to the Carlyle Group, an investment firm whose principals include former secretary of defense Frank Carlucci, former secretary of state James Baker, and former British prime minister John Major, and whose advisers include a former U.S. President, George H. W. Bush.

Born in 1957 in Riyadh, Usama was the seventeenth son and one of the youngest of Muhammad bin Laden's fifty-four children. He was the only son of his father's fourth wife, a Syrian from whom the elder bin Laden was later divorced. (Muhammad eventually had eleven wives, though, in accordance with Islamic law, never more than four at a time.) As their fortunes multiplied, the bin Ladens became one of the kingdom's grand cosmopolitan families. Members settled in Britain and Switzerland and elsewhere to tend to business; many regularly vacationed abroad. In 1967, Muhammad bin Laden was killed in a plane crash. Leadership of the family business passed to Salem, the eldest son and one of several bin Ladens who married Western women, in this case a member of the English upper classes. In 1988, in the second of two aviation disasters to mark Usama's life before September 11, Salem, too, was killed when the ultralight craft he was piloting in Texas was entangled in power cables. Ever since, the Saudi Binladen Group has been run by another brother, Bakr. The family has contributed large sums to endow fellowships at the graduate schools of law and design at Harvard as well as at Oxford and Tufts. On September 11, many family members were in the United States, Britain, and other Western countries; twelve lived in the Boston area alone.[1] After the attacks, most of those in America were flown back to Saudi Arabia by the Saudi government. The rupture in their lives caused by Usama was said to be considerable. "The United States has been like a second home to many members of the family," one family member was quoted as saying in an interview from Saudi Arabia.[2]

Usama, by contrast, has never lived in the West and has seldom, if ever, visited it. According to one family acquaintance, he was the only son not sent abroad for schooling, though exactly why is not clear. His upbringing in Medina, Mecca, and Jeddah, surrounded by prominent Westernized families, royal and otherwise, must have been strange: he would have been enveloped in a private world of sybaritic comfort whose members spent substantial parts of the year in such places as London, the south of Spain, and California. Yet that world was a bubble encased within the most thoroughly religious society on earth. Saudi Arabia has a police squad dedicated to dealing with religious infractions—the Commission for the Promotion of Virtue and the Prevention of Vice—and it metes out traditional sharia punishments, such as death for adulterers and amputation for thieves. Saudi culture is saturated with references to the Quran and Islamic history. Prayer is widely observed at the call of the muezzin throughout the day and, compared with other countries, Saudi Arabia allows few foreign influences to seep through. At the same time, its business culture is one of the most corrupt in the world. Little moves in the country without help from hefty bribes, and the princes of the House of Saud who decide on government contracts are among the most practiced at the art of demanding kickbacks. Although Saudi Arabia has little poverty compared to the rest of the Arab world, the disparities of wealth are enormous, and there is widespread, if muted, criticism of the super-rich. Unlike his peers, Usama would have had no identity outside of Saudi Arabia, no sense of simultaneously being part of the Islamic world and the West. He would have had no insulation from the criticism of his class.

Perhaps it is not surprising, then, that among the few experiences of his early years that bin Laden has recounted publicly is working, as he put it in an interview in 1999 with the Arabic news network al-Jazeera, "at an early age on roads in my father's company."[3] Sweating it out in one of Father's work crews may have been a rite of passage—or beloved myth—for a generation of Americans born to wealth, but it is a safe guess that the young Usama did not spend much time rolling tar in the blazing Saudi heat. There are unsubstantiated stories that in his youth, he visited Beirut, then the fleshpot of the Arab world. It is not surprising that such stories circulate. Bin Laden seems so manifestly a man determined to root out something corrupt—something that touched him—that these stories have the ring of plausibility. But he would have been young for such trips, and it is more likely that the corrosive hatred he developed for his country's rulers and elements of its upper crust was conceived and nurtured at home.

At King Abdul Aziz University in Jeddah, bin Laden studied economics and—like Faraj, the leader of al-Jihad at the time of the Sadat assassination—engineering. (He would refer occasionally to his expertise, noting after September 11, for example, that his training enabled him to make the best prediction in al-Qaeda of the damage that would be caused by two Boeing 767s ripping into the Twin Towers.) After receiving his degree, he worked for a time at the Saudi Binladin Group; business, however, was not to be his métier.

The formative event of Usama's early twenties came with the jihad in Afghanistan. The conflict that followed the Soviet invasion of 1979 riveted the attention of the Muslim world, and both clerics and governments encouraged young men to take up arms against the communist invader. Many young Saudis flew to Pakistan to contribute funds and even to enter the fray, though usually briefly. Bin Laden began his involvement as any rich kid would: bringing useful supplies from the family business, in this case heavy construction vehicles that were used to dig trenches, bunkers, tunnels, and fortifications for the Afghan forces.

Peshawar, the capital of Pakistan's North-West Frontier province, is a short drive from the Khyber Pass into Afghanistan, and it served as command headquarters of the jihad. Bin Laden visited frequently, and it was there that he came to know Sheikh Abdullah Azzam, the leading Islamic ideologist of the campaign against the Soviets. A West Bank Palestinian, Azzam moved to Jordan after Israel's victory in the Six Day War, studied at al-Azhar in Egypt, and rose to be a professor of Islamic law at Abdul Aziz University, where bin Laden may well have first met him. During his time in Egypt, Azzam was influenced by the thinking of the Islamists there. He became a champion of ibn Taymiyya, about whom he wrote a book. Azzam believed that jihad was the greatest obligation upon a Muslim after faith itself and that it was the means for "the reformation of mankind, that the truth may be made dominant and good propagated."[4]

Azzam's thinking about jihad, born of his hatred for Israel, had a powerful impact on his radically minded coreligionists. Against the widespread belief that jihad was a collective duty of the community and that only a legitimate political authority could lead such a fight, Azzam declared the imperative of waging a defensive jihad: Muslim lands were threatened, and every Muslim man must join the fight, an obligation that had priority over everything else, including family and job. With the Soviets overrunning Afghanistan, Azzam's arguments resonated loudly.

An electrifying speaker, Azzam became a dominant figure on the Islamic lecture circuit in the West, visiting the United States more than twenty times to raise funds and recruit holy warriors. Among other stops, he visited a convention in 1989 sponsored by the Muslim Arab Youth Association and the Islamic Association for Palestine in Oklahoma, where he issued vehement calls to support the jihad—and where Wadih el-Hage, who would become bin Laden's secretary, met Mahmud Abouhalima, later one of the conspirators convicted of the first World Trade Center bombing. Videotapes of Azzam's lectures circulated widely. When El-

Sayyid Nosair was arrested in 1990 on suspicion of killing Meir Kahane, a box in his closet was found to be filled with them. (They were only examined years later, when the Kahane murder was included in the federal indictment for the TERRSTOP case.) Nosair's attorneys later described Azzam as their defendant's sheikh, or religious authority, and Clement Hampton-El, the African American hospital worker convicted with Nosair and Sheikh Rahman, also came under Azzam's spell during a stop in Pakistan when he was on his way to fight in Afghanistan.

Azzam became a mentor for bin Laden. The Saudi's belief in the reestablishment of a caliphate through an immediate jihad and his disdain for secular Arab nationalism were undoubtedly fostered by this relationship. Bin Laden's money, which he distributed liberally for the jihadist cause, endeared him to Azzam. Around 1984, the two joined forces: together, they established the Maktab al-Khidmat, the Services Bureau, which would set up a recruiting network for fighters, bring them to Peshawar, put them up in the organization's guesthouses, and dispatch them to training camps. Azzam ran the organization; bin Laden funded it. One of the first offices opened was out of a storefront on Atlantic Avenue in Brooklyn, New York, and Azzam sent one of his protégés, Mustapha Shalabi, to run it.

Through the latter half of the 1980s, bin Laden shuttled between Saudi Arabia and Pakistan. At home, he spoke publicly about the stirring events in Afghanistan and recruited others to join the fight. According to the journalist Peter Bergen, bin Laden was virtually deputized in this role of recruiter-in-chief by the Saudi government, in the person of Prince Turki al-Faisal, the kingdom's longtime intelligence chief.[5] During this time, bin Laden also established himself as an effective fund-raiser for jihad. Giving charity is one of the pillars of Islam, and among the wealthy families of Saudi Arabia, there are traditions about how it is done. Often, these families turn to a trusted third party, who, almost like an investment counselor, channels money to worthy causes. Bin Laden's name would have given him entrée to every clan imaginable, and he used it to advance the cause of the fighters in Afghanistan, either acting as the trusted third party for families or persuading others who also played that role to support his cause. One can almost imagine bin Laden as a version of the younger son of a wealthy American family: outshone by the brother who is gifted at running the family business, he opts instead for good works, running the family foundation or taking up a worthy cause. Bin Laden played this part well, establishing relationships that would keep money flowing into jihadist coffers for years to come.

Much like ibn Taymiyya, who roused the Mamluk warriors from behind the lines to fight the Mongols at Mardin in 1303, bin Laden was more cheerleader than battle-hardened mujahid during the Afghan war. By the late 1990s, when they had been in the field for years, the Arab Afghans, as the foreign fighters were known, were some of the toughest units fighting for the Taliban. In the 1980s, though, they were relatively few in number, unseasoned, and often unserious. To many, participating in the jihad was something akin to a stint in Outward Bound; some stayed in the field for only a matter of weeks. Among Western governments there was snickering at the time about "Jihad Jollies"—the practice of Gulf Arabs who traveled to the region to discharge their obligation to fight in the holy war. The visitors would pay large sums to live in air-conditioned cargo containers that had been turned into motel rooms. When they left the comfort of their lodgings, antiaircraft guns, rocket-propelled grenade launchers, and assault rifles were waiting for them outside, which they would fire even though no enemy was anywhere nearby.

Those who actually made it to the front usually fought in support of the most Islamically radical Afghan commanders, Abdul Rasul Sayyaf and Gulbuddin Hekmatyar, men who were both vicious and ineffective leaders. The Arab Afghans were often considered more of a hindrance than a help. One battle, late in the conflict, was an exception. In fighting at Ali Khel in Paktia province, Arab Afghans stopped Soviet forces from advancing in a fierce battle. Bin Laden took part, and while the details of his actions are clouded by myth, his reputation as a fighter was made there. Towering over most Arabs at about six feet six inches, bin Laden is a commanding figure. That he was known to be a member of a fabulously wealthy family and faced great danger when he could have been living the good life gave this new legend luster. This Galahad-like persona, the ascetic warrior prince holding God's banner aloft, would become the core of the bin Laden myth.

—

The last of the Soviet troops crossed the Friendship Bridge over the Amu Darya and out of Afghanistan in mid-February 1989. The toll over nine years of fighting was fifteen thousand Soviet troops dead or missing in Afghanistan. That was less than a third of U.S. losses in Vietnam. But the number of Soviet soldiers who were sick or wounded was thirty times the number of dead, a staggering figure, and the social, economic, and political costs of defeat were so humiliating that they proved to be an important factor in the undoing of the Soviet Union.

The effect of victory on the Islamists was galvanizing. They believed that all due credit was theirs, and Allah's. Repeatedly in interviews, bin Laden has scoffed at the notion that America's multibillion-dollar contribution in money and matériel, including the vaunted Stinger missile, made any difference to the outcome of the war, boasting that "those who participated in the jihad in Afghanistan bear the greatest responsibility in this regard, because they realized that with insignificant capabilities, with a small number of RPGs, with a small number of antitank mines, with a small number of Kalashnikov rifles, they managed to crush the greatest empire known to mankind." After forty years in which believers had seen the Muslim armies of nationalist rulers defeated four times by Israel in the Middle East and four times in South Asia in the Indo-Pakistan conflict, the triumph was a transcendent event. One prominent jihadist, using language out of ibn Taymiyya and Faraj, would later write that victory in Afghanistan marked a turning point in the history of Islam that was at odds with the intentions of those who poured so much money into it: "The United States wanted the war to be a war by proxy against the Russians, but, with God's assistance, the Arab mujahidin turned it into a call to revive the neglected religious duty, namely jihad for the cause of

God.''[6] A victory, in other words, not only for Islam but for the reformed Islam of the jihadists.

Amid this intoxication, bin Laden began thinking about carrying the struggle forward. In 1989, with those closest to him in Pakistan and Afghanistan, he began organizing the group that would become al-Qaeda. One of the men in this circle was Ayman al-Zawahiri, the leader of a faction of the Egyptian Islamic Jihad (EIJ). A doctor by profession and six years older than bin Laden, al-Zawahiri was a link to the original al-Jihad, the predecessor of EIJ, which he joined in his teens. After the assassination of Sadat, al-Zawahiri was convicted on a weapons charge and spent three years in prison. Another eminence who appeared in Peshawar from time to time was Sheikh Omar Abdel Rahman. How much direct contact the Blind Sheikh had with bin Laden is not clear, but Rahman's ideas were in the air, and two of his sons would eventually join al-Qaeda.

Bin Laden would later claim that he already knew during the fighting against the Russians that his ultimate enemy would be the United States. Yet as they were first articulated, the goals of al-Qaeda, or the Islamic Army as it was also called at the time, resembled those of the Egyptian jihadists: the organization would be dedicated to the goal of toppling existing Muslim governments and establishing a new caliphate—an undivided Islamic realm ruled by sharia. The means for accomplishing these aims would be jihad.

Abdullah Azzam's thinking had heavily influenced bin Laden; but there was a disagreement among the Islamists on how to pursue their goals, and student and mentor found themselves on opposite sides. Earlier in his life, Azzam had turned away from the Palestinian struggle because it was dominated by secular nationalists and leftists, but now he was determined that the next step for the veterans of Afghanistan would be to fight Israel, something he told El-Sayyid Nosair and others. Bin Laden disagreed, preferring, like the Egyptian jihadist, to focus on jahili Muslim regimes. In November 1989, Azzam and two of his sons were killed by a car bomb in Peshawar. In the years since, bin Laden has always heaped praise on Azzam as a great leader of the Afghan jihad and a pathbreaking thinker. As recently as the summer of 2001, a bin Laden recruiting video included footage of the Palestinian cleric speaking. But rumors have long circulated that bin Laden might have been behind the killing. At a minimum, some kind of purge seems to have occurred in the nascent group: in March 1991, Mustapha Shalabi, who also was said to prefer a "Palestine next" strategy, turned up dead in his apartment in New York. Wadih el-Hage, the Lebanese-born convert to Islam who later became bin Laden's personal secretary, was summoned to New York to take over the Maktab al-Khidmat, the Services Bureau. (Sheikh Rahman, who had quarreled with Shalabi on a number of occasions, was also suspected of having a hand in his death.)[7]

From the start, al-Qaeda displayed a grand sense of mission. It required that its recruits swear a special oath of loyalty to the group's "emir," bin Laden, and to the cause of jihad. The signed pledge was called a *baya,* which today can mean simply an oath of allegiance but which originally referred to the homage paid to a new caliph at his inauguration; this implication was well understood by those who joined. Baya, as the al-Qaeda defector Jamal al-Fadl, who swore his oath at the Farouq camp in Khost, Afghanistan, in 1989, later explained, "means you swear you going to agree about the agenda and about jihad, listen to the emir, [that you are ready at all times for] any order and do—whatever work they ask you in group, you have to do it." Asked to be more specific about what the tasks might be, he answered, "They say it's jihad."

Bin Laden assembled a capable leadership team, including many with professional degrees and technical skills. Al-Zawahiri was part of the inner circle from the beginning, and he exerted a strong influence on bin Laden, becoming effectively the number two man in the organization and its chief ideologist. Abu Ubaidah al-Banshiri, a former Egyptian police officer who had distinguished himself as a mujahid in Afghanistan, became the group's "military" chief. Another Egyptian who had been in Afghanistan since the early 1980s, Muhammad Atef, also known as Abu Hafs al-Masry, become al-Qaeda's deputy chief of operations. Mamduh Salim—a.k.a. Abu Hajer al-Iraqi, who taught al-Fadl about ibn Taymiyya—would become an important figure in everything from finances to weapons procurement. On the organization chart, bin Laden was at the top with a shura, consultative council, directly beneath him. Among the shura members were a Nigerian, an Omani, a Yemeni, some Saudis and Egyptians—it was a United Nations of radical Islam. Committees with responsibilities in areas such as military operations, religious affairs, finance, and publicity reported to the council. There was also a cadre of in-house experts: a Libyan named Abu Anas was al-Qaeda's computer specialist; Abu Musab Reuter was the media specialist—the surname Reuter was given to him in recognition of his skills—and published the group's newspaper. Others were knowledgeable about tanks, mortars, and explosives. Along with all these specialists, most of whom would have counterparts in any ministry of defense, there was Abu Muaz al-Masry, whose specialty was the interpretation of dreams. Oneiromancy is taken seriously in al-Qaeda, as was demonstrated by bin Laden's first video after the September 11 attacks, in which prophetic dreams are discussed.[8]

———

With the end of the fighting in Afghanistan in 1989, bin Laden returned to Saudi Arabia and his family's firm while al-Qaeda remained in its camps in Afghanistan and its guesthouses in Pakistan. The withdrawal of the Soviets may have been a crowning achievement, but the various factions of mujahidin still refused to overcome their differences as they fought on fractiously against the Soviet-installed regime in Kabul that was led by the former secret police chief Najibullah. Bin Laden was fed up.

Saudi Arabia was in many regards no more satisfying. The returning soldier who finds himself at odds with society at home is a cliché, but for bin Laden, it had a powerful truth. Those who had fought a holy war came home to no fanfare and little appreciation. After August 1, 1990, when Saddam Hussein invaded Kuwait, bin Laden's disaffection turned to disgust. The takeover and the menacing of Saudi Arabia by the Iraqi army precipitated the worst crisis in the country's history. An oft-reported story tells of bin Laden offering to put his Arab Afghans at the disposal of the Saudi government to defend the country against Saddam Hussein, who, to jihadists, represented the worst kind of Muslim—a blaspheming arch-nationalist. The government declined, instead putting itself in the hands of the U.S. military. The first planeloads of GIs arrived in the kingdom on August 7.

Tradition holds that the Prophet declared on his deathbed that "there shall be no two religions in Arabia," and the injunction has been taken seriously by the al-Saud. Neither churches nor synagogues can legally be erected in Saudi Arabia. While non-Muslims may visit much of the kingdom, Mecca and Medina remain strictly off-limits, a prohibition that has inspired the exploits of travelers such as Sir Richard Burton, who visited the Grand Mosque dressed as a Muslim in 1853. In past decades, Riyadh had maintained a general policy of keeping out foreign troops. An American airfield, a rare exception, was built in the country at the end of World War II and kept in service until the 1960s, when its lease expired.[9] For many in Saudi Arabia, the arrival of the Americans was sacrilege. It exposed the ruling family to criticism on religious grounds and for failing in its responsibility to provide for the defense of the country.

For bin Laden, the arrival of the U.S. forces had the effect of a revelation. No sooner had the Soviet superpower been laid low than the American one reared up to fill the space occupied by its former enemy. As bin Laden would say later, "This collapse [of the Soviet Union] made the U.S. more haughty and arrogant and it has started to look at itself as a Master of this world and established what it calls the new world order."[10] President Bush's famous phrase became code among Islamists for America's purported effort at world domination and the destruction of Islam. After the end of the Cold War, bin Laden believes, "America escalated its campaign against the Muslim world in its entirety, aiming to get rid of Islam itself." This sudden intrusion in the realm of Islam to subdue a Muslim country—even though it was Saddam Hussein's Iraq—confirmed the long-standing belief, handed down from Sayyid Qutb, that the United States was by nature the unalterable enemy of Islam, a demiurge whose values and culture propelled it into a war with the true faith. To Qutb, the West *was* the Crusaders, a force hostile to Islam and indistinguishable in essence from the armies that set out to capture Jerusalem in 1095; to bin Laden, the events of August 1990 confirmed in the most vivid way that America was the modern incarnation of the Knights of the Cross.

Under pressure from the royal family, Saudi Arabia's Council of Senior Ulema, the ranking body of clergy charged with providing religious guidance to the nation, issued a fatwa permitting the stationing of non-Muslim troops in the kingdom. For bin Laden, this exposed the official clergy as irreligious state lackeys, just as the Egyptian ulema were in the eyes of Faraj and Sheikh Rahman. Whatever bin Laden's earlier opinion of his nation's rulers—and his offer to help them defend the borders suggests that it was not always hostile—the House of Saud's refusal to share his Manichaean view condemned it to the realm of the kufr, the infidel.

Among Saudis, bin Laden was not alone in his disgust at the American deployment, and the unprecedented level of dissent that appeared in the kingdom in the months that followed must have strengthened his moral certainty. Two young Islamic scholars emerged as fearless critics of the al-Saud: Sheikh Safar bin Abd al-Rahman al-Hawali and Sheikh Salman bin Fahd al-Awda were both university teachers of sharia who, breaking with the long-standing practice of avoiding public dissent, spoke openly about the errors of the government. Al-Hawali, who had written a book called *Kissinger's Promise,* about the West's treacherous efforts to control Arab oil resources, explained the Gulf War in September 1990 to a crowd in a Riyadh mosque as another step in the conspiracy, saying, "It is not the world against Iraq. . . . It is the West against Islam."[11] Tapes of his speech and a similarly incendiary one by al-Awda were copied and circulated by the millions. The two became known as the *dawa*—religious awakening—sheikhs.

The year following the Iraqi invasion of Kuwait was turbulent. In May 1991, a petition signed by many Islamic scholars—the actual number is disputed—including al-Awda and al-Hawali was presented to King Fahd.

This "Letter of Demands" insisted that the government undertake a broad program of reform to bring Saudi life into accordance with the requirements of sharia, which was violated by, among other things, banks that had "usurious" policies, the unequal distribution of public resources, and a foreign policy that did not advance Islamic concerns. By Saudi standards, the act verged on insurrection. Many signatories were interrogated and some jailed. The Council of Senior Ulema, again under pressure, denounced the letter. The two sheikhs and many like-minded clerics were not intimidated, however, and continued to criticize the regime. In some circles, there was talk about issuing a declaration of takfir, a condemnation of apostasy, against the government, thus making it a legitimate target for jihadist activity. The al-Saud worked to rebottle the genie of antiregime Islamism by using increasingly unhappy senior ulema to pressure the younger ones and having the security services intimidate them. Some activists fled to Britain, where they began writing harsh attacks on the Saudi royal family, such as a "Prince of the Month" feature that was posted on the Internet and mocked members of the royal family for their immorality. "Prince of the Month" recycled British tabloid reports of involvement with call girls and rumors of homosexual affairs, and leveled allegations of drug abuse, neglect of government duties, and, most repetitively, financial corruption.[12] For all the Saudi government's efforts, the criticism was not easily stanched. After several years of warnings and threats, the Awakening Sheikhs were thrown into prison, where they remained for five years.

Bin Laden later referred to the treatment of al-Awda and al-Hawali as a defining instance of the Saudi regime's adherence to man-made laws and disregard for the sovereignty of heaven. Riyadh's actions had an effect on him, and he declared that "when the Saudi government transgressed in oppressing all voices of the scholars and the voices of those who call for Islam, I found myself forced, especially after the government prevented Sheikh Salman al-Awda and Sheikh Safar al-Hawali and some other scholars, to carry out a small part of my duty of enjoining what is right and forbidding what is wrong."[13] This last is an obligation commanded by the Quran that has a place in Islam similar to that of the Golden Rule in Christianity. Bin Laden eventually founded the Advice and Reform Committee, an organization with offices in London and Sudan that devoted itself to anti-Saudi propaganda. Throughout the years, al-Qaeda members have said, bin Laden has maintained a relationship with the Awakening Sheikhs, and they may be counted as both an influence on his thinking and a motivation for his continued efforts to undermine the al-Saud.

—

Stirred by the shock of American troops arriving in Saudi Arabia, bin Laden's ideas about the future of al-Qaeda began to evolve. At the time, he believed that his business in Afghanistan was finished. His determination to overthrow secular regimes was strengthening, as was his anger about American inroads into the Islamic world. He wanted to be more active and to move his forces from the far reaches of Afghanistan closer to the Arab world, where they might directly shape events. But the region was virtually filled with inhospitable nationalist governments, all of which were displaying their anxiety about returning jihadists by harassing and imprisoning them.

SUDAN

The sole exception was Sudan, where a 1989 coup had brought a hybrid military-Islamist regime to power. Even before that, Islamists had been more successful in Sudan than in any other predominantly Sunni country. That record was the accomplishment of a Sorbonne-educated scholar, Hassan al-Turabi, one of the world's leading Islamist thinkers and a onetime dean of the University of Khartoum law school. As the leader of the Muslim Brotherhood in Sudan in the 1960s, al-Turabi engineered the group's metamorphosis into a political party, the National Islamic Front. The NIF had managed to join the government of strongman Gaafar Nimeiry in 1977, with al-Turabi as attorney general.

Using that position and Nimeiry's own turn to religion, al-Turabi pushed through a reform of Sudanese law along the lines of sharia, built up his political base, and established contacts with Islamists throughout the Maghreb, Egypt, Jordan, and the Gulf states. Nimeiry and his government were ousted in 1985, and the NIF's fortunes declined in the latter half of the decade. Determined to reverse the slide, al-Turabi and a military officer, Brigadier General Omar Bashir, spearheaded the coup that deposed Sudan's moderate government. Al-Turabi envisioned turning Sudan into the champion of the Islamist movement, stealing the banner of Islamic leadership from Saudi Arabia, and providing a base for groups that would bring sharia governments to power. After the coup, Sudan flung its doors open to extremist organizations from all over. Al-Qaeda began to ponder relocation to the new center of world Islamism.

Within the group, some were leery of becoming foot soldiers in another man's revolution. A delegation of four of the group's leaders, including Abu Hajer, traveled to Sudan in 1990 to meet with NIF officials and see for themselves how accommodating the country's rulers would be. They were satisfied with what they found and impressed by the erudite al-Turabi. After they returned to Afghanistan and vouched for the Khartoum government, an al-Qaeda migration began. Bin Laden was still in Saudi Arabia; his antiregime agitation and connections with the mujahidin led Riyadh to restrict his travel.[14] But in mid-1991, with public discontent seething and the government eager to rid itself of a problem, bin Laden was expelled from the country. He traveled first to Afghanistan, then joined the al-Qaeda leadership in Sudan.

Bin Laden's decision to move to Sudan was a boon for the ideological aspirations of the regime in Khartoum; it promised an economic shot in the arm as well. Because of its support for Saddam Hussein in the Gulf War, Sudan was short on friends and funds. Bin Laden's personal finances are a continuing mystery, but he clearly came to Sudan with a substantial amount of cash. His inheritance probably amounted to some $30 million, and he may have had more money at his disposal from wealthy donors in the Persian Gulf. His investments in his new home suggest that he was delivering a quid pro quo for the safe haven his group received, but he may also genuinely have shared al-Turabi's hopes for creating a thriving, Islamically pure country. Although the numbers it cites are almost certainly wrong, an article about bin Laden's time in Sudan that appeared in the London-based *al-Quds al-Arabi* newspaper long after his departure relayed that "financial circles in Sudan estimated the money that bin Laden brought with him into Sudan at $350 million. Others said it was more than this. Amid the atmosphere of enthusiasm that prevailed in the reception [for his arrival], Usama bin Laden announced a $5 million donation as an initial fee for his new membership in the Islamic Front." The same report quotes a Sudanese economist as saying that in 1993 the Sudanese government asked bin Laden for "an $80 million loan to import wheat urgently because of an acute shortage of this commodity. The stockpile of wheat was almost consumed and the Sudanese were standing in queues for long hours to get five loaves of bread each that would not be enough for one meal for a middle-size family. Bin Laden immediately responded and spared al-Turabi and his government a critical problem."[15]

Ultimately, though, bin Laden's investments were about providing cash flow for his other activities. After his arrival, he set up a company called Wadi al-Aqiq, named after a valley in Saudi Arabia, that became the umbrella for a panoply of other firms. One of the largest was the al-Hijra construction company, which undertook projects for the government of Sudan, including building a seven-hundred-kilometer road from Khartoum to Port Sudan. (Bin Laden is said never to have been paid for this and other jobs.)[16] He invested heavily in the Islamic al-Shamal bank, which conformed to sharia strictures and did not charge interest. Among the other businesses bin Laden bought, founded, or was given in lieu of payment by the government were a tannery, a heavy-equipment leasing operation, an investment firm called Taba, a bakery, a cattle-breeding operation, and a fruit and vegetable import-export firm. International trading became a major area of activity, much of it under the auspices of Bin Laden International, which exported commodities such as sesame seeds, palm oil, and sunflower seeds and imported much-needed sugar and soap. The group was sophisticated enough to take advantage of the new opportunities for business in a rapidly globalizing world: sales of produce were directed to Cyprus, where entry into the new single European market was possible and there were friendly, no-questions-asked bankers to help out. Bin Laden agents bought heavy equipment and other goods in the Czech Republic, Hungary, and Russia, where prices for trucks and other vehicles were low. The group also purchased farms around Sudan, some very large, which grew corn, peanuts, and other foodstuffs and, more important, were used as camps for training terrorists.

Al-Qaeda quickly developed a close relationship with the National Islamic Front, and, in particular, the Sudanese intelligence service. The government gave bin Laden's organization a couple of hundred valid Sudanese passports. Many al-Qaeda operatives were wanted in other countries for various jihadist activities, so the new fraudulent identities made international travel easier. Members of the group were effectively detailed to the Sudanese authorities to help coordinate the immigration of Islamist radicals, serving as a vetting office to try to prevent unwanted foreign agents from gaining entry under cover.

The mix of business and terror was a hallmark of al-Qaeda's operations in Sudan. The firms provided revenues that bin Laden used to subsidize jihadist groups around the world and to pay for the training camps that terrorists could use as bases between operations. During these years, al-Qaeda laid the foundation for its eventual role as the keystone of international jihad. From its earliest days, al-Qaeda counted Muslims of every nationality within its ranks: Libyans and Filipinos, Nigerians and Iraqis, Saudis, Yemenis, Jordanians, Algerians—whole detachments of jihadist organizations were present in al-Qaeda facilities. Bin Laden's operatives acted as couriers, bringing $100,000 to radicals in Jordan and the same amount to the Eritrean Islamic Jihad. The group dispatched equipment and trainers to the Philippines to work with the Moro Liberation Front and helped found the Abu Sayyaf Group, which would eventually distinguish itself with its penchant for decapitation. In Pakistan, al-Qaeda had ties with a range of extremist groups and was connected to the country's political life through Maulana Fazlur Rahman, leader of a wing of the religious Jamiat Ulema Islamiyya party. The group arranged for radical Tajiks to train in camps in Afghanistan. In supporting Egypt's radicals, the group used both modern and ancient methods: money was funneled into the country by couriers who flew into Cairo, while camel caravans lumbered up from Sudan to the markets of upper Egypt with Kalashnikovs hidden in the saddlebags. Al-Qaeda planted its flag in Lebanon by opening one of its guesthouses there. Using a large vessel that belonged to the group, it shipped arms and explosives from Port Sudan across the Red Sea to Yemeni jihadists then fighting communists after the merger of communist North Yemen and South Yemen in 1990. (Some of these weapons may later have been smuggled into Saudi Arabia for use against American or Saudi forces.)

There was hardly a battle anywhere involving Islamic radicals in which al-Qaeda was not involved. In his capacity as quartermaster for jihad, bin Laden showed a knack for reacting to world events and directing resources where they were needed. When the first Chechnyan war broke out in 1994, al-Qaeda created a pipeline for fighters and matériel that ran through Ankara into Azerbaijan. A nongovernmental organization (NGO) was founded in Baku, the capital, to give cover to al-Qaeda operations involved in moving money, men, and weapons. Fighters were smuggled across the border into Russian Dagestan and then on to Chechnya. The whole operation was done with considerable precision: al-Qaeda calculated the cost of providing an armed fighter to the theater to be $1,500. Operations like these were a critical part of al-Qaeda's activities during its years in Sudan as it created a role for itself as an international clearinghouse and bankroller of jihad. This side of al-Qaeda activities would continue to grow, even as the group's more direct involvement in terror seemed to take the spotlight. Having a finger in every pot served bin Laden well. He may have been more deeply committed to some areas of operations than others. But in return for allying himself with the particular, local agendas of jihadist groups in so many parts of the world, he secured their support for his own evolving vision of the struggle. He was building a coalition, ensuring that he had loyalists operating all over the world as well as fresh recruits streaming into the network for later use.

Life in Sudan suited the group well. Bin Laden lived in a luxury villa and worked in Wadi al-Aqiq's office in Khartoum's business district. He mingled with his troops, holding a lecture on jihad and the al-Qaeda agenda that was attended by all who were in town on Thursday nights after prayers. Operatives could spend time on the group's various farms for rest and relaxation, and the emir himself was said to be happily indulging his own passion for horseback riding, at times with the son of Hassan al-Turabi.[17] For all these advantages, however, the business of the terrorism-and-capitalism conglomerate was not always smooth. The group suffered from sporadic cash flow problems, and its managers complained about a problem that bedeviled international executives of all stripes in the 1990s: the strong dollar was hurting operations, which were conducted in ever-weaker Sudanese pounds. Bin Laden's efforts to cut costs demoralized some of his operatives, and, for all the ideological fervor of the group, there was chronic resentment over low wages, and the lack of money for special needs. (Both of the al-Qaeda defectors who testified at the embassy bombings trial in 2001 left the group over financial issues: al-Fadl pocketed unauthorized commissions and L'Houssaine Kherchtou quit soon after the leadership refused his request for money to pay for his wife's cesarean section.) The money crunch created tensions between different jihadist groups under the bin Laden umbrella as well. At the highest level of the organization, the presence of Ayman al-Zawahiri, Abu Ubaidah, and Muhammad Atef gave the Egyptians particularly strong representation and influence on bin Laden's thinking. Al-Zawahiri's role as leader of the Egyptian Islamic Jihad, and, perhaps, the government of Sudan's machinations against the Cairo government, put the Egyptians in the ascendant. Anger over preferential treatment had flared when the group was still based in South Asia; when Egyptians received better wages, others were resentful. Faced with complaints about money, bin Laden tried to remind his troops that they sought more than profits. "Our agenda is bigger than business. We [are] not going to make [profitable] business here, but we need to help the government and the government help our group, and this is our purpose," he was quoted as saying.

—

If al-Qaeda found itself short on money from time to time, other developments helped it maintain its sense of mission. Religious fundamentalism thrives on a sense of embattlement, and for Islamists in the early 1990s, world events provided frequent and alarming confirmation of a global plot against Muslims. The Gulf War was the foremost piece of evidence: not only had American troops been allowed to "occupy" the Land of the Two Holy Mosques but the United States had gathered into a single military effort most of the hated secular governments in the Islamic world— Egypt, Syria, and Pakistan among them—to destroy another Muslim regime. Bin Laden and his cohorts felt no sympathy for Saddam Hussein, but they were outraged that the West and its servant-regimes would attack a large Muslim country and, in particular, gang up on the one such country that dared to challenge American world control.[18] Iraq won additional sympathy from the Islamists because it was bold enough to work on weapons of mass destruction, which America, in its "arrogance," permitted Israel to develop but forbade Muslim countries from possessing. Once the rout of Operation Desert Storm ended, U.S. troops remained in Saudi Arabia, proof positive of America's desire to subdue the Islamic world. To rub salt in these wounds, much of the coalition that joined in fighting Saddam came together with Israel in an unprecedented Middle East peace conference in Madrid, where Arab governments tacitly accepted "the Zionist entity's" right to exist.

For Islamists, this was a satanic tableau. But the Gulf War and its aftermath were only the tip of the iceberg; violence engulfed Muslim communities on two continents. The breakup of Yugoslavia, beginning in 1991, led to the slaughter of tens of thousands of Bosnian Muslims and a savagery unseen in Europe since the Holocaust. The inability of Europe's peace-

keepers to protect Muslims, the arms embargo on Bosnia, and the failure
of pinpoint aerial strikes to stop the carnage were interpreted by many
Muslims—not just Islamists—as part of a Western stratagem. As Sheikh
Rahman declared in a 1993 speech, "There are two main enemies. The
enemy who is at the foremost of the work against Islam are America and
the allies. Who is assisting the Serbs? And who is providing them with
weapons and food? Europe, and behind it is America, who are providing
them with weapons, money, and food, in order to completely exterminate
the Muslims, and because they declared that they do not want the establishment of an Islamic republic in Europe." Later, more forceful NATO
air strikes, the training of the Bosnian army by private Americans, and the
American-led diplomacy that led to the Dayton Accords and the survival
of the Bosnian state did nothing to puncture the myth that the Serbs were
nothing more than the hatchet men of the West.

More grist for Islamist conspiracy theories was provided by events in
Algeria. In late 1991, when Algerians went to the polls for their first fully
free election since the country gained independence almost thirty years
earlier, they voted overwhelmingly for the Islamic Salvation Front (Front
Islamique du Salut, or FIS). But the army set the results aside, a move
that, not surprisingly, the FIS and its foreign sympathizers viewed as an
anti-Islamic ploy. Civil war broke out. From the welter of competing Islamist groups, the Armed Islamic Group (Groupes Islamiques Armés, or
GIA) emerged as supremely violent. It had an ideology reminiscent of
Shuqri Mustafa's except that instead of withdrawing from a corrupt
world, it viewed violence as justified against anyone who did not support
the group. Arguing that ordinary villagers, schoolteachers, and foreigners
were supporting the regime, it attacked all of them and many others, too.
The GIA's trademark was to infiltrate a village after nightfall and slit
the throats of everyone it could lay hands on. Between the GIA's killing
and the government's brutal efforts to suppress the group, more than
40,000 Algerians have died in the last decade. These events, which were
followed by such tragedies as the first Chechnyan war from 1994 to 1996
and the conflict in Kosovo in the late 1990s, sharpened the Islamist sense
of crisis.

Bin Laden and his followers shared that feeling of world-shattering events going on around them. But set against that notion of crisis was a belief in their own God-given power. *They,* the believers, were the victors of Afghanistan. The umma was in a dire condition—but it was jahili rulers, the agents of America, who were to blame. This juxtaposition is at the heart of bin Laden's thinking. He was gathering in the exiles of jihad, righteous fighters from a score of lands, and not just to confront the swarm of apostates ruling the countries of Islam but to do battle with the force of jahiliyya itself.

Al-Qaeda's future was beginning to come into focus. Bin Laden and the senior leaders turned to thinking about targets to attack, and they issued a series of fatwas spelling out their priorities. In the first one mentioned by Jamal al-Fadl—its date is unknown and no text is extant—bin Laden delivered the message that "we cannot let the American army stay in the Gulf area and take our oil, take our money, and we have to do something to take them out. We have to fight them." At the end of 1992, an elaboration on this theme was presented in a further fatwa on the need to drive the Americans out of Islamic lands.

That the group's policies were set by these edicts reflects a mind-set that is both deeply religious and in its own way revolutionary. As innumerable commentators have pointed out in discussing the 1998 fatwa "Jihad Against Jews and Crusaders," which famously preceded and justified the attack on the U.S. embassies in East Africa, bin Laden lacks the traditional scholarly qualifications to issue a fatwa. Although some of his lieutenants have considerable learning, no clerics are known to have been in al-Qaeda's leadership and no serious appeals to the authority of other ulema are cited. Bin Laden issues fatwas out of a belief that al-Qaeda members and sympathizers require this traditional form to legitimate policy; and, with the official clergy tarnished as the paid, reliable servants of barbarous rulers, he needs no formal credentials. By issuing fatwas, bin Laden and his followers are acting out a kind of self-appointment as alim: they are asserting their rights as interpreters of Islamic law.

In December 1992, U.S. forces arrived in Somalia as part of the UN peacekeeping mission to restore order and provide relief in a country beset by famine. The Americans' appearance in the Horn of Africa was a catalytic event for al-Qaeda, which interpreted the deployment as another unmistakable step in the campaign against Islam. That this was one of the crucial formative moments in the life of the group is an extraordinary irony: for the policy makers of the first Bush administration, the dispatch of forces to Somalia was a move uniquely devoid of geopolitical concerns and expressed only the nation's desire to fulfill a humanitarian obligation. In Khartoum, al-Qaeda issued another fatwa against the Americans, who, it alleged, having established their domination over the Gulf, were now moving into the Horn of Africa, and would soon be headed for Sudan—and presumably, for al-Qaeda itself. At a group guesthouse in the Riyadh City neighborhood of Khartoum, the leaders announced their determination to enlist Somalis into the fight against the United States. Bin Laden declared that the head of the American snake needed to be cut off.

The new fatwa was another step in a fateful turn of events: it signified that al-Qaeda was making the United States its principal target, one it would attack wherever and whenever it could. Earlier jihadists such as Faraj had distinguished between the "near enemy," illegitimate Muslim rulers, and the "far enemy," Israel or the United States. And they had always decided that the near enemy had priority, that Pharaoh must be killed. With this series of Khartoum fatwas, al-Qaeda tacked in the other direction: the desire to topple Muslim rulers had not disappeared, nor would it. But the power that propped up these illegitimate rulers and desecrated the holy soil of Arabia—the ultimate fountain of corruption on earth—was becoming the preferred target.

This resetting of priorities would dramatically distinguish al-Qaeda from all other terrorist groups of the period, and many key aspects of the group's approach to terror would flow from it. Exactly whose idea it was to overturn almost two decades of jihadist thinking is hard to say. From speeches around this time, it is clear that the Blind Sheikh was thinking of a similar strategy, which was laid out in the notebook of El-Sayyid Nosair, and spoke of the imperative to destroy "the enemies of Allah. And this is by means of destroying exploding, the structure of their civilized pillars such as the touristic infrastructure which they are proud of and their high world buildings."

—

Al-Qaeda is hardly the first terrorist group to attack America. Hezbollah, for example, struck America repeatedly and murderously in the 1980s. But its aim was to drive the United States out of Lebanon, not to kill Americans for the sake of killing Americans. Hezbollah calculated correctly that the United States could be prompted to act in a certain way if the costs of its current policy were made too high. Al-Qaeda, some argue, is trying to do the same, to force an American retreat from the Arabian peninsula. But it is ultimately not a single American policy, such as stationing troops in Lebanon, or even in Saudi Arabia, that is the issue. Instead, it is America's very presence in the world, the fundamentals of its relationship with dozens of Muslim countries *and* its relationship with Israel, that arouses the ire of al-Qaeda. America itself, and the essentials of the world order it supports, are what must be attacked. The seeds of this belief can be traced to the deliberations of 1992–1993.

During this time, another development confirmed al-Qaeda's faith in its strategy and in the shift from the near enemy to the far: the repeated failure of jihadists operating at the national level. Not only were the veterans of Afghanistan much harassed at this time, but a growing number of countries were also pursuing harsh policies against Islamists in general. As a result, many were taking flight. The bloodshed in Algeria was the most dramatic, but Islamic movements were under pressure in the rest of the Maghreb and elsewhere. In Egypt, the relatively mild treatment of Islamists in the years after the assassination of Sadat gave way to a harsh crackdown beginning in 1992. The al-Gamaat al-Islamiyya, the southern Egyptian group that grew out of al-Jihad and was most closely affiliated with the Blind Sheikh, was responsible for assassinating Rifaat al-

Mahgoub, the speaker of Egypt's parliament, in 1990 and carried out attacks against police and foreign tourists—in all, the violence of the period
caused more than eight hundred deaths. When the government struck
back beginning in 1992, thousands of Islamists were imprisoned and
many were tortured. Droves fled the country, some obtaining asylum in
Western Europe, others gravitating to Sudan or the training camps of
Afghanistan. The lesson was clear: in national struggles, the jihadists
were overmatched by the security apparatus of the state. With the near
enemy unbeatable on its own turf, the only solution was to wage jihad
against the far enemy. The radicals blamed much of the national authorities' success on U.S. support, which strengthened the desire for a strategy
against the far enemy.

—

Once it turned its attention to America, the group began to innovate and
lay the groundwork for a violent future. Somalia provided the context for
Abu Hajer's discussion of ibn Taymiyya, which Jamal al-Fadl recounted
in the New York courtroom. Al-Qaeda's plans to commit violence against
the United States in a Muslim country inevitably meant that Muslim
lives would also be taken. Abu Hajer instructed that killing noncombatants in the course of attacking those who gave the enemy assistance was
unobjectionable. He constructed a hypothetical case, which al-Fadl recounted: "If the people want to make explosives for building and it's military building and sometimes it could be civilian around the building and
you don't have any choice other than that, you should do it and you don't
have to worry about that." The reason, according to Abu Hajer, was that
"if he's a good person, he go to paradise and if he's a bad person, he go to
hell"—a justification used by, among others, Christian Crusaders and the
Inquisition to exterminate heretics and opponents. The question, so far
as al-Qaeda was concerned, was not whether it made tactical sense to
carry out attacks in which noncombatants might be killed—not, that is,
whether such an operation would anger Somalis who might otherwise be
attracted to an Islamist, anti-American insurgency—the question was

simply whether it was permissible under religious doctrine to carry out such killings.

Al-Qaeda's decision makers were convinced that Somalia was only the beginning of American efforts in the region and that they needed a long-term strategy. The radicals were certain that the United States would come to the aid of Christians in southern Sudan, who had been embroiled in a civil war with the northern Muslims of the Khartoum government for a decade. This would pose a direct threat to Sudan's Islamist regime. After the Somalia fatwa was issued, the shura decided to establish a cell in Nairobi, the crossroads of East Africa, which would serve as the base for operatives on the way to Somalia. The mission was important enough that Abu Ubaidah al-Banshiri, the chairman of the military committee, was sent to oversee its creation. For the tasks at hand in Somalia, Muhammad Atef, then the number two man on al-Qaeda's military committee, was sent twice into the failed state to reconnoiter, establish contact with tribal leaders, and offer them training to carry out attacks.

Mogadishu was dangerous because of the frequent fighting. At the end of one trip, Atef was forced to escape using a small Cessna plane normally used for ferrying khat, the narcotic leaf that East Africans and southern Arabs love to chew. In the months thereafter, there was considerable al-Qaeda traffic to Mogadishu and outlying areas; dark-skinned individuals were chosen for most of the missions because they were less conspicuous. One of those who trained Somalis was Mohammed Odeh, a Palestinian, who years later would play a key role in the bombing of the U.S. embassy in Nairobi. He worked in the southeastern part of the country with the Ittihad al-Islamiyya, a jihadist group that would become a long-term ally of al-Qaeda. Another central player in the embassy bombings, Harun Fazil, spent time in Mogadishu, working on a failed plot to attack a UN building with a truck bomb. Fazil was in the city on October 3, 1993, when gunmen from the militia of Mohammed Farah Aideed brought down two U.S. Black Hawk helicopters and killed eighteen U.S. Army soldiers. It remains unclear whether Fazil had a role in the operation. Later, however, Muhammad Atef would tell others that al-Qaeda was responsible for the killings, and bin Laden would boast about defeating the United States in Somalia.

Whatever al-Qaeda's true role in Somalia, some incidents suggest that, in these early days, the group's reach sometimes exceeded its grasp. To take the fight to the Americans, the leadership decided in 1993 to move weapons stocks from Afghanistan to East Africa. Bin Laden, ever the global operator, arranged to buy a used aircraft in the United States through a former mujahid, Essam al-Ridi, then living in Texas. Al-Ridi found a T-39, the military version of an early jet called a Sabreliner, in the famous Tucson "Boneyard." The al-Qaeda plan called for using the craft to ferry Stingers and other missiles that the group had acquired during the jihad in Afghanistan. To help pay for the operation, the plane would carry sugar to sell in Pakistan.

The saga of the T-39 is a rare amusement in the bin Laden chronicle. Because of a shortage of cash, the Saudi insisted on spending no more than $250,000. What he got was a 1960s vintage aircraft with a range of about fifteen hundred miles. To get the plane from the southwestern United States to Khartoum, al-Ridi had to make a seven-leg journey, beginning in Dallas–Fort Worth and flying via Sault Sainte Marie in Ontario to an airstrip in Frobisher Bay, just below the Arctic Circle, then to Iceland, next to a couple of stops in Europe, on to Cairo, and finally to its destination. Al-Ridi expected the journey to take a couple of days. When he got to Frobisher Bay, −65 degree weather cracked a window and the plane lost its hydraulic system, forcing a stopover. After a week in Canada's frozen north, Air Mujahid was up and running again, and al-Ridi delivered the plane. Al-Qaeda apparently did use the aircraft, though whether the missiles were ever ferried to Sudan is not clear. No U.S. plane was downed by a Stinger in Somalia.

About a year and a half after his epic journey, al-Ridi was summoned to Sudan to fly the plane again. It had been poorly maintained: he arrived at the airport to find that the tires had melted on the runway, the engines were filled with sand, and the keys were missing. After repairs by an airport mechanic, al-Ridi took the plane up for a brief test. He made several circuits around the airport, performed a touch-and-go, and then brought the plane in for a landing. While it was hurtling down the tarmac, all the brake systems failed. Al-Ridi shut off the engines, but with the aircraft still plowing forward at sixty knots, the runway ran out, and the plane slammed into a sand pile. Al-Ridi, an Egyptian who worked for bin Laden as a business matter, not out of ideological conviction, was fearful of being identified with the crash of the Saudi's plane. He sprinted from the runway and caught a flight out of Sudan as soon as he could.[19]

———

During the years in Sudan, al-Qaeda transformed itself from a group whose core was made up of irregular combat fighters from the Afghan jihad into a full-fledged terrorist organization. To do so, the group needed to acquire expertise in the arts of covert operations and sophisticated attack planning. Contingents from different jihadist groups brought with them a store of knowledge about tactics, surveillance, and explosives. Groups like the Egyptian Islamic Jihad had also recruited a number of military personnel and police who contributed their talents.

One person who exemplified how al-Qaeda established its high level of tradecraft was the former Egyptian officer Ali Mohamed—the same Ali Mohamed who helped train El-Sayyid Nosair, Mahmud Abouhalima, and the rest of the Farouq Mosque group in the use of weaponry in the late 1980s. Much of Mohamed's knowledge came from years of service in his country's army. Mohamed, who secretly joined the Egyptian Islamic Jihad in the early 1980s, reached the rank of major before being cashiered by superiors wary of his increasing piety. While still in an Egyptian uniform, he completed a foreign officers' training course at Fort Bragg. He left Egypt in 1985 and the following year enlisted, as non–U.S. citizens can, in the U.S. military, receiving the rank of sergeant. He was again stationed at Bragg, home of the U.S. Special Forces Command. While delivering the occasional lecture on Middle East politics and culture to troops there, he also smuggled out classified documents, including training manuals that later turned up in El-Sayyid Nosair's apartment. Mohamed left the military in 1989 and worked as a computer repairman and security guard in northern California.

Introduced to al-Qaeda through jihadist associates, he was quickly called upon to manage important projects. He helped transport bin Laden from Afghanistan to Sudan in 1991 and taught "intelligence" methods, such as creating cells, the largely self-contained units that terrorists operate in so as to keep information compartmentalized and limit their vulnerability. He also taught operatives how to surveil a target, gather necessary information, photograph targets, develop pictures, and draw structural diagrams. In 1994, after an attempt was made on bin Laden's life, Ali Mohamed was summoned to train bin Laden's bodyguards.

THE MAKING OF A TERRORIST

In the early 1990s, al-Qaeda headquarters were in Khartoum, and the more experienced jihadists had moved to Sudan. But the training camps in Afghanistan, most of which were near the border with Pakistan, were still in operation and provided the point of entry for new members. The fighting in Afghanistan continued after the fall of the communist regime in 1992, with various factions of mujahidin engaged in mindless slaughter. Muslims from outside continued to be attracted to the region, perhaps even more so once the Soviets were defeated and the aura of a historic event became more apparent.

L'Houssaine Kherchtou was one of those drawn to Afghanistan in the early 1990s, and his story is in many respects typical of those who became the rank and file of al-Qaeda. Kherchtou could be called a semi-Westernized Muslim. Born in Morocco in 1964, he graduated from a local high school and a catering school, spending several months working in France as part of his studies. After he finished at the catering school, he moved to France, and worked in bakeries, including one in Corsica, where he lived for some months. He moved to Italy, where, without a visa, he roamed from city to city, settling eventually in Milan. He fell into the orbit of the city's Islamic Cultural Institute and its radical preacher,

Sheikh Anwar Shaban, and was recruited there for Afghanistan. In January 1991, using a visa procured for him by Shaban, who claimed that Kherchtou was attending the annual convention of Tablighi, a million-strong group of itinerant Muslim preachers, he traveled with four other recruits to Pakistan. Among his fellow travelers, he befriended one in particular, a veterinarian who came to be known by the nom de guerre Abu Mohammed al-Masry. (The surname suggests he was Egyptian.) They flew via Karachi to Peshawar and were greeted there and brought to Bait al-Ansar, the guesthouse where bin Laden and Abdullah Azzam housed initiates during the great days of the fight against the Soviets. There, they handed over their valuables for safekeeping, procured Afghan clothes, and received new identities: Kherchtou was called Abu Zaid al-Maghrebi, or Abu Zaid of Morocco. (Later, when he found himself in the company of a jihadist with the same name, he changed his again, this time to Abu Talal. The limited number of noms de guerre, the frequent use of more than one by a single individual, and the common use of the same one by different people have been the bane of those who study the jihadists.) From Peshawar, Kherchtou was driven by minivan to the Pakistani city of Miramshah and then over the border to his first camp, Farouq, near Khost. Told to sleep in a mosque, he was awakened in the middle of the night by a blaze of gunfire—a welcome from the camp that, Kherchtou later recalled, was to let the newcomers know that the life ahead would be difficult and they were not in the camp to sleep.

Kherchtou's next two months were anything but restful. Training was divided into three stages. First, the recruits were instructed on how to handle light weapons ranging from AK-47s to handguns to Uzis. Then they moved on to explosives, including C-3, C-4, and dynamite; grenades; a variety of different detonators; and antipersonnel, antitank, and anti-truck mines. In the final phase, they were instructed in the use of heavy weaponry, such as antiaircraft guns. Throughout the two months, Kherchtou went through a physical training program as well; its rigors can be judged by the fact that he lost twenty-five kilograms—fifty-five pounds—in that time.

Somewhere along the way he undoubtedly received religious instruction; Jamal al-Fadl, for instance, reported that he went through a two-week course. After all this training, Kherchtou returned to the guesthouse in Miramshah, where he was asked if he wanted to join al-Qaeda. Told that it was "a group of Muslims [who] were join[ing together] to fight for Islam, and to do the good things for Islam and Muslims all over the world," he decided he did. He made his baya orally and in writing.

Afterward, Kherchtou spent two and a half months on the front fighting the communist forces of Najibullah's regime. For about a year, he served as a trainer at another camp that gave brief, intensive courses to people who were coming to fight in Afghanistan for a couple of weeks, taking an additional two-week course in explosives along the way. Then, sometime in 1992, the year the Americans arrived in Somalia, the focus of his activities shifted from warfare to acquiring skills useful for terrorist operations. He moved back to Peshawar, and at a meeting in the house bin Laden maintained there, was told by Muhammad Atef, the second-ranking "military" leader, to attend yet another training course. Its subject was surveillance, it would last two weeks, and the instructor was Ali Mohamed. The small group of students were taught how to use a variety of cameras and techniques, such as how to take pictures surreptitiously without bringing the camera up to the eye. They learned how to develop film and how to compile surveillance reports, encode them, and load them onto computer disks. The group cased the Iranian consulate and cultural center in Peshawar—whether for an actual attack or for practice, they were never told. They were taught how to follow an individual; the target they used was a visiting official from the Egyptian embassy in Islamabad. They were instructed on the division of labor in an operation. Four teams were required: one each for surveillance, planning, logistics, and executing the attack. And when all this training was over, Kherchtou spent more than six months studying electronics at a local institute and in a shop where al-Qaeda operatives were working on communications equipment, encryption devices, radios, watches, and other materials that might be used in operations such as bombings. (On the second floor of this workshop, he noticed, visas, passports, and official stamps were being prepared.) After this stint, Kherchtou made the hajj—the journey to Mecca that is one of the chief obligations of a Muslim. On his return, he was told that he would be moving to Nairobi to take flying lessons. Al-Qaeda was investing in its workers.

BUILDING BRIDGES, BUILDING BOMBS

As it prepared itself for an unprecedented conflict, al-Qaeda investigated doing business in unprecedented ways. Could it, for example, make common cause with Shiite terrorists? For an organization led by a Sunni fundamentalist from Saudi Arabia, this was extraordinary. Sunni and Shiite radicals have worked together in the past: Palestinian groups such as Hamas and Palestinian Islamic Jihad have been happy to accept Iran as a sponsor to help advance the common purpose of attacking Israelis. A significant number of Sunnis who fled their native countries to escape the security services—including many Egyptians—found safe haven in Iran and, sometimes, logistical support. But to many who think like bin Laden, Shiites are enemies, heretics who should be slaughtered. In Saudi Arabia, the tension between Sunnis and the Shiite minority can be explosive, and, as the world would see in Afghanistan in the 1990s, radical Sunnis were fully capable of mass killings of Shiites. So for Usama's deputy Mamduh Salim to argue before al-Qaeda, as he did, that Muslims needed to unite to face the common enemy was a daring step. Some of the impetus appears to have come from outside the group. On at least one occasion, members of the NIF and Sudanese clerics visited an al-Qaeda guesthouse to argue for cooperation with Shiites against the West.

Afterward, a small group of al-Qaeda members visited Hezbollah training camps in southern Lebanon, which impressed them. They returned to Sudan with instructional videotapes and recounted being particularly taken with Hezbollah's methods for blowing up large buildings. Eventually, a meeting was arranged in Sudan between bin Laden and Imad Mughniya, Hezbollah's chief terrorist and the architect of the major strikes against America in the 1980s. Hezbollah, the Egyptian Ali Mohamed would later recount, provided explosives and training both to al-Qaeda and the Egyptian Islamic Jihad.[20] The meeting between the two preeminent terrorists of the era reportedly did take place, and there was an agreement to cooperate. But there the record ends; there is little evidence that a long-term bond between the Sunni and Shiite groups was ever formed.

—

Al-Qaeda broached a far greater taboo in its weapons procurement. By early 1994, if not before, the group had begun work on acquiring weapons of mass destruction. Taking advantage of his close ties to the NIF, bin Laden became involved in a Sudanese government operation to produce nerve gas. Khartoum had been fighting Christian rebels in the south of the country since 1983, but government forces in a succession of regimes had been unable to score a decisive victory against their opponents, and hundreds of thousands of lives had been lost. There was frustration in Khartoum; some officials believed that chemical weapons could end the deadlock. Bin Laden secretly invested in Sudan's Military Industrial Corporation, a government-owned firm that was conducting weapons development for the regime.

The group's interest in unconventional weapons did not stop there. Al-Qaeda's leadership was eager to acquire nuclear arms. When word was received that uranium might be available on the black market, a senior al-Qaeda official directed Jamal al-Fadl to meet with the reported seller, a former government minister and military officer named Salah Abdel al-Mobruk. Al-Fadl made contact with al-Mobruk and was told that the uranium was indeed for sale: the price was $1,500,000, plus commissions, which had to be paid outside of Sudan. Al-Fadl reported this to his superiors and was instructed, despite the price tag, to communicate the group's interest and its desire for more information. Eventually, he and a top bin Laden aide, Abu Rida al-Suri, met with another contact, a man named Basheer. They were driven to a house in north Khartoum, where they were shown a cylinder two or three feet high. Engraved specifications on the cylinder indicated, among other things, that it was of South African origin. After further deliberations in al-Qaeda, al-Fadl relayed to Basheer that the group was interested in buying the uranium, subject to testing, which would involve machinery that had to be brought in from Nairobi. Al-Fadl was given a $10,000 bonus for his handling of the matter, and though he heard that the uranium was tested, he knew nothing more about the fate of the deal. It seems likely either that the material was not useful for a weapon or that this was one of many scams that have been perpetrated involving the sale of supposed nuclear material. If the uranium had been weapons grade—and if the group could have created a bomb, which is considered easier than acquiring the fissile material—al-Qaeda would have used it by now.

The combination of terrorists and weapons of mass destruction is the stuff of countless movies and television shows. The reality is otherwise: very, very few groups have ever seriously tried to acquire such weapons. Almost all of those that have—the Japanese cult Aum Shinrikyo is the most notable exception—have sought them primarily for purposes of blackmail. Reading history backward, it is clear that extortion is not part of al-Qaeda's inventory of tactics. Its forays into procuring unconventional arms are an unmistakable sign that al-Qaeda is prepared to cross a threshold never before approached and kill in a way unlike that of any earlier terrorists. The period of this activity roughly coincides with that of the group's decision to focus on waging war against the United States, and it is hard to imagine that the two matters were not linked. It may not yet have known exactly how it would attack the United States, but al-Qaeda was contemplating a kind of terrorist campaign and a level of carnage unlike anything seen before.

TARGETS AND PRACTICE

In late 1993, al-Qaeda was already considering attacking U.S. targets in Kenya. Bin Laden sent Ali Mohamed to Nairobi, where the former U.S. army sergeant cased the American embassy as well as the U.S. Agency for

International Development building, the French embassy, the French
Cultural Center, and British and Israeli targets. He brought back photographs, diagrams, and a report for bin Laden. When the two met in Khartoum, Mohamed would later recall, the Saudi looked at a picture of the
embassy and "pointed to where a truck could go as a suicide bomber."
This occurred well before the Americans left Somalia and *five years* before the embassy bombings. The contemplated attack was meant to punish the United States for its presence in Somalia and to discourage it from
staying in the region. But instead of establishing a long-term presence in
the country, the United States withdrew its forces in March 1994, only
five months after the killing of the soldiers.

Al-Qaeda seems never to have thought about closing down its cell
in Nairobi. As a black African country with a Muslim population but no
history of Islamist violence, Kenya was an opportune place to prepare
attacks against American interests. Operatives settled into Nairobi. Ban-
shiri married a Kenyan woman and started a business importing cars
from the United Arab Emirates, and several other operatives took up residence in the city there as well. Wadih el-Hage eventually came to Nairobi,
and worked in a charity called Help Africa People. To deepen the group's
presence in Kenya and establish a maritime line of communication with
Somalia, a second cell was created in the coastal city of Mombasa in August 1994. Mohammed Odeh, who had trained Somalis, moved there
with his wife. Muhammad Atef came to town a couple of months later and
set Odeh up in business with a large boat, which he sometimes used to
fish and sometimes to haul others' catch to markets along the shoreline.
The boat became the economic mainstay of the cell in Mombasa, which
numbered half a dozen members. Al-Qaeda's sleepers were in place.

In Khartoum, the leadership continued to mull over targets. In 1994,
Ali Mohamed traveled to Djibouti to conduct surveillance on various
facilities, including the U.S. and French embassies and French military
installations. Later that year, he and Kherchtou were ordered to travel to
Senegal, on the other side of Africa, to observe facilities there—for once,
the priority was on French targets, because bin Laden was angry about

France's support for the military regime in Algeria. The trip was scratched, however, when Mohamed received word that the FBI wanted to interview him for the upcoming trial of Sheikh Rahman and his coconspirators. He returned to the United States and told the agents who met him a mixture of lies and partial truths. After reporting on the interview to Atef, he was told not to return to Nairobi, lest he lead American authorities to al-Qaeda's front step.

While al-Qaeda's operational focus in the early 1990s was on anti-American attacks in Africa, the group also weighed attacks in the Arab world. During 1994, Egyptian jihadists suggested blowing up the U.S. embassy in Saudi Arabia, only to find that Saudi members of al-Qaeda objected, perhaps out of fear that such an attack would lead to a more forceful crackdown on dissidents. Bin Laden certainly remained deeply interested in events in the kingdom. He openly backed the Committee for the Defense of Legitimate Rights, in London, an organization created in April 1994 and run by Saudi exiles, which became a leading source of criticism of the regime. Bin Laden set up the Consultative Organization to Defend Islamic Legal Rights in Khartoum, and established the Advice and Reform Committee in London, which was run by Khalid al-Fawaz, who would later arrange the appearance of the 1998 fatwa in *al-Quds al-Arabi*. These offices produced anti-Saudi propaganda in quantity, publishing journals and other materials that called for violence against the regime, which marked bin Laden as one of the al-Saud's most radical opponents. It seems likely that bin Laden supported conspiratorial activities within the kingdom itself. Riyadh's patience with this behavior finally ran out. In the same month that the various antiregime organizations opened for business, the government revoked bin Laden's citizenship and banned him from returning to the kingdom.[21]

For the jihadists, 1995 was a banner year. In June, a team of Sudan-based terrorists from the al-Gamaat al-Islamiyya traveled to Addis Ababa for the annual meeting of the Organization of African Unity. There, they ambushed the limousine of Hosni Mubarak as he drove from the airport. The Egyptian president was saved by his bulletproof vehicle, but several

of the assailants escaped back to Sudan. Five months later, Egyptian Islamic Jihad drove a truck bomb into the gate of the Egyptian embassy in
Islamabad, Pakistan, and detonated it, killing fifteen people and wounding fifty-nine. Egyptian officials accused bin Laden of involvement in the
attack, and, in fact, Ayman al-Zawahiri appears to have played a key role.
(The EIJ leader writes in his memoir that the U.S. embassy in Islamabad
was the original target, chosen in retaliation for a Pakistani crackdown on
veterans of the Afghan jihad, but that it was too well fortified.) In Saudi
Arabia in November, a bomb exploded in central Riyadh, killing five
Americans and two Indians and wounding more than sixty people. The
target was the Office of the Program Manager of the Saudi Arabian National Guard (OPM-SANG). For more than two decades, the SANG had
relied on a U.S. Army program for training and equipment. Despite demands from Washington that U.S. officials be kept informed, the Saudis
quickly shut the door on its investigation. Several groups, none of which
had ever been heard of before, claimed credit; all demanded that U.S.
troops depart the kingdom. Five months later, the country's longtime interior minister, Prince Nayif bin Abd al-Aziz, announced that four suspects had been charged with the bombing. All were in their twenties, and
three of them said they had fought against the Soviets in Afghanistan. In
a televised confession, Abd al-Aziz Fah Nasir al-Muaththam declared the
U.S. presence in Saudi Arabia demanded an act of jihad and denounced
the Saudi regime for not adhering to the sharia. The suspects cited three
radical Islamists who had influenced them, one of whom was Usama bin
Laden.

The combined effect of these events was to turn the spotlight on
Sudan, its sponsorship of international terrorism, and its increasingly notorious guest. The negative publicity peaked in February 1996 when the
United States, citing growing physical danger, withdrew all official personnel from Khartoum; the ambassador moved to Nairobi, from which he
occasionally visited the Sudanese capital. In May, bin Laden left Sudan
permanently, effectively evicted by the NIF regime.

What made the Sudanese change their minds about bin Laden after such a long—and, it would appear, mutually beneficial—relationship? A combination of reasons seems most likely. In the mid-1990s, Sudan was deep in negotiations to develop its oil resources, located primarily in the south of the country. The government recognized that if it wanted investment capital to flow in, it needed a better international reputation, which would be difficult to obtain so long as the country was identified as a supporter of terrorism. Even the relatively small amounts of money already coming in because of oil made bin Laden's financial support less essential. The United States' sharp public criticism of Sudan threatened to discourage investors, which would have prevented that trickle of money from turning into a more reliable stream. Perhaps more important, Saudi Arabia was becoming more insistent that Khartoum force bin Laden to leave, and Riyadh was more likely than Washington to repay a Sudanese favor. Finally, the regime was tiring of its guest. In 2001–2002, John Prendergast, a former U.S. National Security Council official, interviewed well-placed current and former Sudanese officials; they told him that bin Laden was forced out because the Khartoum government felt he was becoming too powerful. With increasing influence over the Sudanese economy and a small private army at his disposal, bin Laden was determined to have his way. "[National Islamic Front leader Hassan al-]Turabi wanted to guide and control bin Laden and other extremist elements. But Bin Laden wanted to guide the Sudanese government, like he did the Taliban," a Sudanese who could only be identified as a Khartoum "legal expert" told Prendergast. Sudan in 1996, unlike the Taliban in 2002, was not about to let the parasite kill the host.[22]

CHAPTER 4

RAIDERS ON THE PATH OF GOD

A CORE TENET of al-Qaeda's strategy is that radical Islamists must gain control of a nation, from which they can then expand the area controlled by believers. Holding a state, in their view, is the prelude to knocking over the dominoes of the world's secular Muslim regimes. "Armies achieve victory only when the infantry takes hold of land," Ayman al-Zawahiri has written. "Likewise, the mujahid Islamic movement will not triumph against the world coalition unless it possesses a fundamentalist base in the heart of the Islamic world." The craving for territory is one reason why al-Qaeda carries out its own terrorist attacks and supports so many national insurgencies. Winning a country will be no easy task, but the stakes are enormous, for only thus can the "Muslim nation reinstate its fallen caliphate and regain its lost glory." Al-Zawahiri cites history as proof: not until Muslim forces in the twelfth century united Syria and Egypt could Saladin—a revered figure among jihadists—defeat the Crusaders at the battle of Hattin in 1187 and retake Jerusalem. "Only then did the cycle of history turn."[1]

Bin Laden and his followers had hoped that this germinal state would be Sudan. The country's leaders may have entertained the same thought, but they ultimately did not share the Saudi's vision of how to make that happen. Bin Laden returned to Afghanistan in May 1996, a disappointed man. If there was a hell on earth, this was it. After seventeen years of war, the country was utterly destroyed—as failed as a state could be. Nearly one and a half million people were dead, and at least two and a half million more were in exile. Afghanistan's irrigation systems were ruined, its livestock herds had shrunk, and much farmland and pasture was unusable because it had been sown with hundreds of thousands of land mines. A bare subsistence was all most people could hope for. Average life expectancy stood at a medieval forty-six years; the infant mortality rate, 147 per 1,000 births, was more than twenty-five times that in the United States. Public order had vanished. Warring armies ranged across the countryside, and gunmen pillaged, raped, and killed with abandon.

One important thing had changed: after years of seesawing battles between rival factions of mujahidin, a new force had emerged determined to end the internecine warfare. The Taliban, literally "the students," was born in 1994. There is no shortage of founding myths about the group, but the one most often cited is set in Kandahar province: two teenage girls had been kidnapped and repeatedly raped by followers of an area warlord. An outraged village cleric, Mullah Mohammed Omar, gathered together thirty students and attacked the camp where the girls were being held. They freed the captives and hanged the group's commander from the barrel of a tank.

Soon, this small band was raiding the camps of powerful warlords, building stocks of weapons and ammunition, and attracting more students. It drew support from the religiously oriented political parties in Pakistan, which are dominated by Deobandi Muslims, who run many of the madrassas, or religious schools, in the Afghan refugee camps and elsewhere. After a series of daring Taliban successes, the Pakistani government began backing the new force as well. Islamabad wanted to break the deadlock among the warring factions that made Afghanistan ungovernable, blocked trade with Central Asia, and kept refugees from going home. The regime also glimpsed in the Taliban the possibility of breathing life into a creature that could aid its own interests.

Within Afghanistan, the Taliban enjoyed a growing popularity. It provided something that ordinary Afghans longed for: a modicum of order. Chaos had reigned for so many years that people had become accustomed to being treated like the chattel of the warlords, or worse. The Taliban vanquished many marauding bands and disarmed trouble-makers.

But stability came at a price: the Taliban enforced an extreme brand of Islamic practice that had evolved in Afghan villages and refugee camps, a fusion between the radical Wahhabism taught by Saudi missionaries and the comparably hard-line Deobandi belief of the Pakistani madrassas, themselves an offshoot of the Wahhabism that had taken root in South Asia in the nineteenth century. Amputations and stonings became common punishments for crimes; due process had little role in the "legal" system. One Taliban specialty was to crush those who committed certain infractions—homosexuality is one example—by knocking walls over onto them. Another effect of the rise of the Taliban was that from one day to the next, women were forced out their jobs, forbidden to appear alone in public, and compelled to wear the head-to-toe burqa. But crime rates fell, and the restoration of some semblance of personal safety in a country that had known none in recent memory, as well as the evident incorruptibility of the Taliban, attracted recruits in droves. Young men and boys flocked from madrassas in Afghanistan and the refugee camps of Pakistan.

After the Taliban's success in capturing Kandahar, Afghanistan's second largest city, at the end of 1994, the group acquired an aura of invincibility. There were occasional setbacks, but with the backing of Pakistan and Saudi Arabia, Taliban fighters—undisciplined but unrelenting—subdued one province after another. In September 1996 they laid siege to Kabul, then ruled by the government of Burhannudin Rabbani and his military commander, Ahmad Shah Massoud. Later that month, when the Taliban broke through, the first thing its soldiers did was hunt down Najibullah, the Afghan communist who had been in power from 1986 until 1992. For four years, since his fall from power, the former ruler had been taking refuge in a UN compound, whose sanctuary the Rabbani government respected. The Taliban was no observer of such diplomatic

niceties: its gunmen broke into the compound, beat and castrated Najibullah, dragged him behind a jeep, shot him, and strung him up from a
traffic post, along with his brother.[2] Pictures of the bloodstreaked and
bloated bodies appeared throughout the world.

———

Ferocious and unburdened by any tactical caution, the Taliban's warmak-
ing was reminiscent of some of the more spontaneous Crusades, when
hermits or lunatics materialized at the head of a great rabble and swarmed
across a continent. Perhaps its strangest personality was its leader: a former mujahid who had lost his right eye in a rocket attack, Mullah Mohammed Omar distinguished himself as one of the world's most reclusive
political figures. He almost never gave interviews, especially not to Westerners, and he never allowed himself to be photographed. He was no
scholar and had done nothing more exalted than run a small madrassa in
his village. But Omar's leadership was unchallenged: he was revered both
as a warrior and a saint.

Omar was uncompromising in his determination that sharia be the
law of the land. In asserting his leadership, he summoned a vision of the
miraculous years of Islam. After the capture of Kabul, he assumed a traditional title of the caliph, *Amir-ul Momineen,* Commander of the Faithful,
and the country was renamed the Islamic Emirate of Afghanistan.[3]

———

Around the world, many believers, including some Islamists in Egypt and
Saudi Arabia, viewed the Taliban with distaste as primitive, unschooled,
and unruly. Even the mullahs of the Pakistani madrassas, who had educated many of the Taliban leaders, would speak of them as well-meaning
but occasionally excessive in their zeal. But if bin Laden had any such
reservations about his new hosts, he never voiced them. He seems to
have settled without hesitation into his life as an honored guest of the
state.

We know little about the ties between him and the Taliban in this period. According to a Pakistani news story that appeared after the first meeting of bin Laden and Mullah Omar, in March 1997, the Afghan leader issued a statement saying that the United States should leave Saudi Arabia "because they risked losing the sympathy of Muslims."[4] It is interesting that the apparent subject of their discussion was bin Laden's issue, not Omar's. And, in fact, al-Qaeda seems to have been surprised that a good relationship was established so quickly with the Afghan regime. Muhammad Atef, who had risen to be chief of military operations after his predecessor, Abu Ubaidah al-Banshiri, drowned in a ferry accident, wrote to members of the group in Africa in 1997: "The situation in Afghanistan has evolved in an unexpected way, and praise to God that this development is to the benefit of Islam." The letter gives a glowing account of the rise of the Taliban and an analysis of geopolitics in South Asia. It was clearly intended to allay the fears of those in the field and correct any misperceptions they might have acquired from the press about the nature of al-Qaeda's new hosts.[5]

But if Omar was welcoming from the outset, he was not typical of his countrymen. As a group, the Arab Afghans, several thousands of whom were still in the country and hundreds more came back with bin Laden, were little liked by the populace, which considered them outsiders and dangerous fanatics. The Taliban was less hostile—much of its funding came from Wahhabi sources in the Persian Gulf—but even so, al-Qaeda devoted considerable energy and money to endearing itself to its new hosts as part of an effort to bend Afghanistan to its own purposes.

The Taliban had numerous needs and one overriding priority: to complete the military conquest of Afghanistan. It had rolled over most of the country's provinces in the mid-1990s only to find itself in a stalemate with the Northern Alliance forces led by Ahmad Shah Massoud, the former military commander of the government the Taliban had toppled. Each year, when winter receded, the two sides would battle each other across northern Afghanistan. But the Taliban could not inflict a decisive defeat on Massoud, a superb general who always managed to hold on to about 15 percent of the country and then, at the end of each fighting season, withdraw to his stronghold in the remote Panjshir Valley. The Taliban received the bulk of its supplies from Pakistan. But bin Laden ingratiated himself with the movement's corps commanders by providing them with additional weaponry and, more important, detachments of fighters.

Much had changed over the many years of combat. The earlier generations of fearless Afghan warriors had faded into memory, and for all their spirit, the Taliban lacked military know-how. The Arab Afghans were now combat hardened, and the Taliban commanders were grateful for their services. Bin Laden's largesse in this regard was so great that high-ranking Taliban officers constituted a hard core of support for him.

His generosity did not stop with the military. He provided Taliban leaders with infusions of much-needed cash, and he imported fleets of Toyota Land Cruisers, the official vehicle of jihad, which he distributed to Taliban worthies. Eventually, his generosity gained him a measure of acceptance from ordinary Afghans. During a time when foreign aid workers were increasingly reluctant to work in Afghanistan because of the restrictions put upon them by the Taliban, bin Laden became a critical source of support, funding hospitals and doling out food. (The refusal of the mullahs to allow Afghan women to work was a major sticking point with nongovernmental organizations, as was the physical danger from attacks after the international community imposed sanctions to punish the Taliban for harboring terrorists.)

—

For bin Laden, as for many jihadists, the present is an echo of the distant past, and his relocation to Afghanistan was nothing less than a recapitulation of the Hijra, Muhammad's own migration to Medina. The Prophet fled Mecca when his community was imperiled by hostile tribes that his followers could not defeat; the Hijra was a retreat in a "time of weakness." In moving to Afghanistan, bin Laden saw himself as making a similar tactical withdrawal, the prologue to a long battle. Throughout his stay in Afghanistan, he described the movement of militants to Afghanistan explicitly as a strategy of hijra, and he implored Muslims to come to the new Islamic emirate. In a recruitment videotape, he declares that emigration stands alongside belief and jihad as articles of faith. "Muslims," he says, ". . . honest scholars, the loyal traders and the tribal sheikhs, must emigrate for the sake of Allah, and find themselves a place in which they raise the banner of jihad, and mobilize the umma in order to preserve their religion and their life." Even at this distant remove, he insists, there is a preserve of true Islam. He reminds the viewer of the importance of pledging fealty to a true leader and, while images of Afghanistan roll by, declares: "This state was established with the grace of Allah. . . . The state of the Taliban. . . . And here is their Emir, the Commander of the Faithful, Mullah Mohammed Omar. This [pledge] has been the duty of the age, for a century. It is a very important duty, that has been absent for a century"— since, that is, the abolition of the caliphate. By imitating the Prophet through emigration and by swearing allegiance to a true leader, bin Laden implies, believers will one day return home in triumph on a wave of unchecked conquest.

Moving to Afghanistan altered bin Laden's sense of his relationship to the world's Muslims. During the years in Sudan, whether by choice or the dictates of the Khartoum regime, he remained largely in the shadows. He was geographically and politically still close enough to the center of the Islamic world that he felt himself to be a presence, known by virtue of his role as the most influential backer of Islamist terror. But in Afghanistan, he needed to declare himself, to come out from behind the curtains as a power in his own right.

Only a few months after arriving in Afghanistan, bin Laden published a fatwa for the first time. "Declaration of War Against the Americans Occupying the Land of the Two Holy Places [Saudi Arabia]" appeared in *al-Quds al-Arabi,* the London-based Arab-language newspaper that al-Qaeda has often used to deliver its messages.[6] The fatwa has come to be known as the Ladenese Epistle; it is an endless list of charges that, in English translation, runs to almost nineteen turgid single-spaced pages. The most prominent grievance is bin Laden's hallmark: the "Zionist-

Crusader Alliance," that amalgam of world infidelity, is waging a war against the people of Islam. So far have matters progressed, he writes, that "the Muslims' blood became the cheapest and their wealth . . . is loot in the hands of the enemies. Their blood was spilled in Palestine and Iraq. The horrifying pictures of the massacre of Qana, in Lebanon [where in April 1996 an Israeli artillery bombardment killed approximately a hundred civilians sheltering at a UN base] are still fresh in our memory. Massacres in Tajikistan, Burma, Kashmir, Assam, Philippines, Fatani [Malaysia], Ogaden, Somalia, Eritrea, Chechnya, and Bosnia-Herzegovina took place, massacres that send shivers in the body and shakes the conscience." All this slaughter is laid at the doorstep of the "American-Israeli conspiracy."

Over and above this titanic bloodshed, the "latest and greatest of these aggressions . . . since the death of the Prophet . . . is the occupation of the Land of the Two Holy Places." Here bin Laden's hatred bursts forth in torrents. He does not stop to explain why the occupation of holy soil is a greater outrage than killing; to him it is obvious that the violation of the sacred is more offensive than the taking of life. But the denunciations of the "Alliance" go on only so long before the iniquitous Saudi rulers are put in the dock for more invective. They are the "agent in our country" of the Americans and Israelis, because they have ignored Muhammad's injunction to "expel the polytheists" from Arabia. Instead, "they permitted [the Crusaders] to be in the Land of the Two Holy Places. Not surprisingly though, the King himself wore the cross on his chest. The country was widely opened from the north-to-the south and from east-to-the west for the Crusaders. The land was filled with the military bases of the USA and the allies. The regime became unable to keep control without the help of these bases. . . . The regime betrayed the Umma and joined the Kufr, assisting and helping them against the Muslims." Bin Laden excoriates the Saudi royal family for failing to defend the country, jeopardizing its resources—especially its oil patrimony, a favorite subject—and not ruling by sharia. He berates them because "the competition between influential princes for personal gains and interest had destroyed the country," and for ignoring and persecuting the critics who sought to correct the government's course. "Through its course of actions," he says, "the regime has torn off its legitimacy."

In the fatwa, bin Laden foresees the destruction of his homeland, and most paranoically, the "Division of the Land of the Two Holy Places, and annexing of the northerly part of it by Israel. Dividing the land of the two Holy Places is an essential demand of the Zionist-Crusader alliance." His prescription for these woes is to drive the "Crusaders" out of the country, "to hit the main enemy who divided the Ummah into small and little countries and pushed it, for the last few decades, into a state of confusion." He quotes ibn Taymiyya, as he often does, as saying: "The people of Islam should join forces and support each other to get rid of the main 'Kufr who is controlling the countries of the Islamic world.' " (Elsewhere in the text, he refers explicitly to the fatwa against the Mongols.) This action, he adds, must be covert: "due to the imbalance of power between our armed forces and the enemy forces, a suitable means of fighting must be adopted i.e. using fast moving light forces that work under complete secrecy. In other words to initiate a guerrilla warfare, where the sons of the nation, and not the military forces, take part in it."[7]

One of the oddest elements of the fatwa is bin Laden's complaint about how he has been treated. He says he has been "pursued in Pakistan, Sudan and Afghanistan. . . . But by the Grace of Allah, a safe base is now available in the high Hindu Cush mountains in Khurasan." He reiterates this location in the dateline with his signature. The reference is obscure and indicative: modern Khorasan, as it is usually spelled, is a province of northeastern Iran. In the Middle Ages, the name stood for that area as well as for Afghanistan and lands that now belong to the Central Asian republics. Khorasan was the land beyond Persia, the farthest reaches of the realm of Islam. Bin Laden uses the archaic name to link himself with the heroic age of Islam, as he often does. In doing so, he connects the struggle of Muslims today to those of the caliphs who fought the Byzantine empire twelve hundred years ago.

For bin Laden, son of a petrodollar kingdom and a fortune built on the global market for high-tech construction, the campaign against the infidel is something out of the great age of Islamic chivalry. The conceit is not just literary. Ensconced in Afghanistan, al-Qaeda reprised a theme out of Islamic history: that of the *ghazis*, or Bedouin raiders. Before the coming of Islam, ghazis carried out brief, brutal attacks on neighboring tribes, capturing women and livestock and showing off their prowess. (The word derives from the Arabic word for "raid," and it lives on in many European languages in which *razzia* means a police raid.) In the Quran, the ghazis become holy warriors. Under Muhammad's leadership, they rode out from Medina against the enemies of the fledgling community of believers. Eventually, these warriors migrated to Islam's embattled borders, protecting against Byzantium in the west and the tribes of Central Asia in the east. They gathered in militant monastic communities called *ribat*, sallying forth to harass the enemy and extend the domain of the faith. They, too, accepted jihad as an individual responsibility, not a communal one.

In fortresses such as Tora Bora and the chain of training camps along the Pakistani frontier, al-Qaeda styled itself an order of modern ghazis. The identification was self-conscious: until it was taken down after September 11, one of the main jihadist websites was www.alribat.com. A passage in the document found after the attack, in Muhammad Atta's suitcase, which never made it aboard Flight 11, reads: "Consider that this is a raid on a path. As the Prophet said, A raid on the path of God 'is better than this world and what is in it.'[8]

—

Creating a hybrid capitalist-terrorist empire à la Sudan would not be possible in Afghanistan. The war-shattered Islamic Emirate of Afghanistan had virtually no infrastructure and no money to build any, little in the way of commodity production for export, no industry, and no economic demand to speak of. Some of bin Laden's companies in Sudan may have continued operating, providing a cash stream. (Their fate remains unclear, though the Saudi did maintain contacts in Sudan

for several years.) More likely, however, the slack in al-Qaeda's finances was taken up by money from outside sources—in particular, by
donations.

How this worked has not been fully elucidated, but some outlines
are clear. Money continued to flow into al-Qaeda's coffers from wealthy
private donors, most of them in Saudi Arabia and the Gulf states; many
of the benefactors presumably had a relationship with bin Laden himself, going back to the war against the Soviets. These funds might
be transferred by hand or deposited in an al-Qaeda-controlled bank
account in any number of countries; Islamic banks were, naturally
enough, special favorites. Another mode of transfer, both for contributions and for shuttling funds to field operatives, involved *hawala*s, the informal Western Unions of the developing world, which rely on family
relations, telephone calls, and a minimum of paper to move money across
continents.

Much of the cash flowed through Islamic charities. Saudi organizations established operations in Afghanistan and Pakistan during the
jihad. After the breakup of the Soviet Union, their offices sprouted up
throughout Central Asia, Bosnia, Albania, and many other countries with
Muslim populations. The goal was to propagate Wahhabi Islam, which
these organizations did by supplying teachers, school materials, and clerics. Large amounts of money came from official Saudi sources, as part of
the kingdom's effort to spread the faith—the mission is considered a duty,
and a source of the ruling family's legitimacy—and was funneled through
official organizations such as the International Islamic Relief Organization and the Muslim World League.[9] Other charities were independently
funded by wealthy individuals. Some cash came from *zakat,* the collection plate, in radical mosques.

Within the organizations handling the money there were rotten veins,
channels through which money could be shunted to jihadists. Radical-
minded executives of nongovernmental organizations gave al-Qaeda
operatives jobs in offices around the world, thus providing a key part
of the infrastructure necessary for terrorist attacks: a shipping address,

houses, identity cards, and a recognized reason for being in a particular place. In this way, Islamic NGOs helped enable al-Qaeda to create the hub-and-spoke structure that has served it exceedingly well.

Another possible source of revenue was the drug trade. When the Taliban came to power, many experts in the West believed the group would discourage narcotics production, because of Islamic injunctions against taking drugs. Nothing could have been further from the truth: during the Taliban's reign, opium production skyrocketed. Poppy cultivation spread, and by 1999, according to a United Nations panel, the country was the source of 79 percent of the world's opium.[10] The glut on the market led to sharp increases in addiction rates in Central Asia and Iran and falling prices in Europe, which receives most of its heroin from Afghanistan. The Taliban's tax on growers became one of its top sources of revenue. (The Taliban embarked on a poppy eradication program in 2000, but the UN panel concluded that this was actually intended to shore up prices, which had plummeted. Stocks of opium were said to be warehoused in Afghanistan.) It has been widely suggested that al-Qaeda had a hand in the drug trade as well. Although this is plausible—in particular, it would not be surprising to find that the group was involved in distribution—so far, there is scant evidence for the hypothesis. It is equally possible that the Taliban considered the opium trade a sort of state-run monopoly in which the Arab Afghans should play no part.

A more likely source of money was al-Qaeda's role as a subcontractor for the insurgency in Kashmir. Beginning in 1994, the Pakistani government sought to increase the pressure in the India-controlled part of the disputed region. Until that time, the fighting was conducted primarily by Kashmiri natives. Eager to increase the tempo of attacks—which would force India to deploy more troops to the region and push the issue of Kashmir up on the international community's agenda—Pakistan began subsidizing the training of militants from other parts of the country. An abundant supply of manpower was available: the collapse of public education in Pakistan had led to the wildfire growth of madrassas, many of which inculcated a radical jihadist ideology. Under the auspices of the

Inter-Services Intelligence (ISI) directorate, the Pakistani military intelligence agency, a kind of terrorist conveyor belt began transporting young radicals from their schools to Afghanistan for training in camps run by or affiliated with al-Qaeda. From there, they were taken to the border with Indian-controlled Kashmir, where they slipped across to launch their attacks. Over time, the number of fighters from outside Kashmir grew until they comprised an estimated 40 percent of those active in the region; two-thirds of the militants were recruited from madrassas. Logistics were handled by groups such as Lashkar e-Tayba and Harakat ul Mujahidin, which was designated by the U.S. government as a foreign terrorist organization for its kidnapping and killing of American citizens. During their training, the young zealots imbibed the ideology of al-Qaeda, and the proof was in an escalation of the violence in Kashmir. As far as ISI was concerned, this was all to the good, and Taliban-controlled Afghanistan became a vital strategic asset for Pakistan.[11] How this training was financed is unclear, but, one way or another, ISI's involvement appears to have defrayed some of al-Qaeda's costs.

The training camps flourished, and the roads of jihad emanating from Afghanistan that had been established in the earlier part of the decade were widened and smoothed. The supply route to the Caucasus continued to carry money, men, and matériel to radical Islamists, such as the renowned Khattab, a native of the border region of Saudi Arabia and Jordan who had migrated to Chechnya to fight there.[12] Members of the Islamic Movement of Uzbekistan, a group active in several Central Asian countries, trained in al-Qaeda camps, alongside the usual assortment of Algerians, Yemenis, Egyptians, Saudis, Filipinos, and others. Recruits continued to arrive from radical mosques, and the group redoubled its efforts to bring aboard Muslims who had American or European passports and could be infiltrated into Western countries.

Much as when L'Houssaine Kherchtou went through his training, different camps provided instruction for different skills. One installation, though, was set apart. At Derunta, fifteen miles from Jalalabad, al-Qaeda maintained a program in special explosives and unconventional weapons.

Here, operatives worked on a variety of poisons and chemical weapons and the means to deliver them. The desire to procure weapons of mass destruction remained a central ambition of the leaders, some of whom undertook risky travel abroad to see what components they could procure.

—

In the eighteen months after the publication of the fatwa, bin Laden, like a novice politician trying to connect with his audience, sought out press coverage and refined his message. He continued to rail against the presence of U.S. troops on the Arabian peninsula, and, although he called them "the shadow of the American presence," he spoke less about Saudi Arabia's rulers. In March 1997 he gave CNN's Peter Arnett the first television interview with a Western broadcaster, in which he declared: "The concentration at this point of jihad is against the American occupiers."[13] In an interview two months later with John Miller of ABC News, he complained that "the truth is that the whole Muslim world is the victim of international terrorism, engineered by America at the United Nations. We are a nation whose sacred symbols have been looted and whose wealth and resources have been plundered."[14] Without taking responsibility for the OPM-SANG and Khobar Towers bombings in Saudi Arabia, he described them as a natural reaction to American depredations. But he pointedly remarked that because of the horrors being inflicted on the umma everywhere, removal of the American troops would *not* stop his campaign: "The driving-away jihad against the US does not stop with its withdrawal from the Arabian peninsula, but rather it must desist from aggressive intervention against Muslims in the whole world." For halting the fight, at least against "the Western regimes and the government of the United States of America," bin Laden offered a piece of advice: "If their people do not wish to be harmed inside their very own countries, they should seek to elect governments that are truly representative of them and that can protect their interests."

With the other half of the "Zionist-Crusader Alliance," the story was different. There, the struggle was elemental and, seemingly, eternal. "The enmity between us and the Jews goes far back in time and is deep rooted," he announced. "There is no question that war between the two of us is inevitable." (While all these radical Islamists are consumed by anti-Semitism, they do not agree on the identity of the driving force behind "world infidelity." To bin Laden, it is the Jews. To al-Zawahiri, "Israel . . . is in fact a huge US military base."[15] Who is the instrument and who the agent interests them little: evil is evil.)

Bin Laden also used these and other interviews to argue, in line with his many Islamist fellow believers, for a textual fundamentalism, asserting that "there is no choice but return to the original spring, to this religion, to God's Book, Praise and Glory be to Him, and to the Sunna [the deeds and sayings] of His Prophet." He was contemptuous of most modern clerics and their ersatz doctrines. And he reaffirmed the radicals' beliefs that "the acme of this religion is jihad. The nation has had a strong conviction that there is no way to obtain faithful strength but by returning to this jihad"—not through the traditional pillars of Islam.[16]

We can only speculate on why bin Laden adjusted his message, concentrating so much of his rhetorical fire on the United States rather than on the al-Saud. His loathing for the rulers of his native country did not diminish, and throughout the 1990s al-Qaeda never ceased to plot against the Riyadh regime. Bin Laden seems to have concluded that anti-American sentiment broadened his appeal among Muslims everywhere, while too much talk about the corrupt leaders of Saudi Arabia—who, after all, seemed hardly more villainous to non-Saudi Muslims than their own rulers did—attracted few new admirers.

That refinement and, perhaps, a far more skilled writer account for the dramatically different quality of bin Laden's second fatwa, issued on February 23, 1998.[17] Here, the language is simple and the metaphors poetic: "The Arabian Peninsula has never—since God made it flat, created its desert, and encircled it with seas—been stormed by any forces like the crusader armies spreading in it like locusts, eating its riches and wiping out its plantations." The indictment is a straightforward one, three counts, each dealing with a different land:

First, the Arabian peninsula:

[F]or over seven years the United States has been occupying the lands of Islam in the holiest of places . . . plundering its riches, dictating to its rulers, humiliating its people, terrorizing its neighbors, and turning its bases in the Peninsula into a spearhead through which to fight the neighboring Muslim peoples.

In Iraq:

[D]espite the great devastation inflicted on the Iraqi people by the crusader-Zionist alliance, and despite the huge number of those killed, which has exceeded 1 million . . . despite all this, the Americans are once [again] trying to repeat the horrific massacres, as though they are not content with the protracted blockade imposed after the ferocious war or the fragmentation and devastation.

So here they come to annihilate what is left of this people and to humiliate their Muslim neighbors. . . .

And in the Middle East:

Third, if the Americans' aims behind these wars are religious and economic, the aim is also to serve the Jews' petty state and divert attention from its occupation of Jerusalem and murder of Muslims there. The best proof of this is their eagerness to destroy Iraq, the strongest neighboring Arab state, and their endeavor to fragment all the states of the region such as Iraq, Saudi Arabia, Egypt, and Sudan into paper statelets and through their disunion and weakness to guarantee Israel's survival and the continuation of the brutal crusade[r] occupation of the Peninsula.

This campaign to oppress, divide, and murder amounts to one thing: "a clear declaration of war on God, his messenger, and Muslims." The response is categorical:

The ruling to kill the Americans and their allies—civilians and military—is an individual duty for every Muslim who can do it in any country in which it is possible to do it, in order to liberate the al-Aqsa Mosque and the holy mosque [Mecca] from their grip, and in order for their armies to move out of all the lands of Islam, defeated and unable to threaten any Muslim. This is in accordance with the words of Almighty Allah, "and fight the pagans all together as they fight you all together," and "fight them until there is no more tumult or oppression, and there prevail justice and faith in Allah."

This, more than any other statement, has become the canonical bin Laden: a call to action to all Muslims, a summons to overcome imposed divisions, a demand that injustices be set right. With the additional signatures of al-Zawahiri and leaders of three other jihadist groups from Egypt, Pakistan, and Bangladesh, it presented the appearance of a consensus. It was an appeal to the discontented of the Islamic world: the presentation of a case, shorn of the usual circular reasoning and obscure references, like no other work of al-Qaeda rhetoric.

———

The fatwa was bin Laden's way of relaunching of himself—a sort of repackaging to create a name brand. Nearly two years had passed since his departure from Sudan and, as far as violence from al-Qaeda-related groups was concerned, that time had been relatively quiet. Bin Laden applauded the 1996 Khobar Towers bombing that killed nineteen U.S. servicemen in Saudi Arabia so loudly that he seemed to want credit for it, but he had nothing to do with it. The outstanding jihadist attack of 1997 was the murder of fifty-eight European tourists and four Egyptians by members of the al-Gamaat al-Islamiyya in Luxor, Egypt, and there is no evidence of an al-Qaeda connection. Moreover, al-Qaeda *was* embarking on something new: at roughly the same time the fatwa was issued, Mohammed Rashed Daoud al-Owhali, the Saudi member of al-Qaeda who had begged bin Laden for a "jihad mission," was sent to receive additional training. Khalfan Khan Mohammed, a Tanzanian, was asked if he wanted to do a jihad job shortly thereafter. Seven months after, al-Owhali jumped out of the Toyota pickup just before it detonated outside the American embassy in Nairobi, and Mohammed drove part of the way to the embassy in Dar es Salaam before getting out of the bomb vehicle and returning to clean up the house where the device was assembled.

Extraordinary goals require extraordinary means, and the bombing of the two American embassies demonstrated that al-Qaeda was acquiring the skills, tactics, and tradecraft it needed. Truck bombs were not new; Hezbollah had used them in Lebanon against the Americans, and in Argentina against the Israeli embassy and a Jewish community center; the Egyptian Islamic Jihad, possibly with al-Qaeda support, had shown its own mastery of the tactic in destroying the Egyptian embassy in Pakistan. But executing two such bombings in two countries at once was novel. More distinctive still was the indiscriminateness of the violence—the large majority of the victims were Africans, including some Muslims. This was another al-Qaeda announcement: the group was broadcasting its desire to achieve a level of destruction greater than terrorists had heretofore produced.

The innovation of multiple, simultaneous, and indiscriminate attacks grew out of the group's worldview. It was conscious, as bin Laden had already noted in the 1996 fatwa, of the greater force available to its enemy, which it considered implacable. Bin Laden may have once believed that Western countries might change their governments to protect themselves from the hostility of jihadists, but his frequent references to "an unspeakable Crusader grudge" suggests that he came to see the West's enmity as an unchanging fact of nature. Al-Zawahiri, always a clearer thinker, would later explain, "The Jewish-Crusader alliance, led by the United States, will not allow any Muslim force to reach power in any of the Islamic countries. . . . It will mobilize all its power to hit it and remove it from power. Toward that end, it will open a battlefront against it that includes the entire world." The West, he said, was acquiring new weapons and new allies and showed no compunction about using all the destructive might it could. Therefore, "we [Islamists] concentrate on the following . . . the need to inflict the maximum casualties against the opponent, for this is the language understood by the West."[18] Inherent in this thinking is the belief that the appropriate fate for these irreconcilable opponents is death. There is no room for bargaining over the sacred. Believer and infidel are separated by an unbridgeable chasm.

Exactly who thought of it is unknown, but the idea of multiple-strike attacks was aired in jihadist circles at least five years before the embassy bombings. Siddiq Ali, the Sudanese who was indicted in the TERRSTOP conspiracy and pleaded guilty early in the trial, was fond of saying to his fellow conspirators as they cooked up bombing plans, "Boom, boom, boom and America is on standby." Emad Salem, the FBI's informant in the case, explained that Ali's thinking was that increasing the number of explosions would multiply the effect: "He said the first one will go boom, everybody will go crazy what's going on. Then five minutes later the second one, boom. Everybody will say, well, what's going on. And then five minutes later, the third one boom, everybody will go crazy and put his hands on his head." Such an attack would have a psychological and material impact far surpassing the kind of theater that terrorists usually seek. Instead of engrossing the audience with a carefully administered dose of violence, two or more strikes would be paralyzing. For some, there would be sensory overload. Others involved in handling the consequences would find that events overtaxed their capacities. The theorists of the new terror aimed at creating a consuming sense of crisis, of destroying the dividing line between the moment of violence and the moment of quiet.

—

The East African embassy bombings were the companion piece to the fatwa. Together, words and deeds were intended to assert the Saudi's claim to be the leader of the umma who would take action to restore its dignity and humble its enemy. But whether bin Laden's actions impressed Muslims or not, the attacks drew the wrath of the United States, and made life for radical Islam's leader-in-waiting much more difficult. After the bombings, the United States launched a cruise-missile strike at training camps in Afghanistan in the hope of destroying al-Qaeda's "command and control," its top leaders. In a country awash in weapons, the group's emir was already used to traveling with a security detail. Now, however, he was forced to become more cautious, because the strikes demonstrated that Washington had the wherewithal to locate him and was prepared to use lethal force to get him. Bin Laden moved constantly from camp to camp and from house to house. He seldom stayed anywhere for more than a day.

As intelligence services worked together around the world to dismantle al-Qaeda operations and arrest operatives, the network suffered serious blows. Were the losses offset by a surge in recruitment and donations from radical sympathizers pleased by the bombings? It is impossible to say. Bin Laden became a household name in many countries; his face adorned T-shirts and placards at rallies in Pakistan, where admirers protested the U.S. missile attacks. Moving money became increasingly difficult as institutions that belonged to the mainstream of global capital markets examined their client lists to avoid trouble with the Americans. But there is a nearly endless variety of ways to move money, including converting it into commodities or stuffing it into a courier's pocket. The group continued to have the resources it needed. Fears about communications being intercepted also led to precautions and innovations. The group encrypted messages on the Internet and used disposable cell phones. As is so often true, low-tech means offered the greatest security: sensitive conversations were often held face-to-face.

Even if its procedures had to be modified to maintain security, the group was not daunted but rather set its sights on ever more ambitious operations. Instead of making the mistakes of earlier jihadists, al-Qaeda did not rush to execute attacks. It maintained its strategy of seeking massive blows, paying at the same time close attention to the symbolism of its actions. In preparing the millennium conspiracies, a bundle of targets was chosen so the attacks would resonate in many quarters. Destroying the Amman Radisson, with all its Christian guests, on the two thousandth anniversary of the start of the Christian era, would have sent an unmistakable message. With the attack on Mount Nebo and the John the Baptist site, al-Qaeda was concentrating violence on the country in the region with the closest ties to the United States and Israel. Jordan had a vocal Islamist minority and a monarch with a relatively weak grip on power; it is not beyond imagination that some jihadists believed that a successful set of attacks would trigger an uprising of the faithful and the toppling of the regime, the scenario that Egyptian and Syrian activists had hoped for in their own countries in earlier decades. The jihadists' intervention in history through these massive attacks might move God to respond. Moreover, Ahmad Ressam's bombing of Los Angeles International Airport would have struck the leader of the Crusader alliance in the midst of its celebrations. The suicide-boat bombing of the U.S.S. *The Sullivans* was to occur in the harbor in Aden on the January 3, the Muslim "Night of Power," when the opening verses of the Quran were revealed to the Prophet.

—

The plot in Yemen that failed in January and succeeded in October with the bombing of the *Cole* gave al-Qaeda something to brag about, and brag it did. Some months after the attack, a recruitment video circulated in the Middle East that opens with footage of the wrecked ship; the caption reads "Destroying the Destroyer *Cole*." The video, complete with adaptations of popular Middle Eastern songs as background music, elaborates on many familiar themes. The travail of the Islamic nation is conveyed by a series of images of suffering from different countries: Palestine has moved almost to the fore, just behind the Land of the Two Holy Mosques. The displacement of Iraq reflects the group's understanding that the al-Aqsa intifada had become the greatest issue of concern for most Muslims. After this grisly tour of injustice comes "The Reasons," the second part of the video, which explains the degraded state of the umma. There are still villains to blame and a parade of them flashes across the screen, beginning with Yasir Arafat, who is condemned for denouncing "martyrdom" operations in Palestine. He is followed by the Saudi foreign minister, President Clinton, King Fahd, and Queen Elizabeth. But a subtitle, "The Love of the Present Life and the Hatred of Death," explains the key problem. Muslims do not want to fight the enemy. Bin Laden explains that this-worldliness is the downfall of the umma: "When we search and closely examine Allah's Book, it becomes clear to us that the hatred for fighting and the love of the present life that have captured the hearts of many of us, are the main reasons for these catastrophes and for this subservience and humiliation." Muslims have averted their eyes from the glory that awaits the fighter. The late preacher Abdullah Azzam appears on-screen and complains that "Jihad has become a word in a quiet, gentle session that starts with Pepsi and ends with rice and meat." The commandment to shed blood, the video suggests, supersedes all else.

—

In the final years of Taliban rule, as international sanctions tightened, bin Laden and the mullahs joined in an unbreakable embrace. Afghanistan was isolated in the world community; only Pakistani intelligence, a scattering of religious radicals in other countries, and bin Laden were supporting the pariah regime. Nonetheless, the Taliban refused to cut bin Laden loose, the one act that might have opened a door for them. Whether or not he had bought into all of bin Laden's beliefs from the first, Mullah Omar came to share his vision. In return, the emir of al-Qaeda paid ever greater deference to the Commander of the Faithful. The two became blood brothers. When a "conference"—actually, a rally several days long—was held, on a field outside of Peshawar in the spring of 2001, to mark the 150th anniversary of the Deoband movement, bin Laden sent a letter of greetings that circulated among the wildly pro-Taliban crowd. In it, he announced that he had sworn baya to Omar.

The ultimate measure of Omar's loyalty to bin Laden and his belief in the cause they shared is illustrated by a story from the Taliban's final days. After September 11, 2001, a succession of Pakistani officials traveled to Kandahar to impress upon the Taliban the need to give up bin

Laden or face the consequences. The last to go was General Mehmood Ahmad, the head of ISI. His orders were to tell Omar firmly that time was up. But Mehmood, a Taliban sympathizer who would later be purged, spoke to Omar more in sorrow than anger, telling him that the Americans meant business and were prepared to use unimaginable force if their demands were not met.

Omar refused, and to a longtime patron, in the most insulting way: The problem with you Pakistanis, he said, is that you have never won a war. And we Afghans have never lost one.

THE REVELATION OF USAMA BIN LADEN

The attacks of September 11 admit of countless interpretations and invite almost as many questions. Perhaps the most important is to what extent al-Qaeda's actions reflect a strategy with intelligible goals and methods. Is the group a rational actor? Some would argue that the answer is yes. Al-Qaeda hijacked four airplanes and used them to inflict harm on the country that it perceived as the greatest enemy of Islam, with the aim of forcing that country to change its policies. In the videotape released on December 27, bin Laden spelled out his thinking. The United States has military superiority, but "there is another way through hitting the economic structure, which is basic for the military power. If their economy is destroyed, they will be busy with their own affairs rather than enslaving the weak peoples. It is very important to concentrate on hitting the U.S. economy through all possible means."[19] These are the elements of a comprehensible strategy. Weaken the enemy, force it to attend to internal needs, compel it to change its behavior.

In light of bin Laden's own "internal" goals—his aims vis-à-vis the Muslim community—the claim can be taken further. He believes that most Muslims share his hatred of the United States. Through these spectacular acts, he attempted once again to make that common antipathy the basis for establishing his leadership of the umma. More extravagantly than it had in East Africa and the bombing of the *Cole*, al-Qaeda tried on

September 11 to set the Muslim world alight with its exploits and show
that its archenemy could be confronted and hurt. The attacks piled symbol upon symbol to strengthen the impression that the forces of jihad
were humbling their opponent—targeting the headquarters of the U.S.
military, the home of the nation's leader, and the architectural icons of
U.S. economic power in New York, a city known for its Jewish population. As bin Laden announced in his first video message in October, the
attack on symbols was central: "The values of this Western civilization
under the leadership of America have been destroyed. Those awesome
symbolic towers that speak of liberty, human rights, and humanity have
been destroyed. They have gone up in smoke."[20]

Hard as it might seem to pack more meaning into one event, al-Qaeda
did exactly that with the destruction of the Twin Towers. The World
Trade Center, of course, had already been the target of the first major Islamist attack against the United States. On September 11, al-Qaeda revisited a failure and turned it into a success, trumpeting its defiance and
showing that it was not only ineradicable but unstoppable. In the second
al-Qaeda video released after the attacks—it appeared on December 13—
bin Laden declared just how the massive damage would boost his standing: "When people see a strong horse and weak horse, by nature, they
will like the strong horse."

———

But is that the sum of September 11—an act of war by a group that defines
itself as a nation without a state, and a play for the loyalty of Muslims
around the world?

Al-Qaeda's rhetoric suggests that more was involved. It is not only the
group and bin Laden that were being advertised, it was also a worldview.
After the hijackings, one note that bin Laden and his surrogates struck
most frequently regarded the war against Islam. The theme was not new,
but the proof of vicious Western enmity was. Bin Laden began his December 27 al-Jazeera appearance like a teacher instructing the uninformed:

Three months after the blessed strikes against world infidelity and the head of infidelity, namely America, and almost two months after the fierce crusade against Islam, it gives us pleasure to speak about some of the ramifications of these events. These events have revealed extremely important things to Muslims. It has become clear that the West in general, led by America bears an unspeakable Crusader grudge against Islam.

Those who lived these months under the continuous bombardment by the various kinds of the US aircraft are well aware of this. Many villages were wiped out. . . . Millions of people were made homeless.[21]

The passage leads into the litany of grievances—Palestine, Iraq, Kashmir, and the rest. And though bin Laden contends that America had "only a mere suspicion" as the basis for "this fierce campaign," and therefore acted unjustly, his reasoning is more than a little surreal. The U.S. campaign in Afghanistan is taken as evidence of the war against Islam. Implicitly, there is no causal connection between the "blessed strikes against infidelity" and the American attacks that followed. The relationship between the events is entirely different: the destruction of the World Trade Center and the taking of three thousand lives allows this Crusader enmity to be seen clearly. The planners of September 11 anticipated the retaliation that would clinch their argument about the nature of the United States. "Regardless, if Usama is killed or survives, the awakening has started, praised be God," bin Laden remarks in the broadcast. "This was the fruit of these operations." The awakening is not merely an intellectual one. It is the step necessary to prod the umma to embrace jihad and the final conflict with "world infidelity." Here, we are in a world where cause and effect lose all meaning.

Action and reaction are disconnected because, for bin Laden, September 11 was a moment that reversed the course of time. It is a stock feature of Muslim apocalyptic literature that a certain sequence of events precedes the end of time. First comes a period of extreme division in the world of Islam, when many Muslims are seduced away from the faith. Then history pivots, and, as if through a shared epiphany, masses turn to Islam. For bin Laden, the period before September 11 was that era of fracture and decay. But after the planes struck the towers, the truth was suddenly revealed. Speaking in the video aired on December 13, he described the performance of the nineteen hijackers as "speeches that overshadowed all other speeches made everywhere else in the world. The speeches are understood by both Arabs and non-Arabs—even by Chinese. . . . In Holland, at one of the centers, the number of people who accepted Islam during the days that followed the operations were more than the people who accepted Islam in the last eleven years." Mass conversion is a sure sign of metaphysical change, and even in America, September 11 had miraculous effects. He relates that he "heard someone on Islamic radio who owns a school in America say: 'We don't have time to keep up with the demands of those who are asking about Islamic books to learn about Islam.' This event made people think [about true Islam] which benefited Islam greatly."

So much of what was heard from al-Qaeda after the attacks sounded to Americans like gibberish that many chords of the apocalypse were missed. Consider some of the first words heard from the group after September 11. In the video broadcast on October 7, bin Laden and Ayman al-Zawahiri appear in front of an outcropping of rock. Before the Saudi utters a word, his deputy is heard to say, referring to Palestine, that they, the jihadists, would not allow a repetition of "the tragedy of al-Andalus." The reference is to Muslim Spain, which disappeared when Christian armies defeated its last enclave in Granada in 1492. It was understood by millions of Muslims—the primary audience—and incomprehensible to most Americans. Similarly, moments later bin Laden compared the sufferings cause by the attacks to the pain endured by Muslims, declaring that "since nearly eighty years we have been tasting this humiliation." The reference was to the abolition of the caliphate in 1924.

These men possess a sensibility completely alien to most people in the West. The avowal that al-Qaeda would permit no new al-Andalus to befall the Islamic nation is a reminder that its leaders inhabit a world where time is compressed, and the catastrophes of yesterday are present as the wounds of today. This belief that all events, no matter how long ago, have moral meaning and urgency, that six-hundred-year-old wrongs can somehow be righted, is the mark of a mind that believes God is near, insistent upon action, and ready to intervene.

For all their technical abilities, their medical degrees, and their engineering training, these men live in a world of signs and portents. Much like characters in scripture—especially those who are given glimpses of the end of time—they find truth revealed in dreams. In the December 13 video, which shows bin Laden surrounded by adoring followers, there is an extended discussion of dreams. A year before the attacks, he relates, a man named Abu al-Hasan al-Masri told bin Laden that he had a dream in which " 'we were playing a soccer game against the Americans. When our team showed up in the field, they were all pilots.' . . . He didn't know anything about the operation until he heard it on the radio. He said the game went on and we defeated them. That was a good omen for us." Someone off-camera mentions another man who knew nothing of the conspiracy and had a vision of a plane hitting a tall building. A Saudi sheikh on-camera says that several other people had the same premonition. Bin Laden recounts that he was in Kandahar when "a brother" told him about another dream in which there appeared a tall building in America and someone teaching karate. "At that point," the master terrorist confesses, "I was worried that maybe the secret would be revealed if everyone starts seeing it in their dreams."[22]

Perhaps the likeness between the attacks of September 11 and the writings of the Arab world's paperback apocalyptics is also no coincidence. These stories focus on destroying New York, which is seen as a city of Jews and the capital of world finance. One stock image is the toppling of skyscrapers in great fireballs. Another recurrent motif is that the final battle, the Armageddon between believers and infidels, will involve nuclear or chemical weapons. Al-Qaeda has worked to procure such tools of mass destruction for a decade, and bin Laden has repeatedly asserted that

Muslims have a right to possess nuclear weapons.[23] In 1999, he went further, telling *Time* magazine that "acquiring weapons for the defense of Muslims is a religious duty. If I have indeed acquired these weapons, then I thank God for enabling me to do so. And if I seek to acquire these weapons, I am carrying out a duty. It would be a sin for Muslims not to try to possess the weapons that would prevent the infidels from inflicting harm on Muslims."[24] It is a remarkable statement: procuring a weapon of mass destruction is an act of piety.

One can imagine that al-Qaeda would try to prevent its enemies from acting against Muslims by threatening to use such a weapon. But for terrorists, a nuclear bomb has limited usefulness as a tool of strategy. If the United States were faced with nuclear blackmail and complied with a set of demands, for example, the terrorists could still never stop threatening. Without their weapon, they would have no guarantee that the United States would continue to act as demanded. And so long as the nuclear blackmail continued, America would seek every opportunity to destroy the terrorists, using means it would otherwise never contemplate. Over the long term, against an enemy without a territorial haven and without a proven ability to launch more than a single nuclear strike, the United States would have a clear advantage. There are reasons why no one has ever seriously tried nuclear blackmail.

More worrisome is the possibility that bin Laden means that the prevention of harm would be accomplished by the destruction of the enemy. As he says in the December 27 video, "God willing, the end of America is imminent." Why should anyone believe al-Qaeda would not inflict the greatest possible damage on its cosmic enemy if it could?

RAIDERS ON THE PATH OF GOD

What did the terrorist attacks of September 11 mean to those who carried them out? What could be going through the mind of someone who hijacks a plane and flies it into a building filled with thousands of people? All of the perpetrators of September 11 knew, bin Laden has said, that they were participating in a "martyrdom operation," though most of them did not know what would be required of them until very late, possibly just before they boarded the planes. Among those in the dark were the "muscle," the ten Saudis who joined the operation in its final months and whose task it was to overcome the planes' flight staffs and those in the aisles so the "pilots" could take control. Others—Marwan al-Shehhi is the prime example—may have lacked the will to do anything but follow orders. For years before the hijackings, al-Shehhi and Muhammad Atta were inseparable. They met and lived together in Hamburg. While in the United States, they moved from one flight school to the next and one apartment to the next, and they were physically together virtually all the time. Rudy Dekkers, the owner of Huffman Aviation, the Florida school they attended the longest, said they were "joined at the hip" and like a "duck with the little ones," Atta in front, al-Shehhi always behind him. Al-Shehhi was incapable of defying his master.

And Atta? An intelligent and disciplined individual, Atta knew what he was doing. That is clear from the five-page document found in his luggage, which accidentally did not make it aboard American Airlines Flight 11 out of Boston's Logan Airport. It is not certain that Atta was the author of the handwritten document—two other copies were found, one in a rental car at Dulles Airport, another in the wreckage of United Airlines Flight 93 in Pennsylvania—but given what is known about him, his piety and his religious knowledge, he is the most likely candidate.

The document was meant to spiritually and practically prepare those who read it for their task. Some of its instructions are mundane—"Tighten your shoes well, and wear socks that hold in the shoes and do not come out." Others, such as "Inspect your weapon before you leave," are obviously meant to prevent errors. Most, however, are intended to concentrate the spirit on the work at hand, laying out readings from Muslim scriptures, setting out a list of invocations to be recited at different points and reminding the reader, for example, "When the [airplane] starts moving and heads toward [takeoff] recite the supplication of travel, because you are traveling to God, May you be blessed in this travel."

The letter testifies to the hijackers' understanding of themselves as warriors, striking against the evil that is the West. The hijacker is told to remember to ask God to "help us against the nonbelievers," that takeoff is the "hour of encounter between the two camps," and that the act will be carried out for the glory of God. The scholars Kanan Makiya and Hassan Mneimneh note that in talking about the killing that will take place on board, the document uses a very specific word for *slaughter*, one that means "slitting the two jugular veins in the throat of an animal" as in ritual sacrifice. For centuries, Muslims have slaughtered a sheep at the Eid al-Adha using this technique as a remembrance of Abraham's willingness to sacrifice his son Isaac to God. When the moment came for the hijackers to make their move, they rushed the cabin crew and, using their boxcutter blades, stabbed them or slit their throats. The crew were being sacrificed, but they were not the only offerings. Ultimately, all those who would die aboard the planes and in the buildings were also being rendered to the deity.

Sacrifices are done for different reasons. Believers may make an offering in thanksgiving for good fortune or to fulfill a requirement of the calendar. (Ancient Israelites made the pilgrimage to the Temple three times a year to fulfill their obligations.) September 11 fits neither category. It was a sacrifice made for the most common reason: expiation, the removal of a sin through an act of giving.

What sins did Muhammad Atta have to atone for? The letter he presumably wrote is unusual for an al-Qaeda document in being introspective, a kind of monologue of the self to the soul of a holy warrior. It provides a single hint about what wrongs Atta was expiating, which comes in the only extended passage about the victims of the sacrifice.

> For all their equipment, and all their gates, and all their technology do not do benefit or harm, except with the permission of God.
>   The believers do not fear them. Those who fear them are the followers of Satan, those who had feared Satan to begin with, and be-

came his followers [illegible]. Fear is a great act of worship that can be offered only to God, and He is most worthy of it. God said, following the aforementioned verses, it is Satan who causes fear in his followers. These are the admirers of Western civilization, who have drunk their love for it and their hallowing of it with the cool water, and were afraid for their weak feeble stomachs. "Fear them not, but fear Me, if you are believers." Fear is indeed a great act of worship offered by the followers of God and by the believers only to the One God who rules over all things, with the utmost certitude that God will annul the treachery of the nonbelievers. For God has said: "Verily God will weaken the treachery of the nonbelievers."[25]

Here, the mask slips. Despite the mention of unbelievers, there are none of the usual rants about Crusaders or Jews, America or the apostate rulers of the Islamic world. It is possible that "admirers of Western civilization" subsumes all these. But, tellingly, the reference is not to the eternal Crusader, the historic violator of the realm of Islam, or to the eternal Jew, who rejects Muhammad's prophecy. Rather, it is to the contemporary admirers of Western civilization, that world armed with equipment and gates: they are what matters.

The young Egyptian had chosen to study in Hamburg, believing that to do so would help him avoid the fate of masses of Egyptian university graduates who cannot find a decent job when they graduate. In the urban planning program at the Technical University in Hamburg, Atta wrote a thesis on the Syrian city of Aleppo and the conflict there between the old, haphazard, organic neighborhoods and modernism, the clearing of the slums and the building of high-rises. He came to loathe the new style.[26] And as time went by in Germany, he seemed more deeply alienated from his surroundings. Many noted his fastidiousness, his refusal to come into close contact with Germans, especially women. In his latter years in Hamburg, he frequently expressed a strong revulsion to the culture around him. No wonder he chose a World Trade Center tower as his target.

Atta was a man flagellating himself. At some point, how and when are not clear, he had a brush with temptation; perhaps he felt he had succumbed. Whatever touched him, he identified with the West. It might have been as simple as a personal desire to be a part of the West that caused him to feel contaminated. His repulsion was powerful, and he felt somehow humiliated.

In this, Atta resembles many of the radicals who take up arms against the West: L'Houssaine Kherchtou, the caterer from Morocco who wandered around France and Italy as an illegal immigrant and eventually, through the mosque in Milan, opted for jihad. The Egyptian Mahmud Abouhalima, one of the conspirators who bombed the World Trade Center in 1993, was living in Germany in the 1980s, where his life was one "of corruption—girls, drugs, you name it." Eventually, he turned to the Quran. After moving to New York, he joined the community of Atlantic Avenue jihadists around Sheikh Rahman. " 'Islam is a mercy,' " he told the scholar Mark Juergensmeyer, ". . . explaining that it rescued the fallen and gave meaning to one's personal life." Abouhalima traveled to Afghanistan in 1988 to show he was "a Muslim, not a sheep."[27] El-Sayyid Nosair, the assassin of Meir Kahane, sat through his trial in a New York courtroom, day in and day out, drawing careful pictures of Princess Diana. These men are descendants of Sayyid Qutb, who recoiled from the woman who accosted him aboard the ocean liner and who at a church social saw a "hall swarmed with legs." All these jihadists react to the taint or seduction they felt by espousing a violent Islamism, as though that overcorrection would erase the sin of their earlier lives.

The novelist V. S. Naipaul has spoken about "half-baked" societies, the developing nations that dangle between modern and traditional, West and East. The pathology is different, but these jihadists have the quality of half-baked men. The societies Naipaul wrote about lurch back and forth, reaching for modernization and then stridently reasserting their traditions in an effort to compensate for a sense of inferiority. The terrorists lurch even more violently. Whether the individual has a buried religious sensibility that is reasserting itself, or has no religious background and is searching for stability and identity in an unwelcoming universe—and many were illegal immigrants in the West at one point or another—the perception of past corruption is real. The remedy is to fight the Seducer and sacrifice his people to propitiate an affronted God.

CHAPTER 5

FIELDS OF JIHAD

LTHOUGH AL-QAEDA WAS badly damaged in the aftermath of the
September 11 attacks, two things are certain. First, even if the organization does not survive the defeat in Afghanistan and continuing worldwide manhunt, some group or groups with the same ideology will follow
it. Second, the United States will continue to be the prime target.

Bin Laden's popularity is remarkable. The Arab street exulted in the
September 11 attacks and acclaimed him a hero in the mold of Saladin.
The mood was encapsulated by Radwa Abdallah, a university student
who, sitting in a McDonald's in Cairo, told a *Wall Street Journal* reporter
that when she heard about the carnage at the World Trade Center and the
Pentagon, "Everyone celebrated. People honked in the streets, cheering
that finally America got what it truly deserved." Op-eds in regional newspapers reflected Radwa's sentiments. Ahmad Ragab, in the Egyptian
government-backed daily *al-Akhbar,* equated the attacks of September 11 with the then impending U.S. strikes on Afghanistan: "The U.S.
and terrorism suffuse a foul atmosphere throughout the world. The
smiles have disappeared from the faces of the peoples, who wait, across
the world, for the disaster that either terrorists or the U.S. will visit upon

them. The U.S. has become like the terrorists." Another Egyptian com-
mentator, Ali al-Sayyed, of the government-owned *al-Ahram al-Arabi*
weekly, wrote, "For many long years, America made many peoples in the
world cry. It was always [America] that carried out the acts; now, acts are
being carried out [against] it. A cook who concocts poison must one day
also taste that poison!"[1] Public opinion in Saudi Arabia, where polling is
difficult to conduct because political self-expression can be dangerous,
matched the Egyptian reaction to the attacks in one survey, where 94 percent of the respondents applauded bin Laden's actions.[2] There is no
doubt that jihadist fish swim in friendly waters.

About a dozen of al-Qaeda's leaders have been killed or captured. Administration sources speak of three thousand, but it is not clear whether this
includes detainees from Afghanistan, or others from the Gulf, Central Asia,
and Southeast Asia. But since intelligence services have only a vague idea of
how big al-Qaeda is, there is no way of knowing how much of the infrastructure has actually been dismantled. Perhaps a dozen senior operatives—
bin Laden associates who know where the sleeper cells are and have the
authority to activate them as well as the logistical and planning skills to equip
and guide them—are unaccounted for.[3] All of them have been implicated in
previous conspiracies, including the attacks of September 11; a few have
been with bin Laden for nearly ten years. Since they can turn the crank on
operations, the fact that they are at large means al-Qaeda is not yet crippled.

Of the group's U.S. network, surprisingly little is still known despite
prosecutions in Detroit and Buffalo and sweeps in Seattle, Chicago, and
Atlanta. The FBI maintained after the attacks that the September 11 ring
acted without help from cells already in the country, but it cannot prove a
negative. There may well have been sleepers who provided logistical
help. It would be more prudent to assume the existence of an al-Qaeda infrastructure that has not yet been detected than to assume the Atta group
was so self-disciplined and resourceful that they carried off the conspiracy with no local assistance—an extraordinary feat, if true.

The group was able to relocate some of its cadres to Pakistan and
some, it appears, to Iran. Others remain in Afghanistan and will either

try to elude foreign forces or cross the border into Pakistan. Most of the prisoners taken from Afghanistan to the U.S. military detention center at Guantánamo Bay seem not to have been connected to al-Qaeda's overseas networks and have so far yielded few valuable clues to the identity and whereabouts of key players.

For the foreseeable future, al-Qaeda will not have the benefits of the safe haven it enjoyed in Afghanistan. It remains to be seen whether the group will reappear in Yemen, where bin Laden had strong links and the government's writ ends at the city limits of Sanaa, leaving large tracts available for secure resettlement. There are other possibilities: Somalia, or the bin Laden–affiliated Palestinian refugee camps in the Lebanese cities of Sidon and Tripoli.

A more salient question is whether al-Qaeda will make the leap from bricks-and-mortar statehood to virtual statehood. In Afghanistan al-Qaeda was, in truth, a state. It controlled territory, maintained an army and waged war, forged alliances, taxed and spent, and enforced a system of law. The de facto sovereignty it enjoyed in Afghanistan offered great advantages: a territorial base, training facilities, and a secure headquarters. But given the possibility that the United States would do in Yemen, Somalia, or Lebanon what it did in Afghanistan, virtual sovereignty holds fewer hazards than reestablishing camps and training facilities where they will attract the terminal guidance sensors of American bombs. Virtuality has its own advantages. A dispersed group is harder to locate and attack. Some elements will inevitably be identified and arrested, but other parts of the network will not be affected. With their Macintosh laptops and encrypted communications, stolen credit cards, access to Internet cafés and disposable cell phones, false passports, and comfort with long distance travel, jihadists can be everywhere and anywhere. With businesses and charities as fronts, they have adequate cover for their money transfers, fax transmissions, and shipments of matériel. To move large sums of money, they can avoid the banking system by using hawala money movers or couriers. Able to move quickly over long distances, the leaders of individual networks can relocate under pressure, or to keep adversaries off balance.

Networks—supple, malleable, invisible—have the advantage over hier-archical organizations, like law-enforcement and intelligence agencies. A virtual enemy is nimble. Moreover, networks can swarm. Their well-developed communications enable them to come together for short peri-ods to launch an offensive, then disperse. It is not only antiglobalization protesters who can use the Net effectively to coordinate the arrival of large numbers of people in the same place at the same time. If al-Qaeda, or its successor, makes this transition, the danger it poses will be vastly greater.

As a network of networks, al-Qaeda is structured to survive multiple amputations, and even decapitation. Its beliefs require members to con-tinue the assault on the United States, wherever and whenever possible. That is the essence of bin Laden's 1998 fatwa, which will remain in effect even if he is gone. The success of the World Trade Center attacks has pro-vided a powerful incentive for al-Qaeda to continue its operations. Strong support from radical ulema with soaring reputations, like the Saudi Safar al-Hawali, and from some Arabic- and Urdu-language print media, which condoned the attacks, reinforces the incentive. The terrorists' dedication is rewarded by the proliferation of stories, still circulating at high velocity through the region, about mass conversions to Islam of Christians in Eu-rope and the United States. There is a grain of truth in these tales. In Europe there has been an increase in conversions, just as there was after the Gulf War. Jihadist mythmaking has transformed this sociological cu-riosity into a sign that Christendom recognized September 11 as a revela-tion of the righteous power of Islam.

The dissenting voices of liberal Muslims or state-appointed clergy tend to elicit contempt among the jihadists. In contrast, *salafi* funda-mentalists who also wish to emulate the earliest generations of Islam, but who oppose jihad—and whose number includes renowned preachers in Egypt, Saudi Arabia, Jordan, and Kuwait—have some limited impact. Their reputation for independence and their devotion to a vision of Islam almost identical to the jihadists' adds to their influence, as does their en-dorsement of jihad by the sword as, in principle, the correct instrument for transforming the world into Dar al-Islam, the Realm of Islam. Only not just yet: unlike the jihadists, this group holds that the time for holy war has not yet arrived, because Muslims are not yet united under the banner of salafiyya Islam. Until that day comes, God will not grant victory to those who wage jihad. Their sacrifice will be in vain and, according to some preachers, might even constitute sin. A jihad that cannot be won will only expose Muslims to the enemy's depredations, and for one Muslim to cause the needless suffering of another is prohibited.

Al-Qaeda recruits will not be seduced by this reasoning. They believe that their thirst for jihad and readiness for martyrdom have clearly won Allah's approval and support. For them, victory is possible. They believe that the realm of Islam has reawakened and its potential is just beginning to unfold. Al-Zawahiri has written that Dar al-Islam

represents a growing power that is rallying under the banner of jihad for the sake of God and operating outside the scope of the new world order. It is free of the servitude for the dominating western empire. It promises destruction and ruin for the new Crusades against the lands of Islam. It is ready for revenge against the heads of the world's gathering of infidels, the United States, Russia, and Israel. It is anxious to seek retribution for . . . the sores of the tortured people throughout the land of Islam, from Eastern Turkestan to Andalusia [i.e., al-Andalus].[4]

This is not a group that will stop attacking American interests as long as it has the power to do so.

Yet, whether al-Qaeda or its successor remains solely fixated on the far enemy, or decides as well to step up action against the near enemy—the secular Muslim rulers it considers illegitimate—remains an open question.[5]

The jihadists lost their revolutionary battle against the state, which proved too strong for them. It deployed effective security services and enjoyed international support, it knew how to divide the opposition, and it doled out small concessions in the area of political reform to siphon off popular anger. In Egypt, the insurgency was decisively crushed. In Algeria, the GIA continues to kill, but with no prospect of victory. In Saudi Arabia, the burgeoning Islamist opposition was humbled in the mid-1990s. In Pakistan, the religious parties were Talibanized, but when the military regime decided to abandon the Taliban, the religious radicals were not able to derail the change in policy. (Among Shiites, revolutionary fervor has died in Iran and holds little appeal elsewhere.) These governments may not have an indefinite lease on life, but for the foreseeable future they have a strategy that will keep them in power.

Does this mean that jihadist Islam has no future in the lands from which it emerged? Can the jihadists inspire a mass movement? Al-Qaeda's consistent clarity about the restoration of the realm of Islam indicates that the jihadists have not abandoned their goals, despite the defeats they have suffered at the hands of the state over the past decade. The jihadists believe that victory over both the far and the near enemies is not only possible, but inevitable. That is why they continue to invest so much into the many "fields of jihad," as Sheikh Rahman has called them—countries where the militants are determined to continue their struggles to defeat the apostates and create an Islamically pure society. Their conviction that they may yet vanquish the near enemy is not entirely delusional. Consider these four factors:

HEARTS AND MINDS

Within Arab Muslim countries, especially those that are vital to regional stability and U.S. interests, the radicals may have lost the war against the state, but they have won the theological debate. In the Middle East and Pakistan, religious discourse dominates societies, the airwaves, and thinking about the world. Radical mosques have proliferated throughout Egypt. Bookstores are dominated by works with religious themes. In Saudi Arabia, nearly one in five undergraduates majors in Islamic studies. In Jordan, a salafiyya form of Islam is surging via informal social networks, eclipsing tamer forms of Islamism. In Pakistan, religious education is supplanting public education and creating a generation of zealots.

The demand for sharia, the belief that their governments are unfaithful to Islam and that Islam is the answer to all problems, and the certainty that the West has declared war on Islam: these are the themes that dominate public discussion. Islamists may not control parliaments or government palaces, but they have occupied the popular imagination.

Strengthening the appeal of radical Islam is the illegitimacy of the governments that oppose it. Egypt is more authoritarian now than it was a decade ago; Saudi Arabia's government is casting about for ways to appear more legitimate without actually expanding political participation; Jordan has delayed parliamentary elections and passed newly repressive laws; Algeria is run, behind the scenes, by its army; and Pakistan is ruled by a military dictator. The political oppression that invited a violent reaction in the 1990s has, in some cases, grown worse. There has been liberalization only in a handful of countries, mostly small Persian Gulf states.

The governments, of course, understand that some form of popular legitimacy is essential to their survival. They also know that the wind is blowing toward Islam. So their quest has led them to burnish their own Islamic credentials. Even Nasser appreciated this need. Sadat understood it better still. He went to mosque, adopted traditional dress, changed the Egyptian constitution to make sharia a source for Egyptian law, and gave free rein to the Islamist groups that ultimately gunned him down. Even as it throws Muslim Brothers in jail, Mubarak's regime is fighting for control of religious discourse by strengthening its grip on the clerics of al-Azhar, licensing and staffing the mosques, and acquiescing to court challenges of family laws that offend the Islamists.

In Saudi Arabia, the king's right to rule is explicitly based on religious credentials. The regime imprisons Islamists who question whether he is fulfilling his Islamic responsibilities, but it also appropriates their language of piety and gives scope to their anti-Western rhetoric. As in Egypt, this deflects popular resentment from the regime and turns it toward the United States. The secular, British-educated general who runs Pakistan uses Islamic language to buttress his credibility in an increasingly strident religious environment. But this strategy of competing with the opposition on its issues cannot be sustained indefinitely. Every flanking movement undertaken by these regimes validates the Islamist agenda. The state's claims to superior religious authority are not taken seriously, and the official clergy are regarded as regime parrots. The game is now played by "ibn Taymiyya rules": apostate governments are illegitimate, and so are the ulema that defend them. In the race to show the people who is more Islamic, the Islamists will win every time. Sooner or later, these regimes will discover that challenging the Islamists at their own game endangers their long-term survival.

In Saudi Arabia, this competition has pitted the ruler's role as patron and defender of Islam against his responsibilities as the leader of a modernizing state. In an earlier time, the demands of xenophobic Wahhabism and responsible internationalism could be finessed. Usama bin Laden has made this much harder to do by exposing the state's compromises. After September 11, for example, the United States—the guarantor of Saudi external security—pressured Riyadh to improve its counterterrorism efforts. But the al-Saud could not do so in any comprehensive way for fear of endangering their religious standing. The Islamists' objections also impede deeper reforms such as economic modernization programs, or improved and expanded secular education. When the regimes boost Islam to create the political space in which they can take unpopular measures—as Egypt has done to maintain peace with Israel—they create even greater barriers to bold secular action.

DAR AL-ISLAM OCCUPIES DAR AL-HARB

When the Islamists recognized that they could not blast through the walls of the state because their groups were easily penetrated and the regimes' use of torture and capital punishment proved so effective, the survivors staged a tactical retreat to the greener pastures of Europe, Southeast Asia, Central Asia, East Africa, and America. In some of these new fields of jihad, weak or nonexistent law enforcement, porous customs and immigration services, and corrupt officialdom enabled jihadists to set up shop.

Where there was a failed state like Afghanistan to exploit, even better. Many Egyptian Islamic Jihad members fleeing Egyptian security forces regrouped in Afghanistan, or redeployed from there to other fields of jihad in the Balkans or Central Asia. Some discovered that Europe provided an ideal staging ground. Civil-liberties legislation and human rights NGOs effectively smoothed the passage of many hardened killers into Europe. They blended easily into that continent's large and growing Muslim community, and they found in it ready recruits.

Throughout Europe, young Muslims are becoming angrier, more radical, and more active. Excluded by racist societies, denied equal opportunity, and denigrated by their own Westernized elites, they have developed an exclusivist mind-set. A vicious cycle has developed, in which the indifference or outright contempt of one side feeds the same emotions of the other. In radical mosques in France, Germany, Belgium, and the United Kingdom young people are told they live in Dar al-Harb—the Realm of War—and that the people around them are the enemies of Islam. Thousands of British youths went to Afghanistan and Kashmir to fight against the infidels. European Muslims increasingly consider themselves Muslims first and foremost, and citizens of their own countries only as an administrative matter. As they begin to articulate their alienation from European society, they come to see themselves as bin Laden sees them: oppressed Muslims whose suffering calls for jihad. In the technologically advanced countries of Europe, they acquire the skills required to wreak havoc anywhere in the world.

If the jihadists run into a dead end in the countries they come from, bin Laden has shown them that they can take the war to the far enemy—whose destruction would in turn bring on the collapse of their near enemy, the countries they fled.

APPEARANCES DECEIVE

Moderate Muslim regimes look solid. But history is a cascade of discontinuities, and the twenty-first century is unlikely to be any exception.

Consider the salient possibilities: U.S. withdrawal from an anarchic Iraq; a succession crisis in Egypt following the aging Mubarak's departure from the scene; a regional war stemming from a calamitous turn in the Palestinian-Israeli conflict; a terrorist attack that kills key members of the Saudi royal family; an economic downturn; or a prolonged plunge in oil prices that significantly worsens the poverty of many people in the region.

In countries where the secular establishment has been weakened, it is far from inconceivable that Islamists will be able to seize power, or at least greatly complicate the consolidation of new governments. We do not know enough, for example, about the scope and nature of the Muslim Brotherhood's organization and reach in Egypt. Consequently, it would be foolhardy to take any particular outcome for granted. American miscalculations regarding Iran in 1979—despite our unimpeded access to that country—provide a sobering confirmation of this reality.

BURGEONING SOCIOECONOMIC PROBLEMS

The delegitimation of regimes and the emergence of religious violence are unquestionably linked to the failure of leaders to cope with massive region-wide socioeconomic problems.

The biggest of these problems is population. Even though fertility rates are declining, the population of the Middle East and North Africa could reach 600 million by 2025; in South Asia, the population of Pakistan alone will break 200 million. Within the next fifteen years, Egypt will grow by 25 percent, to 85.2 million people. Jordan's population will increase by 44 percent, Syria's by 39 percent, Saudi Arabia's by 56 percent, and Palestine's (the West Bank and Gaza) by 64 percent.

Even more alarming is the changing age distribution within these populations. In Iran, Pakistan, and the Arab world, 50 percent or more of the population is under twenty years of age. High concentrations of young people in a society, especially teenagers, correlates well with violence and poorly with stability. From the French Revolution to China's Cultural Revolution and the student movement in Europe and America in the late 1960s, "youth bulges" have accompanied many of history's most dramatic upheavals.

Education and literacy have been spreading, but not quickly enough. Pakistan is worst off, with adult literacy hovering at about 40 percent. Egypt, Morocco, Sudan, and Yemen have achieved rates closer to 50 percent, which is still not enough to propel economic growth, while Algeria, Iraq, Libya, Tunisia, Saudi Arabia, and Syria have reached literacy levels between 50 percent and 66 percent. Iran and Kuwait, where more than three-quarters of adults are literate, have done much better than the rest of the region. All these countries, with the possible exception of Pakistan, are likely to improve in the future. Yet while secondary school enrollment is generally increasing, the pace of enrollment is faster for boys than for girls, which means there will likely be little net diminution in women's fertility or unemployment. Moreover, the quality of the education is often poor. Almost every country in the region emphasizes rote learning and does little to foster the capacity for critical thinking. As a consequence, the region is filled with young men who are too well educated for the lowliest kinds of manual labor, but lack the skills that would enable them to join the globalized economy.

This half-qualified labor force grew at a rate of 3.4 percent per year for most of the 1990s—faster than in any other region of the world. Lackluster economic growth has simply not created a corresponding demand for labor. The mismatch between supply and demand means that unemployment will rise, wages will fall, or both.

In fact, it may not even be accurate to speak of economic growth in the Middle East and North Africa. The economies of the developed world have grown by 1.4 percent per year over the past twenty years, starting from a high baseline. East Asia, apart from Japan, saw its economy grow at 5.8 percent per year. Latin American economies, despite the heavy debt burden of the 1980s, have still managed 1 percent annual growth since 1980. In the Arab world, by contrast, per capita income has been virtually unchanged since 1980; in some countries, including oil-rich Saudi Arabia, it has actually fallen. Real wages and labor productivity are about where they were thirty years ago. Outside the energy sector, trade is at a standstill: the entire region's non-oil exports are smaller than those of Finland. Foreign direct investment in the region adds up to 1 percent of the region's gross domestic product, lower even than sub-Saharan Africa's 1.6 percent. The Arab world has, in effect, disengaged from the world economy.

The misery of economic deprivation and growing unemployment is compounded by living conditions in regional cities, Cairo being an outstanding example. These megalopolises have swelled with 100 million new residents since the mid-1970s. Half of all people in the Middle East, or about 135 million, live in them. This number will exceed 350 million within twenty-five years. The Middle East is not alone in this. Pakistan is experiencing the same urban population explosion and is, if anything, less able to cope. In 1947, Karachi was a city of 1 million. In 2000, it had 11 million. By 2025, its population will approach 20 million. In countries where economic growth is negligible or negative, subsidies are high, and tax collection is uneven, funds are simply unavailable for investment in infrastructure and delivery of public services. As a result, large parts of the urban population lack sewage facilities, clean water, electricity, health care, adequate housing, garbage collection, and efficient transport.

The problem of water supply, already serious, will become much worse in the coming years. In the driest region in the world, the amount of renewable water per person per year in the region dropped from 3,500 cubic meters in 1960 to 1,250 today. By 2025, the average inhabitant of the Middle East and North Africa will have about one-seventh as much water as someone living outside the region. Water quality is also poor. Amman, for example, has periods when sludge, rather than water, is on tap in many households.

If you are poor in this part of the world, therefore, you are also likely to be ill-fed, in poor health, and jammed into squalid quarters. It is no wonder that Hamas in Gaza and the Muslim Brotherhood in Egypt, which fund clinics, charities, and schools in desperate communities, win converts. Nor is it surprising that people are drawn to the mosque—"the one place in the slums which is cool while the outside is hot, the one place which is clean while the outside is filthy, the one place which is calm while the outside is only chaos," as Alan Richards, the dean of Middle East economists, has observed.

In the poorer countries, this situation will be difficult—perhaps impossible—to reverse, because the infrastructure is so bad, the population so ill-educated, and the natural resources so degraded. Governments remain wedded to centralized economic planning, incompetent judiciaries, rococo regulation, and byzantine bureaucracies: these inhibit foreign direct investment as well as development of new business ventures at home.

Even the region's wealthier states face nearly insurmountable problems. Oil-producing countries have failed to develop other economic sectors that might generate new jobs. Years of high wages and incomes have made these countries uncompetitive in manufacturing, while their citizens' skill levels are not up to the requirements of high-technology industries. As a result, governments will use their oil-export revenues to fund nonproductive public sector jobs to absorb the growing number of graduates entering the job market every year. Their resources to do so, however, are shrinking, and are unlikely to increase as the decreasing costs of alternative-energy production keep oil prices down.

In country after country, the scourges of population growth, economic dysfunction, urbanization, and resource scarcity nourish radical Islam.

EGYPT

Egypt, which has been under assault by radical Islamists on and off since the mid-1970s, exemplifies many of these socioeconomic problems.

As we have seen, the Islamist encroachment was made possible by successive regimes that tried to enhance their image as a Muslim government to buttress flimsy claims to popular legitimacy and weaken leftist opponents by making them look like enemies of Islam.

Islamist gains were also made possible by the government's failure to act as a provider of social services, education, and health care. The Islamists saw their opportunity to establish a parallel government that would provide these vital services, however crudely, and crowd out secular authority. They were successful in poor neighborhoods of Cairo, like Imbaba, which acquired the nicknames the Islamic Republic and the Emirate. Their effort was even more fruitful in central and upper Egypt, where Islamic law was imposed, the mosques taken over by radical preachers, and rule by Cairo disregarded.

Mubarak was already concerned by 1992 about the possibility of social unrest because of economic reforms, which were bound to make life even harder for many Egyptians. It seemed prudent to consolidate Cairo's control over areas that might be sources of violent opposition. The *"reconquista,"* as it came to be known, began in Imbaba, which was surrounded by security forces and invaded by thousands of paramilitary police. They moved through the neighborhood block by block, conducting house-to-house searches, seizing weapons, and arresting hundreds for interrogation. Similar operations were carried out in the south. Slowly, central authority was restored throughout the country. But the radicals, descendants of the groups that carried out terrorist attacks in the 1970s and 1980s, struck back, with a campaign of violence beginning in 1992 against public figures, writers, artists, and government officials and the planting of bombs in public places in Cairo and south-central Egypt. A crackdown began to show results in 1996, and by 1998 the government's victory was clear.

The defeat of the insurgency did not eliminate the social, political, and economic conditions that fueled it. Per capita gross domestic product for Egypt is stuck at $1,400. As many as 800,000 Egyptians enter the job market every year; it costs $10,000 to create a new job in agriculture and twice that much in industry. Egypt has nothing like the resources it needs to stem increasing unemployment. Low oil prices, the lingering damage to tourism from the 1997 massacre of tourists and policemen at Luxor, and the Asian economic crisis have all hurt the economy. By the end of 2001 the Egyptian pound had dropped 32 percent from its mid-2000 level, raising the cost of consumer goods for people already hard-pressed to make ends meet. The September 11 attacks undercut the tourist industry, which had finally been recovering from Luxor, and further depressed the economy.

The current economic malaise has dampened hopes for Egyptian economic growth. The government balks at a privatization program and refuses to relinquish its hold on "strategic" industries such as telecommunications. Egypt cannot produce enough food to feed itself.[6] Four and a half million tons of food will be imported this year, a substantial burden for consumers who hold a weakened currency and a government that provides subsidies while the economy is dead in the water. The United States, the European Union, and the international financial institutions are providing balance-of-payments support for Egypt, which should avoid a disaster in the near term. If oil prices hold and the international economy continues to recover, if there are no new terrorist attacks, no regional disruptions related to a war with Iraq, no spiraling Israeli-Palestinian hostilities—then Egypt's economic growth should pick up again in 2004. This is a great deal to hope for.

The grievances that underlie Islamist violence include much more than economics. Egypt's democratic deficit also gives radicals an obvious issue. Mubarak's regime has ruled since he came to power in 1981 under an emergency law that gives the President wide powers—for example, the prerogative to have anyone tried for virtually any felony by a state security court run by military judges appointed by the regime.[7] New laws to further limit political participation have been added to the books in recent years. In 1992, a "parties committee" was established to certify new political parties and thereby approve their participation in elections. It has even prevented the Third Way party, a breakaway faction of the Muslim Brothers that accepts the reality of a secular Egyptian state, from fielding candidates.

Mubarak was elected in September 1999 to a fourth six-year term, with 94 percent of the vote. As the candidate chosen by the People's Assembly, he was unopposed. Low voter turnout and the ever-present irregularities guaranteed that this "angel in the form of a president," as one sycophantic journalist described him, would be approved by an overwhelming margin.

The Muslim Brothers, still the foremost voice of Islamic opposition, fielded an array of candidates in the October–November 2000 elections. The individuals had to run as independents because religiously oriented parties are prohibited by Egyptian law. Their affiliation with the Brothers was known, however, and they won 17 seats. In a 444-seat assembly, this may not seem like many, but given that a thousand or so Brothers were arrested and a greater number harassed prior to the election, it is an impressive achievement. The Brothers are no longer the public firebrands they were before Nasser's purge in 1965. They still run social services outlets and schools, which give them popular appeal, and for the most part, they advocate a political and economic program focused on good government, an end to economic reforms dictated by the International Monetary Fund, and economic protection for certain sectors, especially agriculture. They are combative toward the regime's approach to Israel, peace with the Jewish state being, in their view, un-Islamic.

This is not an extraordinary platform. What sets the Brothers apart is their religious agenda. Article 2 of the Egyptian constitution has been modified twice regarding sharia. Anwar Sadat endorsed the insertion of a provision stipulating that sharia was "a source" for legislation. The Mubarak government, to steal a march on the Islamist opposition, amended this to read "*the* source." Ironically, this had the effect of enabling the Muslim Brothers to assert their right to better treatment by claiming that they sought nothing more then the incremental implementation of the constitution. The Brothers then used the amendment to mount legal challenges to public law that conflicts with sharia, while trying to create pressure for faster implementation of Islamic law. They argue that Islamic sanctions should be applied, which presumably means amputation for thieves, stoning for adulterers, and lashing for those who drink alcohol. Since lavish spending is un-Islamic, laws regulating consumption would also be enforced. Relations with Egyptian Christians would be regulated, which implies the reinstitution of dhimmi— "dependent"—status as called for by sharia. Gambling, music festivals, "un-Islamic" broadcasting and cinema, nightclubs, cabarets, and membership in fraternal organizations, such as the Rotary Club, would be prohibited. All school curricular materials would have to be consistent with Islamic teachings and the state clergy would no longer be appointed by the regime, but elected.

Western analysts do not know how popular the Brothers really are. Signs of greater personal piety are apparent in Cairo. More women wear the hijab and more men have beards but these changes are difficult to interpret. The women could be wearing scarves to discourage unwanted attention on the street. Scarves and loose-fitting robes may be welcome options for girls who do not have money for fashionable clothes. Young men may wear beards because it is cool. But for many, these outward indications reflect a genuine turn to orthodoxy and receptiveness to the Brothers' trademark slogan, *"al-Islam hua al-hall,"* "Islam is the solution."

Mosque preaching supplies much of the voltage for this turn toward religion. The regime, naturally, wants to know what is being said in these mosques and who is saying it. This is a gargantuan task. There are more than eighty thousand mosques in Egypt, and under the law, all must be licensed by the authorities, who appoint preachers, supply the sermons, and monitor their delivery. The government claims it has licensed seventy thousand public and private mosques so far, and intends to bring all the country's mosques under state control. Yet the cost of eighty thousand preachers and the spies to monitor them will be huge. And new mosques spring up continuously in apartments, basements, virtually anywhere. The regime's determination to dominate Islamic discourse in Egypt may turn out to be an impossible dream.

The full scope of the Muslim Brothers' political organization is as much a mystery as the depth of their popularity. The government, of course, would not spend so much energy trying to disrupt their activities if they did not believe that the Brothers had broad appeal and were both popular and well organized. Western diplomats and intelligence officials are effectively blocked from exploring this issue by the Egyptian government, which regards such research as a mere cover for clandestine contacts with an opposition that might one day seize power. These restrictions deprive Western governments, particularly America's, of insights that might provide warning of instability. In 2001, before the September 11 attacks, leading Muslim Brothers would speak cautiously with foreigners. They would tell of plans for incremental change in Egypt fostered by the Brothers' religious outreach efforts and growing presence in the legislature. Former members intimated, however, that the debate within the organization over the use of violence was still ongoing.

If there is unrest—perhaps sparked by an upsurge in Israeli-Palestinian fighting coinciding with Mubarak's departure, by regional tensions that draw the United States into a confrontation with a Muslim country, or by a global recession that creates a local financial crisis—the shock waves will be felt for a long time. The inevitable crackdown will lead to new restrictions on civil liberties and further resistance to democratization, even as the violence deters foreign investment and tourism. A vicious circle will be set in motion, in which intensified poverty spurs more violence, which in turn undermines an already battered economy.

A domestic challenge to the regime is not the only danger. Continued pressure on Islamists means that many young recruits will be drawn to other fields of jihad where prospects for success, or at least survival, are better. Muhammad Atta is the definitive case today, but even before him Egypt exported plenty of real terrorist talent. The A list includes the Blind Sheikh; Yassir al-Sirri, indicted in the United Kingdom for complicity in the murder of the Afghan Northern Alliance commander and Taliban foe Ahmad Shah Massoud; and two of bin Laden's henchmen, Abu Hafs, "the Egyptian," and Ayman al-Zawahiri. The very effectiveness of Egyptian law enforcement in identifying and dealing with terrorists on its own soil creates an exodus of trained and hardened operatives for attacks elsewhere.

SAUDI ARABIA

For Usama bin Laden, Saudi Arabia is the essential field of jihad. It is also increasingly vulnerable. The king's rule is justified by his protection of the Holy Mosques, the propagation of Wahhabi Islam within Saudi Arabia and throughout the world, and distribution of his oil wealth for the welfare of his people. The kingdom has entered a period of transition, however, in which the al-Saud's ability to satisfactorily fulfill these tasks is declining. The presence of foreign military forces casts doubt on the family's power to protect the land of Arabia; Wahhabism at home fuels extremism and impedes modernization, while outside the kingdom it is reshaping Islam in a way that threatens political stability; and rapid population growth, falling oil prices, poor education, and economic mismanagement have raised unemployment and lowered the standard of living.

Economic trends suggest that these challenges will grow. With an exploding population, oil revenue that is unlikely to increase substantially, and an undiversified economy, the kingdom can no longer fund the entitlement and development programs that have thus far helped secure the loyalty of its subjects. Of greater immediate political import is that real gross per capita income has fallen drastically over the past twenty years, from $15,600 in 1981 to less than half that in 2001.

The religious credentials of the al-Saud, their history of conquest, their alliance with Wahhabis, and their responsibility for the Two Holy Mosques endow them with an aura of religious authority that secular regimes in other Muslim countries can never equal. That will secure their survival, at least in the near to medium term. But over the longer run, their reliance for legitimacy on clerical support and public perceptions of their own piety will conflict with other priorities. For example, the al-Saud's implicit endorsement of the radicals' agenda undermines the economic modernization program they hope will defuse political opposition rooted in economic distress. As the leadership continues to deploy its religious authority to outflank the Islamic opposition on the right, it will discover that room in that direction is not infinite and tough choices will need to be made. Such a decision point was reached only recently, when the al-Saud were asked to cut off the flow of money from wealthy Saudis to radical groups. In this telling instance, the ruling family failed the test.[8]

Islam is, of course, integral to Saudi culture in particular and Arab culture in general. It infuses language, thought, and custom. Opposition charges encased in the language of Islam are therefore readily comprehensible and, for many, inherently appealing. The basic arguments put forward provide an internally consistent, Islamic explanation for how Saudi Arabia, poised for international greatness in the 1970s as the world kowtowed to its oil riches, surrendered its sovereignty to America, become entangled in peace talks with Israel, lost much of its wealth, and found itself saddled with Christian troops on its soil preparing to attack another Muslim country. The royal family, it follows, is incompetent and corrupt, disregards the demands of authentic Islam, and is in league with infidels.

The argument is especially persuasive because some of its champions speak with seemingly deep knowledge of the U.S. government and foreign policy process as well as of the deeper forces that have allegedly shaped American society. Arabic-language media reinforce radical assertions about American hostility to Muslims, showcasing statements by fringe journalists or members of Congress that seem disrespectful of Islam or Arabs. Washington's support for Israel, which appears inexplicable in view of American dependence on Arab oil and the obvious injustice of Israel's oppression of Palestinians, becomes understandable once the "fact" of Jewish control over America's government and media is cited.

The acceptance of these views is growing now that fewer young Saudis are studying overseas. Foreign study has dropped off because it is deemed culturally inappropriate and the money to subsidize it is no longer available. Foreign travel once provided a valuable counterweight to the anti-Western indoctrination that has become part of Saudi secondary

education. In mandatory religion classes in Saudi schools—where passing grades are required for promotion—students are taught to show
hostility to infidels and encouraged to view other cultures and faiths,
including Shiite Islam, with contempt. Nor are secular subjects taught as
carefully as they once were, particularly as they relate to Western and especially American history.[9] Without detailed knowledge of these subjects
and with little or no direct experience of American culture and society,
young people lack the tools to assess the logic or content of radical
rhetoric.[10]

Saudi educational practices are creating the conditions for unemployment and political instability not only at home, but also in other countries
where there are Muslim communities to which the kingdom supplies
mosques, clerics, and teachers. The preachers and instructors are drawn
from the droves of otherwise unemployable Islamic-studies graduates of
Saudi universities. And the state pays hundreds of millions of dollars to
support them.* This gigantic missionary enterprise has planted fifteen
hundred mosques, two hundred colleges, and almost two thousand schools
around the world. These institutions are re-creating the forms of Islamic
observance in ibn Abd al-Wahhab's image on virtually every continent,
crowding out other Islamic traditions. Islam's dazzling diversity is being
eclipsed by forms of the rigid and intolerant Saudi piety. These schools
and seminaries are also creating a generation of extremists who are
driven to challenge the validity of their secular—or imperfectly Muslim—
governments, agitate for the exclusion of women and girls from public
life, demand regulation of private behavior, and reject interaction with the
West. These institutions have already had an impact on politics in Central
Asia, the Balkans, and Southeast Asia. By satisfying the clerics' insistence
that they propagate Wahhabism, the Saudi rulers buy their own political
legitimacy at the cost of stability elsewhere.

As in Egypt, the immediate threat is not to the Saudi state. The al-
Saud, who have ruled all or part of Arabia since 1744, have experience on

---

* Only the roughest estimates for Saudi expenditures on this missionary work can be made. It
is known that $220 million has been spent on mosque construction, but numbers for person-
nel and other costs are not publicly available.

their side and can find ways to cope with pressures for change. The consultative assembly that featured so prominently in the Letter of Demands was established in 1994 and has since been enlarged twice to include technocrats and some Islamists. Large-scale displays of state violence are avoided. The few demonstrations in support of the Awakening Sheikhs were not brutally crushed. Senior officers who showed excessive interest in Islamist themes have been retired. Despite the lack of Western-style democracy, informal avenues exist for political participation. Crown Prince Abdullah formed a family council to pressure princes to reduce the surreal scope of their greed and corruption. He is also trying to clean up the justice system and restrain the religious police.[11] At least one constituency, middle-class yuppies, still wants to see change take place within the framework of the existing system. Revolution, they recognize, would not be to their benefit—especially if they are female.[12]

The Saudi kingdom may weather the storms ahead, but the inherent contradictions in the regime will make it more vulnerable to Islamist challenges.[13] The crown prince is keenly aware of these tensions. On November 14, 2001, he convened the grand ulema to tell them that they needed to get a grip on the inflammatory preaching in the mosques that justified the September 11 attackers and, by implication, questioned the Saudi right to rule. But containing the radicals will not be easy. The extremist cleric Safar al-Hawali, who was released from prison in 1999, has released an incendiary "Open Letter to President Bush" that will find many a receptive ear in the kingdom. Al-Hawali says:

In the midst of . . . continuous confusion and frustration, the events of the 11th of September occurred. I will not conceal from you that a tremendous wave of joy accompanied the shock that was felt by the Muslim in the street and whoever tells you otherwise is avoiding the truth. . . .

America will eventually pay for its enormities, because Muslims never forget the wrongs they have suffered and they inculcate hatred for their most ancient enemies in their newest converts. . . . We don't forget our tragedies no matter how much time has passed. Imagine, Mr. President, we still weep over Andalusia and remember what Ferdinand and Isabella did there to our religion, culture and honor! We dream of regaining it. Nor will we forget the destruction of Baghdad, or the fall of Jerusalem at the hands of your Crusader ancestors. . . . It may be a problem for us, but who will pay the price after a while? . . .

Mr. President, if you destroy every country on your list of terrorists, will that be the end or only the beginning? Unless you want to be remembered by history for Armageddon, and in that case there will be no history anyway.[14]

JORDAN

The Jordan Rift Valley, a deep and unstable fissure in the earth's crust, provides a metaphor for the country through which it runs. The Hashemite kingdom of Jordan straddles political fault lines that lie between its largely Palestinian population and the Palestinian Authority on the West Bank, between its Palestinian and Bedouin citizens, between the United States and Iraq, and between the revered and experienced leader, the late King Hussein, and his young, untested successor, Abdullah. If any of these divisions widen, it could bring down the palace roof.

Jordan's importance to the region's stability is far greater than its small size and struggling economy would suggest. A crisis that endangered the Hashemite court would threaten the peace treaty with Israel, pose a grave risk to Saudi security, and draw Syria, Iraq, and Israel into a contest for dominance. This is not a one-in-a-million nightmare scenario, but a powerful triggering event that would have far-reaching implications. The collapse of order in a postwar Iraq, or a Palestinian-Israeli war that sent tens of thousands of West Bankers across the river into Jordan, could leave the country ungovernable, in the hands of an Iraqi puppet, or in the grip of jihadists.

The Muslim Brothers have long been active in Jordan, but they have never challenged the state. Since the late 1970s, however, another Islamist movement has matured.[15] This one coalesced around Afghan war veterans who had drunk from the Wahhabi well during the jihad against the Soviets. They returned to Jordan with a taste for violence and a belief that their rulers were apostates and deserved to be overthrown. This first generation of salafis, fundamentalists who looked to the earliest Muslims for models of behavior, were contemptuous of the Brothers' cooperation with a government whose objectives were antithetical to Islam and that would never make meaningful concessions to the Brothers' demands for a genuinely Islamic society. Their argument—hard enough to answer— made inroads into the younger stratum of the Brotherhood.

The Brothers' decision to participate in the system has allowed the government at times to manipulate and control them. The salafi opposition experimented briefly with public activities licensed by the government, but quickly discovered the risks of such engagement and backed away in favor of a more shadowy form of organization—one based on personal relationships and thus more difficult for authorities to monitor. In 1994, a group of salafis launched a series of bombings in Jordan and planned to murder leading government officials and diplomats negotiating with Israel while also attacking targets they viewed as bearers of Western cultural corruption. Two years later, the royal family was targeted by a group calling itself Obeisance to the Leader, whose leader, Abu Muhammad al-Maqdisi, has an international jihadist following. In 1998, yet another faction, the Reform and Challenge Group, went on a spree of bombing and arson attacks against a luxury hotel, the American school, and police installations. The millennium conspiracy, which Jordanian intelligence detected before it could be put into action, grew out of this turbulent underworld of salafi insurgents. The huge difference in scale between the millennium conspiracy and the smaller plots that played out between 1994 and 1998 was due to the involvement of al-Qaeda. Jordanian success in dismantling the Amman cell and disrupting the operation has not quieted local jihadists. A new campaign was launched in February 2002 with the detonation of a bomb in a car belonging to the wife of Jordan's chief antiterrorism officer, who ran the millennium plot investigation. She would have been killed if she had not altered her schedule on the morning of the attack. Two passersby were less lucky.

The Hashemite kingdom has strengths to fall back on. The king is popular not only with his core East Bank constituency, but with the two-thirds of the population that is Palestinian. His efforts to increase the stake that these non-native Jordanians have in the well-being of his regime seem to be paying off. The "managed democracy" that evolved in Jordan under King Hussein provided a simulacrum of political participation, without providing a platform for public dissent that might spin out of control. The internal security services are loyal and efficient and have good working relationships with the services of neighboring states, as well as with the United States and the United Kingdom. The United States has an especially strong interest in Jordan's stability and will support the kingdom diplomatically and, within limits, economically. The army, the ultimate guarantor of the regime, was home to Abdullah until he acceded to the throne and will stick by him.

Why worry, then? Because sudden changes—shocks on the Israeli or Iraqi front—could overwhelm the king's ability to use all these assets, and even without a drastic swing in Jordan's international situation, trouble could emerge. Press censorship, limits on political speech, and strict controls on public assembly keep things outwardly calm as they drive dissent underground. The salafi networks are growing, hard to penetrate, and show no sign of abandoning their agenda. They *have* shown that they are prepared to carry out catastrophic attacks. This means that the country's intelligence services must be very capable. Jordan's GID (General Intelligence Department) is very capable. But if it is not capable enough, we may find out too late.

PALESTINE

Al-Qaeda has been working hard to gain a foothold in the Israeli field of jihad. Bin Laden had not focused on Palestine until the late 1990s, when he began to exploit links with members of Usbat al-Ansar, a Sunni extremist group in Lebanon. Jihadists affiliated with the group fought in key areas throughout the decade—Afghanistan, Bosnia, Kashmir, Chechnya. Their base of operations in Lebanon is split between two refugee camps, in the south at Sidon's Ein al-Hilweh camp and in the north at the Nahr al-Bared camp, outside Tripoli. They have engaged in pitched battles with Lebanese government forces, planned attacks that got twenty-five members convicted by a Lebanese court on terrorism charges, and provided logistical support for the Jordanian millennium conspirators. Even by Lebanese standards, Usbat al-Ansar is a menace.

Jihadists are ever more eager to carry out attacks in Israel because the Israeli-Palestinian conflict has acquired a religious dimension in recent years that it lacked in the period after Israeli independence in 1948. Israel's main adversaries, Egypt and Syria, were ruled by secular regimes. The dream was of a pan-Arab region rather than a pan-Islamic one, and Israel intruded on that dream. Although there was an explicitly religious violent resistance to Zionism as early as the 1930s, the anti-Israeli impulse among the ruling regimes of Arab states was rooted in anti-colonialism, political need, and self-justification. The June 1967 war, though, unleashed a new religious fervor among Arabs *and* Israelis. Within Israel, an explicitly theological justification for settlements in the West Bank and Gaza was aired while the power of religious parties in Israeli politics was growing. On the Arab side, the scale of the defeat stripped credibility from the secular socialism of Egypt's regime and boosted the prestige of Islam as the "solution." The growing religious content of the conflict is evident in the way it has coalesced around religious symbols, especially the holy places of Jerusalem and shrines like the Tomb of the Patriarchs. Parties on both sides have entwined nationalist passion with religious claims in a way that precludes compromise and provides impetus for mass violence. In May 2002, for example, four settler extremists from a religious West Bank settlement were arrested for plotting to blow up a Palestinian girls' school in East Jerusalem just as the fifteen hundred pupils were arriving for class.[16]

On the Palestinian side, the Hamas charter portrays the conflict in solidly religious terms.[17] "Allah is [Hamas's] goal, the Prophet its model, the Quran its Constitution, Jihad its path and death for the cause of Allah its most sublime belief." At issue is the "struggle against the Jews, who . . . have incurred anger from their Lord, and wretchedness is laid upon them. That is because they used to disbelieve the revelations of Allah, and slew the Prophets wrongfully. That is because they were rebellious and used to transgress. Israel will rise and will remain erect until Islam eliminates it as it had eliminated its predecessors." The document speaks in terms that are both genocidal and apocalyptic. The end of days will be marked by the slaughter of the Jews at the hands of Muslims: "The Prophet, prayer and peace be upon him, said: The time will not come until Muslims will fight the Jews [and kill them]; until the Jews hide behind rocks and trees, which will cry, O Muslim! There is a Jew hiding behind me, come on and kill him!"[18]

In contrast to the absolutism of its doctrine, Hamas has shown a striking flexibility in molding its day-to-day policies to the dictates of survival. The group has had to navigate between Israeli security forces on one side and a more powerful rival, the Palestinian Authority, on the other. Hamas has taken the route Lebanese Hezbollah traveled to garner public support and win converts. The group has developed a mammoth social services and health care delivery system that reaches into the poorest neighborhoods to help Palestinians in ways the Palestinian Authority is too corrupt and inefficient to do.

The energy Hamas devotes to schools, clinics, and welfare activities, the limitations of its violence, and its readiness to participate in what passes for the democratic process in Arafat's Palestinian Authority might suggest that the movement is more moderate than its charter would indicate. Indeed, it is often claimed that Hamas is, in the final analysis, a pragmatic organization. The claim is belied by evidence that the group is beginning to coordinate operations with al-Qaeda. A Hamas activist, Nabil Akil, was recruited by al-Qaeda while studying in Karachi. According to an Israeli indictment, he received training in Kashmir and Afghanistan and agreed to establish al-Qaeda cells within the Palestinian Authority's jurisdiction as well as among Israeli Arabs. (The Israeli Arab contacts were not interested.) He was also given the mission of bombing crowded sites in Israel, including markets and residential neighborhoods, and attacking military installations. Akil never carried out these acts. He was arrested in July 2000 by Israeli forces in the Gaza Strip. (Another bin Laden operative, Richard Reid—the "shoe bomber" who was arrested shortly after September 11 for trying to detonate concealed explosives while on a plane—cased the fifty-story Azrieli Tower, the tallest building in Israel, during a reconnaissance trip.)[19]

Akil is not the only example of operational contact between the groups, and if Hamas and al-Qaeda forge an alliance, the turn will be a fateful one. For Israel, this will mean unending confrontation regardless of any negotiated agreements with the Palestinian Authority on sovereignty, boundaries, and normalization. For the Palestinian Authority, it presages a Hamas attempt to seize power when the opportunity arises. Public opinion polls show that during periods of calm on the Palestinian-Israeli front, Hamas approval ratings hover between 9 percent and 13 percent, despite its social service program. When tensions are high, however, Hamas and Yasir Arafat's Fatah faction run neck and neck, with ratings in the high twenties.[20] Depending on the overall level of Israeli-Palestinian violence and economic despair, Hamas could well acquire enough popular support to challenge the leadership of Chairman Arafat and Prime Minister Mahmoud Abbas. Thus far, the group has not found a charismatic leader to match Arafat's prestige, and its military wing is outgunned by the Palestinian Authority's security services, even though these have been greatly weakened during the al-Aqsa intifada. But Hamas, through its suicide attacks, has shown its ability to destroy any effort to stop the violence between Palestinians and Israelis and return the parties to the negotiating table. If the partnership matures between Hamas and the jihadists, and if truck bombs are used to devastate residential neighborhoods (as Hamas sought to do in 2000) or demolish landmark buildings, there will be no peace for Israel or Palestine.

There may also be less security for Americans. Thus far, Hamas has not targeted Americans. If it draws closer to al-Qaeda, though, it may yet heed bin Laden's injunction to turn the guns of jihad against the United

States. Moreover, Hamas has always pledged not to commit violence against its Palestinian political competitors. Yet al-Qaeda considers the leadership of the Palestinian Authority jahili, and bin Laden has derided Arafat personally. Should Hamas abandon its pledge, the consequences in the Palestinian territories could be disastrous.

ALGERIA

Algeria in the 1990s offers a gruesome vision of a world in which jihadists confronted by a determined state refuse to concede defeat. The violence, which began in 1991 and culminated in a frenzy of slaughter in 1998, is still not over. The Islamist revolt cost at least 40,000 Algerian lives—some reports say as many as 100,000—including women and children, peasants and professionals, soldiers and clerics, government officials and foreigners. Entire villages were essentially put to the sword, massacred by jihadists who favored the knife blade over the gun.

Algeria is no stranger to violence—its late colonial period and civil war were bloodbaths. After Algeria finally became independent in 1962, its society and economy had been mauled by seven years of vicious war. The rebel leadership that fought the French evolved into an oligarchy of soldiers, politicians, and technocrats presiding over a phony democracy. Power struggles within the ruling elite led rapidly to a coup, nationalization of the energy sector, and centralization of the economy. By the late 1980s, socialism and colossal economic mismanagement had burdened Algeria with a massive foreign-debt burden and urban unemployment of 50 percent. When rioting across the country in October 1988 left hundreds dead in the streets, the ruling elite decided to liberalize the political process. Among the parties to emerge from this turbulence was the Front Islamique du Salut, or FIS—in English, the Islamic Salvation Front.

When local elections were held in June 1990, the FIS took 54 percent of the vote, the ruling party just 28 percent. While secular oppositionists were divided, the FIS demonstrated its unity and convinced voters that it genuinely opposed the corruption that plagued Algeria. Then, in December 1991, the FIS won over 80 percent of the seats in the national legislature in the first two rounds of voting. The FIS was certain to win the next round—scheduled for January 16, 1992. While the Westernized middle class, journalists, academics, and technocrats were trying to wrap their minds around this prospect, the regime acted. On January 11, it declared the elections null and void, canceled the next round, and set up an emergency government backed by the army. The FIS was declared illegal and its leaders, along with thousands of party members, were imprisoned.

The FIS turned to violence. Since it had a clear political objective—to return to elections and claim its victory—it calibrated that violence to pressure the regime without sacrificing its hard-won popular support. FIS militants targeted the security forces, policemen, and military units. The following year they added members of the regime.

For some within the movement, this was not enough. Smaller groups with names like Commanding the Good and Prohibiting the Forbidden, Group of the Sunni and Sharia, and even al-Takfir wal-Hijra ("Condemn and Emigrate," like Shuqri Mustafa's Egyptian group of the 1970s), rejected the notion that an Islamic state would ever come about through elections. They also declared that Algerian society was apostate. That meant that everyone not committed to their brand of salafiyya Islam and their vision of a truly Islamic society was also an apostate and under sentence of death. These groups merged under the name Groupes Islamiques Armés (GIA).

"The great tragedy the Muslim community is living in this era is the collapse of the Caliphate," said the first leader of the GIA, "because it is now living an abnormal and disharmonious life due to the separation between its high ideals and principles . . . and the jahili reality imposed upon it."[21]

By 1994, the GIA was busily articulating and implementing these high ideals. In a series of communiqués they demanded that mixed-sex swimming be stopped and mixed-sex tourism banned, that tax and customs inspectors resign or be declared apostate and killed, and that all women married to state employees immediately obtain divorces, since their husbands were apostates and marriages with them contravened sharia. In 1996, they threatened to kill young men who reported for the draft, people who failed to pray five times a day, people who did not pay their religiously mandated alms to the GIA, and any woman who left her house without a head covering. In areas under GIA control, militants shut down beauty parlors and prohibited satellite dishes, cigarettes, French newspapers, and music festivals. Pious Muslims who dared go to a government-funded mosque to pray were liable to be executed. One of the GIA's spiritual leaders explained why these impositions were valid:

> For the whole Muslim community . . . is called upon to join the ranks
> of the mujahidin . . . the issue is one of unity of God versus polythe-
> ism, and a clash between faith and infidelism . . . whoever lags be-
> hind, or cowers . . . has fallen into great danger.[22]

The GIA would not discriminate among its opponents: Algerians were either actively assisting the GIA, or they were apostates to be slaughtered. A farmer tilling his field, or a schoolteacher, was no more or less guilty than the head of the secret police. Thus, teachers and schools became favored targets of GIA attacks. Militants belonging to other armed groups that took a more discriminating approach to murder became targets of GIA killings as well. Between 1995 and 1998, only one-quarter of GIA attacks were aimed at security forces. The majority of victims were civilians.

GIA violence reached a hellish level in late 1996, when it initiated a wave of massacres in Algiers and the countryside south of the city. Jihadists would carry out these assaults at night, slipping into sleeping villages or neighborhoods and using knives and axes to do their work. Whole communities perished in this yearlong onslaught.

As the GIA's violence became more extreme, the FIS abandoned its violent opposition to the regime. The bloodshed of 1996 and 1997 gave killing of any kind, no matter how carefully calibrated, a bad name. The regime exploited the opportunity and opened negotiations with the

FIS. Amnesty was offered to militants who were not implicated in murder or rape. As the broader political situation stabilized and the country's economy began to recover, the insurgency began to disintegrate, leaving a hard core of GIA killers and a bin Laden–financed splinter group still on the offensive.

By the time the GIA appeared on the scene, Algeria had been in the grip of violence for as long as anyone could remember. France had ruled through violence, and violence had stained much of Algeria's post-colonial history. This legacy undoubtedly contributed to Algeria's free fall into slaughter in the 1990s. However, the one indispensable factor— the catalyst that transformed a battle against the state for limited political goals into a jihad gone mad—was the intrusion of radical Islam and "ibn Taymiyya rules." Algeria and its dead offer an object lesson about what awaits a country where takfiris choose to stand and fight.

PAKISTAN

As a state, Pakistan has been failing since birth. Perpetually unable to provide prospects for a better life to its people and beset by a culture of corruption that undermined its institutions, the country limped along, being viewed by outsiders much as people once saw the old Austro-Hungarian Empire, where the situation was always "critical, but not serious." By the end of 2001, it was clear to the entire world how serious the situation was, as the government in Islamabad sought to maintain control while turning its policy 180 degrees to side with America and against the Taliban. Six months later, the stakes had gotten even higher, as radical Islamists pressed for a showdown over Kashmir, one of the key fields of jihad. As nowhere else on earth, the fight over this region is an invitation to the apocalypse. The trigger is meant to be an Indo-Pakistani war over Kashmir, a confrontation between two nuclear powers. Kashmir had the misfortune to be ruled in 1947 by Hari Singh, a feckless maharaja who could not decide whether his mostly Muslim state should become part of Pakistan or India at the time of partition. While he procrastinated, Pakistan invaded with "freedom fighters." India responded by airlifting troops into

Kashmir. When the shooting stopped, Indian forces had pushed the Pakistanis back to what became known as the Line of Control. The outcome left a little more than a third of the old princely state of Jammu and Kashmir in Pakistan's possession. The rest, with the exception of an eastern bulge occupied by China, has been administered by India ever since. A UN-mandated plebiscite that was supposed to enable Kashmiris to decide their own fate was never held. For Pakistan, struggling to establish its identity and demonstrate its integrity as a state, the loss of Muslim Kashmir was psychologically crippling. The defeat became an obsession, which locked the impoverished and fragile state into a never-ending military confrontation with a much larger neighbor confident of its destiny.

In particular, the wound was felt by Pakistan's single resilient institution: the army. Despite its repeated interventions in politics and failed efforts at ruling Pakistan, no party or class has ever managed to identify itself as the guardian of the nation as the army has. Its status and legitimacy became tied to the perpetuation of the effort to take the disputed territory. The army kept the Kashmiri pot boiling by supporting an indigenous insurgency. Initially, this required little; the Indian administration was clumsy and cruel and invited violent opposition. Islamabad committed enough resources to pin down and bleed large Indian army formations that would otherwise have been used to threaten Pakistan elsewhere along the shared border. Pakistani decision makers may also have believed that the steady drip of Indian blood in Kashmir would move New Delhi to negotiate. Over time, though, native Kashmiri opposition waned and Indian rule became less heavy-handed. The guerrilla effort lost steam. The intensity of combat in Afghanistan began to diminish more or less at the same time: the jihad against the Soviets had long since ended, and the Taliban were conducting mopping-up operations in the wake of their conquest of most of the country. Thousands of trained mujahidin were filtering back into a crumbling Pakistan, bringing a taste for holy war and nothing else to occupy them.

The Pakistani army—more precisely, ISI, military intelligence—worked with the religious parties to funnel the Afghan fighters, along with the graduates of the parties' madrassas, into Kashmir to stir things up. Before September 11, 2001, much of the training for new recruits took place in the North-West Frontier province and Afghanistan, far from the media and prying Indian eyes. By the end of 1998, a conflict between India and Pakistan that had been about sovereignty over disputed territory had been transformed into a jihad fought against Hindus by Muslims. The jihadists were determined to spark an Indo-Pakistani war, and their presence changed the face of battle in Kashmir. With no village or kinship ties, with a suicidal audacity and heavy weapons supplied by the Pakistani army, they raised the intensity of violence to unprecedented levels. Presumed collaborators were killed with the same gusto as Indian soldiers. Collateral damage was not an issue.[23]

For the Pakistani military, this was a satisfactory arrangement. With recruitment now taking place nationwide,[24] an array of nationalities represented among the insurgents, and ample funding from wealthy Pakistanis and Saudis flowing through charitable organizations, the army could fight to the last mujahid, pay nothing, and enjoy plausible deniability when India complained. President Pervez Musharraf himself called this campaign a jihad.[25]

Pakistan's rulers believed they controlled events; the country's religious parties and militant organizations took a different view. The government was not using them: *they* were using the government to facilitate a jihad. Although these parties have never done well at the polls—the biggest usually gets no more than 2 or 3 percent of the vote—their power is in the street. From November 3 through November 5, 1999, the radical group Lashkar e-Tayba (Army of the Pure) gathered 200,000 supporters near Lahore to celebrate the Kashmiri jihad, cheer breaking news of the martyrdom of two jihadists in Kashmir—arranged to coincide with the jamboree—and round up new recruits.[26] This festival was followed in mid-April 2000 by a three-day gathering at a village outside Peshawar to mark the 150th anniversary of the founding of the Deobandi movement in India, the wellspring of Wahhabism in South Asia. Attendance was estimated variously at 200,000 to 1.5 million. The conference organizer, Fazlur Rahman, leader of the Jamiat Ulema-i-Islami party, broadcast a recorded greeting from Mullah Omar in defiance of a government order and circulated a letter from bin Laden, who was lionized by a succession of speakers. These demonstrations sandwiched the January 2000 declaration of a United Jihad Front by the heads of the major religious parties, an event made noteworthy by the inclusion of the great "moderate" Qazi Hussein Ahmed, the current leader of the Jamaat i-Islami. He, like the others, sponsors jihadists in Kashmir, but had been trying nudge the rest of the Islamist camp into the mainstream.[27]

Islamist parties of various hues have been a feature of Pakistan's political landscape since the establishment of the state. The liberals who formed the core of the elite in the post-independence period envisioned a democracy with a Muslim identity. The emphasis on Islam owed as much to the rationale for partition from India as to the need for an ideology that might override the conflicting ethnic and confessional interests threatening to tear the country apart after its creation. Islam became the unifying ideology for a country brimming with centrifugal energy.

The prominence of Islam in public life—and the power of parties operating under its banner—was vastly increased by Zia ul-Haq, one of the five generals who have governed Pakistan in its fifty-five-year history. During Zia's years in power (1979–88), his religious convictions and his use of Islamic parties to counter civilian opponents combined to create a privileged space in which Islamism could flourish. The jihad in Afghanistan enhanced these religious movements' prestige and filled their coffers.

The Afghan jihad also engendered close links with armed groups whose recruits were supplied by the madrassas. Zia's civilian successors, Benazir Bhutto and Nawaz Sharif, inadvertently, but disastrously, contributed to the proliferation of these religious schools by squandering resources vital to maintaining a public education system. There are at least eight thousand madrassas now in operation. They appeal to impoverished parents because many are boarding schools that provide food and clothing at no cost to families. A significant minority provide only scanty instruction in secular subjects, focusing almost entirely on scriptural texts and handbooks explaining the superiority of their own form of Islamic belief. The religious parties that subsidize the schools use them to provide activists to propagate the faith and punish opponents.[28] Lashkar e-Tayba, which funnels combatants into Kashmir, runs Wahhabi madrassas whose curriculum glorifies jihad and martyrdom. Its objective is to establish a Taliban-style Islamic state in Kashmir. The Sipah e-Sapaha party and its armed wing, Lashkar e-Janghvi, specialize in the murder of Shiites. (After September 11, the group expanded its target list and murdered *Wall Street Journal* reporter Daniel Pearl, an American Jew.)

———

In his attempt to turn his country around after September 11, Musharraf took a stab at getting the religious parties, their madrassas, and their militias under control. He had little choice. With Pakistan's finances in perilous condition, he was vulnerable to U.S. economic retaliation, and the new Indo-American relationship raised the specter of complete strategic isolation. Musharraf had been down this lonely road already. The year before, he had launched an effort to regulate madrassa curricula, which fizzled, and less than a month before the World Trade Center attacks he had banned the worst of the extremist groups. A bolder move to cut off infiltration into Kashmir and get a grip on the extreme religious parties would be too politically dangerous, since he had abandoned the Taliban at the behest of America and allowed U.S. military forces to operate out of Pakistani bases. The moment called for caution. The religious parties, perhaps in coordination with some Pakistani military sympathizers, drew the opposite conclusion. They stepped up operations intended to force Musharraf into a confrontation with India or be discredited at home.

On December 13, mujahidin of Jaish e-Mohammed—the Army of Muhammad—attacked the Indian parliament in New Delhi, killing six before being gunned down. A greater provocation would be hard to imagine. India's prime minister Atal Bihari Vajpayee responded with a threat to invade Pakistan and put the terrorist training camps out of business. Tensions escalated as Pakistani officials spoke about first use of nuclear weapons. Under intense pressure from the United States, the United Kingdom, and Russia, Musharraf took serious steps to block jihadists from stealing into Kashmir and to close down their not-so-secret camps. Within a day, Vajpayee, who had just been briefed by an American envoy on Pakistan's readiness to use nuclear weapons against India, seized the opportunity to withdraw his threat of war. The crisis was over, for the time being. The militants had come within a whisker of getting the Armageddon they wanted.

Musharraf must now stay alive and continue the work of dismantling the infrastructure of religious terrorism. By leaving the Taliban to face American weapons unaided, cutting off the Kashmiri jihadists, and appearing to bow to Indian demands, Musharraf has established himself as the enemy of the religious parties, their millions of followers, and thousands of armed, frustrated men. An attempt to destroy the American consulate in Karachi with a large car bomb on June 14, 2002, underscored this point. Thus far, the army has proved loyal. But no one knows whether the surge of Islamism in Pakistani society will cause change within the army. All outside analysts can do is count beards in military class photographs, or question officers they meet, usually in Westernized settings. When asked about the issue, General Jehangir Karamat, former chief of the Pakistani army staff, averred that Islamist penetration of the army's ranks would be highly unlikely since the army puts a premium on technical skills that an Islamist would not have. Given the demonstrated capabilities of al-Qaeda and other Islamic terrorists, General Karamat's assumptions should be examined carefully.

The security of Pakistan's nuclear weapons components and nuclear design skills is also open to question. Between October and December 2001, Pakistani investigators interrogated Sultan Bashiruddin Mahmoud, a former nuclear scientist at the Pakistan Atomic Energy Agency (PAEA) suspected of having met with Usama bin Laden in Kandahar. Mahmoud is an eccentric thinker, attracted to theories about sunspots controlling history and moral decadence causing natural catastrophes. He considers himself a disciple of a Lahore-based Islamist radical who believed the coalition attacks on the Taliban had begun "the last war between Islam and the infidels." Mahmoud retired from a thirty-year career at PAEA after being disciplined for insisting that Pakistan should be sharing weapons-grade plutonium and enriched uranium with other Muslim countries. As representative of an NGO he set up called Islamic Reconstruction, he visited Afghanistan regularly between 1998 and 2001.

In his initial interviews, Mahmoud denied contact with bin Laden. The CIA thought he was lying and presented the Pakistanis with their own evidence that Mahmoud and a PAEA colleague named Abdul Majid had met with bin Laden. Under further questioning by Pakistani investigators, the two admitted having met with bin Laden, al-Zawahiri, and two others in Kabul for two to three days in August 2001, and having discussed weapons of mass destruction. Bin Laden, they said, was interested in nuclear, biological, and chemical weapons and sought advice on how to build a dirty bomb, an explosive device that would disperse radioactive material al-Qaeda had either received, or expected to get from the Islamic Movement of Uzbekistan. The scientists described their response as academic rather than technical. Mahmoud also met with Mullah Omar several times, including one occasion after September 11.

A search of Mahmoud's "relief agency" revealed other peculiarities. Among the documents found in its Kabul office were a history of anthrax and details of a Pentagon immunization program, as well as gas masks and diagrams for an aerial balloon system for the dispersal of biological or chemical weapons. Other associates of the "relief agency" were also questioned by Pakistani authorities, including two air force generals, an army general, a third nuclear scientist, the CEO of a Lahore-based engineering firm, and a financial officer. The Pakistanis dismissed the significance of the finds and downplayed the competence of those they had questioned.[29] (The Pakistanis, who released Mahmoud and Abdul Majid without charge in December 2001, described them as "very motivated" and "extremist in their ideas.") Mahmoud's efforts may indeed have been ineffectual. The larger issue, though, is whether the incident was unique, or reveals a seam of Islamic radicalism running through Pakistan's nuclear weapons establishment. It is difficult to know. Like General Karamat's assumptions about the reliability of Pakistan's junior army officers, assumptions about the incompatibility of technological sophistication and religious extremism should be regarded with deep skepticism. The apocalyptic mentality of the terrorists and their fantasies of omnipotence are driving them toward the use of weapons of mass destruction. Pakistan is probably their best potential source of the materials, or of the weapons themselves.

CENTRAL ASIA

Uzbekistan is another country that has been transformed by the extremism of salafiyya religious ideology imported from Saudi Arabia and, before September 11, by bin Laden's money and arms.

The tribes of Central Asia, including those of Xinjiang province in what is now China, were conquered in the mid-seventh century C.E. by Arab warriors storming out of Arabia in the first wave of the Islamic conquest. For centuries, this Sunni outpost of the Arab caliphate, situated astride the Silk Route, thrived economically and culturally. By the fifteenth century, the Muslim khanates, as they were called, were, with a few notable exceptions, in decline. The trade route between Europe and China had shifted northward through Russia, and southward via a sea route navigated by Europeans. To the south, Persia adopted Shiism, ending the cultural interchange that had imparted vitality to khanate society. Orthodox Sunni faith was still strong, however, and the madrassas retained their vigor. The Khanates' military weakness, however, invited Russian incursions. The czars gradually conquered most of these territories, settling Russians there, and destroying mosques and madrassas. The Soviets inherited these lands in 1917 and carved them into separate republics to divide tribes that might cause trouble if they united. The Muslim population resisted Soviet rule as best they could, staging an on-and-off insurgency that drew blood but offered no hope of freedom.

Change came with the 1979 Soviet invasion of Afghanistan. Large numbers of young Muslim men from the Central Asian republics were drafted to fight the mujahidin and found an opportunity for jihad against the enemy—the empire that had trained them. Many soldiers deserted to join the mujahidin and turned their guns on their former comrades. On a larger scale, the Soviet defeat in Afghanistan hastened the end of the Soviet Union and a radical Islamic renaissance.

Religion emerged as a key element in the tumult that followed the collapse of the Soviet Union and the independence of the Central Asian republics. A civil war broke out almost immediately in Tajikistan between the successor government and an opposition that was largely Islamic in inspiration and that drew in combatants from Uzbekistan. Throughout the region, especially in the Fergana Valley, which cuts across the borders of Tajikistan, Uzbekistan, and Kyrgyzstan, popular religious feeling blossomed after years of Soviet oppression. Construction of mosques and madrassas surged. There was also a wave of Islamic influence from the outside. Saudi Arabia financed the spread of Wahhabi Islam, while the Deobandi variant embraced by the Taliban moved north from Pakistan and Afghanistan. The victory of the mujahidin over the Soviets, the experience of many Muslim soldiers who had served in Afghanistan, and, later, the lightning conquests of the Taliban helped spread Deobandism. It was natural that resistance to the autocrats who had taken power when the Russians left should coalesce around religion, especially since the suppression of secular political opposition was virtually total. The ruling regimes had gutted alternative paths of political expression.

The Wahhabi and Deobandi forms of Islam that galvanized the rebels were unlike the kind of Islam that had developed historically in the region. Sufism, a mystical, inward-looking, and essentially tolerant form of Islam, had first emerged in Central Asia and had long been the predominant style of Islamic expression there. Wahhabism had established a toehold early in the twentieth century, but remained distinctly unpopular. Young men, however, were susceptible to the new influences, in part because Soviet rule had cut them off from their Islamic roots, leaving them nothing with which to compare Wahhabism. With Saudi money flowing into mosques and madrassas and extremist preachers taking over the pulpits, it looked to the uninitiated as though Wahhabi Islam were "real"

Islam. Moreover, the militant tone of Wahhabism matched people's anger against their undemocratic governments and over the collapse of the economy. Unemployment and underemployment were rife, and living standards were sinking fast.

In Uzbekistan, the discontents brewing in the late 1980s and early 1990s finally bred a rebellion in 1998 under the charismatic leadership of Juma Namangani, head of the Islamic Movement of Uzbekistan (IMU). Namangani was a Soviet army veteran who had fought in Tajikistan earlier in the decade after fleeing Uzbekistan, where he had succeeded for a time in establishing a miniature Islamic republic in his hometown. He had earned a reputation during the Tajik civil war as an inspiring commander and had only reluctantly dispersed his forces; he had wanted to keep fighting for a full-fledged Islamic state. When he took up arms again, he made it clear that the goal of the two thousand fighters of the IMU was to overthrow the Uzbek government and re-create the fifteenth-century khanate that had encompassed parts of present-day Uzbekistan, Tajikistan, and Kyrgyzstan. He communicated his declaration of war by the detonation of six car bombs in Tashkent, the capital of Uzbekistan, on February 16, 1999. The government's instinctive reaction was to arrest thousands; the authorities were apparently unable or unwilling to distinguish between ordinary Sunni Muslims and the Wahhabis and Deobandis who were in league with the militants. Support for the rebels grew accordingly.

Namangani maneuvered back and forth across Uzbekistan, using Tajikistan and Kyrgyzstan as staging areas, bringing both countries into conflict with Uzbekistan. The size of his force increased steadily, owing to the oafish and brutal tactics of his enemy, the Karimov regime that rules Uzbekistan. Flush with cash from control of a key drug-trade route and riding high militarily, Namangani struck a deal for arms and bases with Usama bin Laden and his Taliban backers in the winter of 1999.[30] Bin Laden supplied tactical helicopters and, eventually, $20 million in cash. Mullah Omar gave Namangani permission to establish bases in Afghanistan and carry out operations from there into Uzbekistan. In return, the IMU would fight with the Taliban against the Northern Alliance. For the next nine months, Namangani's forces, including Muslims from Central Asia, the Caucasus, and China, carried out operations in Uzbekistan and Kyrgyzstan. Namangani's jihad ended in the rubble of Mazar-e-Sharif, blasted by American aircraft and Northern Alliance artillery. He was mortally wounded and several hundred of his fighters were also killed in the siege.[31] The Karimov regime has been strengthened by its military cooperation agreement with the United States, which will continue to want access to Uzbek bases at least until the Afghan campaign is completed and perhaps after that, too.

The Wahhabi- and Deobandi-inspired campaign for an Islamic caliphate in Central Asia did not die with Namangani. The money that supplied the religious indoctrination is still coming in. Just as important, the underlying socioeconomic causes remain: terrible poverty, disastrous economic mismanagement, and, despite recent prisoner releases, notorious and indiscriminate persecution of regime opponents. Other extremist Islamic groups are now moving in for what they hope will be the kill. Hizbat Tahrir, a fanatically anti-Semitic Wahhabi offshoot that seeks to resurrect the caliphate, has established a network of secret cells in Central Asia that will be extremely difficult to find and destroy. Hezbollah—not the Shiite group in Lebanon, but a Sunni organization—has also entrenched itself. Hezbollah is, if anything, more dangerous than Hizbat Tahrir.

Central Asia will continue to be a field of jihad even if bin Laden is gone from the scene. The jihadists smell victory, and with the sustained support of their wealthy funders in the Gulf, they will not stop until enthroned or destroyed.

SOUTHEAST ASIA

The southern Philippines, Indonesia, Malaysia, and Singapore have their own traditions of Islamic militancy nourished by colonial occupation. But the predominant popular approach to religion has historically been relaxed and tolerant. Islam reached these countries through the missionary efforts of Muslim traders before the thirteenth century. These forays paved the way for the establishment of religious schools and mosques, which were tended by holy men from the Middle East. Local rulers, once Islamized, occasionally expanded their realms by force of arms in the name of Islam, but, by and large, the region acquired its Islamic identity peacefully. The Sufi character of Islam in the region fit well with the broader Hindu-Buddhist culture in which the new Muslims were living. The distinctively laissez-faire faith that evolved blended indigenous traditions and practices with the teachings of Islam; it was called "merchant Islam," since it arrived with traders and reflected their need for customers—not enemies—of all faiths.

With the beginning of the Pax Wahhabica, which unified Arabia in the early twentieth century, more and more Southeast Asian Muslims made the hajj, and returned to their native countries enthusiastic about the piety they had seen. At the same time, more young Muslims were studying at al-Azhar University in Cairo, where they absorbed the salafi ideas. As these "reformed" Muslims grew in numbers, Islamic observance in the region began to turn away from the inclusive style of merchant Islam toward sterner views. An influx of Saudi funding for Wahhabi schools and mosques over the past few decades has reinforced this trend.

The new mood of pan-Islamic militancy inspired many young Southeast Asian Muslim men to head for Afghanistan during the war against the Soviets. They returned home radicalized and committed to the fight for an Islamic state—and not just in their own countries. They wanted to unite Indonesia, the Philippines, Malaysia, and Singapore into a single caliphate, ruled by sharia.

The avatar of this movement is thirty-seven-year-old Riduan Isamuddin, an Afghan jihad veteran who goes by the name Hambali. Now in hiding, he leads a group called Jemaah Islamiah, part of the al-Qaeda network that has been connected to both Ramzi Yousef's Bojinka plot and the September 11 attacks. Using graduates of bin Laden's Afghan camps and students he has indoctrinated in his own religious school, he has planted cells all over Southeast Asia's Islamic state-to-be. His work bears the hallmarks of al-Qaeda operations: simultaneous attacks, split-second timing, and pursuit of mass casualties. In December 2000, he launched a series of bombings in Jakarta and Kuala Lumpur that killed thirty-five people; a number of the targets were churches. Provoking hostilities between Muslims and Christians is high on Hambali's agenda.

Hambali's Singapore cells coordinated directly with al-Qaeda leaders in Afghanistan. CIA operatives found plans for one attack, along with a surveillance video in the ruins of Muhammad Atef's house. That attack had not been approved by al-Qaeda headquarters because it was too small. The cell that planned it turned its sights to attacking U.S. naval vessels in Singapore's port in the same fashion that the U.S.S. *Cole* was struck in the port of Aden. Another cell planned to carry out simultaneous attacks against the U.S., British, Israeli, and Australian embassies and possibly the Singaporean Ministry of Defense. The plotters obtained four tons of ammonium nitrate—twice what Timothy McVeigh used in Oklahoma City—and were seeking an additional seventeen tons to arm a fleet of truck bombs that would devastate all the targets on the list. When the cell was broken up in the course of the Singaporean and Malaysian investigations into the January 2000 meeting Hambali had with Khalid al-Mihdhar and Nawaf al-Hazmi, two of the September 11 hijackers who crashed into the Pentagon, they were a week away from conducting at least some of their planned attacks. It was a close call.

Local authorities think they have disabled Jemaah Islamiah, but an enormous quantity of explosives is still unaccounted for, and several plotters may have sought refuge in Indonesia. The Indonesians are reluctant to pick a fight with their homegrown Islamists, Hambali's followers, and have not cooperated fully with either the United States or Singapore. Both countries have cautioned Jakarta not to sacrifice Indonesia's long-term interests in favor of short-term tranquillity. The jihadists, they say, will be easier to tackle now than in five years.

In the meantime, Singaporean authorities arrested at least thirteen of the conspirators. All but one had been born and raised in Singapore—about 15 percent of whose population is Muslim—and attended state schools. Most lived in government-subsidized housing; six were military reservists, and eight had been to Afghan training camps. That citizens of a wealthy, tiny, and tightly controlled state could plan and come so close to executing major attacks shocked even those who thought after September 11 that there were few more shocks to be had.

EUROPE

Western Europe has been al-Qaeda's logistics base and recruiting center; by 2001, it was also a target of operations. The 1998 fatwa "Jihad Against Jews and Crusaders" was announced in London. The millennium and September 11 conspiracies were staged in part from the United Kingdom and Germany. Al-Qaeda conspired to attack the Strasbourg cathedral and the American embassies in Rome and Paris, carry out a massacre in Bosnia, kill the American President in Genoa, and attack British navy vessels in Gibraltar. Al-Qaeda has had a presence in at least a dozen European cities and has recruited many of its operatives on the Continent. Inattentive law-enforcement agencies and a reluctance to intrude on houses of worship have made Europe a congenial place for al-Qaeda operations.

Asylum policies can be changed, houses of worship can be surveilled, and police and intelligence agencies can be reoriented. Reshaping the attitudes of that small but significant segment of Europe's Muslim population that regards the United States—and their own governments—as mortal enemies of Islam is a much greater challenge. Within this subculture, al-Qaeda has found not only recruits but also safe haven, and the best possible camouflage for the network's activities.

Western Europe's Muslim population traces its beginnings to the rush to rebuild the devastated continent after World War II. Countries with surviving colonial possessions in South Asia, the Middle East, and North Africa opened their doors to the manual laborers needed to do the hard work in construction and manufacturing. In Britain, Pakistani Muslims went to the old industrial cities in the north and worked in the textile mills. In France, where a substantial Muslim population had lived for a hundred years, the second wave from Algeria, Morocco, and Tunisia was settled in the heart of the country, where they were used as agricultural workers as well as industrial labor. Having no imperial possessions to draw on, Germany turned to Turkey, where unemployment was high and hard currency in short supply. The Turkish "guest workers" settled in big cities: Hamburg, Berlin, Frankfurt. Italy, which had suffered severe damage along with the rest of Europe, also relied in part on North African labor to provide the muscle power for putting the country back together.

For years, host countries imagined that once these foreign workers earned enough money, they would return home. This did not happen. Political instability and poverty in their homelands gave the laborers a powerful reason to stay where they were and settle in. Living conditions were certainly better than those at home, but were far from ideal. Foreign competition and an obsolete infrastructure led to the closing of British mills, leaving many newly arrived Muslim workers trapped by unemployment and poverty in grimy, decaying cities. In France, immigrants were housed in vast high-rise complexes in isolated, distant suburbs, the *banlieues*. Turks and Kurds in Germany settled in self-contained, tightly knit communities in low-rent neighborhoods.

With few exceptions, European society made little effort to integrate these newcomers. Muslims—as well as black Africans, Asians, and Caribbean immigrants—typically got less in the way of social services, schooling, housing, and jobs than native Europeans. A dynamic evolved in which immigrant communities fell behind socioeconomically, became less able to compete with "whites," and then fell even further behind. The process of alienation, however, affected newcomers and natives both. Some immigrant communities, anxious to preserve their cultural legacies— especially the integrity of their religious practices—shunned the surrounding society. It is still common in Britain for second- and third-generation South Asian men to send "home" for wives.

A toxic mix of "white" prejudice and self-imposed separation has deprived Europe's Muslim communities of a political voice in their countries. There are about 5 million Muslims in France—a bit under 10 percent of the population—but there is not one Muslim representing a region of France in the 577-member Parliament. In Germany, there are 3.2 million Muslims, but just one Turk in the 669-seat legislature. The situation is much the same in Britain, where 2 million Muslims have about half a dozen of the 659 seats in Parliament. No Muslim sits in the Italian parliament at all.

Taken as a whole, roughly half the 12.5 million–strong Muslim population in Europe is under thirty years old. Many of the young men are unemployed or underemployed and are excluded or believe they are excluded from the best French, German, or British society has to offer. They are more likely to have run-ins with the law than their nonminority counterparts. A *Sunday Times* (London) survey revealed that 40 percent of British Muslims believe Usama bin Laden was right to attack the United States. About the same proportion thought that British Muslims had a right to fight alongside the Taliban. A radio station serving London's Pakistani community conducted a poll in which 98 percent of London Muslims under forty-five said they would not fight for Britain, while 48 percent said they would fight for bin Laden.[33] It is hardly surprising that many European Muslims have turned to their religion for a sense of identity and worth.

Some go further. Radical preachers turn alienation and newly acquired religious commitment into hate. In a small number of mosques, worshipers' sincerity and capability are assessed by militant clerics who then facilitate introductions to members of radical groups. In Britain, Sheikh Omar Bakri, a Syrian radical, preaches the downfall of the British government and the murder of the Jews. Abu Qatada, a Jordanian fugitive connected to the millennium plot and now reported to be in the custody of MI5 at an undisclosed location somewhere in Britain, sermonized about jihad and vetted recruits. Abu Hamza al-Masri, a terrorist ringleader who dispatched eight of his recruits to attack British targets in Yemen, has his own mosque, where he whips up his congregants' anger.

Indoctrination and recruitment often take place in prisons, where the Muslim populations are disproportionately large—in the United Kingdom, the number of Muslim prisoners doubled between 1993 and 2000. Potential recruits may be Muslim, but they are unlikely to know very much about their religion, so they are easily persuaded that Islam and the West are at war and that participation in the jihad is every Muslim's responsibility. Richard Reid, the accused shoe bomber, converted to Islam and was transformed into a terrorist at a British jail for youth offenders. In some prisons, Muslim chaplains have done the recruiting, weaving bin Laden's rhetoric into their preaching.

Recruiting also takes place outside of mosques that cater to new converts, where militants hand out leaflets and identify likely targets. Taking advantage of a convert's desire to be the best Muslim possible, they explain that genuine piety requires militancy. The recruits who demonstrate the right mix of passion and piety are soon on their way to a military training camp—perhaps in the United States, where firearms training is legal. In the camp, indoctrination is continued and a sense of confrontation between Islam and Christianity and Judaism is fostered. Wealthy businessmen pay for this through companies like Sakina Security Services, which offers the "ultimate Jihad challenge."[33] Recruitment efforts in the United Kingdom have been enhanced by a videotape made by the Salafist Group for Preaching and War (GSPC), a bin Laden–affiliated insurgent group in Algeria. The tape depicts the massacre of Algerian soldiers by exultant salafis, who are seen cutting throats and beheading their victims. The camera lingers over the neck wounds so that the pumping arterial blood can be seen clearly. To young men looking for a mission in life and seething with resentment against their parents and an unsympathetic society, the images are both mesmerizing and empowering.

Recruitment is not restricted to the young of Europe's immigrant communities. Al-Qaeda also needs ethnic European operatives who can live in enemy territory without arousing suspicion. The small but significant number of converts to Islam makes this strategy possible. In London, Omar Bakri's extremist al-Muhajiroun targets disaffected young Christians for whom the Church of England is a spent force. They are offered an alternative to a consumer society in which satisfaction is beyond their reach, a clear-cut moral code, and a mission. "You look at your average church priest," says one al-Muhajiroun convert, "and what does he do? Who would he go to war with? No one. So how can Christianity claim to be a religion when its followers don't believe in spreading the word? The fact that Western politicians like Blair and Bush are scared of Islam means it's a great religion."[34]

An Islamic army has slowly formed in Europe, the product of exclusion, subversive preaching, and a steady influx of radicals from the Middle East, North Africa, and South Asia. Toughened immigration laws cannot disperse this army, especially as the jihadists fill out its ranks with ethnic Europeans and hone their own infiltration skills. The alienation of minorities in Europe will strengthen the morale of the army and its hunger for victory. It has been mobilized by al-Qaeda for the assault against the Crusaders on their own territory. From the shores of Europe, they will reach the heart of the far enemy. That, anyway, is the plan.

PART TWO

AMERICA

CHAPTER 6

A PARADIGM LOST

B EGINNING SLOWLY—too slowly—after the first World Trade Center bombing, officials in the White House, the CIA, and isolated offices in a scattering of other agencies began to scale a steep learning curve. They struggled to reframe their understanding of terrorism, discard old, deeply held beliefs, and formulate a new notion of what the United States needed to do to confront a fast-changing threat.

This was not easy. Over decades, an unspoken consensus had shaped American policy: terrorists would be dealt with decisively because Americans rightly expected their government to protect them, and every effort would be made to ensure that justice would be rendered when harm was done. Terrorism would be combated vigorously to strengthen deterrence, so no one would conclude that the United States could be taken advantage of with impunity. Wherever possible, America worked with other countries to disrupt terrorist operations, and it used its military might against terrorists when doing so made sense. The United States did not make concessions to terrorists, appease them politically, pay them off, or hustle them out of the country when they were accidentally arrested, as Europeans did in the 1970s and 1980s. The nation had deviated from this policy only once, to disastrous effect: in 1985–1986, the Reagan administration sold arms to Iran, in violation of U.S. law, to secure the release of American hostages held in Lebanon by Iranian-backed radicals. The harm done by this debacle was evident in Iran's continued use of terrorism as a tool of policy. The only country on earth with a tougher counterterrorism policy than America was Israel, which assassinated terrorists when it could locate them abroad. But for all the resolve and resources America devoted to the problem, in the grand scheme of foreign policy, terrorism was a second- or even third-level concern. It was a nuisance to be attended to, not a strategic threat.

Terrorism was not and never had been the kind of issue to provide an organizing principle for America's dealings with the world. For good reason: attacks were sporadic and the damage limited. The death toll from individual attacks rarely broke into the double digits; the annual average of fatalities was twenty-six. Americans were more likely to die from lightning strikes, bathtub drownings, or poisoning by plants and venomous animals than at the hands of terrorists.[1] No major international terrorist organization—not Hamas, Hezbollah, the IRA, or Sri Lanka's Tamil Tigers—placed America at the head of its list of targets. Terrorists, like the poor, would always be with us. But they sought incremental change, not a wholesale revision of the status quo. They wanted to inflict enough harm to be taken seriously, but not so much that their violence would elicit massive retaliation. Terrorists seriously threatened neither American power nor the safety of large numbers of American citizens, and the thinking of the top national security experts reflected that. In the open-session confirmation hearings on the nomination of James Woolsey to be President Bill Clinton's first director of Central Intelligence, the nominee mentioned the word *terrorism* once. In government deliberations spanning decades, counterterrorism routinely took a backseat to other matters—like lining up support for the Middle East peace process, maintaining alliances with European countries, or finding port facilities for U.S. warships.

During the latter half of the 1990s, that began to change. The small group of officials who recognized that al-Qaeda presented a growing, formidable danger to the United States pushed hard to make America's sprawling national security establishment take note of the new threat and respond appropriately. The work was difficult because a government that had never viewed terrorism as a first-tier threat had neither the organization nor the laws to deal with it that way. In many agencies, offices handling counterterrorism issues were bureaucratic backwaters, their managers carrying none of the heft of colleagues who dealt with geographic regions or high-profile issues such as arms control.

Even more daunting for those aware of the emerging threat was the challenge of arguing against a paradigm, a core understanding of a foreign policy issue. There were no dramatic statistics or powerful, graphic evidence; indications of real change in the nature of the danger, while not invisible, were subtle. It took time to sort through intelligence and reconstruct plots, so the origins or motives of an attack might take months or years to understand. And while this new paradigm was being born, the old one of state-sponsored and national-liberation terrorism persisted. The mental universe of America's soldiers, diplomats, and bureaucrats was shaped by history and confirmed by the media, which shared the traditional understanding of terrorism. Without a thunderclap to awaken the sleeping, the recognition that there was a new brand of terrorism did not spread fast enough or forcefully enough to pierce the far reaches of the bureaucracy.

The skeleton national security team had barely begun to unpack in the West Wing of the White House when terrorism first called on the new administration. Shortly before eight A.M. on January 25, 1993, just five days after Bill Clinton's inauguration, a brown station wagon pulled up on Route 123 in McLean, Virginia, near the two-lane queue of cars waiting to be admitted to CIA headquarters. A man carrying an AK-47 rifle emerged from the car and, calmly walking up and down between the lanes, fired some ten times into the idling vehicles. The shooter—he was later identified as a Pakistani named Mir Aimal Kansi—returned to his car and drove off, leaving two Agency employees dead and three others wounded.

A month and a day later, Ramzi Yousef's van filled with urea nitrate exploded in the World Trade Center in what—despite the relatively few casualties—was the worst case of foreign-directed terrorism on American soil to date. In April, the Kuwaiti security services uncovered an Iraqi plot to kill former President George H. W. Bush with a car bomb during his visit to Kuwait. On June 26, the United States launched twenty-three Tomahawk cruise missiles at Baghdad, destroying the headquarters of Iraqi intelligence. It was the first time the Clinton administration used military force and the first such U.S. retaliation against terrorists in seven years. (The last occasion was the Reagan administration's attack on Tripoli in 1986, after the bombing of the La Belle Discotheque in Berlin, where two American servicemen were killed.) After Yitzhak Rabin and Yasir Arafat signed the Oslo Accords in September 1993, Middle Eastern terrorists also intensified their efforts: more than thirty people, including four Americans, were killed in Israel in 1994 by Hamas and the Palestinian Islamic Jihad, as rejectionist Palestinians tried to derail the peace process. In July of that year, Hezbollah bombed a Jewish cultural center in Buenos Aires, killing almost a hundred people. The episode was a near repeat of the group's 1992 bombing of the Israeli embassy in the same city.

In this record, Yousef and Kansi were anomalies; they fit no part of the accepted taxonomy of terror, with its two great phyla, the soldiers of national-liberation groups and the agents of state sponsors. While the United States conducted intensive manhunts for the two—the search for Yousef become frantic after the fire in the Manila apartment revealed what he had been planning—the counterterrorism community's greatest fears still centered on states that employed terror as a tool of foreign policy. Countries with resources and determination could keep up a terror campaign for a sustained period and inflict more harm than any other actors.

History provided the justification for taking state sponsors of terrorism most seriously: Libya's downing of Pan Am Flight 103 in 1988—the culmination of a string of tit-for-tat exchanges between the United States and Libya through much of the preceding decade, including the La Belle bombing and the Tripoli raid—was the most recent attack to register triple-digit deaths. After the Libyan role in the bombing was confirmed, a determination that took more than a year, the Bush administration decided that the existing strategy of military retaliation was futile. "We thought that we weren't likely to get anywhere with another bombing raid and that you couldn't rule out that indeed the Pan Am 103 shoot-down was a consequence of the last bombing raid," Brent Scowcroft, Bush's national security adviser, recalled.[2] Weary of the cycle of killing, President Bush decided to seek a legal solution. The White House redirected its energies into backing UN sanctions against Tripoli in the conviction that the United States did not have an interest in waging an all-out war against Libya and that concerted international pressure provided a better way to change its behavior.[3]

When Clinton came into office, the new approach seemed to be paying off: Libyan terrorist activity had diminished substantially, if it had not entirely disappeared. The administration continued on the course set by its predecessor, remaining vigilant about Libya's behavior and working hard at the UN to keep wayward allies from undermining sanctions. Iraq was another state to worry about: war damage, sanctions, and international isolation had reduced its ability to mount attacks abroad, and its intelligence network was an impoverished shambles. But after the humiliation of Desert Storm, Saddam Hussein still hungered for a violent success. Syria continued to support rejectionist Palestinian groups and, because of its occupation of Lebanon, exercised a powerful influence over Hezbollah. Sudan was the newest addition to the State Department's list of state sponsors of terrorism. The country was so designated in 1993 because virtually every radical group in the Islamic world was operating in the open on Sudanese soil—from Palestinian Islamic Jihad to the radical Shiite group Hezbollah and from the Egyptian al-Gamaat al-Islamiyya to the roving international killer Abu Nidal.

Of all the state sponsors, Iran posed the greatest danger by far. The attacks on the U.S. embassy and Marine barracks in Beirut, which took place in a span of six months during 1983, were both carried out by Hezbollah, acting with the approval of its masters in Tehran. By 1993,

Hezbollah's direct attacks against Americans had stopped, but the two bombings in Argentina demonstrated the group's reach. Ayatollah Khomeini's 1989 fatwa calling for the murder of Salman Rushdie remained in force, and both the Iranian intelligence service, MOIS, and the Revolutionary Guard, the security entity most dedicated to the vision of the Supreme Leader, continued assassinating regime opponents around the world.[4] By this time, Tehran was driven less by the religious fervor of its revolution, during which radical students stormed the U.S. embassy in Tehran and kept its staff hostage for 444 days. Now, geopolitics motivated the mullahs. Through Hezbollah in the 1980s, Iran bloodied America and intimidated it into reducing its presence in Lebanon. Now the hardliners in power wanted the U.S. role in the Persian Gulf, dominant after Operation Desert Storm, diminished so Iran could take its place as the leading power in the region. Under Khomeini's successor, Ayatollah Ali Khamenei, Iran sought to cow Saudi Arabia and the small Gulf states and aggressively advocated a vision in which Persian Gulf security was left to those in the region, which would thus make Iran the hegemon. American analysts feared that the Iranians would strike against the United States to advance their objectives, and had prepared an array of terrorist operations in case America ever took military action.

The blow came on June 25, 1996, when a fuel truck packed with explosives blew up outside the fence surrounding a building housing U.S. military personnel in Dharan, Saudi Arabia. The Khobar Towers bomb sheared off the front of the eight-story building and left a crater thirty-five feet deep and eighty-five feet across. Nineteen American servicemen from the 4404th Fighter Wing, then enforcing the no-fly zone in southern Iraq, were killed, most of them sliced to ribbons by flying glass. It was the largest truck bomb the FBI had ever seen.

Early intelligence pointed to Saudi Hezbollah, a group that drew its members from the kingdom's Shiite minority and enjoyed Iranian backing. As they tried to make sense of the attack and learn about Riyadh's investigation, American law-enforcement officials were frustrated by Saudi evasiveness. Although Saudi Arabia's relationship with Iran at the time was cold, even hostile, Saudi leaders feared that a U.S. attack on Iran from Saudi bases would not be in the kingdom's interest. The Saudis eventually confirmed Washington's suspicions that high-level Iranians were involved and that some of the Saudi perpetrators were thought to be living in Tehran. But the Saudis never delivered enough information, and little, if anything, that could stand up in a courtroom, where the use of intelligence as evidence is problematic in the best of circumstances. With the United States impatient to make indictments, the Saudis balked at cooperating. In a series of meetings between Sandy Berger, then deputy national security adviser, the senior NSC aides for Middle East affairs, and Bandar bin Sultan, Saudi Arabia's ambassador to the United States, the Saudi repeatedly demanded to know what the United States would do with information Riyadh gave it and whether the administration would attack Iran. The U.S. officials said the only thing they could: not knowing what the information was, and unwilling to prejudge future developments, they did not know what decisions would be taken. But before pursuing any action, they promised to consult with the Saudis. For the Saudis, that was not good enough. An elaborate dance began in which FBI officials, including Director Louis Freeh himself, shuttled to Saudi Arabia to increase the pressure. They would extract pledges of help from their senior Saudi counterparts, but after the FBI officials returned to Washington, little that could be called cooperation was forthcoming.

While this went on, Iran continued using terror to advance its goals. In 1996–1997, more than twenty Iranian dissidents were assassinated in various countries. In 1996, during a routine inspection of an Iranian vessel docked in the port of Antwerp, Belgian officials found a "supermortar," a 320-mm device that could send a 125-kilogram projectile half a mile. It was packed in a shipment of pickles and was to be delivered to an Iranian merchant in Germany. Iran continued to provoke the United States, and the *Los Angeles Times* reported that the administration, in a message to Tehran, demanded an end "to Iranian surveillance of American diplomatic facilities in the Persian Gulf, Central Asia and the Balkans."[5]

—

The events of the first years of the Clinton presidency pushed terrorism up the ladder of foreign policy priorities. Clinton arrived in the White House talking of a new agenda in foreign policy, and a key part of that was taking on the growing international disorder created by "nonstate actors"—ever richer and more ambitious drug kingpins and international crime organizations, for example. From early on, Clinton's national security adviser, Anthony Lake, worried about the growing power of these groups and recognized, long before anyone focused on bin Laden and Afghan poppy production, that the clout of each set of malefactors would be multiplied if the different organizations began doing business together. In his speeches, Lake called this agglomeration of bad actors "the nexus."[6] America, he feared, was not ready for such a challenge and would need to reorganize itself.

From early on, the White House recognized the compelling need to get a better grip on all the information that was being gathered in different corners of the government, not just about terrorism but also about such matters as narcotics, counterfeiting, and espionage investigations. A central problem was pooling all the information on these operations, because intelligence represented only a fraction of what was accumulating in the executive branch. The country's seventy federal law-enforcement agencies and nearly ninety thousand agents were constantly collecting material that was potentially not just relevant but crucial for the conduct of foreign policy. The new national security team wanted to gain access to information assembled for prosecutions that were relevant to foreign and security policy—above all by the FBI and the Department of Justice. Therein lay an enormous problem, which grew out of issues of law and also out of the culture of law enforcement, whose officials are deeply reluctant to share information, sometimes even within their own offices or with other law-enforcement agencies. The bar often cited was Rule 6E of the Federal Rules of Criminal Procedure, which forbids disclosure of grand jury material. The rule, the modern incarnation of a principle whose origins can be traced back to seventeenth-century English legal practice, is meant to achieve a number of goals: preventing someone who may be indicted from hearing of the proceedings and fleeing; preventing witness tampering; encouraging maximum candor on the part of witnesses; and protecting innocent individuals who have been accused and are then exonerated.[7] There are limits to the scope of the rule and, at least in theory, ways of sharing national security material that do not violate it. For the FBI, however, Rule 6E is much more than a procedural matter: it is the bulwark of an institutional culture, and as Justice Department lawyers readily admit, it is used by the Bureau far more often than it should be. It is one of the Bureau's foremost tools for maintaining the independence that the FBI views as its birthright.

Eager to resolve the problem in the first year of the administration, Tony Lake and Sandy Berger met with the newly installed attorney general, Janet Reno, and proposed drafting a memorandum of understanding about the handling of such information. Reno agreed immediately and promised to work on it within her domain, including, most critically, the FBI. Although the issue was revisited many times over the next four years, that was as far as matters went. The FBI balked at the proposal, and Reno, although she was Louis Freeh's boss, could never bring him around.

Growing recognition of the terrorist threat did, however, result in legislative movement. Gathering together an assortment of proposals that had languished in Congress for years, the Clinton administration sought to strengthen the government's hand in combating international terrorism by introducing the Omnibus Counterterrorism Act in February 1995. At first, the new bill languished as well. That changed with the Oklahoma City bombing on April 19, 1995. After collecting recommendations from domestic law-enforcement agencies to strengthen the legislation, the administration resubmitted a more comprehensive bill the next month. With the partisan warfare between House Speaker Gingrich's Republicans and the White House then in full spate, the debate on the bill became charged and nasty; by the time a final version emerged, a full year had passed. But the bizarrely named Antiterrorism and Effective Death Penalty Act of 1996 (in the course of modifying the bill, Republicans wrote into it provisions aimed at speeding up appeals in capital cases) was a real improvement on existing legislation. It explicitly banned fund-raising for groups that supported terrorist organizations—hitherto a major weakness in the law, and an indicator of how low a priority terrorism had been for Washington. The new law required that chemical markers known as taggants be added to plastic and some other explosives so they could be tracked, and it toughened penalties for a range of terrorism-related crimes. It also strengthened the government's legal authority to bar terrorists from entering the United States and provided for the creation of an "Alien Terrorist Removal Court," in which classified information could be used without disclosing it to the suspect.[8] Numerous provisions were stripped from the legislation because of objections from the gun lobby and right-wing critics of federal law enforcement: Congress refused to create a penalty for those who knowingly transferred a firearm for use in a felony, refused to lengthen the statute of limitations on prosecuting terrorists who used machine guns or sawed-off shotguns, and refused to put taggants in black and smokeless powder, two frequently used bomb ingredients. Civil libertarians also found plenty to dislike in the bill, such as the procedures of the Alien Terrorist Removal Court, and they joined with conservatives to deny the government authority to seek multipoint wiretaps (taps on all phones a suspected terrorist might use, not just a single one) in terrorism cases, though they were routinely used in organized crime investigations. Still, the law was a breakthrough, making it possible to prosecute a wide range of terrorism-related crimes that had been out of reach for American law enforcement.

—

Another pivotal event occurred in 1995: Aum Shinrikyo released sarin in the Tokyo subway on March 20. This was a double shock for the counterterrorism community. First, when word of the attack arrived, no one could be found in the U.S. government who had heard of Aum Shinrikyo, though the cult boasted thousands of members, was headquartered in the capital of one of America's closest allies, and had an office in New York. The attack also pulled the rug out from under one of the hallowed verities of counterterrorism—namely, that terrorist groups might want to acquire weapons of mass destruction for the sake of bargaining leverage but would not actually use them. Because of the general abhorrence of chemical, biological, and nuclear weapons, it was believed that terrorists would be loath to alienate possible supporters by using them. That kind of mass killing would also harden government attitudes: the only conceivable response to those who used these weapons would be the complete destruction of their group.[9]

After the Tokyo attack, politicians and policy makers were unwilling to rely on that certitude. Working with the Clinton administration, Senators Richard Lugar (R-Ind.) and Sam Nunn (D-Ga.)—the Senate's most prominent security and foreign policy experts—and Senator Pete Domenici (R-N.M.), then chairman of the Senate Budget Committee, introduced legislation to train and equip firefighters, police, emergency services workers, and medical personnel in the country's major population centers to cope with biological, chemical, and nuclear attack. The program, which cost roughly $50 million a year and began in 1997, elicited snickers from critics, who likened it to the duck-and-cover exercises of the 1950s.

The events of the year had a lasting impact on the White House. While Congress was working on the various pieces of legislation, the National Security Council took a hard look at the federal government's ability to sort out the many knotty issues involved in terrorism policy and, in particular, to respond to a catastrophic act of terror. There was a general feeling that terrorism involving weapons of mass destruction might be just over the horizon, and that the country was not ready. The White House embarked on an ambitious effort to end years of ad hoc, reactive behavior and organize the government's efforts. The instrument for doing so was a "Presidential Decision Directive." Every administration, in a display of the narcissism of small differences, gives its own name to these documents: the first Bush administration called them National Security Directives; the administration of George W. Bush calls them National Security Presidential Directives. These directives, which are almost always classified, provide the essential guidelines for broad areas of policy and set out the roles of different agencies.

On June 21, 1995, Clinton signed PDD-39, among the most important of his presidency. It was probably the first major policy document to address head-on the threat of "asymmetric warfare," in which an opponent who recognizes American military superiority tries to attack the nation by targeting civilians with unconventional means. It cut away a thicket of conflicts over agency responsibilities for matters ranging from handling an overseas attack to who should hunt for a terrorist's nuclear weapon. For the first time it delineated the jobs of the different government agencies in "consequence management"—who, for example, would take the lead in Washington, who had responsibility for the care of large numbers of wounded or sick victims, who would deal with the environmental cleanup. The directive brought the Department of Health and Human Services under the national security umbrella for the first time by requiring the Public Health Service to be prepared for a large-scale terrorist attack. It raised the importance of a hitherto obscure working group that supported technology projects related to terrorism, and saved a special military unit that handled chemical and biological weapons from death by defunding. For the first time, it brought all the relevant agencies together for a budget review to see who was doing what. Terrorism had been such a low priority for so long that no one could say what gaps there were in federal capabilities or, for that matter, what overlap. PDD-39 changed that. It was the first major step toward centralizing control over federal counterterrorism policy in the White House. The issue had never required such high-level focus before.

The concentration of authority was recognized by everyone in the "interagency" to be the handiwork of Richard A. Clarke. With the support of the NSC leadership, Clarke used his position as chairman of the CSG (this originally stood for a mysterious "Coordinating Subgroup"

and later for the "Counterterrorism and Security Group") to bring together high-level representatives of the Departments of State, Defense,
and Justice, the CIA and the FBI, and others as needed to drive the administration's efforts. The CSG was one of the oldest interagency groups
in the government, its roots stretching back into the early 1980s. Its original function, however, was to handle crises, not to be a policy forum;
counterterrorism policy discussions were handled by another group,
chaired by the State Department. Early in Clinton's first term, Clarke,
characteristically, threw a bureaucratic elbow at the State Department by
announcing that he would not attend their meetings; from now on, they
would be attending his. PDD-39 formally enshrined that shift of power.

By the mid-1990s, Dick Clarke had become one of the rare career civil
servants in Washington to rise to the uppermost regions of the policy-
making world. He had become an indispensable, if sometimes uncontrol-
lable, figure in the national security apparatus. Clarke was something like
a Whitehall mandarin, one of the demigods of the British civil service
who, in a system with only a handful of political appointees, exercise considerably more influence than any American bureaucrat can aspire to. But
in Clarke there was nothing of the hyperrefined snob that the term con-
jures.

Raised by a widowed nurse, Clarke grew up in working-class Boston;
he attended the Boston Latin School, the University of Pennsylvania, and
MIT, where he earned a management degree. Clarke had little patience
for the fine manners and gentlemanly play of the well-to-do who fill many
of the senior ranks of government. In fact, he had little patience at all. He
began his career as a Cold War defense analyst counting nuclear warheads, and then became a State Department specialist in intelligence and
political-military affairs, the clutch of issues that includes arms control,
regional security, and technology transfers. Clarke became the second
youngest assistant secretary of state ever. Only Richard Holbrooke
climbed faster, and he, unlike Clarke, was a well-connected political appointee. Along the way, Clarke acquired a reputation for bright ideas and
bullying tactics. A rarity in government, he produced a stable of loyal pro-

tégés to whom he gave considerable responsibility, and a horde of antagonistic peers and superiors. In 1992, he ran afoul of Secretary of State
James Baker, who fired him for appearing to condone Israel's illicit transfer of U.S. technology to China. Brent Scowcroft gave Clarke asylum on
his White House staff, where he became a senior director handling portfolios that included counterterrorism, counternarcotics programs, peacekeeping operations, humanitarian interventions, and U.S. relations with
the UN.

In the Clinton administration, Clarke was one of only two senior directors kept on from the old regime. He struck up a friendship with Tony
Lake, whose respect for him grew early on because of the job Clarke did
as chairman of the committee coordinating the military and political operations involved with the U.S. presence in Haiti. He infuriated other
NSC senior directors by refusing to attend the twice-weekly staff meetings and by sending, in bold, red type, e-mail messages that ranged from
the merely snide to the blatantly insulting. Clarke knew everyone, and, to
the chagrin of the Joint Chiefs, delighted in working out of channels to
call the commanders-in-chief at the Central, Southern, or Special Forces
Command when he wanted something done. One assistant secretary of
defense put it cogently when he said, "Dick drove the Chiefs batshit." It is
no exaggeration to say that one person or another at the cabinet or sub-
cabinet level or in the top NSC staff urged the national security adviser to
fire Clarke almost every month. Among the half-dozen executive assis-
tants who served Tony Lake and Sandy Berger during the two Clinton
terms, few sentences were uttered with the same frequency as "This time
Dick has gone too far."

For all the irritation he caused, three qualities distinguished Clarke.
First, he understood as well as anyone in Washington all the levers and
pulleys of foreign policy, from the particular images a specific satellite
could provide, to what hardware could be transferred to a friendly country without congressional approval, to the mechanics of imposing economic sanctions. No one had a better mastery of the repertoire. Second,
he was relentless. Of the top officials who worked with him and recognized his talents, many shook their heads as he overplayed his hand in bu-

reaucratic battles and needlessly alienated people who might have helped him. But even if his abrasiveness did not always lead to the desired results, he delivered considerably more than most. Third, Clarke had a preternatural gift for spotting emerging issues. Whether it was terrorism, money laundering, or protecting the computer-driven infrastructure that kept everything from airports to stock exchanges running, he quickly identified the problem, devised a set of policy options, and took charge. This skill helped Clarke acquire a small bureaucratic empire, and it served the interests of his supervisors, who were eager to stay ahead of the curve of global change. His proficiency in this regard, as well as the growing danger of terrorist attack, would be recognized again three years later in another Presidential Decision Directive, this one numbered 62, which made him America's first national coordinator for counterterrorism. The position provided less power than Clarke wanted but still placed more authority on counterterrorism issues in one set of hands than ever before. The directive also gave the national coordinator a seat at the table when the foreign policy cabinet discussed terrorism. It was the first time an NSC staff member had been so elevated. That created a voice at the top for counterterrorism concerns—an advance over the past practice by which discrete responsibilities were scattered among agencies that historically viewed the issue as a secondary concern.

—

Exactly when the name Usama bin Laden began appearing in American intelligence reports and FBI investigative materials is something we are unlikely to ever learn. During the Soviet war in Afghanistan, the CIA was aware of bin Laden's work arranging travel and training for aspiring mujahidin, but that effort was funded by bin Laden himself, private Saudi citizens, and, perhaps, the Saudi Arabian government. At the time, Washington was keeping its hand in the conflict as well hidden as possible. The Agency maintained a low profile in the region, while Pakistan managed the logistics and operations of the anti-Soviet effort. It is unlikely that any U.S. agent ever came face-to-face with bin Laden.

After his return to Saudi Arabia in 1989, bin Laden's verbal attacks on the al-Saud probably also brought him to the attention of the intelligence community, especially after American troops began massing in the kingdom for Operation Desert Storm. Still, bin Laden would have been just one of many critics of the regime—clerics like al-Awda and al-Hawali were far more prominent—and there was little at that point to indicate how violent his opposition would become. Once he was in Sudan, after 1991, bin Laden loomed larger, a wealthy Saudi who had come to that marginal country, then distinguishing itself as the leading entrepôt for Islamic extremists. Bin Laden's name began to crop up more frequently in 1993. A Saudi-Egyptian investigation found that he was funneling money to Egyptian jihadists. At a time when most Islamic countries were harassing and imprisoning returning veterans from Afghanistan, whom they viewed as dangerous, bin Laden attracted attention by underwriting the travel of as many as 480 mujahidin from Pakistan to Sudan.[10]

In December 1992 Yemeni extremists bombed a hotel in Aden where American troops supporting the UN mission in Somalia were billeted. The Americans were alerted in time and evacuated the hotel without harm; the bomb killed an Austrian tourist and a hotel worker. Later, Yemeni authorities said that those responsible claimed bin Laden had financed the operation, which was the first violent act against Americans that has been linked in any way to the Saudi. But no hard evidence was provided to back up the claim, and U.S. intelligence analysts have long viewed the tie to bin Laden as tenuous.

In the first wave of terrorist conspiracies in the United States, bin Laden was a phantom presence. In the tens of thousands of pages of testimony from the World Trade Center, Bojinka, and TERRSTOP trials, his name appears but once: during the TERRSTOP proceedings Assistant U.S. Attorney Patrick Fitzgerald examined Khaled Ibrahim, who had trained and fought in Afghanistan and was a close friend of El-Sayyid Nosair.

Q. Are you familiar with the person by the name of Osam Ben
    Laden, O-s-a-m B-e-n L-a-d-e-n?

A. Yes.

Q. Have you ever met him?

A. No.

Q. You are sure?

A. Sure.

Q. Have you ever passed messages from Osam Ben Laden to anyone else?

A. No.

The mention on July 13, 1995, is one of the earliest in public by any U.S. official of the name bin Laden.[11] It's a tantalizing hint, but as far as the open record is concerned, the trail stops there.

The investigative record, however, contained plenty of threads that pointed to bin Laden. What is less clear is whether and when they were pursued. When El-Sayyid Nosair was first arrested in 1990, New York police seized a carton full of videotaped speeches by Abdullah Azzam, many of which discussed the cause of international jihad. The tapes sat untouched for more than three years before being examined in preparation for Nosair's 1995 trial, together with Sheikh Omar Abdel Rahman, for the TERRSTOP conspiracy. Azzam's creation, the Maktab al-Khidmat, which bin Laden took over, also never came up at trial, though the organization's New York office, the al-Kifah Center, was a focus of the investigation. Other clues were missed entirely. When Ahmad Ajaj entered the United States with Ramzi Yousef in 1993, he was found carrying a bomb manual that, government translators said, had "The Basic Rule" written on the cover and had been compiled in 1982 in Amman. The manual was entered into evidence at the first World Trade Center trial, in which Ajaj was convicted for his part of the conspiracy. As was later discovered by terrorism expert Steven Emerson and reported in *The New York Times* in January 2001, the manual heading should have been translated not as "The Basic Rule" but as "The Base"—al-Qaeda— and it had actually been published in 1989 in Afghanistan.[12]

Two key bin Laden operatives were well known to U.S. law enforcement years before the East Africa embassy bombings, in which they were implicated. Ali Mohamed, the former Egyptian army officer who wound up in a U.S. uniform and stationed at the Special Forces Command at Fort Bragg, trained El-Sayyid Nosair and other regulars of the New York–New Jersey jihadist circle in the use of firearms in the late 1980s and early 1990s. Documents from Fort Bragg about heavy weaponry and military tactics that Mohamed gave Nosair were among the evidence presented at the TERRSTOP trial. When Mohamed was summoned back from Africa in 1993 to be interviewed by the FBI in connection with the case against Sheikh Rahman and his coconspirators, he convinced the agents that he could be useful to them as an informant. Although he carried out tasks for al-Qaeda in this period, including training bin Laden's bodyguards and surveilling possible targets for bombings, the FBI says he was never caught doing anything illegal by those who handled him. Two months after the embassy bombings in 1998, Mohamed entered into a plea agreement and cooperated—evidently this time in earnest—with federal authorities. Wadih el-Hage, who was also known to the FBI from the early 1990s because of his connection with El-Sayyid Nosair's circle—he had been involved in discussions about weapons procurement for the group—managed to serve as bin Laden's personal secretary for years in Sudan. His office in Nairobi was searched by the FBI in 1997. El-Hage, who had been subpoenaed to testify before a grand jury in New York in 1997, was convicted of perjury in the embassy bombings trial as well as of participating in the broader conspiracy to kill Americans.

After the capture of Ramzi Yousef at the latest, more questions should have been raised about who was backing the "mastermind" of the World Trade Center bombing. When he arrived in America in 1992, Yousef clearly knew where to go to connect with the group around Sheikh Rahman, the spiritual leader of Egyptian jihadists. He traveled first-class, although he claimed he did not have enough money to build the bomb he wanted; that alone should have aroused curiosity. He called Pakistan repeatedly from New Jersey and had a store of identity documents in different names. The apartment that housed his bomb factory in Manila had been paid for by Mohammed Jamal Khalifa, a brother-in-law of bin Laden's. Khalifa is also believed to be a cofounder of the Filipino jihadist group Abu Sayyaf, which is tied to al-Qaeda.

On the plane that carried him from Pakistan to the United States, Ramzi Yousef, despite being advised of his right to remain silent, spoke for six hours about his activities, his goals, and his connections. He did this on the condition that no one tape him or take notes, because he believed he could later deny having said anything. Brian Parr, a Secret Service agent, and Chuck Stern, an FBI agent, sat opposite Yousef in a compartment created by hanging blankets around rows of seats on the specially equipped Air Force 707. Every time they took a break, Parr and Stern went to another part of the plane, out of sight of the terrorist, who was handcuffed and in leg irons, and made notes from memory. Afterward, the notes were put into a formal FBI report that was later entered into evidence. Parr testified at Yousef's trial and mentioned that Yousef said he was trained in explosives in a camp run by Arabs near the Pakistani-Afghan border. It was in this conversation that Yousef mentioned his desire to kill a quarter of a million people, which motivated him in bombing the World Trade Center. Yousef claimed that he had never met Khalifa, saying that one of the other conspirators in the Bojinka plot, Wali Khan Amin Shah, knew him. He added that he had been given Khalifa's card in case he needed help. Yousef also admitted that "he was familiar with the name Usama bin Ladin, and knew him to be a relative of Khalifa's but would not further elaborate."[13] After Yousef's apprehension, Pakistani investigators also reported that he had spent much of the previous three years in a bin Laden–owned guesthouse in Peshawar.[14]

For some time, there was little interest in pursuing these connections or in inquiring further to see who was behind Ramzi Yousef. There is a surfeit of reasons to explain the neglect: from 1995 until early in 1997, there was a lull in work on international terrorism at the FBI and little interest in looking beyond the immediate actors in the terrorism cases related to Yousef and the Blind Sheikh. All terrorism matters, foreign and domestic, were still under one roof, and the Bureau's resources were stretched thin by the Oklahoma City bombing, to which thousands of agents were assigned. Another reason was that a large element of the threat was foreign, and therefore belonged to the CIA. Relations between the two government bureaucracies were historically poisonous. (The FBI chafed at the CIA's unwillingness to allow its intelligence to be used in court, and the CIA was irritated by the increasing number of legal attachés—FBI officers—in embassies. Unwittingly, at times, the LEGATTs, as they are called, were recruiting CIA sources. Tony Lake ultimately had to sit Directors Woolsey and Freeh down for a reconciliation lunch to reduce the infighting.)

Within the Bureau, there was also an unwillingness to believe that there was more than met the eye. The feeling was that Yousef was a one-off, a virtuoso freelancer who wanted to make his mark as the world's greatest terrorist. That was the picture Ramzi drew of himself, and the contrast he posed with others already apprehended for the World Trade Center bombing and TERRSTOP conspiracies validated this thinking. The twelve defendants on trial in New York for plotting to destroy the commuter tunnels were, as one defense attorney later put it, incapable of "blowing up a paper bag," especially without the help of the informant Emad Salem. Bob Blitzer, then the FBI assistant section chief who focused primarily on foreign terrorism, was one of the few senior people reading the intelligence coming in from the CIA, and he argued that the Bureau should be paying closer attention. "Until the day I left international in '96, the community kept saying ad hoc terrorists and loosely affiliated terrorists and I didn't agree," he would recall. "I thought this was some kind of major network. We just didn't have enough of an intelligence base, didn't know how bin Laden and others were commanding it, how they moved people and how they moved money. We didn't have that information sorted out." The image of Mohammed Salameh returning to collect the deposit on the Ryder van used in the World Trade Center bombing left a lasting imprint: no group that relied on someone that stupid could possibly pose a serious threat. Many at the Bureau felt that their job ended when Ramzi entered the courtroom, and, at least at headquarters, they never looked back. It has become commonplace to assume that Yousef had a connection with bin Laden. Yet to this day, the FBI and the CIA maintain that the Yousef–bin Laden relationship has not been elucidated.

Eventually, the indications of a connection to bin Laden were recognized and probed by a new assistant special agent in charge in the FBI's New York field office, John O'Neill, and a group of talented federal prosecutors in the Southern District of New York, led by Assistant U.S. Attorney Patrick Fitzgerald. Their work, which relied on a significant amount of intelligence provided by the CIA, was the basis for an investigation that ultimately led U.S. Attorney Mary Jo White to file a sealed indictment of bin Laden in June 1998, two months before the attack on the U.S. embassies in East Africa. The indictment focused on al-Qaeda's activity in Somalia and its conspiracy to kill Americans. Very few people knew about this indictment—in Washington, no more than a handful in the Terrorism and Violent Crime section of the Justice Department and the FBI. According to one Justice Department attorney familiar with the case, the reason for the "close hold" was that "everyone was so paranoid about leaks," particularly if the State Department got wind of the case. Sandy Berger, who had become Clinton's national security adviser in the second term, was never told about it. Dick Clarke was given a heads-up at the time of the indictment by O'Neill, but by law he was supposed to be informed only if a federal judge approved, and that had not happened. None of Clarke's deputies were told. Thus, as a practical matter, the indictment—and the considerable brain work that had gone into producing it—could have no discernible effect on U.S. national security planning.

—

In the first two years of the Clinton administration, the intelligence community was also slow to examine the growing threat of Sunni extremism to America. For much of this time, the CIA was an unsettled, directionless institution. Clinton's first director of Central Intelligence, James Woolsey, was a failure. At the top of Woolsey's agenda was building a new generation of spy satellites, a project that would serve American military intelligence needs handsomely but do little to protect against emerging transnational threats such as terrorism. "He was obsessed with satellites," said one individual who worked closely with Woolsey. "Every marginal dollar went to technology." Relations between Woolsey and several cabinet-level officials were badly strained. Their overriding complaint was that Woolsey insisted on delivering policy prescriptions, violating the precept that the role of the CIA director is to provide information, not to tell the President how to act on it.

Woolsey's mishandling of the Aldrich Ames espionage case finally tipped the scales against him; he was fired in January 1995. Out of the succeeding thirty months, the CIA was without a Senate-confirmed director for a full year, as the administration struggled to fill the position. First, it took time to get John Deutch, Woolsey's successor, through the confirmation process. Deutch saw the job as a stepping-stone to becoming secretary of defense, but in December 1996, when Deutch was passed over for the Defense post at the end of Clinton's first term, he left abruptly. (During his tenure—perhaps because of his strong interest in defense issues—Deutch further strengthened the Agency's emphasis on supporting the military.) Clinton's next nominee for the CIA job was the outgoing national security adviser, Tony Lake, but he became the target of Senate Republicans who opposed Clinton and his foreign policy. The nomination proceedings dragged on until it became obvious that Lake's opponents were not going to stop digging for material that would kill the nomination. He withdrew in March 1997. Frustrated by the partisanship and concerned about the effects of the nomination struggle on the intelligence community, Clinton turned to George Tenet, who had been the Agency's acting director since Deutch's departure. Before Clinton's election, Tenet had been the staff director of the Senate Select Committee on Intelligence, which made him, in effect, an almost nonpartisan choice. The son of Greek immigrants who owned a diner in Queens, Tenet joined the administration as the National Security Council's senior director for intelligence programs. He was universally liked—a man with a mock-roguish grin who chomped on unlit cigars and played the part of intelligence community insider with a conspiratorial glint in his eye. Even by the standards of the hardworking NSC staff, he put in long hours, and he suffered a heart attack early in the first term. On a Democratic foreign policy team with few experts in intelligence, Tenet had a charmed existence. He was picked to be deputy director of the CIA by Deutch and then, despite a résumé that was short by Washington standards, became the lone salable candidate at age forty-four after the ordeal of the Lake nomination. He was quickly confirmed and sworn in during July 1997. The CIA had been rudderless and undermanaged during much of Clinton's first term, and as far as the White House was concerned, the counterterrorism operations showed it.

———

Washington had concerns about the growth of Islamist violence—it could hardly have been otherwise after the World Trade Center bombing—but much of that anxiety was focused on other countries. Bosnia in the early 1990s had become the newest theater of operations for hundreds of veterans of the Afghan jihad. Emboldened by their success in Afghanistan, these fighters migrated to the Balkans to fight alongside the Muslim forces. Egypt in this period was also enduring its crescendo of violence: in addition to the attacks on foreign tourists and prominent Egyptians, the 1995 assassination attempt on Hosni Mubarak and the bombing of the Egyptian embassy in Pakistan raised fears in Washington about the country's stability.

Egyptian radicalism, while perhaps the most virulent strain, was not the only one. In Saudi Arabia in November 1995—seven months before the Khobar Towers bombing—a bomb exploded in central Riyadh, killing five Americans and two Indians and wounding more than sixty other people. The target was the office of the program manager of the Saudi Arabian National Guard (OPM-SANG). The SANG had relied on a U.S. Army program for more than two decades for training and equipment. Despite demands from Washington that U.S. officials be kept informed, the Saudis quickly shut the door on the investigation. Several groups, none of which had ever been heard of before, claimed credit; all demanded that U.S. troops depart the kingdom. Five months later, the country's longtime interior minister, Prince Nayif bin Abd al-Aziz, announced that four suspects had been charged with the bombing. All were in their twenties, and three of them said they had fought against the Soviets in Afghanistan. In a televised confession, Abd al-Aziz Fah Nasir al-Muahtham declared that the U.S. presence in Saudi Arabia demanded an act of jihad and denounced the Saudi regime for not adhering to sharia. The suspects cited three radical Islamists who had influenced them, one of whom was Usama bin Laden. Less than six weeks after they were apprehended, the four were beheaded. The United States never got a chance to question them.[15] It was hardly news to Washington that some Saudis were deeply opposed to the presence of U.S. troops in the kingdom. But with no help from the host government and little else to go on, the intelligence community could never establish any relationship more definite than "influence" between bin Laden and the OPM-SANG bombers.

Throughout this period, there was little notion that the jihadist movement was coalescing around a single figure or network or that a concerted effort was in the offing to target the United States for supporting the "apostate" regimes of Hosni Mubarak or the Saudi royal family. Philip C. Wilcox, the State Department's coordinator for counterterrorism, delivered the established wisdom when he remarked that "while there are informal contacts among Islamists—especially abroad, where their leaders often find safe havens and fund-raising opportunities—there is little hard evidence of a coordinated international network or command and control apparatus among these groups."[16]

But in the constant drip of intelligence, White House officials were reading enough to make them worry about one name that appeared with disturbing frequency. When CIA briefers arrived at the White House in 1995 to discuss Usama bin Laden, they described him as the Ford Foundation of Sunni extremism. Aspiring terrorists, the analysts said, would approach him with proposals. Bin Laden wrote checks if he found the projects worthy. The drama of Ramzi Yousef's Bojinka plot had shaken NSC officials as no other conspiracy had, and the little that was known about bin Laden's role elicited questions. CIA counterterrorism officials, who took calming down the White House as one of their core tasks, were less agitated. "At first, the CIA thought [bin Laden] was a flake," said one top official with long experience in the intelligence world.

What was known about bin Laden was enough to unsettle Tony Lake and Dick Clarke. The national security adviser raised the issue persistently. "Tony was foaming at the mouth about bin Laden" as early as 1996, said a CIA official who worked with him at the time. Lake, shy and mild-mannered in public, was renowned within the executive branch for his impatient brilliance—"Talk faster," he demanded of his staff—and lightning wit. The same CIA official recalled him saying after a briefing that touched on bin Laden's family background and psychopathology, "Oh, yes, it's the fiftieth-child syndrome."

Lake and Clarke wanted a harder look at bin Laden, so the two drove to CIA headquarters in Langley to meet with the head of the Counterterrorist Center. The two sides of the Potomac may not have seen eye to eye on how dangerous bin Laden was, but the Agency agreed that his role as a financier of terror was intriguing. Money was flowing into counterterrorism programs, and CTC was looking for innovative ways to spend it. The decision was made to focus on bin Laden as a nodal point in the world of terror. To accomplish this, the CIA would create its first "virtual station." Rather than being located abroad and collecting intelligence about a single country, the UBL station, as NSC officials referred to it, would concentrate solely on bin Laden and his organization. By following the money, CTC thought it could find out whom bin Laden was funding and who, in turn, might be funding him; it was hoped that the knowledge might open up new ways to disrupt terrorist operations. "When we started this, we did not expect to find out that bin Laden was who he was. The decision to focus on him was in some ways serendipitous," said one former CTC official. The virtual station began operation in 1996.

As the spotlight narrowed on bin Laden, the picture became alarming. The Saudi was not just underwriting others' operations: he was funding terrorist training camps, had amassed a small business empire that provided him with plenty of cash flow, and was intimately connected with Sudan's ruling National Islamic Front, which shared key elements of his worldview. An essential tool of terrorism is a stock of government papers such as passports, which make possible the creation of false identities, and therefore travel. The prospect that bin Laden had easy access to official Sudanese documents, and might have use of Sudanese diplomatic pouches and the run of the country's embassies, where operatives could be planted, caused deep unease.

While the intelligence on bin Laden was becoming clearer, relations with Sudan were deteriorating. The United States had complained persistently for several years about Sudan's support for terrorism, to no effect. At the end of 1993, the CIA began hearing about a Hezbollah plot to assassinate Tony Lake. A period of quiet followed and then, while he was in New York in the fall of 1995 for a UN General Assembly meeting, Lake was told that new intelligence indicated that the Sudanese were involved as well and that a hit team had been dispatched. He was moved out of his home and into Blair House, the official guest residence on Pennsylvania Avenue, opposite the White House. Later, he moved to a safe house in Washington, finally returning to his own house in the spring of 1996.

In Khartoum, Sudanese thugs believed to be working for the government beat official American personnel, and someone fired shots at the embassy. As Tony Lake recalls, "The CIA came to us first about closing down," saying that the situation was becoming too dangerous for its people in Sudan. Diplomatic Security, the State Department bureau charged with the safety of embassies, wanted to close the embassy. In early February, the embassy's emergency action committee, which comprised the senior officers from the State Department, including Diplomatic Security's regional security officer, and the chief of the CIA station, voted to close the mission. That recommendation came over the objections of Ambassador Timothy Carney, who believed that the United States would lose much of its ability to influence the Sudanese if the embassy closed. But Susan Rice, then the National Security Council's senior director for Africa, and Tony Lake, an Africa specialist by training, distrusted the Khartoum regime and were dismayed by its close ties to Tehran and the rogues' gallery of Islamic extremists in residence. Twenty-three years earlier, a U.S. ambassador had been assassinated in Khartoum by Palestinian guerrillas, and the killing had not been forgotten. Eventually, Secretary of State Warren Christopher agreed that the situation was intolerable. The embassy staff was withdrawn in February 1996, and 2,100 Americans then living in Sudan were urged to leave.[17] The post was nominally left open and relations were not formally broken. Carney moved to Nairobi and monitored—and from time to time visited—Sudan. Weeks after the pullout, Madeleine Albright, then America's permanent representative to the United Nations, delivered evidence to the Security Council of Sudanese involvement in the attempt to kill Egyptian president Hosni Mubarak in Ethiopia.

Throughout the Clinton presidency, when the United States was poised to take action against Sudan or when Khartoum felt its interests were being harmed by American actions, such as sanctions or the shuttering of the embassy, the Sudanese would suddenly express a profound desire to improve relations and cooperate on counterterrorism. Their follow-through never matched their professed eagerness to please. As one State Department official would later recall, when hard questions and requests for information were put to them, the Sudanese "always weaved and dodged." In 1996, the withdrawal of U.S. personnel from Khartoum precipitated one such effusion from the Sudanese. The night before leaving the Sudanese capital, Carney dined with Vice President Ali Osman Taha and they had what the ambassador later described as the first serious exchange on terrorism during his six months in the country. He asked for information on bin Laden's finances, for access to terrorist training camps, and for bin Laden's expulsion from Sudan. The first round of answers from the Sudanese was, as Carney put it, "not satisfactory." After he left for Nairobi, the ambassador continued to push the Sudanese to move.

According to Carney, a second channel of discussions with Sudan about terrorism began in a suite in the Hyatt hotel in Rosslyn, Virginia, on March 3, 1996. Carney and another State Department official, together with representatives of the intelligence community, met with Elfatih Erwa, a senior Sudanese official then in the Defense Ministry. The diplomats made the introductions for the first encounter, which, Carney recalls, "was a get-acquainted meeting. There was talk about [Sudanese President] Bashir's concerns about bilateral relations." In subsequent meetings, the diplomats dropped out. *The Washington Post* has published a list of U.S. demands that was given to Erwa on March 8; at the top was an end to harassment of U.S. personnel in Sudan. Washington wanted surveillance of embassy personnel ended, information on who had been harassing Americans, traces on a number of license plates, access to terrorist training camps, and details about particular individuals associated with terrorism—including bin Laden—and their bank accounts. An explicit request to evict bin Laden was not made.[18]

In later meetings, Erwa, who undoubtedly knew the substance of the earlier exchange between Carney and Taha, upped the ante, saying Sudan was ready to expel bin Laden. They could send him home to Saudi Arabia—would that be acceptable?

The Saudi option was a calculated nonstarter. Riyadh had stripped bin Laden of his citizenship in 1994 for a reason. It would do everything it could to keep him out of the kingdom, where he would have become a magnet for opponents of the monarchy. As the scion of one of Saudi Arabia's wealthiest clans, bin Laden was untouchable. U.S. officials approached the Saudis, but were turned down cold: by the unwritten rules of life in Saudi Arabia, bin Laden was no more likely to be thrown in jail than he was to be declared the Mahdi by King Fahd. The Sudanese undoubtedly knew this. The issue came up again several times over the next few years, but the kingdom's aversion to taking custody of bin Laden remained a stumbling block.

More recently, press reports have alleged that Sudan was also prepared to hand bin Laden over to the United States. No senior U.S. official

is aware of any such offer. From what is known about the close links between Sudanese intelligence and al-Qaeda and the relationship between
Hassan al-Turabi, who in 1996 was one of the two most powerful men in
Sudan, and Usama bin Laden, this claim should be viewed with great
skepticism.

Dick Clarke and the CSG did evaluate at that time whether the United
States wanted custody of bin Laden. The decision was that it did not, for
the simple reason that since he had not yet been indicted the Justice Department had no grounds to hold him. In the unlikely case that bin Laden
was put on a plane to New York, on arrival at Kennedy Airport he would
have been free to catch a connecting flight to Orlando and visit Disney
World, or take the next plane out to Islamabad. The United States had no
interest in that happening.[19]

When U.S. officials told the Sudanese about the Saudi refusal, they
replied that bin Laden would be leaving Sudan. The Americans did not
know where he would go—his choices were limited, because most Muslim governments viewed him as anathema—but the prospect of separat-
ing bin Laden from his archipelago of training camps, his import-export
companies, his construction firm, and his other cash cows, as well as of
putting distance between him and Sudan's passport printing office, was
extremely attractive. Bin Laden departed Khartoum on May 18, 1996,
and returned to the site of his earlier glory, Afghanistan.

—

By the summer of 1996—the summer after Khobar Towers and the relocation of bin Laden—an enduring anxiety about terrorism had taken root
in the top levels of the U.S. government. Perhaps the best indicator of
how seriously a government views an issue is the funding it devotes to related programs. By 1996, the Clinton administration had opened up a
cash spigot that it never closed. Formerly, terrorism was a sufficiently low
priority that the White House Office of Management and Budget did not
even perform a "cross-cut," a compilation of all programs classified as
terrorism-related, so the total being spent was unknown. But beginning in

1996, when the total was some $5.7 billion, the numbers climbed steeply upward.

The ascent began with a bit of legislative subterfuge when the administration decided to take advantage of an aviation disaster. On July 17, 1996, TWA Flight 800 exploded off Long Island, killing all 230 aboard. The administration ruled out terrorism as a cause fairly quickly but used the fears aroused by the disaster as a springboard for a $1.1 billion spending request to Congress, including more than $400 million for aviation security measures—new, high-tech baggage screening devices, "trace detectors" for finding minute residues of explosives, and 140 more customs inspectors. The rest of the money would pay for five hundred FBI counterterrorism agents, better protection for U.S. troops abroad, and other measures.

Congress approved the proposal two weeks later, and in the years to come, the administration kept pushing the numbers up. By the end of Clinton's second term, the figure had almost doubled, to $11.3 billion in 2001. Over four years, money for traditional counterterrorism work increased 43 percent and intensive work began on preparedness for an attack involving a weapon of mass destruction or against America's "critical infrastructure," the computer-driven systems upon which the country's defense establishment, financial systems, telecommunications, and other key sectors rely. By 2001, the weapons of mass destruction and critical infrastructure programs, which had barely existed as areas of government endeavor only a few years earlier, were receiving $3.6 billion in funding. Money was coursing into the FBI's counterterrorism operations, and by the end of Clinton's presidency, the administration would boast that the ranks of its counterterrorism agents had more than doubled. The budget and size of the CIA's Counterterrorist Center swelled, though precise information remains classified and is not included in the figures cited above. Government money would fund a global upgrade of security at foreign diplomatic posts. Assistance to other countries to improve their counterterrorism programs—making them more useful partners for the United States—would also increase. To put all this spending in per-

spective: in an era of flat-line budgets, when the government was wres-
tling to eliminate annual deficits, there was probably no significant—
that is, multibillion-dollar—area of government spending that grew so
dramatically.

The corollary to those spending increases was a level of preventive
activity unlike any seen before. The 1996 Atlanta Olympics were approaching, and the White House, remembering the Munich games
twenty-four years earlier, feared that the event would be an irresistible
target for terrorists. The NSC was put in charge of coordinating arrangements around the many venues and, in a matter of weeks, a security
plan was hammered out that incorporated the FBI, the Secret Service,
Customs, the U.S. military, and the Public Health Service, as well as
numerous state and local authorities. The biggest concerns were a large
conventional bomb or a weapons of mass destruction attack, and extraordinary measures were taken to prepare for these possibilities. Specially
equipped medical teams were positioned around the competition areas.
During one of many visits to Atlanta to meet with organizers and law-
enforcement officials, it dawned on Clarke and one of his deputies that
the Olympic stadium was built over one of the country's largest railroad
hubs. With visions of a trainload of chlorine exploding just a few feet
below street level, they arranged for rail traffic to be rescheduled so that
only conventional cargoes traveled by day; hazardous materials would
pass by at night, when no one was in the stadium.

Five years before Muhammad Atta boarded American Airlines
Flight 11 in Boston, Dick Clarke was worried about an airplane carrying
out a suicide attack on the stadium or releasing a chemical or biological
weapon. He asked the Justice and Defense Departments if anyone under
any conditions had the authority to shoot down a civilian aircraft. The
answer was an unequivocal no. In response, Clarke created an almost
complete "air cap," a closure of the airspace around the stadium. The
FAA agreed to declare the airspace off-limits to all nonofficial aircraft. FBI agents fanned out to every airstrip within a two-hundred-mile
radius and asked airfield operators to report suspicious activity during

the games. Finding and intercepting wayward planes posed a bigger problem because FAA radar could not indicate speed and altitude simultaneously. The problem was solved when the Army provided Patriot radar, which, at Clarke's request, was hooked up to the FAA system and that of a P-3 drug interdiction plane, a mini-AWACS, pulled off customs patrol for the Olympics. Finally, helicopters, also provided by Customs and carrying Secret Service sharpshooters—who are employed by the Treasury Department—were deployed to intercept incoming craft and force them out of the no-fly zone.

All these arrangements were made quietly, out of sight of spectators. Whatever benefit they may have provided was overshadowed by the detonation of a small bomb in Centennial Olympic Park that killed one person and wounded 111, and by the FBI's ham-handed treatment of Richard Jewell, the security guard who was suspected of involvement and then cleared of any wrongdoing. Nonetheless, the security planning operation in Atlanta provided a model for events from presidential inaugurations to the 2002 Salt Lake City Olympics.

The United States also began the long process of improving security at military installations. The investigation following the Khobar bombing revealed a disturbing laxity in "force protection" abroad. To prevent further attacks, four thousand U.S. military personnel in Saudi Arabia were moved out of Dharhan and other population centers and into the remote desert confines of Prince Sultan Air Base, a costly move that left them safer, and depressingly isolated. Even with that relocation and a broad-based tightening of security measures in train, the White House had limited confidence that the Pentagon would follow through on the issue. In early 1997, Sandy Berger asked an NSC official who was traveling to the Persian Gulf to check in on security arrangements at military facilities. He visited installations in five countries and returned with a highly critical memo that cataloged a number of inadequacies—for example, perimeter defenses were not patrolled frequently enough and "setbacks," or buffer zones around buildings, were too small to provide protection from blasts.[20] The memo detailed the vulnerability of ships in port, noting that at the port of Jebel Ali in the United Arab Emirates, swarms of dhows, many of them from Iran, posed a serious threat to American warships. Land access to docked ships was also worrisome, since there was often no more than a drop-down barrier. Sailors on guard duty aboard U.S. vessels carried shotguns, but the heavy machine guns on deck were sheathed. Berger sent the memo to the Pentagon. It was leaked almost instantly to *The Washington Post,* though whether the intention was to embarrass the Defense Department's leadership or provide an example of White House meddling was unclear.

As fears about terrorism rose, the CIA also began to innovate. Its most important step was to vastly increase the number of "renditions" it carried out. *Rendition* is a term of art for the apprehension and transfer abroad, outside the system of legal extradition, of an individual who is wanted for terrorism or other crimes. Renditions may be done for a number of reasons: the country in which the suspect is found may not have an extradition treaty with the United States, yet may wish to cooperate with Washington; or, more often, the country in question is eager to avoid the publicity that extradition would entail. Before the Clinton administration, there had only been three renditions to the United States. Beginning in 1993, renditions became a boom industry for the CIA: in July of that year, Mohammed Ali Rezaq, who helped hijack an EgyptAir plane with Americans aboard in 1985, was rendered from Nigeria. In February 1995, Ramzi Yousef was rendered from Pakistan. Also in 1995, Yousef's associates Abdul Hakim Murad, Eyad Ismoil, and Wali Khan Amin Shah were all brought to the United States. The CIA also stepped up its assistance in renditions between other countries. In these cases, the Agency helped other governments identify terrorists, even entire cells, operating within their borders. The terrorists would be detained and, with logistical help from the United States, delivered to a third country for trial. These operations were kept secret so that the country in which the terrorist was found, or the one he was delivered to, or both, were protected from charges that they were acting as lackeys of the United States. By 1997, the number of renditions grew as more countries, especially in the

Islamic world, recognized that individuals within their borders presented a serious threat to their own security.

—

Renditions were the day-to-day stuff of counterterrorism. Bill Clinton wanted to be apprised of them and of whatever else was happening in that arena. His attention in this period was strongly seized by an over-the-horizon threat: biological terror. The President's interest was sparked by a dinner with Dr. J. Craig Venter, head of the Institute for Genomic Research and eventual co-winner of the "race" to decode the human genome, and by reading Richard Preston's novel *The Cobra Event*. (Clinton even asked the Department of Defense to certify that Preston's scenario was not outrageously far-fetched.) As a result, he came to fear that the next generation of terrorists might well use bioweapons against which America had no defense. A roundtable held in April 1998 in the Cabinet Room and including Venter, the Nobel laureate Joshua Lederberg, and Jerry Hauer, director of emergency services in New York City, confirmed for Clinton the gravity of the threat. The experts urged the President to start a crash program to improve U.S. public health capabilities and build a national vaccine stockpile to cope with the pathogens most likely to be used in an attack. Anthrax was at the top of the list.

At Clinton's request, Dick Clarke convened a series of interagency meetings, brought the Department of Health and Human Services deeper into the national security world, and by early June, had put together an emergency budget supplemental for Congress. The effort revealed important vulnerabilities: there was a woeful lack of vaccine production capacity; the Department of Defense kept a tight hold on its stocks *and* on the only company producing anthrax vaccine (the Pentagon was the only customer for the vaccine in the country); and Congress was reluctant to fund crucial improvements in the decaying public health system. Legislative aides summed up the attitude on Capitol Hill by saying that Congress had forgotten about public health for so long, the members thought trying to fix it now would be like pouring water into sand. The counterargument, that the public health system was the key to providing early warning of a biological attack and limiting the spread of disease, did not move the members. Stockpiling of ciprofloxacin and other antibiotics began, as did an effort to produce new vaccines for anthrax, smallpox, and other pathogens. An administration decision a year later to postpone the scheduled destruction of the world's only known smallpox virus stocks, which are kept at the Centers for Disease Control in Atlanta and a facility in Moscow, was also driven by White House concerns about bioweapons. Fears that there might be undeclared stocks in the possession of rogue nations, coupled with a recognition that the virus might be needed to make new vaccines, convinced policy makers to hold off. An attack involving smallpox—highly contagious and extraordinarily lethal in a population with little or no immunity—would be as catastrophic as anything that could befall the United States. Destroying the declared stocks was to be a crowning moment for the international public health community and a victory for opponents of biological weapons, many of whom saw it as removing history's most deadly virus from the bombs of the future. But Clinton believed that the stocks should be retained if there was any reasonable possibility that they might help with prevention. He was prepared to take criticism—which came—that he was preserving the stocks in order to give America the option of reviving its biological weapons program.

Despite Clinton's concern and Clarke's ceaseless activity, the turning of the U.S. government's attention to the new challenges of catastrophic terrorism would not have gone far if not for Sandy Berger, the man between them on the White House wire diagram. Berger became the national security adviser for Clinton's second term; he had been a successful Washington trade lawyer and, during the Carter administration, deputy director of the State Department's Policy Planning Staff. (Tony Lake had been director.) He and Lake, good friends from their Carter years, were a study in contrasts: Lake skipped dazzlingly from one subject to another and one plane to another. Berger took stock of every inch of the terrain around him, finding every hazard as well as every opportunity.

Lake's four years as national security adviser took a physical toll on the
onetime captain of the Harvard squash team; by the time he left, he was
visibly exhausted and suffering from a host of ailments. Berger, whose
first four years were not much easier than Lake's, had extraordinary
stamina, worked unspeakable hours, and seemed to gather strength as
one aide after another crumpled. The stress of one of the world's most
taxing jobs showed in occasional eruptions of anger in which he told staff
members that their actions would fatally undermine national security. But
he typically called the individual shortly thereafter to apologize, a sign of
humanity in a high place that contributed to the loyalty most NSC officials felt for Berger. He had been Bill Clinton's friend since 1972, and was
one of the very few top officials who actually grew in stature around the
President. He had no qualms about speaking his mind to a man whom
most found an intimidating presence, physically and intellectually. And
because he saw every inch of the landscape—and understood the "due
diligence" that an administration must perform on every issue both for
the sake of national security and to retain public trust—he recognized the
importance of the terrorism issue.

Which was why, in the summer of 1998, Berger and Clarke turned
their energies to forcing the cabinet, and by extension the federal bureaucracy, to begin planning seriously for an attack with a WMD. That July,
after persistent badgering by Berger, a secret "tabletop" exercise was held
in Blair House that brought together the leaders of every agency that
would have any responsibility during such an attack. Merely assembling
the cabinet chiefs, their deputies, and leaders of the uniformed military
and agencies like FEMA to work through such an event was an unprecedented achievement; such prima donnas rarely gather except for photo
opportunities with the President, which, after all, is what most cabinet
meetings are. No one could remember any occasion on which they had all
gathered for several hours of what bordered, in a delicate way, on humiliation. As Clarke walked them through three scenarios involving nuclear, chemical, and biological weapons, those assembled were shocked
to discover how little any of them knew about what to do in such a crisis.

How would one keep the American economy from coming to a halt if all international travel and shipping were stopped because other countries, fearful of contagion, cut travel links? What pressure could be brought to bear on allies to supply needed medications in such a scenario? Who had the responsibility to track down a terrorist with a nuclear weapon? What could the armed forces actually do in a crisis, given *posse comitatus* restrictions against using them for police work? As Berger and Clarke hoped, consciousness of the problem of weapons of mass destruction terror rose almost vertiginously. Recognizing the amount of work ahead of them, the officials who emerged from the darkness of the Blair House reception room and piled into their cars were a shaken group. The gravity of the experience was reflected in the fact that no one leaked a word; despite the fleet of limousines on Pennsylvania Avenue that day, the exercise remained a secret for several years.

CHAPTER 7

THE UNKNOWN WAR

I N THE YEAR before America learned the name Usama bin Laden, the Saudi was a disturbing, enigmatic presence in the world of terrorism. In Washington, bin Laden's fingerprints could still not be discerned definitively on any significant act against the United States or American citizens, but there was growing alarm about al-Qaeda's activities and the company it kept. Throughout, Iran remained the counterterrorism community's top concern; tracking Tehran's undercover activities and jousting in the dark with the Iranian intelligence services occupied much of Washington's energy. Yet, bin Laden was steadily becoming the subject of more scrutiny and apprehension. Around Christmas 1997, the White House decided that the threat posed by al-Qaeda had grown enough that it began pushing executive-branch agencies to increase their efforts to disrupt the network. Bin Laden's fatwa of February 1998, "Jihad Against Jews and Crusaders," a much briefer, more powerful statement than the one from 1996, caused an immediate stir when it was published in the London Arabic-language newspaper *al-Quds al-Arabi*. Its language was determined, direct, and redolent of the Quran. In the months that followed, bin Laden gave more interviews, and a recruitment video circulated around the Islamic world. Beginning in May, meetings were held at the White House on possible action that could be taken against the Saudi. But the obstacles were forbidding: at that point, the United States had no indictment of bin Laden and thus could not bring him to America for trial. No other country wanted custody of him. And there was nothing like a workable plan. At the same time, in the intelligence reporting, there were curious, coded statements that were ambiguous; it was impossible to know what, if anything, bin Laden was up to.

The answer came on August 7, 1998. The Situation Room staff—people detailed from the military and intelligence community, who route diplomatic cables, phone calls, and intelligence reports to White House officials—roused the members of the Transnational Threats Directorate in the early morning with the news from East Africa. Gathered in a conference room in the West Wing basement, they went into permanent session with their colleagues from half a dozen different agencies to work out rescue coordination, an intelligence review, and defensive countermeasures. The initial crisis-management work lasted for several days, with staffers napping on couches when they could, or going home for short breaks.

But amid the nonstop information-gathering phone calls, cable writing, briefing of White House officials, and cajoling of other agencies to move faster, they could not stop glancing at the CNN images on the monitors: in the mountain of tangled rebar, concrete, and glass in downtown Nairobi, the staticky telephone reports of carnage in Dar es Salaam, and the seemingly endless procession of the injured, they saw something qualitatively different from anything that had gone before. No previous terrorist operation had shown the kind of skill that was evident in the destruction, within ten minutes, of two embassy buildings separated by hundreds of miles. Someone at the time was quoted as saying that two such attacks were not twice as hard, they were a hundred times as hard, and that true statement reverberated through the air for weeks. The number of people killed was comparable to the most lethal attacks of the past—241 had been killed in the Beirut barracks in 1983, 270 in the air and on the ground when Pan Am Flight 103 was destroyed over Scotland

in 1988. But in being so indiscriminate, the violence of the African bombings was unprecedented. In addition to the 224 dead, many of whom
were African Muslims, some five thousand people were injured. A rule of
terrorist operations had been to avoid harming those who might sympathize with the cause. These attacks dramatically departed from that practice.

The days after the embassy bombings brought a mixture of successes
and setbacks. The determination that al-Qaeda was behind the attacks
came quickly. A fax claiming responsibility was found on a publicly used
fax machine in London, and there was a sudden spike in phone traffic between organization operatives. At the same time, the slow start to the
search-and-rescue effort in East Africa was an embarrassment. An Israeli
team was first on the ground, freeing victims from the rubble. The official
U.S. aircraft that was to bring a rapid-reaction team of law-enforcement,
intelligence, and diplomatic officials broke down in Europe. American
search-and-rescue teams had trouble finding planes to get them and their
gear to Africa. The FBI's first group of agents did not arrive until two days
after the blast.

The pieces of the conspiracy quickly fell together. Mohammed Sadeek
Odeh was arrested when he arrived in Karachi from Nairobi on the day of
the bombing, carrying a Yemeni passport with a picture that did not
match his face. Doctors in a Kenya hospital noticed that Mohammed
Rashed Daoud al-Owhali had wounds on his back that suggested he was
running from the bomb when it exploded. Wadih el-Hage was picked up
by the FBI on September 15 in Arlington, Texas, and Khalfan Khan Mohammed was found in South Africa using the same alias he had in Tanzania. Some of the men talked at great length, spelling out how the plot was
executed and who was behind it. Bin Laden's involvement was clear.

These successes, however, did little to quell fears that more attacks
were coming. In the face of the damage done in East Africa, the White
House decided that it was imperative to disrupt the terrorists' operations
and preempt possible attacks, including through military means. Action
needed to be taken quickly: in the intelligence "take" after the bombings,

credible reporting showed that other al-Qaeda conspiracies were nearing completion. The White House felt a sense of urgency, because after the performance of August 7, there could be no doubting that al-Qaeda might be ready to strike at any time; more unsettling, there was a fear that sometime soon the group would attempt something far more devastating than truck bombings.

Only weeks before the embassy bombings, CIA briefers came to the White House to inform the National Security Council staff about intelligence reporting regarding al-Qaeda's efforts to acquire weapons of mass destruction. The briefers' assessment was that bin Laden and his colleagues were diligently working to create or purchase chemical and even nuclear weapons. What made this news riveting was evidence that the group might already be preparing an attack with the chemical agent VX, an extraordinarily lethal substance that could be used to kill hundreds of people, or more. Proof came in the form of a clump of dirt—a soil sample collected near the al-Shifa chemical plant in Khartoum. It contained the chemical O-ethyl methylphosphonothioic acid, or EMPTA, which is produced near the completion of the process to synthesize VX. The Central Intelligence Agency concluded that there was no other reason, including accident, for this precursor to be present in the quantity demonstrated in the soil sample, except in connection with the production of this chemical weapon. Faced with the possibility of the use against Americans of one of the most deadly substances ever synthesized, the White House directed that planning begin for a cruise-missile attack against al-Qaeda sites.

"Targeteers" from the intelligence agencies and the Pentagon were ordered to draw up a list of potential targets for a U.S. military strike and made recommendations. Their roster of sites was forwarded to the Principals Committee, as the national security cabinet is known, for final selection.

At least one target, a tannery in Khartoum owned by bin Laden, was struck from the list because there was no evidence of any activity involving weapons of mass destruction. A final group, six terrorist camps in

Afghanistan and the al-Shifa plant, was selected. Within the small circle of officials who knew of the plans, some felt uneasy. Attorney General Janet Reno expressed concern about whether the strikes were proportional and met the requirements of self-defense under Article 51 of the UN Charter, which was how the administration intended to justify them. Others were aware that a decision to attack another country is rarely made on the basis of clandestine intelligence, and the United States has not often pursued a strategy of preempting threats militarily. Yet the perception of imminent danger was powerful enough to overcome these concerns. At the Principals meeting, Sandy Berger asked, "What if we do not hit it and then, after an attack, nerve gas is released in the New York City subway? What will we say then?" Reno declined to vote one way or the other, but the rest recommended unanimously that al-Shifa be destroyed. August 20 was chosen as the date because of intelligence reports that bin Laden and the senior leadership of al-Qaeda would be meeting that day at the camp in Khost. The target list was forwarded to the President, and Clinton approved the strike. On August 19, Dick Clarke assembled a team drawn from the NSC, the CIA, the State Department, and the military; they were told to call home and inform their families that they would be working late and might not make it home. No explanations were given. The group then started work writing cables to embassies around the world, with varying sets of talking points for the ambassadors depending on whether their host countries were close allies, moderate Islamic nations whose further help was needed, or unfriendly regimes that might misread American intentions. A statement explaining the U.S. action was prepared for the United Nations. Fact sheets and talking points were also drawn up for senior officials to use in press briefings. For once, the NSC speechwriters were bypassed completely: Rob Malley, Sandy Berger's executive assistant, drafted a statement for Clinton.

For a brief moment, the operation appeared to be a qualified success. Al-Shifa was destroyed. Six terrorist camps were hit and about sixty people were killed, many of them Pakistani militants training for action in

Kashmir. The Tomahawks missed bin Laden and the other senior al-Qaeda leaders by a couple of hours. This in itself was not a great surprise: no one involved had any illusions about the chances of hitting the target at exactly the right time. The White House recognized that the strike would not stop any attacks that were in the pipeline, but it might forestall the initiation of new operations as the organization's leaders went to ground.

The months that followed, however, were a nightmare. The press picked apart the administration's case for striking al-Shifa, and controversy erupted over whether Clinton was trying to "wag the dog," that is, distract the public from the Monica Lewinsky scandal. *The Washington Times*—the capital's unabashed right-wing newspaper, which consistently has the best sources in the intelligence world and the least compunction about leaking— ran a story mentioning that bin Laden "keeps in touch with the world via computers and satellite phones."[1] Bin Laden stopped using the satellite phone instantly. The al-Qaeda leader was not eager to court the fate of Djokar Dudayev, the Chechen insurgent leader who was killed by a Russian air defense suppression missile that homed in on its target using his satellite phone signal. When bin Laden stopped using the phone and let his aides do the calling, the United States lost its best chance to find him.

On the third floor of the Old Executive Office Building, a permanent crisis mode set in. Intelligence reports on jihadists from around the world began to flood into the directorate's two suites. The East Africa bombings had a catalytic effect on CIA stations, foreign intelligence services, and, it seemed, everyone who had ever peddled information.

The reports that preparations were almost complete for more attacks turned out to be true. Later that August, the Albanian government, working with U.S. intelligence, broke up a plot to bomb the American embassy in Tirana. Concern about such an attack had been so great that some two hundred Marines and a number of plainclothes security men were flown in to evacuate most of the embassy compound. Still, there was no certainty that the worst was over. Other embassies around the world were shut down for varying periods of time because of threat information.

The CSG met frequently, often on no notice, to evaluate information and agree on a response. Within the bureaucracy, the crisis changed behavior all around: now anything remotely worrisome set off alarms. Scraps of intelligence of questionable quality that before August 7 might have prompted a short discussion between colleagues at the NSC and CIA found their way into the President's Daily Briefing, which the CIA prepared for Clinton's morning reading. Not wishing to be caught out, the Agency gave Clinton substantial amounts of threat information that did not require presidential attention. Copies of the PDB would come back to Transnational Threats with Clinton's distinctive reversed check marks and questions in the margins for follow-up. That in turn necessitated multiple calls to the CIA to find out why the threat was not urgent or not credible. Then a memo would be drafted for the Oval Office. The Principals were in constant contact. When they met on September 8, 1998, they were greeted by the good news that a bin Laden lieutenant, Mamduh Salim, also known as Abu Hajer, was in custody in Germany. The bad news was that there were indications Washington might be targeted for attack.

———

That the terrorists might strike within the United States was obvious to everyone, Clarke and his deputies believed. The embassy bombings had made abundantly clear the terrorists' ability and willingness to strike anywhere and at any time. Accordingly, the FBI "checked the locks"—alerts went out to all FBI field offices, and bulletins went to thousands of federal, state, and local law-enforcement agencies, requesting that they enhance protection at public buildings, be especially vigilant about suspicious behavior, and increase surveillance of worrisome individuals. In the months to come, the locks were checked over and again.

The bombings were something Clarke had been preparing for: the moment when a foreign terrorist group demonstrated a capability to operate abroad *or* in America. When he took charge of the CSG, it was evident that the government would have a hard time coping with such a challenge because of the animosity between the FBI and CIA. Clarke had worked to bind the two agencies together by getting them to exchange deputies: a senior FBI agent would occupy one of the top slots at CTC and a CIA official would take an equivalent job in the FBI terrorism section. (A further exchange involving the Department of Defense was planned but killed by congressional objections to having military personnel in law-enforcement positions.) The swap was considered a success and became routine. Clarke's frequent CSG meetings, in which he tried to force as much information as possible out into the open, was also aimed, in part, at breaking down the barriers.

Even in the minds of those who were spending their waking hours thinking of little but the destruction in East Africa, the old paradigm did not die easily. The question nagged: how could any group execute such a pair of attacks without the help of a state sponsor? The intelligence community maintained that it had no indications of any noteworthy relationship between al-Qaeda and a state sponsor of terror, except Sudan. Clarke, a reflexive second-guesser of received ideas, assigned one of his directors to review every piece of intelligence that hinted at any connection whatsoever between al-Qaeda, Egyptian Islamic Jihad, or any other group with bin Laden ties on the one hand, and Iran or Iraq on the other. When the printer finished spitting out intelligence reports, the stack of paper was three feet high. In its pages there was plenty of smoke but no smoking gun. Many Islamists affiliated with the various radical groups were living in Iran or traveling through the country, but that was not the same as saying that they had joined forces. On the contrary, the split between Sunni and Shiite runs so deep that many, if not most, Muslims who espouse a radical Islamism like bin Laden's believe that Shiites are either heretics or not Muslims at all. Among counterterrorism experts there was a presumption that the authorities in Tehran were surveilling the Sunni radicals because state sponsors typically keep a close eye on the terrorists within their borders—to know what their guests were up to. It was even possible there had been passing contacts between some of the Sunni extremists and Iranian officials. But after combing through the pile of intelligence, there was nothing to suggest more than some furtive tapping around in the dark between the Iranian government and al-Qaeda.

The record with Iraq was thinner still. Bin Laden had decried America's treatment of Iraq and gladly repeated the many spurious claims in circulation about hundreds of thousands of Iraqi children dying because of shortages produced by U.S.–backed UN sanctions. He spoke publicly of Iraq as the only country with the military might to challenge the United States. And in Sudan he had invested in chemical weapons production, the technology for which appeared to come from Iraq—an association that was indirect, not even a marriage of convenience. But he was deeply contemptuous of Saddam Hussein. For believers like bin Laden, Saddam was the second coming of Gamal Abdel Nasser, a secular, pharaonic ruler who had destroyed the religion and oppressed the umma. There is little evidence that Saddam viewed bin Laden and his ilk any differently than Egypt's secular rulers viewed Sayyid Qutb, Shuqri Mustafa, and their successors—as religious extremists who would enjoy nothing more than to see secular rule toppled. However attractive their anti-Americanism, they could only be handled with caution. There was nothing in the record to suggest that a central precept of the state sponsors had changed: never get into bed with a group you cannot control. Both the Iranians and the Iraqis appeared to be reluctant to cooperate with an organization that might commit some enormity that could be traced back to them. The NSC analysts found it difficult to accept that al-Qaeda acted alone, but no other conclusion was warranted.

—

In September and October 1998, a set of strategies began to emerge: defensive measures were agreed upon and intelligence, diplomatic, economic, and military initiatives were begun. The disruption of the plot to blow up the American embassy in Tirana was convincing proof that—despite worldwide warnings, heightened security at foreign posts and military bases, and stepped-up assistance from governments in scores of countries—the threat was broad-based and not diminishing. The volume of threat information tripled or quadrupled.

To keep abreast of it all, the NSC initiated a thrice-weekly "threats meeting," at which every credible bit of information about a possible conspiracy would be evaluated. The CIA would conduct the briefing on most of the threat material because it came through their channels; occasionally the Defense Intelligence Agency or State Department sources turned something up. All the Agency representatives at the table would then discuss measures to be taken, including requesting more security from local authorities, temporary closure of the facility, dispatch of emergency security teams, and the withdrawal of dependents and nonessential personnel. In the remainder of 1998 and the early part of 1999, as many as a score of embassies were shut down at one time or another. If an embassy was closed because of threat information, the White House insisted on credible information to show that the threat had been removed, or that the original information had been false, before the embassy reopened. Tempers flared as ambassadors—who often insisted on closures to begin with—were told they could not reopen their posts just because they were tired of the shutdown. Within the CSG itself, irritation built up as the NSC officials who chaired the meetings struggled to keep pace with the volume of intelligence. Agendas were often late, and meetings were called at the last moment. Over time, however, the process brought an order that had not existed before to the oversight of security arrangements at America's overseas facilities. For the next eighteen months, there were no major attacks.

The embassy bombings destroyed the long-held belief that there were regions of the world where American posts were safe and other, more dangerous ones, such as the Middle East, where they were less so. The attacks in Nairobi and Dar es Salaam showed that there were now terrorists capable of hitting the United States *anywhere*—or, as the fatwa put it, "in any country in which it is possible." An implication of the new reality was that the safety of embassy buildings throughout the world was in doubt.

The United States had made a comprehensive reassessment of the security of embassy buildings in the 1980s, after the Beirut bombings, when a commission chaired by Admiral Bobby Inman issued a harsh evaluation of existing conditions. The Inman Report called for new physical security guidelines, and the State Department set a minimum of one hundred feet for setback, the amount of space between an embassy building and public thoroughfares where a truck bomb could be left. New standards for building materials, blastproof windows, armored cars, and the like were also set. The House of Representatives voted for a $4.4 billion, five-year program to replace inadequate facilities, but that figure was quickly pared down in the Senate. For a few years, when the United States needed an embassy, an "Inman box" was constructed. Ugly blocks with small windows, they were loathed by those who worked in them and mocked by citizens of the host country as a sign of American neurosis. The State Department soon undercut the standards, issuing waivers for many existing and new buildings. As the sense of urgency diminished, spending on new, secure facilities tailed off quickly.

Within a couple of weeks of the East Africa bombings, a subgroup of the CSG began meeting to evaluate the vulnerability of U.S. diplomatic posts around the world. Officers from the State Department's Bureau of Diplomatic Security, CIA experts, force-protection specialists from the Department of Defense, and NSC directors spent days hunched over embassy layouts, aerial photographs, analyses of local traffic, and threat evaluations for every foreign post. A list was compiled of some forty facilities that needed immediate inspection, and seven teams with members from the several agencies were quietly dispatched.

When the Embassy Security Assessment Teams (ESAT) returned, a marathon series of meetings was held to determine which posts could be made sufficiently safe through measures such as the construction of security walls or the closure of nearby streets. In the midst of this work, Congress appropriated $1.5 billion for a global security upgrade, which paid for such equipment as radios, surveillance cameras, and armored cars, as well as for more diplomatic-security personnel and improvements in physical security. The number of embassies reporting that they still had regular glass windows instead of blast-resistant ones was shocking. Some posts were put on the fast track for new building construction, though this was often held up by the unavailability of suitable land. At least one embassy was ordered closed immediately, with the staff relocated to another facility made available by the host government. A Persian Gulf post, it had been the subject of several memos to the State Department from NSC staff members who considered it one big "Welcome, Terrorists" sign. After August 7, the message got through.

While the country as a whole was concluding that there was little reason to fear terrorists with chemical weapons, Clarke and his directors still thought the possibility real enough to merit action. In a White House "tasker"—a seldom-used document in which an agency is directed unconditionally to do something—the NSC ordered Foggy Bottom to draw up plans to send MOPP kits ("mission-oriented protective postures," gear to be worn in a chemical or biological weapons attack), decontamination units, and antidotes to posts in the arc of crisis, the region from North Africa through the Middle East, the Persian Gulf, and Central Asia. Al-Qaeda's multiple-strike strategy had worked: the United States had no idea when the attacks might stop, and posts needed to be prepared as soon as possible.

—

If August 7, 1998, introduced America to a new enemy, the months that followed brought reminders that the country also had friends, especially in the Islamic world, where national leaders feared not only a U.S. withdrawal from the region but also the jihadists, who, in reality, threatened their regimes more than they did America. Because of widespread anti-Americanism in these countries, many governments keep their distance in public: the reminders came quietly, in the form of improved intelligence cooperation. Working with the CIA, "liaison services" rolled up one terrorist cell after another in the latter part of 1998 and 1999. In many cases, those caught were tried and incarcerated in the countries in which they were arrested. In others, the United States rendered the terrorists and assisted in arranging transportation to the militants' home countries, where they were usually wanted. Relations that had long been good became better, and a new responsiveness to American concerns appeared. A few terrorist operations that were under way were foiled. That, of course, was the

best outcome. More often, those the United States and its partners apprehended were involved in logistics, fund-raising, and communications—the
infrastructure that bombing teams would connect with when a target had
been chosen and an attack planned. The focus on infrastructure was inten-
tional: there were a small number of bomb teams, they were mobile, and
they were hard to find. But if the infrastructure was knocked out, the
bombers' ability to operate in a particular country was reduced or eliminated, and that made their potential theater of operations smaller.

All the activity had a whipsaw effect on the counterterrorism staff:
e-mails and memos detailing the "takedowns" flew to the West Wing,
where the President and Sandy Berger were keenly interested in the
progress. On one hand, the sheer number of successes suggested that al-
Qaeda operations were being damaged, perhaps significantly. On the
other, it was unnerving how many cells were being discovered. The organization was bigger and more active than anyone had guessed, and no one
could say how deep its ranks were. The intelligence successes also posed
a conundrum: senior officials wanted to underscore the reality of the terrorist threat and show, in the aftermath of the August missile strikes, that
the United States was scoring victories. But the takedowns could never be
discussed in any detail. Leaders in the cooperating countries were fearful
of a hostile reaction from their own people, so the price of their assistance
was silence. At least once before August 7, a newspaper leak had revealed
such joint intelligence work, causing the other country to suspend cooperation for months. Though Berger, Clarke, and other officials spoke
broadly of rolling up al-Qaeda cells, reporters, not surprisingly, declined
to report on something about which they had no specifics.

———

Halfway between the "blackness" of pure intelligence operations and the
visible drama of the military response came the effort to attack al-Qaeda's
finances. The administration publicly announced its first step in this campaign on the day the missiles struck Afghanistan and Sudan. The strategy
was one the Bush administration would duplicate three years later: using
the authority of the International Emergency Economic Powers Act

(IEEPA), Clinton issued an executive order freezing the assets of bin Laden and al-Qaeda. Much as would happen in 2001, the move made news but had little effect; assets in Britain belonging to Salah Idris, the owner of record of the al-Shifa plant, were about the only ones caught immediately. Cutting off the terrorists' finances sounded appealing and played to the public's sense that the world of international finance was one great machine in which every moving piece could be found. The reality was entirely different. As Clarke noted at the time, the "CIA could only guess how much [Usama bin Laden] spends, where his money is from, where it is now, how he moves it." For all the work of the virtual station, the intelligence community largely accepted the notion that bin Laden financed terror out of his own pocket, using either his family money or cash flow from his Sudan businesses.

With the issuance of the executive order, work began to figure out how al-Qaeda functioned financially. The effort was led by Rick Newcomb, a career civil servant who ran the Treasury Department's Office of Foreign Asset Controls (OFAC). Newcomb, who has the gentle demeanor of a village parson, had impressed Clarke over their years of working together by showing an unusual ingenuity and doggedness in investigating international crime and drug operations. Newcomb referred to this period as "building the theory of the case."

It took months, but as information was gathered and evaluated, a picture emerged that was far more intricate than anyone had imagined. Bin Laden's years as a "trusted third party," gathering contributions from wealthy Gulf families and establishing ties with Islamic charities, had paid off for him. Streams of money were circulating out of the Gulf states by way of regional banking centers, especially Dubai, and then being transferred electronically or carried by hand to Pakistan and Afghanistan.[2] From there, funds would be wired or carried to terrorist cells around the world. Some Islamic NGOs were acting as conduits to channel money to al-Qaeda operatives. Rich Arab contributors, it became clear, were providing an important chunk of the al-Qaeda budget. Banks both conventional and Islamic—the latter observed the Quranic injunction against charging interest and functioned as a parallel, unregulated system—were laundering funds for the terrorists as were the informal networks of money changers, the hawalas.

What should be done with all this information? For several years, there had been a running debate in the government about the wisdom of using covert operations to disrupt the finances of terrorists, international crime groups, and even Slobodan Milosevic, the Serb president. Using various technologies, accounts could be frozen and rendered useless. There was one obstacle: Secretary of the Treasury Robert Rubin objected. Rubin, a strong player in interagency battles and a man whose success as chairman of the National Economic Council and at Treasury gave him unrivaled influence, argued that the United States was perceived around the world as the guarantor of the international financial system. If it got out that America, the bulwark of global banking, was conducting covert operations against banks, the loss in confidence could be shattering. It was a tough argument to counter. Sandy Berger believed that the only way to win Rubin over was "not to do this in the abstract" but rather to get pinpoint information that would show that any American action would be limited in scope and not cause a market shock if revealed. The information that would meet that standard was not at hand, however, and the discussion died.

As a result, Newcomb, Clarke, and Will Wechsler, the NSC director who handled the international crime and money-laundering portfolio in the Transnational Threats Directorate, charted a course that would overtly target institutions and individuals by approaching foreign governments with damning information. If governments could be shamed into cracking down on one or two banks, the belief was, terrorists would start pulling their funds out of others for fear of detection. That would deny them the means of laundering money and make tracking them easier. Months were spent working to build a body of information that could be exploited, picking financial targets, and planning approaches to other governments.

—

Meanwhile, the State Department began its effort to pry bin Laden out of Afghanistan and deliver him into U.S. hands. Taliban-run Afghanistan had sunk to unbelievable depths of poverty and backwardness and was virtually forgotten by the world. The Taliban wanted two things: to defeat its opponents, particularly the Northern Alliance, with which it had been waging a seesawing battle across much of the ruined country's terrain for years; and international recognition as the sovereign government of Afghanistan. The sign of acceptance the Taliban craved was that its representative to the UN would replace that of the government of Burhanuddin Rabbani, the last recognized leader of Afghanistan before the mid-1990s collapse into anarchy, and thereafter the political leader of the Northern Alliance. The Taliban was, by the standards of American diplomacy, opaque, and intelligence about the group was limited. No one really knew how decision making occurred, whether there were blocs of moderates and radicals within the group, or how powerful the military commanders in the field were, as compared with the mullahs of the shuras in Kandahar and Kabul. No one could say how strong the tie was between Mullah Mohammed Omar and bin Laden, how ideologically aligned they were, or how much the Taliban relied on the Saudi for money, fighting men, and matériel.

With all those imponderables, no obvious common interests, and a U.S. determination not to reward the Afghans' support for terrorism, only one possible diplomatic equation presented itself: if the Taliban handed over bin Laden, the United States would not block its entry into the international community, which had thus far shunned the Pashtun theocrats because of their bent for warfare and barbarity, their appalling treatment of women, their drug trafficking, and their hatred for all non-Islamic culture. Yet it was not clear that the Taliban was ready to make such a deal. The United States needed leverage and had virtually none. Only three countries maintained diplomatic relations with the Islamic Emirate of Afghanistan: Saudi Arabia, the United Arab Emirates, and Pakistan. Through them, it was hoped, the message could be gotten across.[3]

The first salvo came during the September visit of Prince Turki al-

Faisal, Saudi Arabia's longtime intelligence chief, to Kandahar to discuss with Mullah Omar the fate of bin Laden. There was an irony in the trip: Prince Turki had been bin Laden's patron, helping him get his start as a recruiter for the anti-Soviet jihad in the 1980s. Turki had already visited Omar in June and urged him to bring bin Laden under control. Washington assumed that on this trip the message would be more forceful. The prince arrived in Afghanistan and departed quickly. The Saudis gave no summary of his meetings. This reticence, typical of the Saudis, annoyed but did not surprise the White House. Vice President Al Gore was asked to call Crown Prince Abdullah, the country's de facto ruler since King Fahd's incapacitation by a stroke in 1995.

The report that came back surprised the regional and counterterrorism experts. As Turki would later tell *Time* magazine, he had been unyielding: the Taliban, he said, must take care of the bin Laden problem. The Taliban should either hand over al-Qaeda's emir to a country that wanted him for trial—and Saudi Arabia did not—or the Afghans should resolve the problem in a definitive way. Turki seems to have hinted that the Taliban would be rewarded if it did the right thing. Whatever blandishments were set before him, Mullah Omar was unmoved. Turki was infuriated, and a screaming match ensued. Omar, Turki said, was "spouting bin Laden propaganda against the kingdom. He was very, very hysterical, high-pitched, screaming, gesticulating." The intelligence chief departed. In short order, the Saudis expelled Taliban representatives from Riyadh and withdrew their ambassador from Kabul, downgrading their representation in Afghanistan.[4]

The episode was a foretaste of frustrations to come. The United States had no embassy or diplomats in Afghanistan. But as the administration sought to turn up the pressure, State Department officials spoke regularly to the Taliban, either at the UN, where they had an observer, Abdul Hakim Mujahid, or in Islamabad, where the Kandahar regime had an embassy, or in different capitals with Taliban foreign minister Wakil Ahmed Muttawakil and his deputy Mullah Ahmad Jalil. The assistant secretary of state for South Asia, Karl "Rick" Inderfurth, bore the brunt of this thankless task, meeting with Taliban representatives at least twenty times between the August 1998 bombings and the end of the Clinton administration. Often, he was accompanied by the State Department's special coordinator for counterterrorism, Michael Sheehan, who before being appointed to that position had been a Green Beret and a staffer in Clarke's office at the NSC. The tension in the meetings rose quickly. By early February 1999, the message Inderfurth gave to Mullah Jalil in Islamabad was stern: hand bin Laden over to a country where he would face justice, or the United States "would hold the Taliban responsible" for any act of terror emanating from Afghan soil. (In not specifying the United States, Inderfurth left the door open for the Taliban to send bin Laden to a third country from which he would be packed off to America.) The United States would "respond after the fact or preemptively," as it saw fit. This line remained U.S. policy until the destruction of the Taliban in late 2001.

The Taliban's responses showed it to be possibly the most unsophisticated interlocutor U.S. diplomats had ever encountered. Worse, it appeared as though its leaders thought they could pull the wool over the Americans' eyes. Taliban spokesmen cycled through a sequence of different answers to U.S. demands. So transparent were these dodges that it seemed the Taliban was using a color-coded calendar to indicate which excuse to give on a particular day: bin Laden was a guest, and Afghans place the highest priority on hospitality for guests. The United States had never shown the Taliban evidence of bin Laden's involvement. (The United States gave the Taliban the indictment of bin Laden and a raft of unclassified materials indicating the Saudi's role. When that was not enough, a date was made to show them more evidence, but the Afghans did not show.) Bin Laden would be tried by a sharia court of distinguished Islamic scholars. (This was unacceptable to the United States, which neither trusted mullahs chosen by the Taliban nor was prepared to drop its own prosecution.) Yes, bin Laden was becoming a burden, but he had promised he would leave soon. No one knew where bin Laden was. Bin Laden was under Taliban control, did not have access to communications, and could not organize attacks.

Mujahid, the Taliban representative at the UN, hinted on occasion that he understood the Americans but could not get the leadership in Kandahar to see what was at stake. Faxed messages from Mullah Omar to President Clinton drove home that fact. In one, the Emir of the Faithful stated: "We are not crazy neither are we in love with power. We are in service of God and that's why we are strict in our position. If you have any objection to anything we do you should look at our deeds in light of Islamic principles, and if they are in accordance with Islam, you should know that's why we have to follow that path. How could we change it? Please be a little fair." After that end-of-paragraph whine, Omar also noted menacingly that "if you look at the history of a thousand years, anyone who has become an enemy of Islam has gained nothing other than his own destruction." He closed by saying, "So if despite these clarifications you still say that we are to be blamed, and you think that you are right, what can we say except that only God knows who is really to be blamed and may God punish the guilty with storms and earthquakes." The threat of divinely conjured storms and earthquakes—not something American statesmen face often—was easy to deal with compared to another missive, in which Omar suggested that the bin Laden matter was a foolish misunderstanding and that America and Afghanistan had good reason to join in common cause. Afghanistan, he said, is an Islamic nation and the United States is a Christian one. Therefore, we have a common enemy in the hateful Jews, and that should be the true basis for the relationship between the two nations. Asked whether the letter needed to be forwarded to the President, Sandy Berger pursed his lips. "Not necessary."

Exasperating as they were, meetings with the Taliban continued because of the possibility, however remote, that somehow the calculus would change. (Some in the CSG thought it ironic that the further the United States pursued a policy of international isolation of the Taliban, the more it spoke with Taliban representatives.) One recurrent notion was that increased pressure would open a rift within the Taliban, giving "moderates" more power. The focus of this wishful thinking was a leader in the Kabul shura, Mullah Muhammad Rabbani. But these hopes would rise, crest, and then disappear, while the Taliban position remained unchanged.

At interagency meetings, State Department representatives would repeat what everyone knew: the Taliban was a bunch of village clerics with little education and no understanding of international affairs. "Village idiots," the nondiplomats would say under their breath.

The Emiratis and Pakistanis were pressed to make it clear to their friends in Kandahar that bin Laden had to go; the Emiratis, at least, seemed to do the rhetorical part of the job in earnest. From the outset, however, Pakistan was recognized as the key to any serious effort to bring the Taliban around. Islamabad had supported the Taliban since at least 1994, seeing the group as the vehicle for creating a friendly neighbor, which Muslim Pakistan, sandwiched between secular India and Shiite Iran, has desperately wanted for decades. In an Afghanistan dominated by friendly Pashtuns--also one of Pakistan's largest ethnic groups—and dependent on Pakistani support, the country's military planners saw the realization of their dream of "strategic depth," a region where their forces could safely withdraw, regroup, and prepare a counterattack in the event of an overwhelming Indian invasion. To achieve that aim, Pakistan provided the Taliban with everything from weaponry to training to food. Afghanistan had become an essential part of Pakistan's effort to win its five-decade struggle to undermine Indian control of Kashmir. U.S. officials knew that the Pakistani military's intelligence division had turned Afghanistan into its training ground for the radicals and that the militants' training took place in terrorist camps, many of which, if not all, were run by al-Qaeda. The priority of these two objectives—preserving strategic depth and supporting the insurgency in Kashmir—made Pakistan a hard target for U.S. pressure.

A procession of administration officials made America's case to the Pakistanis year after year. Among them were Inderfurth; State Department counterterrorism coordinator Philip Wilcox and his successor, Mike Sheehan; Ambassador Thomas Simons and his successor, William Milam; and Deputy Secretary of State Strobe Talbott, who regularly visited South Asia to work on nuclear weapons issues. All sought Pakistani assistance in pressuring the Taliban to deliver bin Laden. General Anthony Zinni, the commander-in-chief of the Central Command and one of the few American military officers who had maintained relationships with leading Pakistani officers, made his pitch. Clinton himself spoke on several occasions with Prime Minister Nawaz Sharif, who displayed a passionate, almost abject solicitude. "Yes, Mr. President, anything you want. We are with you one hundred percent. Whatever you need," he would declare when Clinton called.

If Sharif genuinely wanted to deliver—and most senior American officials believed the Pakistani leader said yes when he meant no—there were real obstacles that prevented him from doing so. One was his lack of control over the Pakistani military, which sized him up, rightly, as a corrupt and incompetent politician. Another was that the United States had no carrots to offer. Over the course of two decades, America had taken repeated punitive measures against its Cold War ally for a long list of misdeeds, making Pakistan, as one of its ambassadors put it, the "most sanctioned friend." Violations of U.S. strictures regarding nuclear weapons development and the import and export of nuclear material led to overlapping, congressionally imposed sanctions and a cutoff of military-to-military exchanges. Lifting those sanctions required legislative action for which there was never a glimmer of support. (Over the years, the India Caucus in the Congress swelled to include more than one hundred members; Pakistan could usually count only on the lonely voice of Senator Tom Harkin of Iowa.) Most galling to the Pakistanis was that in the 1980s, they had paid $658 million for twenty-eight F-16 jets only to see Congress freeze the deal because of objections to Pakistan's nuclear program. Under the terms of that action, the U.S. kept the planes *and* Islamabad's money. Pakistan became a textbook case of how congressional involvement in foreign policy tied America's hands and left Washington with no means of advancing its policy other than weak appeals for better comportment.

The third and most important reason for Pakistani inaction was that the U.S.–Pakistani diplomatic agenda was woefully overloaded. As time went on, the logjam worsened. Washington was profoundly worried about the deepening nuclear rivalry between Pakistan and India. Tensions over Kashmir were growing because of attacks by militants who slipped into the Indian-controlled region and threatened to provoke a military conflict. The nuclear issue took on crisis proportions when India conducted five underground nuclear explosions on May 11 and May 13, 1998, its first tests since 1974, and Pakistan responded with five of its own on May 28 and May 30. The shock was that much greater because the U.S. intelligence community missed the signs of the approaching Indian tests.

The tests and much international diplomacy brought the two governments back from the extreme positions they had staked out. In February 1999, Prime Minister Vajpayee of India met Sharif in Lahore for a summit but the respite was short. In the spring, a dangerous military confrontation between the countries erupted in the Himalayan region of Kargil, as Pakistani forces made a surprise incursion across the northern section of the Line of Control. Pakistani and Indian forces had faced off along this border for years, but this time, instead of withdrawing their men for the winter, the Pakistani forces had moved into Indian positions. By the time Indian forces returned, the Pakistanis were well dug in, and, despite furious air, artillery, and infantry attacks, could not be dislodged. India's leaders, who quickly realized that the planning for the Kargil adventure had been going on during the Lahore summit, were in no mood for half measures. A wider war threatened. (There is reason to believe that Sharif himself was partly or entirely in the dark about Kargil; his relationship with the military, led by General Pervez Musharraf, was poor and worsening.)

The prospect of two nuclear-armed enemies losing control of their border conflict caused deep alarm in Washington. The United States pressed hard for restraint on both sides, and officials urged the Pakistanis to pull its forces back behind the LOC. Clinton called and wrote Sharif with the same message. As grave as the situation was in Kargil, Clinton used these occasions to insist to Sharif that Pakistan drop its support of the Taliban and help the United States get bin Laden.

Many have interpreted the Kargil incursion as a Pakistani call for help.

After decades of conflict over Kashmir—a half century in which the country's sense of grievance had grown and many of its other ambitions had been disappointed—the move into Kargil was meant to force international mediation of the dispute, something India had always refused. But when the gambit failed and the United States refused to support Islamabad, Sharif saw his position becoming untenable, and the momentum toward all-out war was growing. He pleaded for an opportunity to come to the United States to make his case. Clinton told him not to come unless Pakistan was prepared to pull back behind the LOC. Sharif insisted. He arrived in Washington on July 4 for talks, which were to be held in Blair House. The White House was surprised to find that he had brought his family along; this was taken to mean that if he did not get what he needed, returning home might be too dangerous.

At the briefing before the first session with Sharif, Sandy Berger told Clinton that this could be the most important foreign policy meeting of his presidency. The Pakistanis, intelligence showed, were readying the missiles that carried their nuclear warheads. A nuclear exchange that would cost millions of lives was probably closer than at any time since the Cuban Missile Crisis.

In the meetings, Sharif was desperate to reach agreement on a path that would allow the crisis to be defused without Pakistan losing face entirely. Clinton did not budge on the demand that the troops be withdrawn behind the LOC. After several iterations of the arguments on both sides, Sharif and Clinton withdrew for a one-on-one discussion, with only Bruce Riedel, the NSC senior director for Near East and South Asian affairs, accompanying them—insurance that Sharif would not later lie about the President's remarks. Sharif repeated his need for a solution with cover. Clinton looked at Sharif and asked him whether he knew just how far things had gone: Pakistan's military was preparing its missiles. Sharif was shocked by the assertion, either because he did not know about the missiles or because the American President did. Clinton threatened that if Sharif did not get the troops pulled back, the United States would issue a statement putting all the blame for the conflict on Pakistan. As Bruce

Riedel recently wrote about the meeting, Clinton then lit into the visitor. "He told Sharif that he asked repeatedly for Pakistan's help to bring Usama bin Laden to justice from Afghanistan. Sharif had promised often to do so but had done nothing. Instead the ISI worked with bin Laden and the Taliban to foment terrorism. His draft statement would also mention Pakistan's role in supporting terrorists in Afghanistan and India."[5]

Eventually, Sharif was worn down. He agreed to issue a joint statement calling for the "restoration of the LOC," a cease-fire, and a resumption of the Lahore Process, the Indian-Pakistani effort at improving their relationship. At the Pakistanis' request, the statement also included a sentence affirming Clinton's "personal interest" in the Lahore Process.

Disaster had been avoided. The hidden cost, however, was that U.S. demands regarding al-Qaeda were partially eclipsed. Clinton never ceased to insist that Pakistan change its tack in Afghanistan. But so long as the issue of nuclear confrontation presented itself, the Pakistanis could ignore other American priorities. They did what countries often do in bilateral talks: they focused on their interlocutors' highest concern and made that the pivot of the relationship. Achieving progress on any other issue was nearly impossible; in fact, Sharif may well have been unable to cooperate on the matter of bin Laden, because the little control he had over his military was weakening. After the July 4 meeting, in calls between the leaders and other officials, the professions of solidarity on the terrorism issue continued, but the Pakistanis' frequent message was that they were doing what they could but had little influence over the Taliban. Appeals for Pakistan to cut off fuel shipments to Afghanistan went nowhere.

With Islamabad providing little cooperation, it seemed that matters could hardly get worse. Yet they did, in October 1999, when Nawaz Sharif tried to fire his army chief of staff, Pervez Musharraf. (Actually, it was more an attempt to exile him: Sharif ordered that Musharraf's plane, then returning from Sri Lanka, not be allowed to land.) The military rebelled, deposing Sharif and jailing him.

The coup was an unwelcome shock for Washington. There was no fondness for Sharif or his feckless government, and no illusion that democracy had been working in Pakistan before Musharraf took over, but the general was a virtual unknown to American policy makers. His record, moreover, had one transfixing blot: he was the architect of Kargil. "This is an impetuous man" was the verdict of one senior American official at the time, expressing the prevalent feeling. Diplomatic emissaries continued to carry the message that Islamabad needed to put pressure on the Taliban, but Musharraf was consolidating his hold on the government. America's problems were not his top priority.

—

From the first days after the August 20, 1998, strikes, Sandy Berger, Secretary of State Madeleine Albright, and several other Principals recognized that there was no banking on a diplomatic solution involving the Taliban. The United States, they believed, had to be prepared to use force again, no matter how relentless the criticisms over al-Shifa had been. The White House ordered Navy vessels armed with cruise missiles to remain on station in the Arabian Sea, ready to fire if credible intelligence arrived concerning bin Laden's whereabouts. The military did not like the mission, which disrupted scheduled cruises and training and left the ships out in the middle of nowhere, hovering in the "basket," the area from which the missiles could reach their targets. When surface ships were briefly deployed there, Pakistani patrol boats motored out to meet them, relaying news of their presence to Islamabad, which likely passed it straight to the Taliban. For the remainder of the Clinton administration, *Los Angeles*-class attack submarines drew patrol duty off the Pakistani coast.

—

Before it is fired, a Block III Tomahawk cruise missile needs to spin its gyroscopes and set its guidance system. Over the next fifteen months, the National Security Council geared up for an attack on bin Laden three times, and missiles were actually spun twice. Clinton was entirely ready to pull the trigger on the man responsible for the embassy bombings.

The first time, the intelligence community received word about an elaborate camp pitched in the desert, replete with elegant tents, a small fleet of Land Cruisers, and a plane parked nearby. The collective feeling was *Bingo!* It had to be bin Laden. Among the handful of people who knew about the intelligence, there was the excitement of an approaching moment of truth. But one more box had to be checked. A second confirmation was required to be certain about who owned the camp. After al-Shifa, no one could face a *real* miss. The order to spin the missiles was held, while the CIA tried frantically to find out more about the camp. Eventually, word came back: the camp belonged not to bin Laden but to a group of wealthy Emiratis who had flown to Afghanistan for a hunting trip, a beloved pastime of Gulf Arabs. The subs were told to stand down. An air of jittery disbelief settled on the NSC. America's relationship with the Emiratis was the best it had in the Gulf, and the administration had devotedly cultivated Sheikh Zayed bin Sultan al-Nuhayyan, the UAE's president and the leader of the country's royal clans. At the moment the Tomahawks were being readied, the United States was in the final stages of negotiations to sell eighty Block 60 F-16s, America's most sophisticated export fighter jets.

The next time the missiles were spun, information had arrived that put bin Laden in one of his compounds in an eastern Afghan city. Again, his presence could not be confirmed, nor was there any way to know how long he would remain there: since the 1998 missile attacks bin Laden had rarely spent more than a night in any one place. After spinning, the Tomahawks required several hours to reach their destination, a long delay if you wanted to hit someone who moved so often. There was one more complication: the compound was near buildings that, at any given time, were likely to be filled with people. Briefing the Principals on the operation, Defense Secretary William Cohen estimated that "hundreds would die." The issue of civilian casualties was not the decisive one in this or any other deliberation on the use of force against bin Laden. But without greater certainty that bin Laden would be hit, collateral damage inevitably became a larger concern. The inability to get good intelligence on bin Laden's movements became a source of unremitting frustration.

—

The Counterterrorist Center was working through its people in the Directorate of Operations, the CIA's actual spies, to develop new sources, and some were promising. But they were chronically unable to provide independent confirmation that bin Laden would be in a particular place at a particular time. In Principals Committee meetings and the more frequent "Small Group" gatherings Sandy Berger held in his office, which brought together only the top representatives of State, Defense, the CIA, and the NSC to explore new options for combating al-Qaeda, George Tenet insisted that one "thread" was not enough. Much as everyone in the room wanted to do something, the realities could not be ignored: the last missile strike had caused an eruption of anti-American demonstrations in Pakistan, and the mood in that country and in other Muslim nations was angry. Another strike would undoubtedly cause a powerful backlash. Getting bin Laden would have made it worthwhile, but there was no room for trial and error.

The intelligence community was coming face-to-face with a set of unprecedented challenges. First, its strength, like every other spy agency's, was in "collecting" against other governments—institutions that have buildings and vehicles, use standard landline telephones and faxes, and, most important, employ large numbers of ordinary people. Al-Qaeda used an ever-growing variety of communications, including untraceable, disposable cell phones and frequent face-to-face contact. The group had little fixed infrastructure and nowhere a spy could place a recording device. In tracking its worldwide activities, signals intelligence—communications intercepts—played an indispensable part, but the limitations imposed by not knowing how much else was *not* being heard was unsettling.

The CIA understood from early on that human intelligence—information provided by an informer—was vital, especially in view of that lack of infrastructure. Yet penetrating a religiously motivated terrorist group that practices a high level of compartmentalization, limiting information to the smallest possible group of those with a "need to know," was nothing like the kind of work the CIA was accustomed to. For decades, the Agency had acquired spies using the customary tools of the trade: money, ideological disaffection, and the exploitation of personal problems, such as professional frustration. Al-Qaeda operatives were not going to show up at diplomatic receptions, and they were likely to be extraordinarily wary of outsiders. They would seldom be tempted by money—it is not something those focused on the hereafter think about much—and many had undergone considerable hardship that resulted at least partly from their shared hatred of America. During John Deutch's tenure, the CIA had instituted rules requiring more scrutiny of "unsavory sources"—individuals who had committed serious criminal acts and human rights abuses—before they could be hired as assets. The experience of having Latin American death squad members on the U.S. payroll had led the Agency to insist that the intelligence value of such individuals be weighed carefully. But terrorism by now was at the very top of the Agency's collection priorities, so those rules were waived for sources who could provide "actionable" intelligence. As far as the White House knew, no terrorism-related source had been rejected because of an unsavory background. Still, there was not much joy at Langley. As Israeli intelligence has found in dealing with the operatives of Hamas and the Palestinian Islamic Jihad, getting someone inside a religiously driven group was an all but impossible task.

—

That a military strategy centered on targeting bin Laden with cruise missiles was problematic came as no surprise, especially after August 20. After the embassy bombings, Sandy Berger had ordered up a larger set of targets for use in case of another attack. As early as November 1998, the White House began asking the Pentagon for more options. Dick Clarke argued for bombing a broad range of sites that would include terrorist camps and Taliban facilities. But when intelligence specialists and the military began looking for suitable Taliban targets, they found not much to whet the appetite. Twenty years of warfare had left Afghanistan with little worth bombing. The frequent, morbid refrain in these discussions, inverting General Curtis LeMay's famous remark, was that an attack would bomb Afghanistan *up* to the Stone Age. Berger was leery of a major bombing campaign; he believed that the odds of getting bin Laden were low and that a failure would make the United States look impotent and its target invincible. There was another problem: in 1998–1999, the United States conducted a war in Kosovo and a sustained bombing campaign in Iraq called Operation Desert Fox. Several policy makers, especially from the State Department, where the foreign criticism of American actions was perceived most acutely, argued that the United States was increasingly seen as the world's mad bomber. Berger was prepared to act when the intelligence was solid, no matter how many theaters America was fighting in. But the background noise of the fighting in Europe and the Persian Gulf could not be ignored.

—

Along with the military, diplomatic, and economic means of dealing with al-Qaeda, there was one other line of attack: intelligence operations. The Antiterrorism and Effective Death Penalty Act of 1996 underscores that "the President should use all necessary means, including covert action and military force, to disrupt, dismantle and destroy international infrastructure used by international terrorists, including overseas training facilities and safe havens." In a 2002 speech, Deputy CIA Director for Operations Jim Pavitt declared that he had people "on the ground in Afghanistan itself . . . well before September eleventh." Any number of newspaper stories have been published regarding what these operatives were doing to disrupt al-Qaeda operations, and their accounts include, as *The Washington Post* put it, working with "surrogate forces in Pakistan, Uzbekistan and among tribal militias inside Afghanistan, with the common purpose of capturing or killing bin Laden."[6] Since the CIA was created, no more than eighteen covert operations have ever been publicly and officially disclosed. A substantive discussion of what, if anything, was going on in Afghanistan will have to await a decision at the highest level of government.

But it is worth noting that, as a matter of law, the actual constraints on using force against terrorists are less than ironclad. The United States has had a ban on assassination since President Ford signed an executive order to that effect in 1976, but as Paul Pillar, a CIA official, has written, "This does not imply an absolute and permanent ban on assassination, however, since whatever is barred by executive order can, of course, be changed or suspended if the president of the day were to sign a new piece of paper—in this case, a covert action finding, or a memorandum of notification if there were an existing relevant finding."[7]

As time went on, the NSC counterterrorism officials wondered why the CIA did not produce—why no new assets were cultivated and why the Agency's paramilitary forces were never even brought into the discussion. (Few knew about the secret paramilitaries—Leon Fuerth, Vice President Gore's national security adviser and a member of the Principals Committee, recalls that they were never mentioned in meetings or briefings; he did not learn of their existence until they appeared in the fighting in Afghanistan in 2001.) Among those outside the CIA who knew about them, they had a reputation as out-of-shape former members of the military's Special Operations Command, and the understanding in the White House was that the Agency did not have great confidence in them. Their performance in Afghanistan suggests that this was not the case.

As for whether the CIA was using all the tools at its disposal to apprehend bin Laden, only its top officials know the answer. To those who dealt with the Agency in 1998–1999, CTC appeared hardworking and committed. Probably nowhere in the government do stress levels rise higher than at the White House, because everyone there knows that virtually all blame eventually finds its way to 1600 Pennsylvania Avenue. So, in the tense months after August 1998, the NSC counterterrorism officials were in touch with their Agency colleagues many times every day, in addition to the regular threat meetings. Whenever a series of disturbing intelligence reports were received, snap meetings were held in the Situation Room, and on plenty of occasions White House officials drove to Langley to discuss issues ranging from terrorist finances to intelligence about weapons of mass destruction. The intelligence world, however, has fences within fences and rooms within rooms that only the most senior White House policy makers may enter; the secrecy is usually for good reasons pertaining to operational security and the protection of sources. Of the areas that outsiders are barred from entering, none is better sealed than the Directorate of Operations' handling of its human assets and the spending of its money. The White House told George Tenet on several occasions that covert operations against al-Qaeda should not be limited because of resources. The CIA would never get everything in the world it wanted—no agency does—but for stopping bin Laden, there would be no stinting. Jack Lew, who was the director of the Office of Management and Budget in the late 1990s, remembers that "the numbers [for covert action] were always small compared to technology and U.S. employee costs," and the message to the Agency was clear: "Money was not the constraint." Whether the message was understood—whether, in fact, the CIA was distributing sufficient cash to enough people—was not something NSC directors or senior directors could ascertain. There is a saying bureaucrats use when the White House becomes too intrusive or inquisitive: "Don't get in our knickers." This was a classic "don't get in our knickers" situation. Whether the Directorate of Operations was making full use of the resources on offer is impossible to say. Some close to the issue today are skeptical.

———

By mid-1999, the understanding in the White House of al-Qaeda was deepening. Something that had not been clear at first was that the movement's strategy embraced not only terror but also territorial conquest. Beyond Afghanistan itself—where, it was becoming evident, bin Laden's organization was backing the Taliban with cash and loaned detachments of fighters—the group also supported insurrections in Central Asia and the Caucasus. Fighters from the Islamic Movement of

Uzbekistan, who had trained in al-Qaeda camps in Afghanistan, skir-
mished in Uzbekistan with troops belonging to the government of President Islam Karimov. On a single day in February, the conflict turned more
ominous when the IMU set off six car bombs, including one that just
missed Karimov himself. That summer, Islamists, including some from
the bin Laden orbit, mounted a surprise rebellion in the Russian region of
Dagestan and called for the creation there of an Islamic republic. When
the Russians had trouble quelling the uprising, the fighting spread to
Chechnya, igniting another round of military action in that republic's
long-running tragedy. Regional experts were taken aback by the events,
because they believed that the Chechens themselves were not eager to
renew hostilities with Russia, but the cycle of attack and reprisal drew
both sides in. The Russians responded with a massive bombing campaign and, eventually, more ground forces. American revulsion at another
wave of Russian brutality in the region caused a chill in relations between
the two countries. The episode provided a lesson in how the Islamist
forces could wreak havoc not only in their immediate surroundings but
also in relations between former Cold War antagonists who were trying to
arrive at a better modus vivendi.

—

At the same time, several elements of Washington's strategy to stop
al-Qaeda were in place and showing progress. Intelligence operations
outside of Afghanistan continued to roll up terrorist cells on several
continents. The $1.1 billion worldwide upgrade of security at embassies
was well under way. Efforts to cut off bin Laden's finances were also pro-
gressing. Having mapped important nodes in the financial network, Rick
Newcomb, Will Wechsler, and others on their interagency team flew to
the Persian Gulf in June to meet with Finance Ministry, intelligence, and
law-enforcement officials in Saudi Arabia and the UAE. The purpose of
the trip was to put the two governments on notice that assistance was
needed and that U.S. pressure to deal effectively with those who fund terrorism would grow. Despite all the intelligence cooperation the United

States was getting, the reception to the delegation's inquiries into financial matters alternated between cool and uncomprehending. The Saudis were particularly recalcitrant. The first conversation the team had with Saudi officials was to let them know what Rick Newcomb's OFAC could do—how it could designate noncooperative entities as being themselves supporters of terrorism. Another meeting made clear that while the message might be getting through, Saudi cooperation was not going to be readily forthcoming. Saudi Interior Ministry officials and bank regulators met Newcomb's team for what the Americans were told was an unprecedented joint gathering—the two Saudi groups never worked together. When the Americans inquired about the Maktab al-Khidmat, they were routinely told that no one had ever heard of it. Everyone the U.S. team met with greeted them with assurances of assistance in the war against terror. But when the conversation got going, the Arab officials would quickly point out that Hamas was a perfectly legitimate organization and nothing would be done to affect its finances. Similarly, they argued, no one should expect that Muslims would stop contributing to those fighting in, for example, Chechnya. The argument that donations for the mujahidin in Chechnya were also funding the terrorists in Afghanistan did not register. The team's initial sense that cutting off al-Qaeda's finances was going to be a challenge was amply confirmed: Saudi Arabia and the UAE had virtually no financial regulatory system and there was no oversight of charities. Even what they thought would have been the clearest of all issues was murky. "In Saudi, the most interesting discussion was a historical one," Wechsler recalls. "It was about the amount of money [Usama bin Laden] got from his parents. They said there was a 'legal' break with the family, but this wasn't Anglo-Saxon law and there were no documents." In other words, the size of bin Laden's inheritance was unknown, and subsequent infusions of family money could not be ruled out. When the discussion turned to other Saudis who might be involved in financing al-Qaeda, says Wechsler, "the more you talked about anyone who had a lot of money, the more freaked out they got."

—

In July 1999, the United States also ratcheted up the pressure on the Taliban. On July 4—the same day he met with Nawaz Sharif—Clinton issued an executive order placing unilateral economic sanctions on the Kandahar regime, freezing its assets, and prohibiting commercial exchange with the Taliban or any entity in the area it controlled. U.S. trade with Afghanistan was almost nonexistent, so the impact was largely symbolic. (The United States imported insignificant amounts of dried fruit and rugs, and the Afghans were trying to buy a cellular-phone system from an American company.) The sanctions did put another obstacle between the Taliban and Afghanistan's gold reserves, which were worth more than $220 million and remained on deposit with the Federal Reserve, no claim by any of the rival Afghan groups having been recognized as valid. When that did not move the Taliban to be more cooperative, the administration issued further sanctions against Ariana, Afghanistan's national airline, for transporting terrorists, their matériel, and their funds. Ariana kept money in a Citibank branch in India, so those accounts were frozen. The impact was magnified when the administration convinced airports around the world that allowing Ariana to land would have serious consequences for them, including possibly designation as a terrorist entity. That inflicted pain on the Taliban because Ariana was its only connection to the Gulf, where Afghan finances were centered and Afghan narcotics—one of the mullahs' few sources of revenue— were shipped. In October, the United States scored a harder blow when the UN Security Council unanimously adopted sanctions identical to those America had in place. The ease with which Resolution 1267 passed astonished the U.S. diplomats who worked on it. The Security Council had been stuck in gridlock for many months, especially on sanctions issues, and such broad agreement from the Russians, the Chinese, and the rest of the Council was a rare, happy surprise. Humanitarian assistance and food were exempted, as they had been under the American sanctions. The Taliban and its supporters quickly signaled their appreciation of the Council's action: on November 12, 1999, when the sanctions went into effect, militants fired rocket-propelled grenades at the U.S. embassy and a UN building in Islamabad. In Afghanistan, protesters overran several UN facilities, burning one office to the ground. Still, the hermit theocracy showed no sign of showing its guest the door.

RESISTANCE

There are few more durable illusions in American life than the omnipotent presidency. For fear of appearing weak, incumbents rarely draw attention to the minimal powers accorded them by the Constitution and established practices of American government. Their critics in Congress and the public avoid mentioning this inconvenient fact because letting the executive off the hook never serves their purposes. Yet anyone who has worked in the White House knows that the office has remarkably little real power, not only when it comes to dealing with Congress and the judiciary but also in running the vast, unwieldy contraption that is the executive branch. A President relies on the loyalty of his appointees in the agencies to overcome the inertia and ingrained predilections of civil servants and the uniform military. That loyalty is quickly tempered: when the political appointee recognizes that only his new agency can make him look good, he cultivates the powers within it even as he tries to hew to the White House line. Hence, when the White House decides that a substantial reordering of policy priorities is necessary, it quickly finds itself confronted with the tremendous task of convincing institutions as large as the world's largest corporations—or, in the case of the Department of Defense, larger—that *their* priorities must change. As one government official put it, "A Presidential Decision Directive is the starting point for negotiations between agencies and the White House."

Even more constrained is the ability of a President or his immediate staff—which constitutes an infinitesimal fraction of the executive branch workforce—to reach down into the workings of the agencies and change attitudes and institutional culture, especially with respect to issues that do not appear on television every night. Only so much crockery can be broken before there is a news story, an embarrassment, and a public brouhaha no one wanted. Firing an official can be done only on exceptional occasions, and even then the dismissal itself may be a long-lived news item, distracting from work that needs to be done. The best chance a President has to change how government works comes when the public spotlight suddenly turns on a newly discovered problem, and change is demanded. That gives the political leadership a window of opportunity. Otherwise, given the tools of leadership—cajolery, empty threats, and the budget—it is surprising that Presidents get anything done at all.

The spotlight did not linger long on the embassy bombings, so reordering government priorities was a struggle. Some agencies and some policy makers got it. Others did not. Bill Clinton did, and in what was left of his presidency, he never lost sight of it. During the NATO Fiftieth Anniversary Summit in Washington in April 1999, he took time out from the pageantry to collar a visiting head of state from one of NATO's "Partners for Peace"—mostly countries that had close military ties to the United States—to pressure him to turn over al-Qaeda materials seized in a raid in that country. Those around Clinton saw to it that counterterrorism issues got to the President quickly. Clinton was always ready to call or write various heads of state, some of whom he hated listening to as they nattered on ceaselessly about pet concerns. At the State Department, Michael Sheehan and Under Secretary Thomas Pickering understood the magnitude of the threat, and at the CIA, George Tenet recognized the danger.

But others in the government only glimpsed the problem. Many thought the loss of an occasional embassy was the price of world leadership; the United States should "button up" where it could, improve security in a reasonable way, and leave it at that. Up to a point, the idea has merit—there are costs to America's role as superpower—but it is essential to prevent as many attacks as possible to preserve the nation's credibility and deterrence. But most of those who argued that the country needed to accept this risk did not fully recognize that a new, far

more lethal kind of attack now threatened. Others never grasped the
dimensions of the threat at all and resisted when the White House demanded action.

Much of the State Department had a hard time wrapping its mind
around the issue. To follow through on the White House order that
the department prepare vaccines, medication, and protective equipment for chemical or biological attacks on embassies where there was
thought to be a persistent threat, the NSC scheduled a series of meeting with State representatives. The meetings were held, the issue was
discussed, nothing moved. The program was shifted from bureau to
bureau—from Diplomatic Security to Political-Military Affairs—and from
office director to office director. Each time, the discussions had to start all
over again. Still nothing happened. The issue was brought up at Principals meetings, to no effect. Eventually, when the backlog of other issues
simply grew too large, the NSC relented. Odd as it may seem, a presidential phone call to convince the State Department to protect its own people
was something no one could seriously contemplate.

More astounding still was the department's handling of embassy construction. As if the evidence on the ground in East Africa was not enough
to spur improved construction, the revelation that Ambassador Prudence
Bushnell had complained about the Nairobi embassy security before the
bombing, and the scathing remarks in the report by Admiral William
Crowe's Accountability Review Board, which investigated the East Africa
bombings, threw an unforgiving light on the department's treatment of
safety concerns. The NSC, Jack Lew of the OMB, and White House
Chief of Staff John Podesta agreed that a major new building program was
a necessity. During the winter of 1998–1999, NSC officials began working with State's Foreign Buildings Office to set priorities for new construction, basing them on the condition of buildings and on threat
assessments for individual countries. (Although the threat was global,
limited resources required that priorities be set according to the severity
of the danger.) OMB's officials are known in the government as "the
abominable no men" for their relentless refusal of requests for money,

but they more than doubled the sum normally allotted for embassy construction in the "passback," their revision of State's planned budget. This brought the construction budget to over $600 million. OMB and the White House legislative affairs officials also agreed to propose a multibillion-dollar five-year program, separate from the regular State appropriation, so planners could think beyond the one-year horizon that made their job well-nigh impossible. When the State Department submitted its final revised budget request, however, all but a token amount—less than $50 million—of the construction money was gone. Beleaguered by years of cuts in the department's budget, the "seventh floor," home to State's top officials, had reallocated the money. Secretary of State Madeleine Albright was reported to have said that there was no sense in defending embassies that had no money to do anything. Only after a meeting in which Lew, a calm man with a lifetime in government, blew up at an undersecretary and an assistant secretary of state were the figures readjusted upward.

Getting the State Department to give in on a money issue—an area in which the White House had real leverage—was one thing. Persuading it to push terrorism far up its priority list was another. The department has an assistant secretary–level coordinator for counterterrorism who, by law, reports directly to the secretary of state. In reality, the counterterrorism bureau has far less pull than the large regional bureaus. Just how little it has became clear in the fall of 1999, when Michael Sheehan tried to take on the issue of Islamic NGOs and their support for terrorism. Sheehan's office wrote a long, forceful cable instructing ambassadors in a number of problem countries to approach their host governments and alert them to the matter. The cable acknowledged that some NGOs played an important role in supporting the development of democracy and civil society, especially in the Middle East and the Islamic states of the former Soviet Union, but, it pointed out, some did not. The message told the ambassadors to press the host governments to ensure genuine oversight of the NGOs.

Despite its acknowledgment of the beneficial work of some Islamic NGOs, the cable still went too far for State's regional bureaus, which demanded that it be killed. Their concerns were not frivolous: many of the countries in question are run by authoritarian regimes that are evolving in the wrong direction. Some NGOs provided the sole source of support for democratization and the only voices of opposition, even if others were up to no good. Compromises were offered, and the counterterrorism officials in State and the White House fought hard to get the cable sent. But after weeks of battle, the regional bureaus won. The cable was spiked.

Dealing with the Pentagon posed a different set of problems. Increasingly skeptical about the use of airpower, the White House began asking for more expansive military options in late 1998. The cruise missiles had the obvious advantage of keeping U.S. troops out of harm's way. But they delivered limited punch, and it took roughly six hours to get a presidential authorization to fire, then program the missiles, spin their gyroscopes, and finally fly them to the target, time in which bin Laden might depart— and all that assumed that the intelligence was reliable in the first place. Clinton wanted to hear about "boots on the ground," plans that put U.S. soldiers in Afghanistan to get the Saudi terrorist. A request for options was made to the Pentagon.

In response, General Hugh Shelton, chairman of the Joint Chiefs, briefed a Small Group meeting in Berger's office overlooking the White House front lawn. The presentation was brisk and comprehensive. Shelton rattled off the factors determining what the military would require to do the job. There was no reliable information about bin Laden's whereabouts at any given time. There was a great deal of uncertainty about the environment that the troops would be entering. There was no good staging area in the region. Closing off a large area would require tens of thousands of troops, and that, in turn, meant lots of "lift"—large transport planes—and therefore a sizable number of air-refueling tankers. Search-and-rescue units would also be required. The list went on. One participant remembered the presentation as the Pentagon's "usual two-division, $2 billion option." Another called it "the canonical option."

It was not what the assembled had hoped for. Hugh Shelton was a former commander-in-chief of U.S. Special Operations Command

(CINCSOC), the first ever to become chairman of the Joint Chiefs. Berger's group had hoped he would want to show what America's special operations forces could do. Instead, Sandy Berger felt he was having déjà vu, reliving the discussions from 1993–1995 about intervening in Bosnia, which the military opposed. This time, Berger felt, the Chiefs had more justification for their position, though he was not happy about where they came out. The absence of a staging area made operating in Afghanistan genuinely difficult. "They didn't want to do it. They weren't crazy. There was just no enthusiasm and creativity. In this case, risk aversion and logic converged."

The episode left a bad taste. The civilian leaders—except Secretary of Defense Bill Cohen, who backed up his chairman—felt that the Pentagon was blowing them off when they badly needed a solution. Shelton was annoyed because he felt that the administration's political leadership was looking to the military to solve a problem of diplomacy and intelligence; unrealistic expectations were being heaped on the uniforms. "It was frustrating for us, and frustrating for everyone. We never had the intel. We knew this would be mistaken for resistance and that drove us up the wall. We'd love to get that frigging guy." Tom Pickering, a man who had held seven ambassadorial posts en route to becoming the most distinguished diplomat of his era and had spent a lifetime working with the military, left the meeting thinking that he had been served "a standard military position—give us forty-eight months and five divisions. These were gold-plated arguments." The Pentagon was reluctant, Pickering thought, "because they didn't see CT [counterterrorism] as their mission. That was a matter of police, FBI, intelligence and diplomacy. . . . They [the military] thought, perhaps with some justification, that the NSC and State wanted to correct every problem with them as cannon fodder."

Within the Pentagon, there was less unanimity about conducting a military mission than Shelton's briefing suggested. Some experienced officers who worked for the Joint Staff (which serves the Chiefs) believed that a mission was both feasible and necessary, though not without risks.

They understood that a "large package," involving a major deployment, was a political nonstarter and would forfeit the element of surprise. They sketched out options that would have been small, stealthy, and lethal and could have been staged from a U.S. base in the region. Shelton was said to believe that the idea had merit, but he insisted on including a "force protection package," which would significantly increase the number of troops involved, but not to the point that the mission would be impractical. But the immovable roadblock came when the notion was put to the Central Command, in which Pakistan falls. Commander-in-Chief Anthony Zinni made numerous objections to the proposal, arguing that an attack on Afghanistan would rock the region, especially Pakistan. The CINCs are enormously powerful—*The Washington Post* has called them "proconsuls"—and under the current organization, they have something akin to bureaucratic sovereignty over their territory. On a closely held issue like this, about which there could be little politicking, it would be difficult for Shelton to turn Zinni around. As a result, the trial balloon sank fast. As was his practice on sensitive matters, Shelton had canvassed only a small number of senior commanders about the options, but no formal planning for a mission to capture the al-Qaeda leadership was carried out—whatever the Principals may have thought.

> *The most effective weapon against crime is cooperation . . . the efforts of all law enforcement agencies with the support and understanding of the American people.*
>
> —J. EDGAR HOOVER (inscription on the J. Edgar Hoover memorial wall courtyard, the J. Edgar Hoover FBI building)

Of the core agencies in the counterterrorism community, the one least troubled by the rise of al-Qaeda was the FBI. The Bureau did one thing very well: investigate crimes that had been committed. After August 7, the FBI was in its element, throwing itself into the investigation of the attacks. Scores of agents were flown to Nairobi and Dar es Salaam and, with the leads provided by Odeh and al-Owhali, the work progressed rapidly. The FBI excels at solving major crimes; it hurtles forward, an unstoppable juggernaut.

The problem was that the Bureau moved only in one direction. There seems to have been no reflection on the fact that Islamist terrorists had bombed American sites on two continents in five years and were showing an unprecedented level of skill, or on the possibility that all these conspiracies might be linked. There was little or no analysis of the phenomenon, and, at least in the Bureau's headquarters, no effort to see the big picture. "We should have gone through every single fricking piece of information and really reconstructed every bit of it, including the court stuff, the intelligence, all of it," says Bob Blitzer who, as one of the Bureau's top counterterrorism officials, pushed for such an effort until he retired in 1998. "I don't think that's ever been done."

On paper at least, the FBI acknowledged its responsibility for tracking and surveilling terrorists in the United States and preventing terrorist acts. This was spelled out in many documents, including Presidential Decision Directives. And in some areas, such as dealing with right-wing extremists after the Oklahoma City bombing, the Bureau took the mission seriously. That was not the case with Islamist terror. Deeply rooted habits came into play, leading the FBI to favor crime solving and not terrorism prevention. Counterterrorism was largely new to the Bureau in the 1990s. It was housed in the National Security Division, which had historically been a small operation compared to the Criminal Division, the dominant force within the institution. An essential part of counterterrorism work involves intelligence gathering, but for a generation of special agents in charge, the barons of the FBI, this was unattractive work: intelligence investigations do not contribute to the statistics—crimes solved, prosecutions generated—that the SACs view as a key component of their individual records. The Bureau was not about this kind of tedious work; it was about what the SACs knew: putting criminals in jail. "It's a culture of guys who are unwilling to change from standard police work to sophisticated counterterrorism and counterintelligence work," explains Blitzer. Those cases "are hard and can ruin your career because of potential fuckups in times of great stress." Agents also do not recognize that terrorism has implications beyond those of, for example, Mob crimes. Matthew Levitt, a leading expert on Hamas who was a terrorism analyst at the FBI until early 2002, says that agents and the institution's leadership "don't understand that they are part of the national security apparatus. To them, a criminal is a criminal, a case is a case. Terrorism is just another case." The FBI does not think retrospectively or project over the horizon. "They don't understand intelligence, and they don't appreciate analysis."

In court records and investigative materials, the FBI was sitting on a trove of information, some of it richer than what the CIA was gathering abroad; the interest of American-based Islamists in Abdullah Azzam is one example. Connections between Ramzi Yousef and the Afghanistan network are another. A third involves the long-standing interest of jihadists in airplanes, and here the record is long. In 1995, the FBI interviewed Abdul Hakim Murad, an accomplice of Ramzi Yousef's in the Bojinka conspiracy. Murad volunteered that he had attended *four* American flight schools, and he told police in the Philippines that a variant of the plot involved flying a plane on a suicide mission into CIA headquarters. It is unclear exactly when the FBI first interviewed Essam al-Ridi and L'Houssaine Kherchtou. Since their testimony dealt largely with the general al-Qaeda conspiracy against the United States—the information that was fed into the June 1998 indictment—it seems likely that the FBI already had a good deal of material about bin Laden's interest in airplanes. Kherchtou discussed how after extensive training in other skills, al-Qaeda wanted him to go to flight school in Nairobi and eventually become bin Laden's pilot. Al-Ridi recounted the story of the plane that bin Laden had him buy and the various missions he undertook for the group. He also mentioned that he had trained and taught at the Ed Boardman Aviation School in Texas. His copilot on the ill-fated flight in Khartoum, in which bin Laden's plane crashed into a sand pile when its brakes failed, was a man named Ihab Ali, who, it was stipulated in the trial, trained at the Airman Flight School in Norman, Oklahoma. In other words, FBI agents had followed up on Ihab Ali and checked with the flight school to confirm that he had attended it. At a minimum, this was a significant demonstration of interest by al-Qaeda in flying and American aviation schools, but the FBI did not pursue the issue further.

The problem was not just that the FBI moved in only one direction; it was that no one from the outside could steer it any other way. Stubborn independence has been a hallmark of the Bureau since J. Edgar Hoover's early days. In the years since Watergate, when the Nixon White House misused the FBI for political ends, that independence has been strengthened by the ingrained suspicion that a close relationship with the nation's political leadership would inevitably taint the Bureau. In the 1990s, this aversion, and the personal inclinations of its leaders, led the Bureau to become extraordinarily unresponsive to the concerns of the White House and, in fact, the entire executive branch. Indeed, the FBI became virtually its own independent branch of the government. It worked hard to please those in Congress, who appropriated its funds, but it seldom did the same for anyone else.

The Bureau's independence and unresponsiveness were reinforced by Louis Freeh. When Freeh was appointed FBI director in 1993 by Bill Clinton, he had a reputation for being fiercely honest and uncompromising, as straight an arrow as America produced. He had been an FBI agent, a federal prosecutor, and a federal district court judge. He had never managed anything remotely like the twenty-thousand-employee Bureau, and that lack of experience became an enduring problem. For most of its history, the FBI had been a highly centralized organization. Since the 1980s, however, power had shifted to the field offices, and the FBI evolved into an anarchic patchwork of fiefdoms. The field offices enjoyed remarkable latitude to set their own priorities and manage their own affairs. Under Freeh, according to Bureau veterans, this tendency continued and accelerated. Freeh was the only person at headquarters to whom the field offices responded. "Fifty-six FBIs and fifty-six little FBI directors" was a complaint frequently heard among those who saw the SACs willfully going their own way, and barely working with one another. Within the Bureau, as Matthew Levitt describes it, "New York doesn't talk to Headquarters. Headquarters doesn't talk to itself. Operations doesn't talk to the analysts. Field offices don't talk to each other." From the inside, the FBI was a disorganized jumble of competing and unruly power centers; from the outside, it was a surly colossus.

—

In the 1990s, an additional factor contributed to the overall problem of dealing with the Bureau: Louis Freeh's animus toward the White House. Throughout Freeh's tenure, White House officials found that the FBI director did not feel that the same rules applied to him as to other top government officials: he refused, for example, to come to meetings on the weekend and, to demonstrate his independence of the nation's political leaders, he turned in his White House pass, saying that he would go there only as a visitor. (The gesture was a strange and hollow one; the Secret Service Uniform Division personnel who guard the White House identify all senior officials by sight and do not require badges.) The relationship between the director and 1600 Pennsylvania Avenue took on the hue of personal antipathy early on. Most within the White House dated the hostility to Clinton's first term, when the special investigation into Whitewater began expanding to include Filegate, Travelgate, and the billing practices at Hillary Clinton's Little Rock law firm. Freeh himself dated much of his dissatisfaction to the White House's handling of the Khobar Towers bombing. He took a passionate interest in the case, and within the Bureau there was admiration for his dedication and some bemusement at the director who had become the case agent-in-chief. The investigation stalled quickly, because the Saudis refused to allow the FBI access to suspects. In mid-1997, the administration was pursuing the Khobar investigation and sending quiet, positive signals to the new, reformist government of Mohammad Khatami in Iran. Reporter Elsa Walsh, with whom Freeh had cooperated for a year, wrote in *The New Yorker:* "Freeh believed that the Clinton Administration had compromised itself in an unforgivable way by seeming to waver in its commitment to resolving the bombing case."[8] The administration believed that America had multiple interests in dealing with Iran, and that the emergence of a moderate government under Khatami—uncertain as that might appear—probably offered the best bet for reducing tensions between the countries and ultimately securing convictions in the case. Freeh, a man with no experience in international affairs and no mandate in that realm, disagreed. His mistrust of the White House grew so strong that it seems to have blinded him and made him susceptible to manipulation.

During this period, Sandy Berger and his senior Middle East aides met repeatedly with Bandar bin Sultan, the Saudi ambassador, to press FBI requests for cooperation. The Saudi continually played to the Americans' belief that the Iranians were behind the bombing but refused to offer assistance—access to suspects the Saudis had apprehended, and investigative materials—without getting a veto over the U.S. response. The meetings became so frustrating that Berger called them a *Groundhog Day* ritual of evasion. At the same time, Bandar was playing Iago to Freeh's Othello, seeking to sow dissension within the government and undercut U.S. efforts to pursue the investigation. The White House, Bandar would tell Freeh, showed no interest in the case and only wanted out of the box it was in with Iran.

Freeh spoke with Berger every other week about the Khobar Towers case and never communicated any dissatisfaction. But the Walsh article depicts a man nursing a secret grudge. Moreover, his assessment of the administration's resolve was wrong: throughout Clinton's second term, the administration viewed bringing those responsible to justice as a high priority. Clinton, Berger, and the cabinet members involved were determined to do what they could to mete out punishment. Proof of that came in 1997 when Canada detained a Saudi named Hani el-Sayegh, who was thought to be involved in the bombing. At the urging of the FBI, the administration had el-Sayegh brought to America with a plea agreement to testify about the bombing, though the foreign policy team worried that he would get here, recant, and ask for asylum. The administration was fully prepared to go wherever el-Sayegh's information led, including to indictments of Iranian officials and perhaps beyond. As feared, however, el-Sayegh reneged on his deal when he got to the United States. Even if they had wanted to sidestep the case—and they did not—senior Clinton officials knew that to duck their responsibilities on a terrorism case involving dead GIs was political suicide.

Thus, when Clinton met with Crown Prince Abdullah in Washington in the fall of 1998 he was, unusually, tougher than his talking points. He told Abdullah that the future of U.S.-Saudi relations would be affected by Saudi cooperation on the case and that the time had come to move forward. At the same time, Bandar continued to feed Freeh's sense that he alone cared about Khobar's dead. He told Freeh, Walsh writes, that the crown prince was persuaded "that the case was no longer of great importance to the United States."

Several weeks after Abdullah's visit, Freeh was summoned to Bandar's estate in northern Virginia and told that the FBI would be allowed to watch through a one-way mirror while Saudi officials put the Bureau's questions to suspects in the bombing. Freeh later attributed this breakthrough to a phone call former President George H. W. Bush made to the crown prince on Freeh's behalf. (The FBI director never requested permission for such a call from the White House, which would have been standard practice.) The supposition that the Saudi leader would help the head of the FBI without a quid for his quo—such as a guarantee that the United States would not take military action against Iran—is implausible. And while former President Bush is much revered by the Riyadh leadership, it is far-fetched to believe that his call was more decisive than the insistence of a sitting President whose actions would determine America's relationship with Saudi Arabia, a country whose defense depends on the presence of U.S. troops.

———

The White House was by no means alone in feeling the sting of FBI obstinacy. The State Department, the CIA, and others all had running battles with the Bureau at one time or another. Worst of all, Janet Reno, who as attorney general was Louis Freeh's boss, eventually confessed to the White House that she simply had no control over the director: he was entirely unresponsive to her requests. Undoubtedly, matters were made worse by the Bureau's string of embarrassments. From the attack on the Branch Davidian complex in Waco, Texas, that left seventy-five cult members dead to the mishandled investigation of Richard Jewell in the Atlanta Olympics bombing, and from the cover-up of inadequacies at the FBI crime lab to the scandalous investigation of Wen Ho Lee, the withholding from defense lawyers of investigative material regarding Timothy McVeigh, and the Robert Hanssen spying case, the FBI was careening from one debacle to another. The FBI director's term is ten years. The one remedy available to the President by law, dismissing Freeh, was a political impossibility. A chief executive who was being investigated by the FBI could not fire the FBI director: it would be another Saturday Night Massacre, the second coming of Richard Nixon. Freeh could not be removed; the Bureau could not be held accountable.

For the national security team, the FBI was at its most difficult in its refusal to share investigative material that had a critical bearing on U.S. foreign policy; as far as the Bureau was concerned, it was not their problem. Rule 6E was the constantly cited bugbear. "They couldn't share information on Chinese political contributions because of Rule 6E," recalls former deputy national security adviser James Steinberg. "They couldn't share information on Russian money laundering because of Rule 6E, and they especially couldn't share anything on counterterrorism." After four years, Sandy Berger gave up trying to sign the FBI on to a memorandum of understanding about sharing information relevant to national security matters. Instead of formal arrangements, he tried informal ones. He, Janet Reno, and Louis Freeh met once a month in Berger's office to discuss issues that fell on the fault line between criminal investigation and foreign policy. "We'd learn a lot of interesting things," Berger recalls, "but it was like pulling teeth." No one outside the Bureau could acquire any sense of the scope of FBI knowledge on a particular issue. The White House could not know what it did not know, so the gravity of the problem could not be assessed. For the NSC staff working on counterterrorism, this was crippling—but how crippling was also something they could not know. Every day a hundred or more reports from the CIA, DIA, the National Security Agency, and the State Department would be waiting in their computer queues when they got to work. There was never anything from the FBI. The Bureau, despite its wealth of information, contributed nothing to the White House's understanding of al-Qaeda. Virtually none of the information uncovered in any of the Bureau's investigative work flowed to the NSC. Nothing retrospective from the cases of the mid-1990s was presented or analyzed. Justice Department attorneys were often seeing the same material, but they said nothing, either. Perhaps this was because of Rule 6E concerns, or perhaps they, understandably, believed that because they were not threat analysts they did not have the expertise to assess the material for that purpose.

Freeh, whose interest in Khobar was renowned inside the government, showed little interest in the growing phenomenon of Sunni terrorism and played no notable role in U.S. strategizing against al-Qaeda. His example undoubtedly influenced his subordinates. Within the FBI, though, one agent who did not share Freeh's attitude about al-Qaeda was John O'Neill, who in the mid-1990s headed the Bureau's foreign terrorism office in Washington and represented it at the CSG. O'Neill was killed on September 11, trying to rescue people inside the World Trade Center, where he had just begun working as the complex's head of security. He has been described often and correctly as larger than life. In Washington, amid the sea of drab suits and Florsheims, he stood out, a tall, tough black Irishman in broad-lapelled double-breasted suits and dainty loafers, with a gun tucked in his waist. In CSG meetings, where bland Midwestern tones and Southern drawls predominated, he punched his points with pure New Jersey gravel.

O'Neill and Dick Clarke took to each other quickly, coming to see each other as the only ones who had registered the true danger of al-Qaeda. Like Clarke, O'Neill was known to have rough edges. During the early stages of the Khobar investigation, he came to believe that Freeh was being manipulated by the Saudis. On a flight back from Saudi Arabia, Freeh remarked about what a productive visit it had been. O'Neill replied, "You call *that* a good visit?"9 O'Neill later applied for the job as the Bureau's assistant director for national security but was turned down; he moved to the New York field office to be head of counterterrorism, playing a central role in several of the major investigations. He was energetic and incorrigibly certain of his views and, like Clarke, he steamrolled those who opposed him. Those qualities turned FBI management against him. In New York, O'Neill was not shy about saying that the Bureau underestimated al-Qaeda and did not have a grip on the group's operations in the United States, and that a domestic attack was coming. O'Neill's conversations with Clarke were the exception to the rule that the FBI provided nothing that informed White House thinking. But his removal to New York and away from the ladder of promotion made him a voice in the wilderness.

In Washington, O'Neill was replaced by Dale Watson, a solid manager who was easy to deal with, though overburdened because he was unusually competent and therefore an easy target for additional assignments. (For this reason and the fact that he responded to her requests, he became a particular favorite of Attorney General Reno.) Watson spent much of his time on the Khobar Towers case and was promoted to be the first assistant director of the newly formed counterterrorism division in late 1999. Although he continued to be brought in during crises, the NSC grew frustrated with the FBI representatives who replaced him. They were uninformed or unhelpful or both.

After the embassy bombings, Clarke grew worried that there were al-Qaeda operatives in the country that the FBI did not know about and, he believed, was not going to find. At meetings after August 7, he began asking the FBI whether the Bureau wanted White House help in getting amendments to the attorney general's guidelines for opening investigations. The guidelines set strict rules for information gathering, and they did not reflect the experience of the terrorism cases of the early 1990s:

they prohibited investigators from attending religious services, bugging houses of worship, or opening investigations without information that criminal activity was planned. So while radical mosques were at the center of the conspiracies to bomb the World Trade Center and destroy the Holland and Lincoln Tunnels, targeting them for investigation was almost impossible. For months, Clarke's question went unanswered, and he continued to badger the FBI. One reason for the inaction, the NSC thought, was that the Bureau, and perhaps the entire Department of Justice, was suffering from a case of political correctness. The Arab-American community had long complained about the FBI's treatment of Muslims; the Bureau's leadership, agents confirmed, was uneasy. Eventually, after being worn down by Clarke's incessant inquiries, the FBI said no revisions of the guidelines were required.

In this episode, as in many with the FBI, the "don't get in our knickers" phenomenon was on display. It would appear again in 1999, when the State Department proposed closer cooperation on terrorism with Russia, then reeling from a series of apartment-house bombings that were believed to be the work of jihadists.[10] The White House agreed that this was a good idea for dealing with a threat against which all help was welcome. The FBI was asked to arrange information exchanges and provide forensic assistance to the Russians. The request was greeted as if it were a demand that Bureau agents exchange their weapons for water pistols. A playground standoff ensued. The FBI refused to make the first move: they were waiting, they said, for specific Russian requests. When a cable finally arrived from the embassy in Moscow describing what Russian law-enforcement agencies were looking for, the Bureau pretended no request had been made.

One incident in this period was particularly memorable. At the end of a CSG meeting in Clarke's office in 1999, an NSC official said to Michael Rolince and Steve Jennings, the FBI representatives, "I've been going through some old intelligence and FBIS stuff [translations from foreign press] and I saw that Ayman Zawahiri was here fund-raising in the early 1990s. I couldn't believe it. Did you know that?"

Wary nods.

"Well, if he was here, someone was handling his travel and arranging his meetings and someone was giving him money. Do you know who these people are? Do you have them covered? There are cells here and we need to know about them."

"Yeah, yeah, we know. Don't worry about it. We got it covered," they replied.

Don't get in our knickers.[11]

A PROBLEM OF DISTANCE

The further one traveled from the center of national security policy making, the more the sense of impending danger diminished. The Immigration and Naturalization Service, a division of the Justice Department largely detached from the mother agency, was nearly oblivious. Immigration, in the view of INS and most of the government, was fundamentally an issue of economics—how many immigrants the United States would admit and how that would affect the labor market. America's borders were known to be porous, and the INS was considered one of the most poorly administered, underfunded, understaffed, and woefully disorganized parts of the government. At the beginning of Bill Clinton's first term, the INS was targeted for reform by Vice President Gore's National Performance Review program and his effort to "reinvent government." But the Internal Revenue Service, which affects all voters' lives, soon became the focus of the more serious overhaul effort. The INS regularly received a list of people who were to be barred from the United States because of their involvement in terrorism, organized crime, or the drug trade—a list that the State Department, which handles visa applications outside the United States, also received. But, as the case of Sheikh Rahman showed, the system was unreliable. The INS did little to improve its own evaluation of entrants to the United States or ensure that those who came here were doing what they said they would.

The issue of terrorists entering the United States had been on the table for two decades. It was first raised after the Iranian hostage crisis

and became a more serious concern after the first World Trade Center
bombing, when it was discovered that Eyad Ismoil, who drove the Ryder
van, had ostensibly come to the United States to study at Wichita State
University but had dropped out and disappeared. Not only were student
visas a ticket to unmonitored activity in the country, but foreigners from
unfriendly nations could show up to study art history and then switch to
nuclear physics or microbiology, acquiring expertise that might help their
governments develop weapons of mass destruction. Falsifying documents
to get a student visa was simple, and INS processing used an antiquated
paper system and hand entry of data. It could easily take two years to detect a fraud, plenty of time for a new entrant to disappear into the population and cause mayhem.

In late 1994, Louis Freeh brought the problem to the attention of
Deputy Attorney General Jamie Gorelick, who ordered the INS to study
the issue and suggest a fix. Congress got involved in 1996, and, as part of
reform of immigration policies, directed the government to establish a
system that would track foreign students.

The job fell to a mid-level INS civil servant named Maurice Berez,
then responsible for student regulations and policy. Berez formed a task
force with representatives from different agencies and officials from an
array of educational institutions that had foreign students enrolled. They
devised a pilot program called the Coordinated Interagency Partnership
Regulating International Students (CIPRIS). Berez's design was impressive: it called for an electronic system that would require student visa
applicants to submit enough personal information—date of birth, nationality, parents' names, all overseas addresses, and detailed financial data—
so it could be run through several government databases of dangerous
individuals. The system would check the student's acceptance and
plan of study with his school, and pass the financial information to
FinCen, the Treasury Department's Financial Services Enforcement Network, to ensure that the source of the student's money was legitimate and
not funneled through institutions used by terrorist organizations. In its
fully developed, national form, CIPRIS would establish whether the application was a fraudulent duplicate of the application of a student already

enrolled, a frequent problem. The system would be accessible on the terminals in overseas consular offices, so if anything suspicious came up, an investigation could be started and a visa denied. If the suspicious applicant was already in the United States, an INS investigator or an intelligence official would be assigned to the case for further investigation. The plan called for approved applicants to receive a visa identity card with a machine-readable code, photo, and fingerprints. Schools would be required to confirm the enrollment and physical presence of the student and to notify CIPRIS of changes in programs. If the student dropped out or disappeared, the visa would be invalidated. If he then left the country and tried to reenter, he would be stopped and handed over to law enforcement. If he stayed in the country and received so much as a traffic ticket, local law enforcement would be alerted of his status through an existing FBI system that carries information on terrorists and others with "wants and warrants."

When the pilot was launched, in April 1997, twenty-one educational institutions and exchange programs in INS's Atlanta district participated. Among them were colleges and universities including Duke and Auburn, other favorites of foreign students such as the ELS Language Centers, which teach English as a second language, and a flight school, the North American Institute of Aviation in South Carolina.

Berez and his task force were pleased with the pilot program, which ran for eighteen months. Top INS officials were less enthusiastic. The program cost about $11 million a year, but the service funded only about a third of that, forcing Berez to trim the effort. The identification card was done away with early on at the insistence of a senior INS official. Knowing that funding would be a problem for the perennially cash-strapped agency, the task force had recommended that the program pay for itself with a user fee; Congress, in its immigration reform, approved a fee of up to $100. First, the INS would not allow the program to collect the fee during the pilot stage; then the plan to have schools collect the money when the entire system was up and running drew sharp criticism from groups of higher education institutions.

With CIPRIS in danger, a senior INS official who dealt with counterterrorism turned to the NSC for help, and a briefing was scheduled. The CSG had discussed the foreign-students issue repeatedly, and the conclusion was always that the problem was too hard to solve. Colleges and universities strongly opposed any regulation that required them to police their students—they viewed it as doing the government's dirty work—and no agency had the political will to force this task on such a powerful interest group. Confronted with Maurice Berez, who has the kinky gray hair and genial demeanor of a figure in a Koren cartoon, NSC aides had low expectations. But once the lights went down in the Cordell Hull Conference Room on the second floor of the Old Executive Office Building, Berez was transformed, delivering a PowerPoint presentation of CIPRIS that, if such a thing can be imagined, verged on rousing.

The NSC officials were impressed. But the appeal for help outside the INS annoyed Berez's superiors, and for all CIPRIS's promise, the INS saw it as a lightning rod for criticism and an administrative burden. On at least two occasions in 1998 and 1999, the INS was poised to kill the program. Both times, the NSC directors contacted the INS leadership to say that the White House wanted CIPRIS continued.

For a while, that kept the program alive. But Berez's imaginative approach had elicited determined opponents. An organization called NAFSA: Association of International Educators, which represents educational administrators who deal with foreign-student programs, dug in against the fee and monitoring, depicting them as an imposition and a threat to a growing business. (There are now some 550,000 overseas students in an estimated $11 billion industry.) At a break in a meeting at INS headquarters, Marlene Johnson, the executive director of the group, said to Berez, "I wonder what would happen to CIPRIS if you weren't leading it?" NAFSA hired a lobbyist and began working to kill CIPRIS. In October 1999, unbeknownst to the White House, Berez was abruptly removed from the program and the task force was dissolved. Four months later, twenty-one senators wrote to the INS asking for a delay in the implementation of the user fee and the program. CIPRIS was reconfigured into a program call SEVIS that would leave the student visa machinery much as it was, a passive database that law-enforcement and intelligence officials could consult, not a system that did a primary screening up front. Berez had originally hoped to get the program implemented nationwide by January 1, 2001, with parts up and running earlier. Instead, he was re-assigned to a position far from the issue of tracking foreign students, running instead the review of the government benefits immigrants could receive.

MILLENNIAL FRUSTRATIONS

In early fall of 1999, George Tenet came to the White House to discuss the possibility of terrorist strikes during the millennium celebrations. He forecast between five and fifteen attacks. Sandy Berger and his aides had long since become accustomed to sudden surges of threat information. As the overloading of the President's Daily Brief showed, the intelligence community was not filtering out much, so great was the fear of being criti-cized for failing to give timely notice. Even by those standards, Tenet's prediction was dramatic.

After the CIA's Counterterrorist Center called Dick Clarke in mid-December to tell him that Jordanian authorities had discovered seventy-one barrels of chemicals for explosives and a large arms cache at a farm outside Amman, the feeling was that even if Tenet's numbers were off, the cumulative threat evaluation was about right: the various subplots—the bombing of the Amman Radisson and the attacks on Mount Nebo and the John the Baptist site—could easily have killed more than a thousand people if carried out. When Customs agent Diana Dean stopped Ahmad Ressam coming off the Port Angeles ferry in Washington State, the shock was tinged with gratitude that the alert system had worked. Other aspects of the investigation revealed more worrisome details, such as the use of twenty-digit encryption on the laptop of one operative, a level of technical sophistication that far exceeded expectations.

The revelations put the administration on a war footing. Almost every

day for three weeks, Sandy Berger met with Tenet, Dale Watson of the
FBI, Janet Reno, and top Pentagon and State Department officials in the
Situation Room to force everyone to share information and coordinate
actions. The lines that ran from Amman and Port Angeles were traced,
the operations were disrupted, and conspirators were apprehended in
eight countries. And still, there was no sense of being out of the woods.
While most of the world was worried about Y2K computer failures,
Berger, Clarke, and the rest of the Principals feared a bombing or worse
throughout the millennium period. Clarke spent the night in a special
command center near the White House. Berger, who was attending the
President's New Year's Eve party, called Clarke compulsively, the last
time at three A.M.

Afterward, the CIA and friendly intelligence services conducted another major dragnet, broader even than in 1998, to roll up terrorist cells
abroad. The Jordanian plot, in particular, had a galvanizing effect on the
Middle East governments, and the results were spectacular: it was the
most successful operation against jihadists to date, with cells broken up in
more than a dozen countries. Once again, the sense of success was mingled with astonishment at how many groups were out there.

—

The millennium experience had the further effect of leaving the counterterrorism community stunned at how many terrorists—or at least individuals connected with terrorists—had turned up in the United States.
The Algerian network in Montreal that Ahmad Ressam was part of had
members in New York and Boston. Most of these were found and de-
ported for visa violations. Reviewing what was learned during the period,
the NSC found itself once again pushing a familiar set of issues. Clarke
wrote to his counterparts in other agencies that widespread immigration
violations posed a serious problem for preventing terrorist attack. He
urged a large-scale coordinated effort involving the FBI, the Secret Service, and the INS to uncover, arrest, and deport potential sleeper operatives. He complained that the millennium had shown again that the federal

government, and especially the FBI, did not have enough translators to cover wiretaps in progress or translate seized materials—this despite budget increases of tens of millions of dollars in recent years. He reiterated that the Justice Department was not bringing any prosecutions for terrorist fund-raising, nor was it using the Alien Terrorist Removal Court that had been created in 1996. And he hammered again at the issue that continued to gnaw at him: "Fear of accusation of ethnic or religious prejudice may be constraining U.S. attorneys and JTTF [Joint Terrorism Task Forces] from bringing prosecutions. Fears of violating the Attorney General guidelines [are preventing the FBI] from developing sources in mosques that are used as meeting places and fundraising facilities by supporters of foreign terrorist groups." To Berger, he declared his certainty that there were terrorist sleeper cells in the United States. The question about attacks was "not a matter of if but when."

Some things slowly began to change. After the millennium, the FBI's Dale Watson remarked that "scales fell from my eyes." He arranged a meeting in Tampa for all the FBI's SACs, and Clarke delivered an unvarnished talk about the jihadist threat. Judging by the level of understanding of the SACs, he thought, "al-Qaeda could have had offices next door to them and they wouldn't have known." In the wake of the Ressam arrest and the Jordan plot, Watson told them, they now had terrorism priorities. The Bureau committed itself to putting an assistant special agent in charge, specifically for terrorism, in every field office. "We thought it was a breakthrough," Clarke said later. "But it was going to take years to turn the culture around." At the same time, FBI headquarters reported to Sandy Berger after the millennium that there was no serious domestic problem. He recalls, "Their post-millennium assessment was that they [al-Qaeda] did not have active cells in the U.S. They said there might be sleepers, but they had that covered. They were saying this was not a big domestic threat."

Ironically, the *foiling* of terrorist attacks did not help the administration persuade people outside the executive branch of the reality of the threat. If anything, it convinced them that the government had the issue in hand. When Rick Newcomb and an interagency group visited Saudi Arabia, the UAE, and Kuwait again in 2000, the effort to close down money conduits was moving slowly. When they did want to act, the governments had few tools, and, particularly in Saudi Arabia, they were reluctant to do anything that would cause them to bump up against any one of the House of Saud's more than six thousand princes. Concerned that al-Qaeda was still laundering its money in places such as the Bahamas, Liechtenstein, and other well-known havens that offer no-questions banking, the administration introduced legislation in March 2000 that would have expanded its authority to ban U.S. residents and companies from doing business with banks in countries that refused to clean up their laws. The bill passed easily in the House of Representatives but was derailed in the Senate because of the opposition of Senate Banking Committee chairman Phil Gramm. The Texas Republican declared that he did not believe that "bureaucrats should have the authority to close down banks." Speaking to a group of international bankers the next year, Gramm crowed, "I killed the [Clinton] administration's anti-money-laundering legislation last year," and he said he would oppose any resurrection of the legislation.[12] The world's greatest deliberative body was not seized by the issue of terrorism.

Some of America's closest allies were also doubtful. The connections of the millennium plots, especially those that led from Ressam's group of Algerians in Canada to a wider network rooted in Western Europe, suggested that help from Islamic governments was not going to suffice in fighting al-Qaeda.

Counterterrorism cooperation had been an issue for Americans and Europeans since at least 1996, when the annual Group of Seven (G-7) summit in Lyons was held just after the Khobar bombing, and the agenda was scrapped in favor of work on terrorism. After the East Africa bombings, the CIA and FBI requested assistance from their European counterparts in investigating and surveilling a group of individuals of concern. Among those discussed with the Germans, for example, were associates of Abu Hajer. Arrests had been made since 1998 in Italy, Britain, and

Germany, but U.S. diplomats and intelligence officials still felt resistance to their requests for better cooperation. The Europeans were skeptical of claims about the size and dangerousness of al-Qaeda, believing that the bombing of al-Shifa was a massive error and the sign of a cowboy approach to foreign policy. They may have also believed—as many in Europe did—that the U.S. government had a psychological need for a new major threat to replace the Soviet Union. At a 1999 State Department lunch for visiting foreign counterterrorism officials, an NSC director discussed al-Qaeda with a woman from one of Germany's domestic law-enforcement agencies. She looked at him disapprovingly and said, "Really, you haven't proven this to us. You haven't made the case."

In early 2000, diplomatic efforts to get bin Laden expelled and the terrorist camps shut down ran aground. The Taliban weathered the shock of UN sanctions and hunkered down, its subsistence economy isolated from the world and nearly impervious to outside pressure. The Pakistanis were still backing the regime in Kandahar with fuel and food deliveries despite the sanctions, and they alone could make a difference. Mike Sheehan put forward a suggestion to come down hard on the Pakistanis. Everything else would be cleared off the bilateral agenda with Islamabad, and the United States would deliver an ultimatum demanding that the Pakistanis cooperate in apprehending bin Laden and shutting down the terrorist camps. If they failed to comply, the United States would move to have the International Monetary Fund cut off its assistance to the all but bankrupt country. The memo underscored Sheehan's determination—and exasperation. But the proposal was doomed from the start. No one wanted to endanger the U.S.–Pakistan dialogue on nuclear issues, out of fear that the Pakistanis might transfer nuclear materials or technology to North Korea or other countries. And no one could seriously contemplate pushing Pakistan over the financial precipice. To the rest of the State Department, Sheehan's plan was a tactic out of *Blazing Saddles* with the United States playing the sheriff who puts a gun to his own head and says, "Stop or I'll shoot!" Plunging Pakistan into the abyss would inevitably cost the United States.

In April 2000, Clinton traveled to India, something he had wanted
to do since his first term in office. It was the first presidential visit in
almost twenty years, and with the Cold War over, he and his advisers
believed there was an opportunity for the world's largest democracy
and its oldest one to improve relations significantly. The problem that
bedeviled the trip planners was what to do about Pakistan. America's
balancing act in South Asia required maintaining some kind of relationship with one country even as it began leaning toward the other.
Pakistan had been Washington's historic friend through the Cold War,
yet circumstances made it a distinctly unappealing stop for Clinton.
Musharraf had toppled the elected but kleptocratic Nawaz Sharif, and
his military government had suspended the country's major representative institutions. Islamabad was making no meaningful gestures of restraint in its nuclear program. A thinly veiled proxy war was being waged
in Kashmir by militants with the clear support of the Pakistani military,
and the smoke from Kargil still hung in the air. Pakistan was abetting the
Taliban and keeping Usama bin Laden safe from American justice. Re-
warding that behavior with a presidential visit did not, on the face of it,
make much sense.

A visit to Pakistan entailed one other challenge: anti-American
jihadists operated in the country with impunity. A plot by bin Laden
or any of a host of other violent actors would put Clinton's personal safety
at risk—the danger would be greater there than anywhere he had ever visited. The Secret Service had only once recommended against a visit during Clinton's presidency. Fearful of Serb forces, which were thought to be
hiding out in tunnels under the Kosovar capital of Pristina, the security
planners argued against a Clinton stop there in 1999. He overrode their
concerns and went ahead with the trip. "If Kosovo was a four on a scale
of ten," said one person closely involved with the trip to South Asia, for
the Secret Service, "Pakistan was an eleven." The South Asia trip was
originally scheduled for 1999; in preliminary meetings then, the Secret
Service argued strenuously against a Pakistan visit. In the preparations
for the 2000 visit, the service dug its heels in, repeatedly confronting the

top NSC officials with horror scenarios. There was danger to Air Force One from ground fire. No one trusted the Pakistani military to keep travel routes in the country secret or secure. The service said it could not perform its mission: it could not protect the President. In a meeting with Clinton, Larry Cockell, the head of the presidential detail, told him so directly.

Clinton still felt he had to go. Skipping Pakistan altogether would widen the rift between Islamabad and Washington—an outcome to be avoided in dealing with an unpredictable nuclear power. Clinton strongly believed the better course was to demonstrate continued American engagement in Pakistan and deliver a stern message about the direction the country was headed in. Whether to go was debated until the last minute; a side trip to a village in Bangladesh was canceled because of information about an al-Qaeda threat, and that did not make the decision easier. Clinton received a euphoric reception in India. It was more than a little strange to slip away to Islamabad in a small G-5 jet belonging to the CIA, while Air Force One flew in as a decoy, drawing a possible attack.

Clinton met twice with Musharraf. In the "expanded" meeting, flanked by a dozen or so aides, the two men discussed a range of issues on the bilateral agenda. Talk of terrorism was kept brief. There was some doubt about Musharraf's hold on power, and Clinton did not want to broach the subject in front of a crowd of people with uncertain loyalties. In the "one-on-one" meeting that followed—Clinton, Berger, Musharraf, and a Pakistani aide were present—the President was more blunt with the Pakistani leader. "He pressed Musharraf very hard and told him to use Pakistan's influence with the Taliban to get bin Laden. He was very tough on that," says Berger. "Musharraf responded by saying, 'I will do as much as I can.' It was positive, but we just didn't know how far he could go."

In the months that followed, Musharraf made remarks that South Asia watchers found encouraging about religious militancy and terrorism, though he also referred to the struggle in Kashmir as jihad, not terrorism. But the government's steps, including its cautious effort to assert some control over the madrassas, were too tentative to make any real dif-

ference. Islamabad made no noteworthy departures in its dealings with
the Taliban.

—

Back in Washington, the sense that the United States was dodging al-
Qaeda bullets rekindled the desire for a military plan to end the bin
Laden problem. At the end of one meeting in the Cabinet Room, Clinton
approached Joint Chiefs chairman Hugh Shelton and said, "You know, it
would scare the shit out of al-Qaeda if suddenly a bunch of black ninjas
rappelled out of helicopters into the middle of their camp. It would get us
enormous deterrence and show those guys we're not afraid." Shelton, a
huge, powerfully built man, blanched. The NSC followed up with a request for a new military plan, a small package that did not require using
the entire 101st Airborne Division.

Some weeks later, Secretary of Defense Cohen and Shelton's deputy,
Air Force general Richard Myers, came to the White House and briefed
Berger and his deputy, General Don Kerrick. The military wanted to
help. Cohen and Myers shared Clinton's eagerness to act, and, as always,
the armed forces would do what they were told. But the answer to the request for a small operation was that "it would be Desert One"—the 1980
attempt to liberate American hostages in Tehran, which resulted in the in-
cineration of two helicopters and the deaths of eight servicemen. For the
most part, military doctrine called for special operations forces to be used
in support of other units; finding SCUD missile launchers behind Iraqi
lines in the Gulf War was a good example of this kind of mission. The
doctrine was supported by the strong inclination—enduringly reinforced
by Desert One—of many military planners and commanders, who are reluctant to use special forces, viewing the risky operations they take on as
prone to disaster, embarrassment, and casualties.

After Desert One, the U.S. military began work to improve its special
forces capacities. In the 1990s, as military theorists turned their attention to
the coming age of asymmetric warfare, large sums of money were poured
into the Special Operations Command (SOCOM). Such units as Delta

Force and the Navy Seals developed into highly skilled, unconventional fighting forces and trained for a variety of terrorism-related contingencies. But the Chiefs and their minions remained extremely cautious about using them: their reluctance to use the operators in Bosnia to capture war criminals, for instance, repeatedly irritated policy makers.

This stance would remain largely unchanged until the war in Afghanistan in 2001. The White House had little recourse; it would not work to order the military to undertake a mission it believed to be suicidal. Tom Pickering recalls worrying "that someone was going to put out the story that the NSC and State wanted to hazard the lives of young Americans in a wild-goose chase. The Pentagon has a great capacity to let things leak to keep from doing them."

Were the Chiefs ducking a mission for which they had no enthusiasm? Military establishments are almost by definition conservative. (General Tommy Franks's first plans for attacking Afghanistan, presented in September 2001, called for five or six divisions to be deployed in an old-style invasion—exactly what the Bush administration did not want.) Without a landscape-changing event, military leaders were unlikely to drastically revise their special forces doctrine. But they were also, according to one former senior political appointee at the Pentagon, particularly unwilling to go out on a limb for Clinton. Much time had passed since his disastrous first year in office, but the watershed events of 1993 and 1994—the decision to end discrimination against gays in the armed forces, the killing of the Army servicemen in Somalia, and the hasty withdrawal of U.S. forces from that country—had not so much receded into memory as been woven into a perpetually troubled relationship between the White House and the military. As this former official put it, "Shelton, like Powell, had eyed up Clinton and decided he didn't have the guts to fight a war. And if you make that conclusion, you're not going to put forward anything in a gray area because you're afraid he's going to wimp out. I think the Pentagon became more nervous and timid because they thought Clinton was—and so they would not put forward risky plans in a serious way. By the end, they just didn't believe. They were so used to pulling their punches, they had written him off taking strong action."

The rotation of submarines in the Arabian Sea continued, the vessels hovering in the basket awaiting intelligence. Once more in 2000, a report arrived that detailed bin Laden's whereabouts for a brief window of time. On a Sunday afternoon while the second thread of intelligence was being pursued, the missiles were spun. George Tenet, who was attending his son's soccer game, called Berger and told him, "We don't have it."

In spring and early summer of 2000, the threat level rose again. A trend first noticed in 1999 appeared to be strengthening: al-Qaeda operatives seemed to be growing in number in the Middle East and attempting to establish ties with indigenous organizations such as Hamas. Beyond rhetorical gestures, bin Laden and his senior leaders had never been much concerned with the Middle East or the Palestinians. But the high drama of the peace process and the marathon Camp David peace talks in July made the area an important theater for al-Qaeda. Also, the Islamic world was being drawn closer together by the electronic media; images of Palestinian suffering were on the televisions and computer screens of Muslims everywhere. Now bin Laden wanted to be part of that picture.

There was a spike in al-Qaeda activity in Lebanon, especially in Palestinian refugee camps. In Syria, which could almost always be counted on to be unhelpful in matters of terrorism, an al-Qaeda cell was uncovered, and the operatives were quickly shipped to Jordan for trial. The country's secular rulers recognized that the group posed a long-term threat to their regime in Damascus, just as it did to the others in the region.

Al-Qaeda also evinced a desire, which would later become a hallmark of the group, to return to the venue of failed operations of the past. The United States embassy in Jordan canceled its Fourth of July celebrations and warned Americans living in the country that there was credible information of a plot to attack the post. During this period, threat information was also received that spoke of attacks on ten embassies at once.

Convinced that the intelligence needed for a cruise-missile attack on al-Qaeda was not going to materialize, the Joint Chiefs decided to see what they could do about the submarine deployments, which struck them as an exercise in futility. Admiral Scott Frye, head of operations for the Joint Staff, was dispatched to the White House to meet with Dick Clarke and tell him that without better intelligence, the vessels should be brought home. Clarke surprised his visitor by agreeing and challenged him to find ways of improving the intelligence. Frye returned to the Pentagon and ordered his staff to draw up a list of possibilities. Like most military options lists, what emerged in early summer of 2000 included ideas that ranged from the unfeasible to the absurd. One of them, however, appealed to Clarke: use a forty-nine-foot unmanned flying drone called Predator, armed with precision video and infrared cameras, to locate bin Laden.

There were myriad objections. Although the idea had come from the Joint Staff, many in the Pentagon disliked the idea of the new battlefield surveillance system being adapted for an intelligence mission. Within the CIA, there were voices of opposition as well. As one senior Defense Department official commented, "They had to cram this down the throat of the Agency. The DO [Directorate of Operations], they go to cocktail parties and recruit spies, and they said this is paramilitary and can screw up my relationship with the host government." But some of the intelligence community's most experienced troubleshooters found the concept intriguing and backed it. To break the logjam, Sandy Berger had Clarke draft a memo for Clinton reviewing the lessons learned from the millennium conspiracies and the ongoing efforts to stop bin Laden. A few days later, as expected, the memo came back, with Clinton's almost indecipherable left-handed scrawl on top: "This is disappointing. Need to do better." Clarke summoned the CSG members to a meeting and used the memo as a cudgel, reciting Clinton's comment. None of those present wanted to answer phone calls from their agency heads about the President's ire. The Predator program moved ahead.

That summer, a first round of tests was conducted in the United States to acquaint the intelligence community with Predator's capabilities. The results were encouraging, and test flights over Afghanistan began in September. On its first outing, the drone failed to take off properly and was damaged. But another was sent aloft, and soon thereafter, Clarke received a call summoning him to the CIA. When he arrived, he was shown a videotape in which a single very tall person in Arab dress was talking to a group of smaller people similarly garbed. The CIA believed the tall person was bin Laden. A CD of the video clip was taken to the White House and shown to Berger and then Clinton.

In all, Predator flew twelve times over Afghanistan. One flight was aborted. Most of the missions were devoted to viewing sites bin Laden was believed to frequent; this intelligence mapping would be essential for a real targeting. Three times, the analysts believed, they spotted bin Laden: twice on film shot by the drone, once in real time, as he emerged from his house at Tarnak Farm outside Kandahar and walked to a nearby mosque. In Washington, a debate began over whether the man really was bin Laden—"a tall guy in robes surrounded by shorter guys in robes" was how one official described the film. During some of the later trials, Taliban radar began tracking the drone, and MiG fighters were sent to intercept it. They failed, flying right past the drone, though they did spook the ground operator, who was watching through the aircraft's camera as the fighters approached at hundreds of miles an hour. The tests ended in mid-October as winter arrived in Afghanistan, and a battle erupted in Washington over the future of the program.

The issue was money. After the first drone crashed, there was a bill to be paid. The CIA had not budgeted for Predator and balked at compensating the Pentagon. The program was suspended. Who would cover further costs—satellite time for relaying pictures, for example—was unclear as well. A Defense Department official who was involved recalls thinking, "We are worried about Usama bin Laden and we are arguing about

$200,000. I couldn't believe it." Finally, in December, Secretary of the Air Force Whit Peters stepped in and found the money. But the future of the program was by no means assured.

—

In the two years after the East Africa bombings, the idea of a "cascading threat" gained currency in national security circles. It was feared that as embassies and military installations were hardened, with more guards on alert and better perimeter controls, al-Qaeda would inevitably search for softer, less fortified targets such as housing complexes, schools, and cultural centers. However, when the next attack came, its target was not an embassy but an even more imposing symbol of American power: on October 12, 2000, a small boat packed with explosives motored up alongside the U.S.S. *Cole,* which was anchored in the harbor of Aden. The blast killed seventeen sailors and tore a forty-foot hole in the $1 billion destroyer, very nearly sinking it. The bombers' audacity was breathtaking. The use of a shaped charge— a bomb fabricated so that its explosive force bursts primarily in one direction—demonstrated a new level of technological skill and resourcefulness.

The attack on the *Cole* demonstrated just how lightly the U.S. military had been taking the threat of terrorist violence. An NSC memo sent to the Pentagon in 1997 and leaked to *The Washington Post* had warned specifically of the dangers surrounding American ships in port. The Navy disregarded these admonitions and the known threat conditions in Yemen, which was second only to Afghanistan on the list of states infested with terrorists. Admiral Vern Clark, the chief of naval operations, conceded after the Navy's investigation of the incident that "the commanding officer of *Cole* did not have the specific intelligence, focused training, appropriate equipment or on-scene security support to effectively prevent or deter such a determined, preplanned assault on his ship." In the words of Vice Admiral C. W. Moore Jr., the commander of naval forces in the Middle East, the *Cole*'s captain, Commander Kirk Lippold, failed to "deliberately plan, deliberately implement and actively supervise a force protection plan." Moore added: "The watch was not briefed on the plan or their responsibilities, the bridge was not manned, service boats were not closely controlled, and there was little thought as to how to respond to unauthorized craft being alongside." The Navy possessed virtually the entire body of intelligence on al-Qaeda and disregarded it so thoroughly that an institution built on the concept of the personal responsibility of the commander decided that no individual should be punished for the security lapses. Equally culpable was the regional commander-in-chief, Anthony Zinni, who approved the decision to refuel in Yemen. A more telling display of the persistent disbelief concerning the threat from al-Qaeda would be hard to imagine.

Responding to the attack on the *Cole* posed another challenge for the Clinton administration. Clearly, jihadists were behind the bombing, including probably al-Qaeda, but no claim of responsibility arrived from any known group and there was no intelligence tying the attack to the leadership in Afghanistan. To launch a military strike against targets in Afghanistan on the basis of nothing more than a strong intuition would have gone well beyond any U.S. military precedent. No information certifying authorship of the attack materialized during the remainder of the administration.

The clock was running out on the Clinton administration, and the United States was in the midst of its closest presidential race in a century. Any military action would have constrained the next President's room for maneuver and committed him to a policy he had not chosen. In eight years, the Clinton White House had never forgotten the unfinished business it inherited from the first Bush administration—in the former Yugoslavia, where Bosnian Muslims were being slaughtered in the worst European violence since the Holocaust; in Somalia, where the Bush administration initiated a humanitarian operation and committed U.S. troops to serve under the aegis of the UN just before leaving office; and in Iraq, where Saddam Hussein continued to build weapons of mass destruction after a war that was supposed to have ended his rule in Baghdad. Bosnia and Somalia provided the two greatest foreign policy traumas of Clinton's first term, and, whether the next President was a Democrat or a Republican, no one thought it was right to encumber him with unfinished military business in Afghanistan. The FBI's investigation in Yemen went forward with John O'Neill in charge, and intelligence collection continued. It was left for the succeeding foreign policy team to decide on an appropriate next move.

CHAPTER 8

THE SHOCK OF THE NEW

O N JANUARY 21, 2001, George W. Bush stood on the steps of the Capitol in a cold rain and took the oath of office. In his inaugural address, the new President made little reference to the world beyond America's borders, except to say, "The enemies of liberty and our country should make no mistake, America remains engaged in the world, by history and by choice, shaping a balance of power that favors freedom. We will defend our allies and our interests. We will show purpose without arrogance. We will meet aggression and bad faith with resolve and strength." The brevity of the passage was in keeping with the campaign, in which neither Bush nor his opponent, Al Gore, spent much time discussing foreign policy.

Bush's national security team boasted an extraordinary amount of high-level experience, and its stars took their seats in the Cabinet Room amid high expectations. Vice President Dick Cheney had served as secretary of defense in the first Bush administration and White House chief of staff during the Ford administration. Colin Powell was on his way to compiling perhaps the most distinguished record in Washington since George C. Marshall: he had been national security adviser under President Reagan and chairman of the Joint Chiefs of Staff under Presidents George H. W. Bush and Bill Clinton; now he was secretary of state. Another former chief of staff for President Ford, a former congressman, and a onetime ambassador to NATO, Defense Secretary Donald Rumsfeld began a second tour in the office in which he had been the youngest incumbent ever in 1975. Only National Security Advisor Condoleezza Rice was relatively inexperienced, having logged just two years as a Soviet expert on the first Bush National Security Council staff, but she was nonetheless highly regarded by both Democrats and Republicans.

The Bush team came into office with clear views about world affairs and a strong disdain for the policies of President Clinton. Their overriding criticism concerned what Condoleezza Rice called "setting priorities," which required focusing on the few great powers that "can radically affect international peace, stability, and prosperity. These states are capable of disruption on a grand scale, and their fits of anger or acts of beneficence affect hundreds of millions of people. By reason of size, geographic position, economic potential, and military strength, they are capable of influencing American welfare for good or ill." In an article in *Foreign Affairs* that served as the campaign manifesto for the Republicans, she argued that a foreign policy was required that "separates the important from the trivial" and took the sitting administration to task for having "assiduously avoided implementing such an agenda. Instead, every issue has been taken on its own terms—crisis by crisis, day by day." China and Russia, she asserted, were what really counted, and Clinton had frittered away American power and prestige by devoting so much time to new second- or third-tier concerns that he had brought into office. Terrorism, she contended, needed attending to only insofar as it was used by rogue states to advance their interests.[1]

In the months before the inauguration, George W. Bush and his advisers seldom spoke about terrorism and then only generically. After the bombing of the *Cole,* Bush told an audience in the Philadelphia suburb of Langhorne, "Let's hope we can gather enough intelligence to figure out who did the act and take the necessary action. . . . There must be a consequence." But when the President-elect's appointees came to the White House for transition briefings, the message they heard was anything but generic.

Sandy Berger wanted the incoming team to be well briefed, and he ordered that issue papers be written and oral presentations be delivered to Condoleezza Rice by every directorate of the NSC. When Transnational Threats gave its review of "why bin Laden is an existential threat," as one directorate member put it, Berger showed up unexpectedly. It was the only one of the briefings he attended. "I'm here," he explained, "because I want to underscore how important this issue is." Berger met with Rice several times to cover the waterfront of foreign policy issues she would face. In the office that he was soon to hand over to the professor from Stanford, he tried to ensure that she grasped the seriousness of the threat. He told her, "You're going to spend more time during your four years on terrorism generally and al-Qaeda specifically than any issue."

In the weeks that followed, Clarke also briefed Vice President Cheney and Deputy National Security Advisor Stephen Hadley. Before the inauguration, Colin Powell worked his way through briefings at the State Department from the many bureaus. The office of the counterterrorism coordinator—Edmund Hull, a Foreign Service officer, now held the job as acting coordinator—brought together the core members of the CSG to meet the incoming secretary. As they went around the table, each one presented his agency's perspective on bin Laden. Powell impressed those present as a careful listener who spoke rarely but asked thoughtful questions. After everyone had their turn and the group got up to leave, Brian Sheridan, the outgoing assistant secretary of defense for special operations and low-intensity conflict, felt a need to underscore the danger. "It was almost like a parting shot from a political appointee who was leaving," he said. Make no mistake about al-Qaeda: "This is a really big thing. It will be a really big problem." At a meeting with Condoleezza Rice, he repeated his message. "I told them this is not an amateur-type deal and you need Dick Clarke. It's serious stuff, these guys are not going away. I just remember her listening and not asking much." Sheridan, a former CIA analyst who had been a business consultant before entering government, let the new team entering the Pentagon know that he was happy to discuss any of the issues his office dealt with—not only terrorism but also counterdrug programs in Colombia and the Caribbean. "I offered to brief anyone, anytime on any topic. Never took it up."

The record of the first months of the new administration suggests that its leaders were preoccupied with other matters. They moved quickly on two issues as soon as they were in office. Their top priority—and the security issue that Bush had campaigned on most vocally—was the construction of a national missile defense. Even before he was sworn in, Bush set about courting key lawmakers to line up support for his vision of a missile shield.[2] During the early months of 2001, administration officials flew thousands of miles to consult with Russia, China, and allies in Europe and Asia over the shape of such a system and its implications, including the scrapping of the 1972 Anti-Ballistic Missile Treaty.

The other issue was China. The Republicans came into office with a strong belief that China posed a long-term challenge to the United States. Their thinking was grounded in their reading of the history of the last century and a half: China at the end of the twentieth century was a fast-developing economic giant and rising military power that, like Germany at the end of the nineteenth century, felt that its present place in the international system was incommensurate with its greatness as a nation. A vision of a looming confrontation became a staple of conservative thinking. Bush himself criticized the Clinton administration for viewing China as a "strategic partner"; both before and after the election, he called Beijing a strategic competitor. While many over the last few decades have espoused similar views of China, the certitude of the new team and the tone it set marked a departure from past U.S. practice. It does not seem far-fetched to suggest that the new administration's position was colored by the China scandals of the 1990s. From Chinese contributions to the Clinton campaign to the Loral–China satellites investigation, and, of course, the Wen Ho Lee case, Washington had gone through a frenzy of China-bashing. In the end, there was much less than met the eye to the latter two episodes; Wen Ho Lee was more likely to have been helping Taiwan than the People's Republic. But the air the new team breathed was filled with deep concern about China.

A series of incidents quickly strained relations between the United States and China: the White House approved a multibillion-dollar weapons sale to Taiwan that included destroyers, submarines, and minesweeping helicopters. There was a flurry of high-level visits to India and strong statements of a desire to accelerate the rapprochement begun under the previous administration. Although the essence of the Bush administration's India policy was little different from Clinton's, the tactics were interpreted by some as an unsubtle effort to encircle and contain China. The collision of a Chinese fighter jet with a U.S. EP-3E spy plane off the northeastern coast of the country and the subsequent standoff over the repatriation of the crew brought tensions to a peak.

An unspoken rule of the new administration was that its policies should contrast sharply with those of the previous administration, which was spoken of with contempt. "Everything that had a Clinton label had to be changed. It was visceral," observed one Foreign Service officer who had been through several presidential transitions.

An interesting case of how the new Bush administration started off on a tack that differentiated it from the Clinton administration involved Iran. Even before the inauguration, there were unmistakable signs of an effort to establish some distance from the Clinton team's position. In foreign policy circles, word circulated that the new team wanted to break the deadlock with Tehran, and oil executives close to the incoming administration confidently asserted that Bush was committed to normalizing trade relations. That would allow American firms to do business in the country, from which sanctions had barred them. Colin Powell's confirmation hearings were seen as setting a new tone: "We have important differences on matters of policy [with Iran]," he said. "But these differences need our—need not preclude greater interaction, whether in more normal commerce or increased dialogue. Our national security team will be reviewing such possibilities." Though Powell mentioned terrorism, no acknowledgment was made of the previous administration's determination, announced fifteen months earlier, that unnamed senior Iranian officials were under investigation for their roles in the killing of Americans at Khobar Towers. The occasion for these remarks was the removal of Hani el-Sayegh, the suspected Khobar conspirator, to Saudi Arabia. In making the announcement, Attorney General Janet Reno said that the United States had not determined whether the bombing was carried out at the instigation of the Iranian government.[3] The United States decided to comply with a Saudi request for custody of the suspect, because once el-Sayegh reneged on his plea agreement, the Justice Department did not have enough evidence to try him. (Powell's only reference to Afghanistan deplored their treatment of women.)

The administration's early posture vis-à-vis Iran must have come as a shock to Louis Freeh, who, Elsa Walsh wrote in *The New Yorker,* was still focused so intently on the Khobar case that he "poured [into it] not only enormous investigative resources but also soul." According to Walsh, Freeh did not believe that President Clinton would make the hard decision to indict Iranian officials for the Khobar bombing; therefore he decided to wait for the next administration to press ahead with the case and, presumably, make those indictments. (Freeh was evidently not troubled by the position of the Justice Department attorneys in the case, who felt they had no admissible evidence to use for such charges.) Freeh announced that he would retire in June, saying that Khobar was his "only unfinished piece of business."[4] After the *New Yorker* article appeared, Freeh was summoned to Condoleezza Rice's West Wing office. The buzz in the corridors of the Old Executive Office Building was that he was given a tongue-lashing, the essence of which was that the FBI director did not make foreign policy.

On June 22, 2001, a few days before the fifth anniversary of the bombing of Khobar Towers, the Justice Department announced the indictment of thirteen Saudis and one unidentified Lebanese. The charges contained references to unnamed Iranian officials who were said to have assisted Saudi Hezbollah, although they were not indicted. Attorney General

John Ashcroft called the indictments "a milestone" and said that the indictment included only "what we believe we can prove in a court of law." But he vowed to pursue charges against the unnamed Iranians, who, he said, "inspired, supported and supervised the attack."[5] This outcome hardly differed from the one the Clinton administration had been headed for when the FBI director began to slow-roll the indictment. Bush's overall Iran policy came to resemble his predecessor's. Freeh, in his hatred of Clinton, had lost touch either with the standards of evidence required in federal courts, or with the foreign policy dimension of the case, or both.

—

The burst of energy from the new foreign policy team on missile defense and China policy contrasted with their inattention to counterterrorism policy. This was not surprising. All new administrations come into office with a short To Do list and need time to think through how they wish to conduct policy on the vast number of issues that played no role in their campaign. They must vet, hire, and shepherd through the confirmation process hundreds of appointees, and they need time to figure out how to operate a policy apparatus that has evolved since they were last in power. Most important of all, they need time to adapt the simplifications of campaign slogans and television talking points to the complex realities of a world with which they have been, to varying degrees, out of touch. The Clinton administration came into office with strong views—about the need for America to act in the world with multilateral backing, about the role of international law, about using force only when sanctioned by the UN, and about expanding humanitarian operations. Its first year was an *annus horribilis* of painful education, memories of which hung over its security policy for years. Though it had a fistful of foreign policy talent, the Bush team, too, had much to learn.

Full-scale policy reviews were undertaken, but day-to-day affairs got stuck in a holding pattern. The State Department went six months without an assistant secretary of state for South Asia. Meetings continued, including one in which a Pakistani general informed his hosts that the United States was not dealing with the Taliban correctly, that it had to be treated like "a special needs child," with care and understanding. No serious initiative could begin until the policy reviews were completed; meanwhile, South Asia experts continued to pray that a rift would appear in the Taliban and their problems would be solved. That faint hope dimmed in April when Mullah Muhammad Rabbani, who was believed to be a moderate compared with Mullah Omar, and the most likely pole around whom Omar's opponents might gather, died of cancer. In other government agencies, stasis—or slippage backward—also prevailed. As of this writing, the Defense Department still does not have an assistant secretary for special operations and low-intensity conflict, and Secretary of Defense Donald Rumsfeld's team made matters more difficult for themselves by clearing out through transfer or demotion all but one of the *career*, nonpartisan deputy assistant secretaries and other senior managers in the department.

In two key offices of the new administration, there was continuity. Many directors of Central Intelligence have wanted to stay in office through a change of administration and party, but George Tenet became the first to accomplish that feat. During his time in the position, Tenet had become popular with many of the CIA's rank and file. He was known for walking the halls and chatting with employees at all levels, eating in the cafeteria, and being unusually accessible. It may be hard to think of the CIA as a love-starved place, but after the reigns of Woolsey and Deutch, both of whom were deeply unpopular, Tenet's embrace of his agency was much appreciated. Among some of the more senior officials, he was quietly faulted for embracing too much and not shaking up an institution still in need of reform. One school of thought also contended that he was too close to the Directorate of Operations—CIA leaders who clashed with the DO have had unhappy tenures—and uncritical of its management. At least in public, Tenet continued to sound the alarm about al-Qaeda. Speaking before the Senate Armed Services Committee in early March 2001, Tenet all but named the group as the foremost national security threat America faced: "Never in my experience has American intelligence had to deal with such a dynamic set of concerns affecting such a broad range of U.S. interests. Never have we had to deal with such a high quotient of uncertainty. With so many things on our plate, it is important always to establish priorities. For me, the highest priority must invariably be on those things that threaten the lives of Americans or the physical security of the United States. With that in mind, let me turn first to the challenges posed by international terrorism. . . . Usama bin Ladin and his global network of lieutenants and associates remain the most immediate and serious threat."[6]

Dick Clarke, surprising almost everyone, survived the change of administration. If records were kept for such things, they might show that he was the only career civil servant to serve as a NSC senior director under three consecutive Presidents and through two changes of party. (Perhaps in earlier, less partisan days, this distinction would not have been so rare.) Clarke had hoped that the new team, which described itself as being hard-headed and decisive, would move quickly to attack al-Qaeda. On his computer, he had an options paper for them that he had first drafted in October 2000. Many of its central elements were already in preparation. What was needed was an executive decision to follow through.

So when Steve Hadley sent all the NSC directorates a request for proposals for Principals meetings in January, Transnational Threats replied with a memo saying that a meeting on al-Qaeda was "urgently needed." This was not, the directorate said, "some narrow little terrorist issue"; a broader "regional policy" was required. A follow-up message noted: "We would make a major error if we underestimated the challenge al-Qaeda poses or overestimated the stability of the moderate, friendly regimes al-Qaeda threatens."

The front office was not persuaded. Rice had been surprised by the small empire of portfolios that Clarke had amassed in the years since she was last in the Old Executive Office Building, and she wanted to consider whether all those issues should be handled by the NSC and whether a national coordinator for terrorism was needed. Instead of scheduling a Principals meeting, they carried out a reorganization of the NSC that diminished Clarke's position, removing him from the seat he had held for three years on the Principals Committee during meetings on terrorism. That position had boosted Clarke's influence on U.S. policy, enabling him to push cutting-edge programs such as Predator and pump up agency counterterrorism budgets. But Rice wanted to consider doing things differently. She asked Clarke to lead an interagency review of U.S. policy toward al-Qaeda and, according to *The Washington Post,* spoke dismissively of her predecessors' handling of counterterrorism policy, saying that the Clinton administration approach was "empty rhetoric that made us look feckless."[7]

Military leaders who remained in office in the Bush administration saw terrorism moving "farther to the back burner," as Hugh Shelton put it. "The squeaky wheel was Dick Clarke, but he wasn't at the top of their priority list, so the lights went out for a few months. Dick did a pretty good job because he's abrasive as hell, but given the level he was at" there was no breaking through into the new team's field of vision.

Under Shelton, the Joint Chiefs had not come up with more military options. There was still a strong belief that al-Qaeda was first and foremost an intelligence problem, but the Chiefs were frustrated by the lack of CIA "information operations"—actually, disinformation operations—to create dissent among the Taliban. In the last year of the Clinton administration, the Joint Chiefs started developing a project of their own, which they planned to launch in 2001. But when they were briefed, the Pentagon's new leaders killed the project. "Rumsfeld [and] Deputy Secretary Paul Wolfowitz were against the Joint Staff having the lead on this," says Shelton. The two had been pruning away tasks that the armed forces had taken on in recent years, but that they did not consider to be *military* missions, and the disinformation project was one of those trimmed. In the early months of the administration, Rumsfeld's attention was on military doctrine, including the existing guidelines that U.S. forces needed to be able to fight two major theater wars, for example in the Persian Gulf and on the Korean peninsula, almost simultaneously. Missile defense and military restructuring were the key issues. According to Shelton, "this terrorism thing was out there," as far as Rumsfeld was concerned, "but it didn't happen today, so [he thought] maybe it belongs lower on the list . . . so it gets defused over a long period of time."

General Don Kerrick, the outgoing deputy national security adviser, spent the first four months of the new administration—and his final ones in uniform—in the Old Executive Office Building. He worried that the new crew had the "same strategic perspective as the folks in the eighties." They did not appreciate new threats such as terrorism that had arisen in the 1990s, and they were fixated on a missile defense system that he, like much of the uniformed military, considered unworkable and unnecessary. As a courtesy, he sent a memo to the NSC front office on "things you need to pay attention to." About the al-Qaeda terrorist threat he wrote bluntly, "We are going to be struck again." He never heard back. "I don't think it was above the waterline," he says. "They were gambling nothing would happen." That remained the new administration's posture even after February 9, when intelligence briefers told Vice President Dick Cheney that the CIA had concluded that al-Qaeda was responsible for bombing the *Cole*.[8]

—

In his policy review, Clarke wanted to push forward three initiatives, all of which were in the options paper he had worked on the previous October. The first was Predator. Despite the successes of the previous fall, the program had not been put on a fast track: the NSC leaders wanted a soup-to-nuts assessment before decisions were made. After the Air Force bailed out the program financially following the damage to the first drone, bickering between the Defense Department and the CIA continued through the winter and spring as the two tried to work out who would pay for lost craft in the future. The CIA insisted that it should not have to.

There was also a change in the nature of the program. After the initial test flights over Afghanistan, discussion began about hanging a weapon on the Predator itself. The attractions of doing so were clear: if the United States could see bin Laden in real time and fire a missile that would take seconds to strike, the problem of launching cruise missiles and not knowing if the target would remain in place for hours would disappear. The CIA was still divided over Predator, but it backed the idea of trying to arm the drone. The Air Force began experimenting with mounting a Hellfire C missile—a laser-guided, hundred-pound air-to-surface missile—on the craft. A consequence of this new approach, however, was that the Predator would not fly over Afghanistan in the spring, as planned, and therefore could not provide the possible second thread of intelligence indicating bin Laden's whereabouts. There were not enough of the drones or technicians to handle them to do reconnaissance and testing at once. The submarines had been taken off station in the Arabian Sea. Any near-term possibility of striking the terrorist with cruise missiles was thus foreclosed.

The "armed Predator" program was originally slated for three years of testing and modifications before the drone was redeployed. Clarke and his deputy, Roger Cressey, who had been detailed from the Defense Department at the end of 1999, worked on the Air Force to compress the program and complete it in three months. Cressey had started work shortly before the millennium conspiracies, and he shared Clarke's impatience to get the Predator into action. Tests for the drone were conducted in the late spring and early summer. At a test site in Nevada, a replica of bin Laden's house outside Kandahar was built and targeted by the drone. NSC staff members do not often attend weapons tests, but Cressey watched the Predator fire from thousands of feet above the desert and score a direct hit. He thought the outcome excellent.

This apparent success was not enough to get the Predator deployed to Afghanistan. Instead, it raised a host of issues that would be chewed over for months to come. Whose finger would be on the trigger when the Predator went after bin Laden—the Air Force's, or the CIA's? If the Predator's control unit was in another country, would that country's permission be required to fire the missile? What was the chain of command for such an operation? Who would issue the decision to fire—the CIA? The White House? If the White House, who at the White House? Could it be someone other than the President? Could there be a list of preap-proved targets, in case the President was not readily available? As hopes increased for the program, so did the number of issues to sort out.

Clarke's second objective was to get a proxy force into the field against bin Laden. In the last year of the Clinton administration, the search for such a force had widened. Uzbekistan, which shared a border with Afghanistan and whose regime loathed bin Laden and the IMU fighters he supported, volunteered to help. The CIA, however, was unenthusias-tic about too close a relationship. Too intimate involvement with repres-sive regimes had caused the Agency much grief over the years, and there was fear that Congress would look askance at the Uzbek connection. Clarke saw no reason not to use available forces, and he hoped that the Bush team would support his position.

The last of the three prongs of Clarke's strategy involved another proxy: he wanted to arm the Northern Alliance forces, then under the control of the legendary battlefield commander Ahmad Shah Massoud. The United States had maintained contact with Massoud over the years; on occasion, he gathered intelligence for the United States and was paid for it. Once, on his own initiative, Massoud had shelled the Derunta camp, where al-Qaeda conducted much of its chemical weapons work.

The possibility of providing Massoud with a major infusion of cash and weapons to support his war against the Taliban was discussed during the Clinton years but went nowhere. The belief among policy makers was that such a move would accomplish little: Iran and Russia—the latter with U.S. encouragement—were delivering plenty of arms and cash to the Northern Alliance. Massoud's problem was, most believed, not resources but the small size of his force. In a war that every year saw murderous campaigning across large swaths of the Afghan countryside, the Northern Alliance never fielded enough manpower to hold on to more than 15 per-cent of Afghanistan at the end of a fighting season. For all of Massoud's charisma and bravery, many of his troops were vicious, corrupt, and deeply unpopular. Assistance, however massive, was not going to turn the tide for the Northern Alliance or make the predominantly Tajik force acceptable to Afghans, of whom only one-quarter are Tajik. Nothing short of a commitment of U.S. air and possibly ground support could make the difference for the Northern Alliance. Few had the stomach to bind America to such an unpredictable bunch. Fewer still wanted to place the United States on what might be a slippery slope to a full-scale war in Asia. Serious as the threat of bin Laden was, there was a mismatch between provocation and this suggested response. No one could imagine presenting the American people with a war over a threat they knew so little about and did not view as critical. At first, after the embassy bombings, Clarke accepted this reasoning; but as time passed, he began to lobby harder for support to the Northern Alliance, believing that if Massoud's forces could tie down more Taliban and al-Qaeda fighters, that could only benefit the United States. He remained in the minority under Clinton. He hoped that would change under Bush.

While the interagency negotiations continued for the policy review, established efforts to counter terrorism were in trouble elsewhere in the administration. At the Treasury, Secretary Paul O'Neill disapproved of the Clinton administration's approach to money-laundering issues, which had been an important part of the drive to cut off the money flow to bin Laden. Prodded by the Clinton administration, the G-7, the multilateral Financial Action Task Force, and the Organization for Economic Cooperation and Development had developed programs that sought to embarrass countries with loose banking regulations into tightening them up, making it more difficult for money launderers. As a result, more than thirty countries began working with these organizations to clean up their banking sectors. But O'Neill and others in the administration, supported by conservatives and some banking groups, opposed the crackdown as "coercive" and contrary to American interests. Nor was there any interest in tracking terrorist assets. Clinton had pushed in his final budget for the creation of a National Terrorist Asset Tracking Center; on paper, the new entity was supposed to be getting organized. Under O'Neill, no funding for the center was provided and the work on terrorist finances slowed.[9]

Other agencies were equally disinclined to spend more money on counterterrorism. Through the late spring and summer, work on the annual budget submissions progressed. Attorney General John Ashcroft asked OMB to seek from Congress increased funding for sixty-eight Department of Justice programs, none of them related to counterterrorism, and the department proposed cutting $65 million from the grant program that assisted communities in buying equipment such as decontamination suits and radios needed for building the capability to deal with terrorist attack. Ashcroft also declined to endorse the FBI's request for $58 million that would have provided some four hundred counterterrorism agents, analysts, and translators.[10]

—

In the early months of the new administration, there was little threat reporting of note. Beginning in late spring that changed, with a sudden surge in activity among known al-Qaeda operatives. As the intelligence community sought more information, other disturbing signs appeared. A reporter from Middle East Broadcasting, an Arabic-language satellite channel, visited bin Laden at one of the camps in Afghanistan, and while the Saudi made no on-air comments, the piece said that his supporters were preparing for attacks against American and Israeli "interests." (When the United States reiterated its long-standing complaints to the Taliban, a Foreign Ministry official replied that bin Laden was under the Taliban's "tight control" and had no facilities for such terrorist activities.)[11] A new training video was also found circulating in radical circles. The tape showed militants rejoicing over the bombing of the *Cole,* and bin Laden inveighing against the United States and calling the faithful to arms. Three years earlier, just before the embassy bombings, bin Laden had also raised his profile through interviews and the issuance of another training tape; the intelligence community noted the parallel with appropriate concern.

It was clear something big was in the offing. The head of the Counterterrorist Center at the CIA, Cofer Black, put the pieces together in late

May. He and his staff believed that a major attack or group of attacks was in the works, and the indications were that Abu Zubayda, who had played a pivotal role in planning the attacks around the millennium, was involved. That news quickened pulses on both sides of the Potomac, because the young Palestinian was thought to be among al-Qaeda's foremost operatives. On the basis of the information at hand, the CIA thought the attack would come overseas. The most likely targets were believed to be in Israel or Saudi Arabia, where U.S. troops might be targeted and bin Laden could advance his goal of expelling America from the Arabian peninsula. Other possibilities included Rome and the Vatican, and U.S. military facilities in Turkey. All these fit with earlier patterns of threat reporting, and the Holy See made sense in light of the Bojinka-related plot to kill the pope. As soon as the CIA drew its conclusions about the data it had collected, the CSG reviewed the intelligence and delivered a warning of a "spectacular," which would be qualitatively different from anything that had come before. George Tenet came to the White House with "his hair on fire," as one staff member put it, to brief Rice and Hadley.

The CSG went through the checklist for impending disasters: the State Department renewed a worldwide caution to travelers and overseas residents about the possibility of terrorist violence, and the diplomatic security bureau asked posts around the world to request that host governments provide more protection. The CIA continued to press other intelligence services for every scrap of information and all possible assistance in tracking down al-Qaeda operatives. In the Persian Gulf, the threat condition for the U.S. military was raised to Delta, the highest level, which can best be described as having troops "lock and load." On the basis of threat information, the Navy's Fifth Fleet put to sea in late June from its harbor in Bahrain. A planned trip by counterterrorism officials to South America was canceled. A warning was issued to all domestic law-enforcement agencies about the possibility of an attack.

For years, July 4 has been a peak moment of anxiety about terrorist attack. In the run-up to the holiday, al-Qaeda operatives were caught in a

Persian Gulf country; their apprehension led to a belief that at least one plot had been foiled. Other events around that time also contributed to a sense that defensive measures were working. Even as the Fourth passed, however, so much intelligence was still coming in that a CSG meeting on the morning of the fifth concluded that a plot was still on. That afternoon, the domestic law-enforcement agencies—the FBI, Customs, the FAA, the Coast Guard, and the Secret Service—were brought in for an emergency meeting to discuss domestic countermeasures. They were briefed again and told that whatever had been planned was still in the works. The FBI was asked again, as it had been in May, to increase surveillance on individuals with al-Qaeda links. Another round of warnings went out, with the FBI notifying eighteen thousand state and local law-enforcement agencies and the FAA contacting every airline and airport. The warnings said that the threats were credible but not specific. In all, between late May and August 2001, domestic law enforcement issued three rounds of such warnings.

As July wore on, the forces in the Gulf were showing signs of fatigue. A level of security that can be difficult to maintain for a few days had been in effect for more than a month. With no more specific information, the threat level was reduced. Washington, however, got more jittery when Egyptian president Hosni Mubarak warned that his intelligence service had received information that al-Qaeda planned to attack President Bush at the annual G-7 meeting, which was being held later in July in Genoa. The scenario called for a plane loaded with explosives to crash into a venue where the President would be. At the insistence of the United States, Italy mounted antiaircraft guns at the Genoa airport, and the airspace around the city was closed.

After Bush returned from Europe, it became relatively quiet. The flow of intelligence died down. No one signaled the all-clear; rather, the last of the three rounds of domestic warnings was issued in August, and both the CIA and the Transnational Threats Directorate reiterated that the threat was still alive. But life began to return to normal. The counterterrorism policy review was ready for the Principals. August is when Presi-

dents take a long vacation, and the cabinet and White House staff, who
are tethered to the commander in chief for the rest of the year, finally feel
safe slipping away. Bush departed on August 4 for a month in Texas.
Originally, the meeting was to be scheduled for the first week of August,
but the NSC leadership decided that this was an issue that the national
security cabinet needed to think about carefully, so instead of rushing the
meeting, it was scheduled for the middle of the month. The State Department, however, objected. Colin Powell would be unable to make it on the
set date, and although deputies substitute frequently for traveling Principals, the department insisted that the secretary be there. The NSC as-
sented. Al-Qaeda would be the subject of one of the first Principals
Committee meetings after Labor Day. Dick Clarke's policy review would
be the center of the discussion.

Typically, by the time an issue reaches the Principals Committee, it
has been the subject of considerable discussion and negotiation at several
levels of the government. The issues are winnowed to a small number,
and for every question the Principals will face, they are given several options to discuss. For the meeting on counterterrorism, the process had
been going on for months. The point of this gathering would be to agree
on a National Security Presidential Directive (NSPD), which would set
out the President's policy. On paper, the administration's approach to al-
Qaeda was growing bolder. The Deputies Committee—all the relevant
second-tier officials—met to make final preparations for their superiors,
and agreed that the goal should not be "rolling back" al-Qaeda but
"eliminating" it.[12]

But the tools for accomplishing this were still being argued about.
Clarke and his team hoped to see the three core elements of their strategy
agreed upon: Predator, arming the Northern Alliance, and mobilizing the
Uzbeks. The CIA continued to put up opposition. It had come to view
the Uzbeks more positively, but the Agency had not changed its mind
about the Northern Alliance.

The Agency's position on Predator had changed. Its apparent enthusiasm for the armed Predator had waned—some said because it had not

taken three years to develop. The leadership in Langley, these individuals say, did not want responsibility for the program, despite the strong advocacy of prominent people inside the intelligence community. The record of this debate remains incomplete, and more of the participants need to be heard from. The version available to us indicates that the CIA threw up a number of obstacles to using the drone. First, it objected that the Hellfire missile had not done enough damage to the mock bin Laden house: bigger ordnance was needed to ensure sufficient destruction. The Directorate of Operations argued that it wanted to use the money to push harder for human sources. That position drew a sharp riposte from the White House, which said that its understanding had been that the DO had all the money it needed for that purpose, as it had said in earlier exchanges when the White House inquired about options for a more aggressive action in Afghanistan.

Finally, the Agency said it was not appropriate for the CIA to operate Predator. That responsibility, it argued, should belong to the Air Force, which deployed aircraft that carried ordnance. In the weeks before the Principals Committee meeting, the head of the Directorate of Operations, James Pavitt, was heard to say that if the Predator was used against bin Laden, and responsibility for this use of lethal force was laid at the Agency's doorstep, it would endanger the lives of CIA operatives around the world. (Whatever the veracity of the rest of the account, that contention about perils to clandestine agents is one made frequently—though not always plausibly—by the DO.) The Air Force reportedly retorted by saying that if it had the mission, it would use B-52 bombers, not some spindly drone. The generals did not say how that would help preserve deniability or, for that matter, how the intelligence to find bin Laden would be produced. There were other issues that needed answers. Where could bin Laden be targeted—for example, could he be hit in a mosque? What about the issue of the placement of the control unit in a foreign country? If it was on foreign soil, the host government's approval would be required, something that all involved recognized as a formidable obstacle. Predator was a hornet's nest.

—

When the Principals convened on September 4 for their first meeting to discuss al-Qaeda, all these issues were on the table. Virtually all the Principals were there, although Paul Wolfowitz sat in for Secretary of Defense Rumsfeld, and Sean O'Keefe, the OMB deputy, took his boss Mitch Daniels's seat. Dick Clarke reviewed the draft NSPD. George Tenet followed by saying, "We really need to aggressively go after these guys." Paul O'Neill cautioned that it was difficult to find terrorists' money. The group quickly came to an agreement of sorts on support for the Northern Alliance and Uzbeks. All voiced their approval for doing something, but the issue of finding the hundreds of millions of dollars to finance the effort was given to the OMB and CIA to figure out—the kind of decision that leaves much undecided, since a government agency that is told to finance a program "out of hide," out of the existing budget, frequently argues back that the issue is not a high enough priority.

These matters were covered in the first quarter of the discussion. Then the conversation turned to Predator. Do we want it? Condoleezza Rice asked. Who is going to run it? Would it do the job? For all the visible damage done in the Nevada desert, the Hellfire missile was not a "penetrator," and there was concern it would hit the roof of a structure and not destroy the target. The monitors the Air Force used scored the test at somewhat below the 85 percent kill probability that was desirable. The Air Force thought more testing would be appropriate—the first shot would almost certainly be the best one the United States would ever get.

The conversation then turned to the question of who would operate Predator. Tenet intervened forcefully. It would be a terrible mistake, he declared, for the director of Central Intelligence to fire a weapon like this. That would happen, he said, over his dead body. The White House officials reeled the conversation back by establishing that the *decision* to fire was not for the DCI but for the President. General Myers, the chairman of the Joint Chiefs, returned to the question of who would carry out the mission. If we do it, he said, we'll do it with cruise missiles. If it is a covert mission, he insisted, it belongs to the intelligence community. Any possibility of agreement was slipping away.

The conversation finally turned to the question of a mission that was only for reconnaissance, putting aside the issue of the armed Predator, whose development had been the focus of the preceding months. Tenet agreed that that was more palatable, but the CIA would still need to review the matter. There was discussion of testing other weapons instead of the Hellfire. The issue of who would fire an armed Predator was deferred. The meeting ended. There was no decision on Predator and no strategy to forward to the President.

—

If September 11 was Usama bin Laden's revelation, the months that followed provided a series of startling disclosures about counterterrorism, the U.S. government, and America's friends.

The identities and origins of the hijackers were quickly ascertained, and their roots in the Hamburg cell were traced. Despite repeated requests for assistance over at least the previous three years, German intelligence and law-enforcement authorities had not taken American concerns about al-Qaeda seriously. The Germans had, as requested, extradited Mamduh Salim (Abu Hajer) in 1998, but they had not delivered the most basic follow-through. Salim had a bank account that was left untouched. A Syrian-born German citizen, Mamoun Darkanzali, had cosigned for the account and, according to U.S. officials, money from it was wired to the September 11 conspirators. Shortly before the attack itself Muhammad Atta sent money back to the account. This occurred despite explicit requests from the FBI to German authorities to monitor Darkanzali's activities.

The inadequacy of the INS's visa system for foreign students was dramatically illustrated. One of the hijackers, Hani Hanjour, who came into the country on an I-20 student visa, would likely have been barred from entry if the CIPRIS system had been operational. Muhammad Atta and Marwan al-Shehhi, the pilots of the planes that struck the Twin Towers, both applied to change from tourist to student status, so their names would likely have been flagged for investigation as well. When Muhammad Atta got a traffic ticket in Broward County, Florida, on April 26, 2001, his only known contact with U.S. law enforcement, he might have been stopped.

Because of a leak, it became known that in July 2001 FBI Agent Kenneth Williams of the Phoenix field office sent a memo to Washington headquarters recommending that the FBI investigate the possibility that Islamist radicals were receiving training at American flight schools. On the basis of his investigation of an Arizona flight school, he determined that one Middle Eastern student there was in touch, perhaps indirectly, with Abu Zubayda, a central figure in the millennium conspiracies.[13] Despite the fact that the FBI knew of at least three jihadists who had received flight instruction, two of them in the United States, the FBI decided that Williams's recommendation would require manpower beyond what the Bureau could spare. The information about the flight training easily qualified as extraordinary and would have received instant attention had it been communicated to the NSC, but it was never forwarded to the White House or the CSG. That Abu Zubayda was in touch with an identifiable individual in the United States ought to have rung every alarm in the law-enforcement and intelligence community—as though bin Laden himself were on the phone. Yet this was never brought to the attention of the White House, either.

In the reporting after the attacks, the government acknowledged that the CIA had notified the INS on August 21 that two of the hijackers, Khalid al-Mihdhar and Nawaf al-Hazmi, should be put on the terrorist watch list. Both had been identified on a surveillance tape meeting with an al-Qaeda operative in Malaysia. The INS informed both the CIA and the FBI that the two were already in the country. The FBI has said that "every attempt was made" to find them. Despite this extraordinary situation, the FBI never notified the White House or the CSG, which had the greatest ability to mobilize all the assets of the federal government, that al-Qaeda operatives—including one suspected of involvement in the bombing of the *Cole*—were in the country.

On a tip from a flight school, Zacarias Moussaoui, a Frenchman of Moroccan descent, was arrested on August 16 outside St. Paul. Moussaoui had offered to pay thousands of dollars in cash for lessons on a jumbo jet flight simulator but only wanted to learn how to steer the plane, not how to land it. At the request of the FBI's Minneapolis field office, the CIA contacted French intelligence, which relayed that Moussaoui was connected with Islamic extremists. When the field office applied for a warrant under the Foreign Intelligence Surveillance Act that would have allowed the agents to examine his laptop computer, FBI headquarters blocked the application from going forward. Had the FBI investigated Moussaoui more thoroughly at the outset, it might have learned that he attended the same flight school in Norman, Oklahoma, that an al-Qaeda operative had attended several years earlier. (In fact, Moussaoui was at that flight school on the day that evidence was presented in New York about al-Qaeda member Ihab Ali's training there.) No word of Moussaoui's arrest was brought to the attention of the White House or the CSG.

After the revelations of FBI failures, many public figures explained that Bureau culture emphasized solving crimes, not preventing them. But they failed to note that in the aftermath of the Oklahoma City bombing, the FBI had effectively dedicated itself to watching the far-right militias and had broken up serious conspiracies—admittedly an easier task than combating al-Qaeda, but a sign nonetheless of the Bureau's understanding of its declared mission.

Within the executive branch as well as in public statements and, especially, testimony on Capitol Hill, the FBI's top leaders regularly asked for more money for counterterrorism. They also regularly received it. Yet after September 11, the FBI acknowledged to senior administration officials that despite hundreds of millions of dollars of budget increases over several years, it had no more agents working on counterterrorism cases than it had in 1996. Although the Clinton administration, using information supplied by the Bureau to OMB, declared on numerous occasions that the number of agents working in counterterrorism had more than doubled, the Bureau had actually assigned most of these new personnel to the National Infrastructure Protection Center, the FBI's cybersecurity unit.

Two weeks after the Principals Committee meeting, the armed Predator was flying over Afghanistan. In November, the drone identified a house where a large meeting of al-Qaeda personnel was under way. Navy F/A-18 fighters were alerted and bombed the house. When those inside emerged, the Predator fired its two Hellfire missiles. Among those killed was Muhammad Atef, al-Qaeda's military chief for nearly a decade. To date, he is the highest-ranking member of the organization known to have died in Afghanistan.

CHAPTER 9

A FAILURE OF INTELLIGENCE

THERE IS NO OBJECTIVE WAY to measure surprise. Looking back over the last century, however, it is difficult to think of any events as shocking—as completely unexpected by the overwhelming majority of people—as those of September 11. For six decades, Pearl Harbor was synonymous with the notion of surprise attack for Americans. But, in fact, on December 7, 1941, the public had been expecting a conflict with Japan for months, if not years, and the base was considered a possible target long before it was struck.

On September 10, ordinary Americans had no conception that one of the bloodiest days in the nation's history would be the work of terrorists, not of another nation. They did not identify Islamist radicals as a group intent on killing thousands. If pushed, they might have named skyscrapers in lower Manhattan as a potential target of attack, but mostly because the Twin Towers had been bombed eight years earlier. They had no inkling that a suicide attack on such a scale was a possibility or that anyone on earth had the wherewithal, or, more important, the desire to carry out such a crime. In fact, most Americans, if asked, would have likely said that their nation had never been more secure. More than a decade after the end of the Cold War, it had become a truism that the world had not seen such a dominant power since ancient Rome.

That a surprise of this magnitude could occur to 280 million Americans living in the information age, surrounded by round-the-clock cable news, daily newspapers, and radio, and afloat on the Internet, the greatest sea of facts and figures in all of history, is astonishing. How could a society so drenched in news and data of every kind have been caught so off guard?

Did the American public, like key parts of the government, miss something that would have alerted it to the growing danger of al-Qaeda? The question should be directed to the institution that keeps Americans informed: the press. Was there a moment that the nation's news-gathering organizations might have recognized that something important had changed in the world, and a new danger was on the rise?

For many of those in the U.S. government who recognized the threat of jihadist terror *before* September 11, the pivotal event was the East Africa embassy bombings. Nothing before that coordinated attack had demonstrated such a combination of skill and murderousness. The indiscriminate violence of those bombings telegraphed al-Qaeda's desire to inflict mass casualties. The evidence appeared on television screens and in newspapers. Why did the media not recognize it or pursue the story more aggressively? Did America have a wake-up call in August 1998, and if so, why did the call go unheard?

———

The key date is not August 7, the day of the bombings, but the twentieth, when the United States struck al-Qaeda targets in Afghanistan and Sudan. The attacks in Africa were seen as pathbreaking, devastating events. But until the twentieth, the news was about the rescue efforts and those who had been killed and wounded. Then Washington launched the cruise missile strike and announced that bin Laden was behind the destruction of the embassies.

The U.S. action against the terrorist camps in Afghanistan was widely accepted by the American press and public, even though the Tomahawk missiles missed the al-Qaeda leadership, hitting shortly after they had departed. It made obvious sense to target sites where those responsible for the bloodshed in Africa might be; explaining the bombing of al-Shifa, thousands of miles from Afghanistan, would inevitably be more difficult. To make their case, government officials spoke definitively about intelligence that indicated al-Qaeda was preparing for more killing and was seeking some of the world's most destructive weapons.

Meeting with reporters immediately after the attack on Khartoum, a senior intelligence official explained why al-Shifa had been demolished:

> First, we know that bin Laden has made financial contributions to the Sudanese military industrial complex [actually, the Sudanese Military Industrial Corporation]. That's a distinct entity of which we believe the Shifa pharmaceutical facility is part.
>
> We know with high confidence that Shifa produces a precursor that is unique to the production of VX.
>
> We know that bin Laden has been seeking to acquire chemical weapons for use in terrorist acts.
>
> We know that bin Laden has had an intimate relationship with the Sudanese government which is a state sponsor of terrorism.
>
> We know that bin Laden has worked with Sudan to test poisonous gases and to finance simpler methods of manufacturing and dispensing gas, methods which would be less time consuming and expensive than prior Sudanese efforts.
>
> Even though he left Sudan in 1996, we know that bin Laden's businesses acquired restricted, high-priced items for the Sudanese military including arms, communications, and dual-use components for chemical and biological weapons.
>
> With regard to the question you raised to the Secretary, why did we do this today? Obviously we felt the information was compelling. We wanted to act quickly. We had compelling evidence—indeed, we have ongoing evidence that bin Laden's infrastructure is continuing to plan terrorist acts targeted against American facilities and American citizens around the world.

Responding to a question, the official added, "We know he has had an interest in acquiring chemical weapons. We know that he himself has talked about thousands of deaths."[1]

———

Before they were banned by an international convention in 1997, nerve agents were the most widely stockpiled chemical weapons among the world's militaries. Pioneered in Germany just before World War II, they were found to be far more effective than the blistering agents, such as phosgene and mustard gas, used in World War I. The weapons work by inhibiting a nerve's ability to stop firing. A class of chemicals—called G-agents because they were developed by Nazi Germany during World War II—were produced in large quantities but never used in battle. Among the G-agents are tabun, soman, and sarin.

In the early 1950s, research on the G-agents led to better protective measures against them and also to the creation of more effective and long-lasting nerve agents. VX, first developed in a British laboratory, was found to be one hundred times as poisonous as the G-agents. As little as a single drop of the oily amber liquid can cause uncontrollable twitching, convulsions, and death within fifteen minutes of being placed on the skin. It was adopted by the U.S. government as its principal chemical weapon and produced in large quantities from 1961 to 1968.[2] There has been no recorded use of VX as a weapon.

Despite the government's assertion that al-Qaeda was working to acquire VX and that bin Laden had spoken of killing thousands, the response to the attack on the al-Shifa chemical plant in Khartoum was entirely different from the response to the strike against Afghanistan. Regarding the former, press coverage about the government's case was not merely skeptical but plainly dismissive. Congress was largely silent about the administration's arguments concerning chemical weapons at al-Shifa. Some members, for partisan reasons, exploited the doubts about the missile strike.

Reporters heard the official quoted above and conclusions that were based on sensitive intelligence, most of which was, at least initially, unavailable to the press. But they also heard charges that Clinton was a "war criminal" leveled by Sudanese strongman Omar Bashir, who had presided over years of fighting in southern Sudan that claimed hundreds of thousands of Sudanese lives. Engineers and businessmen acquainted with the plant also weighed in with their doubts about the link with chemical weapons. Confronted with these contradictory descriptions of al-Shifa, journalists relayed the account presented by government officials as less than credible.

Determined to build up public approval for its actions, the Clinton administration decided to reveal some of the supporting intelligence despite strong reservations about exposing the sources and methods involved. This won over few converts. Intelligence is always incomplete, typically composed of pieces that refuse to fit neatly together and are subject to competing interpretations. By disclosing the intelligence, the administration was asking journalists to connect the dots—assemble bits of evidence and construct a picture that would account for all the disparate information. In response, reporters cast doubt on the validity of each piece of the information provided and thus on the case for attacking al-Shifa.

One of the first aspects of the attack to be criticized was the plant's link to bin Laden. As the senior intelligence official who briefed reporters noted, al-Shifa was part of a larger entity run by the Sudanese government, the Military Industrial Corporation, in which bin Laden had a large financial interest. When no deed of ownership with bin Laden's name on it was produced—hardly surprising—reporters complained that the tie to the Saudi exile had not been proven. This put the administration in a bind: revealing its intelligence, whether from communications intercepts, informants, or other clandestine means, would expose American methods, destroy the ability to continue collecting intelligence. Bin Laden still had deep roots in Sudan; officials concluded that they simply could not afford to reveal more.

The next line of attack dealt with the famous soil sample. The CIA had been reluctant to publicize how it had established that materials associated with chemical weapons were present at al-Shifa: to reveal the sample's existence could endanger the operative who had obtained it and make it impossible for him ever to collect another. Moreover, the Sudanese and other chemical weapons producers around the world would immediately increase security at chemical plants, making it more difficult for the United States to collect samples everywhere. Still, once the sample was discussed on August 24, no amount of explanation would suffice. Some argued that the sample's chain of custody was improper, implicitly disregarding the fact that intelligence operations typically are not and cannot be conducted according to the standards of judicial proof. A single operative with a bag of soil in Sudan would be hard-pressed to demonstrate that it could not possibly have been tampered with while in his control.

Others contended that to have analyzed the soil sample at just one laboratory was shoddy science and that EMPTA, the chemical found in it, could hypothetically have been a derivative of pesticide production. But the CIA's analysis, which reporters were given on August 24, showed that EMPTA had no commercial use anywhere in the world. This conclusion was never refuted; it was also widely ignored.[3] Officials who spoke with reporters also noted that Iraqi weapons scientists had been linked to al-Shifa, and this Iraqi connection was independently underscored by UN weapons inspectors.[4] There are several different methods for making VX, but the only one known to involve EMPTA is Iraq's. Again, this information was never contradicted, but few found it persuasive. As more intelligence was revealed to reporters, the joke circulated among National Security Council staff members that the government was performing the dance of the seven veils but the press was administering death by a thousand cuts.

Even independently reported stories that should have strengthened the government's case skipped off the consciousness of other journalists and the public without leaving a ripple. *Newsday* correspondent Tina Susman reported from Khartoum that the general manager of the al-Shifa plant was living in bin Laden's villa in the al-Riyadh neighborhood of

Khartoum. Osman Suleiman, who had been identified as the manager both by employees at the plant and by the lawyer for the putative owner, moved into the house after bin Laden left it, his neighbors said. When Susman met with Suleiman and asked if he was indeed the manager, the Sudanese "denied this as he sat behind a desk . . . in a downtown Khartoum office whose doors are marked El-Shifa in giant blue letters. Suleiman also denied being Suleiman but eventually admitted who he is." Susman's report was picked up by the *Dallas Morning News* and no one else.[5] Indeed, Sudan itself got something of a free ride during the coverage. In the two weeks following the attack on al-Shifa, *The New York Times, The Washington Post,* and the *Los Angeles Times* printed at least eighty-eight stories that made substantive mention of the strike; only eight mentioned that Sudan was on the State Department's list of state sponsors of terrorism. The *Los Angeles Times* mentioned that fact but once.

Meanwhile, senior officials, in explaining the decision to attack al-Shifa, made errors that badly damaged their own case. Although CIA personnel knew that al-Shifa produced pharmaceuticals, the senior intelligence official who first briefed the press about the plant had said, "Ostensibly, I guess, it's supposed to make pharmaceuticals. We have no evidence, have seen no commercial products that are sold out of this facility." Cabinet officials and the national security adviser, Sandy Berger, all of whom had been referring to it simply as a chemical plant, repeated that point and were caught flat-footed when it became clear that the plant did produce medicines. Berger, for example, referred defensively to the "so-called pharmaceutical plant." The officials repeatedly echoed the mistake of the senior intelligence official in asserting that al-Shifa was involved in producing chemical weapons when the intelligence only demonstrated the presence of the nerve-gas precursor EMPTA, not its actual manufacture. These were critical mistakes, and they were taken as further confirmation of administration incompetence and even malfeasance.[6]

It was not surprising that such errors reinforced skepticism among reporters, but administration officials, still transfixed by the destruction in East Africa, were taken aback by the press's refusal to countenance the government's case. The belief that the nation was genuinely threatened, and that the nature of the threat justified measures such as the bombing, was not getting through. A telling example of the coverage was the headline on a September 21, 1998, *New York Times* story by Tim Weiner and James Risen: "Decision to Strike Factory in Sudan Based on Surmise Inferred from Evidence." They wrote:

> Senior officials now say their case for attacking the factory relied on inference as well as evidence that it produced chemical weapons for Mr. bin Laden's use. And a reconstruction of how the "small group" and the President picked the bombing targets, based on interviews with participants and others at high levels in the national security apparatus, offers new details of how an act of war was approved on the basis of shards of evidence gleaned from telephone intercepts, spies and scientific analysis.

In fact, the attack was based on more than "surmise," and more than "shards" of evidence were involved. Inference was indeed used, but its adequacy—indeed, necessity—as a mode of reasoning by national leaders was something that was never accepted.

—

In its coverage of al-Shifa, though, most of the media did embrace one gigantic inference: by attacking a pharmaceutical plant in Sudan, it was said, President Bill Clinton was attempting to "wag the dog," to distract the American public from a sex scandal just as a war against Albania was used for the same purpose in the eponymous Robert De Niro–Dustin Hoffman movie released eight months earlier. Clinton's grand jury appearance regarding his relationship with Monica Lewinsky occurred three days before the August 20 attack. That event and the universal conviction that life was imitating art swept all considerations of American security aside on the radio and network television and in the daily papers. Within forty-eight hours of the missile attacks, NBC News had broadcast clips from the movie six times, and every other network ran the footage repeatedly as well.

On CNN's *Crossfire,* the satirist Mark Russell led Pat Buchanan and Bill Press in singing:

> If a woman gives you trouble or maybe two or three, and your explanation puts the public in a fog, no problem, pick that red phone up, it's an emergency, and go to war. It's been done before. It's "Wag the Dog."
>
> "Wag the Dog." "Wag the Dog." Go to war, it's been done before, it's "Wag the Dog."
>
> Well, no one will complain with a Hitler like Hussein, and everyone will understand your war. An Afghanistan distraction from your problems and your pain, namely, Monica and Paula and God knows how many more.
>
> "Wag the dog."[7]

The bloodshed in East Africa had been eclipsed by a carnival.

That Clinton would be accused of trying to divert attention from the Lewinsky scandal surprised no one in the policy loop. When the Principals met in the White House Situation Room to approve the operation, Secretary of Defense William Cohen said that the President was going to be criticized for trying to the change the subject from the ongoing scandal. Others in the room were somewhat surprised that Cohen felt this needed to be spelled out, and no one commented on the remark. Later, when Clinton was briefed on the operation in the Cabinet Room, one adviser said that there were certain to be allegations that he was trying to distract the country. "If I have to take more criticism for this, I will," he replied.

Just how much Clinton ultimately had to take was incredible, not only because of the implicit disregard for the bloodshed in East Africa— Exhibit A demonstrating that the United States was in a new game with new rules—but also because of the absurdity of the idea that any President, and especially one with such a famously acute political sensibility, *would actually think* he could get away with wagging the dog. In Congress, however, some believed Clinton was brazen enough to try it. Senator Arlen Specter, the moderate Republican from Pennsylvania, declared, "The President was considering doing something presidential to try to focus attention away from—from his own personal problems." Senator Daniel Coats of Indiana was less restrained: accusing Mr. Clinton of "lies and deceit and manipulations and deceptions," Coats said that the President's record "raises into doubt everything he does and everything he says, and maybe even everything he doesn't do and doesn't say."[8] Throughout this period and the remainder of the Clinton presidency, it is worth noting, no member of Congress ever called the national security adviser to discuss the rising problem of al-Qaeda. (Most of the letters from members during this period dealt with the issue of seizing Iranian assets to compensate victims of Iranian-backed terrorist attacks in Israel.) It is a telling footnote to the entire period that one of the very few phone calls to Clinton about the response to the embassy bombings came from Speaker of the House Newt Gingrich. As Susan Schmidt and Michael Weisskopf recount in *Truth at Any Cost: Ken Starr and the Unmaking of Bill Clinton,* "Gingrich, with his well-known instinct for the jugular, called Clinton to discuss terrorism and ended the conversation with some political advice. The Republicans were riding high in the polls and could pick up dozens of seats. Soon, he said, the president would be hearing from worried Democrats who would want him to step down."[9]

Whether the medium was highbrow print or talk radio, the verdict was virtually unanimous. No less a publication than *The New Yorker* embraced the "wag the dog" explanation, clearing the way for others. The veteran investigative reporter Seymour Hersh used the stratagem of insinuation by indirection, attributing to others a point for which he had no proof: "Some reporters questioned whether the President had used military force to distract the nation's attention from the Lewinsky scandal." His article—essentially a tissue of unattributed quotations—recapitulated the litany of allegations against the al-Shifa intelligence and added a few more verses. After noting, for example, Sandy Berger's public remarks that U.S. intelligence had received "very specific information about very specific threats with respect to very specific targets," Hersh wrote that "some American intelligence operatives, who have spent much of their careers reading and evaluating intercepted telephone calls and other communications, were taken aback that Berger had been so categorical. The specific warnings of future terrorism, one experienced intelligence operative told me, 'came from garbled intercepts and a series of walk-ins'—defectors—'that, while not without merit, are no different from any number of walk-ins that come in all the time.' " Whoever the anonymous intelligence operative was, his remarks were wrong. There was a deluge of information, and, as the foiled plot in Albania—which Hersh never noted—suggests, some of it regarding unfolding matters that were scarily serious. The *New Yorker* piece concluded with remarks about the President from an unnamed "State Department veteran": "Survival is his most important issue. It's always on his mind. If Clinton was not in all this trouble, he wouldn't have done it [authorized the cruise-missile raids]. He's too smart."[10]

For a shrewd manipulator, Clinton certainly took a battering. In fact, one of the supreme ironies of the episode is that the press accounts were so uniformly negative that Clinton himself came to wonder whether the strike was justified. He eventually asked the NSC for a review of all the intelligence on which the decision to strike was based. Those who worked on the memo, which took months of effort, concluded that the call was right. Additional information gathered after August 20, they felt, made the justification for the strike even stronger.

—

The press is in its element when unmasking official folly or malfeasance, and in the al-Shifa reporting, it had a field day. The strike against al-Shifa was woven into the fabric of the impeachment story, and no other interpretation could be admitted. Or, to use a different metaphor, the tale of

Clinton's misconduct became the narrative maelstrom of the period, and all discussion of terrorism was swept into the vortex. So in the midst of it all, no one asked the obvious questions: Why would a President determined to "wag the dog" strike two targets when one would do? The camps in Afghanistan were obviously justifiable targets; striking them alone would have satisfied the public need for retaliation. As the accidental bombing of the Chinese embassy in Belgrade a year later and the 1988 downing of an Iranian passenger plane over the Persian Gulf demonstrate, there are few more damaging events for any administration than a failed or unpopular military strike. Why would a President risk an embarrassing failure by attacking al-Shifa if he wasn't absolutely convinced of the necessity of the action? Would an entire national security team, including Secretary of Defense William Cohen, a Republican, and career military officers, really collude in such a crass maneuver, which cost a guard at the chemical plant his life? It seems not to have been considered that America's intelligence community, to which Congress reportedly appropriates some $30 billion annually, might have gotten the assessment of al-Shifa right and that there was a genuine threat that chemical weapons would be used against Americans. Whether a national leader confronted with the information that Clinton received could afford not to act was a question that no one wanted to address.

In the months that followed, al-Shifa became a byword for the hyping of al-Qaeda. The government's error in striking the plant became a favorite bone that the major dailies and pundits from the right and left could not stop picking. Christopher Hitchens, a contributor to *The Nation* and *Vanity Fair,* proclaimed, in one of more than ten columns in which he raised the subject, that "those who cited *Wag the Dog* may have been acting cynical [*sic*], but even they must now be shocked to hear that it was worse than they thought."[11] The certainty that the United States had gotten it wrong colored reporting about Salah Idris, the owner of record of al-Shifa, and his legal action against the U.S. Treasury, which had frozen his assets following the bombing. When the Treasury released the assets several months later, officials explained that the government was not prepared to reveal additional intelligence in court to maintain the freeze. Disclosing the government's full knowledge of the financial relationships among bin Laden, the Military Industrial Corporation, and al-Shifa would, they said, have destroyed their ability to gather intelligence again about these and similar matters. These statements went largely unreported, and the Treasury's action was widely reported as a concession that the United States had hit the wrong target. Idris himself became a minor celebrity, hiring the politically well-connected law firm of Akin, Gump and the renowned investigators of Kroll International to help him press a suit against the Treasury for damages suffered while his assets were frozen. In the Style section of *The Washington Post,* Vernon Loeb portrayed Idris as Horatio Alger fighting for his rights.

> Idris hardly fits the profile of a terrorist. The son of a tailor from a town in the north of Sudan, Idris, 47, graduated from the University of Cairo's Khartoum branch, moved to Saudi Arabia in 1976 and started working as an accountant at the National Commercial Bank, where he became a protege of the bank's proprietor and chief executive officer, Sheikh Khalid bin Mahfouz. The Mahfouzes are a well-known business family in Jiddah and, through the NCB, have banking connections to the Saudi royal family, staunch U.S. allies who expelled bin Laden in the first place.
>
> Idris formed his own small export firm in 1983 and became ever closer to bin Mahfouz. When his mentor became embroiled in the Bank of Credit and Commerce International (BCCI) banking scandal in the early 1990s, Idris handled bin Mahfouz's personal affairs and basically ran the bank. When bin Mahfouz resumed his duties, he made Idris the bank's manager of international accounts.[12]

What Loeb failed to mention was that Mahfouz was not merely "embroiled" in the BCCI scandal, the largest bank fraud in history, but had to pay a $225 million fine in the matter. More important, the *Post* neglected to note that Idris's patron was deeply involved in Islamic charities that were suspected of funneling money to bin Laden. This was not a secret: two weeks before Loeb's article appeared, ABC News had reported "that a prominent and very wealthy Saudi banker, Khalid bin Mahfouz, is being held by Saudi authorities, accused of using his bank to funnel money to charities and companies that are fronts for bin Laden's organization."[13] The fate of Mahfouz himself is unclear; at least for a time, the British press reported that the Saudi government had confined him in a hospital in the mountain resort of Taif.

—

After August 1998, interest in al-Qaeda and the radicalization taking place in parts of the Islamic world was limited and episodic. The overriding belief was that bin Laden represented a variation on past themes: he hated America, he wanted to kill, and he had shown some skill at it. But he was not fundamentally a new and more dangerous kind of terrorist. By treating him as such, some argued, the United States was only helping him. Mary Anne Weaver, writing in *The New Yorker* in January 2000, suggested that Washington had "mythologized" the terrorist. "And each time the Clinton Administration raises the stakes, and further enhances bin Laden's prominence, more and more disaffected Saudis flock to join the kingdom's militant Islamist underground, of which bin Laden remains a central part. That is one of the most worrisome consequences of America's obsession with one man."[14] Later that year, former CIA agent Milt Bearden and former State Department official Larry Johnson—both long out of government—endorsed this thinking, saying that "American attempts to blast Usama bin Laden out of his Afghan redoubt have elevated him to levels of mystical power in the Islamic world." They criticized the United States for not trying hard enough to negotiate with the Taliban's leaders.[15] In the summer of 2001, Dan Rather, interviewing Sandy Berger for the CBS newsmagazine *60 Minutes II*, said, "Just as FDR's picture is in every home of Americans of a certain age, bin Laden's picture is in every tent and hut in Afghanistan and Pakistan, as a result of your trying to get him."[16] That part of the interview was never broadcast.

Commentators stubbornly preferred criticizing the United States to cred-
iting bin Laden with being a pathbreaking figure and the architect of his
own myth, which was built on audacious attacks, including the destruction of two embassies and, later, the near sinking of a U.S. warship. Another argument, often heard from Europeans, was that the United States
was obsessed with bin Laden because, having lost its longtime nemesis
with the collapse of the Soviet Union, another needed to be invented. As
the German weekly *Die Woche* wrote after the strikes against Afghanistan
and Sudan, "Why open a new [military] front at all? Without a threatening 'Feindbild' [image of the enemy] the Superpower appears to be having a hard time finding its way amid the complexities of the post–Cold
War era. Such a powerful [military] apparatus requires a powerful opponent."[17] These were not the only viewpoints in circulation, but they were
the dominant ones.

—

Clinton himself had been speaking frequently about terrorism for some
time. After the June 1996 Khobar Towers bombing, the United States
had insisted on short notice that the agenda for the July meeting of the
G-7 be scrapped and an emergency session on international cooperation
to combat terrorism be held. The President gave a major speech on the
subject in early August 1996 at George Washington University, and afterward, his speechwriters had a standing order to include warnings about
the rising threat of terror in virtually every foreign policy speech he gave.
These were not just perfunctory mentions: Clinton devoted a significant
portion of his public speaking on foreign policy to the issue, including his
1998 commencement address at the U.S. Naval Academy. (One service
academy each year typically gets a presidential visit at graduation, and it
is the occasion for a major foreign and security policy statement.) Thus,
three months before the East Africa bombings, Clinton spoke about the
task of reorganizing the government to meet the terrorist threat and the
growing danger of terrorism involving weapons of mass destruction and
cyberattacks. A month after the bombings, he devoted his annual address
to the UN General Assembly to the issue, warning that "it is a grave mis-

conception to see terrorism as only, or even mostly, an American problem. Indeed, it is a clear and present danger to tolerant and open societies and innocent people everywhere. No one in this room, nor the people you represent, are immune." During the months that impeachment was hanging in the balance, Clinton did not grant newspaper interviews because of the proceedings, but afterward he gave his first interview to *The New York Times*'s Judith Miller to discuss the threat of terrorist attack with biological weapons, which, of all the different strands within the issue, was the one he cared about most deeply.[18] Whether anyone saw Clinton's efforts as more than an attempt to change the subject is impossible to judge, but they certainly made little impact on reporters. He continued speaking about terrorism, and it became a personal preoccupation. When Clinton gave his final State of the Union address in January 2000, he added, out of the blue, an improvised aside: "I predict to you, when most of us are long gone, but sometime in the next ten to twenty years, the major security threat this country will face will come from the enemies of the nation-state: the narcotraffickers and the terrorists and the organized criminals, who will be organized together, working together, with increasing access to ever more sophisticated chemical and biological weapons." His timing was wrong; the point was right.

NSC officials, ourselves among them, also tried to convince those who would listen that bin Laden was a different kind of terrorist, uniquely dangerous, and that militant Islam posed a growing, serious threat. In the months after the 1998 embassy bombings, this was done, in keeping with White House practice, without attribution by name. Time and again we spoke with journalists and tried to impress on them that al-Qaeda presented a genuine threat to American national security. At a time when it would have been easy to join the masses of government officials who were decrying the bombing of al-Shifa, we and others maintained in conversation after conversation that targeting the plant was the right thing to do. When one of us was asked over lunch by the foreign editor of *The Washington Post* what the most important story was that the press was missing, the answer given was: the rise of radical Islam, especially in South Asia.

After we left the NSC in late 1999 and could speak and write publicly, we tried to sound the alarm. On the *New York Times* op-ed page on January 4, 2000, we argued that after the terror-free millennium celebrations,

> some may have decided that Washington had hyped the prospect of an attack by Osama bin Laden and his allies beyond reason.
>
> But that conclusion is wrong. The danger posed by Mr. bin Laden and like-minded radical Islamists will not fade. . . . These terrorists are highly motivated, not by a cult of personality, but by a world view in which they are the vanguard of a divinely ordained battle to liberate Muslim lands. . . .
>
> The terrorists allied with Mr. bin Laden do not want a place at the [negotiating] table; they want to shatter the table. They are not constrained by secular political concerns. Their objective is not to influence, but to kill, and in large numbers—hence their declared interest in acquiring chemical and even nuclear weapons.[19]

In March, again on the *Times* op-ed page, we warned of "Pakistan's accelerating disintegration" and the dangers to South Asia posed by the graduates of the "terrorist camps in Afghanistan."[20] In the foreign policy journal *Survival,* we expanded our argument:

> The new terrorism has emerged during the Clinton presidency: the 1993 World Trade Center bombings in New York, and related conspiracies; the 1996 Oklahoma City bombing; the 1998 East Africa bombings; and the Tokyo sarin-gas attack in 1995. These attacks were the unmistakable harbingers of a new and vastly more threatening terrorism, one that aims to produce casualties on a massive scale. Although the new terrorism stems from a welter of causes, the face of this phenomenon belongs to Osama bin Laden, the exiled Saudi who has marshaled a network of operatives in more than 50 countries.[21]

Our arguments were rejected by the scholarly establishment—and largely ignored by everyone else—in part because the picture we drew of a new breed of terrorist represented such a departure from the commonly held understandings. We warned against "a heavy reliance on arguments based on historical inference at a time of dramatic change in the ideology of important terrorist groups and rapid technological advances." Al-Qaeda, we reiterated, had "an overriding interest in mass killing."[22] A few journalists took a similar position, among them Judith Miller, whose work a year later on al-Qaeda[23] would help *The New York Times* win a Pulitzer Prize; the columnist Thomas Friedman, also of *The New York Times;* and Neil King and David Cloud of *The Wall Street Journal.* There were other voices from the more official end of the opinion spectrum: several blue-ribbon commissions issued reports at the end of the decade and in 2000 arguing that the United States needed to be better prepared for terrorist attack. Among these were the U.S. Commission on National Security/21st Century (also known as the Hart-Rudman Commission, after the two retired senators who chaired it); the Advisory Panel to Assess Domestic Response Capabilities for Terrorism Involving Weapons of Mass Destruction (the Gilmore Commission, after the Virginia governor who led it); and the National Commission on Terrorism (the Bremer Commission, after the former Reagan administration official who was its chairman). All the reports briefly stirred the pot of public awareness. None discussed at any length the nature of the new threat, and all focused on ambitious bureaucratic measures to strengthen government capabilities, such as combining large agencies to create a superbureaucracy for homeland defense. Both the Clinton and Bush administrations, at least until September 11, avoided serious discussion of the reports because the prescriptions were beyond the realm of reasonable action. The creation of such a bureaucracy would require an enormous investment of energy into legislative work and bureaucratic reform; the decks would need to be cleared of almost all other activity. (The Bush administration found this out after September 11 in its efforts to get a much smaller operation, the White House Office of Homeland Defense, up and running.) The three commission reports were doomed to the nether regions of think-tank libraries.

—

In February 2001, when the trial for the embassy bombings began, another opportunity arrived to take the measure of al-Qaeda. The testimony of the prosecution's first witness, Jamal Ahmad al-Fadl, the al-Qaeda defector, marked the high point of interest in the proceedings. Reports about it were run by *The New York Times, The Washington Post,* and the *Los Angeles Times,* the major television networks, and many of America's other leading news-gathering agencies.[24]

On February 6, 2001, al-Fadl was questioned by Assistant U.S. Attorney Patrick Fitzgerald about chemical weapons that were allegedly made in Khartoum:

Q. Are you familiar with a section in Khartoum called Hilat Koko?

A. Yes.

Q. Did you ever travel to the section of Khartoum called Hilat Koko with any member of al-Qaeda?

A. Yes, I did.

Q. Who did you go with?

A. I remember one time I went with Abu Rida al-Suri, and one time I went with Abu Hajer al-Iraqi. . . .

Q. Tell us about the time you went to Hilat Koko with Abu Hajer al-Iraqi, what you discussed.

A. I learn that in this building they try to make chemical weapons with regular weapons.

Q. Can you explain what you mean by chemical weapons with regular weapons?

A. I remember another guy, he explain more to me about this.

Q. Who was that?

A. Amin Abdel Marouf.

Q. What did Amin Abdel Marouf explain to you?

A. He say the war between the government and the Sudan and the rebels in south Lebanon, it's like thirty years, and always the rebels

during the rain time, they took the Sudanese army to north, and
he say if we use weapons like that, it easy for us to win. . . .

Q. Returning to your conversation with Abu Hajer al-Iraqi, did he
discuss with you who it was that was trying to make the chemical
weapons in the area there of Hilat Koko?

A. He tell me the al-Qaeda group try to help Islamic National Front
to do these weapons, to make these weapons.

A week later, on February 13, al-Fadl was cross-examined by David
Stern, the attorney for defendant Khalfan Mohammed:

Q. There came a time you talked about when you went to Hilat
Koko in Khartoum, remember that time?

A. Yes.

Q. And you went there with Salim [Abu Hajer], didn't you?

A. Yes.

Q. And when you went there, you were going to a place where they
were making chemical weapons, right?

A. Yes, that's what I told—they told me.

Q. And that's what you believed?

A. Yes.

Q. Do you know what chemical weapons are used for?

A. No.

Q. Do you know that they're used to kill people?

A. They say they use it with regular weapons, that's what I hear.

Q. What?

A. They use it with regular weapons.

Q. With regular weapons?

A. Yes.

Q. What did they mean when they said they use it with regular weapons?

A. I really I have no idea about what they mean.

Q. Okay. So I'm asking you, do you know that chemical weapons
are used to kill people?

A. Yes, that's what I hear from them.

Q. You know that, for example, they use gas to kill people, right?

A. Yes.

Q. And whoever is in the area where that gas goes runs the risk of being killed? ·

A. Yes.

Q. And when you went there with Mr. Salim—by the way, what year was that?

A. Maybe during '93.

Q. During?

A. '93 or early '94.

Q. When you went there with Mr. Salim, did you say to him, this is a terrible thing, let's not get involved in chemical weapons production?

A. No, I didn't tell him that.

Q. Did you say, I refuse to get involved in chemical weapons production, I quit al-Qaeda?

A. No.

Q. Just went about your business, right?

A. Yes.

Al-Fadl's testimony provided partial, but striking, corroboration of the Clinton administration's 1998 claim that al-Qaeda was involved in producing chemical weapons in Khartoum.[25] The most astonishing aspect of al-Fadl's testimony about the chemical weapons was the reaction it elicited: none. In the news stories that followed al-Fadl's testimony, much attention was paid to his description of how al-Qaeda is organized, bin Laden's denunciations of America, and the group's murky effort to buy a cylinder of uranium for $1.5 million. But no newspaper or television report gave serious attention to the testimony about chemical weapons, which must have taken several minutes on each of the two days. The issue resurfaced again in another cross-examination of al-Fadl later in the trial. It was raised yet again in closing arguments. Still, no one seemed to notice.[26]

The reporting on the trial betrayed a complacency about the terrorist threat, and some stories left the reader thinking that al-Qaeda was just not all that fearsome. Near the end of the proceedings, under the headline "Trial Poked Holes in Image of bin Laden's Terror Group," Benjamin Weiser of *The New York Times* wrote:

> Before the embassy bombings trial, Osama bin Laden loomed large in the American psyche, a villain of unimaginable evil and sophisticated reach. It was an image fed by destruction done and by American law enforcement eager to drive home the reality of his threat. In some ways, though, it was an image created because so little was known about how he worked.
>
> But the trial, which left many of the details of the bombings un-contested, made clear that while Mr. bin Laden may be a global men-ace, his group, Al Qaeda, was at times slipshod, torn by inner strife, betrayal, greed and the banalities of life that one might find in any office.
>
> "To listen to some of the news reports a year or two ago, you would think bin Laden was running a top Fortune 500 multinational company—people everywhere, links everywhere," said Larry C. John-son, a former deputy director of the State Department's Office of Counterterrorism. "What the evidence at trial has correctly por-trayed, is that it's really a loose amalgam of people with a shared ide-ology, but a very limited direction."[27]

The pooh-poohing continued. Just weeks later, Johnson himself lamented on the *Times* op-ed page that

> Americans are bedeviled by fantasies about terrorism. They seem to believe that terrorism is the greatest threat to the United States and that it is becoming more widespread and lethal. They are likely to think that the United States is the most popular target of terrorists. And they almost certainly have the impression that extremist Islamic groups cause most terrorism.

Of course, if anything like that were the case, there would have been far less shock on September 11. But Johnson continued:

> None of these beliefs are based in fact. . . . The overall terrorist trend is down. . . . Nor are the United States and its policies the primary target. . . . The greatest risk is clear: if you are drilling for oil in Colombia—or in nations like Ecuador, Nigeria or Indonesia—you should take appropriate precautions; otherwise Americans have little to fear.
>
> Although high-profile incidents have fostered the perception that terrorism is becoming more lethal, the numbers say otherwise, and early signs suggest that the decade beginning in 2000 will continue the downward trend.
>
> . . . [I]t is time to take a deep breath and reflect on why we are so fearful.
>
> . . . [T]errorism is not the biggest security challenge confronting the United States, and it should not be portrayed that way.[28]

As a display of sheer idiocy, this was hard to beat, and the article remains an ironic epitaph on a period of almost willful ignorance.[29] There was little interest in opposing ideas. In July, we sought to rebut Johnson with an article submitted to the *Los Angeles Times*. We wrote that it was essential to dispel myths that were taking hold:

> Citing statistics in the State Department's annual review of terrorist activity, some argue that a moderate decline in the number of terrorist incidents since the late 1980s translates into a diminution in the danger. But that overlooks key changes in the motivation and goals of contemporary terrorists . . . who see violence as divinely justified. Unlike their predecessors, these terrorists do not seek to enter negotiations but rather to cause massive casualties.
>
> Looking beyond the numbers, the terrorists' modus operandi tells us a great deal. Unsuccessful operations such as those planned for the

millennium at LAX and in Jordan would have been far more destructive than most, if not all, of the attacks of the 1980s. The bombing of
the World Trade Center—the first major harbinger of the new era—
sought to kill tens of thousands by toppling one tower into another. In
the years to come, religiously motivated terrorists will continue to try
to inflict bloodshed of unprecedented dimensions.

The article was accepted for publication but never appeared. On September 11, it was still sitting in the queue, waiting to be printed.

—

Why did the press—and by extension, the American public—refuse to
take al-Qaeda more seriously? Curiously, polls indicated that ordinary
Americans were deeply concerned about terrorism. That probably had as
much to do with three decades of movies like *Die Hard,* which saturated
popular culture with stories of superterrorist attacks, as with anything
that was going on in the wider world. Indeed, in the 1990s, one could
go to the movie theater and choose among many varieties of catastrophic
destruction narrowly averted: chemical weapons (*The Rock*); nuclear
weapons (*The Peacemaker*); biological weapons (*Outbreak*); and the terrorist hijacking of the President's plane (*Air Force One*), to cite just a few.
One might conjecture that, if anything, terrorism had been so thoroughly
domesticated as a creature of the fictional world of the movies that the real
thing appeared jejune. Yet a Gallup survey in 2000 found that 84 percent of Americans identified international terrorism as a threat to U.S.
vital interests, making it the most often cited concern. Chemical and biological weapons took second place. As New Year's of 2000 approached—
perhaps because of a series of official warnings and the news about the
millennium plot—a poll showed that every second American was changing plans and avoiding large gatherings for fear of terrorist attack.

Undoubtedly, elite opinion makers were to some extent conscious of
the history of terrorism and of the few American lives it had claimed.
More than 150 years ago, Tocqueville observed that "it is an arduous un-

dertaking to excite the enthusiasm of a democratic nation for any theory which does not have a visible, direct and immediate bearing on the occupations of their daily lives."[30] Perhaps evidence of a new kind of terrorism was not visible, direct, or immediate enough to arouse the curiosity of those whose profession it is to inform the public.

The rise of radical Islam came during an era when most of the media elite were focusing on globalization, but in its cheerful aspect—the opening of markets, expanding trade, faster, cheaper communications, easier travel. At the same time, there was an obliviousness to the darker side of the phenomenon—the growth of international crime, regional instability and terrorism, as well as the increasing availability of advanced technology to those who had no intention of using it benignly. But as America grew detached from the world beyond its borders, these dangers remained distant, abstract, and unthreatening.

Statistics tell the story of that drift: on television, the primary source of news for most Americans, international stories accounted for a mere 13 percent of the network news broadcasts in 1997, down from 45 percent during the Gulf War. Driven by cost cutters, exorbitant salaries for star anchors, and market survey data that showed little interest in world events, the networks closed many of their foreign bureaus—ABC was typical in dropping from seventeen to seven over a fifteen-year period. Eventually, no network had a bureau in South America, Central America, Africa, or India. Executives justified this retreat by saying that better travel links made parachuting correspondents into a story a more viable and cost-effective option. But parachute journalism rarely compares in quality to work provided by reporters who know the region where they are reporting.

In the print media, the story was comparably bad. Depending on who did the survey, space accorded to foreign news shrank from 10 percent in 1971 to 6 or 2 percent in 1995.[31] In 2000, the *American Journalism Review* counted 283 foreign correspondents working for American papers, a number that included 107 overseas reporters for *The Wall Street Journal,* the large majority of whom write for the European or Asian editions of their paper and only occasionally are published in the U.S. edition. On September 11, 2001, the *Journal* had not had a permanent correspondent posted in the Middle East for months, despite the al-Aqsa intifada and the growing restiveness of America's allies in Saudi Arabia and other Arab states. The last incumbent had taken a book leave, and since the paper had a hiring freeze, the position was not filled.

The *Journal* was hardly the only paper to trim on coverage. Other distinguished papers such as *The Philadelphia Inquirer*, *The Miami Herald*, *The Boston Globe*, and the Baltimore *Sun* all saw their foreign staffs erode substantially over the decade. *USA Today*, the nation's largest paper, had a mere four correspondents abroad.[32] Only *The New York Times*, the *Los Angeles Times*, and *The Washington Post* maintained a commitment to cover the world. The decline of foreign coverage among the newsweeklies was even more pronounced. The World section of *Time*, which averaged more than ten pages in 1987–1988, was less than five pages a decade later. One third of the newsweeklies' covers carried "a political or international figure" in 1977; twenty years later, only a tenth did.[33]

Insularity, though, goes only so far to explain why the media did not look deeper into radical Islam and the terrorist threat. After all, one voice of warning on the issue, arguably the most important of all, was the U.S. government. The main theater in which the al-Shifa story unfolded was not Sudan but Washington, and reporters there are not thin on the ground. A problem was the disbelief of journalists and editors—the certainty that the U.S. government was peddling a false bill of goods and refusing to admit it.

Undoubtedly, the reporters' confidence in what they were hearing from those who spoke in their official capacity was diminished by the mistakes made in relating the facts about al-Shifa. Those errors weakened the government's case. At the same time, the reporters were not asking themselves hard questions. For example, even if the entire government did not know that al-Shifa made pharmaceuticals, would that be a more important fact than a soil sample contaminated by an extraordinarily rare chemical weapons precursor? Which is the central issue, and which is the peripheral one?

Journalists also found themselves in unfamiliar territory because much of the al-Shifa story dealt with intelligence, which made them uncomfortably reliant on what government spokesmen said. A strong distrust of secrecy has been an American virtue for ages, and it is easy to point to cases in which excessive secrecy has been bad for the country. But that attitude alone cannot explain the blanket dismissal of the government's arguments. A cynicism about the truthfulness of those in office was required as well.

Hostility to political institutions runs deep in America; government is *A Necessary Evil,* as Garry Wills entitled his book on the varieties of American distrust of government. The 1990s were a period in which an epochal political battle was waged between the right and left over government's role in American life—when Ronald Reagan's statement that "government is not the solution to our problem. Government is our problem" was the rallying cry of Republican congressmen and their leader, Newt Gingrich, whose "Contract with America" was a manifesto for shearing away much of the U.S. executive branch. In the midst of this fray, the press, it seems, lost its bearings. Its traditional skepticism hardened into its own kind of antigovernment sentiment—an attitude, a trope of distrust. "Gotcha reporting" flourished. It would be absurd and unjust to suggest that all or even most reporters adopted a purely adversarial stance. But enough did to make relations between press and government poisonous. Another aspect of the phenomenon was the growing investment in large investigative staffs assigned to multipart articles that would be contenders for Pulitzer Prizes. Over decades, this journalistic strategy paid off in some excellent journalism, but it also pushed up the number of journalists looking for the next Watergate, searching for a scandal to break wide open.

In the 1990s, the uncontrollable growth of a culture of scandal crowded out discussion of issues critical to the nation's well-being, including terrorism. It is unnerving to think how much of the nation's attention was devoted to O. J. Simpson, JonBenét Ramsay, Chandra Levy and Gary Condit. But those diversions were inconsequential compared to the many scandals about the nation's government and leaders in which an accelerating feedback loop linked the political arena and the press. This was possible because political life after the end of the Cold War became, as the writer James B. Stewart, put it, "blood sport."

A pattern emerged. Reporters caught a whiff of an audit or internal investigation, a page-one story would appear, and a cycle of outrage would commence, clearing the way for special investigators and congressional hearings. As one inquiry petered out, the authority of a special counsel would be expanded to examine other rumored infractions. Much of this exfoliating reportage came, remarkably, from one journalist, *The New York Times*'s Jeff Gerth. His reporting beginning in November 1992 about the failed Whitewater land deal became the seedbed for a decade of inquiries. In the years that followed, the writ of special investigator Kenneth Starr was expanded to cover the suicide of White House deputy counsel Vincent Foster, Hillary Clinton's alleged involvement in firing seven employees in the White House travel office, White House aides' alleged misuse of FBI files, and in 1998, the possibility that President Clinton committed perjury by denying under oath that he had had a sexual relationship with Monica Lewinsky.[34] The subsequent impeachment of the President left little public room for other issues.

Yet even when the matter of impeachment was finished, another set of connected scandals captured public attention. Beginning in April 1998, again with reporting by Jeff Gerth, a series of articles suggested that Loral Space and Communications and Hughes Electronics had improperly given China classified information that "significantly advanced Beijing's ballistic missile program." Gerth's reports also suggested that Loral's chairman, Bernard Schwartz, a staunch Democrat, had contributed large sums to the party in return for waivers of government regulations that would have prohibited the company from launching its satellites aboard Chinese rockets. The waivers were "quietly" granted by Clinton, Gerth wrote, an action that dealt "a serious blow" to the Justice Department's investigation of the matter. The implication was that Clinton's eagerness to fill Democratic party coffers had led the administration to cut corners on an issue with national security implications. With its echoes of earlier

investigations about campaign contributions to the Democrats from Indonesian businessmen and Chinese sources, the story was picked up instantly by the print and broadcast media, and Republicans in Congress
seized on it. House Speaker Newt Gingrich appointed Representative
Christopher Cox to run a special investigative committee. The *New York
Times* columnist William Safire accused Loral of "the sellout of American
security."

After almost a year of hearings and front-page articles, "Chinasats,"
as the scandal was known in Washington, was eclipsed by an even more
sensational story: on March 6, 1999, *The New York Times* ran a front-
page article headlined "China Stole Nuclear Secrets for Bombs, U.S.
Aides Say." The reporters, Jeff Gerth and James Risen, wrote that Beijing
had achieved rapid advances in its weapons program—especially in
miniaturization—through espionage. A Chinese American scientist at the
Los Alamos National Laboratory was suspected. Wen Ho Lee was interrogated by FBI agents who waved a *Times* article at him and asked him if
he knew "who the Rosenbergs are" and what happened to them. The Department of Energy fired him on March 8, 1999. After months of investigation, Lee was indicted on fifty-nine felony counts and kept in solitary
confinement for nine months. On Capitol Hill, the Cox Committee and
the Senate Judiciary Committee held more than twenty-five hearings, and
Republican lawmakers called for the resignations of Attorney General
Janet Reno and National Security Advisor Sandy Berger. The feedback
mechanism between politics and the press was aptly noted by one *Los
Angeles Times* reporter who observed that the charts the committee used
to illustrate the extent of the spying relied on information culled not from
an investigation of their own but from *The New York Times*.[35]

It is worth revisiting the outcomes of these investigations. After Kenneth Starr resigned in October 1999, his successor, Robert Ray, closed
the Filegate investigation in March 2000 without indictments, saying
there was no credible evidence that Hillary Clinton or senior White
House staff were involved in obtaining the FBI files.[36] In June 2000, he
closed the Travelgate inquiry without bringing charges. In September, he

shut down the original Whitewater investigation, announcing that there was insufficient evidence to indict the President or first lady for their involvement in the tangled dealings of the real estate venture. The House impeached Clinton on one article of perjury and one of obstruction of justice, but when the Senate tried him in February 1999, it imposed no punishment. When his term ended, Clinton agreed to a five-year suspension of his Arkansas license to practice law and a $25,000 fine in exchange for Ray's pledge not to bring a perjury or obstruction indictment.

In its review of the Chinasats case, Justice Department investigators determined that there was not a "scintilla of evidence—or information—that the president was corruptly influenced by Bernard Schwartz" of Loral. The head of the department's campaign finance investigation admitted that Schwartz was "a victim of Justice Department overreaching." The story that emerged was that a low-level engineer had accidentally faxed a document—which he had already scrubbed of classified information—to a Chinese company. The CIA stated that it had no concerns about weapons proliferation as a result of the fax—that U.S. national security had not been affected. Loral later paid a fine to end the matter. Many questions remain about Wen Ho Lee, whose downloading of hundreds of thousands of pages of classified materials continues to be a mystery after the FBI's *three* investigations of him over seventeen years made a hash of the matter.[37] Lee ultimately pleaded guilty to one felony charge of illegally retaining national defense information and was sentenced to time served—278 days he spent incarcerated and denied bail. All of the other fifty-eight counts, many of which carried life sentences, were dropped. Judge James Parker said the government's case had "embarrassed our entire nation." The Lee case did something else as well: it stoked a furious period of China-bashing. Together with the Chinasats scandal, the Wen Ho Lee case heightened suspicions about China, particularly among the foreign policy elite in the Republican party. The Bush administration's determined focus on China in the first half of 2001, during a time when it was conducting its policy reviews on terrorism, undoubtedly was influenced by the atmosphere of heightened mistrust.

The Pulitzer Prize for national reporting was given to the staff of *The New York Times*, with a special mention of Jeff Gerth for his work on "articles that disclosed the corporate sales of American technology to China, with U.S. government approval despite national security risks."

—

Why America became so enthralled by these scandals is something that will keep historians busy for years to come. Part of the impetus was probably unfinished business from the cultural conflict that began in the 1960s, centered on the rapid social changes of feminism, the "permissive society," and legalized abortion. The Clintons were a perfect lightning rod for the resumption of these battles.

However the factors are finally parsed, Americans' fixation on scandal left little space for the perception of new threats. This was a dangerous addiction, especially for the world's sole superpower and therefore the world's primary target of discontent. President Clinton's deeds, for which he was impeached, helped feed this appetite. And in the end, the public commons, the place where the nation deliberates, was covered with the pornography of the Starr report.

—

Laments over the lost opportunities of the last decade and the country's absorption in controversy were beginning to become commonplace even before September 11. The distinguished journalists Haynes Johnson and David Halberstam have both written books in which they decried the decline in journalistic standards. Yet so complete was the occlusion of the terrorist threat from sight that in their compendia of overlooked issues, neither mentions terrorism.[38] The dismissal of the al-Shifa attack as a scandalous blunder had serious consequences, including the failure of the public to comprehend the nature of the al-Qaeda threat. The marketplace of ideas, where truth is supposed to triumph, failed, and the result was the shock of September 11. Some will argue that this was a failure without consequences, that public ignorance made no difference to the war against al-Qaeda, which was conducted exclusively in the shadowy world of intelligence operations. But was it? The conflict broke into the visible world in August 1998 and repeatedly afterward. Had there been a more serious examination of the new terror, perhaps the opportunities for action would have been different.

In 1999 and 2000, there was no glimmer of support in the U.S. public or the Congress for decisive measures in Afghanistan—no one was even thinking about it. It is perilous to imagine realities that might have been, but suppose there had been sustained journalistic reporting on the "new terrorism"—on the evidence that al-Qaeda and others had embraced a strategy of mass killing and were seeking weapons of mass destruction. Had individuals or institutions independent of the government raised concerns about jihadist violence, many things might have changed before September 11. Agencies such as the Immigration and Naturalization Service, which appear to have been largely oblivious to issues of national security, might have taken their responsibilities more seriously if there had been a single investigative effort showing how easy it was for terrorists to enter the country. It is unlikely that so insular an agency as the FBI would have reinvented itself—as it has tried to do since the attacks—with no more stimulus than press interest. But the Bureau is incomparably more sensitive to public opinion than it was to the concerns of the rest of the executive branch, and incremental change would have been a real possibility.

There is a schizophrenia about the power of the press. At times, we still think of it as an objective bystander, narrating events—and many of its leading practitioners portray it this way. In American democracy, however, the press is part of the policy process. As Washington reporters from top newspapers and the networks know well, their personal ability to move the wheels of government equals that of almost anyone in the stone and concrete piles that line Pennsylvania and Independence Avenues. The physicist Werner Heisenberg famously noted that observation changes matter at the subatomic level; it does so every bit as much at the political level. With a public discussion of the threat in the years before Septem-

ber 11, there would have been a chance to talk about sustained military
action against Afghanistan and the use of U.S. ground forces to hunt
down the terrorists. As it happened, no national leader of either party
would publicly suggest such action in that environment. Afghanistan, al-
Qaeda, bin Laden—these concerns were too distant.

—

Could the White House have made a difference? Some will contend that
the lack of public awareness was the result of a failure of presidential leadership, that Presidents Clinton and Bush should have used the bully pul-
pit to instruct the nation about the danger it faced. Perhaps. Unburdened
by the association the public made between the 1998 missile strikes and
Clinton's impeachment problems, the Bush administration might have
begun a new public discussion of the terrorist threat. When the new administration entered office, though, it chose not to raise public awareness
of the danger; there was virtually no public discussion of al-Qaeda by the
national leadership until September 11. As Barton Gellman of *The Washington Post* wrote in early 2002 in a review of the two administrations' efforts to counter al-Qaeda:

> White House officials acknowledge in broad terms that a president's
> time and public rhetoric are among his most valuable policy tools.
> But they challenge the view that Bush's silence on al Qaeda before
> Sept. 11, and his absence from strategy reviews, meant inattention.
> "You didn't deal with al Qaeda by hyping it in presidential speeches,"
> one senior adviser said. "You dealt with it by putting together a plan."
>
> [National Security Advisor Condoleezza] Rice, by this account,
> thought "the last administration had made a major mistake after the
> embassy bombings by saying we're going to war on terrorism and
> then not doing it." And she thought it would be much better to take
> the reverse tack, which was to say nothing and do it.[39]

As for Clinton, after his Oval Office address about the missile strikes
on August 20, 1998, his advisers followed the well-established practice of

passing the task of public explanation of the details to the cabinet and senior White House officials. As we have seen, he continued speaking about terrorism throughout his presidency, though perhaps in more general terms than would have been necessary to change attitudes. Maybe Clinton should have continued to argue strongly in defense of the attack on al-Shifa and revealed more of the intelligence. It needs to be acknowledged, however, that such a tack would have courted even more derision given the tenor of discussion on the issue. Much bolder rhetoric was not likely to have made a difference to those who were singing "Wag the Dog" on CNN or citing the virtues of Salah Idris in *The Washington Post*.

CHAPTER 10

HOW GREAT A FAILURE?

ISTORY, SCHOLARS SAY, is written in three stages: heroic, with the narratives of great individuals and their feats; revisionist, which turns those accounts on their head; and tragic, where we see how events conspired to bring about an end beyond the reckoning of most actors of the time. We may already be able to skip ahead and predict the tragic version of September 11: a civilization unused to thinking about religion as a powerful, potentially violent force in world events was profoundly surprised when a religious ideology erupted violently, taking some three thousand lives. It had been ages since the West last experienced such a fury of killing meant to please a deity. The murderers came out of nowhere—from a milieu that few had any inkling of—and acted in a way that was utterly irrational by the standards we employ. For most, the coordination of the suicide of nineteen young men to achieve such massive killing was unimaginable and therefore could not be defended against. America was the prisoner of an old paradigm for thinking about terrorism, and it could be released only through a revolutionary act of violence.

If this is posterity's verdict, there will probably be a good deal of truth to it. We absolutely need to recognize the impetus—and how alien it is to our way of thinking—behind the mass killing of September 11. This education has only begun. Since the attacks, the administration has enlarged the war on terrorism and concentrated much effort on the "Axis of Evil," states that sponsor terrorism. Removing Saddam Hussein from power in Iraq was said to be "phase two." Our senior policy makers contended that Saddam and other rogue leaders present an intolerable threat because they will work with al-Qaeda and other terrorist groups to attack the United States with weapons of mass destruction. There are very good reasons to have ended Saddam Hussein's brutal reign over Iraq, but terrorism is not one of them. There is little or no history of cooperation between Iraq and al-Qaeda, and, as demonstrated by the U.S. warning to Baghdad against using a weapon of mass destruction during the Gulf War, Saddam Hussein can be deterred and will not court the destruction of his regime. Al-Qaeda, on the other hand, cannot be deterred and must be destroyed. The confusion about these matters and the ease with which the war on al-Qaeda has blurred into a move against Iraq suggest that America's leaders may not yet have taken al-Qaeda's full measure.*

There may also be a great deal of truth in the contention that sharp departures and thoroughgoing change become possible for large countries and their bureaucratic systems only after a tremendous shock that can be felt by everyone. This, too, was said after Pearl Harbor.

Although future generations may be entitled to take such a tragic view, it does not help us much now. It will not prepare the nation for the next attack, which should be regarded as an inevitability. Nor, for that matter, are *we* entitled to the tragic view. The victims in the World Trade Center, in the Pentagon, and aboard the four planes—and their survivors—have a right to see praise and blame assessed and improvements made to the security arrangements that failed them. There were too many missed opportunities, too many missed clues, and too much systemic blindness for America to say that preventing the attacks was too difficult before Muhammad Atta and the others boarded the aircraft.

How great a failure was September 11? The only appropriate measure is Pearl Harbor, where several hundred fewer people were killed and the

---

* In the Afterword, the authors present an update of this prewar assessment from a postwar perspective.

economic losses were minimal but the damage to the U.S. military was considerable. In many ways, the surprise of December 7, 1941, was less excusable. Japan was a nation-state with geopolitical ambitions, a familiar kind of foe. The United States had been expecting hostilities with Japan to commence for more than a year. American military planners expected a confrontation with Japan for years before that, and war games and drills based on the idea of an attack on Pearl Harbor had been carried out since 1936.[1] The reasons why the United States was surprised are complex, but ultimately, the country's political and military leaders were convinced that Japan would attack Southeast Asia or Siberia, and that hostilities would begin when the United States came to the aid of its allies. There was a flat unwillingness to contemplate an opening strike against Pearl Harbor.

Al-Qaeda, by contrast, was the first terrorist organization—a nonstate actor and relatively unfamiliar kind of foe—to carry out an attack that was warlike in its dimensions. The difference is significant. But that, too, does not make the failures of September 11 excusable, because, as with Pearl Harbor, the United States had *strategic warning*. In the first World Trade Center bombing and the other conspiracies of the early 1990s, the nation's intelligence and law-enforcement authorities and its political leaders were put on notice that a new brand of terrorism that aimed at mass casualties had arisen. The threat was made more palpable by the embassy bombings, the millennium conspiracies, and the bombing of the *Cole,* which taken together demonstrated that the United States had a persistent opponent determined to carry out mass-casualty attacks. It is true that between the understanding of that threat and the reality of four planes being used as missiles there is a chasm of incomprehension. But the government failed not because it did not foresee the exact mode of attack. It failed because it did not act against an opponent it knew would like to kill large numbers of Americans, and because it was not alert enough to the signs of an impending operation.

Roberta Wohlstetter, the great historian of the surprise at Pearl Harbor, observed that in sorting through the intelligence and policy documents of the period, "We are constantly confronted by the paradox of pessimistic realism of phrase coupled with loose optimism in practice."[2] The same is true of September 11. Both George Tenet and Louis Freeh called terrorism in general and al-Qaeda in particular the greatest threat America faced. But neither man's agency treated the problem with commensurate seriousness. Much is still to be learned about the CIA's actions in the year before the attacks, and we know no reason to criticize the analytic side of the Agency, except, perhaps, that it did not voice its concerns a bit louder. The clandestine service, however, evidently had other priorities that it felt deserved resources and attention as much as al-Qaeda did. As for the FBI, its record is indefensible; its leadership must bear much of the blame for not preventing the deaths of three thousand people.

America's political leaders also share responsibility. The Bush administration bears no special blame for the shortcomings of the CIA or the FBI. However, in its certainty about the foreign policy realities of the day and contempt for the recommendations of its predecessors and civil servants, the Bush appointees displayed hubris. It is understandable that a new President brings into office a different strategic view of the world. But the Bush administration's certitude about the dangers the country faced—and an aversion to its predecessors that was emotional, not rational—meant that valuable insights were discounted. The development of Predator gave the United States its best new tool for finding and stopping bin Laden, and eight essential months were lost because the new foreign policy team was not persuaded of the nature of the threat. Beyond the implications of this immobility for September 11, it is a sad commentary on the demise of the "foreign policy elite" that there was so little trust and so much animus. President Clinton shares some responsibility as well. Those who blame him for not waging a war in Afghanistan to destroy al-Qaeda have lost touch with the historical context: there was no basis then for such a war, and no honest assessment could show that such a campaign was politically feasible. The U.S. Congress came close to cutting off funding for the war in Kosovo, where mass murder was being carried out regularly and before the eyes of the world. It was inconceivable that a large campaign—since the military was unable, and perhaps too unimaginative, to assemble a small one—would be supported. Clinton was prepared to fire the cruise missiles and put soldiers in the field; he supported the reasonable efforts, such as Predator, that were proposed.

Still, insofar as impeachment became the vortex of public discourse in 1998–1999 and left little room for broader discussion, there is an issue of responsibility. Clinton's actions, setting aside issues of personal morality, created an enormous, consuming public preoccupation. He played into the hands of his enemies, and the country's business was derailed for far longer than was safe. His actions also helped limit his ability to dictate policy priorities to the FBI. But it is equally true that Clinton's enemies—and the press—bear responsibility as well for distracting the nation from more important issues. Different people will allocate blame differently. In light of the record of unrelenting investigations that led nowhere and created a culture of partisan warfare in Washington, we would argue that the greater burden lies with those who carried out a vendetta that a nation serious about its interests could not afford. Many of the failures that allowed September 11 to occur were the obverse side of characteristics of the country that most Americans take pride in. Our government has a high degree of transparency, and its citizens can sway the decision-making process. As a result, a strong lobbying group that gave no thought to national security could press the INS to dismantle the CIPRIS program. Obviously, the INS's leaders bear the lion's share of the blame, but that is our system. Americans have also wanted the federal law-enforcement authority to be independent of politics. No one wanted it to be willful or unresponsive. But that, too, was at least partly an unintended consequence of the legal and cultural insulation that the FBI has been given.

In the face of the devastation of September 11, no one who had any responsibility relating to counterterrorism can claim a clear conscience, and that applies to us as well. We did try to sound the alarm about the danger of al-Qaeda while we were in the White House and afterward. Perhaps we could have done more, for instance to force the FBI to share information and take its responsibilities seriously. We tried, but we did not try harder because, in an environment saturated with fear of impending attacks, we believed that everyone in the intelligence and law-enforcement community shared the general understanding that al-Qaeda sought to kill large numbers of Americans. What followed from that was a further conviction that all the agencies were approaching the subject with a basic level of seriousness. We were wrong. We were, of course, completely shut out from Bureau operations, and, again, we could not know what we did not know. We were also aware that nothing short of a showdown between the President and the director of the FBI could change anything; that was not possible solely on the basis of a strong but still unproven belief in a coming major attack. We were not surprised when the U.S.S. *Cole* was attacked; for all the emphasis on force protection of the late 1990s, the Navy, even with all the intelligence at its disposal, was still far removed from the universe of counterterrorism. But had we been faced with a hypothetical scenario that involved the FBI failing to notify the White House about the presence of al-Qaeda operatives in the United States or the discovery of an individual with radical Islamist ties at an American flight school, we would not have believed it possible. We still cannot imagine that someone in America was in contact with Abu Zubayda, and that the FBI knew this but did nothing about it. It passes all understanding. Perhaps it should not have.

PART THREE

AFTER AFGHANISTAN

CHAPTER 11

TERROR AND STRATEGY

W HETHER IT WAS BECAUSE the total damage was not that extensive or because the event caused a cognitive overload, America shrugged off the attacks of September 11. The dead were mourned, and a short war was fought. But the business of government and of business went on with remarkably little change. Despite the enormous cost to public and private coffers—$16.5 billion—the loss or relocation of 200,000 jobs, and the evaporation of scores of businesses on the morning of the attacks, the U.S. economy suffered no lasting damage.[1]

This was a surprise. First impressions suggested that such a powerful shock to such a complex economy might have caused a cascade of failures. Economists originally predicted a half-point drop in the nation's gross domestic product in 2001 and 1.5 percent in 2002. They also forecast a weakening of international trade, and a total cost to the United States by the end of 2003 of half a trillion dollars. Policy makers deserve credit for preventing much of this from happening. The Federal Reserve acted quickly to make liquidity available and the world's central banks reduced interest rates, which kept investment up and business moving. Congress delivered $40 billion in emergency spending and appropriated

$15 billion in grants and loans for U.S. airlines, the industrial sector hit hardest by the disaster. Within six months, equities were back at their preattack levels and consumer confidence was remarkably robust.

Prolonged political wrangling over legislation that would federalize airport security personnel also showed that Congress, at least, did not view September 11 as a watershed.[2] Traditional partisan concerns on both sides of the aisle about the size and role of the federal government were manipulated by air-carrier and airport-management lobbies to hamstring action on urgent legislation. A far-reaching bill was ultimately passed, but only after the political competition had played itself out.

The new Department of Homeland Security is entangled in its own organization chart even as its creation consumes the energy of officials trying to focus on the prospect of renewed attack. How this new agency will be funded, what precisely it will do, and whether it addresses the causes of America's vulnerability on September 11 are questions being debated in Congress as though the war were on pause.* In the meantime, bureaucratic rivalries are pursued as though nothing had happened. While Treasury and Justice Department officials in charge of finding and cutting off al-Qaeda's funding boycotted each other's meetings, they missed the transfer of bin Laden's assets from bank accounts into precious gems and metals.[3]

The byzantine political and bureaucratic maneuvering that led to the establishment of the Department of Homeland Security left untouched the key government departments—the FBI and the CIA—whose lapses contributed most to the success of the attacks. The FBI has since turned to its default response and pledged to hire nine hundred new agents, although staffing was not central to the Bureau's failures. The Bureau has also established an intelligence analysis center, which, like piling on new agents, does not address pre–September 11 problems. It does raise questions about what FBI representatives in the CIA's Counterterrorist Center have been doing until now and whether a large, independent analytical division at the FBI will contribute to or compete with

---

* The subsequent evolution of the Department of Homeland Security is discussed in the Afterword.

existing structures. The CIA's response to criticism was to expand the Counterterrorist Center at Langley, but with no clear rationale for what new analysts would accomplish when the problem lies mainly in the realm of collection and dissemination rather than analysis.

Reorganization is the classic technique to avoid problems that are too complex or deeply rooted to solve. Some of these problems stem from long-standing societal preferences, rather than the flawed instincts of government departments. Thus, the FBI is not a domestic intelligence agency, like Britain's MI5, because the American people did not want to put their civil liberties at risk by permitting such an agency to entrench itself in this country. Transforming the FBI into MI5, assuming Americans now want to do this, will take time. The Patriot Act—which included the Justice Department's wish list of provisions that legislators perennially rejected before September 11—took limited steps in this direction by reducing court oversight for wiretaps and monitoring of e-mail, Web surfing, and voice mail. Roving wiretaps, which permit eavesdropping on all the phones a suspect uses, are now permitted as well. These new surveillance measures are not permanent. Congress included a sunset provision, which will close off these surveillance options in four years. Federal law-enforcement personnel can now also conduct secret searches and are only required to inform the owner of the premises within a "reasonable time." The law also permits detention of non–U.S. citizens suspected of involvement in terrorist activities for up to seven days without a hearing. An alien determined to be a national security threat may be detained indefinitely.[4] The act also authorized a procedure for sharing of grand jury information for intelligence purposes—to eliminate the "Rule 6E problem"—but months after it was signed into law, guidelines are unclear and barriers persist.

Since the act was passed, the government has taken additional measures to restrict the rights of at least two American citizens: the alleged "dirty bomber," Jose Padilla, and Yasser Esam Hamdi, who was captured in Afghanistan. While they are cut off from legal representation, foreigners such as Zacarias Moussaoui and Richard Reid are getting their day in federal court, as did another American citizen, John Walker Lindh. Depriving U.S. citizens of their civil liberties without a national debate will not inspire confidence in the government's approach; inconsistencies in the application of these curtailments of due process further jeopardize public confidence when it is most essential: in wartime.

The administration's 2003 $47 billion defense increase is intended to fully fund existing programs and provide $10 billion to cover the estimated costs of next year's combat operations in Afghanistan.* Although this sum includes money for new surveillance assets and smart munitions that will be useful for some counterterrorism operations, the huge multiyear funding increase is not a direct response to the emergence of an apocalyptic terrorist threat. For the most part, it will pay for older systems that are already in the pipeline, and for personnel costs that must be borne but have little to do with the new terrorism.

Congress and the executive branch have acknowledged that America's global strategic environment has changed. Their actions reflect an admirable determination and impressive capacity for sophisticated military operations. But these virtues are superimposed at home on a hodgepodge of standard operating procedures, dramatic but ineffective—and possibly counterproductive—actions, and a reluctance to make hard choices. Fortunately, there has not been another attack against the U.S. homeland since September 11. But that has also made it easier not to focus and it has allowed America to get away with it, for the moment.

It is the nature of terrorism for attacks to be unpredictable. Our short attention span is al-Qaeda's advantage. It would be a mistake to think that the absence of big attacks since September 11 means that the group has accomplished its goal or been incapacitated. Al-Qaeda takes its time between spectaculars. The group has consistently set a premium on careful planning and preparation in staging attacks devised by its leadership. There may be a lag of several years between the September 11 attacks and the next big one. Other, smaller attacks will surely occur in this interval, as like-minded groups or individuals lash out against the United States. But the next coordinated, multiple, mass-casualty attacks of the kind that

---

* The administration's 2004 defense budget request is discussed in the Afterword.

al-Qaeda specializes in may not be ready for years, even if planning for them has already begun.

A sense that the worst is over is not just unwarranted but dangerous, since it will slow or sideline actions the United States and its allies need to take to reduce the threat of renewed attack. The senior jihadists who were in Afghanistan have dispersed. Their command and control capability seems intact despite the heavy blows al-Qaeda and its affiliates have suffered. In its first communiqué since the Afghanistan war, al-Qaeda reiterated that it was still in a battle to the death with the United States. The group's spokesman, Suleiman Abu Ghaith, stated that the United States would be punished for its attempt to rule the world in defiance of Allah's clear guidance that Muslims and only Muslims are to exercise world dominion:

> How can [a Muslim] possibly accept humiliation and inferiority when he knows that his nation was created to stand at the center of leadership, at the center of hegemony and rule, at the center of ability and sacrifice? How can he possibly accept humiliation and inferiority when he knows that the divine rule is that the entire earth must be subject to the religion of Allah—not to the East, not to the West—to no ideology and to no path except for the path of Allah?[5]

Abu Ghaith spelled out the price of atonement that America would have to pay for its crimes: the lives of four million Americans. The possibility of a truce would then depend on American recognition of Islam's superiority. Abu Ghaith's statement reflects bin Laden's last instructions before his disappearance at Tora Bora: Muslims must continue attacking the United States, come what may.

—

What if the jihadists renew their assault on American soil?

In the spring of 2002, a Washington think tank convened government officials to consider the effects of a radiological dispersion device (RDD) detonated outside the National Air and Space Museum in Washington,

D.C.[6] An RDD—a "dirty bomb"—is a weapon made of high explosives bundled with radioactive material. In this simulation, the radioactive element was cesium 137, a widely available material that is used in dental X rays. The bomb in this scenario was big, four thousand pounds of TNT encased in a school bus. Its detonation would kill many people immediately and send a plume of radioactive particles into the skies above Washington.

By the time the authorities in this simulation realized the blast was radiological, emergency crews, ambulances, police and fire vehicles, and hospitals had been contaminated. Thousands of people, unaware of the unique nature of the explosion, fled the scene on their own, jamming mass transportation and spreading contamination even farther from the scene. The psychological impact on Washington's population as the news spread about the irradiation of their city was overwhelming. Despite assurances that cesium 137 does not kill those contaminated but only raises the probability of death by various kinds of cancer, workers refused to return to the city. Tourism died, real estate prices plunged, and government operations slowed as the city began the massive task of cleanup. Fears were raised about the effect of radiological debris on the Potomac watershed and whether large buildings whose intakes had sucked in contaminated air could ever be reoccupied.

The detonation of even a rudimentary nuclear device would dwarf the effects of other attacks. This is far less likely a scenario than the detonation of an RDD, but the effects would be exponentially greater. A relatively small—ten kiloton—bomb detonated in lower Manhattan would obliterate three square miles and kill hundreds of thousands instantly. The financial and cultural center of the United States would cease to exist. The metropolitan area would be uninhabitable, living only in the nation's imagination and in aerial footage of the blast zone. America's GDP would fall by 3 percent immediately, and one of its major ports would be closed indefinitely. A successful attack would embolden our enemies and weaken our society. Americans would lose confidence in their social and political institutions. The potential for a breakdown in public order would necessitate the suspension of civil liberties. People would clamor for a major retaliatory strike—but against whom? Populations would desert major urban areas. The vast number of wounded and traumatized people from the New York region, and the shattered national sense of physical security, would precipitate an unprecedented and long-lasting public health crisis. Beyond these immediate consequences, the process of globalization would be halted, perhaps reversed. The current inconveniences of travel would be nothing compared to the complexity of travel after a nuclear attack. Cross-border shipping would slow to a crawl, making just-in-time production impossible. Such things are possible. Despite the resilience and ingenuity of the American people, a nuclear detonation in New York—or Washington, D.C., Chicago, or Los Angeles— could be the defeat that precipitates America's decline.

An anthrax attack like the one that followed the World Trade Center bombing, but launched with the intention of killing hundreds rather than a few high-profile personalities, would have a similar effect. Large areas would be off-limits for months or longer; economic activity in stricken areas would wither, and the cleanup costs would be incalculable. If the investigation proved inconclusive, as it has in the 2001 case, the psychological toll would be profound.

Or imagine that sleeper cells in New York City launched a series of suicide attacks like the ones that have bedeviled Israel for the past year. We know that al-Qaeda attempted to forge links with Palestinian terrorists. It is less well known that Hezbollah, Hamas, and other Palestinian groups that have avoided targeting Americans for tactical reasons now speak of attacking the United States.[7] As a result of ideological convergence we could see intifada-style attacks in American cities. A terrorist group intent on carrying out such attacks will not inevitably rely on such inept operatives as took part in the 1993 World Trade Center bombing— who still succeeded in detonating a huge bomb underneath the Twin Towers. A successor group might look more like the Muhammad Atta ring: disciplined, self-reliant, and self-possessed. A dozen aspiring martyrs could easily be brought into the United States and provide a year's worth of paced carnage in New York City's transportation system, in any number of restaurants and bars, and in houses of worship (including non-radical mosques), which would surely be on the list of abominations to be destroyed. In Israel, urban restaurants have virtually shut down, buses are shunned by those who can afford alternatives, and open-air markets are places of high anxiety. Israel, which has lived with terrorism for decades, is in crisis and emigration is rising.

Americans must assume they will be attacked again. The recruitment of Americans and ethnic Europeans demonstrates yet again al-Qaeda's keen understanding of U.S. vulnerabilities and its imaginative approach to exploiting them. The terrorists intend to make it hard for Americans to distinguish between friend and foe. This is one piece of a larger strategy that not only adapts to the need for virtuality, but makes a virtue of it. Now, converts to Islam recruited in mosques and prisons can blend into Western societies, compounding the challenge for law enforcement. Historically, terrorists have been conservative, unwilling to deviate from customary modes of operation. Al-Qaeda has broken that mold. They are genuinely creative, and their ingenuity and desire to inflict massive casualties will continue to drive them toward the acquisition and use of weapons of mass destruction.

Those planning the war on terrorism also have to grapple with wild conceptual and strategic twists. Throughout the Cold War, the United States concentrated its intelligence warning system on detecting preparations for a Soviet surprise attack against NATO, a strategic nuclear attack against the United States, or both. This made sense, since the Soviets had clearly invested hugely in assembling the force structure to carry out these attacks on short notice. But there is no guarantee against surprise. In 1941, the United States anticipated a Japanese attack but, on the basis of officials' understanding of Japan's strategy and military deployments, assumed it would happen in East Asia. America expected the punch, but was looking the wrong way when the Japanese took their swing.

America's warning dilemmas have now multiplied. Its enemy can strike from anywhere, even from within the United States. The enemy is also adept at turning America's infrastructure against itself, so it need not marshal forces or build stockpiles. Henceforth, surprise attack must be regarded as the natural order of things. This imposes two burdens. American planners must unshackle their thinking and disregard no possibility because it seems unlikely. In the wake of September 11, for example, senior U.S. officials explained that they did not think that al-Qaeda had the ability to attack the United States and that the threat of aerial attack had been considered, but only with respect to small commuter aircraft. The introduction to Roberta Wohlstetter's study of the Pearl Harbor disaster observes that "[t]here is a tendency in our planning to confuse the unfamiliar with the improbable. The contingency we have not considered seriously looks strange; what looks strange is therefore improbable; what is improbable need not be considered seriously."[8] The writer could well have been describing the analytical failure that preceded September 11.

The second burden is to probe the enemy to put him off balance. This is easier said than done, of course, but the United States has carried out clandestine operations against rival intelligence services for precisely this purpose in the past. Al-Qaeda, or whatever replaces it, will be a harder target, but perhaps not an impossible one. Nor do probes have to be covert operations. For example, the United States has the capability to raid al-Qaeda-affiliated camps in Yemen. Without occupying territory, raiders could seize documents, destroy weapons, vehicles, and matériel, plant hard-to-find audio and movement sensors for continuous intelligence collection, and perhaps carry out other tasks as well. These two burdens, "institutionalizing imaginativeness" and probing the enemy, are valuable ways to limit the frequency and scale of the surprises that await us.[9]

There is yet more to the new strategic order. By definition, surprise attacks cannot be preempted. There are no enemy aircraft neatly lined up on the ramp for the United States to destroy, as there were in Egypt when Israel launched its successful preemptive attack in June 1967. Nor are there targets like the Iraqi nuclear reactor that was preventively bombed by the Israeli air force in 1981 just before it went hot. A virtual enemy operating in secret is unlikely to offer such opportunities.

Deterrence is not an option either. An enemy that has no territory to protect and whose forces crave martyrdom will not be deterred by threat of retaliation. At best he may be stymied temporarily if he thinks he cannot achieve his goal because of the defenses he faces. With preemption unavailable and deterrence simply irrelevant, the United States is in deep and unfamiliar waters. A way out of this conceptual cul-de-sac may emerge, but in the meantime, the United States and its allies will be thrown back onto a strategy weighted toward on defense.

This conundrum had already been recognized in 1998 in the Presidential Decision Directive on homeland defense. The preamble to that directive, which summed up the justification for it, stated that the United States was entering an era during which the provenance and nature of threats to national security could no longer be confidently predicted. Attacks could come from any direction and with extraordinary force. Borders were no longer barriers. The PDD concluded that in the face of this diffuse, nameless, and all-azimuth danger, the government must focus less on specific threats than on identifying and remedying the country's vulnerabilities.

Two other radical departures from the past must be understood as America gropes toward a reorientation to the challenge of the new terrorists. The first is that the historic distinction in American strategy between foreign and domestic has been erased. This has implications for law enforcement and intelligence gathering, of course, but also for civil liberties.

The second is that the boundary between the private and public sectors has, in effect, been eliminated. The jihadists are not engaging the American military in overseas battles of maneuver and attrition. Victory for them is killing American civilians, preferably on American soil. If they intend to continue using America's own infrastructure—a cornucopia of opportunities for mayhem—then the defense of that infrastructure will inevitably fall to those who own it. By and large, the U.S. government owns and controls very few of these national assets: transportation systems, computer networks, telecommunications systems, energy production and distribution, food production, water storage. An effective defense will require thoroughgoing cooperation between Washington and the corporations or public utilities and local authorities to whom this infrastructure belongs. The idea of a public-private partnership was broached for the first time only a few years ago, as the Clinton administration sought to draw the computer and telecommunications industries toward a shared understanding of the vulnerability of their systems and the need to work together to ensure their safety. Progress has been slow, but tangible. In the wake of September 11 it will have to advance much faster and on a wider front.

Defense will not be easy because it will come down to finding individuals, the proverbial needles in the haystack. In the Cold War, the United States could peer down from spy satellites at the Soviet Union or its Warsaw Pact allies and see whether they had moved an armored regiment out of garrison or deployed mobile missile launchers. The North American Air Defense Command, using its sophisticated radars, could detect enemy bombers coming over the North Pole from Russian bases. Despite the continuing threat of rogue ballistic attack, those days are over. We are now looking for one guy on a visa line.

Technology and better information sharing within the U.S. government and between the United States and other countries can improve the probability of finding the needle in the haystack from zero to "just maybe." Biometrics, such as facial scanning, can help determine whether the person holding the visa is the one whose name is on the document. Better data storage and retrieval will enable governments to maintain detailed identifying characteristics of vast numbers of individuals and match this information to individuals standing in front of passport control desks at American terminals. Improved artificial intelligence and data-mining software will permit surveillance agencies to single out, translate, and disseminate vital bits of intercepted communications very quickly. That will provide clues on developing conspiracies and make it possible for customs and law-enforcement officers to find dangerous individuals before they find their targets.

These desirable defensive applications of technology raise troubling questions about the right to privacy, especially as the rules limiting surveillance of U.S. residents are loosened. Clearly, the FBI—or whatever agency is created to pick up this responsibility—will have to be reformed and operate in ways that have traditionally made Americans uneasy. Although the death rattle of privacy was already audible before September 11, the combination of technological and legislative responses to the growing threat of devastating attack may hasten privacy's demise. The pervasive implications for American society demand that Congress be fully involved in debating and formulating new rules of the road. If more intrusive police powers become necessary, we will need broad national "buy-in," a tangible sense that democracy is working and that Congress and the White House are committed to protecting people's rights.

Finding people will not be the only challenge. The United States will need to devise ways to block or intercept delivery vehicles for weapons of mass destruction: the shipping container loaded at Antwerp and bound for the United States that contains a nuclear device; the commuter airplane on the ramp at a small airfield in Georgia that has been turned into a remote-controlled crop duster loaded with anthrax; the cargo vessel anchored fifty miles off the East Coast and armed with cruise missiles aimed at inland targets.

The shipping-container problem will require new or improved technologies for bulk cargo screening and tamperproof seals, as well as new procedures, such as loading shipping containers under observation and in "sterile" zones, areas that cannot be penetrated by outsiders. The crop-duster problem will require that security rules governing passenger carriers be extended to general aviation. Conversion kits are now for sale that can turn an airplane into a cruise missile or anthrax sprayer for $75,000; these must be stringently controlled.

Obviously, weapons components themselves must be kept out of terrorists' hands. The largest source of fissile material that could be used to fabricate a nuclear weapon or a radiological dispersion device is Russia. Under a multifaceted program called Cooperative Threat Reduction, the United States has been buying surplus fissile material or helping the Russians use it in ways that make it useless for weapons. In the wake of September 11, the Bush administration, which had not been enthusiastic about this program, embraced it, increasing funding and signaling a clear commitment to deal with the problem of surplus fissile material. Follow-through on this commitment—that is, high multiyear funding—will be essential for American security.

Spotting these materials if they are smuggled into the United States is also vital. Remote detection of nuclear materials is particularly crucial. When the White House receives the phone call saying that a nuclear weapon has been planted somewhere in the greater Washington area and will be detonated unless the United States pledges to remove its forces from Saudi Arabia, emergency response teams will need to be able to find that device swiftly and from a long distance, and to identify its type in order to prepare an assault plan and work out in advance how to render the weapon safe once it has been seized. Likewise, local authorities will need the technology to detect and identify biological and chemical agents that have been introduced into the environment so that they know they have been attacked—and with what toxic agent—before hospital emergency rooms are inundated with very sick people. These analytical methods will have to be complemented by new techniques for rapid development and production of genetically engineered vaccines to stop local attacks from becoming national—and ultimately global—epidemics. Stockpiling pharmaceuticals is not enough. Constitutional law expert Philip Bobbitt advises that the United States should be "stockpiling laws" to cover the sensitive legal issues that will arise in the wake of an attack as, for example, local and federal authorities proceed to enforce essential quarantines. Who, if anyone, has the authority to shoot a person breaking out of, or into, a quarantine zone? Public order and trust in government will depend on these questions having been answered before the inevitable crisis.

Offensive opportunities may be limited in dealing with a virtual enemy, but they are not impossible. They do require impeccable intelligence, however, and this has been difficult to get. Nevertheless, the changing nature of al-Qaeda does not favor only the jihadists. As the group goes virtual and picks up converts to Islam and Muslims who have been long-term residents of Western countries, penetration may become easier. The more they look like us, the more we look like them. Human intelligence— "HUMINT"—may become more easily available to intrepid moles from American agencies or from liaison services in Europe and the Middle East as the jihadists expand their pool of operatives. The presence of John Walker Lindh among the jihadists in Afghanistan—even though he was a mere foot soldier—and Richard Reid's role as a field operative suggest intriguing possibilities for creative intelligence agencies.

The United States should also consider targeted killing, to use the Israeli phrase, of jihadists known to be involved in conspiracies to attack the United States or obtain weapons of mass destruction. As a practical matter, the intelligence value of surveilling such a person usually outweighs the benefits of his death, assuming of course that U.S. or friendly intelligence services could be relied upon to keep him in sight (or earshot). But this will not always be the case. From a legal standpoint, targeted killing under these conditions falls within the right to self-defense. A policy departure of this kind is unsavory and should be thoroughly debated. But in a new strategic context in which jihadists are intent on mass casualties, unsavory may not be the same as unacceptable.

The organizational and technological demands of defensive and offensive measures to counter the new terrorism will cost a great deal of money at a time of an evaporating budget surplus, looming crises in Social Security and health care, and a ballooning defense budget. To complicate matters, the commitment of the Bush administration to missile defense will cost an estimated $238 billion over twenty-five years. This program will compete directly with as yet unknown funding requirements for homeland defense and the war on terrorism. A sustainable homeland defense and war on terrorism will depend on reliable funding that does not crowd out nondefense programs essential to America's quality of life.

Other things being equal, the United States should have an effective defense against ballistic missile attack. The question is whether this is a more likely threat than the jihadist use of weapons of mass destruction—

delivered by plane, train, automobile, or the U.S. Postal Service. George Tenet has grappled with this issue. In January 2002, he released a new "National Intelligence Estimate" stating that U.S. territory was more likely to be attacked by "ships, trucks, airplanes, or other means" than by ballistic missiles. In the realm of missiles, he judged the threat from cruise missiles or unmanned aerial vehicles greater than that from ballistic missiles.[10] The missile defense architecture currently under consideration offers no defense against these kinds of missile attacks.

Americans are capable of self-sacrifice in wartime. However, the long intervals between jihadist attacks and the fact that attacks thwarted by security services will remain shrouded in secrecy will foster the impression that the war is over or in abeyance. When this happens, budgetary commitments to the war on terrorism and homeland defense will be vulnerable to dangerous cuts if they are squeezed between entitlement programs on one side and missile defense on the other. The best way to stave this off is to reorder commitments now in favor of the more urgent and likely threats to American security. Moreover, given the fiscal demands of a struggle against terror that could last for generations, the Congress should reconsider the future—and most expensive—phases of the Bush administration's tax cuts.

ROOT CAUSES

The United States is resented for its cultural hegemony, global political influence, and overwhelming conventional military power. Its cultural reach threatens traditional values, including the organization of societies that privilege males and religious authority. It offers temptation, blurs social, ethical, and behavioral boundaries, and presages moral disorder. America's political weight is seen as the hidden key to the durability of repressive regimes that fail to deliver prosperity while crushing dissent. Its support is cited to explain the power of Israel to oppress Muslims and degrade Islam. American military prowess is used to kill Muslims, as in Iraq, or is withheld to facilitate their extermination, as in Bosnia.

The American cultural challenge to Islamic societies stands for a broader Western commitment to secularization, the relegation of religion to the private sphere, and a focus on the here and now instead of on either a hereafter for individuals, or a messianic era in which the righteous as a collective will partake.

It is not so much the fact of this frontal assault on traditional values as its success in luring Muslims from the true path that angers the jihadists. Led astray by the West, Muslims forsake the beliefs and practices that once won for them world hegemony and would do so again if believers resisted the temptation of secularism and moral relativism and returned to their roots.

The socioeconomic decline of much of the Arab and larger Muslim world plays an indirect role in generating the new terrorism. It contributes to the disparity in power, influence, and prosperity that fuels resentment. But for the most part, the participants in the jihad against the United States have not been poor. This is true of al-Qaeda operatives and, as we have seen, it was true of takfiri renegades in Egypt as well. Some may be the victims of frustrated expectations. Having anticipated a financially secure middle-class lifestyle, they find they cannot attain it in a region that has failed to mesh gears with other globalizing economies. This is economic misery of a sort, but not the relentless, grinding poverty afflicting half the region's population. The link between socioeconomic trauma and terrorism lies in how the imagery of poverty fuels the anger of middle-class terrorists. Revolutionaries from the mid-nineteenth century through the end of the twentieth were similarly motivated.

Despite some success, the industrialized world has done relatively little to alleviate poverty, not just in the Arab and Muslim world, but globally. Indifference is not the full reason. In absolute terms, significant sums are given over to poverty reduction by contributors to multilateral development banks and by bilateral donors. The ineffectuality of aid programs is an equally important explanation for the persistence of poverty. Recipient countries do not have the financial, legal, and social institutions that would allow them to transform financial assistance into lasting economic gains, and donors do not know how to create these institutions. The governments receiving the aid resist the necessary structural reforms because their hold on power is often too fragile to subject their publics to the supposedly short-term pain of reform. The potential recriminations are not worth the uncertain long-term benefits. To the degree that poverty has inspired the terrorists—who almost never speak of it as a factor driving their violence—it will therefore remain an inspiration for a long time. The West, in the meantime, should certainly expand assistance programs and experiment with different approaches to economic reform. The relief of human suffering is a duty in its own right. If, as a side effect, it reduces the pool of recruits for al-Qaeda or its successors, both gratitude and surprise will be in order.

Traditional societies the world over are reeling from the impact of globalization, which arrives wearing the face of American popular culture. Poverty is endemic in Africa, Asia, and Latin America as well as in the Middle East and North Africa. Only al-Qaeda has counterattacked with a campaign of violence that aims for total victory through annihilation of the presumed source of these evils. The catalyst for this campaign, the necessary condition for it, is religious conviction. In this case, the conviction has been shaped by a specific interpretation of Islam deeply rooted in classical sources and emerging from a long tradition of violent Islamic reform movements. This pattern of religious belief has transformed a constellation of cultural conflict, political confrontation, and socioeconomic calamity into a cosmic war between good and evil. The metamorphic process eliminated the possibility of compromise or mundane resolution, because the offended party was Allah. God's partisans cannot bargain over the fulfillment of his will; doing so would substitute man's judgment for the rule of God. So total war is unavoidable.

The fundamental problem is the catalytic reaction of religion and politics. Today, the manifestation of the problem is a variation of Sunni Islam. It was not always this way. In previous epochs, both Christian and Jewish beliefs, equally anchored in the normative traditions of their respective faiths, justified ghastly outbreaks of violence. Over the long run, the current challenge from within Islam will recede as some of its proximate causes fade and the crisis of religious authority that Islam is now undergoing is resolved in favor of more moderate voices. Such voices are heard now, but they are far from enjoying universal credibility within the Muslim world. Not all are necessarily appetizing to secular Western taste, even if they do reject bin Ladenism. Some argue that bin Laden is not acting in accordance with *maslaha,* the welfare of the Muslim umma. Thus, he may be doing things that are consistent with Islam in other respects, such as waging jihad, but in attacking America at this historical juncture he will make matters worse for Muslims without vanquishing the enemy. He should therefore desist. This is a purely utilitarian argument, which does not challenge bin Laden's motivation or underlying legitimacy. Others combine the maslaha argument with Quranic precedents for protection offered by Muslims to infidels under certain conditions. In this case, maslaha is defined in terms of Islam's image in the world, which suffers if Muslims are seen as indiscriminate killers. The practical result is that it is harder for Islam to win converts, a priority for the umma. This of course is also a utilitarian case. Legal precedent for truces or rights of free passage is not rooted in a concept of coexistence or equality but in temporary negotiated arrangements that do not presuppose a fundamental mutual respect or tolerance for its own sake. Still others express a deeply felt horror at the event and demonstrate a convincing sympathy for the victims. Among these there is a sense that religious differences do not necessitate permanent intercommunal competition. For some, however, this sense of common destiny obtains only up to a point—and that point is Muslim-Jewish relations. These are the clerics who deplore the World Trade Center attack but support suicide bombing against Israeli civilians. The debate about jihadism is difficult to sum up because of this complex mix of concern for ethics, advantage, and the scriptural/legal framework in which arguments about the issue are cast. For present purposes, it does not really matter why violence is criticized, only that it is. While it is less than desirable for incipient jihadists to be taught that jihad as warfare is an ideal—but that now is not the time—the fact remains that we are playing for time. Respected Muslim authorities who buy us time are, in effect, on our side. It is worth noting that there are voices that address underlying problems in a useful way. Dr. Abd al-Hamid al-Ansari, dean of sharia and law at Qatar University, argued forcefully against what he calls the "hatred-of-America complex" and demanded curricular reform that would emphasize Islamic traditions of tolerance. There is a debate in the press, as well. Columnists like the Saudis Suleiman al-Nkidan, writing in *al-Sharq al-Awsat,* and Hamad abd al-Aziz al-Isa, writing in the Saudi daily *al-Watan,* have inveighed against their peers who peddle the "news" that the Mossad—or right-wing American militias—destroyed the World Trade Center. These columnists encourage their readers to think beyond rumor, innuendo, and prejudice.*

In the meantime, the West faces a serious threat that could last a generation, and whose causes are multidimensional and difficult to address. The situation is hazardous, but not hopeless. The United States possesses enormous wealth and capable allies, and is at the leading edge of technological development that will be key to survival. An integrated strategy that takes into account the military, intelligence, law-enforcement, diplomatic, and economic pieces of the puzzle will see America through. For the next few years, the objective of such a strategy will be to contain the threat, much as the United States contained Soviet power throughout the Cold War. The adversary must be prevented from doing his worst, while the United States and its allies wear down his capabilities and undermine the support he derives from coreligionists. Success will require bipartisan commitment for this containment strategy at home and the dedication of a strong coalition abroad. These two key ingredients—bipartisanship and prudent diplomacy—must ultimately be supplied by whatever administration is occupying the White House.

---

* The September 11 attacks were assailed as un-Islamic—primarily because the victims were civilians—by prominent authorities, including Sheikh Muhammad Sayyid al-Tantawi, imam of al-Azhar University; Mustafa Mashhur, the general guide of the Egyptian Muslim Brothers; Sheikh Muhammad Hussein Fadlallah, spiritual guide of Hezbollah; Abdul Aziz bin Abdallah al-Sheikh, the chief mufti of Saudi Arabia; and his fellow member of the Saudi ulema Sheikh Muhammad bin Abdallah al-Sabil; and even Ali Khamenei, the Iranian supreme leader.

In developing a sustainable strategy, we need to recognize important distinctions that have been muddied during the first disorienting year of the war on terrorism.

First, Washington should avoid putting Palestinian terrorism into the same rhetorical basket as jihadist violence. Arafat is not bin Laden. Both use terrorism, but there the resemblance ends. Arafat uses it tactically. Bin Laden uses it strategically. One wants to pressure an opponent, the other to wipe him out. Equating them confuses not only the American people but also the allies on whom we depend. This does not mean that Arafat's use of violence should go unanswered, or be accepted as the cost of doing business on the way to a Palestinian state. It does mean that it is not Arafat's terrorism but bin Laden's terrorism that threatens the United States with mass casualties. Palestinian terrorism will presumably diminish when Arafat has departed from the scene and a new, responsible leadership seriously focused on state-building, led by Mahmoud Abbas, the new prime minister, or a younger successor, replaces him. No such outcome is conceivable with respect to the jihadist zealots in bin Laden's camp.

This distinction is so important because America will need partners in the war on terrorism. Most of our allies differentiate between Arafat and bin Laden. They understand the need for cooperation and determination in destroying al-Qaeda, but not Arafat, even if they think he is an obstacle to peace. By equating them, the United States alienates friends who see themselves caught up in a war led by a state incapable of distinguishing between existential threats and tactical ones.

Second, Saddam Hussein was also not bin Laden. Saddam was determined to overturn the regional balance of power. If he had been allowed to, he would have posed a mortal threat to Kuwait, Saudi Arabia, and Israel—and possibly Iran. He could have achieved his dream of hegemony only by deterring American intervention, for which an Iraqi nuclear capability would have been essential. Saddam had to be contained or unseated.

Iraq no doubt deserved its status as a state sponsor of terrorism. But the urgent priority in the war on terrorism is not state sponsors, but failed or failing states. Iraq was in bad shape, but it was not failing. Sudan and

Afghanistan did fail, and when they did they provided an environment in which al-Qaeda flourished. Other countries, such as Yemen and Somalia, could yet provide this too, and still another that might resume the role of host is Sudan. There is *still* little evidence that state sponsors like Iraq and Iran provided al-Qaeda with meaningful assistance, despite the reported prewar presence of the Jordanian al-Qaeda–affiliated terrorist Abu Mussab Zarqawi (see chapter 5) in Iraq and the alleged postwar appearance of a Saudi al-Qaeda operative, Saif al-Adl, and another bin Laden associate, Mahfouz ould Walid ("Abu Hafs the Mauritanian"). Bin Laden was busy establishing terrorism-sponsored states and preparing to destroy the World Trade Center, the Pentagon, and the White House, while state sponsors of terrorism were drawing relatively little American blood.

What makes it so urgent to heed these differences between the Arafats of the world and bin Laden, and between state sponsors and failing states, is the need for international cooperation in countering the jihadist threat. The United States cannot do it alone. This cliché becomes truer every day as American counterterrorism officials survey the foreign ports and terminals that ship cargo and passengers to the United States and as al-Qaeda, or its successor, melts into the population in sixty countries around the world.

Many of these countries will cooperate with the United States because it is in their interest; they don't want jihadists on their soil any more than Americans want them on theirs. Bare-bones cooperation there will surely be. A durable and effective counterterrorism campaign, however, requires something more: cooperation at the political level—that will make clear to the bureaucracies that cooperation with their American counterparts is expected—and coordination of broad military, diplomatic, economic, and security policies that point these bureaucracies in the same direction. This kind of robust political cooperation can produce vital large-scale initiatives: a common diplomatic approach toward problem states; a sustainable program of economic development for the Middle East; changes in domestic policies that lessen the appeal of jihadism to Muslim diaspora communities; improvement of border controls; tightened bonds among justice ministries, law-enforcement, customs, and intelligence agencies; as well as special operations forces on the front lines. Whether this indispensable burden-sharing can work will depend on the give-and-take among the players. Since September 11, the United States has not shown much concern about the sensitivities of its allies and has paid a severe penalty in terms of allied cooperation in the run-up to war in Iraq. At first, the scale of the disaster and the administration's blend of resolve and restraint in the war on terrorism combined to offset the disappointment of America's allies in Washington's go-it-alone posture. But the administration's determination to affect regime change in Iraq brought transatlantic relations to a historic low. As the war on terrorism grinds on, the need for allies will be all the more apparent. The United States might wisely forgo some of its own preferences to ensure allied support in the crises that will inevitably come.

Since 1998, the heyday of the Middle East peace process under Ehud Barak's Labor government, the jihadists have exploited the Israeli-Palestinian conflict to boost their own popularity. This stratagem has worked. The jihadists are seen as sticking up for Palestinian rights, while Arab governments do nothing. Direct, energetic U.S. diplomatic intervention would do much to take the wind out of the jihadists' sails, and by demonstrating American concern for the plight of Palestinians make it easier for regional governments to cooperate in the war on terrorism. The Bush administration has been reluctant to get deeply involved, in part because its officials think Clinton's move to get an agreement at the 2000 Camp David summit was premature and in some undefined way contributed to the outbreak of the present intifada. The current team is pessimistic about prospects for agreement and fears entanglement in a drawn-out, venomous negotiation between irreconcilable parties. This, they worry, will distract them from higher priorities and embroil them in domestic political disputes that will inevitably arise when the Israeli side comes under pressure from Washington. Taken together, these are powerful incentives to stay as far away as possible. Still, the administration has been drawn in by degrees and has announced its support for the creation of a Palestinian state within the framework of institutional reform and democratic elections. If the war on terrorism is now this country's highest priority, then more vigorous—and risky—involvement is required. Concern over the political hazards and distractions of intervention must be subordinated to the more urgent need to defang the jihadist argument that the United States is complicit in the murder of Palestinian Muslims. Governments that suppress political dissent, fail to deliver economically, pander to Islamist activism, and encourage anti-American propaganda to stay in power—states that could fail—are also dangerous. Egypt and Saudi Arabia fall into this category. As a by-product of their own domestic survival strategies, rulers in Cairo and Riyadh have fostered a culture that produced the militants who struck on September 11. Together, with help from other failing or failed states, they have inadvertently produced jihadists who killed thousands more Americans than any of the countries on the State Department's list of state sponsors. Moreover, the close American ties to authoritarian regimes is held against the United States and turns those who otherwise admire American values into critics, or enemies.

There is no easy way for Washington to distance itself from these regimes, if only because the structure of the international system of states requires governments to deal with other governments. Hence the painful reality that Washington will have to continue to deal with the regimes currently in power in Riyadh and Cairo. The United States can, however, try to renegotiate the implicit bargain that underpins its relations with both countries to encourage democratization and redeem, by degrees, America's reputation. Democratization, however hazardous and unpredictable the process may be, is the key to eliminating sacred terror over the long term.

The old bargain went something like this: Egypt supported the American approach to the Middle East peace process, and Saudi Arabia provided oil at a reasonable price and took the U.S. side in its confrontation with Iraq. In return, the United States let these governments run their countries the way they wanted, even if doing so entailed the growth and export of Islamic militancy and deflected criticism away from their regimes and toward the United States and Israel. Now that jihadists are in pursuit of nuclear weapons, this bargain no longer looks very good.

The new bargain would be negotiated along these lines: Cairo and Riyadh would begin to take measured risks to lead their publics toward greater political responsibility and away from Islamist thinking (and action) through greater political participation and encouragement of secular opposition parties. Saudi Arabia would be asked to throttle back on its Wahhabization of the Islamic world. Both countries would be pushed to reform their school curricula and enforce standards that would ensure a better understanding of Western history and encourage respect for other cultures. At the same time, they would focus more consistently on the welfare of their people, with increased financial and technical assistance from the West. The leaders of both countries would use their newly won credibility to challenge Islamist myths about America and the supposed hostility of the West toward Islam. The culture of demonization would be challenged across the board.

In the framework of this new bargain, the United States would establish contacts with moderate opposition figures in Egypt, Saudi Arabia, and perhaps one or two other countries. If the Egyptian government tossed out an American diplomat for talking to the Muslim Brothers, the United States would toss one of theirs. When the government imprisoned a Muslim Brother for talking to an American diplomat, Washington would complain loudly. For the United States, the benefit would be twofold: Washington would get a better sense of what was happening on the ground, while gaining a measure of credibility and perhaps even understanding on the part of critics. This effort would bear little fruit if the United States failed to communicate its efforts by efficient use of the region's media.

Overnight change is not in the cards. The regimes in Cairo and Saudi Arabia face problems that can't be surmounted overnight without serious risks to stability—even if these problems are largely of their own making. The United States has not been entirely free to insist on the new bargain, either, since it required Saudi cooperation with respect to Iraq as long as Saddam Hussein was in power. This gave Riyadh considerable leverage. Nonetheless, change has to start sometime and somewhere. It won't happen without consistent American pressure and persistent attempts to persuade rulers in Cairo and Saudi Arabia that the long-term interests of their countries will be well served by a new bargain. Given the looming demographic, economic, and environmental trends overtaking the region, the sooner these new deals are struck, the better.

At the same time, the United States will have to explore ways to improve the standard of living and the environment in poorer countries in the absence of economic restructuring and reform that are beyond the reach of governments and are doomed in any case by illiteracy and lack of infrastructure. Institution building and the development of basic skills and infrastructure would still be pursued, but not at the expense of despair-reducing assistance.

A dialogue with Muslims both within the Arab world and outside it would be highly desirable. The obstacles, however, are considerable. Trust plays a pivotal role in determining who is listened to in the Middle East and who is dismissed. This is a both a cultural trait and the result of decades of a government-controlled, censored press and of political leaders who lied as a mode of governance. Americans, unsurprisingly, are not on the list of trusted interlocutors. News media outlets that are perceived as "American" fall into this same category. Arabic-language media like al-Jazeera and Middle East Broadcasting (MBC) have prospered in part because the regional audience was hungry for news broadcasting that did not have an overtly Western orientation. CNN achieved prominence in the West during the Gulf War, which was highly unpopular in the region. Americans loved it, but to Arab watchers, who heard a great deal about the accuracy of American munitions and rather less about Iraqi casualties, CNN was not so lovable. To the degree that the new Arabic-language media seek to represent a particularly Arab viewpoint, the U.S. message will have a hard time getting through. And since trust is the issue, it will not suffice to put Arabic-speaking American officials, no matter how eloquent, on al-Jazeera and expect to win converts. This does not mean that the United States should ignore the need to make its voice heard; quite the opposite. But direct discourse will not have a miraculous effect in a region where many people, perhaps a majority, believe the Israeli security service destroyed the World Trade Center.

All of this is daunting and in many respects bleak. But the challenge is not out of proportion to those the United States has confronted, and mastered, in the last century. Hope resides not only in greater vigilance but also in greater ambition. Our first reaction to September 11 is and indeed must be our own self-defense: bolstering homeland security, denying al-Qaeda access to co-optable states and regions, killing and arresting terrorists, and developing a law-enforcement and intelligence network to better cope with al-Qaeda's flat, decentralized structure and the standing threat it presents. Not all vulnerabilities can be plugged, and al-Qaeda need not be successful all the time, just lucky once with a weapon of mass destruction to trigger an existential crisis for the United States and its allies.

We need to convince Muslim populations that they can prosper without either destroying the West or abandoning their traditions to the onslaught of Western culture. That is a long-term project. Our determination in a war against apocalyptic—therefore genocidal—religious fanatics has to be coupled with a generosity of vision about postwar possibilities. That Islam should warmly embrace the West is too stark a reversal to expect in the foreseeable future. But it is feasible to lay the foundation for a lasting accommodation by deploying the considerable economic and political advantages of America and its allies. As of September 11, we are on notice to begin the project.

CHAPTER 12

A WORLD OF TERROR

THE AGE OF SACRED TERROR is not just the age of Islamic terror. In a world turning more religious, more adherents of the great faiths and new, burgeoning cults are placing violence at the heart of their beliefs. The last two centuries in the history of the Muslim world and the sad economic and political state of its many countries have given militants like bin Laden a platform to spread their creed, thus putting radical Islamists at the forefront of those who kill in the name of God. But they are hardly alone, and with increasingly easy access to technologies of mass killing, small groups of believers can inflict unimaginable damage. Jews, Christians, and members of one of the new religions of Japan have used terror strategically in the last decade, some of them killing on a scale without precedent in the recent history of their faiths.

—

Over the last three hundred and fifty years, the West has worked hard to keep religion out of the dealings between states. The banishment of religion from the repertoire of acceptable reasons to wage war has its origins in the famous Treaty of Westphalia of 1648. In recent years, the treaty has been much discussed as the foundation of the modern system of nation-states, entities whose sovereignty within their borders is inviolable. The treaty did not, as is often said, create freedom of religion—though it did establish a new level of tolerance and security for Catholics and Protestants living in lands ruled by princes of the other confession—nor did it provide for any kind of separation of religion and state. Instead, it reaffirmed and clarified the right of the prince to determine the religion of his country. In other words, it made it illegitimate for one country to make war against another for reasons of religion—so that one "true" faith could be imposed on another.

The princes and diplomats who met in the German cities of Münster and Osnabrück established this new order because of the desperate experience of the Thirty Years War. The conflict, which drew in forces from most of Europe, left more destruction behind it than any event since the Black Death. Many reasons lay behind the conflict, but the ferocity of the killing and the devastation that consumed Europe from Alsace to Bohemia was fueled by religious hatred between Protestant and Catholic. Those who wrecked Germany were usually spurred on by cynical leaders, but in their hearts, most of the combatants believed they were carrying out acts of piety. When the war ended, many cities had less than half the people they began with; some towns had only a fifth. Insofar as the conflict left a mark on the West, it was a deep, subliminal sense of the peculiarly horrible nature of religious war.[1]

Religious violence is typically different from any other kind of warfare—for the simple reason that for a true believer, there is no compromise about the sacred. Or, to put it in a more monotheistic key: one God, one truth. Tolerance is not an intrinsic part of any of the monotheistic religions. For some believers, the outcome of a conflict cannot be ambiguous.

When the issues are sacred demands, there can be no bargaining. The believer cannot compromise on the will of God. Killing becomes an end in itself, rather than one instrument arrayed among nonlethal instruments in a bargaining process. Such believers want a lot of people dead and may not care whether a lot of people are watching, as long as God sees what has been done in His name.

Why, looking back over earlier periods, does it seem as though monotheism and violence go hand in hand? Part of the answer lies in the enduring influence of the Hebrew Bible on Christianity and Islam. The great preoccupation of the biblical writers was to take a newly formed people and give them a distinctive identity. The books of the Bible were meant to tell the Israelites who they were and how they came to be. Like societies elsewhere, this community carved out its identity by differentiating itself from the surrounding peoples. One central biblical message to the children of Israel was "You are who you are because you are not the other."

The lesson is reinforced in innumerable ways: the Israelites have a unique covenant with the one God and a territory belonging to them alone; their cultic practices and social customs are different from their neighbors'; they possess true nationhood, unlike others who worship false gods that cannot confer this special status.[2] Nations such as the Amalek, whose claims conflict with those of God's people, are placed under a total ban that requires their complete destruction. "And the Lord said to Moses, 'Write this as a memorial in a book and recite it in the ears of Joshua, that I will utterly blot out the remembrance of Amalek from under heaven.' . . . The Lord will have war with Amalek from generation to generation."[3]

The Bible's division between those who belong and those who do not makes it natural to see life as war. From the viewpoint of the biblical authors, God's role as a warrior is matched only by that of lawgiver and ultimate savior. For the author of Exodus, "The Lord is a man of war, the Lord is his name."[4] The Deuteronomist holds up God as the One "who rides through the heavens to your help, and in his majesty through the skies. . . . Happy are you O Israel! Who is like you a people saved by the Lord, the shield of your help and the sword of your triumph. Your enemies will come fawning to you; and you shall tread on their high places."[5]

Imagery of battle in the Hebrew Bible is bloody and vivid. The Song of Deborah celebrates the Israelite victory over the Canaanites, a victory sealed by the death of the exhausted Canaanite commander whose head is nailed to the ground with a tent peg by a Bedouin woman with whom he seeks shelter. In Genesis, the destruction of the city of Shechem by Jacob's sons in retaliation for the rape of their sister Dinah is equally explicit. The brothers lure the men of Shechem into a bloody trap by offering both their defiled sister in marriage and a political alliance predicated upon the circumcision of the Shechemite males. A deal is sealed, and the men are circumcised, and on the third day, "when they were sore," Dinah's brothers Simeon and Levi "took their swords and came upon the city unawares, and killed all the males. They slew Hamor and his Shechem by the sword. . . . And the sons of Jacob came upon the slain and plundered the city because their sister had been defiled; they took their flocks and their herds, their asses and whatever was in the city and the field; all their wealth, all their little ones, all that was in their houses, they captured and made their prey."

Violent imagery is also part of the earliest Islamic writings. The Quran's matter-of-fact discussion of fighting reflects the desert environment in which Muhammad prophesied. Raiding was common, people were killed, blood feuds were pursued. The early Muslim community struck its enemies and suffered attacks in turn. At the battle of Badr Wells in 624 C.E. God's angels intervene on behalf of the Muslim combatants.[6] A year later, the battle of Uhud led to a defeat for the Muslims. Much of the detail of these battles can be found in *The Life of Muhammad* compiled by Muhammad ibn Ishaq, who was born in Medina within about fifty years of the Prophet's death.[7] Ibn Ishaq recounts the actions of a widow after a Muslim attack on her tribe:

> Hind, the daughter of Utba and the women with her, stopped to mutilate the Apostle's [Muhammad's] dead companions. They cut off their ears and noses and Hind made them into anklets and collars. . . . She cut out Hamza's liver and chewed it, but she was not able to swallow it and threw it away. Then she mounted a high rock

and shrieked at the top of her voice: "We have paid you back for Badr, and a war that follows a war is always violent. . . . I have slaked my vengeance and fulfilled my vow. . . ."

Again, according to ibn Ishaq, when Muhammad turned against the Jewish tribe of Banu Qurayza, he "went out to the market of Medina . . . and dug trenches in it. Then he sent for [the Jews] and struck off their heads in those trenches as they were brought out to him in batches . . . there were 600 or 700 in all, though some put the figure as 800 or 900." Like the Hebrew Bible before it, early Islamic literature is not squeamish.

NEVER-ENDING WAR

The scriptural emphasis on warfare has armed successive generations with powerful mental images of an embattled world. The community of the faithful is perpetually in crisis or at its edge. When a religious group believes that its identity is fundamentally threatened, it may turn to stories of apocalypse that describe the end of earthly history. In Christian apocalypses, Jesus is not the pacifist messiah of the Gospels, but a man of war. The role of angels and demons that intervene in the physical world, uniting the heavenly and earthly battlefields, is especially important in these stories, because it shows that evil is destroyed not just in some metaphorical or symbolic way in the cosmic sphere, but in a parallel, objective sense on earth.

In Christian and Jewish apocalyptic literature—exactly as in the Muslim literature, which is based largely on the earlier-born faiths—the reversal of fortune is a stock theme. The righteous advance from suffering under the murderous rule of a terrible beast to a restored community of believers who enjoy eternal life in the presence of God. The transforming event is the destruction of the beast, followed by the annihilation of Satan and death at the hands of a heavenly figure sent by God. The beast doesn't have to be a bloody persecutor to qualify as the apocalyptic enemy. For the Christian author of Revelation, the very existence of Rome, the beast in that book, was enough to excite visions of fantastic violence.

This is a violence-prone cast of mind, especially when imbued with the belief that the last days are near and a messiah has arisen to usher in the day of judgment. When this way of thinking emerged among Jews in the Roman Empire, it paved the way for two centuries of doomed messianic movements and bloody Jewish revolts that resulted in the annihilation of Palestinian Jewry and the massacre of Jewish communities from Mesopotamia to the Mediterranean.

—

In times of severe social dislocation, political change, and economic upheaval, individuals overwhelmed by radical pessimism may turn to apocalyptic millenarianism. They see the signs that their tradition has identified as portents of the end of time. The tribulation they experience is interpreted as the era of cataclysms that precedes the eruption of a new order and God's reassertion of His beneficent rule. When these individuals merge into groups and find a charismatic leader, or he finds them, they can be stirred to dramatic action intended to force the end of time and the kingdom of God.

While Islamists look to the days of the rightly guided caliphs as a golden age, Jewish radicals hark back to the establishment of the Davidic kingdom in the tenth century B.C.E. or the Hasmonean victory in the second century B.C.E. over a pagan oppressor. The mythologizing of history is a two-way street. Miraculous events of the past are projected onto the future, especially in times of distress. Moreover, current catastrophe is taken as a sign that the emblematic victories of the past are on the verge of being repeated. The misery and humiliation of the present presage the glory and justice of the imminent future. In all the faiths, current and past woes are attributed to the faithlessness and fecklessness of the community of believers.

The last two decades saw episodes of apocalyptic violence or attempts to spark the apocalypse, which were not confined to literature, or to Islam.

Judaism, Christianity, and even an offshoot of Buddhism have each tried to force the end of history: the Israeli religious militancy of the 1980s and 1990s, which nurtured the assassin of Yitzhak Rabin; the Japanese cult Aum Shinrikyo; and the Christian Identity movement, which nourished Timothy McVeigh. Their stories highlight the believers' conviction that their world is in crisis and about to be engulfed, a certainty that a new age is upon them that will bring catastrophe and redemption, and that believers themselves have a role in setting this cosmic process into motion.

JEWISH MESSIANISM

Israel's unexpected and shattering victory in the June 1967 war brought the holiest places in Judaism under the authority of a Jewish state for the first time in almost two thousand years. Not only was the military outcome apparently miraculous, but sudden access to the Temple Mount, the Tomb of the Patriarchs, the city of Hebron, and other sites was packed with religious significance. The emotional and psychological effect of these events was enormous: one consequence was the emergence of a new kind of Zionism.

Classical Zionism was primarily a secular nationalist movement, which aimed to normalize the status of the Jewish people through statehood. Religious faith was subordinated to ethnic identity. After 1967, a more religiously oriented Zionism, which cast the national enterprise as the fulfillment of a biblical promise, began to compete with more secular ideas about the purpose and meaning of the Israeli state. The seeds of this new movement had been planted long before, by a Rabbi Kook, whose seminary in Jerusalem trained the elite of the highly Orthodox Jews in Israel. He preached that the establishment of Israel was due to God's action in history and that the creation of the state was a crucial episode in the unfolding of a divine plan leading to the advent of the messiah. The nature of the 1967 war seemed to many to confirm this worldview.

But the exaltation of 1967 gave way to the grief of October 1973, when Israeli intelligence failed to detect Egyptian and Syrian preparations for a massive two-front assault. The Syrians and Egyptians were driven back in desperate fighting, but Israel was deeply traumatized.

Out of the shock and demoralization of this war, a new political movement arose in 1974: Gush Emunim, "The Bloc of the Faithful." Members focused on gaining political influence and expanding settlements, especially in places associated with biblical heroes and events. This would establish a mutually reinforcing dynamic, through which larger numbers of settlers would have increasing political power, which would in turn win more government support for additional settlements, which would add to the movement's political clout. The strategy seemed sound. When the right-wing Likud party was voted into power in 1977 under Menachem Begin, Gush Emunim activists concluded that ultimate victory was theirs and that Israel would indeed reach the borders promised by the Bible. They were soon disillusioned. Begin almost immediately entered into negotiations with Egypt for the return of the Sinai peninsula and agreed to negotiate autonomy for the Palestinians in the West Bank and Gaza. The resulting Camp David Accord, from the perspective of a number of Gush Emunim activists, was a monumental disaster. How could this happen? How could Israel come so close to the fulfillment of the biblical promise and then be betrayed by the very leader who had seemed destined to take the necessary last steps?

Two Jews in particular were asking themselves these questions in 1978: Yeshua Ben-Shoshan and Yehuda Etzion. Ben-Shoshan was an avid student of the Kabbalah, a group of medieval mystical texts which assert that exile prevents the re-creation of a lost cosmic order and the possibility of redemption. Exile continues and intensifies the cosmic disorder that began with Adam's first sin. The Tetragrammaton, the four-letter name of God, which contains all the emanated worlds, cannot come together into the single, unitary name for God until Jews are restored to their land. The implication for Ben-Shoshan and Etzion was clear: continued Jewish possession of the entire land of Israel is the indispensable ingredient of cosmic order.

In classic apocalyptic mode, these messianists concluded that the tragedy of the Camp David peace agreement between Israel and Egypt was the fault of the Jewish people. Their transgression was to permit the presence of the Dome of the Rock on the Temple Mount. This was an abomination, for which God was punishing Israel by withholding redemption. Not only did the mosque have to be removed, but Israel would have to revert to the kingdom it once was, with its borders between the two rivers of the Nile and Euphrates. According to Etzion, "This kingdom will be directed by the supreme court [the ancient Sanhedrin of seventy sages] which is bound to sit on the place chosen by God to emit his inspiration, a site which will have a temple, an altar, and a king chosen by God. All the people of Israel will inherit the land to labor and to keep."[8] The redemptive power and purpose of removing the great mosque was later described by Etzion as follows: "The expurgation of the Temple Mount will prepare the hearts for the understanding and further advancing of our full redemption. The purified mount shall be—if God wishes— the ground and the anvil for the future process of promoting the next holy elevation."[9]

Etzion, Ben-Shoshan, Menachem Livni (the underground commander), Gilead Peli, and several others began preparations to destroy the Dome of the Rock. During the next three years they stockpiled explosives stolen from the Israeli army, manufactured twenty-eight sophisticated explosive packages, surveilled security arrangements, mapped out the structurally vulnerable points, and determined how to collapse the Dome without damaging the surface of the Temple Mount. The operation was to be carried out by as many as twenty attackers, armed with Uzi submachine guns. Logistical preparations were conducted in tandem with a continuous seminar in the theological and political implications of the act they were intent upon carrying out.

The question of what the conspirators actually thought would happen when the Dome of the Rock was demolished and Israel laid claim to most of the Near East has not been answered in mundane terms. Some appeared to have believed that the destruction of the shrine would force Israel's Arab neighbors to invade, compelling Israel to launch its nuclear weapons in self-defense. The resulting cataclysm would usher in the millennium, as predicted in many apocalyptic narratives. Etzion himself seemed to believe that the very act of bringing down the Dome of the Rock would fundamentally alter the course of history. He said, "For the Gentiles, life is mainly a life of existence, while ours is a life of destiny, the life of a kingdom of priests and a holy people. We exist in the world in order to actualize destiny."[10] With the purification of the Temple Mount, the laws of destiny would take effect and the world would be utterly transformed.

The operation was never carried out, for an important reason. Most religious terrorists want authoritative religious sanctions for their acts. They know that what they are doing is wrong from the standpoint of normal, secular rules and perhaps even repugnant to their own moral sensibility. God's dispensation is essential. As we have seen, the 1993 World Trade Center plotters appear to have sought a fatwa from the Blind Sheikh to authorize their attack. In this case, Menachem Livni approached several prominent rabbis associated with Gush Emunim. Livni disclosed enough about the conspiracy to regard the answer as definitive. The answer was no. Without rabbinical backing, the plotters abandoned the plan. It is hard to imagine what the impact on the Middle East would have been of a different response.

Dr. Baruch Goldstein, another cosmic warrior, shot twenty-nine Muslim worshipers to death and wounded 150 at the Tomb of the Patriarchs in Hebron. Goldstein was a follower of Rabbi Meir Kahane, the proponent of the expulsion of Arabs from Israel and, ultimately, the victim of El-Sayyid Nosair. Kahane saw Jews and Gentiles locked in an existential struggle that had been going on for thousands of years. He justified ruthless action to exact vengeance for the violence done to Jews during the millennia when they were in exile and incapable of self-defense. He also looked back for inspiration and a model to the Hasmonaean kingdom established by the Maccabees, a priestly family that led a successful revolt against Syrians who occupied Judea in the second century B.C.E.

Goldstein was intoxicated by these ideas. For him, the conflict between Jews and Muslims had reached a crisis point. The problem wasn't just the rock-throwing and the tit-for-tat killings. It was bigger than that. The Jews faced a catastrophe. The time for divine intervention had arrived. It was the holiday of Purim, when the Scroll of Esther is chanted before the congregation. Goldstein saw himself and his fellow Jews in the same crisis that had enveloped the Jews of Persia, who in the story faced annihilation. Historical time was drastically compressed, and the ancient narrative of Esther had become his own. He was present at the crescendo of an all-encompassing war that had begun thousands of years before. No rabbinical dispensation was necessary. It was time to strike, and just as in the climax of the Scroll of Esther, "The Jews smote all their enemies with the sword, slaughtering and destroying them, and did as they pleased to those who hated them."[11]

———

A favorable rabbinical ruling *was* issued regarding another religiously motivated terrorist attack: the 1995 assassination of Israeli prime minister Yitzhak Rabin, an event that has had a profound impact on Middle Eastern politics and American interests.

Among the settlers, especially the Gush Emunim movement, hatred of Rabin was intense in the mid-1990s. The prime minister had made no attempt to hide his contempt for the settlers, whom he judged to be a liability for Israeli security and a danger to its larger strategic interests. The religious settlers feared that Rabin would use the army to enforce the evacuation of settlements that were increasingly indefensible, including clusters of settlers and squatters in and around Hebron, which attracted pious settlers because it is the reputed burial place of the biblical patriarchs. In 1993, Rabbi Shlomo Goren, who had served as head chaplain for the Israel Defense Forces and enjoyed considerable authority, wrote that Jews should be prepared to "give our lives in the struggle against the vicious plan of the government of Israel [to evacuate the settlements] and be ready to die rather than allow the destruction of Hebron." A subsequent statement signed by Goren and three other leading lights of the Orthodox rabbinical establishment went further, instructing Jews to "disobey any order to evacuate Jewish settlers from Jewish land." Since the army would be given the task of clearing the settlements, this was an authoritative religious invitation to violence, and a challenge to the legitimacy of the Rabin government. In the meantime, the demonization of Rabin by his radical enemies was under way with wall posters in Israeli cities depicting him as a Nazi.

At the country's Orthodox university, Bar Ilan, student organizations vied with one another in justifying the obligation of Israeli Jews to oppose the policies of the Rabin government by force. A political science professor, Uri Milstein, attained great popularity with his lectures denigrating Rabin's military record. One spellbound student was an intense, Orthodox young man of Yemeni descent named Yigal Amir. The academic affirmation of his views about Rabin reinforced his growing conviction that the prime minister represented an historic danger to the Jewish people. Amir, whose religious training had been thorough, accepted the Orthodox legal assessment of Rabin's policies that was then circulating both in Israel and among some hard-line Orthodox Zionists in the United States. Rabin, in this assessment, was guilty of transgressing Jewish law by jeopardizing Jewish lives and transferring Israel's patrimony to non-Jews. He was therefore liable to two judgments: the *din rodef,* "law of the pursuer," and the *din moser,* "law of the one who hands over." The original application of the din rodef was straightforward: if a murderer is pursuing a victim, it is permissible to slay the pursuer. The din moser was more commonly invoked in Jewish diaspora history with respect to informers (*mosrim*), who would provide information to Gentile authorities for their own aggrandizement or to compromise a hated individual or family. Often, such informers would spark pogroms or massacres that would claim many victims. There is evidence that mosrim were executed at various times and places in Jewish communities in Europe until a few hundred years ago. (The killing of informers is one of the few crimes for which rabbinical authorities have waived the general prohibition of capital punishment since the disappearance of the Sanhedrin, the Jewish supreme court, in 70 C.E. One explanation for this is the clear and present danger that an informer posed to the life and welfare of vulnerable Jewish communities in a hostile Europe.)

In Rabin's case, land, rather than information, was being handed over to hostile powers, with lethal implications for Israeli Jews. More broadly, the surrender of Jewish land endangered the redemption of the Jewish people as a whole. The crime therefore had a metaphysical dimension that made it all the more frightening to people like Yigal Amir. Leaders of the settler community declared, "Should they [government officials] be tried according to the *Halakha* [Jewish law]? And if proven guilty as accomplices to murder, what should their sentence be? Is it not the obligation of the communities' leaders to warn the head of government and his ministers that if they keep pursuing the agreement after the terrible experience of stage one [Oslo I], in all of Judea and Samaria, they will be subject . . . to the Halakhic [legal] ruling of din moser, as ones who surrender the life and property of Jews to the gentiles?"[12]

On the night of October 6, 1995, Avigdor Eskin, a member of Gush Emunim, and some of his companions gathered near Rabin's official residence in Jerusalem to perform the occult rite of Pulsa d'Nura, "Blazing Disks." In the early Middle Ages, it was believed that God used a kind of cat-o'-nine-tails tipped with fiery metal disks to slay wicked Jews. The liturgy of the Pulsa d'Nura is little known among Jews, most of whom have never heard the obscure Aramaic phrase, or have much use for the service, which aims to bring God's lethal wrath down on transgressors within the Jewish community. The rite is said to require ten adult male participants, who gather before midnight in a synagogue or cave lit with black candles. There they chant the names of angels, read the liturgy, and utter elaborate curses. At midnight, the candles are extinguished and the ten worshipers each blow the shofar, or ram's horn. Those gathered on the night of October 6 recited these maledictions:

Angels of destruction will hit him. He is damned wherever he goes. His soul will instantly leave his body . . . and he will not survive a month. Dark will be his path and God's angel will chase him. A disaster he has never experienced will beget him and all curses known in the Torah will apply to him.

I deliver to you, the angels of wrath and ire, Yitzhak, the son of Rosa Rabin, that you may smother him and the specter of him, and cast him into bed, and dry up his wealth, and plague his thoughts, and scatter his mind that he may be steadily diminished until he reaches his death. Put to death the cursed Yitzhak. May [he] be damned, damned, damned![13]

Less than a month later, Yigal Amir walked up to Rabin in a parking facility near a rally Rabin had addressed and shot him to death.

Like the Temple Mount plotters, Amir would not act without explicit rabbinical sanction: "Without believing in God, I would never have had the power to do this—i.e., the belief in the after world. . . . I had to save the people because the people failed to understand the real conditions, and this is why I acted. . . . If not for the Halakhic ruling of din rodef, made against Rabin by a few rabbis I knew about, it would have been very difficult for me to murder. Such a murder must be backed up. If I did not get the backing and I had not been representing many more people, I would not have acted."[14]

Amir felt he had a privileged understanding of the catastrophe that awaited the Jewish people and believed that he could save them. Given these stakes, and the rabbinical guidance, there could be no conceivable constraint on his actions. As Amir expressed this, "Din moser and din rodef is the halakhic ruling. Once it is a ruling, there is no problem of morality. If I were involved now in the biblical conquest of the land, and as said in [the biblical Book of] Joshua, I would have had to kill babies and children, I would have done so regardless of the problem of morality. Once it is a ruling, I do not have a problem with it."[15]

BUDDHISM MEETS CHRISTIANITY AT THE END OF THE WORLD

A preoccupation with cosmic war and apocalyptic violence is not confined to the Judeo-Christian tradition. On March 20, 1995, at 7:45 A.M., five disciples of Shoko Asahara, a messianic pretender and leader of a quasi-Buddhist cult called Aum Shinrikyo, boarded separate Tokyo subway trains at the ends of the five lines that take commuters to the center of the city. All five trains were headed to Kasumigaseki station, underneath the complex of ministries at the heart of Japanese government. The five riders were skilled scientists: a cardiovascular surgeon who had studied in the United States, a former graduate student in particle physics at Tokyo University, two graduates in applied physics, and an electrical engineer. At 8:15 A.M., as the trains converged on Kasumigaseki station, the five used sharpened umbrella tips to pierce plastic containers containing a 30 percent solution of sarin, a nerve agent that kills by blocking the chemical reactions that enable muscle tissues to relax after flexing. It causes death within minutes. If disseminated effectively by aerosol spray, a few quarts would kill thousands of unprotected people. In this attack twelve people were killed and 5,500 were injured, many seriously. The small number of fatalities was due primarily to the way the liquid sarin was packaged and to atmospheric conditions, neither of which favored the rapid, even, and lengthy vaporization required for truly devastating results. As casualties flooded hospital emergency rooms, doctors were mystified by the symptoms they saw. It was not until 10:30 A.M. that an emergency physician recognized the symptoms—pin-dot-sized retinas, vomiting, and respiratory failure—as signs of nerve agent poisoning. And it was not until 1:30 P.M. that the first properly equipped personnel, wearing military chemical-protection suits, arrived at the scene of the attack. No one had expected this horror.

Shoko Asahara was the clerical title taken by a blind huckster named Chizuo Matsumoto. In 1987, he set up Aum Shinrikyo as a school for yoga practitioners and Buddhists. At the time Japan was teeming with syncretistic sects of every description. Some of these new movements are large-scale evolutionary developments within the framework of established religions like Buddhism and Shintoism. Others are new religions entirely, which emphasize magic and the occult as well as more widely accepted patterns of religious practice. These religions do not all remain confined to the Japanese islands. Some have a proselytizing vigor and footholds in foreign countries where there are large Japanese expatriate populations. Aum Shinrikyo, which stressed missionary work, was a good example of this.

Religions have proliferated so swiftly since World War II that Japanese scholars have a hard time cataloging them. As of the 1970s, the category once dubbed "new religions" was already being replaced by a more up-to-date tag: "new, new religions." These consisted mainly of groups with a strong apocalyptic bent, or a mystical approach to religious experience, or both. Depending on how individual observers differentiated between offshoots of established religions and their parent faiths and, indeed, how they defined religion, there were either dozens or hundreds of distinctive religions in the spiritual landscape of 1990s Japan. Secular factors played a role in this explosion of faiths, as they have in the growing diversity of Protestant denominations in the United States. The most important is the competition between religions for new adherents that emerges in countries where there is no official state religion. Where no religion has a monopoly on popular allegiance, each has to show that it has something unique, different, and better to offer than its rivals. Competition therefore encourages diversity. Another factor is tax policy. In Japan, as in the United States, there are significant financial advantages to having official "church" status.

Aum Shinrikyo was just one of many such new, new religions. Its syncretism was typical. In Aum's case, the group's essentially Buddhist orientation meshed with important elements from Christianity, especially an apocalyptic impulse that grew over time, and a belief in a messiah. It was unlike other groups, however, in the degree of its rigid authoritarianism and hierarchical structure. The group was probably enforcing discipline with deadly violence by the early 1990s. By the time it was dismantled in 1995, Aum was organized much like a government, with twenty ministries and even a "Household" ministry analogous to the government bureau that administered the emperor's palace operations. The movement collected taxes, developed a lucrative business network, and cultivated ties with the army and the Yakuza, Japan's criminal organiza-

tions. The recruits came from the best universities and were highly motivated achievers in the hard sciences and law. Many who were willing to
make the break from family, friends, jobs, or school joined Aum com-
munes, or *shukkeshas*. As apocalyptic societies have done since ancient
times, those awaiting the end of time entered seclusion to maintain the
purity that would entitle them to redemption after the great conflagration.

Between 1990 and 1995, the core beliefs promoted by Asahara were
inculcated into the rank and file, although the more radical doctrines
were withheld from the lower orders and revealed only to those who were
in Asahara's immediate circle. Great importance was attached to Nostradamus's elaborate calculations predicting the precise dates on which
great events would occur—including the end of the world—and to the
Book of Revelation. Japan's glory, they believed, was being ground down
by the corruption of the Japanese themselves and cultural pollution from
the West. The situation was made even more dire by the vast conspiracy
that threatened the Aum. Jews, Freemasons, the United States, and "world
government" were determined to subvert and crush the movement. Members believed that Aum could create a race of superhumans through
meditation and that this master race would establish a civilization that
would survive the coming Armageddon. Asahara admired Hitler and his
plan for a thousand-year Reich, which resonated in Asahara's mind with
the millennium of Revelation. Individuals within the organization who
introduced bad karma by expressing doubt or seeking to break with
the group could legitimately be killed. Ultimately, the purified remnant,
the disciples of Shoko Asahara, would survive the inevitable global
devastation.

These astonishing ideas began to coalesce in Asahara's mind in reaction to the collapse of the Soviet Union and the victory of the United
States–led coalition against Saddam Hussein's Iraq. The twin events
seemed to him to be signs of the end time. With socialism eliminated as
an option for human society, there was only the ideological temptation
of materialism. However, all was not lost. In 1992 he declared: "I have
made the following prediction . . . the genuine spiritualists will grow full

and shine like the sun, while Jewish materialists will be collected to be burned." During this period, Asahara became increasingly vocal about the imminence of cosmic war, how it would be fought, and who would survive. He was struck by the effectiveness and power of the weaponry deployed by the United States against Iraq. He obsessed about "ABC": atomic, biological, and chemical weapons, the use of which would dominate the imminent global war. He gave orders to perfect Aum's defenses, even mandating the creation of underwater cities in which his disciples could seek shelter. In preparation, group members were subjected to arduous training regimens, including submersion in water of extreme, though not lethal, temperatures. Asahara also gave the go-ahead to conduct research on weapons of mass destruction for the group's own use. It is possible that he had decided as early as March 1990 to nudge history along and spark Armageddon. While asserting publicly that his enemies were using chemical weapons against him, Asahara had Tsuchiya Masami, an accomplished university chemist, produce sarin for use in the expected third world war. Biological weapons were also fabricated, but never successfully used. The one known attempt was in April 1990, when Aum operatives sprayed the Japanese Diet with botulinum toxin. The group deployed a team to experiment in Australia, where it owned vast stretches of ranchland in the outback. They returned home leaving massive heaps of dead sheep behind them. (Some believe that Aum was mining uranium and somehow caused a huge explosion, which witnesses claimed to have heard from great distances.) Members were dispatched to Zaire to obtain the Ebola virus for cultivation as a weapon. The group's transnational presence, ranging from Russia, the United States, and Germany to Australia and Zaire, made acquisition of chemical- and biological-weapons precursors easier. Links with Russia also provided advanced conventional weapons and commando training.

Aum was also becoming more confrontational with surrounding Japanese society. On occasion they were able to turn these strains to their advantage. The town of Namino Kyushu paid the local Aum Shinrikyo branch about one billion yen to relocate. The constant mantras broadcast over loudspeakers and the twenty-four-hour truck traffic and construction activity drove the inhabitants to desperation. But overall, the group's fortunes were deteriorating through this period. Recruitment dropped as new religions sprang up to compete for converts and donors, while Aum Shinrikyo's reputation became more sordid. Police interest because of the group's disputes with outsiders and reports of disappearances and murders put the group in an even more perilous position. This led to greater tensions as members were pressed to find new sources of funds and new converts. Asahara's fixation on conspiracies grew more baroque as he sought to rationalize the group's accelerating weakness and foster greater internal unity. He tried to have the leaders of two rival cults murdered. The biblical images of the apocalypse he had showcased within the group, which included angels, devils, and pestilential suffering, no longer sufficed to describe the scale of the coming disaster. Mushroom clouds replaced the fiery pit of Hell. Laser weapons, plasma guns, and a monstrous space-based mirror that focused the heat of the sun on the earth studded Asahara's descriptions of the coming catastrophe. These things were to come to pass first in 1996, then 1998. Armageddon was something of a movable feast.

As circumstances grew more desperate, Asahara's ideas about the end evolved further. *Po'a*, a Buddhist term for the rites performed on behalf of a deceased person to facilitate his or her transition to the next world, had already been redefined by Asahara to mean services provided before a person's death to ease the path to the afterlife. His service was to prevent spiritually defective or evil people from accumulating more bad karma than they had already, thereby impeding their own afterlife ascension to more ethereal spheres. Aum could render this service in various ways, but sometimes there was "no other way," according to Asahara, to po'a but to kill the person.[16] By 1994, Asahara was talking about performing po'a for the whole world, instead of just Aum's external enemies and internal malcontents. He put this rhetoric into action on June 27, 1994, when Aum activists drove a refrigerator truck loaded with sarin into the city center of Matsumoto and released the gas. Matsumoto was chosen because it was there that Asahara had been thwarted by the local court in an attempt to acquire land for a large Aum installation. Seven people were killed and 250 were treated for symptoms. The magistrates who had been the prime target were unhurt. Asahara himself publicly emphasized Nostradamus's prophecy that the judiciary will be corrupted in the countdown to Armageddon. Yet Japanese authorities remained oblivious to the threat for nearly a full year, initially misdiagnosing the injuries inflicted by the sarin, then concluding that the cause was insecticide spread by a nearby gardener.

By 1995, events were approaching their climax. The investigation of the Matsumoto attack finally gathered steam. So did police inquiries into the kidnappings and murders Asahara ordered as he understood himself more and more to be operating on a higher plane, no longer subject to human laws. The media began to speculate on how much time Aum had left, just as Asahara was speculating on how much time the world had. The powerful earthquake in the city of Kobe, Japan, combined with increased pressure from law enforcement and Asahara's premonitions of his own death to create the circumstances for the Tokyo subway attack.

It is still not entirely clear what Asahara thought the attack would accomplish. Did he mean it to confirm his repeated claims that chemical weapons were being used by others? Did he expect his followers to interpret it as proof of his apocalyptic warnings? Did he think it would set off the global Armageddon he had been predicting, or cripple Japan's government and thereby open the door to Aum Shinrikyo's government-in-waiting? None of these explanations is implausible, given what is known about Asahara's mental state and worldview in 1995. Nor are they mutually exclusive. In any event, he was ready for anything. The raid on his underground facility uncovered the equivalent of four million doses of sarin, quantities of other chemical weapons, cultures for Q fever and anthrax, and a million doses of LSD.[17]

Asahara's weird blend of messianic Christianity, apocalyptic fervor, and the Buddhist concept of "salvation through death," combined with his recruiting and organizational skills, came frighteningly close to creating hell for his country. The skepticism of law-enforcement and political authorities about the dangers of this bizarre cocktail of beliefs and capabilities mirrored the unwillingness of their European and American counterparts to acknowledge the continuing killing power of religion.

APOCALYPSE NOW

America is a more religious country than it was when it was founded in the late eighteenth century, and judging by public opinion survey returns, church attendance, financial donations, book purchases, and voting patterns, it's becoming even more so. There is also a growing fascination with Christian apocalyptic speculation and with signs that the events depicted in Revelation are at hand. A book series by Tim LaHaye and Jerry Jenkins based on the prophecies in Revelation has sold 32 million copies since the first volume came out in 1995 (not counting the 18 million copies of the illustrated and children's versions). The tenth book in the series appeared in bookstores in 2002 in a hardcover printing of 2.75 million copies. September 11 boosted sales, as it did for the thousands of titles on apocalyptic themes published in the United States. According to a Time/CNN poll, about 35 percent of Americans think about the implications of the daily news for the end of the world. Fifty-nine percent believe that the future will unfold in accordance with Revelation. About 30 percent believe that the September 11 attacks were predicted by the Bible.

A small Christian subculture in the United States strongly believes in the notion of cosmic war. Believers are splintered into a number of small groups, the largest of which is the Christian Identity movement. According to Christian Identity ideology, the British are descended from "Aryan" northern Israelite tribes who migrated to the British Isles in the wake of the Babylonian conquest of ancient Israel. These Aryans are the true Jews of the Bible. This self-serving myth about the genetic superiority of the British people appeared in England in the nineteenth century and quickly died out there, but not before migrating to the United States.

The transplanted version took on anti-Semitic overtones, holding that contemporary Jews, who are assumed to be the descendants of the biblical Jews, are masquerading in that role and may well be the children of Eve and Satan. There are many variations on the core beliefs of the movement, which has now settled in Idaho and also has communities in the southern Midwest. Most adherents believe that mainstream Protestant churches in the United States are unwilling to confront the fraud perpetrated by the Jews, or have secretly been taken over by them. The Catholic Church is also believed to be part of this conspiracy. Identity sympathizers believe that the late-nineteenth-century Czarist forgery *The Protocols of the Elders of Zion,* which purports to disclose the Jewish plan for world domination, is genuine. In pursuit of their goals, the Jews have teamed up, in one or another variation of this story, with the United Nations, the federal government and the Federal Reserve Bank, the Democratic party, Freemasons, African Americans, Asian Americans, and Latinos to thwart the quest of Aryan Christians for liberty and independence. The world is not as it seems: Aryan Christians are the true Jews; the Jews are scheming impostors; ordinary churches are in league with Satan. These convictions are intertwined with an obsession with firearms. In the perilous world inhabited by these Aryans, they will need their weapons to prevent the government from completely subjugating them and enthroning the Jews. Gun control legislation is therefore part of a larger, barely visible conspiracy to enslave white Americans.

Many of these themes run through the plot of *The Turner Diaries,* by the late Christian Identity fantasist William Pierce (who wrote under the pen name Andrew MacDonald). Timothy McVeigh said that this was his favorite book. He hawked it at gun shows around the country, where it is highly popular, and reread it frequently. The novel portrays a guerrilla war waged in the United States by white supremacists, who fight against the federal government's brutal attempt to seize Americans' firearms as a prelude to their complete subjugation. The government's plan is supported by Jews. The insurgents, a monastic, hooded, robe-clad group called the Order, ultimately blow up FBI headquarters in Washington, D.C., using a five-thousand-pound truck bomb, killing seven hundred people. The attackers carry out the assault in order to awaken Christian Americans to their true situation and spur a wider revolt. The campaign includes the assassination of Jews and others and ultimately the obliteration of American cities with nuclear weapons captured from the government. These weapons are then used to destroy Israel and the Soviet Union. When Timothy McVeigh lit the two fuses of the 4,400-pound ammonium nitrate–and–fuel oil bomb in his Ryder truck, just before nine A.M. on April 19, 1995, he was enacting the fictional blow inflicted on the federal government in *The Turner Diaries.* Although McVeigh described himself to others as irreligious, his preoccupation with Christian Identity literature and attempts to link up with Elohim City, a movement commune on the Oklahoma border (Elohim is a biblical Hebrew name of God), suggest an overlap between his worldview and Christian Identity doctrine.[18]

McVeigh's transition from gun show enthusiast and libertarian to adherent to Christian Identity and member of a religiously oriented militia follows an established pattern. Recruits are exposed to these organizations and their ideology in settings where government attempts (real or imagined) to constrain gun ownership, monitor citizens' movements, or impose "unconstitutional" taxes are at issue. Religion is then offered as the way to comprehend what the government is doing and to justify violence as a response. Some, but by no means all, are seduced by the cosmic-war picture painted by militia ideologues. This war concept is at the center of the Aryan Nation creed: "We believe there is a battle being fought this day between the children of darkness (today known as the Jews) and the children of Light (God), the Aryan race, the true Israel of the Bible . . . we believe there will be a day of reckoning. The usurper will be thrown out by the terrible might of Yahweh's people as they return to their roots and their special destiny."[19] A spokesman for the Christian Patriot movement, an assortment of far-right groups dominated by Christian Identity thinking, summarized these apocalyptic expectations in terms that might have come from a textbook on apocalyptic thought: "We are

Christian survivalists who believe in preparing for the ultimate holocaust. . . . The coming war is a step towards God's government."[20] First
the terrible years, then the winnowing, then the establishment of the
Kingdom of God. The underlying image of ancient conflict and a coming
Armageddon is a powerful one in the United States, where a majority of
Americans believe that Jesus Christ will reappear in their lifetimes and
trigger the conflagration, bloodshed, and other horrific tribulations predicted by the Books of Revelation and Daniel. The acceptance of an imminent end-time catastrophe may not be as widespread now in the
United States as it was, say, in fourteenth-century Europe, when scores of
thousands roamed the continent in the grip of an end-of-the-world hysteria that threatened the viability of the Catholic Church and led to the virtual extermination of Jews in Germany and Belgium. But it is a significant
feature of the country's religious landscape and it provides fertile ground
for Christian Identity–like apocalypticism. Even Pat Robertson's 1991
book *The New World Order* partakes of this worldview, particularly in its
reliance on traditional anti-Semitic motifs regarding a global Jewish conspiracy to control governments and world finance.[21]

What distinguishes the Christian Identity movement from the more
traditional theology that informs much (but not all) fundamentalist worship in the United States is its rejection of key events anticipated by mainstream fundamentalists, especially the Rapture and conversion of the
Jews. According to the New Testament, the saved will be "Raptured" to
Heaven before the terrors of end-time "tribulation" commence. *Rapture*
is the term for the ascension of the saved in this scenario:

> For this we declare to you by the word of the Lord, that we who are
> alive, who are left until the coming of the Lord, shall not precede
> those who have fallen asleep. For the Lord himself will descend from
> heaven with a cry of command, with the archangel's call, and with the
> sound of the trumpet of God. And the dead in Christ will rise first;
> then we who are alive, who are left, shall be caught up together with
> them in the clouds to meet the Lord in the air; and so we shall always
> be with the Lord.[22]

For Christian Identity thinkers, Rapture is a repugnant idea, which they deny has any basis in the Bible. They do not intend to be Raptured. They fully intend to be on earth during the tribulation to destroy the enemies of God, who are, of course, the Jews. This conviction justifies their militaristic posture. To fight and survive during the seven years of horrific bloodshed that according to Revelation will characterize the tribulation, they must be well armed, well trained, and well supplied. A well-known Identity figure, Sheldon Emry, wrote in disgust that "the rapture 'doctrine' has done more to disarm and make American Christians impotent than any other teaching since Jesus Christ."[23] The conventional fundamentalist view of biblical prophecies relating to the restoration of Israel is that they refer to Jews of today and to the state of Israel, not to Anglo-Saxons or Aryans who believe that they are the true Jews. Hence the satisfaction many mainstream fundamentalists take in the creation of the state of Israel and in its military successes, the capture of Jerusalem, and territorial expansion, which are taken to be signs of the end time. That most of these Jews will be slaughtered in the tribulation, which commences with a war in the Middle East, is not seen by believers as inconsistent with their pro-Israeli sentiments. In any case, this view of Jews is far too favorable for Christian Identity, which believes it has a responsibility to help God wipe the Jews out during the coming tribulation. There will be no Israelite remnant to be converted in the last days, apart from Identity believers themselves, who are the true Israel.

The self-consciously religious nomenclature and rituals associated with these movements helps them validate their extreme agendas. Leaders and spokesmen for the groups are dubbed "Reverend" or "Pastor." An initiation ceremony described by one observer emphasized these characteristics: it took place in a church, the aisle was lined with rifle-bearing participants, there was a procession, and the service used terms such as "God's soldiers" and "holy war," and stated the importance of killing with love because "God is with us." As for the conviction that the battle has been going on since time immemorial, the Aryan Nation's spiritual leader, the Reverend Richard Butler, in describing his ideological development to a reporter, emphasized an insight he had as a younger man, that "this war has been going on for over 6,000 years between the sons of Cain and the sons of God." Butler explained how this insight had given him a purpose in life.[24] The combination of religion with a belief in an all-or-nothing struggle with evil that will culminate in Armageddon demonizes the other and strips away constraints on violence. The Aryan Nation, according to a U.S. indictment, intended to "carry out assassinations of federal officials, politicians, and Jews, as well as bombings of and polluting of municipal supplies." That was in 1983. The following year, authorities found thirty gallons of cyanide that was supposed to be used to contaminate the water supplies of Chicago and Washington, D.C.[25] The plot was intended to cause massive casualties, as was McVeigh's bombing of the federal office building in Oklahoma City, which was the most damaging terrorist attack on American soil until September 11, 2001. In December 1999, the FBI thwarted a militia attempt to detonate two twelve-million-gallon tanks of liquid propane in Oak Grove, California, just outside Sacramento and about a mile from the nearest housing development. The conspirators, who were subsequently convicted, clearly aimed to cause massive casualties, either through a fireball that would engulf nearby communities, or by means of storage tank fragments that would rocket through vast distances at high velocity.

There is more. A Montanan, David Burgert, was arrested in 2002 for stockpiling machine guns, homemade bombs, and tens of thousands of rounds of ammunition to begin a nationwide revolt. According to the plan, Burgert's militia was to kill twenty-six police and other officials in their corner of the state, defeat the National Guard, and finally spark a nationwide revolt against the federal government when Washington brought in NATO troops to suppress the militia. When the smoke cleared, America would once again be in the hands of white Christians. In the past year, similar conspiracies have been uncovered that aimed at bombing federal buildings in Michigan, assaulting Fort Hood in Texas—among other military bases—by taking advantage of a day when the surrounding community is welcomed into the installation to visit, and destroying a nuclear power plant in Florida.

Events such as these merely hint at what is to come, according to a spokesman for the Church of Israel, an Identity group:

> The fall of the American government is imminent. We are living already in the preparatory throes of a national and world wide revolution . . . as the agents of Satan who head the world wide conspiracy of the anti-Christ, plot and plan the total demise of Christian civilization and of the whole race. . . . A blood bath will take place in the soil of this great nation, that will end only in victory for Christ or Satan.[26]

———

Time, we have seen, is compressed for those in the thrall of apocalyptic ideas. Ancient dramas replay themselves in modern circumstances, and when the believer acts forcefully enough, a reversal in history occurs, wrongs are righted, and injustices are avenged.

Perhaps it is a part of the militants' power that they have compressed time for all of us. It is extraordinary that only twelve years have passed since El-Sayyid Nosair gunned down Meir Kahane in New York, and less than a decade since the first attempted catastrophic attack, the first World Trade Center bombing. Yet within this short span, a new breed of terrorists has emerged and established itself as the preeminent threat to the West. Not only time but strategy has been turned inside out, and we must conjure new ways to defend ourselves against opponents who seek to use the most advanced technologies of the twenty-first century to fulfill imperatives laid down in the seventh century and, in some cases, before. Further, we must now beware of Christians who want to kill thousands, Jews who are prepared to turn the Middle East upside down, and highly educated cultists ready to use taboo weapons for reasons that still remain uncertain.

What is supremely puzzling is: Why now? So many forms of religious terrorism have appeared in such a short time after such a long absence.

We are a long way from taking the full measure of the new terrorists. Those who have committed the most atrocious violence—the jihadists, who are also the most numerous—have done the most to explain themselves. A surfeit of causes lies behind the challenge of bin Laden and his radical Islamists, including frustration with states that fail them politically and economically, a pessimism born of several centuries in which Muslim countries failed to achieve like Western ones, and the deep tremors of an Islamic reformation. Like the European Reformation of nearly five centuries ago, this Islamic upheaval will likely become much more bloody before a new equilibrium emerges. The jihadists are the greatest threat, and will likely remain that. But the shock of their appearance suggests that we should not be surprised if others soon challenge them, and us.

THE WAR THUS FAR: A STATUS REPORT

IN THE SPRING OF 2003, the Bush administration began voicing strong confidence that the war on terror was being won. In May, President Bush, while announcing the end of hostilities in Iraq aboard the aircraft carrier U.S.S. *Abraham Lincoln,* declared, "The war on terror is not over; yet it is not endless. We do not know the day of final victory, but we have seen the turning of the tide. No act of the terrorists will change our purpose, or weaken our resolve, or alter their fate. Their cause is lost."[1] Cofer Black, the former chief of the CIA's Counterterrorist Center, now the State Department's senior counterterrorism official, was quoted soon thereafter in *The Washington Post* as saying that al-Qaeda's leadership losses were "catastrophic" and that the broader network "has been unable to withstand the global onslaught" of intelligence operations.[2] Senior government officials frequently referred to three thousand al-Qaeda operatives who had been detained or killed in counterterrorism operations around the world.

Signs of the new confidence were not just rhetorical. Vice President Dick Cheney, who in the fall of 2002 still shuttled to an "undisclosed location" where he could preside over an emergency government in the

The report of the joint inquiry by the congressional intelligence committees into the September 11 attacks was released on July 24, 2003, too late for its findings to be reviewed here. Although the report details lapses by the CIA and FBI that we did not know about, its broad findings parallel our own conclusions about the failures and mishaps within the government that allowed these events to occur.

event of a major attack, ended his commute. By early June, the nation had gone through four terror-alert cycles in which the official color code was raised from yellow to orange, the second-highest level. But after an episode of panic-buying of duct tape and plastic sheeting in February, Americans grew blasé about the threat; cash-starved state and local authorities shrugged off the later code changes, citing the lack of specific information. In New York City and Washington, where the threat-level change was taken more seriously—in the capital, antiaircraft batteries were occasionally trundled out—the frequency of the alerts still had a numbing effect. Expressions of fear, like that of the senior National Security Council counterterrorism official who in December 2002 wondered whether he should go to the office because he believed that al-Qaeda was "going to kill the White House," ceased to be heard.[3]

Behind the developments lay a substantial record of accomplishment: the United States had scored more significant victories against al-Qaeda than anyone had a right to imagine in the aftermath of the September 11 attacks. American and foreign intelligence and law enforcement agencies, driven by a common understanding of the terrorist threat that had not existed before 2001, disrupted numerous terrorist plots—as many as one hundred, according to FBI Director Robert Mueller. Among these were schemes to destroy ships passing through the Straits of Gibraltar, fire Stinger-type missiles at commercial aircraft flying out of London's Heathrow Airport, crash a plane into the U.S. consulate in Karachi, bomb several embassies in Bangkok, and destroy the U.S. embassy in Beirut. Beginning in January, European authorities broke up a jihadist effort to carry out poisonings using ricin, a castor bean derivative. Progress, U.S. officials reported, was being made in the effort to stem the flow of money to terrorist cells through covert operations and quiet but increasing cooperation from countries in the Persian Gulf.

The banner accomplishments were the arrests or killings of senior al-Qaeda operatives. On September 11, 2002, Ramzi bin al-Shibh, a Yemeni leader of the team behind the attacks of exactly a year earlier, was captured in Karachi. In November, Qaed Senyan al-Harthi, a high-level al-Qaeda official, was killed with five others in a remote area of Yemen by a missile fired from a Predator drone—the same type that had been the subject of a bruising battle within the bureaucracy in the months before September 11. In the same month, Abd al-Rahim al-Nashiri, a Saudi who served as operations chief on the Arabian Peninsula, was apprehended in the Persian Gulf region. In 2003, Walid Baattash, another operative involved in the World Trade Center/Pentagon attacks, was arrested in Karachi.

The pivotal moment in this campaign, however, arrived when the image of a disheveled Khalid Sheikh Mohammed, clad in a grubby T-shirt, hands cuffed behind him, appeared on television screens and front pages around the world following his predawn arrest on March 1, 2003, in Rawalpindi. The uncle of Ramzi Yousef, who engineered the 1993 bombing of the World Trade Center, Mohammed had collaborated with his nephew on the Bojinka plot to blow up a dozen U.S. 747s over the Pacific in 1995 and was an architect of September 11 and other attacks. He was a significant reason why al-Qaeda had emerged as the most tactically imaginative terrorist group in history, and he had eluded capture for almost a decade.

Emboldened by these successes, American officials issued pronouncements about al-Qaeda's fate that at times shaded into boasts. The organization's back had been broken, several claimed, and it would soon cease to pose a serious threat to the United States. President Bush, speaking in Arkansas, claimed, "Al-Qaeda is on the run. That group of terrorists who attacked our country is slowly but surely being decimated. Right now, about half of all the top al-Qaeda operatives are either jailed or dead. In either case, they're not a problem anymore. And we'll stay on the hunt."[4] The perils of such triumphalism were almost immediately demonstrated by coordinated car bombings in Saudi Arabia and Morocco. In Riyadh, an al-Qaeda cell struck three gated expatriate communities almost simultaneously on May 12, 2003, killing eight Americans and seventeen others. (The toll would likely have been much higher if fifty American contractors who worked with the Saudi National Guard had not been on a desert training mission.) Four days later in Casablanca, radicals detonated bombs outside buildings frequented by Westerners and Moroccan Jews, killing another twenty-nine people, including Spanish, French, and Italian tourists, though no Americans. Twenty-one suicide operatives participated in the two multipronged operations.

The May incidents ended, at least for a time, the declarations of impending victory and elicited a brief flurry of news stories on the question "Has al-Qaeda come back?" The query itself was indicative of the American public's difficulty in adjusting to an era in which terrorism poses the preeminent threat to the nation's security—because, in fact, al-Qaeda and radical Islamist violence had never gone away. The May bombings were the latest in a lengthening list of attacks committed by jihadists. Among the victims of these incidents were more than two hundred people killed by the al-Qaeda affiliate Jemaah Islamiya when it bombed nightclubs on the Indonesian resort island of Bali on October 12, 2002. By any measure except that of September 11, Bali was a major attack. In the same month, Chechen rebels led by Movsar Basayev, a protégé of Khattab, a comrade in arms of Usama bin Laden, took some eight hundred theatergoers hostage in Moscow and threatened to blow up the building. A two-day standoff ended when Russian special forces used an opiate gas to render the terrorists unconscious before storming the building. The gas, however, was too potent, and killed as many as 128 of the hostages; the 41 hostage-takers were either killed by the gas or shot.

Late the next month, al-Qaeda's resourcefulness was displayed again in Mombasa, Kenya. A cell there—supposedly cleaned out after the August 1998 bombing of the American embassies in Nairobi and Dar es Salaam—reemerged when suicide operatives crashed a bomb-laden sport utility vehicle into a hotel owned by and catering to Israelis. Ten Kenyan workers and three Israeli tourists were killed. Almost simultaneously, terrorists shot two Soviet-made Strela shoulder-fired missiles at an Israeli charter jet that had just taken off from the local airport for Tel Aviv. The missiles narrowly missed the aircraft, perhaps because the weapons were old or, more likely, because the operators fired them too early, before the plane was within the weapons' minimum range.

These were the largest attacks, but there were many other less spectacular ones, including the bombing of a French oil tanker off the coast of
Yemen, the shootings of American servicemen in the Persian Gulf, the assassination of an American diplomat in Jordan, and a string of bombings
in the Philippines.[5] Rather than being a receding problem, al-Qaeda and
other radical groups were extremely active in the second year of the war
on terrorism despite the enormous pressure on them. In the last half century, only Hezbollah in 1983 came close to this level of killing, when it
bombed the barracks of U.S. Marines and French forces and the U.S. embassy in Beirut, and that still fell significantly short. But the public impression was otherwise. Thomas Friedman of *The New York Times*—who
in 2001 had wondered after the destruction of the World Trade Center,
"Does my country really understand that this is World War III? And if
this attack was the Pearl Harbor of World War III, it means there is a long,
long war ahead"[6]—voiced a common sentiment in April 2003 when he
seemed to dismiss the terrorist threat as a "bubble," a temporary distortion in the market of world affairs, and counseled that "we and the Arab-
Muslim world must now draw the right conclusions. One hopes
Americans will now stop overreacting to 9/11."[7]

Al-Qaeda's failure to carry out a second catastrophic attack in the
United States undoubtedly accounted for much of the growing confidence, as did the fact that the attacks of the period occurred abroad,
which many interpreted to mean that America was becoming impreg-
nable. Analysts and policy makers contended that the group had changed
tactics to concentrate on smaller "soft targets," such as the Bali nightclubs, overlooking the group's proven ability to vary its tactics; the Radisson Hotel in Amman, the pilgrimage sites along the Jordan River, and Los
Angeles International Airport, all key targets in the Millennium conspiracy, were not "hard" targets. Finally, it appeared that Americans were
becoming accustomed to a world in which attacks with casualties in the
double and low triple digits were a fact of life.

Is America underestimating the jihadist threat as it did before September 2001? To be sure, al-Qaeda's capabilities *have* been degraded by
the continued success of intelligence operations. As of June 2003, Usama

bin Laden and his chief lieutenant and ideologist, Ayman al-Zawahiri, have not been captured, and to some Muslims their elusiveness strengthens their implicit claim to represent the divine will. But they are, most likely, constantly on the move and unable to manage al-Qaeda with the kind of control exercised in the past. Still, a terrorist organization—and al-Qaeda in particular—is not a military corps, and the heavy emphasis that U.S. officials have laid on the numbers of leaders and operatives put out of commission may be misleading. If half of al-Qaeda's top leadership is still at large, then a dozen or so individuals remain who have the authority and the know-how to manage a major operation. The significance of the detention of some three thousand operatives is difficult to gauge. U.S. officials have spoken of "tens of thousands" of individuals who were trained in the camps of Afghanistan, and Germany's intelligence chief put the number at seventy thousand,[8] though many were trained as soldiers to fight alongside the Taliban, not as terrorists. Still, the number of operatives at large is probably multiples greater than that of any other terrorist group in memory.

Despite its losses, the organization has also shown an impressive resilience. It has replaced lost leaders, promoting rapidly from within—the organization is on its fourth or fifth chief of operations in a decade—and shows no sign of having exhausted its reserves. A United Nations team in late 2002 reported that al-Qaeda continues to recruit new members and raise funds vigorously, news that was confirmed by intelligence sources.[9] One or two intact cells could, with the right plan, inflict damage of the magnitude of September 11 or greater, and we do not know how many intact cells remain scattered around the globe and are capable of carrying out such an operation.

The dimensions of the threat are further obscured by the habit of viewing attacks such as those in Bali and Moscow as the maximum the terrorists could achieve. Throughout its existence, al-Qaeda has subsidized indigenous Islamist groups in their fight against the "near enemy," central authorities they consider apostate (such as the governments of most Muslim countries) and infidel occupiers (such as the Russians who govern Chechnya), and this network of affiliated groups has become the base for radical Islam's global activity. Attacks against the near enemy represent one track of activity; those against the United States, the "far enemy" that props up these lesser regimes, represent another. The far enemy is so powerful that it must be struck with overwhelming violence—the only message it understands—and those operations require far more time and planning than car bombings that can be orchestrated in a few months or less. It is a mistake to believe that because attacks continue on the one track, they have stopped on the other, slower one. That nearly two years have passed since September 11 without such an attack provides some encouragement but no guarantees.

What has been lost in the war on terrorism, above all, is a realistic sense of al-Qaeda's relationship to the larger environment of the Muslim world and of the long-term threat from radical Islam. In public discussion, the organization has been reified, detached from the broader ideological movement it represents. The metaphors used to describe it are indicative: beyond the implicit, predominant one of an army whose finite number of troops can be systematically destroyed—or "decimated," as the President often phrases it—there is also the beast whose "back has been broken," as officials often intone. Frequently, too, it is the serpent. "Bush has carefully avoided any display of personal interest in bin Laden since the al-Qaeda leader's escape from Tora Bora in eastern Afghanistan in December 2001," one journalist observed. "But a top-ranking adviser said the president's overriding goal is to 'cut the head off the snake,' and Bush asks for constant updates on the 'high value target' list of terrorists on which bin Laden is first of about 36 men named."[10] An unnamed Pentagon intelligence official quoted in *Time* magazine after the Riyadh and Casablanca attacks indicated the problem with these ways of discussing the group when he observed, "They keep likening [al-Qaeda] to a snake, but it's more like a deadly mold."[11]

The truth is that Al-Qaeda is a dynamic ideological movement, part of a growing global insurgency. In this, it more closely resembles international communism before the October Revolution, say, than Napoleon's

Grand Armée disintegrating in a plume across Europe or, as one might sometimes believe from media commentary, a somewhat larger version of the Abu Nidal Group, a terrorist gang that could be wiped out in a kind of St. Valentine's Day Massacre.

If enough damage is done to al-Qaeda, the West may win a pause in the war on terrorism. But in failing to recognize the larger, long-term danger of the group's brand of radical Islam, the U.S. has pursued policies that either ignore the deeper causes of resentment in the Islamic world or, worse, exacerbate them. We have also lost time and the unique political opportunity provided by September 11 to begin addressing these issues.

IRAQ

For the Bush administration, 2003 was also the year in which "phase two" of the war on terrorism was completed. Bringing about regime change in Iraq had been contemplated by the Bush foreign policy team in its first months in office in 2001, when both the Deputies and the Principals committees of the National Security Council met to discuss the issue. Regime change had been the stated goal of the Clinton administration, too, but in the latter part of the 1990s, it found no alternative preferable to the continued containment of Iraq through sanctions, diversion of its oil revenue to a UN escrow account, diplomatic isolation, and, on occasion, military force, which was used to destroy the air defenses and facilities where it was thought that Baghdad was producing weapons of mass destruction.

By the end of the decade, this strategy was threadbare: sanctions had failed to choke off Saddam's revenue but managed to impoverish most Iraqis. Public opinion in the region blamed the United States for their plight, and squabbles over how to fix the sanctions program led to strains among the Atlantic allies and increasing difficulty in maintaining compliance. The absence of UN weapons inspectors after 1998 left a cloud of uncertainty over Saddam's chemical, biological, and nuclear programs, which had provided Washington in the past with unwanted surprises. Viewing the status quo as untenable and Saddam as an intolerable menace to regional security, several top members of the Bush team, including Secretary of Defense Donald Rumsfeld and Deputy Secretary of Defense Paul Wolfowitz, had strongly advocated using force to overthrow Saddam since the mid-1990s. Yet President Bush followed the course of his predecessor and chose to muddle through rather than be distracted from higher priorities—creating a national missile defense, taking a tougher tack in relations with China, and cutting taxes.

September 11 put Iraq back on the table. The story of how Rumsfeld and Wolfowitz broached the issue with the President and argued on September 12—without evidence—for an Iraqi connection to the attacks has been told at length elsewhere. Bush chose to handle Afghanistan first, but then turned quickly to the matter of dealing with Saddam Hussein.

Precisely why the administration decided to wage war in Iraq—as opposed to relying on the UN weapons inspectors who were readmitted to the country in 2002 or using the threat of hostilities to revitalize the containment of the Saddam—is a question that is unlikely to be answered for many years, until the memoirs are written and government records declassified. Whatever the reason, a variety of different arguments were deployed to justify a military confrontation with Iraq to the American public. It became difficult to sort out which of them was uppermost in the minds of the leadership. At first, Vice President Cheney presented it as a certainty that Saddam had revived his nuclear weapons program. In Washington's foreign policy community, this was considered the most salient concern. As former NSC official Kenneth Pollack observes in his book *The Threatening Storm,* Saddam had long shown a determination to use weapons of mass destruction to become the regional hegemon in the Middle East and was a serial miscalculator; the combination made him a threat that could be undeterrable. The administration also cited the threat Iraq posed to Israel. The most determined members of the "war party" of neoconservative political leaders and pundits presented the removal of Saddam as a way to shatter the frozen politics of the Middle East and propel it into a new era of democratization and economic development. With a well-administered shock from the outside—the establishment of a democratic Iraq by the U.S.—an example of a better future would be held up as an irresistible beacon for the region and galvanize a new generation to pursue American-style political reform. War would be necessary, but quick and clean. Victory would endow the U.S. with tremendous prestige, which could be used as leverage elsewhere in the region. The vision was attractive, first in recognizing the need to jump-start democratization in the Middle East and the integration of the region into the global economy. Second, it provided an alternative to the all-too-plausible image of a region locked in political and economic stagnation, a permanent source of instability and danger to America. It may also have been utopian about U.S. capacities and staying power and narcissistic in its assumption that an Americanized Iraq would have a broad appeal.

The administration pressed its case for war most emphatically by arguing that U.S. national security was imperiled by Saddam's ties to al-Qaeda. The argument had the obvious virtue of playing to the public's desire to see the war on terrorism prosecuted aggressively and conclusively. Yet, scant proof of these links was presented. The record showed a small number of contacts between jihadists and Iraqi officials. This was treated as the tip of an unseen iceberg of cooperation, even though it fell far short of anything that resembled significant cooperation in the eyes of the counterterrorism community—as it always had. No persuasive proof was given of money, weaponry, or training being provided. Baghdad's connection with an Islamist group, Ansar al-Islam, which operated in the Kurdish-controlled zone of northern Iraq, out of the reach of Iraqi authorities, was treated as dispositive evidence. But the links were vague, and the group also accepted support and money from Iraq's enemy Iran, suggesting that Baghdad's support, like Tehran's, was opportunistic, intended to strengthen opponents of the American-backed leaders of the enclave rather than boost al-Qaeda's fortunes.

A phalanx of objections by former counterterrorism officials (and, anonymously, some still in the government) was brushed aside. These included the indisputable fact that Saddam relied almost exclusively on his own intelligence service to carry out terrorist attacks that were to serve Iraqi interests—as opposed to, say, paying death benefits to the families of Hamas suicide bombers to boost his reputation—and that he never established a substantive relationship with jihadists because he did not believe he could control or trust them or, for that matter, keep them from turning on him. The further argument that Saddam was exactly the kind of secularist autocrat that Islamist militants loathed prompted Secretary of State Colin Powell to remark at the United Nations that this gave him "little comfort."[12] Perhaps the definitive—and most epigrammatic— argument against those who thought proof of Saddam–al-Qaeda ties would be appropriate before troops were committed was delivered by Donald Rumsfeld, who declared in a February Pentagon briefing that "absence of evidence is not evidence of absence."

In the end, Bush and his advisers fell back on a hypothesis that eliminated the need to demonstrate an Iraq–al-Qaeda connection: Saddam might provide a weapon of mass destruction from his arsenal to terrorists, who would use it against the U.S. Among experts, this too was viewed as implausible. The Iraqi leader had been deterred from using such a weapon against America or its allies in the past by warnings, such as the one Washington delivered before the 1991 Gulf War, that such use would elicit overwhelming retaliation. It was also pointed out that Saddam had recognized since the failed assassination attempt on the first President Bush that state sponsors of terrorism rarely go undiscovered, and for that reason had mounted no further attacks against the U.S. for almost a decade. Press skepticism was fed by intelligence community analysts who fought a rearguard battle, supplying countless blind quotes that cast doubt on the statements of political leaders and pilloried them for politicizing intelligence. To shore up its position, the administration in the weeks before the invasion argued that the Baghdad regime had to be removed because of the suffering it had inflicted on the Iraqi people. The argument, probably the strongest of all, was unusual given the criticism that the Bush team had leveled at the Clinton administration for its various humanitarian missions.[13] Ultimately, though, the American public accepted the administration's reasoning about Iraqi support for terrorism, and many even took it a large step further. By the time U.S. forces began pouring into Iraq, repeated polls showed that a majority of the American public believed that Saddam was behind the attacks of September 11.[14]

—

Whatever its geostrategic value, victory in Iraq delivered the people of that country from the hands of a murderous tyrant. It also yielded several immediate, positive developments for reducing the threat of terrorism. The administration moved quickly to announce that U.S. troops would be withdrawn from Saudi Arabia, whose leaders have said in recent years that such a move would be necessary before the royal family could begin to deal with the growing threat of radicalism in the kingdom; otherwise, the al-Saud would be unable to counter charges that they were beholden to infidel foreigners. It can only be hoped that Saudi Arabia's rulers will now confront the growing existential threat before them. After the Riyadh bombings, the Saudi leadership claimed that they finally "got it," implying that the days when partial crackdowns were accompanied by blandishments to the clerical establishment and influential radicals will end. The much-repeated notion that the May attacks were the kingdom's September 11, the ultimate wakeup call, should be met with some skepticism, since the actual September 11—not to mention earlier, massive plots that had been thwarted in the country—should have had that effect. Radical Islamists will undoubtedly portray the withdrawal of U.S. forces as a triumph for their cause and compare it to Israel's departure from southern Lebanon, but that does not detract from the benefit of removing an irritant in the region. Of course, the presence of 150,000 or more American troops in an occupied Iraq, longtime seat of the caliphate and a central land of Dar al-Islam, will likely prove a far greater irritant to Muslims in general, but the Saudis now must have their day of reckoning.

There were other benefits of the defeat of Iraq. The demonstrated effect of American might greatly increased Washington's leverage with state sponsors of terrorism, especially Syria and Iran, who have a much more sordid history in this respect than Iraq. Hezbollah, the client organization of the two countries, raised its anti-American rhetoric but became more restrained in its behavior. Under U.S. pressure, Syria also moved to lower the profile of the Palestinian terror groups with headquarters or offices in Damascus, though whether the moves heralded a permanent change was impossible to predict. Despite the caution Tehran showed with the terrorists it sponsored, Iran-U.S. relations became even more vexed when Washington charged that al-Qaeda leaders had found a safe haven in eastern Iran, spurring a debate over whether the United States should try to support regime change in Tehran, too. Finally, the destruction of Saddam's regime, together with international maneuvering that led the Palestinian Authority to choose Mahmoud Abbas as prime minister and alternative interlocutor to Yasir Arafat, led to the opening of a small window of hope for renewed negotiations between Israelis and Palestinians. Both sides accepted the "road map" devised by the U.S., the UN, the European Union, and Russia, albeit with many reservations on the Israeli side and failures to meet basic conditions on the Palestinian side. Few outside observers gave the new effort much hope—and a spate of violence immediately followed a summit meeting in Jordan among Bush, Abbas, and Israeli prime minister Ariel Sharon—but if any progress can be achieved, it will help dampen somewhat the potent anti-Americanism in the Middle East and other Muslim countries. As it was before the invasion of Iraq, a reinvigorated peace process will be essential to stemming the tide flowing into the camp of those who hate America.

Against these gains, however, the costs of invading Iraq will be considerable, and possibly of more consequence. Perhaps the greatest one is that the United States has provided the jihadists with what they will portray as definitive proof of their argument. That is, for years to come, the radicals will point to the U.S. military action and occupation as indisputable evidence that America seeks to destroy Islam. We have, in this regard, played into the hands of our most deadly opponents. In an audiotape that surfaced in February, bin Laden made the case bluntly:

We have been following anxiously the preparations of the crusaders to conquer the former capital of Islam and steal their wealth and impose a puppet regime that follows its masters in Washington and Tel Aviv, just like these Arab governments, in order to create what is called greater Israel. This is a war led by the infidels, by America and its spies and agents. . . . We also want to clarify that whoever helps America . . . either if they fight next to them or give them support in any form or shape, even by words, if they help them to kill the Muslims in Iraq, they have to know that they are outside this Islamic nation. Jordan and Morocco and Nigeria and Saudi Arabia should be careful that this war, this crusade, is attacking the people of Islam first. It doesn't matter whether the socialist (Baath) party or Saddam disappear. . . . We want to ask the good Muslims to help in any way they can to join the forces and . . . overthrow the leaderships that work as slaves for America.[15]

Discussion of the tape provided another insight into the administration's determination to see al-Qaeda and the Iraqi regime as twin malefactors. After it was aired, Secretary of State Colin Powell pointed to it as a demonstration of how deeply "in partnership with Iraq" al-Qaeda was. Even a superficial reading of the transcript, however, showed bin Laden's delight at the prospect of a war—one that would underscore America's essential hatred of Muslims—that the Iraqi leadership was trying to avoid. Al-Qaeda recruitment materials pointed to Iraq as another stage of the "crusade attacking the people of Islam." When the military operation was concluded, an audiotape from Ayman al-Zawahiri reiterated this argument: "After dividing Iraq, Saudi Arabia, Iran, Syria, and Pakistan will come next. They would leave around Israel only dismembered semistates that are subservient to the United States and Israel." Al-Zawahiri urged the faithful to fulfill their duty, saying, "The crusaders and the Jews do not understand but the language of killing and blood. They do not become convinced unless they see coffins returning to them, their interests being destroyed, their towers being torched and their economy collapsing."[16]

America's presence in Iraq, which will likely last at least two years and possibly more, may be prompting jihadists to revise their strategy. Though they will continue to target U.S and other Western targets around the world, Iraq itself could become a central theater of activity. This will not simply be a matter of inciting Iraqis to fight the invader. Al-Qaeda believes that the United States will be bogged down in Iraq for years, and so there remains ample time for it to wage guerrilla warfare against the large infidel presence in the region. In a recent analysis of the situation in Iraq, a spokesman explained:

> With guerrilla warfare, the Americans were defeated in Vietnam and the Soviets were defeated in Afghanistan. This is the method that expelled the direct Crusader colonialism from most of the Muslim lands, with Algeria the most well known. We still see how this method stopped Jewish immigration to Palestine, and caused reverse immigration of Jews from Palestine. The successful attempts of dealing defeat to invaders using guerrilla warfare are many, and we will not expound on them. However, these attempts have proven that the most effective method for the materially weak against the strong is guerrilla warfare.[17]

The terrorists are certain to want to bloody American forces to bolster their claims to be the sole true defenders of Muslim interests and will view action in Iraq as a test of their credibility. Since the regime has been overthrown, cooperation between jihadists and the Baathists who are already seeking to foment an insurrection will become more likely than it ever was in the past. With no territory to defend anymore, and therefore no reason to avoid the risk of working with the religious extremists, the Baathists now have an interest in maximizing the violence against the occupation. Intensified attacks against the troops could further set back U.S. work to reconstruct Iraq materially and politically, undermining an effort that is now the key to rehabilitating America's standing in the Islamic world and creating a new Middle East. As the first months of the occupation demonstrated, rebuilding Iraq will not be easy when the provisional government cannot leave its headquarters without heavy security and the troops themselves are in full body armor.[18]

Another potential consequence of the invasion is the spread of weapons of mass destruction to al-Qaeda or other terrorists. As this is written, the fate of Saddam's arsenal of chemical, biological, and nuclear materials remains unknown—and American credibility has been damaged by both the inability to find them and the failure to secure suspected WMD sites early on. Yet certain facts stand out: even if Saddam destroyed the overwhelming majority of his stockpiles sometime between the departure of UN inspectors and their return in 2002, the International Atomic Energy Agency certified that there were highly radioactive materials at the al-Tuwaitha facilities, including partially enriched—though not weapons-grade—uranium. These materials could be used to fabricate one or more radiological dispersion devices—or "dirty bombs," as they have come to be known. Some of these materials appear to be missing—how much remains unclear—and it seems a fair conjecture that someone, perhaps former Iraqi security service officers or scientists who recognized that their prospects in a U.S.-administered Iraq were poor, may have "privatized" these weapons with the intent of selling them to the highest bidder. Ultimately, this material could find its way into the hands of al-Qaeda. It is difficult to imagine a more horrifyingly ironic outcome to the war.[19] It is plausible that Saddam, after so many years of hiding and protecting his unconventional weapons programs, retained the minimum materials needed to reconstitute the efforts after a period of invasive inspections and even armed conflict with the U.S. If this is the case, it is also possible that some biological agents may also be in the wrong hands now.

There were at least two questionable premises underlying the war in Iraq. The first was that ending the threat of catastrophic terrorism requires reforming or eliminating rogue states that support terrorists. The administration has placed heavy emphasis on the "nexus between terrorists and states that are developing weapons of mass destruction," as Secretary Powell put it.[20] While it is tempting to believe that all our enemies are naturally in league together, this approach discounts the fact that even rogue states want to preserve their regimes, and thus have a strong incentive to proceed with caution—something suicidal jihadists will not do. As a matter of public education, the administration's approach brings with it real risks, because, as a result, nearly two years after the September 11 attacks, most Americans still believe that the core problem of contemporary terrorism has to do with states, not the nonstate actors who may be more brutal in their intentions and more capable, as al-Qaeda certainly was compared to Saddam's hapless intelligence service. If jihadists strike again—as we should assume they will—and cause mass casualties, many will wonder how it is that America fought wars in Afghanistan and Iraq and did not eliminate the problem. And they may, in turn, lose confidence in their leaders and their institutions.

The second premise was the one first enunciated by J. B. Kelly, the English historian of the British empire east of Suez, who paraphrased Machiavelli and Hitler before the Gulf War of 1991, saying that it does not matter "whether the Arabs hate us, so long as they fear us." In the debate about this second premise, this same belief that Arabs only understand force was often intoned. Kelly may have been right then, at least about Arab governments. But the certainty of those who believed that American military power could, by itself, be a decisive agent of change blinded them to the gathering momentum of the jihadist movement. Spurred by the earlier Gulf conflict, the movement has fused fear and hatred in a way that breeds violence, not docility. That war was a necessary one for reasons of grand strategy and the maintenance of international order. The war of 2003 was one of choice, and those who led it appear to have forgotten that the fuse that was lit in 1990, when U.S. troops arrived in Saudi Arabia, led to the explosions of September 11, 2001.

METASTASIS

Even if the most optimistic assessments about the damage done in recent months to al-Qaeda prove to be true, the Muslim world's views of the invasion of Iraq on the one hand and Usama bin Laden on the other suggest that the West will face an intensifying, protracted conflict with radical Islam. The most ominous sign of the danger ahead is the accelerating growth of anti-Americanism and anti-Western sentiment. If a paramount aim of bin Laden and his followers is to win the hearts and minds of the world's Muslims, he is achieving real advances, aided unwittingly by U.S. actions.

The public opinion data are unequivocal. A Pew Global Attitudes Project survey released in June 2003 found that "the bottom has fallen out of support for America in most of the Muslim world." Only 27 percent of Moroccans, 15 percent of Lebanese and Turks, 13 percent of Indonesians, 12 percent of Pakistanis, and 1 percent of Jordanians and Palestinians had a favorable view of the United States. (These numbers are broadly consistent with recent surveys of other countries in the region. Just 6 percent of the Egyptian public has a favorable impression of the U.S., while more than half the population has "very negative" views, according to a 2002 Pew study.) The declining popularity of the U.S. has been a fact of life in the region for many years, due largely to the belief that Washington is biased in favor of Israel, employs a double standard that pays little regard to the sufferings of Palestinians, and, in an echo of the jihadist argument, supports corrupt, autocratic regimes. As a result primarily of the invasion of Iraq, the erosion has turned into an avalanche: over the last year, the Lebanese and Turkish figures registered a decline of 50 percent, the Indonesian figure dropped 62 percent, and the Jordanian figure fell 96 percent. Moreover, the antipathy has spread beyond the Middle East to other Muslim countries: the percentage of Nigerians who hold positive views of the U.S. plummeted from 71 percent to 38 percent, and in Indonesia the figure dropped from 60 percent to 13 percent.

With this sudden decline has come a change in the nature of Muslim opinion about America. For many years, Muslims in the Middle East and elsewhere distinguished between their disapproval of U.S. policies and their feelings for the American people. Thus, whatever their government might have done, Americans were admired for their wealth, can-do attitude, popular culture, devotion to democracy, and technological achievements. Increasingly, this is no longer the case. The statistical spread between opposition to Washington's policies and negative attitudes toward Americans themselves has narrowed dramatically, and in many countries a crucial line has been crossed: Americans are increasingly despised as a people. For example, between 2002 and 2003, the number of Pakistanis holding positive views about the American people fell from 39 percent to 16 percent, and for Jordanians from 54 percent to 18 percent. These sentiments are fed by the spreading belief throughout the Muslim world that the U.S. poses a serious threat to Islam. In seven of the eight Muslim populations surveyed, 50 percent or more believed that was the case; only Nigeria, at 42 percent, fell below the line. Most astonishing, significant majorities in seven of the eight—with a near majority in Morocco—worried about a potential U.S. military threat to their countries.

The distance between popular opinion and the jihadist dogma that America is the metaphysical enemy of Islam is growing smaller. Another aspect of this development is the evident need Muslims feel for a powerful figure to stand up for their interests. In six of the populations studied, the Pew research found that 40 percent or more had confidence that Usama bin Laden would do the right thing in world affairs, with a majority of Jordanians (56 percent) and Palestinians (72 percent) placing their trust in the terrorist.

Alongside these opinion shifts, Islamism continues to flourish within these countries. After the defeats of the 1990s, few of the groups that aim to remake their societies according to sharia currently advocate violence, though many have in the past and may come to again. Instead, they continue to work to create an alternative or countersociety to change Muslim countries from within by changing mores and popular behavior through a combination of social services and educational and outreach work. The strategy continues to succeed. As the Israeli scholar Emmanuel Sivan has pointed out, there is no competing ideology, and the Islamists' community work has created a grateful clientele that the state cannot provide for in an era of declining revenues. As result, the state and its subsidized clerics drift toward positions taken by the radicals that push personal piety into the public sphere and preach disdain for the West. Sivan writes, "Governments in various Islamic countries have succumbed to militant pressure, censoring books, plays and films critical of Islam. The Islamist media—notably audio- and videocassettes—is growing, and religious activism is becoming a major avenue for venting protest. Young militants engage in grassroots vigilantism against alcohol, pornography and TV satellite dishes, impose Islamic dress codes and monitor the behavior of non-Islamic tourists."[21] In most Muslim societies there are only two contenders for influence: the authoritarian regimes and the Islamists.

In one key country, Pakistan, the barrier between the two camps has begun to blur. In the October 2002 elections, an alliance of six religious parties polled 11 percent of the vote, putting Islamists into political office and making the group the foremost opposition party in national politics. The parties' strong showing gave them unprecedented control of the provincial government of the North-West Frontier Province and a place in the ruling coalition in Baluchistan. At first the newly installed officials sought to demonstrate their ability to rule and avoided provoking the Pakistani army and President Pervez Musharraf. In June, though, the NWFP legislature enacted a measure to make sharia the supreme law of the land. The move elicited sharp criticism from Musharraf, who warned of "Talibanization" of the province.[22] Pakistan experts warn that if the current national political impasse continues and Musharraf is unable to restore economic growth, answer the calls for greater democracy, or deliver more tangible assistance, the next election could be the occasion of a major breakthrough for the religious parties. In a country perpetually on the edge of a crisis—internally or with India—the prospects are not encouraging. Even cautious analysts fear that Pakistan has perhaps five years to turn itself around before an Islamist takeover becomes a genuine possibility.[23]

THE DEBATE

It is clear who is driving the public discourse in the Muslim world, especially in clerical debate, a central part of intellectual life in these countries. Safar al-Hawali, the Saudi dissident preacher, published a letter in Arabic in April 2003 attached to a bilingual manifesto signed by more than two hundred Muslim preachers in support of a "campaign against aggression." The English-language version of the manifesto, which appeared on the Internet, was tough but restrained in its language. Al-Hawali's letter, though, declared that the Islamic nation should use force if necessary to resist the "beastly teeth" of the "unmasked enemy" and underscored the need to "invest their souls, property, and their words in favor of Allah" in pursuit of victory.[24] The language, intertwining religious concepts with violent imagery, has become commonplace. Indeed, Al-Hawali and other like-minded sheikhs from the heartland of Qassem province are more or less in the mainstream nowadays, one reason why the Saudi rulers released him from jail after five years of imprisonment. Today, he can even be heard as a guest on al-Jazeera talk shows.[25]

While radicals remain true to their message of the last decade, traditionally moderate clerics like Muhammad Sayyid al-Tantawi, the sheikh of al-Azhar—the "parrot" of the Mubarak regime, militants call him—appear to be correcting their course, coming closer to al-Hawali. As war in Iraq approached, Tantawi endorsed fatwas characterizing the U.S. invasion of Iraq as a "Crusader" war and declared that jihad against America was the duty of all Muslims. Under pressure from the Egyptian government, which pays his salary and funds al-Azhar, Tantawi explained that use of the term "Crusader" did not mean he was advocating a war between Islam and Christianity. Yet in a subsequent Friday sermon he whipped up the crowd, saying: "The American aggression against Iraq is not acceptable to Islamic law, and the law [of the land], and the Iraqi people must defend itself, its land, and its homeland, with all means of defense at its disposal, because it is a *Jihad* that is permitted by Islamic law. *Jihad* is an obligation for every Muslim when Muslim countries are subject to aggression. The gates of *Jihad* are open until the Day of Judgment, and he who denies this is an infidel or one who abandons his religion. This is an obligation applying to the nation now, in order to respond to the aggression."[26] The language could have come out of Usama bin Laden's *Sermon for the Feast of the Sacrifice,* which circulated at about the same time.

The convergence of jihadist rhetoric from terrorist hideouts in South

Asia and pronouncements from al-Azhar appears imminent. Extremist views are broadcast widely, and the superstars in the firmament of radical preachers—Sheikh Yusuf al-Qaradawi in Qatar, or Sheikh Abu Qatada in London, now in British custody—have raised the bar for all other imams, who are trying to maintain their credibility in their own mosques. Through the largesse Saudi Arabia devotes to Wahhabi missionary work and the pervasiveness of the Internet, the radical perspective receives a global airing.[27] The spirit of confrontation and religious absolutism has led at least one well-known cleric, a Saudi named Naser bin Hamad al-Fahd, to issue a fatwa on May 21, 2003, endorsing the use of weapons of mass destruction against infidels.[28]

This is not to say that no other opinions are being voiced. No less fiery a preacher than Salman bin Fahd al-Awda, who was incarcerated with al-Hawali and whose name is often coupled with his, has called for a change of direction: less emphasis on demonizing the West and a greater stress on pluralism within the Muslim community.[29] But such countervailing voices are few and their logic is not very appealing. Ahmad Abd al-Hamid Higazi, an Egyptian writer, summed up the clerical approach to moderation in his depiction of Yusuf al-Qaradawi's attempt to talk the Taliban out of wrecking the historic Buddhist Bamiyan statues in Afghanistan. The message was: " 'The timing is not right!' as if saying to them: 'We understand you and appreciate your sentiments, but the evil foreigners are setting a trap for you, waiting for the opportunity to ensnare you. Postpone the destruction of the statues for a while.' "[30]

Radicalization is not confined to Muslim countries. We have written in chapter 5 about the attraction that the jihadist cause holds for large segments of the European Muslim diaspora. The turn to militancy has become increasingly apparent, not only in the number of Muslims who have left Europe to join extremist groups but also in the politics of these communities. The best example was provided in France, where Interior Minister Nicolas Sarkozy spearheaded an effort to give Muslims a greater voice in public affairs and improve state funding for religious activities. Working with moderate members of the country's community of five million Muslims, Sarkozy helped create a Council for the Muslim Religion much like the nearly two-hundred-year-old Jewish Consistory. In the group's first elections, the moderates were thrashed by, among others, the Union of Islamic Organizations of France, a group close to the Muslim Brotherhood, which took nearly a third of the seats.

The tendency to extremism is not likely to diminish any time soon. The French scholar Olivier Roy has described the underlying phenomenon of how the sense of identity of European Muslims—especially the young—is changing, spurred in part by the example of the militants of al-Qaeda.[31] These individuals see themselves less as diaspora Muslims who are tied by bonds of kinship with North Africa, the Middle East, and South Asia than as members of an imagined global community of Muslims. Whether they are citizens of Britain, France, or any other continental country is unimportant to them. For these Muslims, who are simultaneously assimilated and alienated, membership in a supranational Islamic universe provides a sense of belonging otherwise unavailable in their basically homogenous and unwelcoming societies. It also confers a sense of authenticity that trumps the compromised and cramped religion on offer in their parents' mosques.[32] These youths view themselves as modern counterparts of those early Muslims who flocked to strongholds along the borders of the new Islamic empire to defend it against Byzantine or Mongol marauders. This time the enemy is Jews and Crusaders, and the empire is under attack in Kashmir, Chechnya, Palestine, and now Baghdad, the former seat of the caliphate.[33] Omar Saeed Sheikh, the well-off, English-raised and London School of Economics–educated young Pakistani who participated in the abduction and killing of *Wall Street Journal* reporter Daniel Pearl, provided one example of Roy's arguments. They were confirmed again all too vividly in April, when two British Muslims from Pakistani families traveled to Israel to carry out a suicide bombing at a seaside nightclub in Tel Aviv. One man's explosive vest detonated, killing him and three others and wounding fifty more, while the other man's failed; he apparently sought to escape but drowned in the Mediterranean. A *New York Times* reporter who visited the bombers' hometown of Derby found several local Muslims who approved of what the men had done, including one seventeen-year-old who thought suicide attacks might not be the right approach to kill the Jews, but said, "We should find out the best way to kill them, and do that."[34]

It takes little imagination to see how increasing radicalism both inside and outside of Muslim countries could translate into more recruitment, fund-raising, and ultimately terrorism. What is more, one of America's signal achievements in the war on terror, the elimination of sanctuaries in which terrorists could train and plan with impunity—and where al-Qaeda could revitalize or successor groups could form—now looks ephemeral. According to several sources, including France's renowned counterterrorism magistrate, Jean-Louis Bruguiere, terrorist camps in the Caucasus are now serving as replacements for those lost in Afghanistan.[35] Russian and other regional forces may be able to handle that challenge, but terrorist training facilities are cropping up in Southeast Asia, too, especially in areas of the southern Philippines under the control of the rebel Moro Liberation Front.[36]

The most worrisome prospect of all is the reversion of Afghanistan itself into a warlord-dominated state, one in which a well-funded terrorist group could buy itself a safe haven, much as al-Qaeda did when it first moved there in 1996. Eighteen months after the Taliban regime was destroyed, the government of Hamid Karzai is still unable to control the countryside. With the International Security Assistance force of 5,000 troops confined by its mandate to Kabul, a fledgling Afghan army of 6,000, and only 9,000 U.S. troops still in the country, the wherewithal for controlling the resurgent warlords and ethnic factions or destroying Taliban units that are regrouping is limited. Economic assistance and reconstruction have been badly hampered by the lack of security, and opium growing has returned with a vengeance. If it has not happened already, the reappearance of terrorist camps seems inevitable. The United States will destroy the camps when it finds them, but it will have no way to prevent them from being reestablished. Despite Washington's claim that Afghanistan will not be forgotten, this is what is happening. The deterioration so soon after the U.S.-led effort to drive the Taliban from power makes for an ironic counterpoint to the third paragraph of the 2002 National Security Strategy, which emphasizes, "America is threatened less now by conquering states than we are by failing ones."[37]

What might the next round of terrorist attacks look like? Even if al-Qaeda is crippled by the intelligence war that has been waged against it, we may have already had a foretaste of a new kind of terror. The May 2003 attacks in Casablanca appeared to involve radicals who had embraced a bin Ladenist worldview but who hitherto had little or no connection with al-Qaeda. (Moroccan investigators later claimed that al-Qaeda had funneled money to the operatives and that they received training from veterans of the Afghanistan camps.)[38] What distinguishes Casablanca from a classic al-Qaeda attack was the mediocre planning and tradecraft: a Jewish community center was bombed on a Friday night, when no one was inside. Other bombs missed their marks or were used for low-value targets.

Thus, it appears that bin Laden's call for others to take up the struggle is being heeded. Groups with no history of integration in al-Qaeda appear to be adapting their ideologies to focus, like the global network, on the far enemy. As anti-Americanism and anti-Western sentiment grows throughout the Muslim world, the sparks that al-Qaeda threw off could turn into flames in various places around the world. If other groups cannot develop capabilities any better than the Casablanca terrorists, the threat may be manageable, or at least tolerable. But if among the many extremist groups there are some with more educated, more imaginative, and more technically adept members than those who came out of Casablanca's Sidi Moumen slum, the prospect of a dozen or more local al-Qaedas spread around the world is not hard to imagine.

THE ROAD NOT TAKEN

Any comprehensive strategy to deal with the threat of radical Islamism requires, as we discuss in chapter 11, three central elements: intelligence operations to disrupt plots and damage al-Qaeda, homeland security to defend against the attacks that do occur, and a long-term effort to prevent the spread of jihadist ideology and ameliorate some of the root causes that feed the new terror. For intelligence operations, as we have seen, the record has been clear and dramatic. Some critics, including Senator Bob Graham, the former chairman of the Senate Select Committee on Intelligence, have charged that more progress would have been possible if the Bush administration had not chosen to wage war against Iraq. From the perspective of counterterrorism professionals, the war in Iraq was not a continuation but a diversion. It is undoubtedly true that resources for special operations, intelligence collection, and translation were diverted from the effort against al-Qaeda to Iraq-related matters, and clearly the administration believed this was justified by the need to keep Iraq's weapons of mass destruction from falling into the terrorists' control. From outside the government's counterterrorism community—and without access to classified material—it is difficult to say whether this led to missed opportunities. Perhaps the most authoritative answer so far comes from one leading figure from the Bush administration's counterterrorism team who resigned in part because of disenchantment with the focus on Iraq. Rand Beers, who was NSC senior director for counterterrorism and, after serving in the White House of every president from Reagan to the younger Bush, one of the most respected civil servants in Washington, left his position shortly before the fighting began in Iraq. Eight weeks later, *The Washington Post* wrote that Beers believed "the focus on Iraq has robbed domestic security of manpower, brainpower and money. . . . The Iraq war created fissures in the United States' counterterrorism alliances . . . and could breed a new generation of al Qaeda recruits. Many of his government colleagues, he said, thought Iraq was an 'ill-conceived and poorly executed strategy.' "[39]

The state of the two other legs of this strategy is far less encouraging. If one believes, as we do, that the effort to reduce the jihadist threat requires detoxifying relations between the United States and the Islamic world—the global community of Muslims, not simply their governments—

then America is heading down the wrong road. At a minimum, we have staked the future on the reconstruction of Iraq. This is a double gamble: Not only must the occupation succeed by American standards, it also must be accepted as a genuine, well-intentioned effort by Muslims, one that erodes the outrage at the U.S. conquest of an Arab country. For a large number of people who have become predisposed to see the worst in U.S. policy—and view us as the partners of the Serbs in the Balkans, an imperial power that sought a regional foothold in the first Gulf War, and a threat to their faith as a result of the last one—this is a gigantic wager.

In one important sense, America is safer than it was before September 11. Catastrophic terror has been acknowledged as a reality. Hundreds of thousands of law enforcement, emergency services, medical, and other personnel are now alive to the danger it poses and are preparing, so far as possible, to act when they see suspicious activities and to take appropriate steps to minimize casualties when an attack occurs. They may be annoyed by a surfeit of warnings, but the value of their heightened awareness of the threat is inestimable.

That gain was the by-product of the attacks themselves. In homeland security, the government's steps have been haphazard and often headed in a questionable direction. The bureaucratic struggle to set up the new Department of Homeland Security has been as consuming as critics predicted. As an administrative task, the merger of twenty-two different agencies with their own distinctive corporate cultures is an unprecedented undertaking, more ambitious even than the creation of the Department of Defense after World War II. The department's responsibilities include everything from port security to the protection of the cyber networks that drive industries ranging from banking to aviation to health, and from policing borders to checking airline baggage to ensuring the safety of trucks containing hazardous materials. Senior civil servants within the new agency say that the act of conglomeration itself will take at least two years, after which the level of actual security should begin to rise above premerger levels.

Not surprisingly, this has been a troubled infancy. To most Americans, the Department of Homeland Security and its secretary, Tom Ridge, have become known mostly for the bewildering color-coded alerts the agency has issued to reflect variations in the terrorist threat level. The key audience for threat-level changes are the thousands of federal, state, and local law enforcement agencies around the country, which are notified so they can implement specific measures involving security and surveillance. Since it is impossible to notify thousands of anything in the United States without it becoming public, and given the widespread hunger for information, the alert has become a kind of national safety barometer as well. (Its pre–September 11 predecessor was no better in this regard, except that most people paid little attention to it.) As Ridge conceded in June 2003, "Citizens don't have to do anything different"[40] when the threat level goes up, which begs the question of what benefit they derive from knowing about it at all. (In May, the alert level was raised to orange after the Riyadh and Casablanca attacks, confirming what everyone knew: the terrorists had struck.) It is hard to imagine how to fix the system. With any luck, Americans will tune it out enough so that it does not aggravate them, and the government will be more cautious about raising and lowering the alert level.

Over time, the alert system may be refined with the assistance of the Terrorist Threat Integration Center, an innovation that the administration announced to help improve interagency coordination and prevent the failures that paved the way for the September 11 hijackers. Although the TTIC, which will begin operation in 2004, will not gather information of its own—and thus will be at the mercy of other collection agencies—its analysts are expected to help the Department of Homeland Security figure out how to relate specific threat information to the vulnerabilities of American infrastructure and, in theory, enlist the support of the private sector to protect the infrastructure that al-Qaeda seeks to destroy. Making the system work will challenge policy makers, since the larger intelligence community remains a tangle of entities spread across several agencies. Already, there have been rumors that the FBI views the TTIC as a subsidiary of the CIA, reducing the Bureau's desire to cooperate. In a charged arena in which turf fights persist over, for example, who has responsibility for tracking terrorist finances, making the TTIC work will require intensive bureaucratic bullying, and among the officials close to it, there is skepticism that the White House will find energy to make it work. As one senior intelligence official put it, "The heavyweights of the administration are preoccupied from here on in with November 2004. The agenda now has to be domestic economic stuff. Let's face it: No one cares about the TTIC, or the myriad of other little shops that have been set up. Intelligence on terrorism is all so last-year."

On the broader issue of how the United States is investing its homeland security dollar, the record so far suggests that Washington's energy has gone into administrative engineering and not hard thinking about threats and vulnerabilities. Roughly $160 billion in new funds has been poured into national security since the fall of 2001, yet only a small fraction has actually been used to make Americans safer at home. The trends noted in chapter 11 have continued, with the large bulk of the money going to traditional military investments, not confronting terrorism. The President's 2004 budget indicates that there is more of this to come: at $380.4 billion, spending on the military, if approved, will be one-third higher than in 2001, an extraordinary jump by historical standards. At this level, adjusting for inflation, the U.S. is spending about 10 percent more a year than it did in its average Cold War defense budget.[41] (These figures do not include the nearly $75 billion the administration requested to pay for the war in Iraq.) The funding for the Pentagon will be used predominantly to pay for operations and maintenance, higher salaries for soldiers, and such traditional weapons platforms and systems as a new aircraft carrier. These appropriations may be worthy for any number of reasons, but they will do little to help America fight the outstanding national security threat it faces, except in the unlikely event that al-Qaeda hijacks another state, as it did Afghanistan. The U.S. could well face insurgencies in places such as Afghanistan—especially if more assistance is not forthcoming— and the defense budget increases funding for special operations forces by $1.1 billion. But bin Laden's men are unlikely to ever confront the U.S. as the kind of conventional fighting force for which the Pentagon is building up. The administration will also increase 2004 spending on national missile defense to $9 billion. But as the intelligence community continues to believe, America is far more likely to be attacked by terrorists using weapons of mass destruction delivered in a car, truck, or airplane than by a rogue nation with missiles. That assessment evidently has not changed despite growing tensions on the Korean peninsula.

In Washington, most analysis on why defense spending is growing so rapidly falls into two general schools, though they are by no means mutually exclusive. One argument holds that the administration continues to believe that the key to defeating terrorism is to modify the behavior of the states that sponsor terror, and the way to do that is through military might—with the threat or actual use of force. In short, this is another manifestation of the Bush foreign policy team's focus on states, rather than the transnational ideological movement at work. Another school explains the rise in spending as having little to do with the terrorist threat at all. These analysts believe that Donald Rumsfeld's determination to transform the U.S. military into a highly mobile, integrated force of a kind that would be suited to combating new threats was thwarted by the political difficulty of killing large weapons programs. Consequently, he has decided to let these multibillion-dollar projects proceed while also budgeting for the expensive costs of transformation.

By comparison, the funds allocated for security in the United States—through the Department of Homeland Security and other agencies—have been meager. After a sizable amount of money was funneled into this area after the September 11 attacks, the budget for 2004 is basically flat. Major increases since 2001 came in two categories: aviation security and biodefense, into which the administration has put $12 billion, with money for the latter paying for vaccine research and increasing the stockpile of drugs for use in case of a biological weapons attack. Yet even these efforts have been uneven, and not always because of underfunding: when the Department of Homeland Security's top official for intelligence analysis came to brief a House committee on the administration's $6 billion effort to counter the threat of bioterrorism, he arrived with no statement, complaining that he only had one person working for him and insufficient access to classified material to do his job. A Republican congressman afterward described his reaction to the official's performance as one of "shock, depression, outrage, embarrassment, and concern. . . . They're basically acknowledging that they're useless."[42] For aviation security, no comparable security upgrades have been made for U.S. carriers at foreign airports—an inexplicable failure given that the conspiracy devised by Khalid Sheikh Mohammed and Ramzi Yousef to bomb planes over the Pacific would likely succeed today if authorities did not receive an intelligence tip.

Our efforts to prevent the next September 11 in the United States may only prod the terrorists to stage the attack in another region of the world, where their ability to act is generally greater, or to alter the means they employ. To be sure, the task of prioritizing threats is extraordinarily difficult, particularly when the foe is a group as imaginative as al-Qaeda. Should we worry more about propane or gas trucks, discarded radioactive materials from hospitals that could be used in a dirty bomb, the availability of .50-caliber automatic weapons that could take down planes, or individual snipers, like the one that terrorized the mid-Atlantic states in the fall of 2002? The nation has never needed to perform a universal vulnerability assessment before, and there is no algorithm that will tell policy makers where to spend the money.

The administration, though, has barely begun to deal with some types of threats that are not only highly plausible but seem increasingly inevitable. An example is the real and growing danger of an attack using Stinger-type shoulder-fired antiaircraft missiles. The two missiles that barely missed the Israeli plane taking off from Mombasa and the credible warning of a potential attack at Heathrow Airport are frightening harbingers. The world is awash with these Stinger-type missiles, including ones made in the United States, Russia, China, the former Yugoslavia, and North Korea, and many more may have gotten loose during the fighting in Iraq. They have been used dozens of times against commercial aircraft, mostly in African war zones. Twice during the Clinton administration, reports of impending attacks with such missiles caused intense security scrambles abroad. A single hit on an American jet flying over the U.S.,

Europe, or parts of Asia would bring commercial aviation to a halt and cripple the economy. Indeed, a single *miss* in U.S. airspace could well bring air traffic to an indefinite stop.

It is possible to defend against these missiles. Because the projectiles have a ceiling of about 15,000 feet, the danger is greatest for aircraft taking off and landing. While securing every rooftop around urban airports is out of the question, much can be done to map the safest routes for planes and to watch over airports with cameras, patrols, and helicopters. Some of the mapping work has already been done at American and foreign airports, but a global effort is required.

Countermeasures—equipment that uses infrared devices to throw off the missile's sensor—are used on U.S. military aircraft and can also be employed on commercial planes. After Mombasa, Israel started to install this equipment on all its commercial jets. In the late 1990s, the government raised the issue of countermeasures with the airlines. The industry blanched upon learning that it would cost $1 million to $2 million per plane. Airlines today are in worse economic shape, making them even less willing to adopt these measures. But the threat now is no longer hypothetical: weapons are in the wrong hands, and it would not be difficult to smuggle one into the U.S. Legislation has been introduced in Congress to require installation of the countermeasures at an estimated cost of $7 billion. What once was a huge sum seems since September 11 a reasonable amount to pay for a considerable measure of safety.

As a demonstration of halfheartedness about homeland security, the case of the Stinger missiles is hardly unique. Efforts to improve surveillance of the myriad shipping containers that enter the country every day remain sluggish. The money that was to fund training and equipping of first responders around the country was held up in budget wrangling between the executive and legislative branches for most of a year. Other, potentially more taxing threats, such as improvised cruise missiles, are barely discussed. Today, recreational airplanes can be built from kits for a few thousand dollars and converted into remote-control weapons. These planes can take off from a grass strip shorter than a football field and give terrorists an easy means to attack from within America's borders.

A growing number of countries, including Pakistan and Iran, possess antiship cruise missiles that, if stolen or diverted, could be converted into land-attack cruise missiles. These missiles can be transported in nondescript containers and guided by inexpensive Global Positioning System devices to targets mapped with available satellite imagery. Freighters provide the ideal platform for launching these cruise missiles, which can travel more than one hundred miles; al-Qaeda is reported to have fifteen such vessels.[43]

Dealing with this threat would require, to begin with, creating a perimeter at sea to keep suspicious ships out of range. Today, the Coast Guard cannot come close to performing that job, and while a goal of the Department of Homeland Security is to recapitalize the fleet, nothing of the scale needed is envisioned. This upgrade would be easy compared to adapting U.S. air defenses to deal with slow-flying remote-controlled aircraft and terrain-hugging cruise missiles. (Military radar that tracks supersonic aircraft cannot distinguish a terrorist plane or cruise missile from a commercial puddle-jumper; creating a new radar system that knows what to look for would be complicated and expensive—yet it's essential if the United States is to even contemplate shooting down such a vehicle.) A starting estimate of the cost of safeguarding American airspace from these dangers is $40 billion, yet discussion of such a far-reaching effort appears to be all but nonexistent.

If one believes that al-Qaeda is a unique, passing phenomenon, then perhaps it makes sense to avoid spending the money. If, on the other hand, one believes that radical Islamism is an ideology that has made deep inroads, and that the future of regions such as the Middle East is sufficiently bleak that the ideology could persist and spread for years to come, then there is no reason to wait.

—

Ultimately, America's failure to address the rise of radical Islam through its foreign policy is the most ominous shortcoming of the post–September 11 period. We had not thought that the nature of the phenomenon, its character as a dynamic ideology with a broad appeal, could be ignored. Yet, as we have noted, U.S. policy, especially the war in Iraq, seems to have done precisely that, profoundly exacerbating the sense of grievance and antipathy in the Islamic world. In the aftermath of the attacks, there was another direction available for our policy, and, as happens after such rare, historic events, there was an opportunity to take dramatic action.

At the heart of such a policy would have been a renegotiation of the bargain between Muslim states and the United States that takes into account America's compelling security interest in what goes on within the borders of those nations. In return for continued and perhaps expanded economic and military assistance, these countries would undertake reforms aimed at ending the incitement of rabid anti-Americanism and anti-Semitism, improving education, liberalizing their economies, and, finally, democratizing.

In the Middle East and South Asia, democratization is the indispensable measure needed to lessen the appeal of jihad. Democracies are more likely to contain the pressures of radicalism by allowing extremists to vent their discontent instead of becoming a natural magnet for the alienated. They also give Islamists the opportunity to delegitimate themselves through political competition and their inability to provide the social goods—prosperity, education, services—on the universal basis that citizens demand. An understanding of this truth informed the thinking of some administration officials, such as Paul Wolfowitz, who advocated removing Saddam Hussein. If that effort proves self-defeating, it will be because war was pursued in a way that validated the conviction in the region that America's goal was not democracy but the humiliation of Muslims and the plunder of their wealth. Efforts at democratization must be attempted collaboratively, at least at first, with the governments of the region. Pressure will be required, but it needs to be carefully administered; propelling these regimes toward greater anti-Americanism will only undermine our interests. The United States may be able to topple hostile states with ease, but it cannot rule these nations, nor should it want to. Some disagree with this, and one close ally of the administration has suggested that America is fighting another world war and must say "to the autocrats [such as Hosni Mubarak and the al-Saud] who from time to time are, or at least pretend to be, friendly with us: we know, we understand, we are going to make you nervous. But in the last analysis, if you don't change you should be nervous. In that case we want you nervous. We want you to realize that now, for the fourth time in 100 years, this country is on the march. And we are on the side of those whom you most fear—your own people."[44] It is hard to see how, given the limits on America's resources, the public aversion to further warfare, and the danger of further radicalization in the Middle East, this is persuasive.

Pursuing a policy of democratization will be far more difficult today than it would have been in the fall of 2001 or even 2002. U.S. policy on Iraq made support, or at least tacit acceptance, of the confrontation with Baghdad the number one issue in bilateral relations with virtually every Muslim country. A great deal of political capital was expended, capital that we no longer have to push, cajole, or entice these regimes into reform. Nonetheless, there remains no better option than fostering democratization and groping our way toward a dialogue with the Muslim—and especially Arab—world. If we take this road, we must be prepared to cope with three issues:

- The danger that any democratization that moves too quickly will bring to power the very forces we wish to tame, while too tepid an endorsement of democratization will reinforce the perception of America as the problem.
- The need, in crafting our side of a dialogue, to have something to say apart from expressing our commitment to "civilization" and decrying the other side's failure to "modernize." We will need to speak more persuasively to the young technocratic elites in societies where our credibility is at an all-time low.
- The fact that much of the debate within the Muslim world is dominated by Salafi clerics, while intellectuals and moderate clerics—both conservative and progressive—are shying away from the arena.

DEMOCRATIZATION

Democracy is not a cure for all ills. There are intolerant democracies, like Indonesia, and poor ones like India. As our own country shows, democracy does not necessarily lead to wider dissemination of knowledge or a diminution in religious dogmatism. Indeed, democracy may be the cure for only one thing—tyranny. Even that, however, would leave the region's inhabitants far better off. Beyond this basic advance, however, democratization would likely lead to enhanced government accountability, which would in turn lead to better economic governance and greater investment. This could eventually reduce unemployment, increase incomes, and expand the choices available to millions immobilized by poverty. It might also yield more effective environmental protection and thus leave future generations better off. Greater pluralism and political participation would even give an empowered public a sense of control over its destiny. This, in turn, would make America appear less like a malevolent, omnipotent adversary and more like other countries on the international landscape.[45]

For the most part, successful transitions to democracy have come not through decapitation of the country's leadership—though that has occurred in a few cases—but a slow accumulation of trust between reform-minded players within the authoritarian regime and moderate members of the opposition. Each of the parties has to persuade the other that the rules of the democratic game will be obeyed. Regime members need to convince the opposition that they can keep the hardliners in the army and security services under control, and the opposition must show that it can restrain the radicals in its ranks. All the participants in this delicate dance must be confident that democracy is the mutually desired outcome. Such trust-building is a time-consuming, uncertain process.

This pact-making never really got started in the Middle East for three reasons: The military regimes that won independence from the colonial powers were able to claim that their continued monopoly on power was necessary to preserve their countries' hard-won independence, pointing to the conflict with Israel as proof that the battle against colonialism was not over. Second, these authoritarian regimes did not have to depend on their citizenry for resources. The oil-rich states extracted their wealth from the ground, while others extracted it from contending Cold War powers. Egypt, for example, benefited from its serial alliances with the Soviet Union and the United States, while Syria lived off aid from Moscow until the collapse of the Soviet Union, when it began taking advantage of Saddam's largesse and a captive Lebanon. In democracies, there is no taxation without representation; in these states, there was no taxation and therefore no representation.

The last reason for the failure of regional states to make the transition to democracy has to do with the nature of the opposition movements in these countries. As we argue in chapter 5, the best organized, most disciplined, and most ideologically compelling opposition movements are Islamist. These parties or organizations vary in many ways, but they share a uniformity of rhetoric and political agenda—imposition of sharia, disenfranchisement and economic exclusion of females, anti-Zionism, and so forth.[46] Since successful transitions require reformers to trust the opposition party's commitment to democracy and willingness and ability to rein in its radicals, one can reasonably ask how likely it is that Islamists will inspire the necessary trust.

There is another paradox in the tension between the short-term goals of the war on terrorism and the long-term desire for democracy: the United States needs the support of the authoritarian regimes that hunt down and deliver terrorists, in much the same way that America supported such regimes for their proxy services during the Cold War. Every government in the region—including Syria, Egypt, Jordan, Yemen, Saudi Arabia, and Pakistan—has already moved to exploit this opportunity to win points with Washington while ridding itself of troublesome sectors. The cooperation provided by these regimes has helped the U.S. whittle away at al-Qaeda's infrastructure, even as their rulers perpetuate the conditions that have turned so many Muslims against America. The dilemma Washington faces in deciding whether and how to press these governments to share power cannot be taken lightly.

An American strategy to spur democratization must press regional leaders to provide more space for the expression of alternative views and the political participation of those who hold them. The pressure must be exerted publicly, as the Bush administration did when it threatened Egypt with a financial penalty, admittedly minor, for the government's trumped-up conviction of the liberal academic Saad Eddin Ibrahim. We should expect the inevitable resistance to this pressure both from the regime and from the opposition, which will adopt a knee-jerk anticolonial posture even when the outside intervention is clearly in the opposition's own interest.[47] At the same time, the United States must foster more diverse, better-informed opposition movements with sharpened campaigning and negotiating skills. This is easier said than done, but the State Department has taken a step in the right direction with its Middle East Partnership Initiative. This program, which began with $20 million in 2002, aims to support critical pilot projects in areas such as basic education reform, campaign skills training for women candidates, training for new parliamentarians, micro-enterprise programs, and assistance to open markets and eliminate trade barriers. In 2003 and 2004, the amount of money for these efforts is to increase considerably.

The virtue of this approach is that it targets constituencies that have a real stake in staying out from under the thumb of clerical "democratic" regimes as they climb out of authoritarian rule: women and merchants who rely on international markets. By focusing on children's education, the program also aims to reshape curricula as a way of molding a more open attitude toward the "other."

Not surprisingly, the program arouses strong hostility from regional governments—the Egyptian foreign minister denounced it as "the epitome of idiocy"[48]—and populist commentators dismiss it as a Jewish plot to deflect attention from the true source of misery in the region, the occupation of Palestine. Islamists are bound to view the initiative as an attack on an already beleaguered set of values and an adjunct to military conquest, while the left will depict it as a neocolonialist attempt to roll back Arab independence. Nevertheless, there are some who welcome Ameri-

can intervention, arguing that just because Washington is pressing the initiative in its own interest does not mean that there will not be benefits for
Arabs. The liveliness of the discussion so far is one reason to hope for
some positive impact.[49]

More will need to be done, and it is worrying that the Bush administration's new approach to foreign assistance, the Millennium Challenge
Account, appears to target the wrong recipients. The program, which is
to be funded at lavish levels compared to the post–Cold War lean years—
$1.4 billion in 2004 growing to $5 billion by 2006—will benefit countries
that welfare moralizers once called "the deserving poor." These are countries that have undertaken political and economic reforms and improved
their human rights records. Such countries should of course be eligible
for aid, and it is encouraging to know that in these cases, the money will
probably underwrite existing reforms to produce further progress.

The undeserving poor, such as Pakistan, Yemen, and, most urgently,
Afghanistan, will be shortchanged, and it is in these countries that significant sums must be spent to ameliorate the conditions that are the grist for
radicals. Years will pass before they will meet the high standards of the
"Washington Consensus," which holds that only an outward-oriented
and private-sector-led economy can provide the growth, jobs, and exports needed to alleviate poverty and ensure food security. We should
have figured out by now that failing states are the favorite growth medium
of terrorists; turning away from such problems does not make them disappear.

Assistance of this nature will not by itself be enough. Influence is as
crucial as finance. America, however, is ill-equipped for a dialogue with
the intellectuals and technocratic elites who write for newspapers, meet
in cafés, manage large businesses and bureaucracies, and supply the talking heads for proliferating media outlets like al-Jazeera. The current tack,
inherited from the Clinton administration, involves sponsoring radio and
television programs that feature pop music and chat shows so as to seduce Arabic-speaking youngsters into taking the American-engineered
news bits seriously.[50] This Madison Avenue approach to winning the

hearts and minds of Muslims who believe the U.S. to be a superpower under the spell of Jews is not likely to work. Polling data indicates a growing disdain for American culture exports and suggests that this approach, which received nearly $90 million last year, is an expensive mistake.

Focusing on providing news from a Western perspective may be useful, but when it is America's foremost effort in the struggle for hearts and minds it becomes a diversion from the central issue—namely, what do we have to say to Arabs in particular and Muslims more generally? Do we understand what is on their minds? Last year, in an effort to win the goodwill of Muslims overseas, the State Department distributed videotapes of happy American Muslims, explaining that they were not the victims of oppression and that their religious convictions did not conflict with their social and professional roles. Yet subsequent studies, especially in Indonesia, where the tapes were heavily promoted, showed that the country's Muslims were indifferent to the situation of their coreligionists in America. The issue for them and others abroad is not whether American Muslims have made their peace with an aggressive foreign policy and pornographic culture; it is why the U.S.—in their view—seeks political and cultural hegemony in their countries through conquest and subversion. If we are to have a dialogue, we need to be more forthright about our support for unpopular regimes, how we reconcile our insistence on democracy with our own imperious policies, and why we seem to disregard the travail of Palestinians despite the concerns of Arabs and Muslims. We also must be straightforward about how we see the defects of Islamic societies and their failure to take responsibility for their poor performance. At the same time, we need to be prepared for the Muslim critique of our society and its values. This will get harder, not easier, over time.

For a relatively self-absorbed, if not solipsistic, country such as the United States, this is asking a lot. We also must grapple with the problem that so much of the debate about us remains in the clerical arena, where the United States has no voice. If we cannot participate in the religious debate directly, we will have to influence it indirectly. The outcome is too crucial to American interests to watch from the sidelines. This means that Washington will have to find creative ways to channel financial support to moderate clerics and mosques without discrediting the voices we want to amplify. This may mean identifying constructive sermons by eloquent preachers and disseminating them via cassette and the Internet to increase their audience. Or it might mean direct subventions to imams and madrassas. The hazards are great if we approach this delicate project in a clumsy way. But the perils are greater if we step aside.

The issue of whether America can switch tracks and begin to engage the Muslim world in this way raises many questions. One is whether the United States can effect any kind of positive change since it is viewed as the foe by so many. Another has to do with the dimensions of the changes under way. We have described how the changes occurring in the Islamic world resemble a reformation, and if that is the case, it is legitimate to ask whether any outside force can have much effect on a transformation of those dimensions. Our answer is a provisional yes, though it is likely to be limited. More importantly, the United States needs to try to find the road not taken, if only as an exercise in damage limitation. We should not forget that the terror can get worse.

—

The question about the dimensions of change leads to another question, regarding large, impersonal forces: Are we at the beginning of the clash of civilizations forecast by Samuel Huntington, much discussed in the West and obsessively pondered in the Islamic world? We take refuge in the answer Zhou Enlai gave Henry Kissinger when he was asked what he thought about the French Revolution: It is too early to tell. But it is unsettling—and fascinating—to watch the appearance of new cultural energies that seem to be driving events in that direction.

In the last year, the level of raw anti-Islamic sentiment in the United States seems to have risen significantly. The engine has been less the fear of Middle Eastern terrorists in the general public, though there has been some of that, than increasingly frequent denunciations of Islam by Christian evangelical preachers. Some have been simply accusatory, like the claim that Islam is "a very evil and wicked religion," made by Franklin Graham, the son and clerical heir of Billy Graham. Others have been obscene, such as the remarks of Jerry Vines, the former president of the Southern Baptist Convention, who told an approving conference of pastors that "Islam was founded by Mohammed, a demon-possessed pedophile who had 12 wives, and his last one was a 9-year-old girl."[51] Others, such as Jerry Falwell and Pat Robertson, evangelists whose national followings number in the hundreds of thousands or millions, also discuss Islam as metaphysical enemy, thus filling the gap left by the disappearance of the Moloch of Soviet communism with a foe from the Christian Middle Ages. As *The New York Times* reported, "In evangelical churches and seminaries across the country, lectures and books criticizing Islam and promoting strategies for Muslim conversions are gaining currency. More than a dozen recently published critiques of Islam are now available in Christian bookstores."[52] Some of these remarks have elicited rebukes from national evangelical associations. But it is equally clear that September 11 has given some fundamentalists, whose worldview centers on conflict and a sense of beleaguerment, an opening, a chance to convert others to a seductively Manichaean worldview. At this moment, it is impossible to say that Christian fundamentalism will act as the second magnet in the dynamo of clashing civilizations. But it is difficult to feel optimistic about the consequences, nationally and internationally, of this new declaration of sacred conflict.

Ad: a non-Muslim tribe mentioned in the Quran, now thought by some to symbolize the United States.

baya: an oath of allegiance to the Caliph.

Dar al-Harb: the realm of war, i.e., the realm not yet under Islamic law.

Dar al-Islam: the realm in which Islamic law prevails.

dawa: the call to believe in the true faith. The term can refer to missionary activity, as well as preaching to Muslims.

dhimmi: derived from the word for obligation or responsibility, dhimmi refers to "People of the Book"—Christians, Jews, Zoroastrians, and Sabaeans—who do not have the rights of Muslims within Dar al-Islam but have certain privileges. Muslims are responsible, in theory, for the welfare of dhimmis. Dhimmis are required to pay a poll tax and, at various times and places, have been forced to wear distinctive clothing or badges and been barred from certain kinds of employment.

din moser: the Jewish legal doctrine that authorizes the execution of Jewish traitors.

din rodef: the Jewish legal doctrine that permits a murderous pursuer to be killed.

Eid al-Adha: the Muslim festival that concludes the pilgrimage season.

fatwa: a Muslim legal opinion or edict.

ghazi: originally a desert raider, the term has come to mean those who raid the infidel on behalf of Islam.

Gush Emunim: "The Bloc of the Faithful," an Israeli settler movement founded in 1974.

hadith: traditions compiled in the early period of Islam concerning Muhammad's words and deeds.

hajj: the annual pilgrimage that Muslims are obligated to perform once in their lifetime, one of the five pillars of Islamic faith.

Hanbali: one of the four madhdhabs, or Muslim schools of religious thought. Founded by Ahmad ibn Hanbal (d. 855), Hanbali is generally stricter in its interpretations of Muslim law than alternative schools. Ibn Taymiyya was a Hanbali scholar. Wahhabism stems from Hanbali roots.

Haram al-Sharif: literally the "noble enclosure," the term refers to the large stone platform on which the al-Aqsa Mosque is situated. Jews refer to the site as the Temple Mount because it encompasses the ruins of the Jewish Second Temple, destroyed by Rome in 70 C.E.

Halakha: Jewish law. A variant, *halakhic,* means "legal."

hawala: an informal and unregulated system of money transfers that relies on shared codes and trusted emissaries—a way to avoid using the banking system.

Hijaz: the western fringe of the Arabian peninsula, which includes the cities of Mecca, Medina, and Jedda.

Hijra: the flight of Muhammad from Mecca to Medina in September 622.

ijtihad: an independent judgment regarding religious law and doctrine.

Ikhwan: the "Brothers," Wahhabi tribesman who fought on behalf of, and occasionally against, the al-Saud rulers of Arabia.

Islamism: a religious ideology that insists on the application of sharia law by the state. Advocates of Islamism are called Islamists.

jahiliyya: in the jargon of Islamic reformers, this term refers to individuals, or entire societies, that have fallen into a pre-Islamic state of barbarity, especially those where Muslims have forsaken God's law in favor of man-made laws.

Kaaba: literally "cube," it is a structure in Mecca that, according to Muslim lore, was built by Abraham and contains a holy stone given to him by the angel Gabriel. A holy site, it is the object of the annual pilgrimage.

Kharijites: the first Muslim schismatics, the Kharijites battled both Ali and Muawiya, early rivals for the caliphate. Condemned by later generations of Muslims for splitting the umma, they nevertheless spawned a trend of breakaway reform movements within Islam.

kiswa: an elaborately embroidered shroud that is used to drape the Kaaba in Mecca during pilgrimage ceremonies.

kufr: the state of unbelief. A variant, *kafir,* means "infidel."

madrassa: a Muslim religious school.

Mahdi: a messianic figure who will appear at the end of history and restore justice to the world.

muezzin: the person who issues the call to prayer.

Muharram: a lunar month corresponding to October.

mujahid: one who leads Muslims in jihad or participates in jihad. The plural is "mujahidin."

Nejd: the heartland of the Arabia peninsula, which includes the capital of Saudi Arabia, Riyadh.

po'a: in Buddhism, acts undertaken to facilitate the passage of a person through the afterlife.

Pulsa d'Nura: literally "Blazing Disks," the term refers to an obscure and rarely practiced Jewish ceremony during which a sinner is condemned by a quorum of worshipers.

Ramadan: the ninth month of the lunar calendar, during which Muslims must fast during daylight hours.

salaf: an ancestor, an early adherent to Islam.

salafist: a proponent of salafiyya Islam.

salafiyya: an approach to Islam that aims to emulate the way in which early Muslims practiced their religion.

sharia: Islamic law.

shukkesha: a retreat. Aum Shinrikyo sequestered recruits in these retreats.

shura: a council, sometimes used in the phrase "majlis al-shura," meaning consultative council.

Sunna: the proper Muslim life as exemplified by the deeds and sayings of the Prophet.

takfir: to condemn a Muslim or Muslims as infidels.

Torah: the Hebrew Bible or, in some contexts, Jewish law.

ulema: religious scholars.

umma: the community of Islam.

Wahhabi: an adherent of the reformist, puritanical approach to Islam set forth by Muhammad ibn Abd al-Wahhab, an eighteenth-century Arabian preacher.

zakat: the mandatory alms tax paid by Muslims, one of the five pillars of the faith.

NOTES

PREFACE

1. Steven Simon and Daniel Benjamin, "America and the New Terrorism," *Survival*, Spring 2000, 59–70.
2. Daniel Benjamin and Steven Simon, "Defusing a Time Bomb," *Washington Post*, 16 July 2001, A15; and Steven Simon and Daniel Benjamin, "Don't Isolate Pakistan," *Financial Times*, 13 July 2001, 17.
3. "Fourth-Generation Wars," by Abu Ubeid al-Qurashi, identified by the London Arabic-language daily *al-Quds al-Arabi* as "one of Usama bin Laden's closest aides." The article appeared in the Internet magazine *al-Ansar;* the translation by the Middle East Media Research Institute appeared in "Bin Laden Lieutenant Admits to September 11 and Explains Al-Qaida's Combat Doctrine," *Special Dispatch: Jihad and Terrorism Studies,* no. 344 (10 Feb. 2002).

CHAPTER 1: DAYBREAK

1. Susan Sachs and David Kocieniewski, "Kahane Slaying Fit into Larger Puzzle," *Newsday*, 23 July 1993, 4.
2. James C. McKinley Jr., "Islamic Leader on U.S. Terrorist List Is in Brooklyn," *New York Times*, 16 Dec. 1990, 44.
3. Jim Dwyer, David Kocieniewski, Deirdre Murphy, and Peg Tyre, *Two Seconds Under the World* (New York: Ballantine, 1994), 34.

4. Barbara Rogers, to whom Salem was married for a number of years, was his equal. She introduced herself as a doctor when, in fact, she was a secretary.

5. It would later be revealed that there had been not one but two tests. In December 1994, Wali Khan Amin Shah, one of Yousef's fellow conspirators, who was later arrested in Malaysia, bombed a Manila movie theater using one of the devices.

6. Al-Qaeda has a remarkable knack for turning its enemy's needs and practices to the group's advantage. In May 1997, when bin Laden decided that he needed a new battery for his satellite phone, his organization arranged to have it brought to him by a man named Tariq Hamdi. A bin Laden follower who lived in northern Virginia, Hamdi was then working as a fixer for ABC News, which wanted an interview with the terrorist chieftain. The visit of the news crew to Afghanistan, accompanied by Hamdi, provided the opportunity for delivering the battery. The irony of the world's first truly global terrorist piggybacking his operations on the television news division of the Disney Corporation speaks for itself.

7. Ayman al-Zawahiri, *Knights Under the Prophet's Banner,* as printed in *al-Sharq al-Awsat,* 2 Dec. 2001 (FBIS-NES-2002-0108).

8. Judith Miller, "Dissecting a Terror Plot from Boston to Amman," *New York Times,* 15 Jan. 2001, A1.

9. After the attacks, the Federal Emergency Management Agency and the Structural Engineers Institute of the American Society of Civil Engineers assembled a building performance assessment team. The group received assistance from a group of federal, state, and city authorities and professional organizations. The distillation of their draft report appeared in the May 2002 issue of *Civil Engineering* magazine and is the best analysis we have found of the physical events involved in the attacks. This account is based largely on that article, which appears at www.pubs.asce.org/ceonline/ceonline02/0502feat. html. Other sources are noted as necessary.

10. Marc Fisher and Don Phillips, "On Flight 77: 'Our Plane Is Being Hijacked,' " *Washington Post,* 12 Sept. 2001, A1.

11. Eric Lipton and James Glanz, "First Tower to Fall Was Hit at Higher Speed, Study Finds," *New York Times,* 23 Feb. 2002, A1.

CHAPTER 2: IBN TAYMIYYA AND HIS CHILDREN

1. Elias Canetti, *Crowds and Power,* trans. Carol Stewart (Middlesex, England: Penguin Books, 1973), 166.

2. Al-Fadl said that before approaching the Americans in 1996, he went to Syria, Jordan, and Lebanon, trying to raise money to start an opposition

party to the National Islamic Front, the ruling party in Sudan. He said he also considered going to Israel to gain support, but did not. He visited Eritrea and Saudi Arabia as well. See also Benjamin Weiser, "Ex-Aide Tells of Plot to Kill bin Laden," *New York Times,* 1 Feb. 2001, B3.

3. Emmanuel Sivan, *Radical Islam: Medieval Theology and Modern Politics,* enl. ed. (New Haven: Yale University Press, 1990), 101.

4. A. Chris Eccel, "Alim and Mujahid in Egypt: Orthodoxy Versus Subculture, or Division of Labour," *Muslim World* (July-Oct. 1988), 189–208.

5. John Calvert, "Sayyid Qutb in America," *Perspectives* (www.isim.nl/ newsletter/7/features/3.html); see also John Calvert, "'The World Is an Undutiful Boy!': Sayyid Qutb's American Experience," *Islam and Christian-Muslim Relations,* vol. 11, no. 1, 87–103.

6. Karen Armstrong, *The Battle for God* (London: HarperCollins, 2000), 240.

7. Nazih N. Ayubi, *Political Islam: Religion and Politics in the Arab World* (London: Routledge, 1991), 139.

8. David Zeidan, "The Islamic Fundamentalist View of Life as a Perennial Battle," *Middle East Review of International Affairs,* vol. 5, no. 4 (Dec. 2001), accessed at meria.idc.ac.il/journal/2001/issue4/jv5n4a2.htm.

9. Ayubi, *Political Islam,* 140.

10. Ibid.

11. Carole Hillenbrand, *The Crusades: Islamic Perspectives* (Edinburgh: Edinburgh University Press, 1999), 603.

12. Alfred Guillaume, trans., *The Life of Muhammad: A Translation of Ishaq's Sirat Rasul Allah* (London: Oxford University Press, 1955), 231–33.

13. Zeidan, "The Islamic Fundamentalist View of Life."

14. Ibid.

15. Ayubi, *Political Islam,* 143.

16. When the verdicts were announced at the conclusion of the trial of Sheikh Rahman and his coconspirators, Victor Alvarez, the somewhat mentally handicapped Puerto Rican convert to Islam, jumped up and yelled, *"Takfir!"* before being taken away by marshals. Reporters, missing the poignancy of the moment, thought it was a call to prayer. See Patricia Hurtado, "Sheik & Co.: Convicted: All 10 Guilty of Plotting Urban Jihad," *Newsday,* 2 Oct. 1995, A5.

17. V. S. Naipaul, *A Bend in the River* (New York: Vintage, 1989), 14.

18. Gilles Kepel, *Muslim Extremism in Egypt: The Prophet and Pharaoh,* trans. Jon Rothschild (London: Al Saqi Books, 1985), 219–22.

19. Ibn Taymiyya described the Alawites as "more infidel than Jews and Christians, indeed more infidel than many polytheists, and their harm to the com-

munity of Muhammad is greater than that of the fighting of infidels such as the Tatars or Franks" (Ayubi, *Political Islam*, 88).

20. Al-Utaybi entered the building wearing the traditional costume of the Ikhwan (Brothers), the ferocious tribes of the Nejd who brought the al-Saud military victory in the eighteenth century and were vital in consolidating the dynasty's control over most of the Arabian peninsula in the twentieth. But their belli-cose puritanism and territorial ambition made them at times an uncontrol-lable force within the Saudi camp. During the final push to extend Saudi control over the Hijaz, the region that contains Mecca and Medina, in 1929, the Ikhwan massacred three hundred inhabitants of the hill town of Taif to punish heresy and assert their own control of the area. Neither the al-Saud nor their supporters, the British, could tolerate this. The Ikhwan were sup-pressed and, to keep them in line, absorbed into the National Guard. Ibn Humayd Sultan bin Bijad, an Ikhwan leader in the revolt against the al-Saud, was killed in 1929 at the battle of Sabila, the climactic engagement of the war. Now bin Bijad's grandson Juhayman al-Utaybi stood in the Grand Mosque in a shin-length robe and headdress without any black rope circling it— because this, scripture led the Ikhwan to believe, was how Muhammad had garbed himself.

21. These pamphlets were eventually published in Kuwait. Their content was ultimately given a sympathetic but thorough elaboration in a 1980 book by an author using the pseudonym Abu Dharr, an allusion to Abu Dharr al-Ghifari, a sainted companion of Muhammad's who personified the ideals of nonconformity and piety and suffered for it at the hands of the caliph.

22. The best account of the siege and of al-Utaybi's ideology is contained in two articles by Joseph A. Kechichian: "Islamic Revivalism and Change in Saudi Arabia: Juhayman al-Utaybi's 'Letters' to the Saudi People," *Muslim World*, vol. 86 (Jan. 1990), 1–16; and "The Role of the Ulema in the Politics of an Islamic State: The Case of Saudi Arabia," *International Journal of Middle Eastern Studies*, vol. 18, no. 1 (Feb. 1986), 53–71.

23. Abdullah Yusuf Ali, *The Holy Qur'an: Text, Translation and Commentary* (New York: Tahrike Tarsile Qur'an, Inc., 1987), 46:21–26.

24. "O mankind! Fear your Lord! For the convulsion of the Hour [of Judgment] will be a thing terrible!" (Ali, *The Holy Qur'an*, 22:1).

CHAPTER 3: THE WARRIOR PRINCE

1. Marcella Bombardieri and Neil Swidey, "American Prepares the Personal and Political: In Cambridge, a bin Laden Breaks Family Silence," *Boston Globe*, 7 Oct. 2001, A1.

2. Alison Leigh Cowan, Kurt Eichenwald, and Michael Moss, "A Nation Challenged: The Relatives—bin Laden Family, with Deep Western Ties, Strives to Re-establish a Name," *New York Times,* 28 Oct. 2001, A9.

3. Usama bin Laden, interview with Jamal Ismail in Afghanistan, 10 June 1999; accessed at www.terrorism.com/terrorism/BinLadinTranscript.shtml.

4. David Zeidan, "The Islamic Fundamentalist View of Life as a Perennial Battle," *Middle East Review of International Affairs,* vol. 5, no. 4 (Dec. 2001).

5. Peter Bergen, *Holy War Inc.: Inside the Secret World of Osama bin Laden* (New York: Free Press, 2001), 55.

6. Ayman al-Zawahiri, *Knights Under the Prophet's Banner,* as printed in *al-Sharq al-Awsat,* 2 Dec. 2001 (FBIS-NES-2002-0108).

7. Mary Tabor, "Slaying in Brooklyn Linked to Militants," *New York Times,* 11 Apr. 1993, A28.

8. The name of the dream reader, which appears in testimony, is identical to one of the aliases of Ayman al-Zawahiri. Judging by how dreams are treated for their prophetic, as opposed to psychological, content, it does not appear that he is working in the tradition of Freud.

9. Timothy Noah, "Why U.S. Military Bases Are Good for Mecca and Medina," *Slate,* 15 Oct. 2001 (www.slate.msn.com).

10. Usama bin Laden, interview with Peter Arnett, Afghanistan, CNN, Mar. 1993.

11. Joshua Teitelbaum, *Holier Than Thou: Saudi Arabia's Islamic Opposition* (Washington, D.C.: Washington Institute for Near East Policy, Nov. 2000), 30.

12. Accessed at www.miraserve.com/englishnew.htm.

13. Usama bin Laden, interview with Peter Arnett.

14. U.S. State Department, "Usama bin Ladin: Islamic Extremist Financier," U.S. State Department Press Release, 14 Aug. 1996.

15. "Part One of a Series of Reports on bin Ladin's Life in Sudan: Islamists Celebrated Arrival of Great Islamic Investor: Front Offered Him Membership. Isam al-Turabi: Sudanese Government Parties and United States Arranged Departure of Saudi Oppositionist," *al-Quds al-Arabi,* 24 Nov. 2001, 13 (FBIS-NEW-2001-1124; www.fas.org/irp/world/para/ladin-sudan.htm).

16. Robert Block, "In War on Terrorism, Sudan Struck a Blow by Fleecing bin Laden," *Wall Street Journal,* 3 Dec. 2001, A1.

17. "Part One of a Series of Reports on bin Ladin's Life in Sudan."

18. Sheikh Rahman summed up the jihadists' antipathy to the opposing Gulf War camps. Answering a question after one of his speeches about what punishment those who were fighting Iraq should receive, he replied, with charac-

teristic eloquence, "Both [those] who are against and the ones who are with Iraq should be killed."

19. Al-Ridi cooperated with the federal authorities and appeared as a witness at the embassy bombing trials. Although he conducted business for bin Laden, he did not sympathize with him and, he said, criticized him to his face. Afterward, he was treated poorly by the United States and appallingly by his native Egypt. See Judith Miller, "A Witness Against Al Qaeda Says the U.S. Let Him Down," *New York Times*, 3 June 2002, A1.

20. *United States of America v. Ali Mohamed*, S (7) 98 Cr. 1023 (LBS), NY Sup. Ct., 20 Oct. 2000 (cryptome.org/usa-v-mohamed.htm).

21. Teitelbaum, *Holier Than Thou*, 76.

22. *God, Oil and Country: Changing the Logic of War in Sudan* (Brussels: International Crisis Group Press, 2002), 78.

CHAPTER 4: RAIDERS ON THE PATH OF GOD

1. Ayman al-Zawahiri, *Knights Under the Prophet's Banner*, excerpts as printed in *al-Sharq al-Awsat*, 2 Dec. 2001 (FBIS-NES-2002-0108).

2. Ahmed Rashid, *Taliban: Militant Islam, Oil and Fundamentalism in Central Asia* (New Haven: Yale University Press, 2000), 49.

3. On April 4, 1996, to underscore the aspirations of Taliban rule, Omar made a rare appearance in public in the conquered capital. He brought with him a relic that had been in safekeeping in a shrine and had not been seen for sixty years: a cape believed to have belonged to Muhammad. In a gesture that might have been presumptuous to the point of blasphemy if committed by another, he donned it in front of a large crowd. The Pakistani journalist Ahmed Rashid wrote that the event was a political masterstroke, for by cloaking himself with the Prophet's mantle, Mullah Omar had assumed the right to lead not just all Afghans but all Muslims. Rashid, *Taliban*, 42.

4. Rahimullah Yusufzai, "Afghanistan: Omar, bin Laden Demand Ouster of U.S. Forces from Saudi, Islamabad," *News in English*, 27 Mar. 1997, 12 (FBIS-NES-97-061).

5. The letter was found on the computer of Wadi el-Hage in Nairobi. It was exhibit 300B-T in the embassy bombings trial.

6. "Declaration of War Against the Americans Occupying the Land of the Two Holy Places" was issued on 23 Aug. 1996; accessed at www.washington post.com/ac2/wp-dyn?pagename=article&node=&contentId=A4342-2001Sep21.

7. Bin Laden occasionally refers to other Islamic authorities, and some individuals, such as Sheikh Rahman and Muhammad Abd al-Salam Faraj, make

use of a variety of sources in their argumentation. By and large, however, jihadists rely heavily on ibn Taymiyya as well their own understanding of the Quran and hadith for support, but very little else. They dismiss the work of some of the greatest Muslim thinkers as un-Islamic, but rarely on the basis of any serious study. Meager knowledge of the riches of Islamic thought is one of the striking characteristics of these radicals.

8. Kanan Makiya and Hassan Mneimheh, "Manual for a Raid," in Robert B. Silvers and Barbara Epstein, eds., *Striking Terror: America's New War* (New York: New York Review of Books, 2002), 324.

9. David B. Ottaway and Dan Morgan, "Muslim Charities Under Scrutiny," *Washington Post,* 29 Sept. 2001, A1; Judith Miller, "A Nation Challenged: The Money Trail—Raids Seek Evidence of Money-Laundering," *New York Times,* 21 Mar. 2002, A19. The IIRO and the Muslim World League deny that they purposefully funded any militant group, although they do not deny that some of their funds may have made it into the hands of militants without their knowledge.

10. Edith M. Lederer, "U.N. Panel Accuses Taliban of Selling Drugs to Finance War and Train Terrorists," Associated Press, 25 May 2001.

11. Daniel Benjamin and Steven Simon, "As a Conflict Intensifies, It's India's Move," *New York Times,* 15 Mar. 2000, A29.

12. Khattab was a resilient force in the region until his death, which was reported on 25 Aug. 2002. The death of the other major Islamist leader in the region, Shamil Basayev, suggests that Russia scored a major intelligence coup that allowed it to target the two, which it had been unable to do before.

13. Usama bin Laden, interview with Peter Arnett, Afghanistan, CNN, Mar. 1997 (www.anusha.com/osamaint.htm).

14. Usama bin Laden, interview with John Miller, Afghanistan, ABC News, May 1998 (www.pbs.org/wgbh/pages/frontline/shows/binladen/who/miller.html).

15. Al-Zawahiri, *Knights Under the Prophet's Banner.*

16. Usama bin Laden, interview with Peter Arnett.

17. "Jihad Against Jews and Crusaders," World Islamic Front Statement, 23 Feb. 1998 (www.washingtonpost.com/ac2/wp-dyn?pagename=article& node=&contentId=A4993-2001Sep21&notFound=true).

18. Al-Zawahiri, *Knights Under the Prophet's Banner.*

19. Accessed at www.fas.org/irp/world/para/ladin_122701.pdf.

20. Usama bin Laden, interview with Tayseer Alouni, Afghanistan, al-Jazeera, Oct. 2001; translation accessed at www.cnn.com/2002/WORLD/asiapcf/south/02/05/binladen.transcript/.

21. "Al Jazirah TV Broadcasts bin Laden Recorded Statement," al-Jazeera, 27 Dec. 2001, accessed at www.fas.org/irp/world/para/ladin_122701.pdf.

22. In June 2002 several al-Qaeda operatives were arrested in Morocco. One, a Saudi, said he knew the emir well and that until September 11, bin Laden had increasingly adopted the mantle of a prophet, preferring to speak through senior aides rather than interact directly with his followers. In late August, speaking to followers through an aide, bin Laden was beginning to talk of a dream he'd had, a Moroccan official said. "He said he saw America in ashes. It was like announcing a prophecy." Peter Finn, "Arrests Reveal Al Qaeda Plans: Three Saudis Seized by Morocco Outline Post-Afghanistan Strategy," *Washington Post,* 16 June 2002, 1.

23. Bin Laden, it is increasingly clear, is by no means alone in seeing his struggle as part of an apocalyptic drama. On July 10, 2002, al-Jazeera interviewed several leading Saudi dissidents. Speaking by telephone, Sheikh Safar al-Hawali declared, "The relations between America and us differ from the relations between us and all the other peoples or nations. These are relations between two [very] different nations: One is a nation that was chosen by Allah, who tested it and purified it with disasters so that it will atone for its sins. Allah is using that nation in order to wave the banner of truth and justice on the face of the earth. This is our nation. There is also a tyrannous and evil nation that Allah is manipulating, unbeknownst to it, until it reaches the end to which it is sentenced—the same end that was the lot of all the nations of heresy, tyranny, and aggression such as the peoples of Noah, 'Aad [Ad], Thamud, and Pharaoh." Translation by Middle East Media Research Institute, *Saudi Arabia/Jihad and Terrorism Studies,* no. 400 (19 July 2002).

24. "Conversation with Terror," *Time,* 11 Jan. 1999, 38.

25. Robert B. Silvers and Barbara Epstein, eds., *Striking Terror: America's New War* (New York: New York Review of Books, 2002), 322–23.

26. John Cloud, "Atta's Odyssey," *Time,* 8 Oct. 2001, 64.

27. Mark Juergensmeyer, *Terror in the Mind of God: The Global Rise of Religious Violence* (Berkeley: University of California Press, 2000), 65.

CHAPTER 5: FIELDS OF JIHAD

1. Quoted in Daniel Benjamin and Steven Simon, "Islam's War of Words," *Time International,* 12 Nov. 2001, 35.

2. "Saudi Government Opponent Predicts Overthrow, Says Bin Ladin Is Alive," *Der Spiegel,* 4 Mar. 2002, 138–39 (FBIS-NES-2002-0304).

3. David Johnston, Don Van Natta Jr., and Judith Miller, "Qaeda's New Links Increase Threats from Far-Flung Sites," *New York Times,* 16 June 2002, A1.

4. Ayman al-Zawahiri, *Knights Under the Prophet's Banner,* as printed in *al-Sharq al-Awsat,* 2 Dec. 2001 (FBIS-NES-2002-0108).

5. Emmanuel Sivan, "Why Radical Muslims Aren't Taking Over States," *Middle East Review of International Affairs*, vol. 2, no 2 (May 1998); meria.idc.ac.il/1998/issue2/jv2na2.html.

6. The more food is produced locally, however, the more scarce water is consumed. For poor countries, the trade-offs are unforgiving.

7. Eberhard Kienle, *A Grand Delusion: Democracy and Economic Reform in Egypt* (London: I. B. Tauris, 2001), 94.

8. David B. Ottoway and Dan Morgan, "Two Muslim Charities Under Scrutiny: Saudi-Funded Groups Deny Ties to Terrorist Networks but Cite Vulnerability," *Washington Post,* 30 Sept. 2001, A12.

9. Neil MacFarquhar, "Anti-Western and Extremist Views Pervade Saudi Schools," *New York Times,* 19 Oct. 2001, B1.

10. Ministry of Education, Saudi Arabia, accessed at www.mohe.gov.sa/stat/index.asp.

11. International Institute for Strategic Studies, "Saudi Arabia's Political Dilemmas," *Strategic Comments,* vol. 7, no. 10 (Dec. 2001), and David Butter, "Keeping Up the Momentum," *Middle East Economic Digest,* 23 Nov. 2001, 4–5.

12. Mai Yamani, *Changed Identities: The Challenge of the New Generation in Saudi Arabia* (London: Royal Institute of International Affairs, 2000). This is the conclusion drawn by a Saudi social scientist who has interviewed (in Arabic) dozens of Saudis between fifteen and thirty years of age.

13. Daniel L. Byman and Jerrold D. Green, "The Enigma of Political Stability in the Persian Gulf Monarchies," *Middle East Review of International Affairs,* vol. 3, no. 3 (Sept. 1999). Mamoun Fandy also stresses the familial and tribal differences that influence Saudi Arabia's politics.

14. Safar al-Hawali, "Open Letter of Sheikh Safar Hawali to President Bush," 15 Oct. 2001, accessed at www.as-sahwah.com.

15. Quintan Wiktorowicz, "The Salafi Movement in Jordan," *International Journal of Middle East Studies* 32 (2000), 219–40.

16. Suzanne Goldenberg, "Israel Thwarts Jewish Bomb Attack on School," *The Guardian,* 13 May 2002, 13.

17. The Hamas charter can be accessed at www.palestinecenter.org/cpap/documents/charter.html.

18. This quotation from a hadith is cited frequently by bin Laden, including in the recruitment videotape circulated in 2001 before September 11.

19. Richard Reid and Usama bin Laden were not the only parties interested in bringing down the Azrieli Tower. The Palestinian Front for the Liberation of Palestine was preparing to destroy the building in late September by detonating an explosives-packed vehicle in the underground parking facility. That

conspiracy was broken up by a 24 September 2001 Israeli raid on a safe house in the West Bank town of Qalqilya.

20. In July 2000, Hamas's approval rating was 27 percent, against Fatah's 28 percent. In January 2001, Hamas was at 25 percent, with no change to Fatah's rating. Survey results were accessed at www.pcpsr.org/survey/index.html.

21. Mohammed M. Hafez, "Armed Islamic Movements and Political Violence in Algeria," *Middle East Journal,* vol. 54, no. 4 (Autumn 2000), 581.

22. Ibid., 587.

23. Jonah Blank, "Kashmir: Fundamentalism Takes Root," *Foreign Affairs,* Nov.-Dec. 1999, 36–53.

24. Ghulam Hasnain, "Inside Jihad," *Time Asia,* 5 Feb. 2001, 157.

25. "Pakistan in Crisis," IISS Strategic Comments, vol. 6 (3 Apr. 2000).

26. Anthony Davis, "Inside Jihad International," *Asiaweek,* 19 Nov. 1999, 44.

27. A few months later, a leader of the United Jihad Front, Maulana Sami ul-Haq, told us in an interview at the Haqqaniya Mosque near Peshawar that the government was jahili and had to go.

28. Pervez Hoodbhoy, ed., *Education and the State: Fifty Years of Pakistan* (Karachi: Oxford University Press, 1998), 241–46.

29. Steve LeVine and Saeed Azhar, "Nuclear Scientist Denied Knowing bin Laden—Investigators Find Nothing Objectionable," *Wall Street Journal Europe,* 5 Nov. 2001; Douglas Frantz and David Rohde, "2 Pakistanis Linked to Papers on Anthrax Weapons," *New York Times,* 28 Nov. 2001; David E. Sanger, "Nuclear Experts in Pakistan May Have Links to Al Qaeda," *New York Times,* 9 Dec. 2001; Kamran Khan and Molly Moore, "2 Nuclear Experts Briefed bin Laden," *Washington Post,* 12 Dec. 2001; Toby Harnden, "Pakistani Scientists Gave bin Laden Nuclear Advice," *Daily Telegraph,* 13 Dec. 2001; Farrah Stockman, "A Disenchanted Researcher's bin Laden Tie," *Boston Globe,* 16 Dec. 2001; Peter Baker, "Pakistani Scientist Who Met bin Laden Failed Polygraphs, Renewing Suspicions," *Washington Post,* 2 Mar. 2002.

30. Ahmed Rashid, "They're Only Sleeping: Why Militant Islamicists in Central Asia Aren't Going to Go Away," *New Yorker,* Internet edition, posted 7 Jan. 2002.

31. Rumors in Tashkent that Namangani is still alive and in hiding continue to swirl. Ian Traynor, "War in Afghanistan: Al-Qaida Ally Reported Killed," *The Guardian,* 26 Nov. 2001, 4.

32. Melanie Phillips, "Britain Ignores Angry Muslims Within at Its Peril," *Sunday Times* (London), 4 Nov. 2001.

33. Nicholas Le Quesne, "Islam in Europe: A Changing Faith," *Time Europe,* 24 Dec. 2001, 44.

34. Burhan Wazir, "Essex Boys Sign Up for Holy War," *Observer*, 24 Feb. 2002.

CHAPTER 6: A PARADIGM LOST

1. Bruce Hoffman, "Testimony on Security Threats to Americans Overseas," Hearing on Protecting American Interest Abroad: U.S. Citizens, Businesses, and Non-governmental Organizations, Subcommittee on National Security, Veterans Affairs, and International Relations, 3 Apr. 2001; and *Odds of Death Due to Injury, United States, 1998* (Washington, D.C.: National Safety Council, 1998); www.nsc.org/lrs/statinfo/odds.htm.

2. John Lancaster, "Compromising Positions," *Washington Post Magazine,* 9 July 2000, 10.

3. While Clinton was in office, Libya wound down its support for terrorism, expelling groups, such as Abu Nidal's, that had been operating out of Tripoli. Eventually, Libya agreed to a United States–United Kingdom proposal to try those indicted in the case in a Scottish court sitting in the Netherlands. One of the two Pan Am 103 defendants, Libyan intelligence agent Abdel Basset Ali Megrahi, was convicted on 31 January 2001. The United States continues to insist that Libya accept responsibility for its actions, cooperate with the continuing investigation, and pay compensation to the families of the victims. For more, see Daniel Benjamin and Steven Simon, "Pan Am 103: Keep Up the Fight," *Washington Post,* 1 Feb. 2001, A21; and Daniel Benjamin and Steven Simon, "Seeking Justice for Pan Am 103," *Christian Science Monitor,* 5 June 2000, 9.

4. This was typical Iranian behavior. "A Western official who follows the movement of the Islamic volunteers said there has been a pattern during the last few weeks of increased video surveillance of NATO installations, many of them American, by some of the volunteers. He said the volunteers were closely allied with the Iranian intelligence agency and were poised to strike at NATO forces in Bosnia. Iranian officials have denied any link.

   " 'If this situation is not cleared up it becomes a policy disaster,' he said.

   "A senior NATO official agreed. 'This is a time bomb waiting to go off,' he said. 'These mercenaries are all well trained, both as fighters and terrorists. While they are being kept under wraps now, the moment they are given the order to set off car bombs or carry out assassinations this whole mission could go up in smoke. These guys should be rounded up and put on a bus out of here.' " Chris Hedges, "Outsiders Bring Islamic Fervor to the Balkans," *New York Times,* 23 Sept. 1996: A1.

5. Iran's surveillance, which began before Khatami's surprise election in May,

exceeds "the normal spy vs. spy stuff," the senior administration official said. Some activities by Iranian agents, such as monitoring where U.S. personnel park cars and their travel routes, could be interpreted as preparation for attacks. See Robin Wright, "Iranian Leader Plans to Address the U.S. on TV," *Los Angeles Times,* 31 Dec. 1997, A1.

6. Anthony Lake, *Six Nightmares: Real Threats in a Dangerous World and How America Can Meet Them* (Boston: Little, Brown, 2000), 50–65.

7. Charles Alan Wright, *Federal Rules of Criminal Procedure,* 2nd ed. (St. Paul, Minn.: West Publishing, 1982).

8. At least until the end of 1999, the Justice Department declined to use the Alien Terrorist Removal Court because it never felt it had a case that would stand up to judicial review and believed precedent was all-important in determining the further use of the court. As a result, the department was self-deterred.

9. This orthodoxy prevailed among scholars of terrorism, many of whom saw the Aum as a freakish exception until September 11.

10. Department of State, "Usama bin Ladin: Islamic Extremist Financier," State Department fact sheet, 14 Aug. 1996.

11. Ironically, the only earlier one that shows up in Nexis searches is from the 1994 annual human rights report, where it was noted that Saudi Arabia had stripped bin Laden of his citizenship. See U.S. Department of State, *Saudi Arabia Human Rights Practices, 1994,* Feb. 1994 (www.state.gov/www/global/human_rights/hrp_reports_mainhp.html).

12. Stephen Engelberg, "One Man and a Global Web of Violence," *New York Times,* 14 Jan. 2001, A1.

13. FBI Form FD-302: Investigation on 2/7/95 and 2/8/95 by Special Agent Charles Stern, FBI, and Brian G. Parr, USSS.

14. Much later, during his 2001 testimony, Jamal al-Fadl claimed that he had seen Yousef in the Khalden training camp in Afghanistan in the late 1980s, one of many citations linking Yousef with the camp.

15. Joshua Teitelbaum, *Holier Than Thou: Saudi Arabia's Islamic Opposition* (Washington, D.C.: Washington Institute for Near East Policy, Nov. 2000), 73–77.

16. Robin Wright, "Islam in the '90s: A Study of Diversity: Despite Pervasive Stereotypes, Major Islamist Groups Differ Widely in Tactics and Tenets," *Los Angeles Times,* 7 Feb. 1995, A1.

17. Thomas W. Lippman and John M. Goshko, "U.S. Begins to Withdraw Personnel from Sudan: Staff Vulnerable to Attacks, State Dept. Says," *Washington Post,* 1 Feb. 1996, A4.

18. "1996 CIA Memo to Sudanese Official," *Washington Post,* 3 Oct. 2001,

accessed at www.washingtonpost.com/wp-srv/nation/specials/attacked/
transcripts/sudanmemotext_100301.html.

19. Since September 11, one much-repeated allegation has been that the Clinton
administration missed a key opportunity in the mid-1990s to improve relations with Sudan and learn more about the terrorists, including bin Laden,
who had been sheltered there. Had the United States done that, critics contend, it could have prevented the attacks on the World Trade Center and
Pentagon.

The chief proponents of this argument are Mansoor Ijaz, a New
York–based investment banker, and Timothy Carney, the former U.S. ambassador to Sudan. Carney has sharply criticized the Clinton administration for
what he says are critical mistakes in its policy toward Sudan. In the 1990s,
Ijaz made sizable contributions to the Democratic Party and met once with
National Security Adviser Sandy Berger at the request of White House political personnel. Berger heard out Ijaz's argument that the United States should
engage more with the Sudanese. Despite repeated requests, Berger declined
to meet Ijaz again. (The White House had been harshly criticized for meetings between officials and businessman Roger Tamraz, who wanted assistance in getting a pipeline built to carry Caspian basin oil, and Ijaz presented
a comparable case since he has investments and ties to firms in the energy
sector, some of which may have been interested in oil development in
Sudan.) Ijaz, a Pakistani-American who has advertised his close ties with
governments in South Asia and his ability to make progress on the Kashmir
conflict, was viewed by other NSC officials as an unreliable freelancer, someone who was pursuing his own interests and fancied himself a grand strategist. Jointly and separately (and Ijaz much more frequently), Carney and Ijaz
have made their case in the *Los Angeles Times, Vanity Fair,* and *The Washington Post* and through numerous television appearances.

They adduce several pieces of evidence to support it. Ijaz, in particular,
often cites correspondence from Sudanese leaders professing a desire to
cooperate on counterterrorism that he personally delivered to U.S. officials.
They refer to an offer to hand bin Laden over to U.S. authorities, as they
wrote in *The Washington Post* on June 30, 2002. (See Timothy Carney and
Mansoor Ijaz, "Intelligence Failure? Let's Go Back to Sudan," *Washington
Post,* 30 June 2002, B4.) And they claim that Ijaz was shown sensitive intelligence on terrorists tracked through Khartoum by the Sudanese intelligence
chief. They argue that the administration was blinded by its preconceptions
about Sudan and refused to engage with the Khartoum regime.

The notion that the United States missed a great chance is belied by the
facts. There was no break in diplomatic relations even though the U.S. em-

bassy in Khartoum was closed. U.S. and Sudanese officials met numerous times, including, as Carney and Ijaz note, in Virginia in early 1996. The Sudanese were not shunted off to low-level officials but met with Undersecretary of State Thomas Pickering. They had ample opportunity to provide genuine intelligence cooperation, and they did not do so. The U.S. government declined Ijaz's services because there was nothing he could achieve that America's diplomats could not. In fact, Ijaz's involvement could add nothing to relations except provide Khartoum with an opportunity to manipulate him. And that is exactly what has happened, whether he is wittingly complicit or not.

An example is Ijaz's claim to have seen sensitive intelligence: How could Ijaz possibly know what constitutes sensitive intelligence? What expertise does he have in terrorism? How could he know anything about the value of the paper in front of him beyond what the Sudanese told him? What kind of perspective did he have on years of Sudanese dissembling about its support for terror and its dealings with the United States?

A further example of the thinness of this story is the claim that Khartoum offered to hand bin Laden over. Setting aside the issue of whether the United States could take custody of bin Laden, against whom it had no indictment at the time, no senior government official from the Clinton administration is aware of any such offer, nor has any record of one surfaced. It is hard to find anyone who has made this claim other than Mansoor Ijaz. In fact, in an interview on May 2, 2002, in Washington with one of the authors, Timothy Carney said that he "was not aware of any option to send [bin Laden] to us." One has to wonder what suddenly convinced him that there was such an option.

At the heart of the argument that Washington botched its dealings with the Sudanese government is the implicit contention that in 1996 and after, the Khartoum leadership was well-meaning but misunderstood. Again, this is belied by the facts. Sudan continued to harbor and support terrorists long after bin Laden left. As the embassy-bombing trial transcripts show, Khartoum kept close watch over the terrorists within its borders, knew them well, and cooperated closely *with them,* not with the United States. Senior bin Laden operatives continued to visit Khartoum, undoubtedly with the acquiescence of the regime, months after the bombing of the East Africa embassies in 1998. The Sudanese knew precisely what they needed to do to improve relations with the United States. They refused because they shared many of the goals and ideology of the terrorists and, at a minimum, wanted to keep their involvement with these groups safe from scrutiny. Sudan never provided any serious cooperation with the United States because to do so would have revealed its complicity in numerous acts of terror.

It is also worth remembering something about the character of the Sudanese regime: through unrelenting warfare, it is responsible for inflicting unspeakable suffering on Sudanese citizens in the south of the country that, in the opinion of scholars and government officials in many countries, amounts to genocide. That Ijaz and Carney have been able to help the Sudanese leaders improve their public image is a testament to widespread ignorance about the record of the Khartoum regime.

20. Bradley Graham, "NSC Aide Warned White House of Gulf Facility Security Gaps," *Washington Post,* 20 Mar. 1997, A21.

CHAPTER 7: THE UNKNOWN WAR

1. Martin Sieff, "Terrorist Is Driven by Hatred for U.S., Israel," *Washington Times,* 21 Aug. 1998, A1.
2. According to *The New York Times,* "The Central Intelligence Agency has obtained evidence that Mr. Bin Laden has been allowed to funnel money through the Dubai Islamic Bank in Dubai, which the United Arab Emirates Government effectively controls." See James Risen with Benjamin Weiser, "U.S. Officials Say Aid for Terrorists Came Through Two Persian Gulf Nations," *New York Times,* 8 July 1999, A1. Also, the *Los Angeles Times* wrote that "millions in Al Qaeda funds cascaded through the freewheeling financial institutions of the neighboring emirate of Dubai." See Judy Pasternak and Stephen Braun, "Emirates Looked Other Way While Al Qaeda Funds Flowed," 20 Jan. 2002, A1.
3. Prince Turki al-Faisal Saud, the head of the Saudi General Intelligence agency, managed the Saudi contribution, aided by Prince Salman, the governor of Riyadh. Bin Laden worked closely with Prince Turki during this period, effectively operating as an arm of Saudi intelligence. Peter L. Bergen, *Holy War, Inc.* (New York: Free Press, 2001), 55. See also Ahmed Rashid, *Taliban* (New Haven: Yale University Press, 2000), 131.
4. Scott Macleod, "The Near Misses: Saudi Arabia's Ex-intelligence Chief Tells *Time* About the Failed Efforts to Bring in Osama," *Time,* 19 Nov. 2001, 57.
5. Bruce Riedel, *American Diplomacy and the 1999 Kargil Summit at Blair House,* Policy Paper Series 2002 (Philadelphia: University of Pennsylvania, 2002); www.sas.upenn.edu/casi/reports/RiedelPaper051302.htm.
6. Barton Gellman, "Struggles Inside the Government Defined Campaign," *Washington Post,* 20 Dec. 2001, A1. Speaking in 2002, well after he had left office, former President Clinton mentioned in passing about having "contracted some people in Afghanistan to go get [bin Laden], because we

thought he was dangerous." See also Wolf Blitzer, *CNN Late Edition with Wolf Blitzer,* CNN, 19 May 2002.

7. Paul R. Pillar, *Terrorism and U.S. Foreign Policy* (Washington D.C.: Brookings Institution Press, 2001), 123.

8. Elsa Walsh, "Louis Freeh's Last Case," *New Yorker,* 14 May 2001.

9. Several months before he died, O'Neill discussed the Walsh article with one of the authors. Asked about the fact that Freeh withheld information from the White House because he had a loss of trust in Clinton, he said, "You know, I used to think that if you didn't have confidence in the President, you resigned."

10. Soon after the explosions, rumors circulated that the government of newly appointed Russian Prime Minister Putin, and not jihadists, had arranged the bombings to rally public opinion and distract from numerous domestic problems. At the time, the number of analysts who believed that Russian officials would carry out such operations was small. More recently, that has become a more widely held opinion.

11. The individual handling al-Zawahiri's travel in the United States was Ali Mohamed, the former U.S. Army sergeant and bin Laden aide. At the time of this conversation, he would have been in federal custody, having made his plea agreement. Whether any of the FBI representatives knew that is impossible to say, but they provided no information on Mohamed or any of his contacts to the White House.

12. Rob Garver, "Launder Law Looks Like an '01 Washout," *American Banker* 7 May 2001, 1. A little less than a month after September 11, legislation carrying similar provisions passed in the house by a 412–1 vote. The Democratic-controlled Senate included similar provisions in a broader counterterror bill that was approved October 12 on a 96–1 vote. Senator Gramm, however, stuck to his argument. "I was right then and I am right now," he declared in opposing the bill, which he called totalitarian. He added, "The way to deal with terrorists is to hunt them down and kill them."

CHAPTER 8: THE SHOCK OF THE NEW

1. Condoleezza Rice, "Promoting the National Interest," *Foreign Affairs,* Jan.-Feb. 2000, 45.

2. Eric Schmitt with Steven Lee Myers, "Bush Courts Key Lawmakers for Support on Defense Goals," *New York Times,* 9 Jan. 2001, A1.

3. Deputy Attorney General Eric H. Holder, "Statement on the Justice Department's Decision to Remove Hani el-Sayegh," 4 Oct. 1999 (Washington, D.C.: FDCH Federal Department and Agency Documents).

4. Elsa Walsh, "Louis Freeh's Last Case," *New Yorker,* 14 May 2001.

5. Dan Eggen and Vernon Loeb, "U.S. Indicts 14 Suspects in Saudi Arabia Blast," *Washington Post,* 22 June 2001, A1.

6. George J. Tenet, Statement by the Director of Central Intelligence George J. Tenet for the Senate Armed Services Committee, 7 Mar. 2001, "The World-wide Threat 2001: National Security in a Changing World."

7. Barton Gellman, "A Strategy's Cautious Evolution: Before Sept. 11, the Bush Anti-Terror Effort Was Mostly Ambition," *Washington Post,* 20 Jan. 2002, A1.

8. Ibid.

9. Adam Cohen, "Banking on Secrecy," *Time,* 22 Oct. 2001, 73, and William F. Wechsler, "Follow the Money," *Foreign Affairs,* July-Aug. 2001, 40.

10. Adam Clymer, "How Sept. 11 Changed Goals of Justice Dept.," *New York Times,* 28 Feb. 2002, A1.

11. Amir Shah, "Taliban Reject U.S. Concerns on bin Laden's Threat," Associated Press, 24 June 2001.

12. Gellman, "A Strategy's Cautious Evolution."

13. Eric Lichtblau and Josh Meyer, "Terrorist Ties Cited in Memo," *Los Angeles Times,* 23 May 2002, 1.

CHAPTER 9: A FAILURE OF INTELLIGENCE

1. Accessed at www.fas.org/man/dod-101/ops/docs/x08201998_x820bomb. html. Compare James Risen and Stephen Engelberg, "Signs of Change in Terror Goals Went Unheeded," *New York Times,* 14 Oct. 2001. The authors refer to a plan in an al-Qaeda communication intercepted last year to carry out a "Hiroshima." Citing unnamed officials, they write:

> *Looking back through the prism of Sept. 11, officials now say that the intercepted message was a telling sign of a drastic shift in the ambitions and global reach of Al Qaeda during the last three years. Clearly, the officials agree, the United States failed to grasp the organization's transformation from an obscure group of Islamic extremists into the world's most dangerous terrorists. (p. A1)*

The senior intelligence official's remark suggests that was not the case. For more on the issue of how government officials assessed the intentions of al-Qaeda, see Daniel Benjamin and Steven Simon, "The New Face of Terror-ism," *New York Times,* 4 Jan. 2000, A19; as well as Simon and Benjamin, "America and the New Terrorism," *Survival,* Spring 2000, 59–75; and "America and the New Terrorism: An Exchange," *Survival,* Summer 2000, 156–72.

2. See www.opcw.nl/chemhaz/nerve.htm; www.mitretek.org/mission/envene/

chemical/history/nerve_history.html; and www.bt.cdc.gov/Agent/Nerve/VX/VX.pdf.

3. In his excellent book *Terrorism and U.S. Foreign Policy* (Washington, D.C.: Brookings Institution Press, 2001), Paul R. Pillar, former deputy chief of the Counterterrorist Center at the CIA, writes that "a sample of soil collected outside the [al-Shifa] plant—unlike samples collected at other suspicious sites in Sudan—contained a chemical that is a precursor to the nerve agent VX (there are other conceivable reasons for the chemical to exist, but none that was a plausible explanation for it to be present at this location in Sudan)" (p. 108).

4. According to David Kay, a former United Nations weapons inspector, traces of VX were found on SCUD missiles in Iraq following the Gulf War. He says Iraq may even have helped build the al-Shifa plant in Sudan. "Sudan is not a state that you'd normally expect to understand by itself the intricacies of the production of VX," Kay said. "I think most people suspect there was Iraqi help in this." CNN, 21 Aug. 1998. Iraq is also the only producer of VX that uses a method involving EMPTA.

5. Tina Susman, "Bin Laden Link/El-Shifa Factory Chief Lives in House He Used to Occupy," *Newsday,* 27 Aug. 1998, A3. The article was also run August 28, 1998, in the *Dallas Morning News,* p. A9.

6. Writing before the attacks on the World Trade Center and the Pentagon, Paul R. Pillar observed in *Terrorism and U.S. Foreign Policy:*

> *U.S. intelligence performed the same role in August 1998 that it always performs in supporting military targeting: namely, providing everything known about a large number of sites that are associated with the adversary and that could be reviewed by military planners and senior decisionmakers for possible selection as targets. The intelligence did not show what role, if any, al-Shifa may ever have played in any VX program (production, storage, occasional transshipment, or whatever), nor did it point to any specific plans by bin Laden to use chemicals in a future attack. The intelligence also did not deny that the plant was engaged in the legitimate production of pharmaceuticals (chemical weapons programs elsewhere, as in Iraq, have had such dual-use facilities).*
>
> *The issue was thus not one of bad intelligence but rather whether, based on the partial information and still unanswered questions about al-Shifa, hitting the plant was prudent in view of the costs of doing so.*
>
> *Those costs included the public relations battering that the United States suffered from the al-Shifa strike itself, as well as the broader*

*blow that the episode inflicted on the perceived integrity of U.S. intelli-
gence and U.S. counterterrorist efforts generally. (p. 108)*

Perhaps, after the events of September 11, the calculus looks different.

7. *Crossfire,* CNN, 7 Sept. 1998.

8. Todd Purdum, "U.S. Fury on 2 Continents: Congress; Critics of Clinton Support Attacks," *New York Times,* 21 Aug. 1998, A1.

9. Susan Schmidt and Michael Weisskopf, *Truth at Any Cost: Ken Starr and the Unmaking of Bill Clinton* (New York: HarperCollins, 2000) 261–62.

10. Seymour Hersh, "The Missiles of August," *New Yorker,* 12 Oct. 1998.

11. Christopher Hitchens, "Minority Report: Monotheist Notes from All Over— Salman Rushdie Persecution; Immoral Bombing of Sudan by U.S.; and Other Items," *The Nation,* 19 Oct. 1998, 7.

12. Vernon Loeb, "Salah Idris," *Washington Post,* 25 July 1999, F1.

13. *World News Tonight with Peter Jennings,* ABC News, 9 July 1999.

14. Mary Anne Weaver, "The Real bin Laden: By Mythologizing Him, the Government Has Made Him Even More Dangerous," *New Yorker,* 24 Jan. 2000, 32.

15. Milt Bearden and Larry Johnson, "A Glimpse at the Alliances of Terror," *New York Times,* 7 Nov. 2000, A29.

16. Interview with Samuel R. Berger. CBS declined to allow its raw footage of the interview to be seen.

17. Sabine Rosenblatt et al., "Krieg der Zukunft" (War of the Future), *Die Woche,* 4 Sept. 1998, 22.

18. Judith Miller and William J. Broad, "Clinton Describes Terrorism Threat for 21st Century," *New York Times,* 22 Jan. 1999, A1.

19. Daniel Benjamin and Steven Simon, "The New Face of Terrorism," *New York Times,* 4 Jan. 2000, A19.

20. Daniel Benjamin and Steven Simon, "As a Conflict Intensifies, It's India's Move," *New York Times,* 15 Mar. 2000, A23.

21. Daniel Benjamin and Steven Simon, "America and the New Terrorism," *Survival,* vol. 42, no. 1 (Spring 2000), 59.

22. "America and the New Terrorism: An Exchange," *Survival* (Summer 2000), 156–72.

23. See especially Stephen Engelberg, "One Man and a Global Web of Violence," *New York Times,* 14 Jan. 2001, A1; Judith Miller, "Dissecting a Terror Plot from Boston to Amman," *New York Times,* 15 Jan. 2001, A1; Judith Miller, "Killing for the Glory of God, in a Land Far from Home," *New York Times,* 16 Jan. 2001, A1.

24. Al-Fadl supplied prosecutors with so much detailed information that they asked him, at the beginning of the trial, to provide jurors with a general ac-

count of bin Laden's organization as it developed over six years. During the trial, some of the details he provided were contradicted by succeeding witnesses. In view of the high degree of "compartmentalization" practiced by al-Qaeda, and the large number of people in its network, this is not surprising.

25. In his testimony, al-Fadl never mentioned al-Shifa, where the CIA's soil sample was collected. Hilat Koko, the neighborhood described by al-Fadl, is in the northern part of Khartoum. According to Sudanese exiles, including some who had served in the government, the country's National Security Agency maintains a large, secure compound there. Al-Fadl's testimony raises the possibility that the United States struck the wrong target when it hit al-Shifa, something that some opponents of the National Islamic Front regime argued after the 1998 missile attack, though they conceded that they were not privy to all NIF weapons activities and were suspicious of other plants as well. But the high level of EMPTA in the soil sample at al-Shifa, which is a few miles from Hilat Koko, cannot be disregarded. EMPTA could have been produced at one of the two sites and then transferred to the other for storage, the completion of the chemical process that would turn the EMPTA into VX, and perhaps the loading of the agent into weapons. In view of al-Fadl's testimony and the chemical analysis of the soil sample, the most plausible explanation is that both plants were involved. Both therefore would have been appropriate targets for attack.

26. We have found only two passing mentions of chemical weapons in the press, the first during al-Fadl's testimony, the second after the cross-examination. Colum Lynch wrote in *The Washington Post,* 8 Feb. 2001, "The testimony appeared to be aimed at supporting the government's contention that bin Laden's group—known as al Qaeda, Arabic for 'the Base'—planned terrorist acts and sought to acquire chemical and nuclear weapons in a crusade to drive American forces out of the Islamic world. But U.S. weapons experts cautioned that there is no evidence that Sudan or al Qaeda has ever possessed nuclear materials." Benjamin Weiser, in *The New York Times* of 21 Feb. 2001, reported that al-Fadl "testified that there was moving of weapons and explosives and attempts to buy uranium and to get chemical weapons."

27. Benjamin Weiser, "Trial Poked Holes in Image of bin Laden's Terror Group," *New York Times,* 31 May 2001, A1.

28. Larry C. Johnson, "The Declining Terrorist Threat," *New York Times,* 10 July 2001, A19.

29. If ever there was an example of the rewards for getting it wrong in American public life, Johnson's post–September 11 career is it. He became probably the most frequently interviewed terrorism expert in America, with appearances on scores of television shows and quotations in hundreds of newspapers.

30. Alexis de Tocqueville, *Democracy in America,* trans. George Lawrence (New York: Harper and Row, 2000), 642.

31. "Global Blinders: The End of the Cold War Hastened a Retreat from Foreign News," *Colombia Journalism Review,* supp., fortieth anniversary issue, 110.

32. Nicholas Bender and John Giuffo, "Hard Numbers: Overseas Bureaus," *Columbia Journalism Review,* Jan.-Feb. 2002, 53.

33. Thomas Ginsberg, "Rediscovering the World," *American Journalism Review,* Jan. 2002, 48.

34. Howard Schneider and Ruth Marcus, "White House Supports Starr: Despite Misgivings, Aides Express Acceptance," *Washington Post,* 9 Aug. 1994, A1.

35. Lucinda Fleeson, "Rush to Judgment," *American Journalism Review,* Nov. 2000, 20.

36. Jerry Seper, "No Evidence to Back Filegate Prosecution, Report Says," *Washington Times,* 29 July 2000, A2.

37. For an extraordinary account of the FBI's mishandling of the Lee case, see the declassified version of the Final Report of the Attorney General's Review Team on the Handling of the Los Alamos National Laboratory Investigation, written by Randy I. Bellows: www.fas.org/irp/ops/ci/bellows/.

38. Haynes Johnson, *The Best of Times: America in the Clinton Years* (New York: Harcourt, 2001), and David Halberstam, *War in a Time of Peace: Bush, Clinton, and the Generals* (New York: Scribner, 2001).

39. Barton Gellman, "A Strategy's Cautious Evolution: Before Sept. 11, the Bush Anti-Terror Effort Was Mostly Ambition," *Washington Post,* 20 Jan. 2002, A1.

CHAPTER 10: HOW GREAT A FAILURE?

1. Roberta Wohlstetter, *Pearl Harbor: Warning and Decision* (Stanford, Calif.: Stanford University Press, 1962), 68.

2. Ibid., 69.

CHAPTER 11: TERROR AND STRATEGY

1. The tax cut enacted by Congress in the first year of the Bush administration complicates the calculation of long-term effects. Certainly, in the absence of a tax cut now, the future economic impact of the September 11 attacks would be measurable, but not significant.

2. Daniel Benjamin and Steven Simon, "A Homeland in Search of Security," *New York Times,* 13 Nov. 2001, A17.

3. Karen DeYoung and Douglas Farah, "Infighting Slows Hunt for Hidden Al Qaeda Assets," *Washington Post,* 17 June 2002, accessed at washingtonpost.com/wp-dyn/articles/A1813-2002jun17.html.

4. Congressional Research Service Report for Congress, "Terrorism: Section by Section Analysis of the USA Patriot Act," Library of Congress, 10 Dec. 2001.

5. " 'Why We Fight America': Al-Qa'ida Spokesman Explains September 11 and Declares Intentions to Kill 4 Million Americans with Weapons of Mass Destruction," 12 June 2002, accessed at memri.org/bin/articles.cgi?Page=archives&Area=sd&ID=SP38802.

6. Center for Strategic and International Studies, "Report on the Greater Washington, D.C., Crisis Planning Workshop," 21 Mar. 2002, accessed at www.csis.org.

7. U.S. citizens have been among those killed in attacks against Israeli civilian targets.

8. Roberta Wohlstetter, *Pearl Harbor: Warning and Decision* (Stanford, Calif.: Stanford University Press, 1962).

9. Dennis Gormley, "Enriching Expectations: 11 September's Lessons for Missile Defense," *Survival,* vol. 44, no. 2 (Summer 2002), 23. Gormley, an influential defense and intelligence adviser to the U.S. Congress and Department of Defense, here quotes the famous Harvard economist and strategist Thomas Schelling. Gormley also coined the term "institutionalizing imaginativeness."

10. The unclassified National Intelligence Estimate is at www.cia.gov/nic/pubs/other_products/Unclassifiedballisticmissilefinal.htm. Tenet's testimony on these issues is at www.cia.gov/cia/public_affairs/speeches/speeches.html.

CHAPTER 12: A WORLD OF TERROR

1. The sense that religious conflict is worse than other kinds was rekindled for many in the West in the 1990s by the horrifying violence between Christians and Muslims during the fighting in the Balkans.

2. Regina M. Schwartz, *The Curse of Cain: The Violent Legacy of Monotheism* (Chicago: University of Chicago Press, 1997).

3. Exodus 17:14–16. See also Numbers 24:20, Deuteronomy 25:17–19, and I Samuel 15:7–8. According to the Bible, the Israelites did not succeed in extirpating Amalek until the reign of Hezekiah, several hundred years later; see I Chronicles 4:41–43.

4. Exodus 15:3.

5. Deuteronomy 33:26, 29.

6. Francis E. Peters, *Muhammad and the Origins of Islam* (Albany: State University of New York Press, 1994), 218–19.

7. Alfred Guillaume, trans., *The Life of Muhammad: A Translation of Ishaq's Sirat Rasul Allah* (London: Oxford University Press, 1955).

8. Ehud Sprinzak, "From Messianic Pioneering to Vigilante Terrorism: The Case of the Gush Emunim Underground," in David Rapoport, ed., *Inside Terrorist Organizations* (Portland, Ore.: Frank Cass, 2001), 206.

9. Sprinzak, "From Messianic Pioneering," 206.

10. Ibid., 207.

11. Esther 9:5.

12. Ehud Sprinzak, *Brother Against Brother: Violence and Extremism in Israeli Politics from Altalena to the Rabin Assassination* (New York: Free Press, 1999), 254.

13. Ibid., 275.

14. Ibid., 277.

15. Ibid., 280.

16. Ian Reader, *Religious Violence in Contemporary Japan: The Case of Aum Shinrikyo,* Nordic Institute of Asian Studies Monograph Series No. 82, 2000, 19.

17. Bruce Hoffman, *Inside Terrorism* (London: Victor Gollancz, 1998), 125.

18. Lou Michel and Dan Herbeck, *American Terrorist: Timothy McVeigh and the Oklahoma City Bombing* (New York: Regan Books, 2001), 167, 304.

19. Ibid., 113.

20. Ibid., 116.

21. Michael Lind, "Rev. Robertson's Grand International Conspiracy Theory," *New York Review of Books,* 2 Feb. 1995, 21–25.

22. I Thessalonians 4:15–17.

23. Michael Barkun, *Religion and the Racist Right: The Origins of the Christian Identity Movement* (Chapel Hill: University of North Carolina Press, 1997), 105.

24. Mark Juergensmeyer, *Terror in the Mind of God: The Global Rise of Religious Violence* (Berkeley: University of California Press, 2000), 155.

25. Hoffman, *Inside Terrorism,* 115

26. Barkun, *Religion and the Racist Right,* 110.

AFTERWORD: THE WAR THUS FAR: A STATUS REPORT

1. Remarks by the President from the USS *Abraham Lincoln* at Sea off the Coast of San Diego, California, 2 May 2003, http://www.whitehouse.gov/news/releases/2003/05/iraq/20030501-15.html.

2. Walter Pincus and Dana Priest, "Spy Agencies' Optimism on Al Qaeda Is Growing; Lack of Attacks Thought to Show Group Is Nearly Crippled," *Washington Post,* 6 May 2003, A16.

3. Barton Gellman, "In U.S., Terrorism's Peril Undiminished: Nation Struggles on Offense and Defense, and Officials Still Expect New Attacks," *Washington Post*, 24 Dec. 2002, A1.

4. Remarks by the President on the Jobs and Growth Plan, Little Rock, Arkansas, 5 May 2003, http://www.whitehouse.gov/news/releases/2003/05/20030505-4.html.

5. If one were to add the many victims of violence in Chechnya, the tally would grow considerably.

6. Thomas L. Friedman, "World War III," *New York Times*, 13 Sept. 2001, A27.

7. Thomas L. Friedman, "The Third Bubble," *New York Times*, 20 Apr. 2003, D9.

8. The authors are indebted to Dr. Bruce Hoffman of the RAND Corporation for this reference. Compare, as well, the Dutch General Intelligence and Security Service's Report, *Recruitment for the Jihad in the Netherlands: From Incident to Trend* (The Hague: Ministry of the Interior and Kingdom Relations, December 2002).

9. "Al-Qaeda Remains a Global Threat: UN," Agence France Presse, 17 Dec. 2002.

10. Barton Gellman and Susan Schmidt, "U.S., Pakistan Intensify the Search for Bin Laden: The Debate: To Kill or Capture," *Washington Post*, 7 Mar. 2003, A1.

11. Michael Elliott, "Why the War on Terror Will Never End: Bomb Attacks in Riyadh and Casablanca Suggest That Even on the Run, al-Qaeda Is a Resilient Threat to the West," *Time*, 26 May 2003, 26.

12. Secretary Colin L. Powell, Remarks to the United Nations Security Council, New York City, February 5, 2003, http://www.state.gov/secretary/rm/2003/17300pf.htm.

13. Indeed, after the hostilities were over, Deputy Secretary of Defense Paul Wolfowitz told a reporter that the humanitarian argument was "a reason to help the Iraqis but it's not a reason to put American kids' lives at risk, certainly not on the scale we did." Interview with Sam Tannenhaus, *Vanity Fair*, 9 May 2003. Transcript accessible at http://www.defenselink.mil/transcripts/2003/tr20030509-depsecdef0223.html.

14. See, for example, the Pew Research Center poll of February 2003, http://people-press.org/reports/display.php3?ReportID=173.

15. "Purported bin Laden Message on War Against Infidels," 12 Feb. 2003, http://www.cnn.com/2003/WORLD/meast/02/11/binladen.excerpts/.

16. "Al-Qaeda Statement: Full Text," 21 May 2003, http://news.bbc.co.uk/2/hi/middle_east/3047903.stm.

17. "Al-Qaeda on the Fall of Baghdad, Guerrilla Warfare: 'Is the Most Powerful

Weapon Muslims Have, and It Is the Best Method to Continue the Conflict with the Crusader Enemy,' " MEMRI Special Dispatch Series, no. 493, 11 Apr. 2003; accessed at http://www.memri.org/bin/articles.cgi?Page=archives&Area=sd&ID=SP49303.

18. Daniel Benjamin, "In the Fog of War, a Greater Threat," *Washington Post,* 31 Oct. 2002, A23.

19. The issue of a potential proliferation crisis arising out of a war in Iraq should not have come as a surprise to the administration. See Benjamin, ibid.

20. Secretary of State Colin Powell, Testimony Before the Senate Budget Committee, Washington, D.C., 11 Feb. 2003, http://www.state.gov/secretary/rm/2003/17620.htm.

21. Emmanuel Sivan, "The Clash Within Islam," *Survival,* Spring 2003, 25–44.

22. "Musharraf Wades into Islamist Heartland with Anti-Talibanisation Campaign," Agence France Presse, 10 June 2003.

23. Stephen Philip Cohen, "The Jihadist Threat to Pakistan," *Washington Quarterly,* summer 2003, 7–25.

24. Reuven Paz, " 'Global Campaign Against Aggression': The Supreme Council of Global Jihad?" Global Research in International Affairs (GLORIA) Center, Project for the Research of Islamist Movements (PRISM), Occasional Papers, vol. 1, no. 6 (May 2003).

25. "Leading Islamic Clerics Come Out for Reform in Arab-Islamic Society," MEMRI Special Dispatch Series, no. 386, 5 June 2002. In his al-Jazeera appearance, Sheikh al-Hawali explained, "The relations between America and us differ from the relations between us and all the other peoples or nations. These are relations between two [very] different nations: One is a nation that was chosen by Allah, who tested it and purified it with disasters so that it will atone for its sins. Allah is using that nation in order to wave the banner of truth and justice on the face of the earth. This is our nation. There is also a tyrannous and evil nation that Allah is manipulating, unbeknownst to it, until it reaches the end to which it is sentenced—the same end that was the lot of all the nations of heresy, tyranny, and aggression such as the peoples of Noah, 'Aad, Thamud, and Pharaoh." Thamud and 'Aad are tribes that were supposedly destroyed by God for resisting Muhammad's call and frequently stand in for the United States or other powers whose obliteration is foretold in contemporary apocalyptic stories (cf. chapter 2).

26. Yotam Feldner, "Sheikh Tantawi's Positions on Jihad Against Coalition Forces, Saddam's Resignation, and the War in Iraq," MEMRI Inquiry and Analysis series, no. 130, 8 April 2003, http://memri.org/bin/articles.cgi?Page=archives&Area=ia&ID=IA13003.

27. "Intergrating Muslims," *The Economist,* vol. 367, no. 8323, 10–16 May 2003, 22–25.

28. Sheikh Fahd has his own website, which has been translated by Reuven Paz. See "The First Islamist *Fatwa* on the Use of Weapons of Mass Destruction," PRISM Special Dispatches, vol. 1, no. 1 (May 2003).

29. Salman bin Fahd al-Awdah has a slick website in English and Arabic, the tone of which is generally liberal within an essentially religious framework.

30. "An Egyptian Intellectual Campaigns to Change the Religious Discourse Led by al-Azhar," MEMRI, http://www.memri.org/bin/articles.cgi?Page= archives&Area=sd&ID=SP43602.

31. Olivier Roy, "EuroIslam: The Jihad Within?" *The National Interest,* spring 2003, 63–73.

32. The responsibility for reversing this dangerous trend lies with European governments. The U.S. can do nothing about its underlying causes. Europeans, however, have been in denial, insisting, as Americans did for many years, that its minority population was equal under the law and therefore had no cause for resentment. With over one hundred arrests in a half-dozen countries since September 11, this complacency is on the wane. One option would be to adopt a European version of the affirmative action program pursued—with partial success—by the United States. Public funding (along German lines) for Islamic houses of worship, schools, preachers, teachers, and prison chaplains would help limit the influence of Wahhabi-financed radical mosques and madrassas and slow down the recruitment of Muslims in jails. And a more receptive attitude toward Turkey's application for accession to the European Union might help inculcate a greater sense of Europeaness in young Muslims who feel cut out. See also Daniel Benjamin and Steven Simon, "A Place at the Table," *Time Europe,* 16 Dec. 2002, 56.

33. In chapter 5 we discuss the large number of jihadists from Great Britain who went to Afghanistan and Pakistan in the 1990s.

34. Sarah Lyall, "What Drove 2 Britons to Bomb a Club in Tel Aviv?" *New York Times,* 12 May 2003, A3.

35. Don Van Natta, Jr., and Desmond Butler, "Threats and Responses: Terror Network: Anger on Iraq Seen as New Qaeda Recruiting Tool," *New York Times,* 16 March 2003, A1.

36. Raymond Bonner, "Threats and Responses: South Asia: Philippine Camps are Training al Qaeda Allies, Officials Say," *New York Times,* 31 May 2003, A1.

37. The National Security Strategy of the United States of America, http://www. whitehouse.gov/nsc/nss.html.

38. Elaine Sciolino, "Aftereffects: North Africa: Moroccans Say al-Qaeda Masterminded and Financed Casablanca Suicide Bombings," *New York Times,* 23 May 2003, A16.

39. Laura Blumenfeld, "Former Aide Takes Aim at War on Terror," *Washington Post,* 16 June 2003, A1.

40. John Mintz, "Ridge Seeking Fewer Changes in Terror Alerts," *Washington Post,* 6 June 2003, A11.

41. Steven Kosiak, "Analysis of the FY2004 Budget Request," Center for Strategic and Budgetary Assessments, http://www.csbaonline.org.

42. Siobhan Gorman, "Bioterrorism Project Falls into Intelligence Gap," http://www.govexec.com/dailyfed/0603/061603nj1.htm.

43. John Mintz, "Freighters Believed to Be Linked to al Qaeda; U.S. Fears Terrorists at Sea; Tracking Ships Is Difficult," *Washington Post,* 31 Dec. 2001, A1.

44. R. James Woolsey, "World War IV," *Journal of Counterterrorism & Homeland Security International,* winter 2003.

45. The authors are indebted to Professor Alan Richards of the University of California at Santa Cruz for his insights into the political economy of democratic transitions.

46. Emmanuel Sivan, "The Clash Within Islam," *Survival* 45, spring 2003, 25–44.

47. For a fascinating explanation of this behavior, see John Waterbury, "Democracy Without Democrats? The Potential for Political Liberalization in the Middle East," in Ghassan Salame, ed., *Democracy Without Democrats? The Renewal of Politics in the Muslim World* (London: I. B. Tauris, 1999).

48. See Foreign Minister Ahmed Maher's reaction at http://memri.org/bin/articles.cgi?Page=archives&Area=sd&ID=SP46503.

49. A sampling of views on the initiative can be accessed at http://memri.org/bin/articles.cgi?Page=archives&Area=ia&ID=IA11502; http://memri.org/bin/articles.cgi?Page=archives&Area=ia&ID=IA11603; and http://memri.org/bin/articles.cgi?Page=archives&Area=ia&ID=IA11703.

50. Vanessa O'Connell, "Radio Mogul Heads U.S. Arabic TV Network," *Wall Street Journal,* 26 March 2003, B1.

51. *Biblical Recorder,* 14 June 2002, accessed at http://www.biblicalrecorder.org/content/news/2002/6_14_2002/ne140602vines.shtml.

52. Laurie Goodstein, "Seeing Islam as 'Evil' Faith, Evangelicals Seek Converts," *New York Times,* 27 May 2003, Page A1.

INDEX

Islamaya, Jemaah, 450
Islambouli, Khalid Ahmed Shawqi al-, 75–76, 82–83, 94
Islamic Army, 103
  see also Qaeda, al-
Islamic Association for Palestine, 99
Islamic Cultural Institute, 124–25
Islamic Jihad, 222, 223
Islamic Movement of Uzbekistan (IMU), 146, 204, 207, 286, 338
Islamic National Front, 369
Islamic Reconstruction, 204
Islamic Salvation Front (FIS), 116, 195–96, 197–98
Islamism, 490
Ismoil, Eyad, 7–8, 11, 251, 308
Israel, 63, 78, 102, 115, 189, 210, 232, 359, 400, 401, 406, 410, 412, 458, 494n, 501n
  Azzam's hatred of, 99
  in bin Laden's fatwas, 141, 142, 460
  Camp David Accords and, 426, 427
  Christian views of, 443
  counterterrorism policy of, 220
  East Africa embassy attacks and, 258
  Egyptian peace with, 73–74, 182, 426, 427
  Iraq and, 455
  Jewish Messianism and, 425–32
  in 1967 War, 192, 425
  in 1973 War, 425–26
  Palestinian conflict with, 103, 127, 189, 191–95, 223, 414, 426, 500n
  al-Qaeda and, 103, 148, 149, 340, 459
  religion in Palestinian opposition to, 192–93
  settlers from, 426–31
  U.S. support of, 186, 464
Italy, 213, 314
Ittihad al-Islamiyya, 121

jahiliyya, 56–57, 63, 64–65, 66, 490
Jaish e-Mohammed, 202
Jalil, Ahmad, 272, 273
Jamaat al-Jihad, 73–75
  see also Tanzim al-Jihad
Jamaat al-Muslimin, al- (takfiris), 70–73, 74, 77, 196, 408
Jamaat i-Islami, 60–61, 201
Jamiat Ulema i-Islami party, 113, 200–201
Jansen, Johannes J. G., xiii
Japan, 400
  Aum Shinrikyo and, ix, 129, 228–29, 425, 433–38
  new religions in, 434
Jazeera, al-, 98, 157, 417, 467, 485, 499n
Jemaah Islamiah, 209, 210
Jenkins, Jerry, 439
Jennings, Steve, 306

Jerusalem, religious symbols in, 192
Jewell, Richard, 250, 303
Jewish Consistory, 469
Jewish Defense League, 4
Jews, 58, 208, 213
  Christian Identity and, 440, 441, 443
  Muslim views on, 66–68, 92, 93, 410, 480, 484, 486
  New York and, 157, 160
  al-Qaeda and, 148, 186
  Taliban and, 274
jihad, 46, 63, 104, 459, 463, 464, 467–68, 480
  apostasy as reason for, 50
  Azzam on, 99
  domestication of, 54–55
  ibn Taymiyya's views on, 48–52, 55n
  Maududi on, 60
  meaning of, 5
  Mustafa on, 73
  Quran and, 48–49
  Qutb on, 65
  Rahman on, 16–17, 84
  salafi view of, 170–71
  as sixth pillar of Islam, 77–78, 81
  Sunni view of, 49
"Jihad Against Jews and Crusaders," 117, 211, 256
John Paul II, Pope, 20, 21–22, 341
Johnson, Haynes, 380
Johnson, Larry C., 363, 371–72, 511n
Johnson, Marlene, 310
Jordan, 176, 451, 493n
  bombings in, 190
  Islamists in, 172, 189–91
  millennium conspiracies in, 30–32, 153–54, 190, 311, 312, 313
  al-Qaeda in, 30–32, 112, 320
Judaism:
  apocalyptic literature of, 423–24
  Messianism in, 425–32
  violence and, 421, 423–32
Juergensmeyer, Mark, xiii
Justice Department, U.S., viii, 226, 227, 231, 239, 307, 331, 340, 394, 395

Kaaba, 490
Kaaba, Operation, *see* Nairobi embassy bombing
Kach party, 4
Kahane, Meir, 165, 428, 445
  murder of, 3–7, 15, 19, 100
Kansi, Mir Aimal, 221, 222
Karachi, 448
Karamat, Jehangir, 203, 204–5
Kargil, 277–78, 280, 316
Karimov, Islam, 287
Karzai, Hamid, 470

Tantawi, Muhammad Sayyid al-, 411*n*, 467
Tanzania, *see* Dar es Salaam embassy bombing
Tanzim al-Jihad (Tanzim Muhammad Abd al-
    Salam Faraj), 75–86, 98, 119
    Copts attacked by, 81–82
    Egyptian government attacked by, 82–86
    recruitment to, 76–77
    structure of, 76–77
    see also Jamaat al-Jihad
Technical Military Academy, 70
Tel Aviv, nightclub attack in, 469
Tenet, George, xii, 240, 286, 291, 311, 312,
    320, 333, 341, 345, 387, 407
terrorism:
    changing nature of, ix, 220–28, 365–82
    fund-raising for, 228, 452
    future scenarios of, 397–401
    government papers needed for, 244
    ignored in media, 365–82
    information sources on, xii–xiii, 226–28
    in movies, 373
    NGOs in support of, 293
    nonstate actors in, 226–28
    political vs. religious reasons for, ix
    religious sources for, ix, 38–94, 408, 409,
        419–46
    socioeconomic origins of, 408–9, 417
    state sponsorship of, 222–25, 457, 458, 459
    types of, 222
    weapons of mass destruction sought for,
        128–29, 147, 161, 202–4, 229, 230, 248,
        249, 252–55, 259, 264, 267, 292, 338,
        365, 366–70, 381, 398, 404, 405, 415,
        433–39; *see also* Shifa, al-, chemical plant
    see also counterterrorism; *specific individuals
        and groups*
Terrorist Asset Tracking Center, 339
Terrorist Threat Integration Center, 474–75
TERRSTOP, 18, 152, 234, 235, 238
Thirty Years War, 420
Threatening Storm, The (Pollack), 455
Time, 161, 272, 453
TNT (Directorate of Transnational Threats),
    vii, viii, 257, 262, 270, 328, 342
Tocqueville, Alexis de, 373–74
Tomb of the Patriarchs, 428–29
Tora Bora, 143, 453
Torah, 491
Travelgate, 300, 377, 378–79
Treasury Department, U.S., 269, 308, 394
Tripoli, 169, 192
    U.S. attack on, 222, 223
*Truth at Any Cost: Ken Starr and the Unmaking
    of Bill Clinton* (Schmidt and Weisskopf),
    359
Tunisia, 177, 212
Turabi, Hassan al-, 109–10, 111, 114, 133,
    247

Turkey, 212
Turki al-Faisal, Prince, 271–72, 506*n*
Turks, 212, 213
Turner Diaries, The (Pierce), 440
TWA Flight 800, 248

ulema, 491
umma, 47, 491
Union of Islamic Organizations, 469
United Airlines, 21
United Airlines Flight 93, 35–36, 162
United Airlines Flight 175, 33
United Arab Emirates, 130, 251, 271, 275, 281,
    287–88, 314
United Jihad Front, 201
United Kingdom, *see* Great Britain
United Nations, 145, 245, 260, 271, 273–74,
    324, 332, 355, 364–65
    Afghanistan sanctions and, 289, 315
    Libya sanctions in, 223
    weapons inspectors of, 454–55, 462
United Nations building, 16, 18
United States of America v. Eyad Ismoil, xiii
*United States of America v. Mohammed A.
    Salameh et al.,* xiii
*United States of America v. Omar Ahmad Ali
    Abdel Rahman et al.,* xiii
*United States of America v. Ramzi Ahmed
    Yousef, Abdul Hakim Murad, Wali Khan
    Amin Shah,* xiii
*United States of America v. Usama bin Laden et
    al.,* xiii
USA Today, 375
Usbat al-Ansar, 191–92
Utaybi, Juhayman bin Muhammad bin Sayf al-,
    87, 88, 89, 90, 94, 495*n*
Uzbekistan, 205, 206, 207, 208, 284, 286–87,
    338, 343, 345

vaccines, bioterrorism and, 252, 476
Vajpayee, Atal Bihari, 202, 277
Vanity Fair, 361, 504*n*
Venter, J. Craig, 252
Vines, Jerry, 488
VX, 259, 352, 353, 355

Wahhabis, 52–54, 59, 144, 190, 202, 208, 491
    Saudi missionary work for, 185, 187, 206–7,
        209, 468
    Taliban and, 136, 138
Walbert, Cal, 22
Walid, Mahfouz ould, 413
Wall Street Journal, 202, 367, 374–75, 469
Walsh, Elsa, 300–301, 331, 507*n*
"Washington Consensus," 485
Washington Post, xi, 246, 251, 284, 296, 323,
    335, 356, 362–63, 365, 368, 375, 382,
    383, 447, 472, 504*n*